A New History of Yachting

A New History of Yachting

MIKE BENDER

Foreword by Tom Cunliffe

THE BOYDELL PRESS

First published 2017
The Boydell Press, Woodbridge

ISBN 978 1 78327 133 7

The Boydell Press is an imprint of Boydell & Brewer Ltd
PO Box 9, Woodbridge, Suffolk IP12 3DF, UK
and of Boydell & Brewer Inc.
668 Mt Hope Avenue, Rochester, NY 14620–2731, USA
website: www.boydellandbrewer.com

A CIP catalogue record for this book is available
from the British Library

The publisher has no responsibility for the continued existence or accuracy
of URLs for external or third-party internet websites referred to in this
book, and does not guarantee that any content on such websites is, or will
remain, accurate or appropriate

This publication is printed on acid-free paper

To Ally, Emma, Amy and Jakub

Awaking suddenly, he listened, started up and sat listening.

Florence asked him what he thought he heard.

'I want to know what it says,' he answered, looking steadily in her face.

'The sea, Floy, what is it that it keeps on saying?'

Charles Dickens, Dombey and Son, p. 123

Contents

Illustrations

The author and publishers are grateful to all the institutions and individuals listed for permission
to reproduce the materials in which they hold copyright. Every effort has been made to trace the
copyright holders; apologies are offered for any omission, and the publishers will be pleased to
add any necessary acknowledgement in subsequent editions.

Foreword

Tom Cunliffe

I first crossed tacks with Mike Bender back in 1982. He was studying for the RYA Yachtmaster examination at the National Sailing Centre, West Cowes. I was playing truant from my job there as an examiner. More specifically, I was preparing for a voyage in the wake of the Vikings from Norway to North America in *Hirta*, my Bristol Channel pilot cutter. Mike remembers that, for some reason now lost in the mists of time, I was dragging *Hirta*'s huge flax mainsail through the main building with a couple of 'willing volunteers'. My four-year-old daughter danced ahead clearing our passage, announcing to any who would listen that the deadweight of canvas was going to take her across the Atlantic.

Many tides have ebbed and flowed since then. Today, we can look back on the 1970s and 1980s as halcyon days in British yachting. We sail in leaner, more worrying times for our favourite sport and, as is so often the case, the best we can do to secure its future is to learn what we may from its past.

It is a lifetime now since histories of yachting were published by such luminaries as Peter Heaton and Douglas Phillips-Birt. This book is different. The old texts generally concentrated on big racing yachts with large professional crews, owned by the landed aristocracy or, at a pinch, captains of industry. Whilst undoubtedly important, this glamorous approach was incomplete. It tended to see yachting as a discrete subject outside the general flow of history. Always excepting the colourful arrival of Kaiser Bill before the First World War, wars tended to feature mainly as inconveniences that held up design development for a few years. Mike Bender's *New History of Yachting* places the subject in a fuller historical context. His story involves far more than political events, taking in industrial and technological revolutions as well as changes in transport systems, such as the boom in yachting havens created by the railways. He even discusses how the arrival of the motorway system has opened up hitherto distant waters.

The traditional big-yacht approach to history often sets aside much of the hands-on reality enjoyed by many over the decades. By far the commonest vessel for leisure sailing is the dinghy, operating often on reservoirs and rivers with heroes like Jack Holt rather than Watson or Fife. Dinghy sailing is far less well recorded than yacht cruising or racing, and the author has clearly laboured long and hard to uncover original material.

Dinghies for sport came in around the 1890s. Their affordability encouraged people with a much wider range of incomes to enjoy them, while the lightness of the gear allowed women to compete as equals. Sometimes, much to the chagrin of Edwardian racing gents, the ladies shone as superiors.

Another gap filled by this book is the social history of yachting, and how it related to class and gender. The class origins and exclusiveness of yacht clubs across the centuries are carefully described, along with their reaction to women sailors. Until the 1960s, the author declares, ladies tended to appear on committee agendas under the same heading as dogs, both of which most members would prefer to have kept outside the premises.

Despite what one hopes are their best efforts, nearly all historians show a tendency to colour their conclusions in the image of their own humours. For the serious student or the more casual reader, the only way to keep a check on this is to study the author's references. These have often been absent in previous volumes on the subject, but not here. The copious notes in Mike's book are fascinating. They will not only be useful to those with an academic interest, some of them will even help the sailor wanting to learn more about a local club or river.

To conclude, I cannot bang the drum often enough in praise of the richness of yachting literature, a passion I have tried to share through my recent compilation *In The Wake of Heroes*. Since Mike has spent the last fifteen years studying the subject, to the extent of being awarded a Ph.D. on the topic, he and I sing from the same chanty book.

This work is a lot more than a mere recitation of facts and a thumping good read. It leads us to understand that knowing where we have come from enriches our enjoyment of the sea and of sailing as it is today.

Tom Cunliffe FRIN

Acknowledgements

This book has been so long in its development and went through many drafts, and the manuscript, with its many footnotes, needed so much preparation, that I must start by expressing my gratitude to my wife, Alison, and to Kay Harding for their help.

I also want to thank my editor, Peter Sowden of Boydell & Brewer, for his encouragement and patient support.

I wish to record my thanks to those who encouraged me when I was getting started, some fifteen years ago, in my attempts to understand the place and the importance of yachting and yachting literature: Dr Robert Lawson-Peebles of the English Department, Exeter University, who supervised both my M.A. and Ph.D. research into the literature of yachting; Maldwin Drummond, one-time Commodore of the Royal Yacht Squadron and key figure in the founding of the Association of Yachting Historians; Mike Duffy, Professor of Maritime History, Exeter; Dr Peter Davies, Emeritus Professor of History, Liverpool University; and David Clements, founder member of the South West Maritime History Society and the long-time editor of its journal *Maritime South West*. Hal Sisk has given me invaluable advice concerning the history of Irish yachting, and W. M. Nixon kindly found time to talk to me at short notice when I was sailing up the Irish coast in July 2016. I must also record the encouragement I received from Theo Rye, supremely talented marine architect and historian, who died at the tragically young age of forty-eight in October 2016.

I owe a particular debt to Roger Ryan, for his continued support, and for providing detailed criticisms on this and previous manuscripts. Barbara Farquahason and John Torrance kindly also commented in depth on a previous draft of this book.

Conversion from Imperial to Metric Measures

Imperial	Metric
One inch	2.54 cm
One foot (12 inches)	0.30 metre
One yard (36 inches)	0.91 metre
One ounce	28.39 grams
One pound	0.46 kilogram

Introduction

This book is about yachting, which is usually understood as *leisure sailing, in which wind power is the major form of propulsion*. So, this history covers all forms of yachting, including dinghy and keelboat sailing. It does not include motor yachts nor windsurfing, since this sport seems to relate more to the use of boards rather than boats.

Yachting has played an important part in this nation's leisure. It has long been a major, socially significant leisure activity. It proffered status, signified by yacht ownership and membership of yacht clubs. As part of our cultural and social history, leisure sailing can illuminate the wider society of which it is part – its values, its beliefs and its paradoxes.

Additionally, yachting has a much wider range of literature than other sports. Tom Cunliffe, introducing his *In the Wake of Heroes* puts it well: 'Those of us who go down to the sea, whether for leisure, war or commerce, are incomparably blessed with good reading matter. Indeed, I believe no other sport or form of transport is so richly endowed.'[1]

Other sports have their 'How to' books, autobiographies and biographies, but yachting has also generated thousands of accounts of passages and voyages, as well as some major fiction. More than other prestige sports, it has been represented in other media, such as painting and music.

Why a New History of Yachting is Needed

There has not been a history of yachting published for many years. The standard yacht histories, such as Heaton's *Yachting: A History* (1955) or Phillips-Birt's *The History of Yachting* (1974) are now some fifty years old.[2]

---

[1] Cunliffe, *In the Wake of Heroes*, p. 2.

[2] Mention should also be made of Peter Johnson's *The Encyclopedia of Yachting* (1989) and Robin Knox-Johnston's *History of Yachting* (1990). These are more pictorial, coffee-table tomes. However, the comments I make on previous histories also apply to these texts.

Theirs was the 'big history' approach: important, rich owners, often public figures, owning large racing yachts, designed and built by the top yards, with large, professional crews, taking part in prestigious yacht races, being organised by the long-established 'royal' yacht clubs for large, silver cups, in one of the major yachting centres, such as Burnham-on-Crouch, the Clyde or the Solent, especially Cowes.[3]

In short, these histories concerned the events that the prestigious rich felt were worthwhile, so areas that they did not consider worthy of attention, or events that might show them in a negative light, were backgrounded. So, this was the history of the rich at play, written up by contemporary yachting journalists, and memorialised by yachting historians. Their accounts of the rise of the sport were usually lavishly illustrated by fine oil paintings and photographs of large yachts racing, often with the Needles in the background, to which only a little explanatory text needed to be added.

Such accounts required a number of major distortions. They over-focussed on yacht racing, especially the racing of large yachts, a relatively small, if very visible, part of the totality of yachting. In addition, yacht racing, as opposed to the much more popular yacht cruising, requires organisation, so there was an emphasis on yacht clubs.

This focus leaves out all the people sailing small boats for pleasure, especially after the 1880s, when dinghies started to appear in large numbers. So, in this book, I have adopted a philosophy of 'one sailing boat, one vote' in terms of what needs to be foregrounded. Or, since larger yachts inevitably get more attention and more is known about them, perhaps 'one sail, one vote' would be more accurate, but this will still result in a major re-balancing of the story of yachting.

I have mentioned the over-concern of previous histories with sailing in the Solent. In contrast, this book describes the development of yachting across the United Kingdom, and also the Republic of Ireland, particularly until its independence in 1922. Some of the earliest developments in yachting occurred in the Cork area and the western loughs of Ireland, such as Lough Dergh. Similarly, the pre-eminence of the Clyde yacht builders, such as Fife and Watson, will draw attention to developments in Scotland. I will also

---

[3] This kind of history is what Mary Beard calls 'big books by blokes about battles' ('Move over History Boys'). 'History' as the selection and foregrounding of certain narratives, mostly those selected by the powerful, is discussed in Beverley Southgate, *History Meets Fiction*. For example, as John Arnold, in *History: A Very Short Introduction*, p. 82, points out, 'big history' is rather weak on women and their contributions.

describe the export of yachting to British colonies and trading centres, such as Gibraltar and Bombay (Mumbai).

Perhaps most crucially, previous writers had little interest in analysing the context in which yachting activity was taking place. There was the odd mention of major events like the Industrial Revolution, the Napoleonic Wars and the World Wars. In place of a more encompassing history, yachting history was presented as progressing through a series of well-defined stages: introduced as the sport of kings by Charles II, little happened then till 1815 and the creation of the Yacht Club that was to become the Royal Yacht Squadron. There then followed a gradual diffusion downwards that stopped with the newly created prosperous middle classes in the last quarter of the nineteenth century.

Instead of this simplified march-past, we need to look at the changing social position of yachting and yachtsmen, and later on yachtswomen, across time. We need to see yachting as part of the larger culture of contemporary society, as well as a (sub-)culture with its own beliefs and practices.[4] So, this book will examine:

- *The historical, economic and political contexts* in which yachtsmen made their decisions and their attitudes were formed. For example, right through till after the Second World War, the exclusionary politics of the yacht clubs kept out people engaged in trades or marine professions, and, to a large extent, women. I will examine how these attitudes were supported or undermined by the wider society.
- *The organisational structures, the hierarchies of prestige, and the methods used to maintain them.*
- *The belief systems* – the values, decision paths and attitudes shared by members of the yachting fraternity at any given period. Within any given group, there are unstated assumptions. As the philosopher, Alfred North Whitehead put it: 'There will be some fundamental assumptions which adherents of all the variant systems within the epoch unconsciously presuppose. Such assumptions appear so obvious that people do not know what they are assuming because [they have] no other way of putting things'.[5] These assumptions are often not written down as they are so obvious that they do not merit recording or discussion. So the historian has to make intelligent guesses about these unspoken assumptions.

---

[4] Anthropology students will recognise Clifford Geertz' idea that it is insufficient to describe behaviour independent of the context of that behaviour, i.e. to provide a 'thick description' (See Geertz, 'Thick Description: Towards an Interpretative Theory of Cultures').

[5] Alfred Whitehead, *Science and the Modern World,* p. 71.

- In a sport as complex as sailing, *technological change* is a key driver of change. However, the adoption of these changes depends on the response of the relevant sectors of society to the possibilities raised by these changes.
- *The forms of communication and recording that the society is using.* A narrative is not just carried by words. Oil paintings and engravings have played an important part in memorialising yachting. (One summer, I sailed into Ramsgate and called in at the Royal Temple Yacht Club, founded 1857. I asked a member if there was a history of the club. 'It's on the walls' was the reply).
- The media by which we communicate and transmit information are important in determining how we actually see the world and behave in it. A possible schema is:

   Pre-1720: horse-delivered letter and diary

   1720–1830: newspaper and coffee house

   1830–1890: development of rail network and steamship services

   1890–1920s: photography, telegraphy, telephone, postcard

   1920s–1950s: gramophone, record, radio

   1950–1980s: television

   1990s–present: satellite communication, mobiles, e-mail, instant messaging and networking sites.

- *The representations of the sea and sailing.* There have been a number of ways in which people have related to the sea and sailing. When a particular mode of relating dominates a time period, we can consider it the dominant mode. Thus, in the second half of the eighteenth century, as Corbin documents in *The Lure of the Sea*, the health-giving properties of sea water and sea air were 'discovered' by Georgian society. Then, the aristocracy used the sea in the first half of the nineteenth century to flaunt their wealth through their conspicuous consumption. In the latter half of the nineteenth century, upper middle-class professionals saw sailing as a gladiatorial competition with the sea and wished to show their ability to dominate the sea in any weather. So, each of these groups 'saw' and understood the sea and its properties in different ways. One of the features of yachting that I also want to demonstrate is that these ways of relating to the sea live on, even when they are no longer the dominant mode.[6]

---

[6] Jonathan Raban puts this notion well in his *Passage to Jeanneau*: 'I thought it might be possible to think of a sea as the sum of all the reflections it had held during its history. You'd never know the half of them, of course, but in the clashes and contradictions of image against image you

- *Making sense of yachting in terms of other social sciences.* History seems to exist in splendid isolation from anthropology, sociology and psychology. While only claiming expertise in psychology, I attempt to indicate a wider range of perspectives within which to make sense of the history of yachting.

One last difference between this and previous histories is that these earlier histories did not indicate where they got their information from. No historian can prove their narrative to be correct, but they can try and indicate clearly the supporting evidence, so that future researchers can assess for themselves the material the writer was drawing on. For this reason, wherever possible, I have given references to back up my statements.

To sum up, leisure sailing is an important part of British social history, and it deserves to be seriously analysed and documented. We need to look not only at the changing conditions and the changing technologies that determined how the sport developed, but also at people's understandings – their perceptions – of the world they lived in.

This book is about the different ways that yachtsmen have used the rivers and seas of this country and the stories they have told about their exploits.

---

might at least catch something of the provocative power of the sea, which has meant so much, so variously, to us' (p. 35).

CHAPTER ONE

Stirrings and Beginnings

Dating the beginning of the sailing narrative is inherently problematic since people have sailed for pleasure since there were boats to sail, so a fisherman, the captain of a commercial vessel, or a harbour pilot might well sail for pleasure on high days or holidays, and they had no reason to record their experiences in a permanent form.

Leisure use of yachts is recorded from ancient times.[1] W. M. Nixon goes back to 600 BC and the Roman poet Catullus, 'proud owner of a 30ft seagoing yacht, planked in pitch-pine on oak frames … with a somewhat cumbersome lug-sail', he sailed from his home water of the Adriatic to Greek ports, and 'on his most ambitious cruise, of all, the Black Sea'.[2]

An early example of the use of yachts for royal leisure is shown by Harold, king of Norway, presenting a 'king's ship' to the English king, Athelstan (924–939); and King Edgar (944–975) enjoyed 'sommer progresses and [his] yerely chiefe pastimes were the sailing round about this whole isle of Albion'.[3] 'When King Robert Bruce of Scotland lived in his castle at Cardross near Dumbarton "his chief amusement was to go upon the river [Clyde] and down to the sea in a ship which he kept for his pleasure. In 1326 six men were paid 2s for crossing in his yacht to Arran."'[4]

Brian Lavery in *The Island Nation* tells how 'A fifteenth century manuscript in the British Library shows three people in a small boat partly covered with an awning, playing musical instruments and drinking from a jar'.[5] I point out the continuous association of sailing and drinking at various points in this

---

[1] For pre-literate uses of the sea and voyaging, see Brian Fagan, *Beyond the Blue Horizon*.

[2] W. M. Nixon, *To Sail the Crested Sea*, pp. 2–3. Nixon goes on to add the voyage of St Columba of Derry, who sailed from Derry to the Hebrides to establish Iona and who, in AD 563, wrote 'What joy to sail the crested sea and watch the waves beat white upon the Irish Sea'.

[3] Tony Dalton, *British Royal Yachts: A Complete Illustrated History*, p. 3.

[4] George Blake and Christopher Small, *Cruise in Company*, p. 168. This is not a very early use of the term 'yacht' but a later translation of a Gaelic manuscript.

[5] Brian Lavery, *The Island Nation*, p. 125.

book; and also the link with music, and often singing, especially after 'a few jars', as seems to have been the case on this occasion.

Representations of the Sea

We need to pay attention to the various 'meanings' of the sea, since these inform leisure sailing and define the various types of pleasure and purpose to be gained from it.[6]

The oldest and most primeval representation of the sea was as being *a source of terror* – a hostile, uncontrollable and dangerous environment, and *The Odyssey*, written at the end of the eighth century BC, is perhaps its greatest canvas.[7] St Paul, in Acts 27, describes a storm of many days duration, due to sailing too late in the season. Such a perspective was, in large part, rational. Ships were so unwieldy that they really were at the mercy of the sea. Until the Middle Ages, the need for a keel to prevent leeway was not properly understood.[8] Certainly, until the nineteenth century and the advent of the Bermudan (fore-and-aft) sail, the square sail, set horizontally across the ship, was the commonest form of sail. With such a sail configuration, boats were unable to sail close to the wind. This meant that, if sailing near to a coast, a wind shift could trap them and drive them onto the shore (becoming *embayed*). In addition, the British coast had very few navigational beacons before 1850 to warn of dangers, such as reefs and sandbanks. The fear of the sea and its unpredictable nature was reified into tales of sea monsters, which illustrated the primitive maps and charts of the Middle Ages.[9]

The sea continued and continues to cause terror at its potential ferocity – when Defoe toured Great Britain in 1726, 'half the houses along the Norfolk coast were built from the wood of shipwrecks';[10] witness the storm scene, the shipwreck and deaths by drowning in Dickens' *David Copperfield*, published

---

[6] W. H. Auden compares the sea and the desert to the city in *The Enchafed Flood*. For ethnographic meanings of sailing, see John Mack, *The Sea: A Cultural History*. For a more discursive discussion, see Raban, *Passage to Jeanneau*.

[7] The same fear was true of mountains. See Marjorie Hope Nicolson, *Mountain Gloom and Mountain Glory*, '... one of the curious paradoxes in the history of literature: that mountains, upon which modern poets have lavished their most extravagant rhetoric were for centuries described – when they were described at all – at best in conventional and unexciting imagery, at worst in terms of distaste and repulsion' (p. 17).

[8] 'Leeway' refers to the sideways drift of the boat caused by the wind.

[9] See Chet Van Duzer, 'On the Origins of Sea Monsters'.

[10] John Blake, *Sea Charts of the British Isles*, p. 112. He is quoting Daniel Defoe, *A Tour through the Whole Island of Great Britain*, 1724–26.

1849–1850;[11] Conrad's *Typhoon*, 1903, and again in Arthur Ransome's *We Didn't Mean to Go to Sea*, 1937. The 1953 East Coast floods were yet another reminder, if needed. It is an attribute used to this day in the charity appeals of the RNLI.

Equally clearly, from very early on, the sea was seen as *a means of mercantile trade*. So, the fear of the sea co-existed with the flourishing of maritime trade from many centuries before the birth of Christ – across the Mediterranean by the Phoenicians, the Greeks and the Romans; on the Indian Ocean and the China Sea.[12] Hayle, a port on the north coast of Cornwall, was a neolithic centre of the tin industry, trading with the Irish, the Bretons and the Phoenicians, from around 9000 to 3000 BC. Much later, 'the Venetian galley fleet came annually to Southampton en route for the Netherlands till the end of the fifteenth century'.[13] By the Middle Ages, there was an active trade between North and South Europe in metals, wine and wool.

The sea was also, of course, from the earliest times, *the location of fishing*. By Elizabethan times onwards, fishermen from Dartmouth and Teignmouth, in southwest England, voyaged each year across the Atlantic to catch and dry cod in Newfoundland.

Likewise, ships had long been used for *naval warfare*. The Battle of Actium, where Octavian defeated the combined fleets of Mark Antony and Cleopatra, was in 31 BC. An early English example is the Battle of Swanage Bay, where Alfred defeated the Danes in 877. They were also used to *transport armies*. 1147 saw 164 ships and 13,000 troops leave Dartmouth for the Second Crusade.[14] 1190 saw 34 ships leave from there for the Third Crusade.

They were also used as *a means of exploration leading to the discovery of new lands*. De Souza suggests that:

> The end of the fifteenth century and the beginning of the sixteenth mark a watershed in the history of the seafaring civilizations of the world. It was in this period that several European nations began to expand their maritime networks across the Atlantic, Indian and Pacific oceans … This expansion is impressively symbolised by the famous voyages of Columbus, Vasco da Gama, Magellan and others.[15]

---

[11] Dickens, *David Copperfield*, Chapter 55: 'Tempest'.
[12] Philip de Souza, *Seafaring and Civilization*.
[13] James Dunning, *The Maritime History of Southern England*, p. 6.
[14] Forced by bad weather into Porto, Portugal, they then agreed to take part in the siege of Lisbon, held by the Moors. After a successful siege, most of the army settled in Lisbon.
[15] Philip de Souza, *Seafaring and Civilization*, p. 5.

The English were not to be left out of the list of great explorers. In 1589, Richard Hakluyt (1553–1616), a member of the clergy, wrote his chief work *The Principall Navigations, Voiages and Discoveries of the English Nation*, using eyewitness accounts as far as possible. Between 1598 and 1600, he expanded this work into three volumes, indicating the Elizabethan desire for new trading opportunities.

Elizabethan and Early Stuart Times

'In 1588, Queen Elizabeth caused "a pleasure ship" to be built at Cowes [then known as Shamford]. This craft was called the *Rat of Wight*. She was 80 tons burden, and carried a crew of seventy men, under the command of Gilbert Lea.' We can see flexibility of use – for royal transport and by the navy – 'she was one of the volunteer fleet of Lord Charles Howard, which defeated the Spanish Armada'.[16]

Richard Ferris' Sail from London to Bristol, 1590

Possibly the earliest small-boat pleasure voyage recorded in detail was that of Richard Ferris, whose dates, according to the *Oxford Dictionary of Biography*, are 1561? to c. 1613. In 1590, he wagered that, with the defeat of the Armada in 1588, English command of the Channel was so complete that a wherry could make a safe passage from London to Bristol. He took a friend, Andrew Hill, and a skilled Thames waterman, William Thomas, which was a wise move since Ferris wrote that he himself 'was neuer trained vp on the water'.[17] Ferris refers mainly to his rowing, but he makes it clear that he chose the wherry for both its rowing and sailing capacity:

> The boate wherein I determined to perform my promise was new built, which I procured to be painted with greene, and the oares and sayle of the same colour, with the red crosse for England and her Maiesties armes ...[18]

His Victorian editor adds that 'the Gravesend wherries ... were generally safe and powerful boats, rigged with a foresail and mainsail, and they not unfrequently went out into rough water'.[19] Except for the Thames

---

[16] Arthur Clark, *History of Yachting 1600–1815*, p. 238.
[17] Richard Ferris, *The Most Dangerous and Memorable Adventure of Richard Ferris* (1590).
[18] Richard Ferris, *The Most Dangerous and Memorable Adventure of Richard Ferris*, p. 3.
[19] J. Payne Collier, Introduction, Richard Ferris, *The Most Dangerous and Memorable Adventure of Richard Ferris*, p. 1. Collier (1789–1883) was exposed as a forger of Shakespearian documents, but I have not read of any suggestion that the Ferris voyage is a fake.

passenger-carrying wherry, all wherries had sails. Their characteristic sail was a 'high-peaked sail set upon a long gaff with the mast forward'.[20]

Even so, there were considerable risks. They would have carried no charts as these were not marketed before the 1670s.[21] Instead, they would have received pilotage information ('local knowledge') about the next stretch of water from locals at each port they visited. Even so, they experienced difficulties at North Foreland, the Solent, St Aldhelm's, Portland and off Minehead. The seas were not quite as safe as he believed, because they only narrowly avoided pirates off Land's End by going inside the Runnelstone.[22] They were well received by the citizens of Dartmouth and Bristol, and the naval officers of Plymouth. The account was published in 1590 and included 'some very ordinary verses' – to quote Collier – by James Sargent, such as:

> From London cities this wager sure,
> Was for to bring his wherry small
> On surging seas, if life endure,
> From port to port, happe what happe shall,
> To Bristowe citie of worthie name,
> Where Ferris now hath spred his fame.

The aficionado of bad poetry had not long to wait for more, for Peter Heaton, in *Yachting: A History*, tells of:

> John Taylor, the 'water poet', who wrote long (and at times it must be admitted, tedious) poems about his coast-wise cruises. John Taylor, whose 'Pegasus' was a wherry, and … [who] flourished in the latter part of the sixteenth century.[23]

Taylor (1578–1653) was, for most of his life, a Thames waterman, and obviously was capable on the water, as one of his passages was from London to Queensborough on the Medway, 'in a paper boat with two stockfish tied to canes for oars', described in *The Praise of Hempseed*.[24] With a crew of three watermen, he rowed and sailed a wherry from London to York in 1622. He

---

[20] David Bray, *The Story of the Norfolk Wherries.*

[21] The first charts to be marketed were created by John Seller, a cartographer and scientific instrument maker based in Wapping. He published *The English Pilot Books I and II* in 1671–2 (John Blake, *Sea Charts of the British Isles*, p. 26).

[22] The Runnelstone is a drying rock one mile south of Gwennap Head. Gwennap is a short distance south of Land's End.

[23] Heaton, *Yachting: A History*, p. 49.

[24] http://en.wikipedia.org/wiki/John_Taylor_(poet); the references for *The Praise of Hempseed*, is www.Lumnarium.org/renascence-editions/taylor1.html. It is some fifty nautical miles from London Bridge to Queensborough, on the River Medway, a long way in a paper boat. (A nautical mile is 1.15 land miles.) I would assume the 'paper' to be papyrus reed, but it still

used a working wherry, took a compass and spare oars and tells us he was well victualled. He worked his way using the tides to Boston, Lincolnshire and then up river. In 1623, he made a passage from London to Salisbury, Wiltshire.

Phineas Pett and the *Disdain*

Next comes the much more substantial autobiography of Phineas Pett (1570–1647), a member of a long-running and extensive family of royal boat-builders from the time of Henry VIII, who, in 1543, had appointed Peter Pett a Master Shipwright.[25] Educated at Emmanuel College, Cambridge, Phineas, his second son, kept a journal. Like Pepys, he apparently transcribed it in chunks from his more frequently kept diary; and as with Pepys, it was proba-bly kept as an aide-memoire, for when his enemies, in those turbulent times, tried to do him down. (There is a long account of an inquiry against him in 1608–1609.)[26] His autobiography runs from 1570 to September, 1638. In early 1604, when Pett was a shipwright at the Chatham dockyard, James I ordered a small yacht for his first born, his ten-year-old son, Prince Henry (1594–1612):

> … about the 15th of January, being at Ratcliff with my wife, to christen her sister Simonson's daughter Martha, there was, unknown unto me, a letter sent post to Chatham from my Honourable Lord Admiral Howard, commanding me with all possible speed to build a little vessel for the young Prince Henry to disport himself in above London bridge, and acquaint his Grace with ship-ping and the manner of that element, setting me down the proportions and the manner of her garnishing, which was to be like the work of the *Ark Royal*, battlement wise.[27]

His instructions were to build a miniature of a ship of the line – the *Ark Royal* , which had fought gallantly against the Armada.[28] Pett built the boat with all possible speed, because there were only a limited number of master boatbuilders appointed by the Crown, a rank he had yet to achieve.

---

leaked very seriously. Stock fish are dried, unsalted fish, nowadays associated with northern Norway.

[25] Pett's journal was transcribed by Pepys. An abbreviated version, edited by Rev. S. Dunne, ap-peared in *Archeologia*, Vol. 12, 1796. A full version, edited by W. G. Perrin, was published by the Naval Records Society in 1918.

[26] *The Autobiography of Phineas Pett*, pp. 32–68.

[27] Ratcliff was a hamlet between Shadwell and Limehouse. It is now in the borough of Tower Hamlets, south of Stepney.

[28] John Rousmaniere, *The Luxury Yachts*, p. 20.

This little ship was in length by the keel 25 foot, and 12 foot in breadth, garnished with painting and carving both within board and without very curiously, according to his Lordship's directions. I laid her keel the 19th day of January, wrought upon her as well day as all night by [flaming] torch and candle lights under a great awning made with sails for that purpose.[29]

The Navy List for 1618 records her as being rated as 30 tons burden. The 'burden in tons' represents the net wine-carrying capacity of the ship in Bordeaux casks (i.e. 'tuns').[30] The 'tonnage' was an additional allowance equal to one-third of this; the 'ton and tonnage' representing the gross burden'.[31]

He launched the ship on 6 March and sailed out of the Medway and up the Thames:

On Wednesday, being the 14th day of March, by my Lord Admiral's commandment, we weighed from Limehouse, and anchored on the 14th March, by order of the Lord Admiral, moored right against the Tower before the King's Lodgings ... The 16th day, being Friday, we unrigged and shot the bridge, and the 17th we rigged again and received both ordnance and powder from the Tower.[32]

The bridge was London Bridge, the only bridge across the river in London throughout the seventeenth century. To get under it, he had to take the mast down.

On Sunday, in the afternoon, being the 18th day, fitted with a noise of trumpets and drums and fife, we weighed and turned up with the wind at southwest as high as Lambeth, with multitudes of boats and people attending upon us. As we passed by Whitehall, I saluted the Court with a volley of small shot and our great ordnance ...[33]

As was to be the case over the next 200 years, yachts were routinely furnished with cannon. These could be used for the purposes of self-defence or aggression, and, throughout the Caroline and Georgian eras and into mid-Victorian times, were also used for decoration, pomp and celebration.

On Thursday morning, being the 22nd day I received a commandment from the Lord Admiral to prepare the ship and all things fitting to receive the young prince aboard of us in the afternoon; who accordingly presently after dinner

[29] *The Autobiography of Phineas Pett*, p. 21.
[30] A 'tun' was a cask holding 252 gallons of wine (four 'hogsheads').
[31] W. G. Perrin, Footnote, *The Autobiography of Phineas Pett*, p. 96.
[32] Pett, *The Autobiography of Phineas Pett*, pp. 21–22.
[33] *Ibid.*, p. 22.

1 *The Embarkation of the Elector Palatine and Princess Elizabeth in the 'Prince Royal'
at Margate, 25 April 1613* by Adam Willaerts. The vessel to the left of the *Prince Royal*
is traditionally identified as the *Disdain*, built by Phineas Pett for James 1's son,
Prince Henry, in 1604.

came aboard us in his barge accompanied with the Lord High Admiral, Earl
of Worcester, and divers other noblemen. We presently weighed and fell
down as far as Paul's Wharf, under both our topsails and foresail, and there
came to anchor; and then his Grace, according to the manner in such cases
used, with a great bowl of wine christened the ship and called her by the
name of the *Disdain* ... [34]

Already at this early date, we see the memorialising of yachts in oil paint-
ings. The *Disdain* is traditionally identified as one of the smaller vessels in *The
Embarkation of the Elector Palatine and Princess Elizabeth in the Prince Royal at
Margate, 25 April, 1613* by Adam Willaerts.[35]

So popular was this little vessel with the royal children that a much more
substantial vessel was ordered from Pett.

About the middle of June [1612], by the commandment of Prince Henry, I
began to make ready a frame for a small new ship, who was to be as a pinnace

[34] *Ibid.*, pp. 22–23.
[35] James Taylor, *Yachts on Canvas: Artists' Images of Yachts from the Seventeenth Century to the
Present Day*, p. 19.

to the great ship, the *Prince*, in which the Prince's Highness did purpose to solace himself sometimes into the Narrow Seas; and therefore she was appointed to be fitted with a very roomy cabin and all other accommodations for that purpose; the keel of which ship was laid in the launching place at the old dock at Chatham the last day of June, being in length of 72 foot, in breadth 24 foot and to draw 11 foot water, of the burden 250 tons and tonnage, or thereabouts.[36]

A pinnace was, usually, a small, two-masted craft, using both sail and oars, to carry dispatches between naval vessels. This is much larger, which suggests that the king wanted to demonstrate his wealth.[37] 'The Narrow Seas' are the English Channel and the North Sea.

Pett record his last meeting with his sponsor, on the first of August of the same year, 1612. They had discussed various matters, presumably concerning the new vessel:

> … In conclusion, upon my parting with a most princely loving gravity, he gave me a farewell in these words 'Go on cheerfully' saith he 'in that which I entrust you with and let not the care of your posterity incumber you any ways, for you shall leave the care both of yourself and them to me, who have a purpose carefully to provide for you'; which gracious speeches took such impression in me, that when I came to kiss his Highness' hands at parting I could not choose but shed some tears, though I little thought (as God knoweth) that had been the last time I should have seen him alive, and those the last words that he ever spake unto me.[38]

Henry appears to be saying that he is so satisfied with Pett's work, that, in the event of his not being able to look after his relatives, say, through death, or possibly, by being accused and found guilty of corruption, he had no need to worry as he, Henry, would make sure that they were cared for. However, the Prince died, aged eighteen, of typhoid fever that winter, 1612, and the boat was never finished.

Pett also talks of a 'yoathe' in 1613. He was part of a royal fleet that visited Holland. He records in his *Autobiography*:

> The 28th day [April, 1613] we weighted about noon, and anchored thwart of Sluce [Sluis], where came on board us with yoathes [yachts], the Prince of

---

[36] Pett, *The Autobiography of Phineas Pett*, p. 96.
[37] I discuss ostentation in yacht ownership in greater length in Chapter 5.
[38] *Autobiography of Phineas Pett*, p. 98.

Orange, Grave [Count; Dutch 'Graaf'] Maurice with a great train of gallantry and followers, who all lay this night on board the Admiral.[39]

This is one of the first uses of the term in English, and it is not surprising that he uses it when in Dutch waters, since, as mentioned, the Dutch had been using yachts for various purposes for decades.

It was to be another fifty years before yachting re-surfaced. The dispute between Charles I and his Parliament, culminating in the Civil War (1642–1651), was too serious to allow for the development of aquatic sport.

[39] *Ibid.*, p. 109.

CHAPTER TWO

Restoration Yachting and Its Purposes

Charles II introduced yachting into this country and the sport was taken up by a few high prestige individuals outside the Royal family, such as Sir William Petty and Roger North.

Charles II and His Yachts

Up to the end of the eighteenth century, the word 'yacht' had much wider definitions than being only a leisure craft. As early as 1599, an Antwerp dictionary defined 'jaght schip' or 'jaght' as 'a swift, light vessel of war, commerce or pleasure'.[1] This definition reflected the use by the Dutch of yachts for transport and business on Holland's shallow lakes and inland seas. These uses of yachts were introduced into England by Charles II in the middle of the seventeenth century.

In 1646, when his father was losing the Civil War, his son, the future Charles II, fled from Falmouth to the Scillies, and thence to Jersey. He passed the time learning to sail in these locations and, in the summer of 1646, had a boat built at St Malo, borrowing the money from the Governor of Jersey. He then left for France where his mother was living. In 1648, he moved to the Hague, Holland.

As already mentioned, yachts had an important place in Dutch political and economic activity. Heaton wrote:

> The Dutch did not race their yachts, but by the seventeenth century they were using them for many other purposes. There were yachts employed on Government business; passenger-carrying yachts; Admiralty yachts in the service of the Navy; dispatch yachts and many privately owned yachts,

---

[1] Gordon Davis, *Dartmouth Royal Regatta*, pp. 2–3. 'The first nautical dictionary was written as early as the 1620s by Sir Henry Mainwaring and published in 1644. It incorporated both the technical language of seamanship and … sailor's slang' (Mack, *The Sea: A Cultural History*, p. 190).

magnificently painted, sporting lofty sterns and high bowsprits, belonging to
the wealthy citizens of Amsterdam, Rotterdam and other towns.

For the Dutch, by the middle of the seventeenth century 'a yacht was a
normal possession of a person of wealth and rank', an ostentatious way of
demonstrating that status, but also 'an essential of life in a country where
water was always nearby'.[2]

We are indebted to the contemporary diarists, John Evelyn (1620–1706),
and, especially, his lifelong friend Samuel Pepys (1633–1703) for much of
our information about Charles' yachts.[3] Sadly, Pepys, usefully positioned as
Secretary to the Naval Board, only kept his diary for nine years (1660–1669),
before, fearing he was going blind, taking his doctor's advice to stop his
record.

Charles was in Breda when he was proclaimed King of England at
Westminster Hall on 8 May, 1660. Pepys accompanied his master and cousin
Admiral Lord Montague, later created the Earl of Sandwich, as his secretary,
to escort Charles back from his exile.

The Dutch, in a nice demonstration of their wealth, offered thirteen
yachts to take the gentlemen of the Court through Holland to the coast.[4]
Also, as Adrian Vlackett recorded in a contemporary account written in 1660:

> Each yacht had her own steward, cooks and officers who were in charge of the
> pantry, kitchen and wines, and those yachts which had not suitable kitchens
> on board were accompanied by other vessels, wherein stoves for the kitchen
> had been provided, also ovens for baking and there had been made great pro-
> vision of so great a quantity of all kinds of food, game, confitures, and wines
> and all the tables were so fully served, that the stewards of the English lords,
> though accustomed to abundance were astonished thereat, and confessed
> that they could not conceive by what means twenty or twenty-five great

---

[2] Heaton, *A History of Yachting in Pictures*, p. 8.
[3] We must thank the nineteenth-century thirst for archival research for the publication of these
journals. Evelyn was first published in 1818. Pepys had left his extensive library, 3,000 books
and six volumes of his diary to his old college, Magdalene, but there they stayed (Claire Tomalin, *Samuel Pepys*, pp. 378–386).

Stratford Canning, the diplomat, wrote in his diary for 3 June, 1820:

I called on [William] Gifford [editor of the *Quarterly*] ... we talked of his *Review* ... He told me
he had lately seen a curious journal kept by a person named Pepys, who had been Secretary to the
Admiralty in Charles II's time ... Part of it will probably be published by Murray.

This was the rather poorly transcribed Braybrooke edition, published in 1824 – Pepys was
rather sexually active with ladies of the lower classes, an embarrassment to the Victorian biographer. See Latham and Matthews' chapter on 'Previous Editions' in their complete transcription of Pepys' diaries (Pepys, *The Diary of Samuel Pepys: A New and Complete Transcription*).
[4] Clark, *The History of Yachting*, p. 52.

dishes for each table could be prepared on board the yachts and with the motion of the water.[5]

Charles had expressed his pleasure at the fine vessel he was loaned and said that 'he might order one of the same style as soon as he should arrive in England'. The Burgemeester (Mayor) of Amsterdam, Cornelis Van Vlooswyck, in yet another show of wealth, said that 'lately a yacht had been built in Amsterdam which was almost of the same size and at least as handsome, and he took the liberty of presenting it to his Majesty'.[6] The Dutch delivered their present, the *Mary*, to Charles in London in August, 1660.[7]

The *Mary* was 52 foot long on the keel, with a breadth of 19 feet and a draught of 7 feet 7 inches. She carried lee boards in the Dutch manner.[8] Thirty men and eight guns were crammed aboard England's first true yacht.[9]

Charles was eager to see if his shipbuilders could improve on the *Mary*. Pepys, by then the Secretary to the Naval Board, entered in his diary for 8 November, 1660:

> In the afternoon, Commissioner [Peter] Pett [son of the Phineas Pett who built the *Disdain*] and I went on board the yaght [*Mary*], which endeed is one of the finest things that I ever saw for neatness and room in so small a vessel. Mr. Pett is to make one to out-do this for the Honour of his country, which I fear he will scarce better.[10]

Pepys was impressed by its neatness, for he was comparing the use of space on the yacht with that of a warship. Yacht building cannot have been alien to the English shipwright if Pett was immediately expected to be able to improve on the Dutch yacht.

When Pepys went to check how Pett was getting on with the *Catherine*, his confidence in her superiority increased:

---

[5] Maldwin Drummond, *Salt-Water Palaces*, p. 12.

[6] Clark, *The History of Yachting*, p. 51.

[7] It may seem strange that within five years, Holland and England were at war, but John Torrance (personal communication, September 2015) points out that this was a period of intense rivalry between the two countries, whether expressed by giving extravagant presents or by actual war; and, of course, within thirty-five years, a Dutch king was on the throne of England. Incidentally, this was the second Anglo-Dutch war, the first being 1652–1654 in which the Commonwealth defeated the Dutch navy.

[8] *Lee boards* were two pivoting boards fitted to the side of a flat-bottomed boat. The leeward board is lowered to provide lateral resistance and prevent sideway drift. The windward board is raised to prevent it twisting and being damaged.

[9] Drummond, *Salt-Water Palaces*, p. 12.

[10] *The Diary of Samuel Pepys*, Vol. 1, pp. 286–287.

> January 13th, 1661: … So to the Globe to dinner, and then with Commissioner [Peter] Pett to his lodgings there (which he hath for the present while he is building the King's yacht, which will be a pretty thing, and much superior to the Dutchman's.)[11]

The King's brother, the future James II and the Admiral of the Fleet, had a yacht, the *Anne*, built at Woolwich by Christopher, another of the clan of shipbuilding Petts, being a son of Peter, the commissioner.

These first two yachts – the *Catherine* and the *Anne*– were fairly close copies of the Dutch present, the *Mary*. The *Catherine* had a length of keel of 49 feet, a breadth of 19 feet, depth 7 feet and 94 tons burden. We know the estimated cost of the *Catherine*. In the Admiralty Papers of 3 November, 1660, it is recorded '… estimate by Peter Pett of the charges of building a new yacht of 80 tones for the King at Deptford; total 1,335 pound sterling'.[12] It is worth bearing in mind that, despite their ostentation, the King's yachts were coming out of the Naval budget, and, as such, belonged to the Navy. They were routinely armed with guns.

The *Anne* had the measurements: length of keel 52 feet, breadth 19 feet, depth 7 feet and 100 tons burden, at a cost of £1,815. 2.4. Each carried 8 guns and a crew of 30 men. Their sails were of 'Holland Duck … the best canvas for sails for the Duke of York's pleasure yacht now building [at Woolwich], the same as is to be bought for the King's new yacht now at Deptford'. Both were named after the owners' wives.

In 1661, the Dutch gave Charles another yacht as a present – the *Bezan*. Smaller than the *Mary*, her length of keel being 34 feet, the *Bezan* was used as the standard against which to measure the speed of new yachts being built for the king.[13]

Perhaps the first yacht race in England, certainly the first one to be recorded, took place on 1 October, 1661, between Charles' *Catherine* and his brother, James' *Anne*, from Greenwich to Gravesend and back for 100 guineas. Pepys makes no record of this event, perhaps because he wasn't invited. Fortunately for posterity, John Evelyn was on hand, on board the *Catherine*.[14]

---

[11] *The Diary of Samuel Pepys*, Vol. 2, p. 12.

[12] Heaton, *Yachting: A History*, pp. 35–37. Clark, in his *The History of Yachting*, p. 61, states that this is the first recorded spelling of 'yacht'.

[13] There is a 1661 painting of the *Bezan* by B. C. Kleeneknecht is in the Sheepvaart Museum, Amsterdam.

[14] Evelyn was closer to the King than Pepys. While Pepys had been sympathetic to the Roundhead cause, Evelyn, as a devoted Royalist, had thought it prudent to spend the Civil War abroad. The quote that follows is from *The Diary of John Evelyn*, Vol. 3, pp. 296–297.

2 *Calm: The English Yacht 'Portsmouth' at Anchor*, by William Van de Velde the Elder. The use of oil paintings, from the earliest days of yachting, to memorialise the owner's yachts and to show how no expense has been spared, is clearly shown in this picture, where the ornate scrollwork is highlighted. *Portsmouth*, named after Charles' mistress and confidante, Louise de Keroualle, whom he created the Duchess of Portsmouth, was built at Woolwich Dockyard in 1674 by Phineas Pett.

The opening remark in the passage below shows the novelty of yachting in England at that time:

October 1. I sailed this morning with his *Majestie* (on) one of his Yaachts (or Pleasure boates), Vessells newly known amongst us, til the *Duch* [East India Company] presented that curious piece to the King [the *Mary*], & very excellent sailing Vessels. It was on a Wager betweene his other new *Pleasure boate* [the *Catherine*], built fregate-like, and one of the *Duke* of Yorks [*the Anne*]; the wager 100 pounds. The race from *Greenwich* to *Gravesend* and back: The King lost it going, wind Contrary, but sav'd stakes returning. There were divers noble Person(s) and Lords on board: his Majestie sometimes steering himselfe: There attended his *Barge* and Kitchin boate: I brake fast this morning with the King, at returne in his smaller Vessell [the *Bezan*], he being pleasd to take me & only foure more, who were Noble-men, with him; but dined in his *Yacht* where we Eate together with his *Majestie*.

Evelyn is obviously pleased to enjoy such exclusive company. Generally, Charles preferred cruising to racing. 'Lord Arlington records that he would steal away from Windsor on any pretence and board his fleet at Sheerness for a cruise to Plymouth or other ports along the South Coast';[15] and also along the Essex and Suffolk coast, sailing from Harwich to Aldeburgh on a Sunday afternoon in 1668.[16]

Charles had at least twenty-six yachts built during his reign with fourteen built between 1671 and 1677.[17] They were all named after women – wife, sisters, mistresses. The yacht *Portsmouth* was named after his favourite mistress, Louise de Kérouaille, whose advice he gave most weight to, and whom he created Duchess of Portsmouth. When she put on a bit of a weight, the second yacht named after her was called *Fubbs* ('Fubby' signified 'plump' or 'chubby').

On one of his last sails, Charles II took the *Fubbs* along the Kentish coast and it got so rough that the King and his brother, the Duke of York, had to help man the ropes to preserve the vessel. The king had requested that John Gostling, a subdean at St Pauls, accompany them because of his fine voice. The King himself had a fine tenor voice and would join in on the easier songs, while at times the Duke of York would accompany them on the guitar.[18] The association of singing and yachting, especially once the anchor is safely down, is a long one.

Charles' queen was the Portuguese princess, Catherine of Braganza. Sir Anthony Deane built a yacht for her at Portsmouth, called the *Solalis*, a vessel of 180 tons burden, with which she sailed to Lisbon in 1670.[19] She also owned a smaller yacht, the *Sandadoes*, 86 tons, built for her at Deptford in 1670. She sailed in it to Portugal in 1672–73, and also used it for pleasure excursions on the Thames.[20]

Charles clearly built his yachts to demonstrate his wealth:

All were visions of opulence, with elaborately gilded bulwarks and soaring poop decks. Some had ornate figureheads, usually in the form of a bird's

---

[15] Clark, *The History of Yachting*, p. 110.
[16] Frank Hussey, *Old Fitz*, p. 6.
[17] Rousmaniere, *The Luxury Yachts*, p. 25; Phillips-Birt, *The History of Yachting*, p. 15.
[18] Clark, *The History of Yachting*, p. 114.
[19] Ibid., pp. 103–104.
[20] Janet Cusack, 'The Rise of Aquatic Recreation and Sport', p. 318.

head. Nearly all mounted guns, mostly for decoration and for firing salutes; many of the gunports were encircled by wreaths of gilded woods. Besides the customary signal flags, the royal yachts carried a full inventory of large silk ceremonial flags; they accounted for more than 10 per cent of the yachts' cost. And belowdecks, Charles's yachts were almost as sumptuous as his palaces. Bulkheads were panelled in mahogany; crimson damask hung at the portholes and around the beds. Such appointments as Holland quilts and pewter chamber pots added to the ambiance – and to the price.[21]

Such opulence needed to be memorialised. The oil painting was the main means of recording contemporary events, even if only for the eyes of the owner and his circle, and it was the chief mode of representing yachts and yachting till the advent of the camera in the late nineteenth century. These pictures were reconstructed by the artist to illustrate the scene desired by his patron – paintings are constructed creations, not elaborate photographs.

On 20 February, 1674, Charles instructed the Treasurer of the Navy to pay salaries to two artists:

> We have thought fit to allow the salary of one hundred pounds per annum unto WILLIAM VANDERVELDE the Elder, for taking and making of Draughts [drawings] of Sea Fights; and the like Salary of One Hundred pounds per annum unto WILLIAM VANDERVELDE the younger, for putting the said draughts into colours [oil paintings] for Our particular use.[22]

The Dutch economy was depressed in the early 1670s, due to the French invasion of 1672, which had decimated trade. Willem van de Velde the Elder (1611–1693) and his son, Willem the Younger (1633–1707), the two most outstanding marine artists of their generation, accepted this generous offer, which included studio space in the Queen's House, Greenwich.

To be considered talented, a maritime artist had to understand how boats were put together and how they sailed – i.e. their pictures had to achieve realism. This skill had to be married to the ability to present the boat at its most attractive. Thus, quite often, the ornate stern of these yachts was given prominence, which also emphasised the ability of the owner to afford such wealth. In many pictures, the ship was depicted twice, once from the stern, and one from broadside under sail. That the van de Veldes were men of substance who sailed themselves is shown by plans that have been found for a yacht built for them, with their own coat of arms.[23]

[21] Rousmaniere, *The Luxury Yachts*, p. 25.
[22] Oliver Warner, *An Introduction to British Maritime Painting*, p. 10.
[23] Heaton, *A History of Yachting in Pictures*, p. 11.

Major works of theirs included the Elder's *Calm: The English Yacht 'Portsmouth'*, in 1675. Charles had purchased the brig *Surprise*, which had taken him to safety after the battle of Worcester. He had it anchored off Westminster, renamed it the *Royal Escape*, and opened it to royal visitors, making it perhaps the first museum ship. [24] It was duly painted by van de Velde the Younger.

The royal use of yachts and their patronage of the Van de Veldes undoubtedly gave maritime art and seascapes a boost in prestige, and widened the demand for such works. So the tradition of memorialising yachts was started long before there were many yachts being built.

Naval Uses of Charles' Yachts

It is important not to see Charles solely as using yachts for leisure. He only kept one or two yachts at any one time for his leisure sailing. Despite their opulence, these yachts were armed with cannon and had multiple State uses. For example, Pepys noted: 'this day [21 November, 1662] came the King's pleasure boats from Calis with the Dunkirke money, being 400000 pistols' (The money was paid by France in exchange for Dunkirk.)[25] His first yacht, the *Mary*, recorded as the first yacht of the Royal Navy, was being used to run his senior civil servants between Holyhead and Dublin when it was wrecked on the Skerries, rocky islands outside Holyhead, on 25 March, 1675.[26]

Some of the top echelon of the king's servants had yachts. 'The Lord Lieutenant of Ireland, the Commissioners of the Dockyards and the Governor of the Isle of Wight all had yachts attached to their appointments.'[27]

The yachts were given to the Navy for the duration of the various wars with the Dutch. During the Second Dutch War (1665–1667), all the Royal yachts were handed over to the Navy for the duration as fast despatch vessels to the fleet.[28] The *Fanfan*, 55 feet long, was built for Prince Rupert of the Rhine, a senior admiral under Charles II, by Sir Anthony Deane and was involved in the St James Day Battle off Lowestoft in 1666, even harassing De Ruyter's flagship, the *Seven Provinces*. Another royal yacht, the *Henrietta*,

---

[24] Drummond, *Salt-Water Palaces*, p. 11.

[25] *The Diary of Samuel Pepys*, Vol. 3, p. 262.

[26] The wreck was located and the artefacts dug up and analysed by a team led by Professor Peter Davies of Liverpool University in 1971. See Peter Davies, 'The Discovery of the *Mary*, Charles II's Yacht', and 'The Discovery and Excavation of the Royal Yacht, *Mary*'.

[27] Dalton, *British Royal Yachts*, p. 20.

[28] Ernle Bradford, *Three Centuries of Sailing*, p. 30.

was sunk in the Battle of Texel by the Dutch in 1673, the same year that the *Catherine* was captured by them.

By improving *yacht design*, Charles hoped to improve *naval* vessels. Pepys, a shrewd judge, commented in 1662 on the quality of the build, and this was shown by the very long lives of some of the yachts. The *Mary*, built at Chatham in 1677, was finally broken up in 1816. The *Fubbs*, built in 1682, lasted till 1781 and the *Augusta*, built as the *Charlotte* in 1677, was sold in Deptford in 1818.[29] So, British yachts got a reputation for excellence of construction.

Charles' Encouragement of Navigational Science

Recognising the importance of the Royal and Mercantile navies for the nation's well-being, Charles saw how yachts could be used to advance the knowledge of the sea and ships'.[30] In the Second Dutch War, 1665–1667, it had become clear that the Dutch had better charts of British waters than the British did.[31] Charles, accordingly, authorised Captain Greenville Collins to make the first comprehensive survey of the British coastline.

Two of the royal yachts – the 53 foot *Merlin*, from 1681 to 1683 and the 52 foot *Monmouth*, from 1683 to 1688 – were lent to Collins who 'with inadequate funds and equipment, prepared 120 plans of harbours and stretches of open coast, forty-eight of which were engraved'.[32] This took Collins seven years from 1682 to 1689. *Great Britain's Coasting Pilot*, published in 1693 by the chart sellers Mount and Page, ran through nineteen editions and was sold till 1792.[33]

A group of scientists had begun meeting in the mid-1640s, and formed themselves into 'a Colledge for the Promoting of Physico-Mathematicall Experimentall Learning' after a lecture by Christopher Wren on 28 November, 1660. This became the Royal Society in 1662, when Charles granted it a Royal Charter. Early members included the chemist, Robert Boyle, the physicist Robert Hooke and Sir Christopher Wren. They followed Francis Bacon (1561–1626) in believing that the application of the scientific method could,

---

[29] C. G.'t Hooft, 'The First English Yachts', *Mariner's Mirror*, 5 (1912), pp. 108–123.

[30] Drummond, *Sea-Water Palaces*, p. 18.

[31] A large proportion of the charts in *The English Pilot*, published by the King's Hydrographer, John Seller in 1671, were copies of Dutch charts.

[32] 'Greenville Collins', in Kemp, ed., *The Oxford Companion to Ships and the Sea*, p. 181.

[33] John Blake, *The Sea Chart*, p. 39. Collins 'dedicated the first accurate chart of the Harwich Harbour regions to Samuel Pepys', who, as First Secretary to the Admiralty, had commissioned the work (Hussey, *The Royal Harwich: A Short History of the RHYC*, p. 3).

and, in due course, would, solve all problems.[34] Thus, the development of better and faster sea-going vessels was seen as clearly amenable to experimentation and improvement. John Evelyn was elected a Fellow in 1663, and Pepys in 1665, the same year that he received 'a very neat silver watch' as a bribe from 'one Briggs a Scrivener [a man who draws up legal contracts] and Solicitor'.[35] Pepys was so delighted with this amazing innovation that he walked from Greenwich to Woolwich several times, finding that the time taken only varied by two minutes.

In the Royal Society, members were quick to see that time, rather than distance, might be used to measure longitude, and Pepys helped his Fellows by getting hold of the logs of captains who were using Huygens' pendulum watch.[36] The results, however, were not encouraging, as the watches did not keep good enough time, a problem not solved till Harrison's spring-regulated timekeeper nearly a century later.[37]

A year later, in 1666, Pepys learnt from the Harwich shipbuilder, Sir Anthony Deane, how a vessel's displacement could be calculated, which allowed one to estimate its draught, an important step in scientific shipbuilding.[38]

Charles commissioned the Royal Observatory in 1675, and it was completed in 1676, the first astronomer royal being John Flamsteed. The accurate plotting of the movement of the planets and stars allows one to find one's position at sea by means of a sextant and 'reduction' tables that convert the angles recorded to the position of the boat at the time the sight was taken.

Sir William Petty and the *Experiment*

Catamarans (from *catta* meaning 'tie' and *maram* meaning 'wood' in Tamil) did not become popular till after the Second World War, but were developed

---

[34] Ashley (*England in the Seventeenth Century*, pp. 156–157) lists many of the original members.

[35] We know it was a bribe because Pepys was angry with his wife 'for receiving, or at least for opening the box wherein it was, and so far witnessing our receipt of it as to give the messenger 5s for bringing it. But it can't be helped and I will endeavour to do the man a kindness – he being a friend of my uncle Wight' (17 April, 1665). Corruption and backhanders were rife throughout this period. It is likely that Pepys was involved in these processes (J. D. Davies, *Pepys' Navy*).

[36] Christiaan Huygens, FRS (1629–1695) was a multi-talented Dutch scientist. He invented the pendulum watch, which kept time far more accurately than any other watch or clock for its time.

[37] Dava Sobel and William J. H. Andrewes, *The Illustrated 'Longitude'*.

[38] Deane wrote a pioneering work on how to design a warship. He also built fast yachts, such as the *Cleveland* of 1671 and the even faster *Charles* of 1675 (Brian Lavery, Introduction, in Deane, *Deane's Doctrine of Naval Architecture, 1670*, pp. 25 and 16).

in Charles' time. Sir William Petty (1623–1687), civil servant, a pioneer in census techniques, and a founder member of the Royal Society, designed a 'Double Bottom' ship, a prototype catamaran, called by himself the *Invention*. Petty had probably heard of such craft from sailors' accounts of catamarans off the coast of India, seen when they were working for the East India Company.

Petty built a number of catamarans, the first in 1662. Interest was so great that a committee was appointed by the Royal Society to examine the vessel and to organise a race in Dublin Bay against all comers. Three other boats competed with the catamaran on January, 1663, and Petty's vessel won easily.[39]

Adrian O'Connell suggests that Petty was aiming 'to prove that he would be able to transport the Royal Mail across the Irish Sea to Anglesey at over twice the speed of the then Mail boat'.[40] Petty therefore built a second, much bigger vessel, *Invention II*.

Pepys, in a diary entry for 31 July, 1663, carefully notes its technical details and achievement:

> Before I went to the office, I went to the Coffee-house where Sir J Cutler and Mr. Grant came. And there Mr. Grant showed me letters of Sir Wm. Pettys, wherein he says that his vessel which he hath built upon two Keeles (a modell whereof, built for the King, he showed me) [*Invention II*] hath this month won a wager of 50*l*. [pounds] in sailing between Dublin and Holyhead with a pacquett-boat, the best ship or vessel the King hath there; and he offers to lay with any ship of the world. It is about 30 Ton in burden and carries 30 men, with good accommodacion ... This carries also ten guns, of about five Tons weight.
>
> In their coming back from Holyhead, they started together, and this vessel came to Dublin by 5 at night, and the pacquett-boat not before 8 the next morning; and when they came they did believe this vessel had been drownded, or at least behind, not thinking she could have lived in that sea.
>
> Strange things are told of this vessel ...[41]

The *Experiment* sailed to London, but Petty was subjected to ridicule and mocking, among whose numbers was the King. The vessel sank in 1665, during a storm in the Irish Sea, when returning to Dublin. Petty, who had

---

[39] The Yachtsman, *British Yachts and Yachtsmen*, p. 72 ff.
[40] Adrian O'Connell, 'Royal Western Yacht Club of Ireland – Club History'. 'The first packet boats began to sail out of Holyhead in the 1570s' (Jamie Owen, *Magic Islands*, p. 64).
[41] *The Diary of Samuel Pepys*, Vol. 4., pp. 256–257.

fanatical faith in his design, built a number of 'double-bottom' ships – three in 1662–1664 and a fourth in 1684 – but was too far ahead of his time.[42]

Yacht Owners in Charles' Reign

Several high-ranking personages had their own yachts. Among these were Francis, Lord Dacre of Herstmonceaux and Pevensey, Sussex, who had a pleasure boat in the early 1640s. The household accounts for Herstmonceux Castle, in the year 1643/4, show 'the sum of £6 paid to George Richardson for making a dock at Pemsie [Pevensey] for my lord's yought'.[43]

The *Charlotte* was owned by the Surveyor to the Navy, Sir William Batten. Pepys again:

> 3. [September, 1663]: ... and then to Sir. W. Batten who is going this day for pleasure were going to the Downes [off Deal]. I eat a breakfast with them, and at my Lady's desire with them by coach to Greenwich, where I went aboard with them on the *Charlotte* yacht. The wind very fresh, and I believe they will be all sick enough – besides she is mighty troublesome on the water.

The troublesome 'she' is Lady Batten, and Pepys' prediction was correct:

> 5. [September] ... I hear this day that Sir W Batten was fain to put ashore at Quinbrough [Queensborough, Isle of Sheppey] with my Lady, who hath been so sick shee swears never to go to sea again.[44]

Not the last sailor's wife to make that vow.

Other private yacht owners included Colonel Francis Wyndham, who Pepys described as only sailing for pleasure, not for duty.[45] 'In 1667 an artist called John Griffiere, or Griffier, purchased 'probably a smack or small hoy' and made her his floating studio, cruising in the Thames, sketching as he went. One account is that he was wrecked off Holland.[46] In 1671, the yacht *Industry* took Charles Fox and a party of Quaker Friends to Maryland, USA, by way of the West Indies.

In 1677, Captain Jeremy Roch of the King's Navy sailed from Plymouth to London and back in, to quote him, 'a little boat' for pleasure. At Cowes, he resolves 'to give my bones some ease in a good feather bed for one night'. The next morning, 'having replenished the bottles', he takes on board 'un

---

[42] *The Diary of Samuel Pepys*, Vol. 5, footnote 3, p. 256; Drummond, *Salt-Water Palaces*, pp. 16–17.
[43] Dalton, *British Royal Yachts*, p. 19.
[44] *The Diary of Samuel Pepys*, Vol. 4, pp. 296 and 298.
[45] Pepys, *The Tangier Papers of Samuel Pepys*, p. 110.
[46] 'The Yachtsman', *British Yachts and Yachtsmen*, pp. 68–69.

povre franchman dat want de passage de Londra… thinking that he might be serviceable in rowing if need were, but instead of that, he only served to devour our meat and drink'.[47] He was aware of the uniqueness of this voyage for at the end of his record, he bursts into poetry:

> Thus Ends a Voyage none e'er perform'd before
> In such a Boat to Coast Albions Shore!
> From Plymouth to London and back agen
> Is a great Wonder to the Sons of Men
> And may in future times be deemed as Strange
> As those with Ships that Round the World did range.

Roch is contrasting his *Boat* with much larger *Ships*, sea-going vessels.[48] In 1678, he sailed in the *Mercury* yacht, again from Plymouth towards London. On the return passage, he was caught in a ferocious storm off Deal. He upped anchor and ran before the storm and was wrecked at Sandforde, Holland, 4 miles from Haarlem.

Roger North and the Pleasures of Sailing

The best record of yacht cruising in Caroline times was written by the Honourable Roger North (1653–1734).[49]

Like Pepys a Cambridge man, North rose to be King's Counsel in 1682. We find the use of the yacht for prestigious entertainment and the consumption of large amounts of alcohol aboard ship:

> On of the last seal day [Motion Day in the Court of Chancery], wee top practicers in chancery, as usuall, made merry together, in a frolik wold goe to sea, as I use to call it. I sent for the yacht, which had layne all Trinity terme in the heat, uncawkt, so that her upper work was open, tho (her) bottom was as tight as a dish. Wee went aboard, and when the vessel began to heal, the water came in at her seams, and flowd in the cabin where the company was, who were too warme to perceiv such an inconvenience till at last they were almost up to the knees, and then they powdered out [rushed out]; wee called for boats, and went ashoar, and the yacht was run ashoar, to prevent sinking downright. This made much merryment when wee came together againe, discovering what a present wee had like to have made to our freinds

---

[47] Roch, 'The Journals of Jeremy Roch', p. 91.

[48] Joachim Schult, in *The Sailing Dictionary*, gives two relevant definitions of 'ship': '1. A sea-going vessel, larger than a boat. 2. Strictly, a three-masted *full-rigged sailing ship* with a full set of *square sails* on each mast' (p. 253) (Schult's italics).

[49] North's *Notes of Me* was first published in 1887.

at the barr, by sinking and drowning, the primier practisers and so making way for the rest.[50]

The cause of the near-disaster, was that the boat was 'uncaulkt'. Having been out of the water, the seams between her planks had dried out in the sunlight and opened up. They should have been filled by caulking – forcing oakum (tarred fibres) into the seams with a mallet.

The relevant definition of 'warme' in the *OED* is 'Of persons. Glowing with exertions or exercise, with eating or drinking, etc.' The juxtaposition of yachting and drinking, usually good quality wine or spirits, is one that continues throughout the history of yachting; as does minimising the dangers of mixing drinking and sailing.

North was, like Pepys and Evelyn, a 'virtuoso', which is defined in the *OED* (giving the seventeenth-century meaning) as 'one who has a general interest in arts and sciences, or who pursues special investigations in one or more of these, a learned person, a scientist, savant or scholar'.[51] The opening line of the quote below, with its juxtaposition of sailing with 'mathematicall enterteinements' is very characteristic of the virtuoso:

> Another of my mathematicall enterteinments was sailing. I was extream fond of being master of anything that would saile, and consulting Mr John Windham about it, he incouraged me with a present of a yacht, built for himself. Which I kept 4 years in the Thames, and received great delight in her ...

> This yacht was small, but had a cabbin and a bed-room a-thirt-ships, aft the mast, and a larg locker at the helme; the cook-room, with a cabin for a servant, was foreward on, with a small chimny at the very prow. Her ordinary sail, was a boom mainsail, stay foresail and gibb. All wrought aft, so wee could sail without a hand ahead, which was very troublesome, because of the spray that was not, (sailing to windward) to be endured.

> ... She was no good sea-boat, because she was open aft, and might ship a sea, to sink her, especially afore the wind in a storme, when the surg breaks over, faster than her way flys. But in the river she would sail tolerable, and work extraordinarily well. She was ballast with cast lead. It was a constant

---

[50] Roger North, *Notes of Me*, p. 102.
[51] Pepys' curiosity was wide-ranging – naval matters, science and music. Evelyn experimented with horticulture and laid out a beautiful garden at his house in Sayes Court, Deptford. North developed a system of natural and moral philosophy.

enterteinement to sail against smacks, and hoys, of which the river was all-
wais full.[52]

This reads remarkably well, and translated into more modern English,
would pass for a description of a yacht's qualities today. North is commenting on water coming aboard, filling the cockpit and thereby causing the boat
to founder. This was because the yacht did not have a self-draining cockpit.

His account of the pleasures of sailing, again, has a contemporary ring:

> When I prepared for one of these voyages I used to victuall my vessel, with
> cold meats in tin cases, bottles of beer, ale, and for the seamen brandy. ...

> For the day proved cool, the gale brisk, air clear and no inconvenience to
> molest us, nor wants to trouble our thoughts, neither buissness to impor-
> tune, nor formalitys to teas us; so that wee came neerer to a perfection in life
> there, then I was ever sensible of otherwise ...

He is representing sailing as a mode of relaxation and cutting oneself off from
work.

'Brisk gale' meant a 'fresh breeze'. Thus in *The Taming of the Shrew*, Act 1,
Scene 2, line 48, Hortensio asks Petruchio 'What happie gale Blowes you to
Padua heere, from old Verona?'; and in 1626, Captain Smith, in *An Accidence
for Young Seamen or the Pathway to Experience Necessary for All Young Seamen*,
p. 17, lists wind strengths as 'A calme, a brese, a fresh gaile, a pleasant gayle, a
stiffe gayle' (*OED*).

North cruised the London River and in 1675 went as far as Harwich. He
recounts that he had a crew of 'a man, and a boy, with my self and one servant,
and ... a pilott' 'who understood the northcours out of the river well; being
used to carry lampreys into Holland'.[53]

> At Harwich, wee were askt if wee had left our souls at London, because wee
> took so litle care of our bodys. For our vessel was not storme proof ...[54]

Clearly, this sail had elicited much shaking of the head by the Essex maritime
professionals, doubtless to North's satisfaction.

---

[52] Roger North, *Notes of Me*, p. 101. 'A-thirt-ships': nowadays 'athwartships', across the beam of
the boat, not along the length of the boat. 'All wrought aft': all the sheets (the ropes that control the sails) were brought aft into the cockpit, so that they did not have to be handled on the
deck, which would be more dangerous.

[53] North, *Notes on Me*, p. 101. The 'northcours' or north course, would have been a channel in the
northern part of the Thames Estuary.

[54] *Ibid.*, pp. 105–107.

They returned to the Thames, and anchored not too far ahead of four great East India Men, in the King's Channel. It was a balmy night:

> ... at midnight in the air, the eating cold meat, and bread; and drinking small beer, was a regale beyond imagination, I can say I scarce evere knew the pleasure of eating till then, and have not observed the like on any occasion since.[55]

This is an early account of the satisfaction of a meal when the sailing is done and the anchor safely down. In modern English, it could come straight out of 1930s account of creek crawling in Essex.

Another modern touch is the possible use of the yacht to avoid customs. The pilot asks whether they could take on some contraband from the [East] India men that are anchored near them, North refuses:

> Considereing that if I was caught smugling as they call it, I should be laught at for being condemned to forfet my vessel at the custome hous, where my owne brother, was a ruling commissioner, as he had certeinly done.

Concluding, North apologises for the length of his account, saying:

> And I must needs recommend it to all persons, that are fond of pleasure, to gratifie all inclinations this way, which makes health, the chief good wee know, rather then those of weomen, or of the belly, which weaken nature and destroy health.[56]

He may well be contrasting the health-giving properties with high living and permissive ways of the Court.

Frank Hussey, in his history of *The Royal Harwich*, after mentioning North's sail from the London river to Harwich, comments: 'Vivid, too, are Thomas Bowery's log entries of 1694 to 1701, made while cruising in the *Duck* yacht of the burthen of about fourteen tons' in the Thames estuary. In 1698, he cruised in the Low Countries.'[57] Bowery chartered his yacht for a £1 a day. He earned a massive £109 in 1705–6 for 109 days' hire to the Marquis of Carmarthen.[58] The Marquis was an enthusiastic yachtsman and yacht designer, who had been made aide to the Tsar, Peter the Great, during his visit to England in 1698. The British government wanted trade privileges with Muscovy, including a monopoly on the American tobacco trade. When

---

[55] *Ibid.*, p. 107.
[56] Ibid., pp. 107–108.
[57] Hussey, *The Royal Harwich*, p. 58.
[58] Cusack, 'The Rise of Aquatic Recreation and Sport', p. 36, quoting from Bowery, *The Papers of Thomas Bowery, 1669–1713* ed. Richard C. Temple.

the Tsar granted the latter, he left for home with the gift of the experimental yacht *Royal Transport*, largely devised by Carmarthen.[59]

Maritime painting records the end of the Stuarts. The *Fubbs* was painted by van de Velde the Younger in 1689. She is accompanying the royal yacht *Mary* which was bringing William and Mary to the English throne after the successful invasion by the Dutch, with 53 warships, carrying 1,700 canon, 20,000 soldiers, seven thousand horses and 5 fireships to discourage any counter-attacks. His excuse was an invitation by a handful of high-class traitors. This invasion has been re-framed and re-named 'The Glorious Revolution'.[60]

---

[59] W. F. Ryan, 'Peter the Great's English Yacht: Admiral Lord Carmarthen and the Russian Tobacco Monopoly'.

[60] Having for very many years, believed the 'official' narrative that the last successful invasion of England was in 1066, and that William of Orange was invited by the British people, it was encouraging to read that Linda Colley was also taught this 'in some of the patriotic history books I was forced to read as a child'. She gives the figure of 500 ships and over 21,000 Dutch, German and Scandinavian troops (*Acts of Union and Disunion*, p. 25). No wonder the burghers of Exeter 'welcomed' him. William also hired a good Public Relations firm, since a 'revolution' is defined as strife among the citizenry. Yet, since no-one fought for James, for the very good reason that they would inevitably lose against this formidable Dutch army, it cannot have been a revolution.

CHAPTER THREE

The Development of Yachting
in the Eighteenth Century

PART ONE
The Seaside Towns

The eighteenth century is usually characterised in yachting histories as a period of inactivity. McCallum, for example, evidently drawing on such sources as Phillips-Birt's *The History of Yachting*, writes that 'records show that in 1812 there were about 50 pleasure yachts afloat in Britain'.[1] In fact, there is clear evidence, which this chapter will present, of an increasing level of yacht ownership and activity across the eighteenth century.

This increasing visibility of yachting was due to a number of factors, including the need of the Hanoverian monarchs and their families to 'commute' between England and Hanover, and the widespread use of yachts on state business. I will discuss these in the first part of this chapter before moving on to the growth of yachting as a leisure sport, most obviously in Cork Harbour, in the South of Ireland, and later on the Exe in Devon. The growth of seaside resorts, at the expense of the inland spa towns, then led to the development of yacht regattas.

The Industrial Revolution's dates are usually given as 1760–1830, but by 1760, it already had a clear momentum. Pioneers had been working on the inventions that underpinned it from much earlier. For example, Thomas Savery had a steam engine to raise water in mines working in 1698. Abraham Darby smelted iron using coke at Coalbrookdale in Shropshire from 1709. A long beam (steam-powered) 'atmospheric' engine was built by Newcomen in 1712, the first practical use of steam, with the engine being used in Cornish mines. Newcomen's engine was much improved by James Watt by 1769.[2] However, the first mills relied on water-power and were therefore built in

---

[1] May McCallum, *Fast and Bonnie*, p. 26.
[2] An example of the engine can be seen in Dartmouth, Devon, Newcomen's home town.

the countryside, along fast-flowing streams and rivers, upstream of harbours and ports. These harbours imported the raw materials the mills needed for the production of their goods, and exported the finished products. So, wealth was coming into ports and harbours from the early eighteenth century.

State Uses of Yachts

> YACHT, a vessel of state, usually employed to convey princes, ambassadors, or other great personages from one kingdom to another.

> ... The royal yachts are commonly rigged as ketches, except for the principal one reserved for the sovereign, which is equipped with three masts like a ship. They are in general elegantly furnished and richly ornamented with sculpture; and always commanded by a captain in his majesty's navy.

> Besides these, there are many other yachts of a smaller kind, employed by the commissioners of the excise, navy and customs; or used as pleasure-boats by private gentlemen.[3]

The Yacht as Royal Transport

Queen Anne reigned from 1702 to 1714, and when she died in 1714, the throne passed to her eldest son, George, the Elector of Hanover. The Hanoverian monarchs were therefore kings of both Great Britain and of Hanover and other German lands.[4] George I 'was constantly returning to Germany, and for these yearly expeditions he employed his Royal yachts'.[5] So it is not surprising that Falconer, in his dictionary, first published in 1769, gave one of his definitions of a yacht as '*a vessel of state*, usually employed to convey princes, ambassadors and other great personages *from one kingdom to another* ... always commanded by a captains in his majesty's navy' (my italics).

[3] Falconer's *An Universal Dictionary of the Marine*, 1780. William Falconer (1732–1770), born in Edinburgh, had a career as a seaman in both the Royal and the merchant navies. He made his name with his maritime poetry, most notably *The Shipwreck* (1762) and published his *Universal Dictionary of the Marine* in 1769. The next year, he was drowned whilst on the East India Company frigate, the *Aurora*, which was lost off the coast of Madagascar. Falconer's *Dictionary* was well received, and was updated in 1771, 1776, 1780, 1784 and 1789; an 850-page edition, written by William Burney, was published in 1815.

[4] A situation that only changed with the accession of Queen Victoria, who, as a woman, was barred from succeeding to the throne of Hanover (Linda Colley, *Acts of Union*, p. 46).

[5] Heaton, *Yachting: A History*, p. 55.

The *London Gazette* reported Court and Parliamentary events, as written by the Civil Service, its tone being invariably fulsome. On 22 May, 1713, it noted:

> On Saturday, the 17th inst., His Majesty went on board the *Caroline* Yacht at Greenwich about one in the afternoon, and set sail with a fair wind … On Wednesday evening a Messenger brought the welcome news that His Majesty arrived at Helvoetsluys on Tuesday at six in the morning. And God be praised in perfect health.

In 1749, Lord Anson conveyed George III's Queen-to-be, Princess Charlotte Mecklenburg-Strelitz back from Stade, a town between Hamburg and Cuxhaven on the Elbe, in the *Royal Charlotte* (the *Royal Caroline*, renamed in her honour). The royal yacht was nearly driven north to Norway by successive southwesterly gales, and a contemporary account records:

> Notwithstanding the fatigue of the voyage, the Princess amused herself with playing the harpsichord and continued in good spirits and health, endearing herself to all on board by her fascinating manners.[6]

Besides the respectful reporting, this voyage generated considerable artistic activity:

> The voyage of Queen Charlotte was perhaps the most picturesque and certainly the most pictured event in which a fleet of royal yachts was concerned. Dominic Serres captured the scene as the five yachts and their kitchen boat sailed into Orwell Haven and John Cleveley's panorama shows them coming to anchor in the Stour off Harwich. Three prints by Canot show the original departure from Harwich, the scene in the Elbe at Stade when the Queen embarked and the fearful storm encountered during the return voyage.[7]

This quote indicates that maritime art had become a profitable career, with the yachting artist often passing on their trade within their family. Dominic Serres (1722–1793) with his son John Serres (1759–1825) served as marine painter for George III. John Cleveley (1712–1777), and his twin sons, Robert Cleveley (1747–1809), marine painter to the Prince Regent, and John Cleveley the Younger (1747–1786), were all painters of yachts.

---

[6] Drummond, *Salt-Water Palaces*, p. 18. Original reference not given, presumably the *London Gazette*.

[7] Hussey, *The Royal Harwich*, pp. 3–4. Pierre Charles Canot (1710–1777) was a maritime engraver.

Naval and Trinity House Yachts

From 1674, the Admiralty maintained yachts at Portsmouth. In 1716, it placed one in Chatham and, in 1718, located the *Queensborough* at Sheerness.

> The earliest yachts used in South Devon were Royal Naval vessels. The *St Lo*, presumably named after Captain George St Lo, Commissioner of Plymouth Dockyard between 1695 and 1703, was built at Plymouth Dock in 1700 … The Dockyard, or Admiralty yachts were used for official business, the entertainment of distinguished visitors, and private pleasure by the Commissioners of the Dockyard. For instance, in 1762 Sir Frederick Rogers, Commissioner, lent his yacht to take Dr Johnson out to see the Eddystone Light.[8]

The Eddystone Lighthouse, which had been completed by John Smeaton in 1759, was something of a tourist attraction as it represented a major advance in lighthouse building. Samuel Johnson (1709–1784), famous for his wit as well as his dictionary, used yachts on several occasions to move around the Hebrides, which he visited with Boswell in 1773. Both he and Boswell wrote accounts of this tour.[9]

Voyages of Exploration

The search for new lands with which to trade ushered in a period of exploration, map making and charting in the second half of the eighteenth century, with Captain Cook's voyages (1768–1780) as the prime exemplar.

These voyagers, of course, did not use yachts – Cook, in his four voyages (1768–1780), used colliers built in his home town of Whitby, Yorkshire. Their relevance to us is the huge sales of accounts of these voyages, as was the case with one of the first narratives, William Dampier's *New Voyage Around the World*, published in 1697, which had very large sales.[10]

To prevent unauthorised accounts:

> When a ship returned from a long voyage, pirated editions – often embellished with sensational adventures – were produced with a rapidity and regularity … To curb such aggressive if specious pursuit of best–sellers, standing orders routinely directed captains, including Cook, to collect all log books

---

[8] Cusack, 'The Rise of Aquatic Recreation and Sport', pp. 71–72.

[9] Samuel Johnson, *A Journey to the Western Islands of Scotland*, 1775; James Boswell, *The Journal of a Tour of the Hebrides*, 1785.

[10] Philip Edwards, *The Story of the Voyage*, Chapter 2. Richard Hakluyt (1552–1616), with his *Divers Voyages*, 1582, and *The Principall Navigations, Voiages and Discoveries of the English Nation*, 1589, preceded him, as did Samuel Purchas' *Purchas His Pilgrimes*, 1625, but it was Dampier's text which created the fashion for voyage narratives.

and journals from officers and crew at the end of the voyage and deliver them
to the Admiralty.[11]

The reading public had a near insatiable thirst for voyage narratives. Philip
Edwards estimates that 'Perhaps two thousand works would be a reasonable estimate of published voyage-narratives in the eighteenth century'.[12]
So established was the genre that, in 1725, Defoe (1660–1731) wrote a mock
voyage – *A New Voyage around the World*.

It has always been the case that books about sailing are predominantly
not bought by sailors. A list of subscribers for an unofficial account by Pascoe
Thomas, 'teacher of the Mathematicks on board the *Centurion*' of Anson's
circumnavigation in the *Centurion*, published in 1745, is extant and shows
that while many subscribers were mariners, others were clergymen, schoolmasters, surgeons, attorneys-at-law and several merchants.[13]

Trinity House, incorporated by Royal Charter by Henry VIII in 1514, carried out its responsibilities for lighthouses and buoyage by means of sailing
tenders or yachts.[14] It set up a Yacht Establishment, distinct from the dredgers
and lighters of the Trinity Ballast Office during the first half of the eighteenth
century. Richard Woodman found documentation concerning a Trinity
Yacht for 1745, when the Board of Trinity House 'ordered that Mr Widgeon
go down in the Trinity Sloop to clean the buoys in the South Channel'.[15]
There is a painting of 1778: 'The Trinity House Yacht approaching the River
Humber to inspect the new lighthouse on the Spurn Point on 17th April 1777'.
In Scotland, the Northern Lighthouse Board, created by Parliament in 1786,
employers of generations of Stevensons, also used yachts for the same tasks.[16]

The Trinity House yachts played an important role in suppressing the
Nore Mutiny of 1797. (The Nore is the area of the Thames at the mouth of
the Medway.)[17] The Admiralty was worried that the mutineers would sail the
fleet to a foreign power. Trinity House used its yachts to destroy the Thames
buoyage; and, later, in 1803–1805, to block the Thames against invasion.[18] Its

---

[11] Robert Foulke, *The Sea Voyage Narrative*, p. 103.

[12] Philip Edwards, *The Story of the Voyage*, p. 2.

[13] Edwards, *The Story of the Voyage*, pp. 8 and 56. The text by Pascoe Thomas was titled *A True
and Impartial Journal of a Voyage to the South-Seas and Round the Globe in His Majesty's Ship the
Centurion*, 1745.

[14] It was only given a monopoly of lighthouses by the Parliamentary Act of 1836, which effectively nationalised lighthouses.

[15] Richard Woodman, *Keepers of the Sea*, p. 13.

[16] Bella Bathurst, *The Lighthouse Stevensons*.

[17] Woodman, *Keepers of the Sea*, Chapters 2 and 3.

[18] *Ibid.*, pp. 20–25.

Yacht Establishment was only disbanded by the replacement of sailing yachts by steam vessels.[19]

The Water Club of the Harbour of Cork

The first yacht club in the British Isles, if not the world, was the Water Club of the Harbour of Cork, which was created in 1720.[20]

The membership appears to have been the well-off Irish, for as Guest and Boulton point out, 'many typical Irish names appear in its list – Inchiquins, O'Briens, O'Neals, Mitchells ...'.[21] However, Catholics were not allowed to own land (or even a horse), so the 'Irishness' of the names means relatively little, as the Protestant Ascendancy – the colonisers, who had been given the land – after settling in an area, often changed their names into Irish equivalents.[22]

We have a near-contemporary account, from the seaman, William Spavens, published in 1796 to earn the money needed for his survival after being crippled in action. He is writing of the 1750s and 1760s:

> Cork may, in some respects, be called the second city in the kingdom, and in point of commerce, perhaps the first. It is far inferior to Dublin, yet it is large and populuous ... Its manafactures are poplins, lines & c. and in the adjacent parts of the country there are kept large dairies for butter, some of the graziers keeping 150 or 200 cows; and great numbers of horned cattle and hogs are bred and fed. They slaughter and cure abundance of provision, and export beef, pork and butter, for the supply of great part of our West Indies islands, his Majesty's royal navy and the East India company's ships, &c.[23]

Cork, then, was a major victualling centre for both ocean-going trading vessels and for naval vessels servicing the campaigns and wars that were a near continuous feature of the eighteenth century, such as the War of Spanish Succession, 1701–1714, the Seven Years War, 1756–1763, the American War of Independence, 1775–1883, and the Napoleonic Wars, 1792–1815.

So it is probable that the members of the club were the food producers and victuallers, supplying the ships and/or offering related services.

---

[19] *Ibid.*, p. 61.

[20] Barry Pickthall states that Peter the Great founded the first yacht club, the Neva Yacht Club, in St. Petersburg on 12 April 1718 (*A History of Sailing in 100 Objects*, p. 48).

[21] Montague Guest and William B. Boulton, *The Royal Yacht Squadron: Memorials of its Members*, p. 15.

[22] Seamas Mac Annaidh, *Irish History*, p. 123; see also Wallace Clark, *Sailing around Ireland*.

[23] William Spavens, *Memoirs of a Seafaring Life*, pp. 181–182.

At its inception, the Club drew up a detailed set of rules and codes of conduct. It appears that these rules, spelt out by the Water Club for the first time, were almost socially 'hard wired' because they reoccur so frequently in the rulebooks of later yacht clubs. Some of the features of these rules are:

- *Exclusivity*: Membership was limited to twenty-five captains (Rule 13) through ballots. There was also a rule that no non-member could be invited to take part in the cruise in company who had not slept at a member's house the night before. Thus, any visitor had to be acceptable to at least one member, who was responsible for their 'good' behaviour.

  This exclusivity was further enhanced geographically by their headquarters being situated not on the waterfront of the city of Cork, but on the Island of Haulbowline in the harbour.

  The Water Club's cruises in company acted as an advertisement for the club's prestigious status.

- *Links with Royalty*: Murrough O'Brien, created 1st Earl of Inchiquin in 1654 and his son, the 2nd Earl, were part of the group associated with Charles II.

- *Links with the Navy*: The organisation of the club mirrored that of the Navy – 'admirals', 'captains', uniforms, etiquette, procedures. Officers of the navy were honorary members of the club.

- *Patriotism (towards England)*: The superiority of the colonial rulers over the indigenous population was made manifest in the ensign. 'Rule 5: Ordered that the Secretary do prepare a Union Flag with *the Royal Irish Harp and Crown* on *a Green Field in the Centre.*'

- *A structure designed to strengthen the group*: The original constitution established meetings for sailing and dining once a fortnight during the season, i.e. fortnightly between April and September. Members had to entertain the whole club to dinner, in accordance with a rota. Failure to do so, or to appoint a deputy to do so, was cause for expulsion (Rule 27).

- *Use of arcane procedures and rituals*: 'Rule 14: Resolved: That such members of the Club, or others, as shall talk of sailing after dinner be fined a bumper [of champagne].

In-group identity was further encouraged by:

- *Concern with dress and dress codes and uniforms*: 'Rule 9: Ordered. That no long tail wigs, large sleeves, or ruffles be worn by any member of the club.'

  These procedures and dress codes distinguished members from non-members; in addition, the uniforms created a group (a 'we') identity; and

- *A signals book exclusive to the members* – their private language.

Cruising, not racing, was the major activity of the Club. Members were expected to Cruise in Company (Rule 18). Such Cruising in Company, with its complicated manoeuvring at the commands of the annually elected Admiral, drew on naval manoeuvres and the seventeenth-century mock naval battles practised by the Dutch citizenry, for example the one witnessed by Peter the Great on his visit to Amsterdam in 1697.[24] These Cruises in Company reached a climax once each year when the Water Club flotilla, in stately line of battle, sailed a few miles out to sea to hold a grand annual review.[25] Some of the Sailing Orders for the event were as follows.[26]

Sailing Orders for the Water Club Fleet, 1720

The fleet to rendezvous at Spithead on club days by the first quarter Ebb, any boat not being in sight by the time the Admiral is abreast of the Castle in Spike Island, to forfeit a British half-crown for gunpowder for the fleet.

When the Admiral hoists his foresail half up, it is for the fleet to have a peak upon their anchor,a and when the foresail is hoisted up and a gun fired, the whole fleet is to weigh [anchor].

Observe that if the Admiral wants to speak with any of the fleet he will make the following signals.

- If with the Vice-Admiral he will hoist a white flag at the end of the gaff or derrick, and fire two guns
- If with any private Captain he will hoist a pendant at his derrick, and fire as many guns as the Captain is distanced from him and from the same side.
- When he would have the fleet come to anchor, he will show double Dutch colours at the end of his gaff and fire a gun.

Notes

a *a peak upon their anchor': to pull in the anchor chain or rope till it is straight up and down, i.e. ready to break out of the bottom.*

b *double Dutch colours': The national flag of Holland after 1596 consisted of three horizontal red, white and blue stripes. Double Dutch colours would be a flag of six stripes, the Dutch flag repeated twice.*

W. R. Chetwood, in his *A Tour through Ireland, 1748*, witnessed a Cruise in Company:

---

[24] Heaton, *Yachting: A History*, p. 23.
[25] Rousmaniere, *The Luxury Yachts*, pp. 43–44.
[26] Heaton, *Yachting: A History*, p. 61.

A set of worthy Gentlemen, who have formed themselves into a Body, which they call the Water-Club [of Cork. Ireland], proceed a few Leagues out to sea once a year, in a number of little Vessels ...

Their Admiral, who is elected annually, and hoists his flag on his little vessel, leads the van ... The rest of the fleet fall in their proper stations and keep their line in the same manner as the King's ships. The fleet is attended by a prodigious number of boats which, with their colours flying, drums beating and trumpets sounding, forms one of the most of the agreeable and splendid sights.[27]

Note 'a prodigious number of boats' following the Cruise. Yachting in Cork Harbour was clearly not confined to the boats of the Water Fleet. Additionally, these manoeuvres, watched by large crowds ashore, were memorialised in oil paintings by one of the first *British* marine painters of note, the London-born Peter Monamy (1681–1749), who had gradually established himself as successor to Willem van de Velde the Younger, who had died in 1697.[28] He already had a considerable reputation as a landscape and marine painter, when he painted at least two pictures of the Water Club fleet in 1738.

'Some storm seems suddenly to have burst upon the gay fleet', for the Club seems to have disappeared in 1765.[29] The East Monkton Pic-Nic Club(!) took over the Haulbowline building and there are no records of the Water Club from 1765 till 1805, probably because the complicated manoeuvres of the Water Fleet required open water outside the harbour; and, around this time, there could be no guarantee that the waters outside Cork Harbour were safe from foreign naval vessels and privateers.[30]

The Water Club did differ in one important way from the senior clubs that came later. Around the time of the re-formation of the club, in 1807, a new rule was passed: 'That the wives and daughters of the members of the club, be also considered members of the club, and entitled to wear its uniform.' This

---

[27] *Ibid.*, pp. 58–59.

[28] Peter Kemp and Richard Ormond, *The Great Age of Sail*, p. 67.

[29] R. T. Pritchett, 'Irish Clubs', p. 102. Such waxing and waning of even senior yacht clubs is by no means uncommon as I show in 'Concerning the Fragility and Future of Yacht Clubs'.

[30] Privateers were ships licensed by the State to attack vessels of enemy countries. The Americans sent privateers to English waters during the American War of Independence (1775–1782) and again during the War of 1812 with the UK, which lasted till 1814. The French used privateers during the Napoleonic Wars (1792–1815). Also, the French encouraged insurrection in Ireland, sending fleets in 1796 and 1800, and supported Wolfe Tone's rising in 1798, which was bloodily put down. Marilyn Butler, in *Romantics, Rebels and Reactionaries: English Literature and its Background 1760–1830*, points out that during the Napoleonic wars, 'England committed twice as many troops in Ireland as she ever engaged on the Continent' (p. 55).

3 *Yachts of the Water Club of the Harbour of Cork, 1738.* Created in 1720, the Royal Cork claims to be the oldest yacht club in the world (but the Neva Yacht Club, founded by Peter the Great in St Petersburg in 1718 probably is). Peter Monamy, one of the earliest English painters of yachts, is demonstrating a cruise in company, the favoured form of yachting activity in the Georgian clubs. Note the prominence given to the Royal Ensign – the Irish members clearly showing their loyalty to the British Crown.

apparently 'was passed in compliment to the great interest in the proceedings of the club exhibited by the ladies in question, who, it is added, fully acknow-ledged the courtesy, by appearing at club dinners in nautical costume.'[31] Resistance to women's presence inside yacht clubs continued till after the Second World War, so this encouragement of their participation is some 150 years ahead of its time.

[31] Clark, *The History of Yachting, 1600–1815*, p. 235.

The Growth of Seaside Resorts and Regattas
in the Eighteenth Century

In the mid-eighteenth century, a new way of relating to the sea developed –
seeing the sea as health-giving, rather than a source of terror, or a means of
trade.[32] This led to the growth of seaside towns, and with their growth, an
increase in yachting activity in wider sections of society.[33]

In 1750, Dr Richard Russell, FRS published the first edition of his influential *Dissertation on the Use of Sea Water in the Disease of the Glands* – good
health was furthered by a medically supervised regime of being dipped in the
sea. Invalids should also *drink sea water* 'as a cure for all manner of "human
ills", including glandular problems, tumour and eruptions … kept the head
clear and the bowels regular …'.[34] 'A pint a day', he enthused 'will give three
or four sharp stools'.[35] He built a mansion by the water's edge in Brighton to
minister to his patients.

Further west, Dr John Crane, author of *Cursory Observations on Sea-
Bathing*, 1795, built up a practice at Weymouth, and his proselytising attracted
the attention of George III, who, attempting to cure his undiagnosed por-
phyria, visited each summer between 1789 and 1805. These medical opinions
helped create the movement of the aristocracy away from the inland health
spas, such as Tunbridge Wells, Harrogate and especially Bath, to coastal
resorts, such as Scarborough, Lyme Regis, Weymouth, Sidmouth and most
notably Brightelmstone (Brighton).[36]

According to Dr John Ingenhousz, in his 1780 paper to the Royal Society
entitled *On the Degree of Salubrity of the Common Air at Sea*, it was sea *air* not
sea water that was the therapeutic ingredient.[37]

---

[32] This development of outlook and practice is well described in Alain Corbin's *The Lure of the
Sea.*

[33] John K. Walton, *The English Sea Side Resort.*

[34] According to Alan Chedzoy's *Seaside Sovereign*, drinking seawater was an improvement on
'murky [inland] spa water, which smelt of sulphur' (p. 8).

[35] Christopher Horlock. *The Neat and Nippy Guide to Brighton's History*, pp. 7–9

[36] These beliefs seemed to have been held by all layers of society. In 1795, John Aiken, in *Description of the Country from 30 to 40 Miles Round Manchester*, reported that many poor people were
visiting Liverpool 'for the purpose of washing away (as they seem to suppose) all the collected
stains and impurities of the year'; and in 1814, Richard Ayton, in *A Voyage Around Great Britain*, reported from Blackpool on the same phenomenon – poor people seeking 'a physic from
the sea'. See James Walvin, *Leisure and Society 1830–1950*, p. 14.

[37] John F. Travis, 'Devon Seaside Tourism and the Coastal Environment 1750–1900', pp. 160–179.
The belief in the curative properties of sea air, with its valorising of ozone, continued into the
twentieth century. By 1909, the 'Fresh Air Fund', launched in 1892 by C. Arthur Pearson, had
financed day trips for more than two million children to the coast and countryside (Walvin,
Leisure and Society 1830–1950, pp. 122–123).

One of the specific claims for the health-giving properties of sea air was as a cure for consumption (tuberculosis). This belief was important in the rise of South Devon resorts, such as Teignmouth, Dawlish, Exmouth and Torquay, whose milder climate was considered kinder to consumptives in winter than London with the smoke from its industries and from domestic fires, a situation getting ever worse as the Industrial Revolution accelerated.[38] These resorts were winter resorts – hence the *winter* gardens. Keats' brother, Tom, was attracted to Teignmouth, hoping it could cure his consumption. Keats, a doctor before he became a poet, came to the town to nurse him, but his brother died in 1819.[39]

The Fete Marine on the Exe, August 1772

On 8 July, 1772, a social club, not a yachting club, was set up 'by [the second] Lord Courtenay of Powderham Castle and Sir Lawrence Palk, creator of Torquay as a resort, both yachtsmen, with members of the nobility, gentry and clergy', at Starcross on the west bank of the Exe.[40]

Lord Courtenay was a member of the top London club, White's. He must have witnessed a Cruise in Company by one of the many sailing clubs that were starting up in London (see next chapter) and took the idea back to the Exe. Obviously, other members of the Starcross social club also owned yachts for, in early August, Courtenay organised a Fete Marine – a Cruise in Company to Teignmouth and back for splendid entertainments, a ball with illuminations and fireworks, in the grounds of his castle, Powderham. This was a lavish affair, which was reported on at length in the *Exeter Flying Post* for August 14:

> On Monday last the Gentlemen of the Starcross society gave an entertain-ment to their friends at that Place, under the Denomination of a Fete Marine – At eight o'Clock in the morning the Exmouth yacht, accompanied by a Band of Music, came from thence, withy several Members of the Society, and having saluted the King's Cutter, and the Village of Starcross, anchored opposite the Octagon Building in Lord Courtenay's park [Powderham] and join'd his Lordship's Yacht, and several more of the Members' – As soon as the Tide serv'd they were joined by the Bee Yacht and several other Vessels

---

[38] London's industry was to the East of the city, so that smoke and toxic discharges were blown away from the city by the prevailing southwesterly winds. However, in winter, when there is high pressure over central Europe, the weather system creates easterlies which blow across London.

[39] Keats, who may well have caught the disease from his brother, died in Rome from tuberculosis in 1821.

[40] Johnson, *Yacht Clubs of the World*, pp. 79–80.

from Topsham, Lympston, and that Neighbourhood, about twenty in Number, and full of Company ... they all proceeded to sea, sailed as far as Teignmouth and back ... At six the Ladies and Gentlemen invited to partake of the Evening Entertainment, came, as soon as it was dark, very curious Fire-works and Illuminations were displayed, close to the Waterside ... At 9 the Ball was open'd and a handsome cold supper provided at twelve o'Clock. The Whole was conducted with great Regularity, and the company departed about 3 ... The Fire-works were mostly prepared and conducted by Sig. Paulo Colpi, and did him great credit.

As with the Cruises in Company of the Water Club in Cork, the number of accompanying onlooker boats indicates how much yachting has taken off:

... On Wednesday, the 26th ult. was given, at Starcross (by the Members of the Starcross Club) a Regatta, supposed to have been the completest ever given in this county. In the morning Lord Courtenay's yachts, in which were a number of the Nobility and Gentry, sailed over the bar [at the mouth of the Exe], with a band of music & c. accompanied by an incredible number of yachts, cutters, pleasure boats, & c. a general salute of cannon taking place immediately as they got under way ...

They returned about four in the afternoon, and were again saluted by the cannon from the shore, which was lined by an amazing concourse of people, and every boat and vessel in the harbour was filled. The compliment was returned by the yachts [i.e. they fired their cannon] ...

This was clearly a very major attraction.

[Again a ball and fireworks] ... It was supposed that there were near 10,000 spectators attended, and a vast number continued in boats, & c on the water the whole night. In short every thing seemed to conspire to render the scene delightful.[41]

South Devon was predominantly agricultural, except for Exeter and a number of small ports and fishing harbours. If accurate, 10,000 people watching the regatta, and standing outside the grounds in which a ball is being held, is an amazingly large crowd. But more important for our purposes is 'the incredible number of yachts, cutters, pleasure boats &c.' that accompanied the Club's boats. Clearly, leisure sailing had arrived and was flourishing on the Exe long before 1772.

Despite its success, the Fete Marine on the Exe was not repeated. George III enjoyed sailing his yacht, which was kept at Weymouth. When

[41] Quoted by Johnson, *Yacht Clubs of the World*, pp. 161–162.

he visited Plymouth, the *Exeter Flying Post*, 20 August, 1789, reported that 'their Majesties, in rowing up the Catwater [the mouth of the Plym], received salutes and huzzas from upwards of 200 yachts and pleasure boats'.[42] Again, note the number of boats.

Fanny Burney in Teignmouth, 1773

Teignmouth was one of the first towns to be promoted as an all-year round resort. The *Grand Gazetteer* of 1759 commented:

> Teignmouth of late has been much beautified with diverse and handsome buildings; the air being very wholesome especially in the summer season whereof it is much visited for health and recreation.[43]

A contemporary account of the pleasures of this seaside resort is given in the letters and journals of Fanny Burney (1752–1840), famous novelist, diarist and playwright.[44] Burney wrote letters, later collected, to her favourite sister when she was staying at Tingmouth [Teignmouth], with her stepsister in 1773.[45] She wrote one of the first accounts by a woman of pleasure sailing.

After an easy sail with the vicar of Drewsteignton, who 'is as fat as Falstaff', his wife and crew, to Torquay to view the fleet in Torbay, she records:

> The Wind was against us – & we were hardly out of the Harbour, before we found the sea terribly rough – I own I was not very easy, as our Boat, though a large one for the Thames, was very small for the sea ... it was no sport for me to be Danced up & down, & find the Waves higher & rougher every instant: especially when I saw Mr Hurrel, who had hitherto guided us quit the Helm to the Boatswain, & exclaim 'We shall run foul of these Rocks'!

Burney indicates a fair amount of aquatic knowledge. The daughter of the famous musicologist, Charles Burney, she had obviously taken part in the new fashion – boating on the Thames (see next chapter) – for she knows the difference between a river boat, compared with what is needed at sea; and is, rightly, worried when the owner hands over to the crew. She finishes the tale with a nice piece of humour. Mrs Hurrell, not surprisingly, very frightened:

---

[42] Cusack, 'The Rise of Aquatic Recreation and Sport', p. 130.

[43] S. F. Thomas, *A History of the Teignmouth Corinthian Yacht Club*, p. 7.

[44] Burney's major novels were *Evelina* (1778), *Cecilia* (1782) and *Camilla* (1796).

[45] Writing letters for later publication was a technique used up to Edwardian times, e.g. Lord Dufferin's letters to his mother became *Letters from High Latitudes*, 1857; Erskine Childers' letters to his sister from the Boer War became *In the Ranks of the C.I.V.* [City of London Imperial Volunteers], 1900. They had the merit of apparent spontaneity.

... burst into Tears – & cried vehemently, 'for the lord's sake – for mercy's sake – Mr Hurrel, pray let us go back to Brixem ...'

'But where are we to Dine?' cried he.[46]

The Development of Leisure Yachting in the United Kingdom

The take-up of yachting was a nationwide phenomenon. Martin Black notes: 'The National Archives of Scotland have an account for wages for 1703 due from the Duke of Argyll to James Gordon, master of his Grace's yacht, *The Jockey*. The Archives also have a copy of F. M. Mackenzie of Seaforth's accounts for 1786 to 1792 relating to his yacht, *Mary of Seaforth*.' In 1803, Scotts of Greenock had launched the 44 ½ ton *Roebuck* for Colonel John Campbell. By then, Fife's of Fairlie has started building fishing boats, and also the occasional yacht, namely the *Comet* in 1806 for James Smith, who was to be a founder member of the Royal Northern Yacht Club, and who cruised her to the Hebrides in 1807.[47]

From the 1740s onwards, there was considerable sailing activity on the Thames, as will be documented in the next chapter, where we shall meet William Hickey, man about town. In the April of 1768, he had become friends with a Mr Smith of Battersea, a successful stationer who came into an inheritance, and purchased 'from a Mr. Clark in Christchurch, in Hampshire, a beautiful yacht, about fifty tons burthen ... the *Lovely Mary*'. They went on a ten day cruise in her, leaving from Battersea.[48]

On the East side of the country, Lord Orford, his mistress and two friends explored the Fens for three weeks in 1774.[49] All three of the men wrote brief accounts.[50] Orford seems to have been most concerned to set nets to catch fish. They visited a race meeting. Clearly, sailing was just one of the pleasures available to the Lord and his friends. Additionally,

> As for the Broads, it was possible to hire a Dutch yacht at Yarmouth as far back as 1766. She was 'commodiously fitted up with two Cabbins, Fireplaces

---

[46] *Journals and Letters of Fanny Burney*, pp. 281–284. Where to eat is still a problem in Brixham today.

[47] Martin Black, *G. L. Watson*, pp. 32–37.

[48] Hickey, *Memoirs*, Vol. l, pp. 72 and 86–88.

[49] Orford was known as a rake, being a member of the notorious Hell Fire Club. He was also an enthusiast for agricultural improvement.

[50] Lord Orford, *Lord Orford's Voyage round the Fens in 1774*.

and bed places, capable of carrying 14 or 15 Persons completely on a Party of Pleasure in our Roads, along the Coast or up our Rivers.'[51]

Miss Elizabeth Chudleigh, an interesting lady, masqueraded as a maid of honour at the Court of the Princess of Wales. Her double life included bigamy. When, after a trial in the House of Lord in 1776, the order went out for her 'to be burnt on the hand as a bigamist and an impostor, she left these shores in a private yacht of her own.'[52]

In 1788, aged 20, Uxbridge, later the Marquess of Anglesey, writing during his Grand Tour from Lausanne, Switzerland, complained that 'there is not one pleasure boat on the finest piece of water imaginable ... how I should enjoy myself here if I had but the little skiff that I used when in Angelsea ...'. He inquires after his father's yacht: 'I am very anxious to hear about the *Mona*, I hope she did not lose her golden druid and harp [figure head?] during the Equinox [gales]; I rather suspect she had; I advised them *to take a spare one*'.[53] Guest and Boulton suggest that the Menai Straits had seen a number of yachtsmen before the turn of the eighteenth century and that yachting was well-established as a leisure activity among the local gentry around the Menai:

> A correspondent of the *Sporting Magazine* of 1853 made an interesting communication to that journal which point to the growth of yachting on the Welsh coast quite early in the century. 'Before Waterloo I can call to mind an amateur fleet, where Lord Uxbridge in the *Liberty*, with Assheton pere, the very beau ideal of the squire of olden time, the Messrs. Williams, father and son, an Irish gentleman of the name of Gavin *cum multies aliis*, tempted the tides among the treacherous Swillies.[54]

Cusack found a report that Sir John Aubyn of St Michael's Mount lost a 'yott' stranded in a gale in 1749, and replaced it by a yacht bought from Reginald Pole of Stoke Damerel [a ward of Devonport]. A bill has survived for repairs to a leaking yacht owned by the Rashleigh family [near Fowey] in 1745 and family accounts show that John Buller of Morval [two miles north of Looe] bought a 'yatt' in 1776, and spent a considerable amount of money on fitting her out.

---

[51] Hussey, *Old Fitz*, p. 7.
[52] Guest and Boulton, *Memorials of the Royal Yacht Squadron*, p. 9.
[53] The Marquess of Anglesey, *One-Leg: The Life and Letters of Henry William Paget, First Marquess of Anglesey*, p. 35.
[54] Guest and Boulton, *The Royal Yacht Squadron: Memorials*, pp. 35–36.

Another sign of yachting activity was advertisements of yachts for sale. Cusack identified '203 yachts used or sold in South Devon between 1700 and 1815, and an additional 334 between 1816 and 1827, these figures being certainly an under-estimate'.

There was clearly a *national* market for yachts. Cusack analysed advertisements in regional papers for yachts in South Devon for the period 1754 to 1827, and found 45 advertisements for yachts for the period 1730 to 1815. Between 1786 and 1815, she found that eighteen out of forty-one yachts over 15 tons registered in its harbours were sold out of the area.[55]

The *Sherborne Mercury* was one of the first regional papers, being started in 1737 by Robert Goadby (1720/21–1778).[56] It had a circulation from Wiltshire down to Cornwall, being carried by hawkers known as 'Sherbornes'. In the *Sherborne Mercury*, 8 October, 1770, Cusack found this advertisement for a substantial yacht:

> Burthen between 30 and 40 tons, clench work, built with mast, boom and gaff, bowsprit, sails etc. Compleat with four bed-places, copper stove, beasets in each side, and lockers round the cabin. A fire place forward with four cabins, a sail room, and many other conveniences. The reason for her being sold is that the gentleman for whose use it was kept, is lately deceased. Enquire of Mr. Peter Simmons, shipwright, at Little Falmouth, near Falmouth in the county of Cornwall.[57]

To show the national nature of yacht selling and brokerage, she quotes one from the Ipswich area.

> The *Lion* yacht of about 36 tons was advertised in 1757 for sale in her dock near Freston Tower. Her gear included masts, bowsprit, bomb [boom], gaff-yards, mainsail, foresail, topsail, topgallant sail and crossjack.

Yachts 'genteely fitted up', which meant they were already leisure craft, were also advertised in the Ipswich press. The phrase 'fit for a gentleman's pleasure boat' described boats suitable for conversion from their previous use as a fishing boat or a commercial craft.

---

[55] Cusack, 'The Rise of Yachting in England and South Devon', pp. 127–131. The French and American privateers did not apparently greatly affect *English* coastal sailing, probably because the English coast was more effectively defended or defendable than the South Coast of Ireland.

[56] Known as the *Western Flyer* or the *Sherborne and Yeovil Mercury* from 1749.

[57] Cusack, 'Yachting in Cornwall before the First World War', p. 308. 'Little Falmouth' is part of Flushing, on the other side of the Penryn river from Falmouth.

Yachts were advertised for a wide variety of purposes. For example, they were often equipped for trawling: '… in 1789, a 14-ton yacht "in good repair, with small boat, trawl etc." was sold in Exmouth.[58]

A yacht that could sail fast, especially to windward, would be suitable for smuggling light, but valuable cargoes, such as tea and spirits. During the eighteenth century, smuggling was considered by much of the population as a fair response to heavy taxation on many items.[59] Smuggling vessels were built side by side with revenue cutters in the same yard; and, if captured, could be sold by the Customs for leisure use. So, the eleven-ton sloop *Fanny* seized, condemned and sold for smuggling in 1816, was bought from the Customs by Augustine Seller, a gentleman of Fowey, Cornwall. Mr Seller employed a captain for the first season, but thereafter acted as his own master.[60]

This flexibility is shown in the following advertisement:

> The copper-bottomed brig *L'Impromptu*, taken by H.M.S. *Triton* in 1799 was offered as suitable for 'Pacquet, Guineaman, Yacht or any other purpose'. Also the lugger privateer *L'Enterprise* captured by the *George*, armed cutter in the same year was 'calculated for a Plesure Yacht or Guernsey Employ'.[61]

The range of possible uses suggested in this advertisement is remarkable. A 'pacquet' carried the Her Majesty's mail to the colonies and Lisbon, a 'guineaman' was a slave ship, and 'Guernsey employ' indicates its potential as a smuggling craft.

Towards the end of the eighteenth century, there were long-distance voyages. In 1784, Mr Shuttleham took his 10-gun, 140 ton *Lively* to Florida and then up to Hudson Bay, where he cruised. John Stanley, aged 23, hired the brig *John* for his pleasure trip from Edinburgh to Iceland in 1789.[62]

---

[58] Cusack, 'The Rise of Aquatic Recreation and Sport', p. 106.

[59] This taxation was necessary for a country that was practically continuously at war during the century. The American War of Independence, being fought at such a great distance from England, was particularly ruinous; but the ambivalent, if not negative, attitude of the majority is shown in collusion by the Custom officers, the active involvement of the landed gentry at the very least by purchasing smuggled goods, and the difficulty in achieving a conviction from local magistrates, and by the preferred term 'free trade'. This ambivalence is nicely shown by the fact that the best quality spirits were landed at the Crow Link Gap in Sussex and 'for many years wine and spirit merchants in London openly advertised their Hollands gin as 'Genuine Crow Link'. Incidentally, smuggling was two-ways – English wool, being in demand on the continent was taxed, so smugglers ('owlers') shipped it out of Kent and Sussex (William Webb, *Coastguard!*, pp. 4 and 3).

[60] Cusack, 'Yachting in Cornwall before the First World War', pp. 291–292.

[61] Cusack, 'The Rise of Aquatic Recreation and Sport', pp. 77–78.

[62] Clark, *The History of Yachting*, p. 202.

The gradual increase in the importance of yachting is shown by the publication of *Naval Architecture* by Marmaduke Stalkartt in 1781. It is in seven
books, on such topics as 'Of the Forty-Four-Gun- Ship'; and 'Of the 74-Gun
Ship'; 'Of the Frigate', but also a twenty-eight page book 'Of the Yacht'
(pp. 28–57).[63]

There were a number of chart publishers, whose origins date back to the
late eighteenth century – Laurie dated originally from 1746; Imray has origins
going back to 1781; and Norie and Wilson date back to 1793.[64]

The Development of Regattas

Another indication of the growth of yachting is their participation in regattas, although we do need to exercise caution. 'Regatta' today suggests yacht
racing. However, this is misleading. Even today, yacht racing forms a very
small part of any town regatta, which are, and were, primarily town fairs. The
regatta may well have been an expansion of a market, or hiring, fair whose
origins are lost in the mist of antiquity. The Dartmouth regatta almost certainly grew out of Dartmouth Fair, an annual event for the sale of animals and
hiring of farm workers, on the quay.[65] Harbour towns encouraged regattas,
as they brought hundreds, if not thousands, of people into town from their
hinterland, intent on enjoyment and ready to spend their money.[66]

The town fete would offer sports, such as rowing, swimming, tug-of-war
and the greasy pole. There may have been a race or races for working boats.

Exmouth held its first regatta in 1775. There were regattas at Teignmouth
and Starcross in the 1770s. Torquay held its first regatta in 1811. The Teignmouth
regatta may have been particularly attractive as the competitions were
between women. Because the men were away cod fishing in Newfoundland,
the women did all the marine work – the ferry up to Newton Abbot, pilotage,
wheeling bathing machines into the sea and hauling in the seine nets.

Emphasising the point that it was races among *working* boats that characterised eighteenth century regattas, Dominic Serres painted the Cowes
Pilots' Regatta in 1774. Cowes was the main port of the Isle of Wight with a
number of pilots. At its regatta, the pilots performed a parade of sail followed
by racing between the fastest vessels for money prizes. The first yacht race

---

[63] *Ibid.*, p. 201.

[64] Camilla Herman, 'From Bluebacks to Chart Apps'. The three firms, faced with the growing
success of UK Admiralty charts, amalgamated in 1904.

[65] Davis, *Dartmouth Royal Regatta*, p. 97. Davis compares it to Tavistock's Goose Fair.

[66] There were no Bank Holidays till the late nineteenth century, so feast days were rare and to be
enjoyed to the full.

organised by the Squadron did not take place till 1826. Cowes Week, dedicated to yacht racing, was started in 1834.

Austin states that 'pilot boats have raced in Swansea Bay since the 18th century ...'[67] Races for working boats were held in Southampton regattas in 1790, 1798 and 1802.[68]

Sometimes, the regattas were organised by local grandees. For example, a race for Essex fishing smacks was organised by Bradwell's parson, Bate-Dudley, and held in the Blackwater in 1783. It was imitated a few months later, when Captain Hopkins of Wivenhoe, on the nearby Colne, organised a similar event for smacks belonging to Wivenhoe, Rowhedge, Brightlingsea and Mersea, which raced for a silver cup and a suit of colours. This became a regular event.[69]

Running separate races for local, working boats and for 'gentlemen's boats' occurred towards the end of the eighteenth century and then gathered pace. Reasons included the fact that the owners and crew of large yachts spent money in the town, and they brought prestige to the regatta.

The first regatta on the Deben, Suffolk took place in 1784, 'following a sailing race on the Blackwater in the previous year, and there soon came sailing matches on the Orwell and the Colne which attracted far greater interest than they would today' wrote Frank Hussey in 1974.[70] In 1788, there was a regatta on Windermere, attended by the young William Wordsworth (1770–1850), back home from Cambridge. In 1796, the yacht *Peggy* sailed from the Isle of Man to the mainland and was dragged to Newby Bridge, at the foot of the lake, to be refloated and win her races.[71]

In the southwest, 'the first Devon yacht races took place on the River Exe between 1786 and 1802'.[72] Fifteen yachts raced at Starcross in 1802 for a silver cup donated by Lord Courtenay.

The *Exeter Flying Post*, under the heading *Teignmouth* for 22 September, 1807 reports:

> The Sailing Matches fixed for Thursday 1st October and Friday 2nd October are expected to be particularly entertaining. There will be several matches between boats of various descriptions.

[67] Ronald L. Austin, 'Yachting in Swansea Bay', p. 205.
[68] Cusack, 'The Rise of Aquatic Recreation and Sport', p. 39. From *Sporting Magazine*, 8 (1796), 269; *The Times*, 5 October 1790, 2 October, 1798, 17 September, 1802.
[69] John Leather, *The Northseamen*, pp. 85–86.
[70] Hussey, *Old Fitz*, pp. 6–7.
[71] Showing the flexibility of use we have already commented on, *Peggy* was almost certainly used for smuggling.
[72] Cusack, 'Yachting in Cornwall before the First World War', p. 310.

> On Friday there will be a grand match between ten gentlemen's yachts for a substantial silver cup. An elegant and numerous assemblage of the nobility and gentry, it is expected will be present ...[73]

An advance review of the Teignmouth regatta of 1808 stated that ten gentlemen's yachts had entered.[74] There were separate races for fishing boats and for yachts in 1812.

Torquay, conscious of its need to attract the well-heeled visitor to recoup the cost of its development, worked hard to attract the upper class and visiting yachts. It had joint races in 1812. From 1813, the regattas were organised by the Torquay Royal Regatta Committee. In 1814, they separated races, 'the main race, for vessels between 20–40 tons [i.e. sizeable], was restricted to "yachts of the first class to be the real property of reputed gentlemen only", and a second contest was held for boats under 14 tons "the property of any individual who may care to send them".[75]

While, by this stage, yacht havens and yacht clubs were trying hard to attract racing yachts, their attempts were not very successful. A major problem faced by regatta committees was that most yacht-owners, both visiting and local, regarded regattas as social events and occasions for display, and had no intention of racing, despite the town's efforts to attract racing yachts by offering valuable prizes. Cusack's figures for the Southwest suggest low turnouts. She found only 395 yachts reported racing at South Devon regattas during the fifty-five years between 1775 and 1827, but these are *entries*, not separate vessels. Since some owners raced enthusiastically and frequently, this suggests relatively few entries for these races, except for special events such as the peace celebrations in Plymouth Sound in 1817 or the visit of the king to Plymouth in 1827.[76] It is clear that the eighteenth century yachtsmen went cruising, not racing.

As indicated in my Introduction, the 'big history' accounts of the development of yachting suggested that there was little leisure sailing before 1815 and the arrival of the Squadron. In actual fact, yachting expanded as the Industrial Revolution developed and accelerated, creating surplus wealth not just in factories but also in agriculture to feed the expanding population.

---

[73] Davis, *Dartmouth Royal Regatta*, p. 2.
[74] Cusack, 'The Rise of Aquatic Recreation and Sport', pp. 410 and 81.
[75] *Ibid.*, p. 110.
[76] *Ibid.*, pp. 82–83.

I can take little credit for showing that yachting was certainly a well-established leisure pursuit well before the end of the century. I am drawing on the detailed research work of Janet Cusack. Sadly, she died before she had time to write up her thesis into book form. But the conclusion is clear: much more research needs to be undertaken into eighteenth-century yachting, and in other areas of the country besides the Southwest.[77]

It is undeniable that the development of yachting was hindered by Britain being on a near continuous war footing throughout the eighteenth century, and by the presence of enemy ships and privateers in home waters.[78]

However, it is clear that, despite these obstacles, by the last half of the eighteenth century, there were a large number of yachts, especially around resorts that were also yacht havens. Probably, during the season, there were slow 'whirlpools' of yachts on a local circuit, e.g. Plymouth–Salcombe–Dartmouth; Dartmouth–Teignmouth–Exmouth; Falmouth–Fowey–Plymouth, and similar circuits elsewhere, for example in the Menai Straits and in the East and the West Solent, as there are to this day. The yachts moved around to regattas to take part in the merriment offered ashore, and to watch the few racers on the water. There was a flourishing yachting scene, with brokers ready to offer you your ideal boat at a bargain price. Yachts had already become part of the landscape of leisure and recreation.

---

[77] Such research is made easier by the arrival of newspapers at the beginning of the eighteenth century. Amanda Vickery in 'From Whigs to Wigs', concluded:

> For most of the 17th century, only one, semi-official newspaper [the *London Gazette*] had been tolerated. The first daily paper [the *Daily Courant*] appeared in London in 1702; by 1792 there were 16 London papers circulated in the provinces, but local newspapers also sprang up in almost every major provincial town by the 1730s (p. 8).

[78] For example, during the American War of Independence (1775–1783), the *Hawke*, a boat belonging to an early Cumberland Fleet member (see next chapter), was chased by an American privateer into Calais, a neutral port in 1777 (Rousmaniere, *The Luxury Yachts*, p. 46).

CHAPTER FOUR

The Development of Yachting in the Eighteenth Century

PART TWO
Yachting in Boom Time London

The Start of the Industrial Revolution and Yachting's First Golden Period

Henry Fielding, the author of *Tom Jones* (1749) sailed from London to Lisbon, in the vain hope of a cure for his jaundice and dropsy.[1] As his ship sailed down the Thames in August 1754, he recorded in his journal:

> When we have passed Greenwich we saw only two or three gentlemen's houses, all of them of very moderate account, till we reached Gravesend …

> And here I cannot pass by another observation on the deplorable want of taste in our enjoyments, which we shew by almost totally neglecting the pursuit of what seems to me the highest degree of amusement; this is, the sailing ourselves in little vessels of our own, contrived only for our ease and accommodation, to which such situations of our villas as I have recommended would be so convenient and even necessary.[2]

Fielding was proposing a greater take-up of yachting. He also wanted a greater, more ostentatious display of wealth along England's most important trading river, the symbol of English greatness and history. He may well have had in mind how Capability Brown (1716–1783), the great landscape gardener, was defining how a country mansion and its parkland should look. So, Fielding imagines vistas of Georgian mansions along the lower Thames, with the owners' yachts lying alongside their private quays. This was certainly

---

[1] Before he left the Thames, he had the eminent surgeon, Mr Hunter, come aboard and draw off 10 quarts (20 pints). Not surprisingly, reaching Lisbon did not achieve the desired result. He died on 8 October of that year, and is buried in the British Cemetery, Lisbon.

[2] Henry Fielding, *The Journal of a Voyage to Lisbon*, pp. 212–213.

happening to some extent, since an engraving of 1751 shows Mr Baptist May's yacht under sail in front of his house.[3]

Within a few years, Fielding's aspirations were to come true. Britain and her allies won the Seven Years' War (1756–1763), which resulted in France losing most of her colonies. The war ended with the thirteen British colonies on the eastern seaboard of North America and the British possessions in India secure; and with Canada, Florida and many Caribbean islands acquired. Britain was now the leading maritime power in the world, thus fulfilling what Thomas Arne and James Thomson had seen as the national destiny when they penned their ode 'Rule Britannia' in 1740: 'Rule Britannia, Britannia rule the waves'.[4] These gains gave Britain a crucial advantage in overseas trade, essential for exporting the surplus of goods created by the Industrial Revolution which was starting to get underway – surplus to what the indigenous population of these islands could consume.

We are now entering the first period when yachting has a centrifugal importance, generating social, cultural and political impetus. Yachting was entering its first of three golden periods::

Necessary Conditions for a Golden Period in Yachting*

A golden period of yachting occurs when:

- the prospect of continued social advancement and increased wealth appears realistic for a large number of people
- there is a period of growth and economic expansion and consumer optimism for a number of years
- yachting has cultural centrality, so that it matters to people whether they sail or not
- many people want to actively participate
- and yet many more want to keep themselves informed about it
- and the media respond to that desire for information
- the upper classes and the aristocracy also want to be involved

---

[3] A yacht would also have been a more convenient and more pleasant means of transport into London, whose roads were unmade and crowded.

[4] A strange pair to write such a patriotic song. Arne was an English Catholic composer, and James Thompson a Scottish Presbyterian poet and playwright (Linda Colley, *Acts of Union and Disunion*, p. 24). Hal Sisk has pointed out to me that this British mastery of the seas was incomplete. The British loss of the War of Independence (1775–1783) was due to an important extent to the success of the French fleet being able to blockade British reinforcements when supporting the American rebels.

- as does the monarchy
- its cultural centrality is shown by its use by artists and musicians.

---

* Note that these conditions are necessary but not sufficient, as a yachting boom may not occur during every such period, because the demonstration of wealth and rising status may take other forms of activity and expenditure.

Events relating to this first golden period were mainly located in London and on the Thames, although, as we have seen in the previous chapter, there was steady growth elsewhere. During this century of near continuous war, London was where the government, the War Office, the Admiralty and most of the provisioning companies' headquarters were, as well as the service industries, such as the banks and the law.

This golden period occurred mainly in the first phase of the Industrial Revolution – of machinery turned by *water power*, and the growth of canals, as opposed to the second stage of *steam-driven power* and the railways, that arrived after the 1830s.

There was also at this time a great improvement in the transport infrastructure. Turnpike trusts improved roads – the first Turnpike Act was passed in 1706. Between 1750 and 1790, 1,600 turnpike roads, for which the user paid a fee, were created, introducing macadamised and cambered roads giving a harder and drier surface than that of the previous roads which became impassable mud baths in winter. But the most important advance in transportation was the creation of the canal system. 'The canal age' is usually taken as lasting from 1760 to the early nineteenth century. Josiah Wedgwood opened his potteries in Etruria, Staffordshire in 1759, and he encouraged James Brindley (1716–1772) to build the Trent and Mersey – 'the Grand Trunk Canal' – from Derbyshire to the Irish Sea, which was constructed between 1766 and 1777.

The surplus wealth of the late eighteenth and the nineteenth centuries has traditionally been linked to the creation of *industrial* wealth. An alternative view is provided by William Rubinstein. He investigated British wealth-holders over a number of years and argued in *Who Were the Rich?* that the key factor was the development of *financial services*:

> the modern economic era began in Britain not with the emergence of industrial capitalism and the industrial proletariat, but with the arrival of financial capitalism and the financial bourgeoisie. The modern age dated not – as the Victorians had supposed – from the 18th century, when England became the

workshop of the world but from the 17th century when London became the world's money market.[5]

This view is interesting as it pushes back the start of the modern era into the *seventeenth* century, giving a long run-in of prosperity *and* the prospect of continued prosperity that I have suggested are necessary for the growth of yachting and yachting centres.

This explains why the first English yacht club, the Cumberland Fleet, was created in 1775 *by people successful in the service sectors.* The growth of investment in transport infrastructure and industry, with the resulting growth of cities, required provisioning, banking and legal services to support it. It was from these professions that the London yachtsmen predominantly came.[6]

The Cumberland Fleet, 1775

William Hickey (1749–1827) was a man about town, rake and, later in life, author of a four-volume autobiography, which is very informative about club life.[7] He records how around 1768:

> A new source of expense now sprung up. Rowing ceased to be the fashion: every young man who could afford it, and many that could not, got sailing boats. Of the latter description I certainly was, nevertheless I must have one, commencing with an open skiff carrying only a single sprit sail, but by degrees I rose to a half decked vessel with boom and gaff main sail, fore sail and jib ... In this boat I used to cruise in Chelsea reach when blowing hard, so much so that the people on shore often stood watching me expecting every moment to see me upset.[8]

Masculinity is one of the central attributes of yachting, and it is interesting to note how demonstrating one's masculinity moved from rowing to sailing.

Hickey described the formation in the 1760s of a dining club of London businessmen who had boats.[9] Clubs came out of coffee houses; a 1739 survey records fifty-one coffee houses.

---

[5] John Pemble, 'Golden Dolly. Review of William Rubinstein, *Who Were the Rich?*', p. 24.

[6] London was also a major industrial centre, in 1805 producing 22 per cent of the UK's total output (Linda Colley, *Acts of Union and Disunion*, p. 63).

[7] Hickey, *Memoirs*, 4 vols.

[8] *Ibid.*, Vol. l, pp. 297–298.

[9] Coffee was first imported from Mocca into Venice in 1615. The first coffee house in England was opened in Oxford by a Turkish Jew, called Jacob, in 1652. Since they encouraged free conversation, they were initially seen as subversive and Charles II tried, unsuccessfully, to have them closed.

Clubs were a key part of Georgian London life and there were clubs for almost every specialised activity. Particular coffee houses were meeting places for these clubs. One may be worth describing, as it shows how different the position of women was in Georgian, compared to Victorian times. *Almack's* in King Street was a women's club, with balls and suppers once a week during the season. It was 'rigidly exclusive and dominated by the current *grand dames*. Men were admitted as guests only if they were good dancers – and only if they were attired in formal knee breeches.'[10] Hickey describes the setting up of another club, this time for yachtsmen, some time before 1773:

> Amongst the earliest of the gentleman sailors were the Honourable Mr. Dillon, Mr. Templar, now Master of the King's Bench, Mr. Howorth, Mr. Adair, Recorder of London, & c. &c. Having formed ourselves into a club, we dined together once a week at the Swan tavern in Chelsea. In a short time, it was resolved to have an anniversary of the establishment, upon which day a subscription silver cup should be sailed for, to be presented to the proprietor of the successful boat. This match always attracted a multitude of spectators. When over, we dined at Smith's Tea Gardens, finishing the night at Vauxhall.[11]

Apparently, there were several such clubs on the Thames.[12] Phillips-Birt believes that one of these clubs 'came to the attention of the Duke of Cumberland, obtained his patronage, and adopted the title of the Cumberland Fleet';[13] and it would appear that this was the one that Hickey belonged to. On the second anniversary of its formation, the Duke put up a cup for a race between Westminster and Putney Bridges.

Cusack researched the background of the early members of the Cumberland Fleet:

> The Thames yachtsmen, members of the Cumberland Fleet and the Thames Yacht Club which succeeded it, while wealthy enough to own pleasure boats, were rarely aristocrats. Many Thames sailors were in fact merchants, bankers, senior members of the Livery Companies, lawyers and such-like ... [the club included] Mr James Bigger of the East India Company, Alderman Kirkman, Mr. Templer, later to be Master of the King's Bench, and Mr. Adair Recorder of London ... Mr. Smith of Smith's Tea Garden, and Mr Fairbrother the

---

[10] Rousmaniere, *The Luxury Yachts*, p. 46.
[11] Hickey, *Memoirs*, Vol. l, p. 298. The Vauxhall Gardens, very fashionable leisure gardens at Kennington, on the banks of the Thames, opened in 1732.
[12] Cusack, 'The Rise of Yachting in England and South Devon Revisited, 1640–1827', p. 116.
[13] Phillips-Birt, *The Cumberland Fleet*, pp. 10–12. It would have been one of these clubs' boats on the river, either racing and/or cruising in company that Lord Courtenay observed and decided to create the Fete Marine, described in the previous chapter.

sailmaker … Mr. Condell, winner of the 1786 Jubilee Cup was 'of the opera band'. The Cumberland Fleet was a middle class organisation, which is probably emphasised by their respect for craftsmanship, so that major cups, before presentation, were paraded by water around the fleet, held by the silversmith.[14]

The main activity of the Fleet was cruising in company. The ever-diligent Cusack found out that of all races on the Thames between 1786 and 1809, as recorded by surviving race sheets and newspaper reports, forty-six vessels only sailed in one race, eleven in two, and four in three, concluding that racing was a *rare* event for most of the Cumberland yachtsmen.[15] Further evidence is provided by Thomas Taylor, the second Commodore, who held office from 1780 to 1816. He wrote 'Amusement being the principle Business of the Society … ' (i.e. cruising); and in 1779, he produced a set of signals. These related solely to cruises in company and his notes made no reference to racing.[16]

Like the Cork Water Club, from the very beginning of the club, much attention was paid to club uniforms, such as buttons for the captains' jackets.[17]

The Growth of Yacht Racing on the Thames

There was a well-reported race from Greenwich to the Nore, at the mouth of the River Medway, and back in August 1749.[18] It was the first race between more than two boats and between commoners.[19]

The Nore is a sandbank in the Thames extending from Shoeburyness on the north side towards Sheerness on the South. It was probably chosen for its convenient lightship, the first ever established in English waters in 1732, as the turning mark. Twelve yachts took part in this twenty-four hour race, for a cup presented by the young Prince George, the Prince of Wales (the father of the future King George III).

[14] Cusack, 'The Rise of Aquatic Recreation and Sport', p. 58. 'Master of the king's bench' and 'recorder' are types of lawyers.

[15] Cusack, 'The Rise of Yachting in England and South Devon Revisited, 1640–1827', p. 117.

[16] Phillips-Birt, *The Cumberland Fleet*, pp. 21–23; Clark, *The History of Yachting*, p. 231.

[17] E. W. Castle, R. Castle and R. T. Pritchett, *The Thames Clubs and Windermere*, p. 155. For those who wish to explore yacht club buttons in detail, see Roger Revell, *Yacht and Rowing Club Buttons for the British Isles, 1750–1950*.

[18] Heaton, *Yachting: A History*, Chapters 1 and 2.

[19] There had been a private wager match for 50 guineas in 1726 between two small yachts, one English and one Dutch-built, sailed with three hands, from the Tower to Greenwich. The English yacht won. *Brice's Weekly Journal*, Exeter, 14 October, 1726. Quoted in Cusack, 'The Rise of Aquatic Recreation and Sport', p. 41.

The *Gentleman's Magazine* for that month, August, 1749, gives an account.

[The cup was won] by a boat built on purpose, called the *Princess Augusta*, belonging to George Bellas, Esqr., a Registrar in Doctors Commons, who on receiving the prize generously gave the value of it among the men that work'd the boat ... she came in first by ten minutes, which was the next day at forty minutes past two in the afternoon. The Prince of Wales, with five or six attendants in his Chinese Barge and the rowers in Chinese habits, drove gently before for some time and a crowd of boats about him, the people frequently huzzaing, at which he pulled off his hat. It was almost a perfect calm and not the least damage happened, though the river seemed overspread with sailing yachts, galleys, and small boats.[20]

A number of features of this race are worth commenting on. For twelve boats to be at the starting line, yacht racing must have been going on for some years beforehand to build up a racing fleet of that size (which, as we have seen, would have included many boats that did not race that day). So, once again, it is clear that yachting took off early in the eighteenth century, not the nineteenth, congruent with Rubinstein's earlier dating of the growth of wealth in the British economy.

The race had obviously been taken seriously (and advertised well in advance), for the winner to have a boat specially built. To go to those lengths suggests a well-established yacht racing fraternity.

These yachtsmen were skilled and had access to skilled crew, such as Thames watermen, because a twenty-four race on a busy river, obviously involving night sailing, is not to be undertaken lightly.

Royalty was obviously keen to be involved, and since with a race of this length, one cannot know exactly when the winner will arrive, gilling around is required, as the report notes. This level of involvement is quite different from that of Charles II, who enjoyed his sailing, as did his brother, but there is no evidence that they encouraged leisure sailing among their subjects. In contrast, the future king was furthering *yachting as a leisure sport* and making sure his presence was noted. One reason that has been proposed is that the Hanoverians monarchs were insecure, being unpopular German imports, necessitated by the end of the Stuart line in 1714, and so they deliberately sought popularity.

Finally, the very large crowds of spectators were a feature of races on the London river throughout this period.

---

[20] Quoted by Heaton, *Yachting: A History*, pp. 62–63. 'Doctors Commons' was the society of lawyers practising civil law in London.

4 *The Fleet of the Cumberland Sailing Society Racing on the Thames.*
The Cumberland Fleet, made up of small yachts skippered by their owner, was
evidence of the wealth being created by the burgeoning Industrial Revolution
in London.

The newspapers, reporting on yachting, did not know quite what to make
of this high-class novelty:

> Some of the expressions used in the newspapers about the different matches
> are very curious; in one paper it is called 'Fluviatic and Fresh Water Frolics,'
> in another 'Thamesian Pleasantry,' and again 'Water-racing Galloways,' but
> the best of the lot is in the 'Morning Post' of [26 July] 1782, where the race is
> described as 'a Fluviatic Cavalcade'.[21]

It was the yacht races, rather than the cruises in company, that attracted most
public and press attention, and it is worth bearing in mind that these yachts
are not billowing white clouds of sail. Rather, the confined waters of the

---

[21] Castle, Castle and Pritchett, *The Thames Clubs and Windermere*, p. 157.

Thames meant that boats had to be kept small, and were therefore, relatively affordable.[22]

> Most of the yachts raced on the Thames were under 10 tons, and the larg-est vessel shown on race sheets for the years 1828 to 1831 held by the Royal Thames Yacht Club was 23 tons.[23]

For example, Thomas Taylor, the Club Commodore from 1780 to1816, won the Cumberland Cup in 1776 with *King's Fisher* – 20 foot long, indicative of the small size of boats in the racing fleet.

I will look at one race in a bit more detail. In the summer of 1775, the Duke of Cumberland presented a cup. As announced in the *Public Advertiser* for 6 July:

> A Silver Cup, the gift of His Royal Highness, the Duke of Cumberland, is to be sailed for on Tuesday, the 11th instant, from Westminster Bridge to Putney Bridge and back, by Pleasure Sailing Boats, from two to five tons burthen, and constantly lying above London Bridge. Any gentleman inclined to enter his Boat may be informed of particulars by applying to Mr. Roberts, Boatbuilder, Lambeth, any time before Saturday Noon next.[24]

This race is of some importance, as it is an open race – you did not have to be a member of any particular yacht club to enter. Ward suggests that the Duke of Cumberland, the brother of the reigning monarch, got involved as he was an Admiral and was an outcast in the Royal Family, because he had married without the King's consent.[25]

The owner had to helm and was only allowed two 'assistants'. The 'cap-tains' (owners) must have known each other, since, according to the *Morning Post* of 10 July, 'the Gentlemen, about 18 or 20 in number, who sail for the prize have come to a resolution to be dressed in aquatic uniforms'.

> The racing boats were anchored in line, with their sails furled; their places having beforehand been determined by lot … handicapping was an unknown quantity in those days, and the boat which succeeded in passing the winning-post first claimed the cup … The victorious Captain was then taken aboard the Commodore's barge, and with great ceremony introduced

---

[22] However, the Thames was wider than it is today, before the construction of the wharfs and docks. This would be particularly the case at high water, when crossing at least some of the mudbanks would have been feasible.

[23] Cusack, 'The Rise of Aquatic Recreation and Sport', p. 58.

[24] Phillips-Birt, *The Cumberland Fleet*, p. 11. A picture of the rather fine cup is shown on p. 32 of *Robin Knox-Johnston's History of Yachting*.

[25] A. R. Ward, *Chronicles of the Royal Thames Yacht Club*, p. 15.

to his Royal Highness. In the meantime the Duke's butler had filled the cup with claret and handed it to his Royal Highness, who thereupon drank to the health of the winner, and then presented him with the cup. The captain then drank to the Duke and Duchess, with three cheers; the whole ceremony having been performed amidst the strains of martial music, salvos of artillery and the huzzas from the crowds upon the river and its banks. The fleet then proceeded up the stream to Smith's Tea Gardens, which lay where the gasworks now are … and dined together. The Duke himself was very often present at these festive gatherings, and later on the evening they all visited Vauxhall Gardens and made a night of it.[26]

'Anchored in line': at this time, yachts in a race would be moored or anchored until a gun fired for the start. After the 1860s, 'the flying start', used today, across a defined start line – either two posts in line or a point on the shore and a committee boat – was introduced.[27] Handicapping was not introduced till the 1830s. Smith was the first Commodore of the Fleet from 1775–1779, and the racing started and ended at Smith's Tea Gardens.

The account talks of music and singing which were an integral part of the post-race activities. Drinking songs to commemorate a racing victory were composed. There is evidence of a song written for the celebrations at the end of the 1786 race. By the 1820s, we find a 'popular song-sheet "Thames Yacht Club"' (see next page).[28]

The chorus is surely a constant refrain; the name of the yacht, in the verse, would commend the winning yacht of that year's race.[29]

The consumption of alcohol seems to be socially hard-wired into yachting.[30] Veblen, in his *Theory of the Leisure Class*, considers drinking and inebriation among the upper classes as 'honorific', a badge of status:

---

[26] Castle, Castle and Pritchett, *The Thames Clubs and Windermere*, pp. 155–156.

[27] Leather, *The Northseamen*, p. 105.

[28] Phillips-Birt, *The Cumberland Fleet*, p. 30.

[29] Pierce Egan, *Book of Sports and Mirror of Life*, p. 105. The *Don Giovanni*, 7 Tons, was owned by Captain J. M. Davey, who joined the newly established Thames Yacht Club in 1823.

[30] A yacht club cruise will invariably include a *vin d'honneur* at a yacht club they visit. 'Vin d'honneur' is defined by the *Oxford English Dictionary* as 'wine formally offered in honour of a special guest', so it is noteworthy that a banquet is defined by its alcohol. Any account of such a cruise will invariably include 'humorous' remarks concerning a party that leaves some of the yachtspersons 'with a sore head'. Excessive alcohol consumption by yachtsmen is rarely commented on, because it is lower-class drinking ('lager louts' etc.) that is to be frowned on and prevented. Upper-class drinking is framed as 'high spirits'. An example of this selective attention is Brian Harrison, *Drink and the Victorians 1815–1872*, in which he focuses exclusively on working-class drinking, and pays no attention to the heavy drinking of wines and spirits by the upper classes, especially in Georgian times. The over-indulgence in alcohol is a continuous feature of yachting history, and in order to avoid repetition, I take it as a given, rather than mention it time and again.

Thames Yacht Club Song-Sheet 1827

The song-sheet concerns a 'crack boat of her day' the *Don Giovanni*, and ends:

> Now toast the *Don Giovanni*'s crew, who bear the prize away
> And may they always sail as well as they have sail'd to-day!
> Then fill each glass with sparkling wine, and bumpers let them be,
> And drink to Captain Davey's health – his health with three times three:
>> For the cup is won, the match is done
>> And settled in the rub;
>> Let mirth abound, and glee go round,
>> In this – the Thames Yacht Club

Drunkenness and the other pathological consequences of the free use of stimulants therefore tend in their turn to become honorific, as being a mark, at the second remove, of the superior status of those who are able to afford the indulgence.[31]

These races were discussed beforehand and reported in detail by the papers, at least in part, to offer information to gamblers. Besides needing information and detailed descriptions of yachts before a race, punters needed post-race analysis of the vessels' performances. This was provided in such journals as the *Sporting Magazine*, started in 1792. In the same year, *The Times* discussed a proposed wager race between the yachts *Phoenix* and *Troliopus*, and noted that current betting was five to four in favour of the *Phoenix*. *Bell's Life in London* discussed contestants in a later, 1824, race: 'The *Fortitude* is a washing tub looking affair, [she] can therefore do little if it blows hard, but while she can carry full sail ... she goes through the water at a surprising rate ... her owners are somewhat deficient in spirit ... *Venus*, hatch boat, the swiftest below London Bridge, but not calculated for the highest part of the Thames ... *Mentor*, formerly a good sailor, but now old.'[32]

Explanations: in a blow – strong winds – 'a washing tub' with its flat bottom, would make lots of leeway when beating, and be blown sideways

---

[31] Veblen, *Theory of the Leisure Class*, p. 70. This is a feature of most prestige sports. 'Such conviviality lay at the heart of much Victorian sport. For the upper classes, hunting, shooting and fishing, alongside horse racing, remained as much social activities as sports' (Mike Huggins, *The Victorians and Sport*, pp. 103 ff.). In golf, drinking is such a part of the game that the club bar is referred to as 'the nineteenth hole'. In yachting circles, post-sailing drinking is often referred to as 'a beer or three'.
[32] Cusack, 'Yachting in England', p. 119.

off course; the Cumberland/Thames necessitated the owner to helm, and if 'deficient in spirit' would probably not be ruthless enough to win races; while 'a hatchboat' was primarily a fishing vessel, with a deck composed almost entirely of hatches, so probably needing fairly strong winds to get moving, conditions less likely to apply further up a river.

The popularity of these races was remarkable. The *Morning Chronicle* report on the Cumberland Sailing Match twenty-guinea race, that took place on the 19 July, 1786 gave an attendance figure of 200,000. London's population was 750,000 in 1760 and 900,000 in 1800, so that, if the attendance was anything like the figure given, a quarter of the total population watched the match, and this on a Monday. Not surprisingly: 'All the pickpockets in London attended, and several of them got safe lodgings for the night in the custody of the Bow Street Officers of Justice'.

Without crowds to witness this pomp, and without newspapers to broadcast it, there would be little point in the Duke seeking this publicity.[33] So, royal involvement was made worthwhile by the cheering crowds. The Duke of Cumberland gave an annual cup from 1776 to 1782.

The Napoleonic War did not stop the Fleet's activities. Jonathan Tyers, the proprietor of the Vauxhall Gardens provided an annual cup from 1786 till 1810, with a special cup every seventh year. The Vauxhall Gardens failed in 1811, so the State Lottery stepped in(!). In 1812, the New Ranelagh Gardens presented a cup. So, it is clear that racing continued throughout the Napoleonic War and newspapers were reporting on them.

The Creation of 'the Yacht Club' (The Royal Yacht Squadron)

One feature missing from the early part of this golden period was the involvement of the aristocracy in sailing. To helm one's own boat would seem dangerously close to the forbidden activity of work; and besides, it lacked ostentation. But as sailing's visibility grew, the involvement of the aristocracy was perhaps inevitable and came towards the end of this first golden period. Its involvement was to crucially reshape yachting.

The English aristocracy is made up of those of noble birth, holding hereditary titles (duke, marquess, earl, viscount or baron, and baronet). Since this is a fixed number of families, it follows that the only way to join the aristocracy

---

[33] In the same vein, the pageantry we now associate with the coronation was only worthwhile the bother for the new monarch when it could be photographed, i.e. starting with Edward VII. See David Cannadine, 'The Context, Performance and Meaning of Ritual: the British Monarchy and the "Invention of Tradition", c. 1820–1977'.

is to marry into it (or, much more rarely, be adopted by a member of it). *Debrett's Peerage and Baronetage* first appeared in 1802, so it became easy to find who was and who was not in the aristocracy.[34]

As David Cannadine has shown in *Aspects of Aristocracy*, at the beginning of the nineteenth century the landed aristocracy occupied almost all the important sources of power: seats in the Commons, bought commissions in the army and the navy, and the senior positions on the bench and in the church.[35] The system was referred to by contemporaries, such as the radical journalist, William Cobbett, as 'Old Corruption'.[36] Their wealth was augmented by ruthless enclosures of common land, agrarian experiments and industrial ventures, as well as investment in overseas trade.[37] In addition, they did very well out of the first phase of the Industrial Revolution, which required plentiful supplies of clean, running water to power mills, i.e. upstream rivers; and, when the steam engine arrived, the coal it needed was under their land. The canals, and later the railway, might well go across their land, requiring the canal and railway companies to make expensive purchases.

Industrial advances included John Kay's flying shuttle of 1733, which was in general use in Yorkshire's woollen industry by the 1780s. Hargreaves invented his spinning jenny in 1764. Richard Arkwright's water frame was patented in 1769. Its size was too large for home spinning and required a mill. Samuel Crompton's mule (1779) revolutionised textile spinning; and James

---

[34] This aids quick scene-setting in many of Jane Austen's novels, most notably in *Persuasion*, where, in the opening paragraphs, Sir Walter Elliot's perusal of the *Debrett's [Peerage and] Baronetage* told the contemporary reader that he is not in the peerage, but is the holder of a hereditary title. You could become a Knight by outstanding works or outstanding generosity towards the party in power, but this was, and is, a personal, not a hereditary title.

[35] Buying commissions in the army only came to end with the Cardwell reforms of the army in 1871. Edward Cardwell was the Secretary of State for War (1868–1874) under Gladstone. Lord Cardigan had paid £40,000 for the Colonelcy of the 11th Hussars and his incompetence, as witnessed by the Charge of the Life Brigade (1854), during the Crimean War (1853–1856) and his unpopularity (sleeping on his luxury yacht, whilst his soldiers endured terrible conditions on land), aided this change.

[36] Cannadine, *Aspects of Aristocracy*, p. 18. William Cobbett (1763–1835) is best remembered for his accounts of agricultural poverty in his *Rural Rides*, published in the *Political Register* from 1821, and in book form in 1830. His *Political Register*, called, because of its low price, the *Twopenny Trash*, was a main source of news information for the working class and orators. It ran from 1801 to 1817, when Cobbett, who had already spent two years, 1810–1812, in prison for treasonable libel, hearing that he might be arrested for sedition, fled to America.

[37] Butler, *Romantics, Rebels and Reactionaries*, esp. pp. 100 and 179. Enclosures of common land had been undertaken by landowners since the Middle Ages, ending the rights of peasants to keep their livestock on this land and therefore rendering them much poorer. The pace of enclosures greatly increased between 1760 and 1820 and they were undertaken brutally and on a large scale in the countryside, with forced evictions and burning of dwellings. The resulting rural depopulation was deplored in Oliver Goldsmith's poem, *The Deserted Village* of 1770.

Watt patented his rotary steam engine in 1786.[38] These innovations required factories, with a large labour supply housed nearby, leading to the rapid growth of industrial towns and cities, especially in the North. As the cities developed, the urban land usually belonged to the nobility.[39]

These aristocrats, owning large acreages, should be distinguished from the less prosperous 'squires', a distinction of some importance, as the squire did not attend the London season.[40]

For men of such wealth, the problem of what to do with their time was ever present, especially for the younger generations. As C. Brookes described them: 'a group of people who possessed almost infinite amounts of time and money to devote to the cause of leisure';[41] as well as being unable, in order to maintain their superior status, to be seen to be doing any work. How were they to pass their time?

The commonest demonstrations of their leisured wealth were travel, sport and gambling. Guest and Boulton explain aristocratic preferences:

> Young men of condition, from the days of the Revolution [1688] to those of King George the third [1760–1820] at least, spent their leisure in cards and hazard rooms, hated the country as a place of banishment, and looked upon moors and mountains as outrageous wildernesses which separated cities like Paris and Milan, where alone rational enjoyment was to be found.[42]

The young aristocrat was expected to travel for a year or more to the lands of classic art – the glories of Rome and Greece on the 'Grand Tour';[43] but now they were imprisoned in this country by the Napoleonic Wars, which people thought would go on for ever – which is why Jane Austen barely mentions it. This left only London life – the London sporting clubs, such as Boodle's and White's, with their emphasis on social acceptability, maintained by blackballing; and the ostentatiousness of their gambling for high stakes.

This was not a very satisfactory diet. One way of passing time was suitable hobbies. In West Cornwall, buying rare specimens of plants from returning sea captains and skippers of the packets (carrying the royal mail) and trying to grow them in this country was popular. If successful, the plant became a

---

[38] Jeremy Black, *A History of the British Isles*; Butler, *Romantics, Rebels and Reactionaries*, p. 100.

[39] In the early eighteenth century, Manchester had 9,000 inhabitants; by 1801, it had 90,000; Birmingham went from 25,000 in 1740 to 73,000 in 1801 (C. P. Hill, *British Economic and Social History 1700–1964*, 3rd edn, p. 3).

[40] Thomas Hughes (1822–1896) draws a contemporary portrait of a squire as the father of Tom Brown, in *Tom Brown's Schooldays*, 1857.

[41] C. Brookes, *English Cricket*, p. 40.

[42] Guest and Boulton, *Memorials of the Royal Yacht Squadron*, p. 2.

[43] Geoffrey Trease, *The Grand Tour*.

British species and could be named after the grower in the Linnean classification. In other areas, nobility were amateur scientists or collectors of art.

A far more favoured aristocratic activity was horse-breeding. The five classic races were established in this period: the Oaks in 1779 and the Derby in
1780 at Epsom; the St Leger in 1788 at Doncaster; and the 2,000 Guineas in
1809 and the 1,000 Guineas in 1814, both run at Newmarket.[44] The sport was
accompanied by heavy gambling.

Before 1800, the only *outdoor* sport practised on a large scale by the upper
classes was game shooting. There were only about six packs of foxhounds
before 1800. It was only into the nineteenth century that a number of outdoor sports, such as fly-fishing, fox-hunting, shooting parties and yachting,
became established as sought-after, prestigious leisure activities.[45]

In 1815, two yacht clubs were formed. A group of yachtsmen 'banded
themselves together into a club' at Chester, and formed the Dee Yacht Club,
with a membership limited to sixty and which was granted the royal warrant in 1847 by Queen Victoria.[46] In London, on 1 June, the Yacht Club was
formed at a meeting in the Thatched House Tavern, St James, with forty-two
founder members, most of whom were members of White's. Napoleon had
escaped from his imprisonment on Elba and created a new army, so this was
two weeks before the battle of Waterloo, on the 18th, but as Ernle Bradford
points out: 'War in those days, unlike our own were things that were left to
professionals.'[47]

Forty members were present at this inaugural meeting. The Earl of
Uxbridge was commanding the cavalry at Waterloo. (For his valour and
ability on the battlefield, where one of his legs was shot away, he was made
Marquess of Anglesey). Forty-one were landed aristocrats. The 42nd, Sir
William Curtis, the Lord Mayor of London, had the contract for ship's bis-
cuits with the Navy. He was on board his yacht heading for St Petersburg.

---

[44] John Ford, *This Sporting Land*, p. 28.

[45] Guest and Boulton, *Memorials of the Royal Yacht Squadron*, pp. 1–2.

[46] We do not know much about the Royal Dee's early days as its records were destroyed in fires
in 1884 and again in 1929. Roger Ryan, 'The Emergence of Middle-Class Yachting in the North-
West of England from the Later Nineteenth Century', p. 153, describes it as 'largely defunct by
1850'. Limiting the membership to a few dozen was quite a standard practice, although, if the
club was successful, the permissible number of members was usually revised upwards.

[47] Ernle Bradford, *Three Centuries of Sailing*, p. 41. Additionally, reports in newspapers were delayed
because journalists did not go out to seek news; and the news was first received, digested and
then released by the government. See Brian Cathcart, *The News from Waterloo*.

He was reported to spend £1,600 a year on his yacht, which was 'the finest pleasure vessel belonging to any British subject'.[48]

Most of those who signed up to the Yacht Club were summer visitors to the Isle of Wight, and therefore were already meeting informally. Cowes was the main port of the island, and, at its regatta, its pilots performed a parade of sail followed by racing between the fastest vessels for money prizes. Diana Harding, the late RYS archivist, wrote '1814 saw a new spectacle – yachting gentlemen got together, and followed the pilots with a parade of yachts. From this was probably born the idea of the Yacht Club.' They probably met at other yacht harbours informally during the season.

For all these forty-two members to already own yachts, they had to have been sailing them for some years previously, so 1815 does not magically see the start of aristocratic yachting. Uxbridge (1768–1854) had owned *Pearl* and based her at Cowes for some years, and had been sailing since his youth.[49] Likewise, the grandfather of Edward Fitzgerald, translator of the The Rubbaiyat of *Omar Khayyám,* was a founder member of the Squadron, and it is likely that he, the grandfather, was sailing on the south coast by 1802.[50] Again, Joseph Weld, of Lulworth Castle, and Mr. Sturt of Branksea Castle (on Brownsea Island, Poole Harbour) had raced against each other in September, 1800.

The Yacht Club's rules were simple. Members may have resented White's fierce and capricious blackballing policy but they copied it:

> Regulations. Fourth – that no person be hereafter admitted as a member without being balloted for at a general meeting consisting of less than ten members. The candidates to be proposed and seconded by two members of the club. Two black balls to exclude.[51]

---

[48] 'Recollections of J. A. Gardner', *Navy Records Society*, p. 41, quoted in The Yachtsman: *British Yachts and Yachting,* p. 105.

[49] The reader will come across Uxbridge in a variety of names. His father Henry Bayly was the son of an obscure Scottish baronet. Through his marriage and some unexpected bequests, 'in middle age he found himself one of the richest peers in the country' (Anglesey, *One Leg,* pp. 19 ff.) and, within three years of his marriage, the title, Lord Paget. The Earldom of Uxbridge had been created for the seventh Lord Paget, so Henry Bayly became the ninth and 'Henry Bayly's metamorphosis was complete' (p. 21). But not that of his oldest son, Henry Paget, the tenth Earl of Uxbridge who was made the first Marquess of Anglesey after Waterloo. His main home was Beaudesert on the Cannock Chase, Staffordshire, but he retained great affection for another of the family's home, Plas Newydd, on Anglesey, where the family had sailed when he was a lad. Nearby is a column, built in 1817 to commemorate Waterloo. After the Marquess' death, a statue of him was placed on top of the column in 1860.

[50] Frank Hussey, *Old Fitz,* p. 17.

[51] Ian Dear, *The Royal Yacht Squadron 1815–1985,* p. 18.

Exclusion at two black balls was set far too low and gave no end of trouble as a small number of members could vent their dislike of an applicant, or amuse themselves with whimsical decisions, such as the wind was in a certain direction, or the colour of the applicant's tie etc. resulting in painful rejections.

Article Six of the original 1815 Regulations indicated the not very demanding expectation that the members would attend two meetings a year, one at Cowes in August, and one at the Thatched House on the first Saturday in May, at which they would ballot concerning new members.[52]

Another rule was that a member had to own a vessel of ten tons or more. In fact, the minimum tonnage for membership was soon revised upwards, so that we can see how the Yacht Club differentiated itself from the Thames yachtsmen: their boats were far bigger, seagoing vessels, rather than being restricted to river sailing.[53] Such vessels required a professional crew. Given their cost, they became objects of ostentation, a point I will elaborate on in the next chapter.

The Yacht Club members were clearly looking ahead to the Channel becoming safe for sailing again. The Napoleonic Wars (1793–1815, with a year's peace in 1802, created by the Treaty of Amiens) had rendered the English Channel unsafe due to the presence of French warships but also, and probably more dangerously, French and American privateers. When G. A. Fullerton ventured beyond the Needles in his 55 ton cutter *Zephyr* in 1806, he was nearly captured by a French privateer. When George I wished to sail his yacht, *Augusta*, off Weymouth in 1801, this required an escort of two frigates, *Hydra* and *Fortune*, passing on opposite tacks.[54] True, the third Lord Courtenay of Powderham Castle, son of the organiser of the 1772 Fete Marine, having to leave these shores in a hurry in 1811, embarked in *Dolphin*, a 70-tonner, built by the second Lord. He set sail for America and duly arrived.[55]

---

[52] Note the lack of a club house at either venue. Until the mid-century, it was quite common for nobility to use public houses for meetings of associations or clubs – this, despite major turmoil from the Chartists and the movement for electoral reform. This mixing of the classes in taverns is an important plot link in Dickens' *Nicholas Nickleby*, published in 1839.

[53] The tonnage required for membership rapidly rose from 10 tons in 1815 to 20 tons in 1817 to 30 tons in 1825, till this ostentatiousness gave rise to the rhyme: 'Nothing less than 40T may ever race with our burgee'.

[54] Drummond, *Sea-Water Palaces*, p. 19.

[55] According to the Powderham Castle website, 'the Third Viscount led a rather flamboyant lifestyle. He was a homosexual, and was forced to live abroad in consequence, first of all in the United States where he owned a property on the Hudson River in New York State, and later in Paris where he died in 1835.' This is presumably correct, although homosexuality was not a crime till the 1890s.

The original aim, then, was unambitious: to formalise their informal get-togethers by agreeing to meet twice a year, once in London and once in Cowes. The Squadron's historians noted: 'It is quite clear that at first the club was merely a social gathering of those gentlemen who found Cowes a convenient summer resort, and regarded sailing as a pleasant incident of their visit.'[56] It is not even certain when the club was formed, for 'the seal of the yacht club bears the date of 1812.'[57]

As we will see in the next chapter, this formalising of gatherings of aristocratic yachtsmen who already knew each other and who came across each other in the Solent was low-key and unambitious. What was to change it into the most prestigious yacht club in the world was the need of the Georgian monarchs to ingratiate themselves with members of the Club.

With all this activity, with its fashionability, the active support of the royal family, and its huge popularity as a spectator sport – with spectators in boats on the water and huge crowds lining the shore, a goodly number who may have had a gamble, and therefore likely to be knowledgeable about what was happening on the water – this was the first 'Golden Period' of yachting.

Racing on the Thames, and yachting more generally, in London, gradually died out. The Cumberland Fleet changed its name in 1823 to the Coronation Sailing Society to celebrate the coronation of George IV, when in the July of that year, there was a dispute over a protest in a race, due at least in part to the personality of the rule-bending (and worse) of one Captain Bettsworth, 'all too often the centre of controversy'.[58] Forty members of the Fleet resigned and formed the Thames Yacht Club. The resolution forming the new club notes that 'river sailing … has of late years fallen off …'

By 1827, the Thames had 200 members while the Coronation Society had withered. The Thames got its royal warrant in 1830, and, of course, its buttons had to be changed from TYC to RTYC. It adopted the long pennant of the Cumberland Fleet and also the date of the Fleet's founding, 1775, instead of its own less remarkable but accurate, 1823.[59]

---

[56] Guest and Boulton, *The Royal Yacht Squadron*, pp. 69–70.
[57] Heaton, *Yachting: A History*, p. 75.
[58] Ward, *The Chronicles of the Royal Thames Yacht Club*, p. 21.
[59] Phillips-Birt, *The Cumberland Fleet*, p. 32. By moving the date, it also avoided the problem that the Thames was formed at the behest of a racing yachtsman of dubious ethics. 'In a TYC match in August 1825 he [Bettsworth] was accused of dumping ballast … in August 1829 [Bettsworth's] *Spitfire* entered a Clarence Yacht Club match in which she became involved

More bridges were built across the river in the nineteenth century as the city, especially south of the river, expanded.[60] The Pool of London became increasingly busy with large, heavily laden vessels, anchored in the river, being loaded and unloaded by lighters, making racing impracticable. Also, in the absence of any sewage facilities, the use of the Thames as a sewer detracted from its suitability for aquatic recreation.[61]

Yachting would have to leave London, first of all down river and then to the East coast, most usually Harwich or Burnham-on-Crouch; or to the Solent.

These were gradual changes, but the end of the first golden period can be taken as the victory at Waterloo. This time, Napoleon was locked up properly on St Helena. Peace returned and with it came the shrinking of a war economy that had been running at full speed for quarter of a century, mass unemployment for the 300,000 demobilised men, and political unrest at the ways of the ruling 'Old Corruption' that they had fought for and so many of their comrades had died for.[62] Yachting's first golden period was at an end, and as Chapter 6 will show, growth would be slow for the next fifty years.

---

in a protest and counter protest situation based on accusations of handing off another boat' (Ward, *The Chronicles of the Royal Thames Yacht Club,* p. 21).

[60] Putney, 1729; Westminster 1738 ('Upon Westminster Bridge' composed by Wordsworth in 1802), Blackfriars, 1769 and Waterloo 1817.

[61] London did not have an integrated sewer system till the 1860s, required after 'the Great Stink' of the effluent in the river in the summer of 1858.

[62] C. P. Hill, *British Economic and Social History 1700–1964,* 3rd edn, p. 67. Butler states that the Napoleonic campaigns have been estimated to have cost more lives as a proportion of the British population than the 1914–1918 war (*Romantics, Rebels and Reactionaries,* p. 115).

CHAPTER FIVE

The Landed Gentry Take Up Yachting

Mr Herbert Weld, who was elected to the Squadron in 1924, owned the Big Class cutter *Lulworth* which he raced very successfully. Or to be more accurate, his crew raced very successfully … The papers were always delivered to Lulworth about half an hour before the race was due to start. Weld would then go below with a copy of *The Times* tucked under his arm and would not reappear until the race was well under way. 'Hullo!' he would say, casually looking round him. 'We've started'.[1]

Cowes Becomes Yachting's Capital –
the Squadron's Early Years

We left an informal grouping of yacht-owning aristocrats at the end of the last chapter who had agreed to meet twice a year, once in London and once in Cowes. Two questions merit answering. Firstly, why meet at Cowes, and, secondly, how did this informal group become the most prestigious yacht club in the United Kingdom, if not the world? In the final section, I will examine the America's Cup, first raced for in 1851, and its subsequent history.

I described in Chapter 3 how, during the second half of the eighteenth century, inland spa towns had gradually lost favour to seaside resorts, as doctors began lauding the merits of seawater, seawater bathing and sea air. Besides, inland resorts were becoming 'invaded' by members of the 'lower classes', seeking to join in the promenades, the dances and the meetings.[2] Royalty and the Aristocracy moved their socialising away from the inland spas to coastal spas.

Already, before the turn of the century, grand properties were being built along the Solent Coast around Cowes and along the Medina River. The swelling of its summer population was reported on by the *Hampshire Courier* and

---

[1] J. B. Atkins, *Further Memorials of the Royal Yacht Squadron*, p. 179.
[2] Cf. Corbin, *The Lure of the Sea: The Discovery of the Seaside 1750–1840*.

the *Hampshire Telegraph*, 'two papers which may be regarded as the archives for the first period of English yachting, of the fine company which gave an increasing prosperity to Cowes before the nineteenth century had run into its teens'.[3]

Travel to the Island was improved by the introduction of the paddle steamer, *Prince Cobourgh*, on the Southampton–Cowes run from 1820.

Brighton had become fashionable thanks to the Prince Regent building the Royal Pavilion there. In 1819, the Prince Regent greatly added to the success of the Cowes season. He had intended to sail from Brighton to Plymouth in his yacht, the *Royal George*, 'but was so delighted with the beautiful scenery of the Isle of Wight, Southampton River, and the view of the New Forest', that he ended his cruise in the Solent.[4] Then, in 1821, as the recently crowned George IV, he bought a cottage on the sea-front.

There can be little doubt that it was royal involvement that, within fifteen years, changed an informal social grouping of aristocrats into the premier yacht club.[5]

The Prince Regent had been appointed as acting monarch in 1811, due to the poor mental health of George III. He had an additional reason to court the upper classes. He had become involved in a lengthy, messy and unpopular attempt to disown and divorce his wife, Caroline. He sought nomination in 1817, within two years of the Club's creation.

Because its structure was so informal, the Yacht Club had incurred little expense and subscriptions had been allowed to lapse. The cost of binding the Prince Regent's signal books in red morocco leather led to the re-imposition of an annual subscription. In the following Spring, the Royal Princes, the Dukes of Clarence and Gloucester, joined the club.

Faced with this upsurge in prestige, the club began to tighten up its regulations. As mentioned, the tonnage required for membership rapidly rose from 10 tons in 1815 to 30 tons in 1825 and soon 40 tons, which is sizeable.[6] Yachts of such size needed a professional skipper and crew of some fifteen, or more, men. (The owner never worked the boat.)

The club's social ascendancy was further emphasised when, on being crowned in 1820, the Prince Regent, now George IV, agreed to a petition to change its name to the Royal Yacht Club, and to become its patron.

---

[3] Guest and Boulton, *Memorials of the Royal Yacht Squadron*, p. 32.
[4] Guest and Boulton, *Memorials of the Royal Yacht Squadron*, p. 59.
[5] The exact nature of a 'senior' club is a little vague. Formed before 1875, permitted to call itself 'Royal' and to fly a defaced ensign would be three important attributes.
[6] Not of the weight of the boat, but the weight of a theoretical cargo.

Cruising in company, like the Cork Water Fleet and the Cumberland Fleet before them, was the preferred method of the members meeting on the water. The members cruised in company off Cowes, with an annual procession around the Brambles – a sandbar off Southampton Waters. By 1822, these processions had become so popular it was resolved:

> that on the first and third Mondays of each month the yachts be assembled in Cowes Roads at 10am for the purpose of sailing together under the directions of the Commodore appointed for the day.[7]

The first such procession was on 1 July, 1822. The arrangements were practically identical with those of the Cork Water Club, excepting that the Solent did not require that meetings should happen at the time of Spring tides, and there were no penalties for non-attendance.

There were tensions concerning these sedate processions. A missive to the members from the Committee, after the event, notes:

> The original proposition of assembling the vessels of the club upon certain days under the direction of a leader having being made with a far different view from that of racing and showing superiority of sailing, that inconvenience and danger arise from irregularity, and that it would tend to the comfort of all, and particularly the ladies who may honour the meeting with their presence, if order were preserved.[8]

The ladies' presence and dress provided evidence of 'vicarious display' – they were displaying the owners' wealth. It would not do if they were frightened off by their husband feeling he had to compete.

Once again, there was ongoing discussion regarding the appropriate uniform. In 1826, the *Southampton Town and County Herald* noted that:

> the club uniform of a common blue jacket and white trousers was far from being unbecoming, provided the wearer was not 'too square in the stern'.[9]

Buttons, however, were the subject of several resolutions during the next few years.[10] And again, a signal book provided a secret language spoken only by members. The 1817 signal book 'contains a simple vocabulary of nearly 3000 different signals, which would rise to 6500 words, 2000 sentences, 900 Christian and surnames … and a list updated annually of naval ships …'

---

[7] Dear, *The Royal Yacht Squadron 1815–1895,* p. 26.

[8] *Ibid.,* p. 26.

[9] Changes were made again in 1827 and 1831 (Dear, *The Royal Yacht Squadron 1815–1985,* pp. 33–34).

[10] Dear, *The Royal Yacht Squadron 1815–1985,* pp. 34–35.

Sentences included 'Can you lend me your band', 'three hundred oysters' and 'even included what signal to fly if one member wanted to borrow from another as many as fourteen types of wine!'[11]; and this list was available two years after the club's formation.

Going South

The Squadron members were the first group of yachtsmen to have boats of sufficient size to entertain the reality of long-distance cruising, especially as they could afford to hire sufficient, competent sailors. The boats were also large enough to carry cannons, useful for attacks from pirates. Their destination was invariably the South, most usually the Mediterranean. Besides the better weather, sailing in the Mediterranean had echoes of the pre-Napoleonic war 'grand tours', as it permitted visits to the sites of classical antiquity.

As Cusack states:

> By 1851 the Mediterranean, from Gibraltar to Constantinople, had become the most widely used cruising area. The Mediterranean offered yachtsmen a pleasant climate, health presented no major problems in this region, and while some yachts encountered cholera, this disease was not unknown in England, for instance affecting Plymouth in 1849.[12]

The 150 ton yacht, *Falcon*, was often sailed by the first Commodore, the Earl of Yarborough, down to the West of France and Spain to pick up wines.[13] The stocking up with wine from France and Spain was a favourite pursuit of members, as boats of the Royal Yacht Club, being treated as equivalent to naval vessels, did not have to pay custom dues or harbour charges. This may well have been part of the motivation for a more ambitious club cruise by twenty Squadron yachts to Cherbourg in 1833: a 'booze cruise'. 'This cruise aroused considerable public interest, and the yachts were escorted by a fleet of small craft, occupied by sightseers and newspaper reporters.'[14]

We can put figures to this clear preference for the South. In the RYS scrapbook compiled by Montague Guest are listed the destinations of 48 RYS members cruising in 1851. Forty-one had gone South, with only seven going North, all to Norway. A further 'large number' were in or going to Gibraltar.[15]

---

[11] *Ibid.*, pp. 19–20.
[12] Cusack, 'The Rise of Aquatic Recreation and Sport', p. 187.
[13] Johnson, *The Encyclopaedia of Yachting*, p. 28.
[14] Cusack, 'The Rise of Aquatic Recreation and Sport', p. 62.
[15] *Ibid.*, p. 187. A few went both North and South. Sir Thomas Dyke Acland cruised Ireland and Northern Spain in 1833, and circumnavigated England, calling at St Kilda in 1834 with

Perhaps the most dramatic aristocratic presence in the Med. was that of the second generation of Romantic poets – the titled Byron and Shelley, and Keats.[16] Shelley, with two others, sailed his eight-metre schooner, *Don Juan*, from Lerici in the Bay of Spezia, Italy, where he was staying with Byron, to Livorno, to meet Leigh Hunt to discuss the creation of a new radical journal. On the return leg, they were hit by a violent squall and the boat foundered. Richard Holmes suggests that 'the sail to hull ratio was far too high; it was ballasted with too much pig iron, and it floated with too little freeboard'. Freeboard – the distance from the waterline to the top of the deck – is particularly crucial on an open boat, as it is liable to be flooded, also the crew are at risk of being thrown out of the cockpit by a large wave. According to Holmes, the designer, Captain Roberts, helped by Edward Williams, who was also lost, refitted it in the month before this voyage with a view to increasing its speed and made it even more unstable. For example, they fitted new topsails which could not be taken down without going up the mast, obviously a dangerous manoeuvre in a rough sea.[17]

Some members ventured further afield:

> … Captain Corry sailed his 58-ton cutter to Jamaica with a crew of only four, surely the first time a private yacht had accomplished a crossing of the Atlantic. … In 1832 J. Leveson Gower's *Albatross* was en route for Madeira … And in 1839, Sir James Brooke took his 142-ton schooner *Royalist* to the Far East.[18]

James Brooke was attacked off Borneo by pirates. A few broadsides from the *Royalist*'s guns soon saw them off. He also helped quell a rebellion in Sarawak against the Sultan of Borneo, who, in gratitude, made him the 'White Rajah' of Sarawak. Not all the members' interactions with Pacific islanders were so positive. Ben Boyd, cruising the Solomon Islands in 1851, went ashore for a spot of game shooting, but ended up being eaten by cannibals.

In 1833, Royalty acted proactively. The new king, William IV, declared that the club was to be known as the Royal Yacht Squadron, of which 'his Majesty is graciously pleased to consider himself the head'.

---

his family and a piano on board. In 1835 and 1836, his *Lady of St Kilda*, 136 tons, 70 foot long, made two voyages to the Mediterranean, allowing the family to overwinter there in 1835 (*Ibid.*, pp. 208–209).

[16] Wordsworth and Coleridge, with their *Lyrical Ballads* (1798) were the first generation.

[17] Richard Holmes, 'Death and Destiny'. Whilst persuasive, Holmes gives no references, so it is unclear what sources he is quoting and their reliability.

[18] Dear, *The Royal Yacht Squadron, 1815–1985*, pp. 44–45.

It is clear that successive monarchs were actively engaging in what they saw as a benevolent circular process – increasing yachting's prestige, most especially the Squadron's, and, by doing so, increasing their own, by achieving greater acceptance among the aristocracy.

The first clubhouse on the Parade was acquired in 1825. (It moved to its present premises, the Castle at West Cowes, in 1857.) Cowes became an even more prestigious resort after Queen Victoria found Brighton too crowded with the arrival of the railway from London in 1841. Prince Albert designed Osborne House, to the east of Cowes, which was built between 1845 and 1851. However, the opening of the London to Southampton Line in 1840 and the London to Portsmouth line in 1850 gave a major boost to yachting in the Solent.

In 1829, the Admiralty had granted the use of the White Ensign to the Royal Club, and the few other extant yacht clubs who chose to apply for it.[19] This allowed freedom from custom dues when abroad and use of the buoys reserved for naval vessels, if empty. As mentioned in the last chapter, smuggling was widely tolerated and there were complaints of abuse of the White Ensign. Consequently, the Squadron's prestige was further increased, when, in 1842, the Admiralty withdrew the right to fly the White Ensign from all clubs except the Squadron.[20]

The Squadron Starts Organising Races

It was racing, organised by the Club after 1826, that made it the focus of popular attention and 'Cowes Week' an important part of the social calendar.

Before then, those members who wanted to race had to look elsewhere. The southwestern harbours gained from the slow start to racing at Cowes. For example, at the Royal Western, Plymouth, the racing was under Royal Yacht Club rules. Dartmouth Regatta was a convenient location, and Yacht Club boats took part from 1822. By 1825, the *Exeter Flying Post* was noting that

---

[19] Guest and Boulton, *Memorials of the Royal Yacht Squadron*, pp. 269–273. It is worth noting that two of the insignia of a senior yacht club come from different sources. The right to call oneself 'Royal' is granted by the monarch; the right to fly a defaced ensign by the Admiralty. Some yacht clubs have a defaced ensign but are not 'royal'. Examples are the West Mersea Yacht Club and the Cruising Association.

[20] Adrian O'Connell, 'Royal Western Yacht Club of Ireland – Club History', 2004. O'Connell suggests that this was because it was difficult at a distance to distinguish a naval vessel, say a revenue cutter, from a large yacht, if both flew ensigns of the same colour, the yacht club's emblem defacing it being hard to recognise at distance. The Admiralty forgot to tell the Royal Western Yacht Club of Ireland, and it is a fine point whether the present club could fly the white ensign.

there were 'only 5 or 6 yachts from Cowes', suggesting that this was a regular event but a poor year.

Another way was by privately arranged matches. Much interest was aroused when, in 1825, Captain J. M. Davey, with his crack Thames Yacht Club craft, *Don Giovanni*, issued a challenge to any boat of her tonnage. Captain Lyons, in the Solent, had *Queen Mab* specially built. It appears that Davey, arriving at Cowes, looked across at the opposition, didn't like what he saw and refused to race. *Queen Mab* sailed the course and won the £200 stake (equivalent to about £30,000 in 2016).[21]

Usually, the races were between much larger, crewed vessels. The aristocratic owner, as John Leather put it, 'regarded the yacht carrying his colours in the season around the coast rather as racehorses are still owned – one does not expect the owner to train and ride the horse'.[22] Very few members actually raced – the same names: Weld, Anglesey, Assheton-Smith and Belfast occur repeatedly in the early years of the Squadron races.

Joseph Weld had been left both Lulworth Castle and a considerable fortune when his older brother entered the Catholic priesthood. In 1815, he entered a three-race match of his *Charlotte* with Mr Thomas Assheton-Smith's *Elizabeth*. The tone of reporting the activities of the rich by the *Hampshire Telegraph*, like other local papers, was obsequious:

> A match was made on Monday last for 500 guineas is as likely to afford as much sport as any race that was ever contested by the highest-mettled coursers at Newmarket. Both yachts are of beautiful model and construction, and of celerity as quick sailers, and each gentleman confident of his vessel's superiority.

Apparently, there was widespread betting on the outcome. Unfortunately, for at least some of them, it was over all too soon, for 'a very severe puff of wind' – to use Guest and Boulton's phrase – dismasted the *Elizabeth* off St Aldan's Head during the first race, and she was withdrawn from the contest.

The Marquess of Anglesey in his quest for fast, racing yachts had sought out Philip Sainty, a Colneside shipbuilder, in 1809, to build *Emerald*, which with a local crew was unbeatable in yachts of her size.[23] When, after Waterloo, in 1815, he went back to North Essex, he found that Sainty was in jail for smuggling. He talked to the son, inside for the same offence, who did not

---

[21] Guest and Boulton, *Memorials of the Royal Yacht Squadron*, pp. 72–73.

[22] Leather, Introduction, *Yachts and Yachting*, by Vanderdecken, p. vi.

[23] Sainty also built him *Liberty*, before he built him *Pearl*, but Leather (*The Northseamen*, p. 88) does not give the date of the build.

let on that he was not talking to the father. Anglesey procured a pardon from the Prince Regent, with whom he was on good terms, for the Sainty he had seen. Then he had to get Sainty, the father, out and he in turn demanded the release of two other relatives. When this had all been done, it was worth the string-pulling. Sainty delivered *Pearl*, a fast and good-looking craft.[24]

That recklessness of betting was a pleasurable activity in itself – to show that losing money would be of little import – is evident in the next race account. In August 1825, Joseph and James Weld challenged the Marquess of Anglesey to a two-race bet of 300 guineas. The Welds' *Arrow* was twenty tons lighter than Anglesey's *Pearl*, but as Guest and Boulton remark:

> Nothing is more remarkable in the history of yachting than the cheerfulness with which the owners of small boats took the odds of tonnage and sail area without the slightest hesitation or without a single thought for time allowance.

Lord Anglesey, in accepting it, remarked 'If the *Pearl* should be beaten, I will burn her as soon as we get back.'[25] Not surprisingly, the *Pearl* won easily.

In 1826, a meeting of the Club acknowledged that racing was popular with some members, and that races between the Cowes pilots were watched by large crowds. So, it unanimously resolved that:

> A gold cup of the value of £100 be sailed for by vessels belonging to the club, of any rig or tonnage.

As usual, there was no handicapping. It was won by Joseph Weld's *Arrow*.

The race generated such enthusiasm that the next year, 1827, the townspeople suggested a second regatta of two races, one open and one for yachts not exceeding 70 tons.

Once again, the monarchy must have been monitoring the situation, for the open race was sponsored by George IV, who 'repeated his well-known attachment to the club, and was pleased to direct that a cup of the value of 100 guineas be sailed for by the yachts of the Royal Club annually on his birthday, the 12th August.'[26]

In the account of the main 100 guineas race in the *Sporting Magazine*, Georgian acceptance of a violent free-for-all in a sporting contest is manifest.[27]

---

[24] Leather, *The Northseamen*, pp. 87–90.
[25] Guest and Boulton, *Memorials of the Royal Yacht Squadron*, p. 58.
[26] *Ibid.*, p. 104.
[27] The 'folk stage' phase concerned games that were played by very large numbers of the local males and involved much roughness and violence, and rules specific to that community (John

Weld, in the favourite, *Arrow*, had scant regard for giving priority to boats on the starboard tack (i.e. the wind is coming over the boat's starboard side.)

When only a few miles from home, the distance sailed being nearly eighty miles ... the *Arrow* had the temerity to cross the *Miranda* on the larboard [port] tack, and had not Captain Lyons taken the helm just in time she must have been run down.[28] As it was, the two vessels became entangled, and a scene of much violence took place ... The gallant Sir James Jordan, who was on board Mr Maxse's, had a narrow escape from a dreadful blow aimed at the back of his head by one of Mr Weld's men with a handspike.

... He avoided the blow by ducking his head, and hitting out right and left, a la Spring, floored the rascal with such tremendous violence that Captain Lyons told me afterwards he thought he was done for.[29]

Yacht racing created industries that were needed to support it. Ratsey and Lapthorn, sailmakers at Cowes, date from 1796, and the fore-runners of Camper and Nicholson were certainly building yachts by 1821.

The absurdity of yachts of vastly different sizes racing without handicap soon became apparent – the ambitious racing owners commissioned ever bigger yachts: Weld moved up from the 60 ton *Charlotte* in 1811 to the 193 ton *Alarm* in 1830; Assheton-Smith from the 60 ton *Elizabeth* in 1815 to the 180 ton *Menai*; Belfast from the 96 ton *Harriet* in 1815 to the 162 ton *Louisa* in 1828.[30] The first attempt by the club to regularise racing came with the division by tonnage into six different classes in 1829. Another scheme by a RYS member – the Ackers Graduated Scale – was introduced in 1843. This first attempt by the Squadron to introduce a handicap system was tried out in the regatta that year, the first to which royal clubs throughout the kingdom were invited. The next year, 'in 1844, fourteen Royal Thames cutters sailed to the Solent to challenge the South Coast fliers for a cup open to yachts under

---

Horne *et al.*, *Understanding Sport*, Chapter 1). Yachting was showing the violence that was typical of this 'folk stage'.

[28] The boat who was sailing on the starboard tack, i.e. had the wind coming over the starboard side and with the mainsail, therefore, on the port side, had the right of way.

[29] Dear, *The Royal Yacht Squadron, 1815–1985*, p. 37. 'A la Spring': A reference to Tom Spring, bare-knuckle fighter and Heavyweight champion of England from 1821 till his retirement in 1824. Another example occurred in an 1829 race, when Lord Belfast's *Louisa* and Mr Weld's *Lulworth* collided. '... Lord Belfast's crew drew their cutlasses. They cut through the lacing of *Lulworth's* boom as well as her reef pendant, leaving her disabled. Mr Weld's crew now began to hack at the rigging of Lord Belfast's *Louisa*. A subsequent decision in the club produced the deservedly famous ruling that '... the use of axes to cut away rigging was unjustifiable' (Bradford, *Three Centuries of Sailing*, p. 41).

[30] Data extracted from Guest and Boulton, *Memorials of the Royal Yacht Squadron*.

25 tons'.[31] The Thames boats were impressed by the Ackers system. So 'time allowances were endorsed and thereafter persisted'.[32]

Links with the Navy

The Squadron saw itself as an adjunct to the Navy. The Yacht Club as early as 1816 resolved:

> Officers of the Navy shall hereafter be eligible as honorary members of the club, but that the resolution respecting entrance and annual subscriptions shall not be considered as applicable.

Sir Thomas Hardy, Nelson's Captain at Trafalgar, 'headed a short list of distinguished naval officers granted immediate honorary membership'.[33]

Many of the Yacht Club's vessels, but also the vessels of other prestigious non-members, carried armament that made them look like vessels of the Royal Navy.[34] In 1847, 102 yachts of the Squadron carried 1,600 men and 400 guns (cannon). Additionally, members liked to claim that their crews represented a naval reserve, ready to be called on in times of war. Optimists hoped that 'these amateur tars [would] add to the security of England'.[35] George Bonner, in 1845, reported:

> The Editor of 'Bell's Life' tells us, That in case of war, there would be upwards of 5,000 able bodies seamen who are now employed in noblemen and gentlemen's vessels; the discipline in which is equal (if not superior) to any man of war cutter. He mentions an instance, that the Gannymede Yacht, R.S.Y.C., on a late occasion fired a royal salute in honour of the Princess Alice's birthday, with four guns, at six seconds time, or ten guns a minute.[36]

The uniform of the club emphasised its links with both the Navy and its patriotism. Ryan points out that 'adoption of naval type dress, customs and ranks, with a commodore leading each club, identified the British yachtsman as a loyal supporter of the crown'.[37]

---

[31] Guest and Boulton, *Memorials of the Royal Yacht Squadron*, p. 186.

[32] Peter Johnson, *Yacht Rating*, p. 21.

[33] Dear, *The Royal Yacht Squadron 1815–1985*, p. 20.

[34] *Ibid.*, p. 8.

[35] Roger Ryan, 'Identifying the British Yachtsman, 1815–1939', p. 66. The quote is from a letter to the Editor of *Hunt's Yachting Magazine*, Vol. I, 1852, p. 340; see also Leather, *Northseamen*, p. 100.

[36] George Bonner, *The Yachting Season of 1845*, p. 113.

[37] Roger Ryan, 'Identifying the British Yachtsman, 1815–1939', p. 66.

The Club's doings were being widely reported in the local and national papers. The Club agreed with the public perception that, with their resources and access to the best designers, they had the duty of being the test bed for designs that could be useful for the navy.[38] 'Trunnion', in 1822, complains of the Club's inadequacy 'in the production of any new models of swift sailing'.[39]

As racing became more fashionable among members, so heed was taken of Trunnion's (and doubtless others') complaint. By 1827, John Fincham, Superintendent of the School of Naval Architecture at Portsmouth Dockyard, was writing about six of the Squadron's yachts – *Falcon, Pearl, Coquette, Emerald, Nautilus* and *Dolphin*. When he published his findings in book form in 1855, *The Royal Yacht Squadron: Its Yachts and a Scientific Basis for Their Improvement*, he added seven more yachts belonging to the Squadron.[40]

A Club member, Commander Symonds, became Surveyor of the Navy in 1832. The *Pantaloon* (323 tons) was built to his design and sailed with great success with the Experimental Squadron in 1831 and was eventually bought by the navy.

The most famous prototype was Lord Belfast's brig *Waterwitch*, (330 tons), built by Joseph White of Cowes in 1832. For his amusement, he would have the boat lying off Portsmouth and then, *under shortened sail*, it would outrun the unfortunate Naval vessel proceeding out of the Solent. Her trial against naval vessels was commemorated by the leading maritime artist W. J. Huggins' painting *Trial of Lord Belfast's Waterwitch on 5 September 1832 off the Scilly Isles, with HM Ships Vernon, Dougal, Stag* and *Snake*. The painting tells the story – the naval vessels are so slow, compared to *Waterwitch*, that they are disappearing into the mist behind the foregrounded *Waterwitch*. Having shown herself to be so superior to existing naval brigs, the Admiralty was forced by the public clamour to buy her in September 1834.[41]

Making Sense of the Squadron

There are only a few written accounts by Squadron members of their voyages. These few concern journeys to the Mediterranean and to other sunny climes.

---

[38] Guest and Boulton, *The Royal Yacht Squadron*, Chapter 7: 'The Royal Yacht Club as a School of Naval Architecture', pp. 126–148.

[39] 'Trunnion', *Sporting Annals*, October, 1822; quoted by Dear, *The Royal Yacht Squadron, 1815–1895*, p. 27. 'Trunnion' took his nom de plume from Commodore Trunnion in Tobias Smollett's *The Adventures of Peregrine Pickle*, 1751, rev. 1758. Smollett is usually credited with creating 'the sailing novel' with *The Adventures of Roderick Random*, 1748, his first novel.

[40] Dear, *The Royal Yacht Squadron 1815–1985*, p. 41.

[41] Guest and Boulton, *Memorials of the Royal Squadron*, pp. 142–147.

5   *Trial of the R.Y.S. Squadron Brig 'Water Witch' on the 5th September 1832 off the*
Scilly Islands with H.M. Ships 'Vernon', 'Donegal', 'Stag' and 'Snake'. The public
expected the Squadron to develop yacht design to aid the Navy. Lord Belfast
agreed with them. Huggins was an artist highly regarded for his accuracy. Here
he demonstrates the manifest superiority of Belfast's yacht by showing the Naval
vessels so far back as to be only visible in outline.

As Diana Harding, RYS archivist, remarked, these accounts 'tend to record
the places (and people) they visited or the number of tigers they shot'.[42]
The earliest book written by a member is *The Narrative of a Yacht Voyage to
the Mediterranean during the Years 1840–41* by Earl Grosvenor. 'It is in two
thick volumes, but the subject of sailing is hardly touched upon', presumably
because the author left that to his crew.[43]

   This lack of written texts does not mean that members did not wish to
memorialise their expensive possessions. Rather, the primary mode, as
before with the Water Club of Cork a century earlier, was the oil painting.[44]

[42] Personal communication, June 2006.
[43] Dear, *The Royal Yacht Squadron, 1815–1985*, pp. 45–46. Francis Gower, afterwards Lord Elles-
    mere, was another early long-distance cruising yachtsman. Guest and Boulton (*Memorials of
    the Royal Yacht Squadron*, p. 67) note that 'In the *Owen Glendower* or the *Menai,* he was often
    in the Mediterranean, and has left record of his cruises called *Mediterranean Sketches.'* This was
    published in 1843.
[44] James Taylor, *Yachts on Canvas*, pp. 46–49.

As early as the 1827 Cowes Regatta, Turner was commissioned by John Nash to paint two pictures.[45] A large number of Turner's paintings were seascapes, and he owned and sailed boats. Turner stayed with Nash from the end of July till the second week of September, and drew nine sketches and the two oil paintings. The two paintings were *East Cowes Castle, the seat of J. Nash Esq.; the Regatta beating to Windward*, and *East Cowes Castle, the seat of J. Nash, Esq.; the Regatta starting from their moorings* (the standard way of starting a race at the time). Both were exhibited the following year at the Royal Academy but Turner was too abstract, too concerned with light and form, to be considered a good ship portrait painter – owners didn't want an impression, they wanted detailed accuracy.[46]

Squadron members hired a well-known marine artist, like Huggins or Nicholas Condy junior, to memorialise their yachts in oil paintings, often prominently featuring in a race and/or against a well-known landmark, such as the Needles. Nicholas Matthews Condy (1818–1851) was the official marine painter to the Royal Thames and to the Royal Western, Plymouth. His father Nicholas Condy (1793–1857), who outlived him, had been employed by his principal patron, the Earl of Mount Edgcumbe.[47] The Yacht Club appointed John Shekty as their marine painter in 1826. This kind of painting is equivalent to a Gainsborough or a Reynolds depiction of the owner and his wife in her finery, perhaps fanned by a young, black servant, with the backcloth of his country house and the park. What was different was that the owner of the yacht was not in the picture. However, this was also the case with a Stubbs (1724–1806) of the owner's favourite racer.[48]

---

[45] John Nash (1752–1835) was a town planner, who built much of Regency London, including the famous Nash terraces. He had built himself a neo-gothic East Cowes Castle (not to be confused with the Castle at West Cowes, the home of the Squadron after 1857).

[46] There must be space for an anecdote by John Ruskin, the most eminent Victorian art critic: 'Some years ago I happened to stand longer than pleased my pensioner guide before Turner's "Battle of Trafalgar", at Greenwich Hospital; a picture which, at a moderate estimate, is simply worth all the rest of the hospital – walls – grounds – pictures and models put together. My guide, supposing me to be detained by indignant wonder at seeing it in so good a place, assented to my supposed sentiments by muttering in a low voice: "Well, sir, it is a shame that that thing should be there. We ought to 'a 'ad a Uggins, that's sartain"' (*The Harbours of England*, p. 33).

[47] C. H. Ward-Jackson, *Ship Portrait Painters*, pp. 37–39.

[48] A rare exception is 'The Yacht *Guerrilla*' by the younger Condy, showing Captain Charles Ward and his family. Ward was on the Squadron's list from 1827 to 1833 (Taylor, *Yachts on Canvas*, p. 79).

Cowes Week

By the end of the 1820s, membership of the club demonstrated the person's presence at the top of the social pinnacle. The membership was and has continued to be restricted to around 400. But it was racing, dovetailed into the seven days of Cowes Week, started in 1834, that made yachting a key part of the social season.

Events in 'the season' included the Oxford and Cambridge Boat Race, first run in 1829 over the four-mile course on the Thames from Putney to Mortlake every April. The Eton vs. Harrow cricket match, first played in 1805, has been held annually at Lords in June since 1822.[49] Henley Regatta, in July, began in 1839. There was horse racing at Epsom (first recorded race, 1661) and at Ascot (founded by Queen Anne, who gave Her Majesty's Plate, worth 100 guineas, for the winner of the first race, 11 August, 1711). The first meeting at Goodwood, on the Duke of Richmond's grounds, near Chichester, where it is still held, was in 1802. Goodwood preceded Cowes. Cowes Week's dates – the first week of August – were apparently chosen to give the owners time to get up to Scotland for 'the glorious twelfth' – the opening of the grouse shooting season.[50]

Janet Cusack, following Thorsten Veblen (1857–1929), the Norwegian born American economist, argues that much of what the Squadron did and the way that they did it had the purpose of ostentatiously flaunting the members' non-productivity. She suggests that the procedures and activities of the Club can be best understood by the application of Veblen's *A Theory of the Leisure Class*, published in 1899, whose main ideas are summarised by Horne *et al.* in *Understanding Sport*:

> For Veblen, status is not passively linked to wealth. On the contrary, 'wealth or power must be put in evidence, for esteem is awarded only on evidence … In short, in order to maintain their status, the ruling class has to be seen to be busy, spending both time and money, doing nothing …'[51]

Veblen suggests that the leisure class is made up of those who control government, warfare, religion and sports, and this was certainly true in the first

---

[49] The MCC, the Middlesex Cricket Club, which had a goodly proportion of titled members, concluded their season at the beginning of August, so as not to interfere with the opening of the grouse shooting season (Huggins, *The Victorians and Sport*, p. 23).

[50] Yachting had to take its place alongside the other aristocratic sports. To give just one or two examples, Anglesey was a keen grouse shooter, Assheton-Smith and James Maxse enthusiastic fox-hunters (Guest and Boulton, *Memorials*, pp. 47–48 and 66). In contrast, later in the Victorian era, yachting was competing with the upper middle-class sports of golf and tennis.

[51] Horne *et al.*, *Understanding Sport*, pp. 36 and 98.

part of the nineteenth century, for the simple reason that this class controlled and owned almost everything (although this was less true for sports, as these were still emerging from the community-organised 'folk game stage'). Furthermore, entry into the key occupations was reserved for the current occupants' offspring.

The 'evidence' of their excess wealth was demonstrated by *conspicuous consumption*. Veblen described two types – conspicuous consumption of *time* and the conspicuous consumption of *objects*.[52]

We may see conspicuous consumption as *ostentation*. They did not work, they did not need to work; *but they did need to show the world that this was the case*.

So, an ostentatious display demands an audience to appreciate the display. Veblen suggested that there were two target audiences for ostentation. It has the purpose of impressing one's peer group – one's friends and, especially, one's competitors – with evidence of one's status. The other audience is the wider world, represented by the crowd on the Parade. For example, in 1829, the *Southampton Herald*, now called the *Hampshire Advertiser*, reported on the firework display that ended the regatta:

> All the yachts were illuminated with blue lights, producing an effect of almost inimitable grandeur ... Then followed rockets, wheels, serpents etc., and the Parade was illuminated by a beautiful display of pieces by the club's pyrotechnical artist, Jones, whose exhibition excited universal approbation from as numerous an assemblage as ever was collected on and around the Parade.[53]

This relationship is *a two-way process*. Ostentation only has purpose when it can demonstrate social superiority. This requires an audience to concur with the efficacy of that demonstration. Further confirmation is provided by the reporting of the ostentatious activity for those who cannot be present.

What is of interest in the accounts of the Squadron is how much of it concerns gossipy tales about the members and their ladies. Gossip seems almost the main form of information transmission about the Squadron.

The *Hampshire Courier*, the *Hampshire Telegraph* and the *Southampton Town and County Herald*, saw creating a 'gossip stream' as a serious business.[54]

---

[52] J. A. Mangan, in *Athleticism in the Victorian and Edwardian Public School*, p. 100, added a third type: consumption of *conspicuous resources*, such as underused playing fields, or empty yacht club moorings in an otherwise crowded harbour.

[53] Guest and Boulton, *Memorials of the Royal Yacht Squadron*, p. 115.

[54] *Ibid.*, p. 32.

It was a sure sign of the increasing importance of the club as a social institution that the prominent gentlemen of the Press in London found it worthwhile to attend the annual festivities in Cowes, and to favour their readers with their impressions. Among those gentlemen, who were the professional ancestors of the society [gossip] journalists of our own day, Mr. C. Westmacott, the 'Bernard Blackmantle' of the *English Spy*, was not the least eminent.[55]

Mr Blackmantle's, and the paper's, efforts were rewarded in 1827 when the paper was permitted to assume the additional title of 'The Royal Yacht Club Gazette'. 'Blackmantle', earning his crust, records:

the evening promenade is unusually brilliant in all the attractive features of wealth, beauty, and fashion. Among the leading stars are the Ladies Pagets, Ellenborough, Ashbrook, Thomas, Listowels, Frampton, Rivers, Vivian, Mrs Sturges Bourne, Corbett, Lloyd, and a host of bright eyes and graceful forms.[56]

These fine ladies must promenade for their husbands' 'vicarious consumption' to be noted.

In 1857, the Squadron moved into the Castle, West Cowes. The ladies watched the races from the Squadron's gardens, which were without seaward walls. So the public, gathered on the esplanade, the Parade, had a clear view of these important personages 'gazing at the elite on the lawns [of the RYS], picking out their pet celebrity, sometimes with awe, but just occasionally with ribaldry ...'.

A final point about ostentation is that it is only effective if it attracts an audience, but, at the same time, that *audience must not be acknowledged,* because that might suggest that these onlookers were necessary and their presence noted.[57]

We should not devalue the various social functions of gossip.[58] When social exclusion is very marked, it may be that gossip is a strategy for the

---

[55] *Ibid.*, p. 61.

[56] *Ibid.*, p. 63.

[57] Similarly, in paintings and, later, in photographs of rich men and women posing on yachts or in yacht clubs, their gaze is not towards the observer/lens, but to the middle distance; whereas crew, in pictures after a successful season, look at the camera.

[58] It was around this time that 'silver fork' novels were all the rage. For example, John Peck. *War, the Army and Victorian Literature*, p. 8 notes 'tales of upper-class licentiousness both appeal to the envious traits of middle-class readers and bolster their self-confidence by confirming their worst suspicions about the class above them ... "Silver Fork" novels that were in vogue from the mid-1820s to the mid-1840s, novels that portray, with a mixture of excited envy and moral disapproval, the manners of post-Regency society'. See also Alison Adburham, *Silver Fork Society: Fashionable Life and Literature from 1814 to 1840.*

poorer members of society to handle their non-inclusion. Perhaps it allows people to feel closer to their betters, while simultaneously proving 'they're just like you and me'.[59]

Derogatory gossip allows us to feel superior concerning those of higher social status. During the Crimean war, Lord Cardigan had given 'great offence by living in luxury on his yacht off Balaclava, served by a French chef, at the time when his men were enduring great privation'. So, it was recorded that his skipper asked him 'Will you take the helm, milord?' to which he replied 'No thank you, I never eat between meals'. So, this piece of gossip, demonstrating his complete ignorance of sailing despite owning a large yacht, gratifyingly takes him down a peg.[60]

More rarely, gossip can make us feel closer to the rich, because it helps justify their status. Lord Brassey, first member of the Squadron to circumnavigate the globe in the *Sunbeam*, was unusual in that he held a Master's certificate and, even more unusually, was a hands-on owner.[61]

> On one occasion just after *Sunbeam* had been fitted with some studding-sail booms, one of the crew began grumbling about the awkwardness of handling them aloft. 'I wish the old [bastard] was up 'ere 'isself,' he shouted to a mate. 'The old [bastard] is up here', a voice shouted back and the startled hand turned to see the owner coming out along the yard's footropes.[62]

Maldwin Drummond, who served as Commodore of the Squadron, concluded: 'Such stories are the very stuff of which clubs are made and a good reason to have a meeting place ashore, even if members had their palaces afloat'.[63] This indicates another function of gossip – to increase intragroup cohesion by increasing the sense of 'we-ness' (and the 'otherness' of the non-members).[64]

---

[59] The proliferation of gossip magazines in recent years may indicate the severity of current social exclusion. Eric Foster undertook a review of 'Research on Gossip', 2004, and considered its four main functions: the gaining of information, entertainment, intimacy among the gossipers and maintaining moral standards, both by criticising the objects of the gossip and reinforcing the standards of the gossipers. For those in a power group, gossip reinforces the we-ness of the group, even if highlighting (and delighting in) scandalous behaviour of other members, and also maintains the group boundary against non-group members.

[60] Dear, *The Royal Yacht Squadron 1815–1985*, p. 65.

[61] Other rare examples were Lord Dunraven, who held an Extra Master Mariner ticket, as did T. B. Davis, owner of *Westward* between the World Wars.

[62] Phillips-Birt, *The Cumberland Fleet*, p. 84.

[63] Drummond, *Salt-Water Palaces*, p. 42.

[64] cf. S. Haslam, *Psychology in Organisations*, which outlines his Social Identity theory that our identity is not that of a monad, but is made up of the groups we belong to.

So far, all the gossip has only been about men, which is not surprising since women were only granted associate membership in the 1960s and full membership in 2014. Anthony Heckstall-Smith tells of 'a certain fascinating lady called Mrs. Perkins',

> the wife of a London brewer who owned several yachts, used her husband's vessels 'as so many barouches or landaus for her morning visits.' In 1845, this lady 'arrived at Cherbourg in one of her yachts to call upon a lady of her acquaintance.

> They gossiped over new novels and new Irish melodies, and in the sequel Mrs Perkins kindly offered to return to England and fetch some new songs … One morning shortly afterwards, Mrs Perkins again made her appearance with a roll of music in her hand.

> 'You positively must stay and dine with us,' said her fair friend, whom she had exerted herself to oblige.

> 'Can't indeed, my dear,' replied the yachting lady. 'I must be off immediately; I have promised the wife of the British Consul in Cadiz and I know she is expecting me'; and away went Mrs Perkins to Cadiz and back to London.[65]

This rare piece of gossip about a woman in RYS circles serves to show that her husband has so much money he can afford her gallivanting life-style. Note also the conversation is reported as if it was witnessed and recorded, which is clearly not the case.

One other woman must be noted. Flora Condy, the widow of marine artist Nicholas Condy, the younger, was invited on a cruise from Cowes to Plymouth at the end of the 1852 Cowes week, on board the 69-ton cutter, *Ganymede*, owned by the martinet J. H. W. Smyth-Piggott. She wrote a humorous account of the passage, the high point of which is his attempt to hold a service in high wind, an event that required the flying of the church pennant at the peak. This required the raising of the mainsail, at which point the boat rocked uncontrollably. Condy's *Reminiscences of a Yachting Cruise*, published in 1852, is far funnier than the later and far more famous *Three Men in a Boat*.[66]

---

[65] Anthony Heckstall-Smith, *Sacred Cowes*. 2nd, rev. edn, 1965, pp. 27–28. Mr Perkins was one of the owners of the great brewing firm Barclay, Perkins and Co., and was elected to the Yacht Club in 1819.

[66] In *Reminiscences of a Yachting Cruise*, the *Ganymede* becomes the *Anona* and Smyth-Piggott 'Mr Matsell'.

The America's Cup

The arrival of the yacht *America* in the summer of 1851 is very much part of the Squadron's narrative. In addition, it allows us a final look at the role of gossip in the Squadron: its use for disinformation.

Arthur Clark in his *History of Yachting*, describes an engraving of 1717 which showed Colonel Morris' *Fancy* of New York.[67] America at that time was a British colony. Before that, it had belonged to the Dutch, who Clark thinks had introduced yachts as a means of transport in the seventeenth century.[68] The New York Yacht Club (the NYYC) was founded in 1844 and Lord Wilton, the Commodore of the RYS, offered members of the NYYC the opportunity 'to become visitors of the clubhouse at Cowes'. Stevens, the NYYC Commodore, wrote that he was commissioning a new schooner, which he would sail to England with a view to racing against RYS members' yachts.[69]

There was something of a decline in the quality of British yacht racing in the years before *America's* victory, with even talk of the demise of the Squadron's regatta.[70] So, the Americans were arriving with a newly designed, newly built boat to race against a rather undistinguished Squadron racing fleet.

On 31 July 31, 1851, *America* came in from Le Havre and anchored opposite Osborne House. She was described by the yachting correspondent of *Bell's Life* for 17 August, 1851:

> She has a low black hull, two noble sticks of extreme rake without an extra rope … her bow is as sharp as a knife blade, the side gradually springing out- wards as round as an apple … Her stern is remarkably broad, wide and full.[71]

Innovative features included: her cotton sails, which held their shape better than the flax sails used by the English yachts; her long fine bow, which cut through the water better compared to the bluff bows characteristic of the Squadron boats; and her raked masts which were a visually startling inno- vation.[72] However, it is still rather puzzling why the myth has grown up that

---

[67] Arthur Clark, *The History of Yachting*, p. 36.

[68] *Ibid.*, p. 42.

[69] '*America* was designed by George Steers, whose father, a Devonshire man, had learned his trade in the Royal Dockyard, and emigrated in 1819' (George Blake and Christopher Small, *Cruise in Company*, p. 96).

[70] Dear, *Royal Yacht Squadron, 1815–1985*, p. 56.

[71] Stella Archer and Peter Pearson, *The Royal St George Yacht Club*, p. 105.

[72] Black, *G. L. Watson: The Art and Science of Yacht Design*, p. 34.

6 *The Yacht 'America' Winning the International Race,* by Fitz Hugh Lane.
Winning a race around the Isle of Wight against Squadron yachts
started this long-running competition.

America was a very advanced yacht. We have the story of Lord Anglesey, out for a sail in his *Pearl*, followed by *America*.

> Under mainsail and jib alone, the Yankee passed *Pearl* easily. His Sailing Master said to the Marquis, 'Your Lordship knows no vessel with sails alone could do that'. When the two yachts came to anchor, the Marquis went aboard *America* and leaned so far over the stern looking for the propeller that the owner, Commander Stevens, had to seize his leg to prevent him going overboard. [Later, she was hauled out at Portsmouth, and, of course, had no propeller].[73]

This passage neatly shows how gossip is constructed. There are various 'factual' details – the verbatim wording of the remark of the Sailing Master and the antics of the Marquess – so that we are encouraged to believe it. Then there is the visually striking picture – Stevens holding onto Anglesey by his one good leg.[74]

How do we know this is made up? Firstly, an engine makes a noise and needs an exhaust pipe above the waterline, belching easily visible smoke. Secondly, it is quite unbelievable that the Marquess would be so insultingly rude as to accuse Stevens of cheating. Stevens was no upstart. He was a founder member and the Commodore of the New York Yacht Club. Besides, it would have been easy for Anglesey to check out any suspicions with other members of the Squadron. Guest and Boulton tell us that Stevens 'conducted many hundreds of visitors over the *America* as she lay in the roads … we read of the Commodore taking a distinguished party for a sail', who would have also seen the coal store, had there been one.[75]

There is another piece of gossip bolstering the superiority of *America*. Guest and Boulton make it clear that Stevens was not prepared to race against cutters, a wise move as we shall see from the actual race. Stevens, having no takers for a schooner match, issued a second challenge: 'This time he offered to match the *America* against any type of yacht, stating that he was prepared to lay down a ten thousand pound stake on the outcome.' £10,000 is, at a conservative estimate, worth £1 million pounds in 2015 terms, and, as Adrian Morgan puts it, was a 'staggerer', proposed by Stevens, an inveterate and heavy gambler, 'to frighten away competition and allow him to return home with his reputation intact'.[76] The lack of takers for this sum was interpreted as

---

[73] Henry Boylan, *White Sails Crowding*, p. 84.
[74] He obviously could not hold him by the 'peg leg' that Anglesey used after Waterloo.
[75] Guest and Boulton, *Memorials of the Squadron*, p. 220.
[76] Adrian Morgan, 'The Schooner *America*', p. 70.

indicating that the members of the Squadron were bad losers. *The Times* com-pared 'the British yachting fraternity ... to a flock of pigeons paralysed with terror at the appearance on the horizon of a sparrow-hawk'.[77] If, however, it was clear that the knowledgeable members of the Squadron recognised the boat's superiority, their hesitation becomes defensible.

The incorrect narrative then goes out that the Squadron hurriedly organ-ised a race for a £100 cup to quash this accusation of its members' cowardice. In fact, at the May meeting at the Thatched House, the members, knowing that *America* was coming over for the 1851 season, had agreed to ask Garrards to create a new cup, 'the Royal Yacht Squadron Cup', value £100, 'one of the ordinary prizes of the Royal Yacht Squadron', for a race open to foreign owned yachts, east about round the Isle of Wight, to take place on 28 August. This decision was long before *America's* arrival on 31 July.[78]

America was entered along with seventeen other yachts. She crossed the line some twenty-one minutes before the next yacht, *Aurora*. The Squadron, wanting to encourage links with the NYYC, had waived 'the already accepted principle of time allowance for tonnage'. Otherwise, *Aurora* would have won by some thirty minutes.[79]

The manifest superiority of *America* was hardly evident. Her inability to compete with cutters is shown by the fact that 'the *Wildfire*, a cutter of 48 tons, [which] had accompanied and led the field. Yet, *America* displaced 179 tons.'[80] As 'the Yachtsman' in *British Yachts and Yachtsmen* caustically remarked, 'one can find but little merit in a vessel of 170 tons beating another of 47 tons by 21 minutes over a course of 53 knots'.[81] Guest and Boulton con-cluded that 'the victory of the schooner [*America*] proved very little ... the owners of the *America* made no pretensions to compete with cutters, and that she was greatly superior to the English schooners who started against her, which, however, were all built as comfortable cruisers, in which racing qualities were of secondary consideration' which, if true, shows the minor quality of the race.

---

[77] Lipton, *Leaves from the Lipton Logs*, pp. 238–239.
[78] The Yachtsman, *British Yachts and Yachting*, pp. 122–124; Morgan, 'The Schooner *America*', p. 70.
[79] Guest and Boulton, *Memorials of the Squadron*, pp. 226–227; Morgan, 'The Schooner *America*', pp. 72–73.
[80] Guest and Boulton, *Memorials of the Squadron*, pp. 227 229. A *cutter* is a single-masted boat with a mainsail and more than one foresail. A *schooner* is a sailing ship with two or more masts, rigged fore-and-aft (i.e. not with square sails). Cutters usually are the faster boats.
[81] Yachtsman, *British Yachts and Yachtsmen*, p. 124. *Aurora* was a cutter, but with such a huge difference in tonnage, that should not have mattered.

It is not clear that *America* should have been given the cup. There was a
protest that *America* and some of the other yachts had not rounded the Nab
light [off the east coast of the Wight]. By going inside, they saved distance
and time – some one hour, twenty minutes.[82] 'Since the notice of race and
the sailing instructions were contradictory, the protests were withdrawn'.[83]
This 'withdrawal' does not mean the protestors 'saw reason'. Rather, given
the high status of the members, business at the Squadron had (and has) to
be conducted through consensus. So, it would have been quietly explained
to them that, because it was such a tinpot prize, it was not worth the protest
committee having to be heavy handed, when they could be gracious to their
American visitors.

What was smart was that the winning syndicate renamed the rather ordinary cup they had won – most senior yacht clubs boasted far larger, more
expensive and more ornate specimens – after the yacht: the *America's* Cup,
engaging national pride.[84] There were a large number of pictures, painted
from imagination by American artists, of the schooner during the race, jubi-
lant at beating their ex-colonial masters.

Because of the embarrassment this trumpeting caused, and the attempts
to get the Cup back across the decades, the significance of the 1851 race has
been re-written backwards to give it extra importance. There was no challenge
till 1870, the American Civil War (1861–1865) intervening. The challenge
came from James Ashbury, in his schooner *Cambria*, from the Royal Thames,
not – as might have been expected – from the Squadron.[85] (The challenge
has to come from a yacht club, not from the yacht's owner.) Similarly, Sir
Thomas Lipton, the millionaire tea and grocery shop merchant, is estimated
to have spent two million pounds of his money on America Cup challenges.
(For the 2015 equivalent, multiply by a thousand.) Yet, in 1899, the Squadron
refused his application, thereby rebuffing the Prince of Wales (later Edward

---

[82] Morgan, 'The Schooner "America"', p. 72. He is quoting from a pamphlet 'The Phoney Fame
of the Yacht America and the America Cup' by A. E. Reynolds Brown.
[83] Johnson, *Yacht Clubs of the World*, p. 65.
[84] Lipton, in his *Leaves from the Lipton Logs*, describes the cup as 'a piece of silver of the intrinsic
value today of considerably less than five hundred dollars!' (pp. 235–236). The most casual
glance at the trophies cabinet of any senior yacht club will show a number of cups of far greater value and ostentatiousness. The reader can compare the America's Cup with the 'priceless
collection' that Lipton won (opp. p. 236 of *Leaves from the Lipton Logs*). For another example
of far more impressive cups, see Leather, *The Northseamen*, p. 162, for two 'pots' won by the
racing cutter, *Ailsa*, in 1894.
[85] Bob Fisher, *The Great Yacht Races*, p. 13.

VII), then the Commodore, who proposed his application.[86] Lipton used the Royal Ulster for his five challenges.[87]

This is not to say that America Cup Challenges did not excite patriotic fervour, especially on the Clyde and on the Colne. Because of the eminence of Watson and Fife, many of the challengers were built on the Clyde. 'The excitement in Scotland during the [1887] races [*Thistle* challenger] had been intense, with newspaper offices being besieged for the latest news'. 'Despite rainy weather, a crowd of several thousand turned out to wave *Valkyrie III* on her way as she set sail for New York' on 27 July, 1895'.[88] The next table lists all the British challenges.

British Challenges to the America Cup

	Date	Name of yacht	Name of owner and designer	Name of sponsoring yacht club	Name of winning American yacht
1	1851	RYS racing fleet (14)		RYS	*America*
2	1870	*Cambria*	James Ashbury Designer: Michael Ratsey	Royal Thames	18 New York YC boats, winner *Magic*
3	1871	*Livonia*	Captain W.P. Douglas Designer: C. & R. Pollen	Royal Thames	*Columbia; Sappho*
		1876: Canadian challenge: *Countess of Dufferin*; 1881: Canadian challenge, *Atalanta*			

[86] Strictly speaking, Lipton was never blackballed, as, once it was clear he would not be admitted, his application was withdrawn. The Prince of Wales, the Commodore, told the members in 1900 that in the last twelve years, ninety-five candidates had been blackballed, and proposed that the power to admit should be vested in a committee. The members refused to change their rules (Anthony Heckstall-Smith, *Sacred Cowes*, 2nd, rev. edn, p. 45). Lipton was eventually elected in 1931, when it was clear his health was failing, and the members wanted to make clumsy amends. Lipton, who was sailing in the Solent that summer, refused to enter the Castle, the club house. He died in the October of that year.

[87] His parents left their home in County Monaghan to escape the Potato Famine and went to Glasgow, where Lipton was born. He wanted the first *Shamrock* to be built by Hartland and Wolff in Belfast, but they declined, having no experience of building yachts (*Leaves from the Lipton Logs*, pp. 24–25 and 242).

[88] Black, *G. L. Watson*, pp. 149 and 245.

4	1885	*Genesta*	Sir Richard Sutton Designer: J. Beavor-Webb	RYS	*Puritan*
5	1886	*Galatea*	William Henn, RN Designer: J. Beavor-Webb	RYS	*Mayflower*
6	1887	*Thistle*	John Bell & syndicate Designer: George Watson	Royal Clyde	*Volunteer*
7	1893	*Valkyrie II**	Earl of Dunraven Designer: George Watson	RYS	*Vigilant*
8	1895	*Valkyrie III*	Earl of Dunraven Designer: George Watson	RYS	*Defender*
9	1899	*Shamrock*	Sir Thomas Lipton Designer: William Fife, Jr	Royal Ulster	*Columbia*
10	1901	*Shamrock II*	Sir Thomas Lipton Designer: George Watson	Royal Ulster	*Columbia*
11	1903	*Shamrock III*	Sir Thomas Lipton Designer: William Fife, Jr	Royal Ulster	*Reliance*
12	1920	*Shamrock IV*	Sir Thomas Lipton Designer: Charles Nicholson	Royal Ulster	*Resolute*
13	1930	*Shamrock V*	Sir Thomas Lipton Designer: Charles Nicholson	Royal Ulster	*Enterprise*
14	1934	*Endeavour*	T.O.M. [Thomas Octave Murdoch] Sopwith Designer: Charles Nicholson	RYS	*Rainbow*
15	1937	*Endeavour II*	T.O.M. Sopwith Designer: Charles Nicholson	RYS	*Ranger*
16	1958	*Sceptre*	Hugh Goodson & syndicate Designer: David Boyd	RYS	*Columbia*
	1962	Australian challenge: *Gretel*			
17	1964	*Sovereign*	J.A.J. Boyden Designer: David Boyd	Royal Thames	*Constellation*

* *Dunraven had started building Valkyrie I in 1889 when the Squadron, the challenging yacht club, considering the NYCC's conditions unacceptable, withdrew their challenge.*

The America's Cup was a game with very few players. Dunraven (2), Lipton (5) and Sopwith (2) account for nine of the sixteen English challenges, and Bob Bond accounted for three Australian challenges before he won it at the fourth attempt, while it was his skipper, John Bertrand's, fifth involvement in the Cup. From 1901 up till the Second World War, only three designers (Fife, Watson and Charles Nicholson) were used. Only three yacht clubs – the Squadron (7), Royal Thames (3) and Royal Ulster (5) – sponsored the challenges. On the American side, the Herreshoff Manufacturing Company built eight of the American yachts. Nat Herreshoff designed six of them.[89] Thomas Ratsey (1851–1935) was directly involved in seven Cup challenges, and his firm of sailmakers in West Cowes was involved in providing sails for ten challengers and four defenders – he set up a sail loft in City Island, New York in 1901. Finally, many of the crew came from the North Essex villages. During the 1893 series, between *Valkyrie II* and *Vigilant*, 'Post Offices on Colneside displayed telegrams telling how the racing was going'.[90]

After 1964, the next six America's Cup challenges came from Australia. In 1983, *Australia II* defeated *Liberty* to finally wrest the cup from the New York Yacht Club. The Australian skipper, John Bertrand wrote a best-selling account of how *Australia II* won the series, stealing the series 4–3 in the final race.[91]

From 1983, challengers had to compete against each other for the Louis Vuitton Cup, to decide which yacht was to challenge the holder of the America's Cup. The British yacht, *Victory 83*, got to the finals of the Louis Vuitton but was beaten 4–1 by the eventual America's Cup winners, *Australia II*.[92]

That there was no successful British challenge was not surprising. The Americans held fierce trials for the right to defend the Cup, contested by the millionaire owner members of the NYCC, hiring the best crews, so the chosen boat was highly tuned by the time of the first race; whereas they required that a single British boat was named as challenger, preventing such sharpening of selection. Secondly, until 1937, the challenger had to sail to the competition 'on its own bottom', i.e. could not be transported on a steam vessel, requiring the boat to do quite different types of sailing – inshore racing and an Atlantic crossing in August, to be in time for the September

---

[89] L. Francis Herreshoff, *Captain Nat Herreshoff, the Wizard of Bristol*.

[90] Leather, *The Northseamen*, pp. 246–247.

[91] In a nice piece of continuity, Bertrand's great-grandfather, Thomas Pearkes, had been one of Lipton's main engineers, working on Lipton's Cup Challenges (John Bertrand, *Born to Win*, p. 10).

[92] The challenge had come from the Royal Burnham on behalf of Peter de Savary. For an insider's account of the British challenge and the complications involved, see Frank Kember, 'To Us It's Sport … To the Americans It's War'.

races, which is close to the hurricane season.[93] Finally, the British owners were amateurish.[94] Watson was involved in designing three of the challengers, but, unlike Herreshoff, allowed the owners to interfere with the designs. The British boats often came to the line woefully under-prepared. Dunraven took *Valkyrie III* to the 1895 challenge after only four races in one week in Scottish waters.[95] When, in 1920, the crew of *Shamrock IV,* probably his best chance, demanded more money, Lipton sacked them and replaced them with amateurs. Sopwith, after similar crew trouble, did the same with *Endeavour* in 1934, which he skippered himself.[96] Leather summarised the difference: 'When the skipper ordered 'All hands on the mainsheet!', within a second there were thirty powerful men hauling in unison and with a practised power which amateurs can never attain on a canted and heaving deck'.[97]

   Martin Black, in his *G. L. Watson*, analyses all the challenges from 1887 to 1903 in detail. It is a continuous, hair-pulling, saga of British incompetence; and of turning up in New York with basically unraced boats. This resulted in contests that were so one-sided that in at least two races, the American yacht was kept under-canvassed, in order not to demonstrate its actual superiority. It was the familiar British mixture of incompetence, arrogance ('who needs professionals and professionalism? Amateurs are just as good, and you can take them into the yacht club without embarrassment'); and 'it'll be alright on the night'. But it never was.[98] Hopefully, Ben Ainslie and the Land Rover BAR (Ben Ainslie Racing) team will improve on this record in 2017.

---

[93] For example, the 1888 challenger, *Thistle*, carried a very heavy main mast for the ocean crossing, which penalised her in the lighter airs of the American coastal waters (Black, *G. L. Watson*, pp. 148 and 150, n. 7).

[94] The Watson designed *Shamrock II* was faster than *Columbia*, but *Columbia* was skippered by the redoubtable Charlie Barr, a Scottish sailor who got his break in America and became a naturalised American (Black, *G. L. Watson*, p. 129).

[95] Black, *G. L. Watson*, pp. 243–244.

[96] Lipton offered the crew a bonus of £8 a week and they sought a bonus of £15. In the context of the overall cost of the campaign, this was a tiny percentage. For Sopwith, see Leather, *The Northseamen,* p. 250. Even more dismay-making is that Charles Nicholson, the designer of *Shamrock IV*, was not familiar with the Universal Rule the boats were racing under, so *Shamrock IV* had to give the defender, *Resolute*, 7 minutes 1 second on the 30 mile course. The key race was a dead heat, which meant that *Resolute* was the winner on corrected time (Johnson, *Yacht Rating*, pp. 73–74). Sopwith's incompetence with regard to *Endeavour* is particularly galling, as Leather (*The Northseamen,* p. 250) reckons that 'handled by her original crew she might well have brought back the Cup as she was acknowledged to be the faster yacht …'

[97] Leather, *The Northseamen,* p. 142.

[98] Perhaps to this list of British attributes should be 'inability to learn'. Leather points out that the 1964 challenger, *Sceptre*, was underprepared and also had an amateur crew (*The Northseamen*, p. 250). She produced the poorest results of any challenge.

In the long run, the cost of the Squadron life style meant that it was never going to be the way forward for leisure sailing; but first, there had to be greater political and social stability and that would only occur in the second half of the nineteenth century.

CHAPTER SIX

The Slow Expansion of Yachting in Britain, 1815–1870

There are at the moment a score of Yacht Clubs in the United Kingdom, containing altogether about five thousand subscribing members ... A national sport ... ought certainly to have a Magazine, to register the regattas, cruises, crotchets, inventions, deeds, discussions, and opinion of its supporters.[1]

The Lack of Political and Social Stability Needed for Yachting to Develop

The growth of yachting and yacht clubs in Great Britain was rather laboured after 1815 until the 1860s. To understand the reasons for this slow growth, we need to try to specify the conditions necessary for a yachting community to develop. [2]

The Conditions Necessary for a Yachting Community To Develop

- The use of the sea for leisure purposes requires political stability, so that people feel safe to invest in non-essentials
- There is economic and political confidence and optimism: potential boat owners must believe that these favourable conditions will continue into the future

---

[1] Preface to the first issue of *Hunt's Yachting Magazine*, August 1852. The 5,000 members was an over-estimate of the number of yachtsmen, as many members did not sail; and many of those who did belonged to more than one yacht club, so are being counted more than once (discussed later in this chapter). A 'crochet', besides its usual musical connotation, has an alternative meaning 'a whimsical fancy'

[2] These conditions draw on my 2009 article 'Leisure Sailing on a Hostile Shore: Yachting in the Bristol Channel, and Its Mudhole Yacht Clubs'. They are different criteria from the requirements for a yachting boom or golden period, discussed in Chapter 4

- The potential boat owner considers that sailing and the role of being a yachtsman relate to a way of life they value and wish to achieve
- There are a sufficient number of potential sailors for the would-be sailor to feel part of a community of like-minded souls
- A sufficiently large group within a society have surplus wealth
- *and* surplus time. 4) and 5) are not the same, as the creators of new wealth may spend all their time working, so it may well be the *second* generation of a newly rich family who become yachtsmen
- They have sufficient time and motivation to learn how to sail, to use the boat, and maintain it (or have it maintained), and to enjoy their chosen leisure pursuit
- There are a sufficient number of potential yachting havens, capable of providing safe moorings for a number of yachts
- There is easy access from the yachtsmen's homes, which are likely to be in a city, to these yacht havens
- The seas around these havens provide protected waters within which to sail
- The water is clean – free from sewage and pollution
- And free of industrial and urban character and congestion
- Peter Johnson adds: Access to foreign or other land within a few hours.*(This is surely a bonus, rather than a requirement.)

---

* Johnson, *Boating Britain*, p. 158.

These conditions were not present in the period between 1815 and 1850, which was one of high political tension and social instability.

The speed of replacement of rural home industries by machinery in city-based factories led to the smashing of the new, steam-driven machinery in Luddite riots, 1811–1816, in the lace mills of Nottingham and the wool and cotton mills of the North. The Corn Laws, 1815, by restricting imports, made bread – the staple food of the poor – prohibitively expensive. In 1816, income tax was abolished to be replaced by indirect taxes on goods, thus making the everyday goods that the poor needed more expensive, whilst the rich became wealthier.

In August, 1819, 80,000 people gathered to hear Orator Hunt in St Peter's Fields, Manchester. The magistrates panicked and sent in the cavalry, killing fifteen and seriously injuring 400–700 attenders, including 100 women. The government responded to this unrest with increasingly repressive measures. Habeas Corpus – no imprisonment without a trial – was suspended from 1816–1818. The Peterloo Massacre led to the Seditious Meetings Act of 1819, making all meetings of more than 50 people illegal without permission. The Six Acts Law rendered any meeting for the purposes of reform a treasonable act. Spies and agent provocateurs, capital punishment for 200 offences, and the extensive use of transportation meant that England had descended into a police state.[3]

These measures were not effective in quelling discontent. On 15 September, 1830, the Prime Minister, the Duke of Wellington, participated in the first running of a passenger train – from Liverpool to Manchester. On arrival at Manchester, the train was pelted with rotten vegetables by the crowd, forcing the Duke to order the train's return to Liverpool. In 1831, anger at the refusal of the Lords to pass the Reform Act, widening the electorate, caused the Queen's Square Riot in Bristol, which, as the result of a cavalry charge by the 3rd and 14th Light Dragoons, resulted in four dead and eighty-six wounded. This meagre toll did not satisfy the authorities, who court-martialled the commanders of the two companies, Captain Warrington and Lieutenant-Colonel Thomas Brereton, for leniency. Brereton shot himself before the conclusion of the court-martial.

For a decade from 1836, the Chartists became a very strong working class movement. Their aims were votes for all men; a secret, not an open, ballot;[4] and an end to rotten boroughs – seats with very few voters, which, with no secret ballot, could easily be controlled.[5]

Gradually, Parliament responded to the sources of discontent. The hours worked by women and children under 18 had started to be controlled by the Factory Acts of 1833 and 1847 (the Ten Hour Act). The Corn Laws were repealed in 1846, resulting in cheaper bread. In 1848, there were revolutions in a number of European countries, but not in Britain.

Historians generally agree that political stability was only created after 1850. The success of the Great Exhibition of 1851 in the Crystal Palace, erected in Hyde Park, has often been regarded as symbolic of Victorian society's new found self-confidence. This optimistic account is retrospective since, on the opening day, the Government was sufficiently nervous to bivouac regiments

---

[3] Six Dorsetshire labourers – the Tolpuddle Martyrs – were transported to Australia in 1834 for meeting and 'taking an oath of secrecy'. There were massive protests at this sentence across the country and the Martyrs came home in triumph in 1836.

[4] Only achieved in 1872 with the Ballot Act.

[5] Rotten boroughs were removed through the Reform Acts of 1832 and 1867.

in the suburbs and several Guards battalions in Hyde Park itself and to mobilise 6,000 police.[6] In the event, over six months, not even a flower was picked in the Park, and 6.2 million visitors had entered the Exhibition.[7] It was in the period of 1850 to 1870 that Britain became 'the workshop of the world' and the nation's prosperity increased dramatically.[8]

'Aristocratic' Yachting

'Aristocratic' changed its meaning during the course of the nineteenth century. Over the course of the century, the source of the nation's wealth changed from agriculture and land to manufacturing. This is shown by W. R. Rubinstein's research.[9] He analysed nineteenth-century wills to locate millionaires, and came up with the following figures. Between 1809 and1858, 181 millionaires made their money from the land, 5 from manufacture and 3 from commerce. During 1858 to 1879, the corresponding figures were 117; 13 and 16. The number of landed millionaires dying between 1880 and 1899 had shrunk dramatically to 38, while there were now 22 from manufacture and 23 from commerce. This dramatic shrinkage of landed wealth is not surprising, given that rent-rolls fell by 20 per cent between the late 1870s and the late 1890s – in the South of England by 40 per cent – and land prices fell as well.[10] The price of wheat fell by half between 1874 and 1896.[11] Clearly, across the century, great wealth was being accumulated in manufacture and service industries, rather than agriculture.

Eighteen yacht clubs were set up before 1855 and strived to follow the Squadron's example.[12] However, given the unfavourable circumstances, at least half of these had folded by 1860. I have already discussed the demise of the Cumberland Fleet, formed in 1773 and disbanded in 1823. The Royal Dee, Chester, formed in 1815, never seems to have thrived. The Royal Warrant, granted in 1847, was removed in 1879, when only two club yachts were flying the defaced ensign.

I will discuss Irish clubs in the next chapter. Here, we only have to note that the Northern Yacht Club, Belfast, formed with its twin on the Clyde

---

[6] Sir Robert Peel, Prime Minister, created the Metropolitan police force in the Metropolitan Police Act of 1829.

[7] François Bédarida, *A Social History of England 1851–1975*, pp. 4–5.

[8] David Thomson, *England in the Nineteenth Century*, p. 83.

[9] W. D. Rubinstein, *Wealth and the Wealthy in the Modern World*, p. 60.

[10] Jose Harris, *Private Lives, Public Spirit: Britain 1870–1914*, pp. 102–103.

[11] Bédarida, *Social History*, p. 126.

[12] Hussey, *The Royal Harwich*, p. 11.

7 The Schooner Yacht *Wyvern* passing under the Menai Suspension Bridge, Menai Straits, by Nicholas Matthew Condy. This picture illustrates that paintings do not accurately reflect reality: the yacht is apparently about to proceed under full sail through the dangerous Swellies. But it nicely shows the unity of the growth of yachting with a major symbol of the Industrial Revolution – the suspension bridge built by Thomas Telford to cross the Menai Straits, opened in 1826.

in 1824, was dissolved in 1830. The Royal Western at Kilrush, founded in 1827, had 201 members in 1837, and by the 1850s, had clubhouses in Cork and Dublin and a floating clubhouse in Dun Laoghaire. Yet, by the beginning of the 1860s, it had ceased to exist.[13]

The existence of the first Royal Irish, Kingstown (Dun Laoghaire), formed 1831, was even briefer. James Lyle, in an 1865 article in *Hunt's*, wrote: 'With this [1840] Regatta ended the life of the old Club which had been in a failing state and heavily in debt for some time, its yachts fallen off and members resigned'.[14] It was re-formed in 1846.

The Royal Eastern Yacht Club of Leith and Edinburgh was formed in 1835 (although there is a painting, *Royal Eastern Yacht Club Regatta, Leith Roads,*

---

[13] http://www.westernyachtclub.com/cons/index.php?page=club
[14] Boylan, *White Sails Crowding*, p. 12.

1834 by Edmund Thornton Crawford). Bonner records it as 'never properly supported after 1836 … it would appear that the Scots have no taste for aquatic sports', hardly a very satisfactory explanation.[15] It was defunct by the late nineteenth century and was incorporated into the Royal Forth in 1969. According to the latter's website, although the Royal Eastern had a clubhouse in Granton on the Firth of the Forth, its main practical purpose was organising the annual 'Royal Forth Regatta' and its main base was a club house in Princes Street. So, it would seem to have been primarily a social club.

On the south coast, the Royal Southampton, founded in 1838, according to Bonner's *The Yachting Season of 1845*, collapsed within two years because it admitted 'undesirables'.[16] This club was re-created on the Hamble as the Royal Southern in 1840.[17]

Similarly, the Eastern Yacht Club was formed in 1843 on the Orwell near Ipswich, but:

> … although a successful Eastern Coast Regatta followed in September, 1844, the absence of progress as a club soon brought about a reconstitution. This was arranged by William Knight, a well known yachtsman who was a also a barrister, and he successfully obtained for the members not only their Royal Patronage but also the Admiralty Warrant to wear the Blue Ensign and various foreign port privileges. From that point, the Royal Harwich Yacht Club, as it as renamed, went from strength to strength'.[18]

We need to be careful about assuming that the other clubs had an untroubled run, as many have not published a history. Giving them all the benefit of the doubt, the 'continuous' clubs are the Squadron (1815); the Arundel (1838) later renamed the (Royal) London, and based at Cowes from 1883; the Deben Yacht Club, Woodbridge, Suffolk (1838); the Royal Mersey, Birkenhead (1844); the Royal Kingstown, Dublin (1845), renamed the Royal St George in 1847; Royal Victoria, Ryde, Isle of Wight (1845); Royal Welsh, Caernarfon (1847); and the Royal Yorkshire, Bridlington (1848). Even if all progressed smoothly, it is clear that the conditions were not right for a steady development of yachting during these years.

We can easily see the weakness of the 'Aristocratic' model: the desire that these clubs should be solely for aristocrats. For example, the Royal Dorset,

---

[15] Bonner, *The Yachting Season of 1845*, pp. 150–151.

[16] *Ibid.*, pp. 111–112.

[17] By changing its name, so people had to be (re-)elected, and doubling the subscription, the 'undesirables' could be removed (*ibid.*, p. 113).

[18] Hussey, *The Royal Harwich*, p. 11. The coy 'lack of progress' is typical of yacht club histories covering up negative or unpleasant events.

formed in 1875, had, in its original list, '2 royals, 1 duke, 4 marquises, 12 earls, 12 lords (assorted), 1 count, 1 viscount, 14 baronets, 2 knights bachelor, 2 admirals, 4 generals and 16 members of parliament'. But this fine list totals a mere 71, when the desired membership was 400.[19] The Royal Dorset, helped by being near the Solent, did survive, but as the above list shows, many early clubs did not.

Whether their path was rocky or smooth, once a yacht club had come into existence, it would follow in the path of the earlier clubs at Cork, the Thames and Cowes, not just in slavish imitation, but because these were the practices in prestige sports clubs. For example, shortly after formation, two or three uniforms would be specified for the various types of occasion. The Royal Welsh, founded in 1847, specified in its club rules what constituted 'dress, undress and dinner dress'.[20] Mead, in his history of the Royal Cornwall, gives two pages to the niceties of the various kinds of dress. e.g. 'Undress, for normal yachting wear, consisted of a blue serge, double-breasted jacket with four black horn buttons on either side; blue (or white) waistcoat with six small buttons' and so on for another five lines.[21] The Royal Northern was established with club houses in Belfast and on the Clyde in 1824, because the two areas shared the Irish Sea as a cruising ground. It saw itself as a very patrician organisation, and 'more formal than its Southern counterparts, with a rigid dress code that fined members who did not appear at dinner in the prescribed blue, crimson-lined jacket, white or black pantaloons, or breeches and silk stockings'.[22] There was strict enforcement of this code: 'Members who appeared at dinner without wearing the full dress uniform of the clubs were fined 10s', then a very hefty sum.[23]

Dining together and the Cruise in Company featured in the Royal Western (England), Plymouth, formed in 1833.[24] By 1847, members dined with the Commodore and the Vice-Commodore once a week during the sailing season, and, after the dinner 'went off to their yachts and the Flag Officer

[19] Geen, *The Life and Times of the Royal Dorset Yacht Club*, pp. 4–5.

[20] Caernarfon Record Office, XM/923/59, 63, 56, *Royal Welsh Club*, quoted by John Lowerson, *Sport and the English Middle Classes 1870–1914*, p. 50.

[21] Mead, *History of the Royal Cornwall Yacht Club*, pp. 165–167.

[22] Rousmaniere, *The Luxury Yachts*, p. 48.

[23] Heaton, *Yachting: A History*, p. 82. To see yacht club dress codes in a wider context, see James Laver, *A Concise History of Costume* or Lucy Adlington, *Stitches in Time: The Story of the Clothes We Wear*, among many others.

[24] Cusack, 'The Rise of Aquatic Recreation', p. 200. The club had to specify 'England' as the Royal Western (Ireland) was extant.

in command took the squadron to sea and put it through sailing evolutions, much on the lines of the sailing evolutions of the Royal Navy'.[25]

We see a feature that would become very marked in Victorian yachting – the fear of competing with a maritime professional. In the Teignmouth Regatta of 1824, '... disputes arose about the winning vessels ... and it was reported that the Yacht Club [the Squadron] were so offended that they declared that they would never visit the Devonshire Coast again'. This was because, as *Bell's Life in London* reported, the 'principal contest was between Mr Tucker's *Nymph* and Captain Quantock's *Fawn*, which was won by the former, but the prize was awarded to the *Fawn*, the *Nymph* not being considered a gentleman's yacht'.[26] Mr Tucker was a Shaldon boatbuilder.

There are figures regarding the number of yachtsmen and yachts during this period. *British Yachts and Yachtsmen* gives the Squadron's fleet in 1850 as having 100 vessels, the Royal Thames 130, the Royal Western, England about 80, and the Royal Western, Ireland 47.[27] Leather states that 'In 1857 there were 780 British yachts, totalling 30,000 tonnes; including 511 cutters, 138 schooners, 75 yawls, and 37 'other rigs'; but there were only 19 steam yachts.[28] This is a confident assertion, but he gives no reference, and the Royal Northern, on the Clyde, held a race for steam-powered yachts in August, 1827, so the figure for the steam yachts seems low, which then makes one doubt the other figures. Cusack has calculated that in 1863, there were a mere 113 races in Britain, and by 1875, it was still only 305.[29]

Anthony Trollope, journalist as well as novelist author of the *Barchester Chronicles*, writing towards the end of the period covered by this chapter, surveyed yachting in his *British Sports and Pastimes*, and estimated:

> In 1867 there were thirty-one yacht clubs in the United Kingdom, – and, with two exceptions, sea-going yacht squadrons, – bearing the Admiralty warrants;[30] and about 1,740 yachts, of which 240 only were under twelve tons' admeasurement. The total tonnage of these yachts amounted to about 55,700.

---

[25] *Ibid.*, p. 205. Presumably 'dinner' means 'lunch' as the Cruises in Company were undertaken in daylight.

[26] *Ibid.*, p. 112, quoting *Bell's Life of London*, 22 August, 1824.

[27] The Yachtsman: *British Yachts and Yachting*, pp. 117–118. Phillips-Birt in his *The History of Yachting*, p. 15, estimated that there were only 500 yachts in British waters in 1850, but this is clearly an underestimate.

[28] Leather, *The Northseamen*, p. 107.

[29] Cusack, 'The Rise of Aquatic Recreation and Sport', p. 216.

[30] Trollope presumably means that thirty-one clubs have permission to fly a defaced ensign. This figure seems on the high side.

Allowing one man for every ten tons, we find here a force of 5,700 men, – and boys, – employed in yachting service.[31]

If the great majority of yachts are over twelve tons, then yachting must still have been primarily for the very wealthy. Trollope's assumption that these yachts are crewed reinforces this conclusion and suggests how socially limited the growth of yachting was during this period.

However, there are real problems in taking these as accurate estimates. Multiple club memberships of the 'senior' (early) yacht clubs was probably the norm, rather than the exception. A yacht owner would patronise his local club on a social basis, or as a place to discuss business. He would join other yacht clubs, if he had his boat moored elsewhere, or if they were on the race circuit of regattas his boat took part in, he wanted to watch the regatta, or he regularly cruised there.

Yachtsmen, whether club members or visiting yachtsmen, preferred to sleep ashore and the yacht clubs had bedrooms, a bar and a restaurant.[32] One needed to be a member to use these facilities, or for one's club to have reciprocal arrangements. So, it was easier if one was a member.

Cusack details how, in 1868, only ten members of the Royal Dart were members of only that club; 17 belonged to 2 to 4 clubs; 5 to 5 or more. In 1870, 12 members belonged just to the Royal Dart; 21 to 2 to 4 clubs; and 6 belonged to 5 or more. In 1875, the respective figures are 27, 53, 32. She provides similar data for the membership of the Royal Western. In 1845, 32 members are only members of the RWYC, and 35 of 2 to 4; but in 1875, there are 18 RWYC only members, 21 belong to 2 to 4 clubs, and 18 to 5 or more.

Cusack suggests that, as more clubs came into existence, so multiple membership increased accordingly.[33] So, the actual number of yachtsmen belonging to yacht clubs is probably less than a third of the total membership of those clubs.

There were not that many yacht-owning members in yacht clubs to start with. Cusack calculated the percentage of yacht-owners in a number of yacht clubs in 1845. They ranged from 21 per cent at the Royal Victoria, Ryde through 29 per cent at the Royal Western, England to 57 per cent at the Squadron.[34]

---

[31] Trollope, *British Sports and Pastimes*, pp. 201–202.

[32] E. E. Middleton, in *The Cruise of the 'Kate'*, which describes his circumnavigation of the United Kingdom, via the Bowling (now called the Firth & Clyde) Canal, in 1869, always rowed ashore to find a hotel, despite the quite frequent dangers of doing so.

[33] Cusack. 'The Rise of Aquatic Recreation and Sport', pp. 151–157.

[34] *Ibid.*, p. 139.

The number of yachtsmen sailing at this time will always be a matter of guesswork, given multiple membership of clubs, and because many yachtsmen did not belong to any yacht club. What is even more troubling is trying to estimate the number of yachts. If members of senior yacht clubs were, in fact on average, members of some four or five other clubs, they would have registered the same yacht four or five times.

The usual problem remained concerning yacht racing. Many came to regattas to watch, but few to race. In Dartmouth, by 1836 there were 'numerous gentry in yachts to view the contests'.[35] Cusack found that, in 1843, the Royal Yacht Squadron brought 23 yachts to the Devon regattas, but at Torquay, 'the main race was abandoned as there was only one entry …'. She gives figures for Plymouth regattas: 1859: 20 attended, 13 raced; 1860: of 26, 13 raced; 1863: 20 raced of the 39 attending etc.[36] As a rough rule of thumb, only half the yachts that were visiting a regatta raced.

Other Signs of Growth

Cusack considering only South Devon, gives 'figures of 203 known yachts between 1730 and 1815, and 334 between 1816 and 1827, [which] are almost certainly underestimates'.[37]

In 1828, in Swansea Bay, the proprietors of the *Palmerston* (steam packet vessel of 200 tons, 80 h.p.) offered the public the opportunity 'to enjoy the enchanting scenery of the bay and the manoeuvres of yacht and boat sailing for a variety of prizes'. By the early 1830s, yachts were coming from Milford Haven and the Bristol Channel to compete.[38]

There were early buds of Corinthian yachting – the hairshirted battle with the waves characteristic of yachting after the 1870s (see Chapter 9). A rare yachting text before 1860 was *Two Summer Cruises with the Baltic Fleet in 1854–5. Being the Log of the 'Pet' Yacht, 8 tons, R.T.Y.C* [Royal Thames] by Rev. Robert Hughes (1855). This is an account of two cruises to the Baltic in the 8 ton cutter, 33 foot long *Pet*, with two crew. In his first voyage, he went from Lowestoft to the Aaland islands and back. The second voyage took them into the Gulf of Finland. Less well-known is S. R. Graves' *A Yachting Cruise to the Baltic*, 1863. This attraction for the North predates the better known voyages of E. F. Knight and Erskine Childers.

---

[35] Davis, *Dartmouth Regatta*, p. 11.
[36] Cusack, 'The Rise of Aquatic Recreation and Sport', p. 219.
[37] *Ibid.*, p. 86.
[38] Austin, 'Yachting in Swansea Bay', pp. 205–206.

An early club, termed 'Corinthian', was the Prince of Wales, formed in 1852 to encourage racing between yachts of no more than eight tons on the Thames. Biddle commented that it 'was the first to open the season, the red burgee with snow white plume was generally the last to be hauled down, when the shortening days and chilly nights gave indications that the yachting season was drawing to a close'. Biddle does not explain why the club ceased to exist in 1879.[39]

Offshore and ocean racing started in a small way. There was a Dublin–Cork race in 1860. In 1863, a race from Ryde to Cherbourg was organised by the Royal Victoria Yacht Club of Ryde, Isle of Wight.[40] In 1864, the Royal Mersey organised a Liverpool to Kingstown Race to coincide with the Royal St George Regatta;[41] and in 1870, a race from Cork to New York and in 1887, New York to Cork.[42]

There were technical advances. Faced with the fact that the French had better charts than his Navy – Nelson used French charts at Trafalgar – George III set up the Hydrographic Office in 1799. Thomas Hurd, Chief Hydrographer from 1808–1823 and Admiral Beaufort, creator of the wind strength scale, Chief Hydrographer from 1829–1855, set up an ambitious scheme to use redundant Naval vessels to chart the waters of the world, over which the British empire now extended, and to undertake a complete survey of the waters of the British Isles.[43]

On the water, the spinnaker sail, such a feature of photographs of big yachts racing with the great sail boomed out in front, replaced the square sail for running.[44] It is named after the 47 ton *Sphinx*, who used it to remarkable effect in the Royal Victoria regatta of 1866. Leather attributes the innovation to Dan Hatcher, builder, and Captain Tom Diaper (senior), racing skipper, working on *Niobe*, a couple of years earlier.[45]

The form of ballasting a boat changed from moveable ingots inside the hull to outside the hull in the form of metal keels, increasing a boat's stability. Galvanised iron wire replaced hemp for standing rigging. It was stronger and less likely to deteriorate. After the success of *America* during the 1851 season, her cotton sails, which kept their shape better, were imitated and replaced flax canvas ones. While all these innovations took time to be accepted – for

---

[39] Tyrell E. Biddle, *The Corinthian Yachtsman or Hints on Yachting*, p. 5.
[40] The Yachtsman, *British Yachts and Yachtsmen*, pp. 142 and 155–156.
[41] Archer and Pearson, *The Royal St George*, p. 92.
[42] Nixon, *To Sail the Crested Sea*, pp. 17–18.
[43] Blake, *The Sea Chart*, p. 40.
[44] *Running*: when the wind is coming from directly behind the boat.
[45] Johnson, *Encyclopedia of Yachting*, p. 280; Leather, *The Northseamen*, p. 109.

example, moving pig iron ingots from the bilges to lighten a stranded boat is part of many late Victorian accounts – yacht materials were clearly being developed in response to the increased demand.

Yacht building, as an industry, was certainly developing from the first decade of the nineteenth century on the Clyde and on the Colne in Essex.

John Fife (1743–1831) opened a yard to build fishing boats at Fairlie, a small Ayrshire village on the Firth of Clyde. He gave his son, William (1785–1865) the unprofitable, embryonic yacht building side. His first real yacht was a 51 ton cutter, *Lamlash*, built for James Hamilton in 1812, for extended cruising. She went down to the Med. in 1819.[46] She was obviously well built because, under new ownership, she left Scotland for Van Diemen's Land (Tasmania) and the Sandwich Islands. Another pioneering build was *Gleam*, a 30 ton cutter, launched in 1832. Having established his reputation, he built a succession of successful racing yachts. The 53 ton *Cymba*, built 1852, won the Queen's Cup on the Mersey. Other crack racers from his yard included *Stella* (1848), *Onda* (1852), *Fairy Queen* (1857) etc. By 1858, Fife was building six to eight yachts a year because, already by the mid-century, the entrepreneurs of Glasgow's expanding industries, such as shipbuilding and thread making, wanted to demonstrate their good taste and wealth in their crewed racing yachts.[47]

On the Colne, Sainty's yard was taken over by Thomas Harvey in 1832, who continued building yachts. He obviously prospered because, in 1849, he opened a second yard in Ipswich.

By this time, there must have been a fair amount of yachting activity around the Colne and Blackwater, because in June 1850, John Griggs of Brightlingsea was sending yacht owners a card regarding laying up facilities, in good time for the following winter:

> The yachts can be laid up in perfect safety, the sails and rigging will be stored, and the boats, spars and ballast can be protected from the weather if required … John Griggs has had twenty-five years experience as a master of yachts …[48]

Bell's Life in London and Sporting Chronicle, started in the early 1830s, included a weekly roundup of news from the yachting world in its 'Aquatic Register'.[49]

[46] Martin Black, *G. L. Watson*, p. 33.
[47] McCallum, *Fast and Bonnie*, pp. 1–27; Martin Black, *G. L. Watson*, p. 77, n. 7.
[48] Leather, *The Northseamen*, pp. 184 and 277–278
[49] Archer and Pearson, *The Royal St George Yacht Club*, p. 37; Boylan, *White Sails Crowding: A History of the Royal Irish Yacht Club*, p. 25.

Hunts, a firm of commercial printers' first venture into yachting was *Hunt's Universal Yacht List*. It was set up on a subscription basis – the owner paid to have his yacht listed – in 1848 and it ran till 1914, eventually being outdone by the more prestigious *Lloyd's Register of Yachts*, founded 1878. Hunt's brought out the first magazine devoted to yachting, *Hunt's Yachting Magazine*, available only on subscription, which began publication in 1852. The magazine ran till 1887, when he died. *The Illustrated London News* started in 1862 and included some yachting coverage.

The slow development of yachting in the first half of the century was inevitable, given that key conditions – political stability, and the ability of city dwellers, with surplus wealth to use on aquatic leisure, to easily access the coastal towns and fishing ports that would become yachting harbours– did not become a reality till the second half of the century. What developments there were, were led by the very wealthy, often the new industrialists.

CHAPTER SEVEN

The Development of Yachting
in Ireland and the Colonies

'Am I,' Mr Michael Shaughnessy, a barrister, asked himself incredulously, surveying these ghastly scenes [of famine in Ireland] in 1848, 'am I in a part of the British Empire?'[1]

Hunters for gold, or pursuers of fame, they had all gone out on that stream [the Thames], bearing the sword, and often the torch, messengers of the might within the land, bearers of a spark from the sacred fire.[2]

This chapter describes, how, in contrast to the slow growth of yachting in the United Kingdom during this period, there was a more rapid diffusion of the sport in Ireland and the colonies.

The Development of Yachting in Ireland

The number of yacht clubs in Ireland formed in the first part of the nineteenth century is remarkable, as it is almost as great as the number in England.

Ireland, till its independence in 1922, was, of course, part of the United Kingdom. Yet, if we equate colonising with occupation, Ireland, with its desire for independence and its frequent, albeit unsuccessful, revolts, was effectively a colony. Rebellion in Ireland was feared throughout the nineteenth century and Ireland had to be heavily occupied by garrisons and patrolled by the Navy. Ireland could not be given independence, partly because of the fear that it might welcome a foreign power, and because it proved impossible, towards the end of the nineteenth century, to get 'Home Rule' through the two houses of Parliament.

The need for the Crown to defend Ireland led to the building of the road from London to Holyhead (the A5), a remarkable feat of pioneering

---

[1] James Morris, *Heaven's Command*, p. 155.
[2] Joseph Conrad, *Heart of Darkness*, p. 7.

engineering across the Welsh mountains, by Thomas Telford. The road was completed by the building of the Menai Suspension Bridge in 1826.[3] The breakwater at Holyhead, begun in 1845 and completed in 1871, is 1.7 miles long, thereby providing excellent shelter. The early dates of the founding of the Royal Dee at Chester, 1815, guarding the entrance to North Wales and a route to Holyhead, and the Royal Welsh at Caernarfon, 1847, may be, at least in part, due to the need for local suppliers and contractors.

Because of the lack of relevant research, it is difficult to know with any certainty why yachting developed so early in Ireland. There were probably a variety of reasons. Where there were military or naval bases, there were service personnel needing suitable recreation. A related source of people with the money and time to enjoy yachting would be the administrators of the colony and the civil servants. These groups required food and drink, so their presence created a large number of wealthy farmers, and the wholesalers and the retailers who sold their produce. Yet another group would be the local entrepreneurs who provided for the services' needs in terms of ordnance and equipment. A final group would be those who maintained and repaired the services' equipment – in the case of the Navy, shipwrights, sailmakers etc. It is likely that all these groups contributed to the growth of yachting.

The successful creation of the powerful Catholic Association by the lawyers Daniel O'Connell and Richard Lalor Shiel caused the prime minister, the Duke of Wellington, who had been brought up in Ireland, to push the Catholic Relief Bill through Parliament ('Catholic Emancipation') in 1829. This removed all penal laws and restrictions against the employment of Catholics, except for the highest offices of government and state. As a result, the number of Catholic middle class entrepreneurs increased, but the wealth remained with the Protestant Ascendancy.[4]

Yachting occurred primarily in four areas of Ireland: Cork, the West coast and Shannon, Dublin, and Ulster.

Cork: the large, natural harbour of Cork, and its ability to provision Naval and mercantile ships (see p. 33) made it the centre of English naval activity, based at Cove (Queenstown). The supply depot of the Royal Navy had been

---

[3] Better known bridges by Isambard Kingdom Brunel were some decades later. The railway bridge across the Tamar was completed in 1859, the Clifton Suspension Bridge, after his death, in 1864, its building delayed by Bristolian anxieties as to its stability.

[4] Mac Annaidh, *Irish History*, pp. 151–154.

at Kinsale from 1694, but was moved to Cork in 1805. Cork was, from the 1840s, the home base of the Irish Squadron.[5]

The first 'ocean yacht race' was organised by the revived Royal Cork. It was between Kingstown (Dun Laoghaire) and Cork in July, 1860. Seventeen yachts took part. The winner was *Sybil* from *Peri* by three minutes.

The Munster Model Yacht Club was founded in 1872 as a corinthian or amateur yacht club to provide amateur racing, as opposed to large yacht racing for monetary prizes. It became the Royal Munster, later to amalgamate with the, yet again near dormant, Royal Cork, in 1966.

The West Coast and the Shannon. The UK's longest river, 230 miles long with 8 loughs, going deep into the heart of the Ireland, the Shannon required patrolling. If there was an invasion, it would not be on the well-defended East coast but the sparsely populated West with its many inlets and harbours, so this area had to have garrisons, as well as naval surveillance.

The easiest way for the landed gentry of the West of Ireland to return from visits to Cork or Dublin was by yacht. The island's topography allowed even those with homes far inland to use this mode of transport, and so, from the eighteenth century, yachts were quite common. Colonel John Bateman Fitz-Gerald, the Knight of Glin, built both Glin Castle and the yacht *Farmer* in the 1780s. He would sail this 18-gun cutter up and down the West Coast complete with volunteer band, till he sold her in 1803. His son then owned the cutter *Reinvelle*.[6]

The Lough Ree Yacht Club claims to be the second oldest yacht club in the British Isles, founded in 1770 as the Athlone Yacht Club, and renamed in 1895. Lough Ree is a large inland lake on the Shannon above Athlone. Downstream, the Lough Derg Yacht Club was established in 1835. Further into the Northwest, the *Impartial Observer* reported the starting up of racing by returning naval officers at Enniskillen, at the bottom end of Lough Erne, in 1818; while the Lough Erne Yacht Club, founded in 1820, claims to be the first yacht club in the world created specifically for yacht racing.[7] Sligo Yacht Club, which used the inland Lough Gill, claims to have run the oldest continuous sailing trophy, the Ladies Cup, since 1821.[8] The formation of these clubs relates to the prosperity of the Protestant Ascendancy landowners.

---

[5] Jerome Devitt, The 'Navalizaton of Ireland'.

[6] Drummond, *Salt-Water Palaces*, p. 40. Glin Castle is on the south side of the Shannon estuary.

[7] Alfred and Vincent Delaney, *The Water Wags 1887–2012*, p. 83.

[8] A 'Ladies' Cup' usually means a cup donated by ladies, not raced for by ladies. Occasionally, it means the cup for the winner of a ladies' race, for example, the Ladies' cup given by Joyce

Ireland was devastated by the Famine of 1845 to 1851.[9] For two years, 1846 and 1847, the English government provided no aid, arguing that free trade would, somehow, solve the problem. The famine was accompanied by the diseases of malnutrition such as dysentery. James Morris' chapter on the famine in *Heaven's Command*, based on observers' accounts, reads like the Belgian Congo of Conrad's *Heart of Darkness*.[10] One million died and two million emigrated. The great famine hit the rents of the land owners very hard.

> After the Great Famine of 1844/1846 … many boats lay rotting in the small harbours all around the coast with nobody to sail them. Their owners, mainly Irish or Irish-Anglo gentry had bankrupted themselves as a result of the loss of Tenant revenue and in a lot of cases as a result of their attempts to help, feed and nurture their Tenants. They lost their estates … their properties being taken over by often absentee Landlords from more wealthy areas of the UK who used their Irish residences as summer holiday homes rather than permanent bases.[11]

The situation stayed grim for decades after the famine. In the 1860s, Mark Hutton sailed to Ireland to expose the starvation, poverty and misery of the majority of the people in those parts. His *The Cruise of the 'Humming Bird' or Notes near Home* was published in London in 1864. It opens with the author arriving at Galway on the West Coast:

> 'Charity! In the honour of God, yer Honour! I'm a Claddagh woman with five small childer – Gold help'em the crathurs. And one lying stritched in the house beyant.'

> The speaker was one of a group of ragged and wretched-looking women who were crowding around the entrance of the hotel in which, after landing from a small yacht, which was for the time my nominal home, I had temporarily taken up my quarter.[12]

The Great Famine probably accounts for the demise of the Royal Western Yacht Club, Ireland, formed in Kilrush in 1827. By 1837, its membership was 201, with 82 sailing vessels. This membership was based across ports in Ireland and by the 1850s, as well as being on the Shannon in the west of Ireland, it had

---

Anderson in 1951 to Whitstable Yacht Club (Geoff Bush, *Of Merlins, Mirrors and Darts*, p. 2).
[9] The standard work is Cecil Woodman-Smith's *The Great Hunger*.
[10] Morris, *Heaven's Command*, Chapter 8: An Act of God, pp. 152–174.
[11] O'Connell, 'Royal Western Yacht Club of Ireland – Club History', p. 3.
[12] Hutton, *The Cruise of the 'Humming Bird'*, p. 1. Note the irony in '*near* Home'.

clubhouses in Cork and Dublin and a floating clubhouse in Dun Laoghaire. By the beginning of the 1860s, it had ceased to exist.[13]

Dublin: By the first half of the nineteenth century, Dublin was known as 'the second city of the Empire'. It was a major trading centre and a prosperous metropolis, long before the Industrial Revolution created the massively wealthy cities of Belfast, Glasgow and Manchester in the second half of the century. In 1796, in the first, water-powered, phase of the Industrial Revolution, a flotilla of yachts was present when the Lord Lieutenant, Lord Camden, on the vice-regal yacht, *Dorset*, opened the Grand Canal Dock in Dublin.

Entering the port of Dublin required negotiation of the dangerous bars and sandbanks of the Liffey. So, the small nearby port of Dun Laoghaire in Dublin Bay was expanded by the construction of extensive breakwaters between 1817 and 1842. (When visited by King George IV in 1821 to see the work in progress, the name was changed to 'Kingstown', a name it retained till 1922 and Irish independence.) Its increasing importance is shown by the mail boat's destination moving from Howth to Kingstown in 1826.[14] In 1828, the first major sailing event, the Dublin regatta was held.

The railway to the harbour of Kingstown, built in 1834, was only the second passenger-carrying railway in the world. (By contrast, Dublin and Belfast were not linked by rail till the 1870s.) The railway now gave a substantial, prosperous middle class access to a large, sheltered harbour. It also gave access to clean water. In both the Thames and the Clyde, yachtsmen were pushed several miles downstream by the filth and sewage in the rivers. For the Dublin sailor, a harbour with clean water, and immediate access to the open sea, was practically on their door step.

By 1848, the steam packet from Holyhead was bringing the London papers to Dublin on the day of publication.[15] In 1859, Carlisle Pier was built for a new fleet of mail boats, which linked directly with the rail network; but the harbour's military, as well as administrative, importance is shown by the fact that there was always a guard ship in the harbour and a battery on the East Pier, built in 1859.

The first yacht club in Kingstown was the Royal Irish, created in 1831. A club made up of high profile dissenters, Catholics and Quakers, was problematic. The Royal Irish collapsed in 1840 but was revived in 1846.

---

[13] http://www.westernyachtclub.com/cons/index.php?page=club
[14] Howth is a few miles north-east of Dublin and was initially developed as Dublin's sea port.
[15] Archer and Pearson, *The History of the Royal St George*, p. 35.

The top yacht club, the Kingstown Boat Club (the Royal St George from 1847) was the establishment club, formed in 1838.[16] The Royal St George would not accept Catholics or non-conformists, such as Quakers, and this determined the social and religious composition of these two clubs.[17] By 1843, the Royal St George was claiming to have 'some four hundred Irish Noblemen and Gentlemen', all of them Protestant of course.[18]

It had a purpose-built yacht club house by 1848, which lays claim to being the first of its kind in the United Kingdom, if not the world.[19] In 1845, George Bonner, in *The Yachtsman's Annual and General Register*, was reporting that the Royal Kingstown (the St George) had 503 members.[20] This is far more than any other yacht club he surveyed, the Royal Thames having 325 and the Royal Western, Plymouth, 260. But, in contrast to those clubs and the Squadron, the Irish club had only 29 yachts on its books, so that owners accounted for a mere 6 per cent (in contrast to Royal Thames YC 38 per cent, Royal Western YC 29 per cent and the Squadron 57 per cent).[21] The high percentage of social members of the Royal St George suggests that it was essentially providing a suitable social club for English administrators, serving officers and, more widely, the Establishment around the court of the Lord Lieutenant of Ireland at Dublin Castle.

Its colonial position is nicely demonstrated in an incident in 1870, when a Mr Dalton brought a non-member, a Mr Hawksworth, into the club, which was against the rules. In their letter to him, demanding an apology, Mr Hawksworth is referred to as 'a native Irishman', which is presumably one step up the evolutionary ladder from 'an Irish native'.[22]

There must have been some relaxation of the religious embargo, as Mr Dease, MP for Louth and a Catholic, was elected a member in 1851.

---

[16] Bonner's *The Yachting Season of 1845*, pp. 159–181, refers to the Royal St George as the Royal Kingstown Yacht Club. The Boat Club came out of the Pembroke Rowing Club.

[17] Winkie Nixon (personal communication, 14 July, 2016) related that doctors and lawyers were also excluded from the Royal St George, an excellent strategy to prevent the confident presentation of self being undermined by those who know the actual state of your inner workings. Hal Sisk (personal communication, 11 July, 2015) pointed out to me that the link with the Quakers could make life difficult for the Royal Irish, as they refuse to engage in activities of war, and it could not ask for a defaced ensign on the grounds that the club's yachts' crews would be useful in times of war. Fortunately, the Admiralty could also grant the use of a defaced ensign to aid the fishing fleet, and it was on this ground that the defaced ensign was sought and gained in 1846.

[18] Archer and Pearson, *The History of the Royal St George*, p. 19.

[19] In terms of a meeting place, it can go back even further, since the Kingstown Boat Club did have a club house, but nothing as grand as the Georgian splendour of the present club house.

[20] If you add up Bonner's list of members, it comes to 519.

[21] Cusack, 'The Rise of Aquatic Recreation and Sport', p. 139.

[22] Archer and Pearson, *The Royal St George Yacht Club*, p. 55.

Unfortunately, he sadly abused his position, when, in 1870, waiting for the departure of the mailboat, he went into the St George club accompanied by a Catholic priest, who was not a member! He then compounded his unacceptable behaviour, for 'again and again the Secretary endeavoured to elicit a reply and all his communications being treated with contemptuous disdain'. Also, 'had he expressed regret of the violation of the rule, the whole matter could have been quietly settled'. What probably infuriated the members most was that the matter had become public – it is, of course, possible that this was what the MP had wanted in the first place. He was expelled.[23]

The Dun Laoghaire branch of the dying Royal Western Yacht Club was re-formed as the Kingstown Model (as in 'exemplary') Yacht Club in 1857, which subsequently changed its name to the 'Prince Alfred Yacht Club' in 1864 and to 'the Royal Alfred' in 1870.

The Royal Alfred, a club for racing yachtsmen in Dublin Bay, organised most of the racing in the Bay. The club, which did not have a club house, was near the top of the league of British yacht clubs in terms of the value of the prizes offered in the 1870's. The Irish Sea was the scene of nearly half the yacht races run in Great Britain in that decade.[24]

Hal Sisk names the key figures in the development of racing in Dublin Bay and the Irish Sea as 'Vanderdecken' (William Cooper, 1824–1872), who we shall meet as a leading yachting journalist in Chapter 8; George Thompson (1837–1923), wine merchant; Henry Crawford (1817–1909), solicitor, leading figure in the Royal Irish, the Royal Alfred and the Royal Ulster; and James Lyle, who wrote under the pseudonym 'Red with White Maltese Cross', another solicitor.[25]

Yet another key figure was T. B. [Thomas Benjamin] Middleton, a Dublin solicitor, of Shankill Corinthian Sailing Club, who saw the advantages of a one-design (identically built) racing dinghy, rather than handicapping the entrants in various types of dinghies. The first One Design dinghy in the UK was the Water Wag, established in Dublin Bay in 1887, its design modified in 1899, and still going strong today.[26] This area also claims the oldest one-design

---

[23] Ibid., pp. 57–59.

[24] Hal Sisk, Dublin Bay: The Cradle of Yacht Racing, 2nd edn, pp. 29 ff.

[25] Ibid, pp. 4–5. It was bad form for doctors or solicitors to advertise, hence the pseudonym. Similarly, Howard Sinclair, the Ulster-based doctor, winner of the (Royal) Cruising Club Challenge Cup for three years running, 1896–1898, wrote as 'Diagonal White'.

[26] Alfred and Vincent Delany, The Water Wags 1887–2012. This claim can be disputed since the Clyde Canoe & Lugsail Club commissioned G. L. Watson to produce a small one-design yacht in 1886 and three were built by R. McAllister and Son at Sandpoint, Dumbarton and named Red, White and Blue. Middleton placed the order for his first Water Wag, Eva, with the same builders. The Clyde Boats are referred to as the 17/19 class – 17 feet on the waterline, 19 feet

keel-boat class: the Howth 17, 17 feet on the waterline, cutter-rigged with jackyard tops'l.[27]

Ulster: Yachting was taken up later in Ulster than in the south. The huge wealth of Belfast, later in the century, centred around linen and shipbuilding, was reflected in the growth of yachting in Belfast Lough.

The Royal Northern was formed in 1824, the next club to be formed after the Squadron, with club houses in Belfast Lough and the Clyde. The Irish branch, being premature in terms of the Industrial Revolution, had become defunct by 1830. The link between the armed services and yachting is shown by G. A. Henty, the boys' story writer. He was in the Purveyor Department of the Army, when he was stationed in Belfast at the end of the 1850s, and took up yachting.[28]

The Holywood Yacht Club, on the County Down shore of the Lough, was formed in 1862, but information on its early days seems scarce. The Ulster Yacht Club was formed in 1866 at Bangor, after the railway from Belfast reached that town in 1865. It was 'Royal' by 1869. By 1875, it demonstrated its rapid growth by heading the list of yacht clubs' prize moneys for races. It offered £874 for thirteen races in 1876. The Squadron's fund for that year was a mere £455.[29] Later, it was to challenge for the America's Cup on behalf of Sir Thomas Lipton (see Chapter 5). Bangor Corinthian Sailing Club was formed in 1880; after its demise, the Ballyholme Sailing Club was started the next year and became the leading dinghy club on the Lough. The North of Ireland Yacht Club, at Holywood was formed in 1899 by an amalgamation of the Ulster Sailing Club with the Cultra Yacht Club. In 1902, King Edward VII was graciously pleased to command that the Club be henceforth known as 'The Royal North of Ireland Yacht Club'.

Regarding membership criteria, there were no Catholic yacht clubs.[30] It seems likely that the Ulster Victorian yachtsmen, certainly those who were members of yacht clubs, were almost totally drawn from the Protestant community.

---

overall with a sail area not exceeding 530 square feet. Incidentally, the Water Wags changed from the lug rig to the more efficient gunter rig in 1900 (Dear, 'Leisure Sailing in the Twentieth Century', p. 138).

[27] Johnson, *Yacht Clubs of the World,* p. 141. Howth Yacht Club was formed in 1895. See W. M. Nixon, *Howth: A Centenary of Sailing.* See also Daniel O'Sullivan, *Dublin Bay: A Century of Sailing.* A dinghy has no fixed keel, the keelboat has.

[28] Guy Arnold, *Held Fast for England: G. A. Henty, Imperialist Boys' Writer,* p. 7.

[29] James Nixon, *Royal Ulster,* p. 12.

[30] Hal Sisk, personal communication, 2 August, 2016.

This section indicates how pioneering Irish yachting was, some decades before yachting took off among the English middle classes. On the west coast, yachts were being used for transport from the eighteenth century by the prospering Protestant Ascendancy landowners. With a different topography from mainland Britain, the loughs of the west and northwest Ireland provided wide, yet sheltered, waters, on which small boat racing could safely take place. The suitability of Dun Laoghaire for sailing, and its early rail link to the prosperous city of Dublin, were important factors in the innovations, such as the first one-design and the development of racing in the Irish Sea. The British government was always fearful of a successful revolution by the Catholics – the vast majority of the population – perhaps supported by their fellow Catholics, the French, or the revolutionary American Fenians, radical Irish immigrants, during the nineteenth century. The yachting correspondent, Anthony Heckstall-Smith recorded this conversation at the start of Cowes week, 1914, about the declaration of war with Germany:

War had been declared

I remember my mother in anxious conversation with Philip Hunloke, groom-in-waiting to the King. I recall him telling her not to worry.

'It will be quickly over' he assured. 'The Irish question is far more serious'.[31]

There is still much to study in reaching an understanding of the development of yachting in Ireland. *Pace* Joyce's *Dubliners*, let us imagine two children standing at the end of the West Pier at Kingstown [Dun Laoghaire] in the summer of 1900, one child Protestant, the other Catholic, watching the Water Wags racing of a weekend.[32] The Protestant child might see his father, owner of a business in Dublin, enjoying his well-earned leisure time, the Catholic child the oppressors wasting money on ostentatious leisure, that could have been better used paying their workers a decent wage. Much research is still needed to make sense of the combination of so much pioneering development, within the context of English suppression and colonialism.

Another key outpost was *the Channel Islands*, far closer to France than England. Perpetually at risk of a French invasion, their main towns were massively defended – St Helier by Elizabeth castle and St Peter Port by Castle

---

[31] Anthony Heckstall-Smith, *Sacred Cowes*, rev. edn, pp. 82–83. Hunloke was the King's Sailing Master, i.e. responsible for the navigation, on *Britannia* (see Douglas Dixon, *The King's Sailing Master*).

[32] *Dubliners* was written in 1905, but publishers kept wanting to leave out some of the stories. It was eventually published in 1914.

Cornet. Heaton dates the formation of Royal Channel Islands Yacht Club as 1855.[33] In 1862, Queen Victoria had designated Jersey Yacht and Rowing Club as 'royal' and in 1869, it assumed its present title, with members in both Jersey and Guernsey.[34]

Similarly, in the Mediterranean, yacht clubs were founded early in the nineteenth century. The Royal Gibraltar was founded in 1829, and is the oldest commonwealth yacht club. Formed by the captains of two cutters, they invited members of the Garrison to join. The Royal Malta states its origins go back to 1835. It was given an Admiralty warrant in 1875.

The Development of Yachting in the Colonies[35]

Following the British victory over Napoleon and the Treaty of Paris in 1815, the nineteenth century saw a huge expansion of the British empire, maintained by its naval supremacy. Between 1815 and 1914, around 10,000,000 square miles (26,000,000 square kilometres) and roughly 400 million people were added to the British empire.[36] By 1897, there were about 72,000 regular British officers and men in India, and some 32,000 in other colonies.[37] Yachting spread dramatically and quickly to the colonies and major trading posts as the sport of officers, colonial administrators and senior traders.

The Rise of Athleticism as the Dominant Empire Narrative

The philosophy of the colonisers was Athleticism, a philosophy they had absorbed in their public schools and at university. The pioneers of Athleticism were public school headmasters, Charles Vaughan at Harrow, 1845-1859, and G. E. L. Cotton of Marlborough, 1852–1858, who deliberately used sport as a means of diverting schoolboy energy and aggression – Cotton's predecessor had resigned after a school riot.[38]

It had two major, overlapping components: *Muscular Christianity*, which encouraged group sports, the valorising of pluck, and strong bonding to the

---

[33] Heaton, *Yachting: A History*, p. 108.

[34] http://rciycjersey.com/about-rciyc/, accessed 6 April, 2015.

[35] Useful texts are 'Colonial Yachting' in The Yachtsman: *British Yachts and Yachtsmen*, 1907, pp. 307–362; Heaton, *Yachting: A History* and Peter Johnson, *Yacht Clubs of the World.*

[36] There were further additions after the Great War, so that by 1922, the British empire covered 13 million square miles (33,700,000 square kilometres) and 458 million people (Timothy Parsons, *The British Imperial Century 1815–1914*).

[37] Huggins, *The Victorians and Sport*, p. 220.

[38] J. A. Mangan, *Athleticism in the Victorian and Edwardian Public School,* Chapter 2.

institution (the house/the school); and *Social Darwinism*, arguing for the natural state of competition between races, which provided a justification of the 'white man's burden'.[39]

Before the 1850s, sport was held in little esteem at public schools. This is shown by the Doctor, the headmaster, leaving the school for his holidays before the start of the Cricket match against the M.C.C. at the end of *Tom Brown's Schooldays*, published in 1857.

In the 1860s and 1870s, sport came increasingly to dominate the public school timetable, and the virtues of group sports, such as rugby and cricket, were highlighted. J. A. Mangan, in *Athleticism in the Victorian and Edwardian Public School*, has shown that public schools were happy to valorise *Muscular Christianity*, with its emphasis on team sports as a way of getting rid of excess adolescent energy, that might otherwise become indiscipline. Riots at public schools in early Victorian times by pupils had, on occasion, become so serious as to require the intervention of the military.[40] Hugh Cunningham added that there were yet other benefits: 'sport encouraged team spirit, fostered qualities of leadership, especially valuable in the administration of empire, it took boys' minds off sex, and it was the best training for war'.[41]

Thomas Hughes 'claimed Christ himself for the league of muscular Christians in his book *The Manliness of Christ*' (1879);[42] but the imparting of Muscular Christianity could be cruel. Arthur Ransome, born 1884, went to the Old College, Windermere, at around the age of ten. Ransome was extremely short sighted, a difficulty not corrected till he went to Rugby. He recalled in his *Autobiography*:

> Our headmaster was a muscular Christian. He had been a good boxer himself and loved nothing better than to pick a brace of small boys, fit them with boxing gloves and teach them the elements of self-defence. When I was thus set to battle, it meant merely that I was continually battered in the face, blow after blow coming which I could not foresee or counter ... [I] used to welcome the bleeding of my nose because as the blood poured down, my turn at fighting came to an end. The headmaster called me a coward. The other boys jeered at me and knowing my utter inability to retaliate used to attack me at any odd moment just for fun.[43]

[39] Term first used in a poem of that name by Kipling, published in 1899.
[40] Vivian Ogilvie, *The English Public School*.
[41] Cunningham, 'Leisure and Society', p. 297.
[42] Jeffrey Richards, 'Passing the Love of Women', p. 103.
[43] Ransome, *Autobiography*, p. 47.

Physical fitness and hardiness were highly valued, as was the ability to suffer and ignore pain, inevitable, given the highly physical nature of games such as soccer and rugby. This ability to accept pain was referred to as *pluck*, and also entered the military vocabulary. Physical fitness was useful in countries where the colonisers were at high risk of contracting diseases, such as malaria. What was also being taught or imbibed was unthinking loyalty to an institution: the boys belonged to the best house in the best school, and this was an analogy for England as the best country.[44] Arthur Clough, a pupil, founded *The Rugby Magazine* in 1837, and in his first editorial, wrote 'O all-wise God … let thy purifying influence so continually dwell in me, … that I may seek in it not the selfish gratification of my own desires, but the increase of reputation to this *my* school' (Clough's italics).[45]

After the 1870s, *Social Darwinism*, expounded by T. H. Huxley and by Herbert Spencer, in his *Progress: Its Law and Cause*, published in 1857, two years before Darwin's *Origin of Species*, became an increasingly influential.[46] 'The survival of the fittest', in Darwin's writings, is between species so that Huxley and Spencer's usage as meaning competition between nations or races, is incorrect.[47] However, this interpretation resonated well with Victorian competitiveness, with its proposition that man must instinctively compete to survive. This exonerated a laissez-faire policy with regard to any casualties – in terms of injuries, ill-health, poverty or starvation – either at home from industrialisation, or abroad, through colonial activity, while proposing that 'natural' competition between nations makes wars inevitable.

Social Darwinism had a pragmatic use in the public school context. Any difficulties in terms of sexual activity or bullying could be rationalised as teaching the unmonitored, and probably unmonitorable, schoolboys the lesson of the 'survival of the fittest'.

Social Darwinism needed a superior, the 'fittest' race, that deserved to rule the world. Newbolt and writers of his ilk, such as William Henley (1849–1903), influential editor of the *National Observer*, and G. A. Henty (1832–1902) author of a copious number of boys' stories about the empire,

---

[44] Cf. Peter Parker, *The Old Lie*. The statistical absurdity that each and *every* house could be the best house, and therefore be representative of England, seems to have gone unnoticed.

[45] Ian Hamilton, *A Gift Imprisoned: The Poetic Life of Matthew Arnold*, p. 35.

[46] Darwin had developed, but not published, his ideas on Natural Selection as early as 1838. Spencer, in fact, draws more on Malthus' 1798 work, *An Essay on the Principle of Population*, than on Darwin, but his critics called him a 'Social Darwinian'.

[47] See Mangan, 'Social Darwinism and Upper-Class Education in Late Victorian and Edwardian England'.

created an artificial race of 'the English'.[48] The 'English race' was 'pure', unsullied by the countless waves of immigrants and the conquests as late as 1685. It was 'Northern', whose racial supremacy included a superior ability in fighting and war over lesser nations. In Charles Kingsley's *Westward Ho!*, 1855, the English captain shouts at his Spanish counterpart: 'Do you not see that you are but fifty strong to our twenty?' The Spaniard foolishly does not realize the hopelessness of these odds, and fires a pistol at him. Of course, being Spanish, he misses. The English captain knocks him out, being 'unwilling to shed needless blood; on which all the crew yielded … and the prize was taken'.[49] All so easy and so cheap in terms of British life and limb.[50]

One of the central features of Henry Newbolt's poems – very popular in the twenty years before the Great War – was the superiority of men educated at public schools. Those who attend such schools are a superior race, born to be leaders of men and to rule over other inferior races. In his *Clifton Chapel*, published in 1908:

> This is the Chapel: here, my son,
> Your father thought the thoughts of youth
> Henceforth the School and you are one
> And what You are, the race shall be.[51]

The utility and relevance of Athleticism was not just on the playing field, study or dormitory. What was being imbibed was a philosophy framing the

---

[48] Henty wrote two or three books a year, such as *With Clive in India* (1884), *With Kitchener in the Soudan* (1903) etc.

[49] Charles Kingsley, *Westward Ho!*, p. 324.

[50] This unequal value of non-English nationalists continued till at least the First World War. In the May, 1908 issue of *The Captain*, a Mr R. van Eeghen, clearly a foreigner, complained that 'After fourteen or fifteen years perusal of "piffle" written apparently for edification, the young Englishman leaves home and country with the very firm idea in his head that he, personally, is equal to two or more Frenchmen, about four Germans, an indefinite number of Russians, and any quantity you care to mention of the remaining scum of the earth' (Arnold, *Held Fast for England*, p. 22).

[51] *Clifton Chapel and Other School Poems*, 1908. Like much of Newbolt's writings, this is disingenuous. It was unlikely that many of the pupils' fathers stood in the chapel, as Clifton was only founded in 1862 with seventy boys. And the poem did not apply to Newbolt – he sent his son to the more prestigious Winchester. Newbolt's representation of Clifton is actively misleading. John Percival, headmaster from its opening in 1862 till 1879, was an important educational innovator. He opened a house for Jewish boys. He advocated science teaching, when most public schools still shunned it, and four science teachers went on to become Fellows of the Royal Society. He encouraged music teaching. Sport had its place, but for the purpose of physical well-being. Clearly, he was trying to create the 'well-rounded' scholar, a quite different goal from Newbolt's. In Newbolt, there is not just a dislike of intellectual ability, but a distrust of it too, for he wasn't very bright, but he was very mean-spirited. See Derek Winterbottom, *Henry Newbolt and the Spirit of Clifton*. Newbolt worked for the War Propaganda Bureau during the war, a position for which he was excellently qualified.

rightfulness of British world domination. What was also being taught was a way of acting, or performing, as an Englishman, and therefore a member of the highest race on earth. Quick, decisive action – the Victorians used the word 'promptitude' – could be necessary in dealing with unruly natives; and if that action, however inept, resulted in injury or death, it was always a 'glorious death'.[52]

The universities – Oxford and Cambridge – encouraged Athleticism, despite its overt anti-intellectualism. If relating to other 'races' was by domination, learning and erudition was hardly necessary, and deliberation might interfere with the exercise of force.

The universities' role was not just one of passive acceptance. Their role was crucial as it was from these universities that the colonial administrators and the civil servants were selected. They added value by handing out 'blues' to the best athletes and sports players of their year. These were excellent additions to a CV of the would-be colonial administrator, and in the world of business generally. The Sudanese Political Service, set up in 1889, recruited from those who had been recommended by a limited number of dons, and Sudan was referred to as 'a land of blacks ruled by blues'.[53]

Not surprisingly, academic creativity in the old universities in this period was limited.[54] Jesus College Cambridge, head of the river for eleven consecutive years from 1875, was said to be 'nothing but a boat club'. Richard Holt, presumably with a touch of irony, says this is not quite true, as the College excelled in other sports too. During the Victorian period, there was hardly a major academic advance at English universities.[55]

---

[52] These values can be seen in the dozens of schoolboy and Empire yarns by G. A. Henty.

[53] Roger Ryan (personal communication, September 2015) suggests that banks and insurance companies would also have favoured applicants with a sporting, rather than an academic, background.

[54] It is not clear whether this was a change in level of intellectual activity. Ashley (*England in the Seventeenth Century*, p. 158), writing of Charles II's times, wrote 'this was not a specially lively time at Oxford and Cambridge, although they had not yet sunk into the torpor of the eighteenth century'.

[55] Richard Holt, *Sport and the British: A Modern History*, pp. 66–67. The only major nineteenth-century English scientific creation – the theory of evolution – was created by Darwin and Alfred Russell Wallace. Neither held a university post. Barely a single major figure in Victorian literature went to university – Dickens, Thackeray (who started a degree but did not complete), Trollope, Shaw, Conrad, Kipling, Hardy and, of course, George Eliot (a woman, Mary Ann Evans, who would not have been admitted), had not a degree between them, a pattern only broken in the new century by E. M. Forster (King's College, Cambridge, 1907–1911). It is the case that the Victorian era was one of unparalleled developments in engineering. The age's great engineers, such as Brunel, Smeaton and Telford, and 'the Lighthouse Stevensons' were not products of English universities. They were of a Celtic background and education – Watt and Stevenson from Scottish education, Trewethick from the Cornish mines, while Brunel's

The Athleticism Narrative seemed to harden after the 1870's. This may have been a result of the 1857 Indian Mutiny, showing that the oppressed were ungrateful for the British civilising force, and the accompanying exaggerated horror story, if not invention, of the Black Hole of Calcutta, that was supposed to have happened in 1856, allowed for a greater degree of force to enter the narrative. This hardening was in line with the increasing jingoism of the Imperial Narrative.[56] As James Morris noted in *Heaven's Command*, after 1870, and accelerating thereafter, there was 'a coarsening dogmatism too, a trace of arrogance and contempt ... the British ... had been called to terrible but noble duties. They were not made to be loved: they were made to rule the world for its own good'.[57]

Athleticism was the dominant belief system concerning masculinity for some fifty years up to the First World War – for which it prepared the ground, with its worshipping of the mindless obeying of orders, and the devaluing of the individual's right or ability to think for themselves, and of reasoned discussion.[58] Lord Curzon, Chancellor of Oxford between 1907 and 1925, stated in 1907 that 'compared with German scholarship and science, the education offered by the University seemed amateur and superficial', but was unable to get the University to accept his reforms.[59]

Athleticism was the working philosophy that imbued all aspects of colonial life, including the yacht club; and yachting was very congruent with its central values of physical fitness and the ignoring of pain ('pluck').

---

father, Marc, was French. This situation was not always the case. Arthur Quiller-Couch, Professor of English at Cambridge, 1912–1944, in *On the Art of Writing*, p. 32, names the great poets of the first part of the nineteenth century as Coleridge, Wordsworth, Byron and Shelley, who all went to University and Keats was trained at Guy's Hospital.

[56] Guy Arnold notes the same trend in Henty's later books around 1900. 'There is a cold efficiency about these later heroes (*Hold Fast for England*, p. 36).

[57] Morris, *Heaven's Command*, pp. 301 and 405. An alternative view is that this hardness came with the emergence of the 'Empire' ideology at the turn of the century. Bernard Porter argues in *British Imperial: What the Empire Wasn't*, that the ideology of empire, with the world map displaying large splodges of pink, did not emerge till 1900. Interestingly, in Conrad's *Heart of Darkness*, Marlow seeks to explain his wanderlust: 'Now when I was a little chap I had a passion for maps ... At that time there were many blank spaces on the earth ...'(p. 11). Note how Marlow sees blank, not pink, spaces. Marlow is 'talking' in 1902, so his childhood would have been around the 1860s. Ferdinand Mount points out that imperial art was never seen as high art and artworks 'were soon relegated to provincial regimental museums and their painters seldom became R.As [Royal Academicians]' ('Lumpers v. Splitters', p. 31).

[58] The power of the narrative is shown that '2.5 million men from the U.K. enlisted in the armed forces without any form of legal compulsion [at the start of the First World War]' (Tracey Loughran, 'Masculinity, Trauma and "Shell-Shock"').

[59] Cannadine, *Aspects of Aristocracy*, pp. 96–99.

In successful colonisation, the threat of overwhelming fire power quells most indigenous unrest, at least for a while. Once the native population believes it can successfully fight against the colonisers, unless there are over-whelming economic benefits from staying, the colonisers will usually leave. (The glaring, and tragic, exception to this principle is, of course, Ireland). Until then, a successful occupying force has plenty of spare time on its hands for sports.

In the forces, there were separate sports for officers and men. In the col-onies, officers, often at considerable personal expense, engaged in cricket, yachting, polo, big game hunting and pig sticking; the men soccer and box-ing.[60] Huggins, in *The Victorians and Sport*, points out that 'successful partic-ipation had positive social and professional importance for officers' careers, especially after the abolition of purchase [of commissions] in 1870'.[61]

These prestige sports were for the enjoyment of officers and, in some countries, the very top of the indigenous social system, whose cooperation was required if the country was to be run quietly. There were three other groups attracted to colonial sport. 'As the empire spread, newly recruited administrators were increasingly expected to be sportsmen. Sports learnt on public school playing fields supposedly taught them the moral values and character necessary for effective imperial administration ...'[62]

School magazines, such as the *Eton Chronicle*, the *Haileyburian* and the *Cheltonian*, would regularly carry reports of the exploits of ex-pupils, as sol-diers, players or administrators, carrying out whatever needed to be done to bring civilisation to the world.[63] This was not just a matter of 'keeping in touch' with the old school. The news of successful individual military and sporting exploits provided role models for adult life and glamorised colonial careers.

And no longer were the colonies an unpredictable matter of months away, reachable only by a sailing ship dependent on the weather and wind direction, making communication difficult. Telegraphy created fast long distance communication.[64] The steam ship was almost always quicker than

---

[60] Morris, *Pax Britannica*, Chapter 15, 'Consolations', pp. 281–301. Where a sport attracted a varie-ty of classes and races, there would geographical separation, e.g. the grandstand for the whites. Huggins, in *The Victorians and Sport*, has a useful chapter 'The Wider World', pp. 219–247.

[61] Huggins, *The Victorians and Sport*, p. 221.

[62] *Ibid.*, p. 221.

[63] Mangan, *The Games Ethic and Imperialism*, p. 59. It is interesting that at the end of Kipling's *Stalky and Co.*, 1899, Kipling, having made the masters look fools, tells us of Stalky, now a General, and his exploits in defending India against the Indians. So, the schoolmasters' efforts were not wasted. See also Huggins, *The Victorians and Sport*, pp. 224–226.

[64] Michael Robbins, *The Railway Age*, p. 11.

a sailing ship, was considerably more comfortable and its arrival time more reliable. The term 'liner' came into use because the ship could sail directly in a line between two ports, and not be at the mercy of the wind. The early steam ship companies, such as P&O, formed in 1822 for the Iberian trade, and Cunard, running regular services across the Atlantic by the 1840s, were given subsidies for carrying the royal mail (and, when necessary, troops), as they were expensive to run, due to their coal consumption; but the government recognised the vital role that the mail played in colonial administration and social life.[65] A career in the colonies became both excitingly desirable and a practical choice.

Another group were missionaries. The Christian Missionary Society was founded in 1799, the British and Foreign Bible Society in 1804. As Huggins in *The Victorians and Sports* points out 'As the sea of faith receded in Britain in the later nineteenth century ... The evangelical movement made particular efforts to recruit the "hearties" and "bloods" of the public schools and universities, purveying new forms of manly "missionary" muscularity ... Anglican clergy were likely to be middle class and public school and Oxford educated.'[66]

The last, and largest, group were Britons who came out to trade or maintain the infrastructure. Between 1850 and 1880, three million English and Scots left for the new Anglo-Saxon colonies. Three out of five were male.[67] Sport 'integrated British new arrivals, through its recognisable rituals, its common language and convivialities, into the small British colonial social world'.[68]

Huggins summarises both the attraction and the importance of sport in the colonies as 'imperialistic cultural diffusion in which British sports and their association with manliness, the games ethic and athleticism variously became a cultural bond, a moral metaphor and potent symbol of British power'.[69] So, yachting and the yacht club, which allowed the ex-pats to be with 'their own', was a badge of prestige and ethnic superiority, and provided a unifying place and code of conduct.

The British in India could follow sport at home, albeit with a severe time lag, through the *Indian Sporting Review*, Calcutta in the 1840s, and the *Indian Field* from the 1850s, both of which carried much British material; and in

---

[65] Richard Woodman, 'A Brief History of Cargo Liners'.
[66] Huggins, *The Victorians and Sport*, p. 221.
[67] Bédarida, *A Social History of England*, p. 15.
[68] Huggins, *The Victorians and Sport*, p. 227.
[69] Ibid., p. 226.

Australia, through the weekly papers, such as the *Englishman's Magazine, Bell's Life in Sydney and Sporting Reviewer*, started in 1845, and followed by similar publications in Victoria, Tasmania, Adelaide and New South Wales. The telegraph linked England to India in 1866 and to Australia in 1872. The underseas telegraph came ashore in Darwin, in Northern Australia. An overland telegraph link was then made across the desert to Port Augusta in South Australia in the same year. The arrival of the telegraph allowed the newspapers to carry much more up-to-date sporting news from 'Old England'.

The Development of Yachting in African and Asian Colonies

Where there was a large indigenous population, the yacht club, besides representing the top stratum of colonial society, had the additional function of visibly representing the rulers of the land; and invariably excluded the ruled. John Torrance termed their self-image as 'a kind of illusory aristocratic status'.[70]

In the West Indies, the Royal Bermuda Yacht Club was formed by 'a party of thirty gentlemen who 'met together at Moore's Calabash tree near Walsingham' and consisted largely of army officers. It held a large regatta in 1845.[71] It was instrumental in early offshore races. One was held between a Bermudan yacht, *Pearl*, and the American yacht, *Brenda*, in 1849. The Royal Jamaica Yacht Club was formed in Kingstown in 1887.

In Africa, the Royal Natal Yacht Club, Durban (originally the Durban Regatta Club) was formed in 1858.

What is noticeable is the willingness of the English monarchy and its admiralty to acknowledge and encourage these clubs and give them prestige. This keenness to incorporate the colonies and their institutions in the 'traditions' of the home country is indicated by the large number of colonial yacht clubs declared 'royal' during Victoria's reign.

In the East, the Royal Bombay started in 1846; the Royal Hong Kong Victoria Regatta Club, either in 1845 or 1849, becoming the Royal Hong Kong Yacht Club in 1887; and the Royal Colombo Yacht Club, Ceylon (Sri Lanka) in 1898.

---

[70] And, similarly, he terms the Protestant Ascendancy as 'a second class peerage' (personal communication, September 2015).

[71] Heaton, *Yachting: A History*, p. 98. The biennial Newport, Rhode Island-Bermuda race started in 1906. Heaton ranks it, alongside the Fastnet and the Sydney–Hobart, as one of the three great ocean races of the world.

The Royal Bombay Yacht Club, Mumbai

The history of the Royal Bombay has been well documented in Gulshan Rai's *The History of the Royal Bombay Yacht Club*. We can therefore use it to examine its development as a fairly typical colonial yacht club.

The first regatta in Bombay harbour was in 1830, and, as was usual, came out of the leisure pursuits of the occupying forces and the British traders. 'The Royal Engineers Yacht Club formally came into being at Chatham, in 1846. In India, for a while, the Royal and Honourable East India Yacht Club existed but it merged with the Royal Engineers Yacht Club' to form the Bombay Yacht Club. It was declared Royal in 1876 .[72]

The club's racism was evident in 1900, when the Indian yacht owner of *Eileen IV*, Mr N. N. Wadia, offered 3 cups to the club, but was not welcome at the Club. As a member of the Royal Mersey and the Royal Clyde, he could enter his yacht 'provided said yacht was not sailed by the owner'. As a member of prestigious senior English clubs, he obviously would have been allowed if he had been white. Nor could he present his cups to the winners on club premises.[73]

Some Indian states were ruled by Indian princes, rather than directly by the British. In such states, the top Indians raced and, because the English needed to stay on good terms with them, they would race against them. 'A crack racer', Capt. J. J. Welch, Master of the Bombay Port pilot boat *Sunbeam*, raced in his Tomtit, 'a Linton Hope-designed 18 ft centre board sloop', *Clutha*, built in 1902. He won a cabinet-full of prizes. The one he was most proud of was the princely state of Bhopal's General Obaidullah Trophy, which he won against a wider ethnic range of opposition than was possible in Bombay. His account gives a flavour of the times, and shows the take-up of the sport by the top Indian echelons:

> Just for fun I took the *Clutha* to the Bhopal regatta and glorious times we had too. There I was pitted against the latest types of Tomtits ... rigged with beautiful Ratsey sails. 'Gopal', I said to my *tindal* (paid deckhand). 'We have got to make a show', and I sewed a strengthening piece of cloth into my main sail where it was a bit shaky in the luff and I started racing against my friends General Obaidullah Kham, the Hon'ble W. S. David, Capt. E.Y. Watson and others. When Gopal saw the lovely sails on the Bhopal boats, he said, '*Ky karega Sahib, bohut nawa hai*' (I am helpless Sir, their sails are brand new). 'All right, Gopal', I said, 'you just *tanao* (tighten) that main halyard and we will

---

[72] Rai, *The History of the Royal Bombay*, p. 26.
[73] *Ibid.*, pp. 64–65.

get going' and off we went to windward. The wind was usually fresh in Bhopal and I could keep *Clutha* driving ahead all the time seldom easing sheets, and in this way, I pulled off several races and won the Trophy.[74]

The club continued to be all-white even after India gained its independence in 1947.[75] The first Indian member was not elected to the RBYC till November, 1959, and the first Indian Commodore, K. N. Naoroji was elected in 1961.[76] The history of the Royal Bombay is telling, as yachting could have been a means of demonstrating the generosity of the British character and the wonders of their technology. Instead, the need to maintain social distance in terms of race, class and gender, was seen as paramount – 'the blatant racism of "Greater Britain" created social, racial and cultural barriers'.[77] Yachting seems to reflect a fundamental flaw in the English psyche – the need to maintain status at the cost of understanding and humanity, a theme that was repeated within British society (see Chapter 9).

The Development of Yachting in Dominion Colonies

A number of today's Commonwealth nations were originally a group of separate colonies.[78] The formation of yacht clubs in the various colonies started early. Since the major city of the colony was invariably a seaport, yachting must have seemed a natural leisure pursuit. The Royal Hobart Regatta Association stems from 1838. The Port Phillip Yacht Club, at Williamstown, the port of Melbourne, was formed in 1853, changing its name to the Royal Yacht Club of Victoria when it gained royal consent in 1887. The Royal Geelong Yacht Club, also in Victoria, was formed in 1859 and what is claimed to be Australia's first ocean race – from Queenscliff on the western side of Port Philip Bay to the

---

[74] *Ibid.*, p. 69. The regatta was held on Naina Tal Lake, Bhopal State.

[75] Similar Canute-like behaviour is to be found in Ireland. The town council changed Kingstown's name back to Dun Laoghaire in 1921. The Dublin Bay Sailing Club took till 1926 and the Royal St George till 1930 to recognise this change (O'Sullivan, *Dublin Bay*, p. 66; Archer and Pearson, *Royal St George Yacht Club*, p. 117).

[76] Rai, *The History of the Royal Bombay*, pp. 174–176. This appears to have provoked a racially prejudiced response on the part of the Royal Thames, which, in 1966, terminated its reciprocal arrangements with the RBYC, on the grounds that 'they cannot offer hospitality on the scale previously offered without severely prejudicing the interests of our members' (*Ibid.*, p. 180). The use of the term 'severely prejudicing' is an interesting Freudian slip.

[77] Huggins, *The Victorians and Sport*, p. 238. Ryan (personal communication, November 2015) points out that French, German and American colonisers show similar exclusive behaviour.

[78] So there was an early yacht match between New South Wales and Melbourne, Victoria (The Yachtsman, *British Yachts and Yachtsmen*, p. 324). Upper and Lower Canada were united in 1840; New Zealand became a single state in 1854, Australia in 1856 and the Cape Colony in 1872 (Thomson, *England in the Nineteenth Century*, pp. 93–94).

mouth of the Tamar River, Tasmania – took place on Christmas Day, 1907 in the Australian summer. This development occurred because the editor of the American yachting magazine, *Rudder*, Thomas Fleming Day, was in contact with the Commodore, T. A. Dickson, a contributor to *Rudder*. Day had organised the first offshore race in America from Brooklyn to Marblehead in Massachusetts and wanted to encourage offshore sailing more generally.[79]

England could no longer transport criminals to America after it lost the War of Independence in 1773. The transportation of criminals to Botany Bay, which is part of Sydney, began in 1787, with the First Fleet consisting of eleven vessels from Portsmouth, six of them convict ships with 799 convicts on board (743 alive on arrival). Transportation to Botany Bay was suspended in 1840 and abolished in 1850.[80] Sydney developed yachting as it moved away from being a penal colony towards becoming a trading city. The first regatta was in 1827 and thereafter there were 'Anniversary Regattas' to celebrate the founding of the colony. The Royal Sydney Yacht Squadron was created in 1862 and clearly modelled itself on the RYS. The DictionaryofSydney website proudly recounts that 'the Sydney organisation was the first yacht club outside the British Isles to be permitted to fly the prestigious blue ensign of the British Navy' and goes on, 'The pseudo-naval ceremonies and displays associated with English yachting were replicated on Sydney harbour'.[81] Modelling itself on the RYS, it would not admit members owning open boats. As a result, Royal Prince Alfred Yacht Club, Sydney, was formed in 1867, the Sydney Amateur Sailing Club in 1872 and the Sydney Flying Squadron in 1891.[82]

Sydney was the destination of a number of yachts from England. The 72 ton schooner *Chance* left Cowes on 13 January, 1862 and arrived at Sydney on 3 June, stopping at the Cape. The same passage was made in 119 days by the 25 ton *Vivid* in 1864–1865. *Alerte*, a 56 ton cutter, leaving in May, 1865, took 108 days out from Falmouth. She returned safely to England in 115 days. Her owner was the Sydney Squadron's first commodore, William Walker.

---

[79] Geoff Heriot, 'Australia's First Ocean Race'. Day really is the father of ocean racing, creating the 600-mile Newport, Rhode-Island–Bermuda Race and the 2,250-mile Transpac (Los Angeles–Honolulu), both first run in 1906, defunct by 1912, and, after the First World War, revived in 1923 (Dear, 'Leisure Sailing in the Twentieth Century, pp. 137–140).

[80] The other main destination of transported prisoners was Van Diemen's Land (Tasmania) from 1803 to 1853. The destination of the last transport ship from Dun Laoghaire, which left on 2 June, 1853, was to Fremantle, Western Australia (Dun Laoghaire Harbour Co. 'The Construction of Dun Laoghaire Harbour', download, n/d).

[81] www.sydneydictionary.org, accessed 29 March 2015.

[82] Useful information on the development of yacht racing in Australia can be found in McCallum, *Fast and Bonnie*. Chapter 8: 'Down Under', pp. 58–64.

John Henry Want was a prominent Australian lawyer, and also a keen
yachtsman, a member of the Sydney Squadron and the Royal Prince Alfred,
of which he was Commodore from 1877–1881. He came to England in 1883
to buy a fast yacht to take back home. Instead, he purchased the ageing
Mignonette, built 1867, a 52 foot long cutter. He arranged for her to be sailed
back to Sydney, hiring Tom Dudley as skipper. In 1883, Dudley hired two sailors and a boy from his home village of Tollesbury on the Essex Blackwater.
The ship foundered in the South Atlantic and the crew took to a small dinghy.
Running out of food and water, they killed the weakened boy, drank his blood
and ate him. Rescued, they were brought back to Falmouth and sentenced
to death at Exeter in a celebrated case that is still taught to law students.
However, it is clear that there was never any intention that the death sentence
be carried out, since it was considered acceptable to resort to cannibalism in
such situations. They were released after six months in prison.[83]

Joshua Slocum arrived in Sydney from Newcastle, New South Wales
in October, 1996, during his single-handed navigation. Down the pontoon
came 'a young gentleman … with brass buttons enough to sink him … it
had been decided by his club [probably the Royal Sydney Yacht Squadron]
that *Spray* could not be officially recognised, for the reason she brought no
letters from yacht clubs in America'. The delivery of this message of social
superiority was rather spoilt by the messenger stepping into a barrel of water
that Slocum was coopering and nearly drowning. Slocum was treated better
by the Johnstone's Bay Flying Squadron, who gave him a new set of sails.[84]

The Royal Perth, Western Australia, formalised in 1865, traces its history
back to 1841. Its website tells us it was 'just 12 years after Captain Fremantle
arrived to establish the Swan River Colony, when a group of sailors staged a
modest regatta to celebrate Foundation day'.[85] The Royal Freshwater Yacht
Club followed in 1896.

Similarly, the Colony of South Australia was proclaimed at Glenelg,
Holdfast Bay, Adelaide on December 28, 1836. There was a major yachting
regatta at Glenelg, to celebrate Prince Edward's (the future Edward VII)
eighteenth birthday in 1859. The Royal South Australian Squadron was
formed in Adelaide in 1869. The Glenelg Yacht Club was formed in 1874, to

---

[83] A detailed account of the whole episode and its aftermath is given in A. W. Brian Simpson,
Cannibalism and Common Law. Dudley emigrated with his family to Sydney in 1885, and set up
a business in yacht sails and rigging. In 1900, the bubonic plague reached Sydney from Hong
Kong, and Dudley was the first man to die of it on Thursday, 22 February, 1900, at the age of 46.
[84] Joshua Slocum, *Sailing Alone around the World*, pp. 312–313.
[85] www.bestclubs.com.au/was/perth-royal-yacht-club/default.aspx

be followed in 1883 by Holdfast Bay Yacht and Boat Club and the Glenelg Dinghy and Aquatic Club in 1898.

Other Australian clubs formed before 1900 were the Royal Yacht Club of Tasmania, 1874; and the Royal Brighton Yacht Club, Middle Brighton, Victoria, 1875. The Royal Melbourne Yacht Squadron, previously named the St Kilda Sailing Club, was created in 1876 and the Royal Queensland Yacht Squadron, Brisbane in 1885.[86]

In New Zealand, a regatta was held in Auckland waters in 1840; the Auckland Yacht Club, from 1902 known as the Royal New Zealand Yacht Squadron, Auckland, whose early records are lost, was certainly functioning in some form before 1887. Heaton suggests 1871; the Royal Port Nicolson, Wellington, 1883; and the North Shore Sailing Club, now the Royal Akarana Yacht Club, 1897.[87]

The use of the term 'squadron' in so many of the Australasian yacht clubs indicates the prestige of the Royal Yacht Squadron that they were seeking to emulate.

In Canada, again, whether on the Great Lakes or on the coast, there is a royal yacht club at the main colonial locations. The Royal Canadian Yacht Club was formed in Toronto 1852, becoming 'Royal' in 1854. Again, the Services' influence was evident. Heaton writes about the objectives leading to its formation:

> The object was for the members' yachts to meet every Saturday afternoon in the season, draw lots for a leader, who would head the fleet to the garrison Wharf and back, after which the yachts dispersed. Like the Royal Yacht Squadron and other British clubs of the time, some of the activities were considered as training for the navy in time of war, or for experiments in naval architecture and ship handling for defence. (There had been naval engagements between Canada and the USA on the Great Lakes, barely forty years earlier).[88]

As in Australia, each major settlement had its early yacht club. The Halifax Yacht Club, founded in 1837, became the Royal Nova Scotia Yacht Squadron in 1873. The Royal Hamilton, Ontario was formed in 1854, the Royal Saint Lawrence, Montreal in 1891, the Royal Victoria, British Columbia in 1892, the strangely named Royal Kennebecassis Yacht Club, Milledgeville, New Brunswick in 1894, and the Royal Vancouver on the West Coast in 1901.

---

[86] Johnson, *Yacht Clubs of the World.*
[87] Heaton, *History of Yachting,* p. 174.
[88] *Ibid.,* pp. 61–62.

It was not necessary that there were military personnel for yachting to start up. A strong trading presence was enough. Egypt had long been an overland route to Africa by transhipment from the Mediterranean to the Red Sea. The opening of the Suez canal in 1869 made Egypt a vital link in the control of the empire. In 1875, Disraeli bought the shares of the ruling Khedive, who had fallen on hard times. The British then stayed as important players in Egyptian politics till being thrown out by Nasser in 1956. The Royal Yacht Club of Egypt, in Aqaba, had been formed in 1901. The British built and controlled rail transport, banking and meat production in Argentina. The Yacht Club of Argentina, Buenos Aires, was founded in 1883.

Wherever there were enough well-off British personnel in a trading centre with suitable sailing waters, be it a colony or an independent country, a yacht club would be set up, and this process was well underway before yachting really took off in the home country.

CHAPTER EIGHT

The Enthusiastic Adoption of Yachting by the Mercantile and Professional Classes after 1870

PART ONE
The New Men

The love of boating is inherent, more or less, in the heart of every British boy, the more so if brought up within the sight of salt water

… careful papas and anxious mamas would do well to throw no obstacle in the way if master Harry or Tom show any predilection for yachting.[1]

As yachting became increasingly popular among the members of the rapidly expanding middle class with surplus income to spend on leisure, so the composition and structure of yachting and yacht clubs changed, and the Corinthian style of yachting grew. The key factors in this growth were political stability and the creation of a railway network linking the cities to the coast.

Regarding political stability, the working class moved away from radicalism towards cooperation, friendly societies and trade unionism.[2] Abroad, the Navy was establishing a *Pax Britannica* that lasted from the Crimean War (1853–1856) to the First World War.

With the advent of the railways, 'the countryside seemed to shrink perceptibly, as the iron rails swiftly formed connections between the cities, linking

---

[1] Tyrell Biddle, *Amateur Sailing in Open and Half-Decked Boats*, 1886, p. 1.
[2] Bédarida, *Social History of England*, p. 67. He points out that Marx lived in London almost unknown: 'at his death [14 March, 1883 in London] it was the *Times* correspondent in Paris, who cabled the news to his paper in London' (p. 80).

town and country, city and coast, and bringing together the far extremities of the land'.[3]

Who Were the New Participants in Yachting?

As Ryan has pointed out, yachting expands as the middle class expands, and it was expanding fast.[4] We can distinguish three overlapping but distinct groups.

Firstly, there were those involved in manufacturing or the production of raw materials, such as coal. It was among these new industrialists, the manufacturers and their managers, that new yachtsmen were recruited; and if not from them, because they were too concerned and too anxious about maintaining their new found status and wealth, from their sons.

These men were, very predominantly, based in and around the cities, created by the Industrial Revolution. In the second half of the nineteenth century, Manchester, Salford (the location of Engels' *The Condition of the Working Class in England in 1844*), Birmingham, Leeds, Sheffield, Newcastle, Hull, Bristol and Glasgow all doubled or trebled their population. New cities grew from towns, created because they were suitable for a particular product or process like Leicester (engineering, joinery, traditional hosiery), Stoke-on-Trent (pottery), Cardiff (coal export), Middlesborough and Barrow-in-Furness (ironworks), and Crewe and Swindon (railways).

Most of the industrial cities were not on the coast, but near the source of either the raw materials, such as coal, or where the relevant skilled workers were congregated. Cities that were on a navigable river had the problem that the water was filthy and used as a sewer. The yachtsmen therefore needed the advent of the railways to reach clean water. In the case of Belfast, this was to Bangor, Belfast Lough (1865). For Glasgow, the yachtsman used both rail and steamer to access the Lower Clyde: rail to Gourock, opened 1889, thence by ferry to Hunter's Quay, near Dunoon, home of the Royal Clyde, and other yachting havens on the Forth of Clyde, such as Rothesay, on the Isle of Bute, the home of the Royal Northern Yacht Club till 1937.[5] For Liverpool, this meant the Menai Straits (rail link to Chester 1847; Chester–Holyhead 1850). From London, trains reached the Lower Thames at Gravesend in 1849 and Southend in 1856.

---

[3] Walvin, *Leisure and Society*, p. 18.
[4] Ryan, 'The Emergence of Middle-Class Yachting in the North-West of England from the Later Nineteenth Century'.
[5] when it moved to Rhu, on the Gare Loch.

By 1851, there were over 6,000 miles of rail track in Britain. By 1870, this had expanded to 13,500 miles and, by 1913 to 20,281 miles.[6] After 1870, the city-based cruising man could quickly reach his boat. He could sail from his home port to a large number of small ports and fishing villages, leave the boat there in the care of a local boatman, take the train home and pick his boat up the following weekend.

The second new group were the middle-class professionals needed to service the Industrial Revolution. Professions, in the second half of the nineteenth century, were growing rapidly both in terms of numbers, and also in terms of professional organisation. To the old 'learned professions' – Divinity, Physic (medicine) and Law – were added officers in the army and navy, and members of the newer professions, such as architects, engineers of various sorts, accountants, actuaries etc.[7]

But it was the older professions that were seen as providing a leadership role, and as challenging the hegemonic power of the landed aristocracy. In an 1858 article, titled 'Liberalism, Patriotism and English Liberty', published by the influential periodical, the *Edinburgh Review*, Fitzjames Stephen commented on these new leaders:

> They are the leaders of everyday English life – what we may well call the non-commissioned officers of English society ... the clergy, the lawyers, the doctors, the county squires, the junior partners in banks and merchants' offices, men who are in every sense of the word gentlemen, though no one would class them with the aristocracy.[8]

Implicit in his comments is that these members of the middle classes *never* gained their income from trade or manual labour and were paid a salary or fee – for example, for a medical consultation – not a wage, differences that were to become crucial in deciding membership of yacht clubs. Their households

---

[6] Robbins, *The Railway Age*, pp. 31 and 40.

[7] Bédarida, *A Social History of England*, pp. 50–51. Buying commissions in the army came to end with the Cardwell reforms of the army in 1871. Edward Cardwell was the Secretary of State for War (1868–1874) under Gladstone. Lord Cardigan had paid £40,000 for the Colonelcy of the 11th Hussars and his incompetence, as witnessed by the Charge of the Light Brigade (1854), during the Crimean War (1853–1856) and his unpopularity (sleeping on his luxury yacht, whilst his soldiers endured terrible conditions on land), aided this change. So, now, becoming an officer became open to a wider socio-economic range.

[8] Fitzjames Stephen, 'Liberalism, Patriotism and English Liberty', p. 37. This new elite was also visible in politics. Before 1867, the old aristocracy ruled, through such men as Lords Grey, Russell, Derby and Palmerston and half the cabinet ministers were in the Lords. After that date, Melbourne, Gladstone and Disraeli, all prime ministers, did not belong to aristocratic families (Thomson, *England in the Nineteenth Century*, p. 123).

had servants; and this general societal definition of a 'gentleman' would be fiercely implemented by yacht clubs.

If the industrialists were the key energisers of the growth of yachting, It is three of the older professional groups – lawyers, medical practitioners and the clergy – that provided many of the important figures of this expanding Victorian sport.

Figures are hard to come by, but another Victorian prestige sport, mountaineering, had only one organising club, the Alpine Club, founded in 1857. A full 28 per cent of their membership in 1857–1863 were lawyers.[9] It is less easy to get equivalent figures for yachting. Key figures in Irish yachting history include the solicitors, Henry Crawford and James A. Lyle, who were leading lights in the development of the Royal Alfred and racing in Dublin Bay and the Irish Sea. T. B. Middleton, in Dublin, the inspiration behind the creation of the first one-design class, the Water Wags in the 1880s, was another practising solicitor as was Harry Donovan, founder member of the Irish Cruising Club in the 1920s. In England, pioneers such as MacGregor, E. F. Knight, G. Christopher Davies, advocate of sailing on the Broads and author of a number of early how-to books, and Erskine Childers, were all legally trained. Of these, only Davies practised in the legal profession. Childers worked in the Houses of Parliament. Knight was a journalist. MacGregor, the son of General Sir Duncan MacGregor, had independent means. Arthur Underhill, a practising barrister, was a key figure in the creation of the (Royal) Cruising Club, in 1880. The membership never exceeded 300 and entry was by recommendation. The club had a strong legal presence, with committee meetings in members' chambers.[10] An explanation could be that the law is well-paid and has long holidays, especially in the summer.

Medical practitioners included H. L. Jones, the surgeon author of *Swin, Swale and Swatchway*, published in 1892. His cruising companion was another surgeon, Charles Barrett Lockwood. Claud Worth, author of the magnum opus, *Yacht Cruising*, 1910, and Harrison Butler (1871–1945), famous yacht designer in his spare time, were both ophthalmic surgeons.[11]

---

[9] Peter H. Hansen, 'Albert Smith, the Alpine Club, and the Invention of Mountaineering in mid-Victorian Britain', p. 310. The development of mountaineering, among Victorian sports, mirrors the development of yachting. See Fergus Fleming, *Killing Dragons: The Conquest of the Alps*, and Ann Colley, *Victorians in the Mountains*.

[10] See Sir Arthur Underhill, *A Short History of the Royal Cruising Club MDCCCLXXX–MCMXXX*; Alisdair Garrett and Trevor Wilkinson, *The Royal Cruising Club 1880–1980*.

[11] Claud Worth, *Yacht Cruising*, 1910; Harrison Butler's *Cruising Yachts: Design and Performance*, was based on his inter-war work, but was only published in 1945.

At the inaugural meeting of the revived Royal Irish in 1846, of the 28 present, there were five barristers and four solicitors.[12] Of the seven founder members of the (Royal) Burnham Yacht Club in 1895, three were lawyers and one was a doctor.[13]

The other notable profession was the clergy. Among those who wrote accounts of their voyages were the Reverend Robert Hughes, skipper of the *Pet*, who voyaged to the Baltic in 1854 and 1855. The Rev. Edward Lyon Berthon designed the Collapsible Rescue Boat and formed the Berthon Boat Company and built it in Romsey from 1860 till 1892. The Rev. A. G. L'Estrange was the author of a number of cruising accounts. Rev. William Forwell recounted the voyage he took with his son in *A Thousand Miles' Cruise in the Silver Cloud from Dundee to France and Back in a Small Boat* (1879). The Rev. C. Wilkinson wrote under the pseudonym of 'Diagonal White', while the Rev. Albert J. Van Straubenzee was the first Vice-Commodore of the Cruising Club.[14]

The Public School Origins of Corinthian Yachting

Squire Brown is considering his final words of advice to Tom, before he leaves for Rugby:

> Shall I tell him to mind his work, and say he's sent to school to make himself a good scholar? Well, but he isn't sent to school for that – at any rate, not mainly. I don't care a straw for Greek particles, or the digamma; no more does his mother. What is he sent to school for? ... If only he'll turn out a brave, helpful, truth-telling Englishman, and a gentleman, and a Christian, that's all I want.[15]

We need to turn our attention to the public schools. It was their philosophy of Athleticism that was focussed and re-shaped to become Corinthian yachting. Yachting developed as a prestigious sport because the old and new elites had a shared set of values and beliefs that many of them had experienced

---

[12] Boylan, *White Sails Crowding*, p. 15.

[13] Royal Burnham Yacht Club, *A History of the Royal Burnham Yacht Club*, p. 2.

[14] Robert Edgar Hughes, *Two Summer Cruises with the Baltic Fleet, 1854–5, Being the Log of the "Pet" Yacht*, 1855. The Rev. A. G. L'Estrange, *Yachting around the West of England. 1865; From the Thames to the Tamar*, 1873; Rev. William Forwell, *A Thousand Miles' Cruise in 'Silver Cloud' from Dundee to France and Back in a Small Boat*, 1879; Diagonal White, *By Ocean, Firth and Channel; Amateur Cruising on the West Coast of Scotland and North of Ireland*, 1894.

[15] Thomas Hughes, *Tom Brown's Schooldays*, pp. 73–74.

and learnt at their public schools. In addition, the Victorian yacht clubs drew heavily on the 'traditions' and rituals created in these schools.[16]

The second half of the nineteenth century saw a rapid increase in the number of public (private, fee-paying) schools. Marlborough opened in 1842, Radley 1847, Lancing 1853, Clifton and Haileybury 1862, as the aspiring middle-class professionals wanted to give their male offspring the best chances in life.[17]

Vivian Ogilvie suggests that Arnold of Rugby was aiming at the new rich – the merchants from the North and the manufacturers from the Midlands – who wanted a family makeover, a class laundering, so that their sons could go to the old universities – Oxford and Cambridge – and thereby be admitted to the elite. The professional middle class likewise sent their sons to improve their career chances.[18]

Crucially, as the century progressed, the landed aristocracy moved away from home tuition to sending their sons to public schools. Thus, both upper-class and upper middle-class sons were receiving the same education – and induction of values – at public schools. The result was a powerful unity. Leonore Davidoff comments:

> The unique feature of Victorian society is that these essentially middle-class patterns were grafted on to the honorific code of the aristocracy or gentry to produce the widened concept of 'gentility' which was, without doubt, one of the most effective instruments for social control ever devised.[19]

Asa Briggs, in *Victorian People*, points out:

> It was difficult to resist the attractions of a graceful and effortless country gentleman's society. In the battle between the self-made man and the gentleman, the self-made man won in England only if he became a gentleman himself, or tried to turn his son into one.[20]

This joining of the old and the new elites in a common education had an important effect in yachting as it meant that both classes had been inducted into a similar value system, concerned with four central, intertwined, values, which would be transferred across to sailing. It is important to understand

---

[16] Cannadine, 'The Context, Performance and Meaning of Ritual: The British Monarchy and the "Invention of Tradition", c. 1820–1977'.

[17] The 'sacred nine' – Winchester, Eton, Westminster, Rugby etc. were all established much earlier.

[18] Ogilvie, *The English Public School*, Chapter 10: 'Arnold and the Modern Public School', pp. 139–168.

[19] Davidoff, *The Best Circles*, p. 36.

[20] Briggs, *Victorian People*, p. 142.

that all these terms, while retaining their central importance in British society, changed their meanings over time.

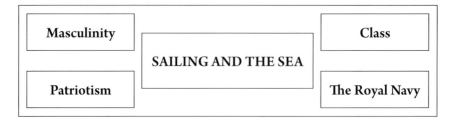

We may start with a consideration of *patriotism*. The love of 'the house'
and 'the school' was converted into *patriotism and duty to one's country, especially to the Navy.* [21]

The concept of yachtsmen as naval reservists – officers in waiting – was
frequently pronounced. With regard to patriotism, we may ask: *patriotic to
what?* The answer surely is 'to England'. 'Britain' is only invoked when there
is a war looming or happening and the Celtic poor are needed for cannon
fodder. For example, the icon of patriotism, Nelson, born in a vicarage in
Burnham Thorpe, Norfolk, is primarily an *English* hero, not a British one.
The United Kingdom was in existence, after the union of England and Wales
with Scotland by the accession of James I in 1603, and the four kingdoms were
united into one United Kingdom by the Act of Union of 1707.[22] So, why not
'*Britain* expects …'? After all, that signal would have used the same number
of flags.[23] This elision of English and British seems almost unconscious.
R. L. Stevenson's family was Scottish and had become famous for building
Scottish lighthouses. He was educated in Scotland and attended Edinburgh
University. Yet in 1878, in the *Cornhill* magazine, he wrote:

> The sea is our approach and bulwark; it has been the scene of our greatest
> triumphs and dangers; … We should consider ourselves unworthy of our

---

[21] I discuss these values at greater length in 'Written on the Waves: British Yachting Literature
and Codes of Masculinity 1888–1945'. We have observed these values before, e.g. William
Hickey preferring sailing to rowing to demonstrate his masculinity (p. 53); and the Squadron seeing one of its roles as developing prototypes of fighting ships (p. 79), but these values
would become much more centre stage in the Corinthian philosophy of yachting.

[22] England and Wales had been united under Henry VIII in 1543.

[23] The reader who wants to go further into the complexities of national identity should consult
Benedict Anderson, *Imagined Communities* and Linda Colley, *Britons* and her more accessible
Acts of Union and Disunion.

descent if we did not share the arrogance of our progenitors and please our-selves with the pretensions that the sea is English.[24]

One of the stereotypes of the Victorians is that they had a fixed and unchanging understanding of 'masculinity'. However, this is incorrect in two important ways.

Firstly, writings on 'masculine identity' have been almost solely focussed on gender relationships. This is not a useful way of understanding 'identity', especially in the Britain of the Victorian empire. It incorporated far more aspects of living and one's values than merely one's sexuality, such as one's relation to one's family, to different social classes, to other nations etc. So, the person's code of masculinity affected and controlled all aspects of their life.

Secondly, during the Victorian and Edwardian period, there were a number of competing models of masculinity, exercising various degrees of dominance, depending on the date and the group under consideration. So, we need to bear in mind the multifaceted and changing nature of 'masculin-ity' or 'manliness', the Victorians' preferred term.[25]

The first conceptualisation of 'masculinity' in Victorian times was *Manly Virtue*, expressed by Thomas Arnold, headmaster of Rugby. Arnold was rendered a Christian icon to his contemporaries and later Victorians by A. P. Stanley's *Life and Correspondence of Thomas Arnold, D.D.* (1844), which went through five editions in its first year of publication, and which, by 1890, 'had sold hundreds of thousands of copies in at least fifty editions'.[26] Arnold's teachings were fictionalised by an old Rugbeian, Thomas Hughes, in *Tom Brown's Schooldays*, 1857, which sold 11,000 copies in its first year of publication.[27]

Arnold's *Manly Virtue* was a very active Christianity, in which a person is continuously being guided by God in his decisions. During Arnold's

---

[24] R. L. Stevenson, 'The English Admirals', *Cornhill Magazine*, 38, July 1878, p. 36. Quoted in Mack, *The Sea: A Cultural History*, p. 82.

[25] 'manliness': ... As interpreted by the early Victorians it represented the virtues of seriousness, self-denial and rectitude; as understood by the late Victorian, it denoted robustness, perse-verance and stoicism' (Mangan, *The Games Ethic and Imperialism*, p. 18). I discuss Victorian manliness at greater length in my 'A Brief History of the Yachting Narrative', 'A Brief History of the Yachting Narratives, Part Two' and 'Written on the Waves'. It is worth pointing out that the meanings of 'masculinity' and 'femininity' are continually mutating in our times, just as much as in Victorian times.

[26] James Eli Adams, *Dandies and Desert Saints: Style of Victorian Masculinity*, p. 65. Adams gives Michael McCrum, *Thomas Arnold, Headmaster: A Reassessment*, p. 153n. as his source. It was common for ambitious Victorian headmasters and bishops to publish their sermons.

[27] Huggins, *The Victorians and Sport*, p. 160.

headship, 1,500 boys came into contact with him and 300 took Holy Orders.[28] This religious content of masculinity is shown by two of the pioneer yachtsmen, MacGregor and E. E. Middleton, who distributed religious tracts at the various ports they entered. MacGregor, in addition, was a very active philanthropist, setting up numerous organisations to help London's beggars and poor, such as the Ragged School Shoeblack Society.[29] A third, McMullen, wrote Protestant tracts. All three represent a very active, proselytising Christianity, close to Arnold's. However, across the Victorian era, religion markedly diminished as an active ingredient of masculinity and became more of a ritualistic act. By the time of E. F. Knight's sailing writings in the 1880s, there is no mention of Christianity.[30] And this remained the case. In such popular novels as Childers' *The Riddle of the Sands* or, later, in Ransome's *Swallows and Amazons* series, religion is noticeable by its absence.

Manly Virtue was replaced by the philosophies of Muscular Christianity and Social Darwinism, which were amalgamated into Athleticism, as discussed in Chapter 7. Later alternative and popular forms of masculinity were Aestheticism associated with Aubrey Beardsley and Oscar Wilde, with its celebration of beauty and art, and Baden-Powell's Empire Pioneer.[31]

Since those who attended public schools and went on to university would usually have come from wealthy families, they would have been over-represented among the elite of yacht clubs. It is useful to see if the behaviours and values of public schools can be discerned in yacht clubs.

The Victorian public school was a *total institution*, a term the sociologist, Erving Goffman, used to analyse mental hospitals.[32] The difference was that, in the case of public schools, it was not the staff who ran the institution, but the inmates. And their rules, enforced by the older boys, were arbitrary and

[28] J. R. De S. Honey, *Tom Brown's Universe*, p. 27.
[29] In *A Voyage Alone in the Yawl 'Rob Roy'*, there is a picture of MacGregor 'distributing tracts' in his skiff to a rather puzzled Frenchman on horseback in the water of a French port (p. xx) and passing one to a lad through a porthole (p. 88), so MacGregor was keen to demonstrate his evangelising. For a Victorian biography, focussing on his good works, see Edwin Hodder, *John MacGregor* (1895).
[30] A loss mourned in the lines of Malcolm Arnold, Thomas' son, in 'Dover Beach', lines 21–26: 'The Sea of Faith/ Was once, too, at the full and round earth's shore/ Lay like the folds of a bright girdle furl'd/ But now I only hear/ Its melancholy, long, withdrawing roar/ Retreating.' The poem was written during, or inspired by, his honeymoon in Dover in June, 1851.
[31] Representative texts are – for Manly Virtue: Thomas Hughes. *Tom Brown's Schooldays*, 1857; Muscular Christianity: Charles Kingsley. *Westward Ho!*, 1855; Social Darwinism: Jack London. *Sea Wolf*, 1904; Athleticism: Erskine Childers. *The Riddle of the Sands*, 1903; Aestheticism: Oscar Wilde. *The Picture of Dorian Gray*, 1891; Empire Pioneer: Robert Baden-Powell, *Scouting for Boys*, 1908 and Ransome's *Swallows and Amazons*, 1930–1947.
[32] Erving Goffman, *Asylums: Essays on the Social Situation of Mental Patients and Other Inmates*, 1962.

their application equally arbitrary. So, Flashman, having taken an intense dislike to Tom Brown, attempts to roast him alive. For once, this is such a serious assault that staff have to be called, but take no action – it is left to the boys to sort out.[33] It was a purely male environment, with the only women being the masters' wives or matron. Boys learnt how to cope in an all-male environment, but only in an all-male environment, and with almost no women at university, this was true also for those who became undergraduates.

The head of house/school can be equated with the commodore and the prefects with flag officers.

Also, as Huggins points out, uniform allowed a comforting continuity between the public school and life outside, for at public school: 'caps, scarves, stockings, ties, badges, braid and blazers all symbolised sporting achievements. Uniform or special kit functioned as a badge of belonging, and as a way of excluding';[34] and for advertising status.

Finally, there can be little doubt that homosexual experiences – in any variety from deep adolescent passions to rape – were common. Homosexual experiences are referred to in fictionalised autobiographical accounts of Victorian schooldays.[35] The same is true of the old universities. Hermione Lee refers to the '"golden glow of homosexuality" that suffused Cambridge in those days [the 1900s]'.[36]

How did these experiences affect the graduates on leaving these all-male environments? Unfortunately, this question is impossible to answer. In the 1880s, the zeitgeist turned against gay men. Homosexuality first became the crime of 'gross indecency', with the passing of Section 11 of the Criminal Law Amendment Act of 1885.[37] (It was this legislation that was used against Wilde

---

[33] Hughes, *Tom Brown's Schooldays*, Chapter 8, pp. 182–186.

[34] Huggins, *The Victorians and Sport*, p. 194.

[35] Such as *Maurice*, written by E. M. Forster in 1914, but not published in his lifetime; *David Blaize* by E. F. Benson, 1916; *The Loom of Youth*, by Alec Waugh, 1917. With regard to Athleticism and homosexuality, see Jeffrey Richards, 'Passing the Love of Women: Manly Love and Victorian Society', Norman Vance, 'The Idea of Manliness' and Jeffrey Weeks, *Sex, Politics and Society*.

[36] Hermione Lee, *Penelope Fitzgerald: A Life*, p. 13. Both types of institution had a problem in that they lauded the Classics, and the Greeks saw homosexuality as superior to heterosexuality. Older men taking young men as lovers, to help them towards maturity, was part of the culture. De S. Honey has documented that the early public school headmasters, when they railed against sexual evil, had masturbation in mind. During this period, homosexuality was not a crime and they were not very interested in sodomy, as they considered it to have few health implications (De S. Honey, *Tom Brown's Universe*, pp. 167–194).

[37] The term 'homosexuality' was first used by the Professor of Psychiatry at Strasbourg University, Richard von Krafft-Ebing, in his *Psychopathia Sexualis* published in 1886. Although disliking the term, Havelock Ellis used it in his *Sexual Inversion* in 1897. Translated into English by 1889, Krafft-Ebing had discouraged lay readers of his medical text by writing parts of it in Latin;

in his trial in 1895.) So clearly, after that date, gay men were not going to declare their orientation. Also, in Victorian times, it was common for upper-class men who were primarily homosexual in orientation to marry, for two reasons: first, to deflect attention from their primary orientation, and second to provide an heir.[38]

Which New Sport to Choose?

So how did this new, emerging power group use its leisure time?

By the 1870s, the professional classes had surplus income and surplus leisure time. Many lived in the 'leafy suburbs', to which the expanding middle class migrated, commuting to work by rail, or, in London, by underground (the Metropolitan line was opened in 1863 and, by the next year, worked with the District Railway to complete the Circle Line). Their pleasures were often pursued locally, at the tennis club and on the nearby golf course. Yachting would have required additional income.

Victorian entrepreneurial initiative ensured that they had a range of new sports to choose from. We need to bear in mind two features of prestige sports in the second half of the nineteenth century.

Firstly, *the Victorians took up games that were newly created*. Lawn tennis, badminton, field hockey, croquet, cycling, snooker, table tennis and water polo were all mid-Victorian creations, while golf was brought south from Scotland.[39]

Secondly, *Victorian upper-class males often, if not usually, played more than one sport, and so were members of more than one type of sports club*. The expansion of sport and the creation of new types of sporting activities can be clearly seen in three classic Victorian boating novels: Jerome K. Jerome's *Three Men in a Boat*, 1889, features punting, fishing, sculling, rowing and sailing; Erskine Childers' *The Riddle of the Sands*, 1903, tells of duck shooting, large yacht cruising, steam yachts, small yacht cruising, rowing and dinghy sailing; while in *The Wind in the Willows*, 1908, Kenneth Grahame, mainly

---

and a bookseller was prosecuted for selling Ellis' book, so it is unlikely that either had a great influence among the public.

[38] Even when homosexuality was decriminalised in 1997, the silence in yachting literature and yacht club histories as to the existence of men who were or are gay continued, excepting the occasional mention of the Gay Sailing and Cruising Association. The history of gay men and women, and their contribution to yachting, is unwritten.

[39] Lowerson, *Sport and the English Middle Classes 1870–1914*, Chapter 8: 'Sport as Business', pp. 225–260, details how developments in rubber technology were important in the development of tennis, golf and cycling (and, through contraceptives, for the decline in the birth rate in late Victorian and Edwardian times).

through the medium of the easily bored Mr Toad, describes punting, sailing, houseboating, wager-boating, caravans, cars and motorboats. E. F. Knight's *Sailing*, published in 1889, is part of the All-England series, which also published volumes on *Cricket, Boxing, Lawn Tennis, Golf, Mountaineering, Rowing and Sculling, Cycling, Cycling Touring, Gymnastics, Dumb-Bells,* and *Indian Clubs*.

Tennis and golf clubs expanded rapidly in number after the second half of the nineteenth century. In 1850, there were 17 golf clubs in the United Kingdom. By 1898, there were 1,460 clubs, with slightly over half of them in England.[40]

Rowing and sculling on the upper Thames were favoured activities of public school boys and varsity students, with the first Henley Regatta taking place in 1839.[41] As a prestige aquatic sport, the Regatta was regularly attended by the Queen's Consort, Prince Albert. Rowing expanded hugely in the second half of the nineteenth century.[42]

The benefits and rituals were similar across the various prestige sports clubs. As Lowerson points out:

> Within themselves the clubs sought to create 'tradition' … Ceremonial conduct, titles, insignia and chains for officers, the opening of the first match of the season, uniforms and badges were wrapped in specialised language … the new sportsman moved into a world distinguished by arcane and dedicated terms offering him separateness and a bond with the elect, even in humour.[43]

Bonding was furthered by a favourite Victorian institution – the 'smoking concert', an evening of music and discussion, attended only by men. These winter get-togethers generated income for the club, and kept the membership together.

---

[40] Lowerson, *Sport and the English Middle Classes, 1870–1914*, p. 126. 'The Cyclists Touring Club, founded in 1878 with 142 members, had 60,000 by 1899' (Huggins, *The Victorians and Sport*, p. 8).

[41] Patricia Burstall, *The Golden Age of the Thames*; Christopher Dodd, *Henley Royal Regatta*, 1981; Richard Burnell. *Henley Royal Regatta: A Celebration of 150 Years.* Contested aquatic space is a feature in Jerome's *Three Men in a Boat*, where the clerks compete for the same water as Oxford University scullers and rich owners of steam yachts (see my 'Angry Voices on the River Bank: A Reinterpretation of Two Aquatic Classics').

[42] In *Winning Waters*, Aylwin Sampson usefully lists the founding date of all clubs affiliated to the Amateur Rowing Association. Taking 'B' for example, 15 rowing clubs beginning with 'B' were formed between 1847 and 1892: Bedford RC 1886, Berwick ARC 1869, Bewdley RC 1877, Bexhill RC 1890, Bideford AAC 1870, Bideford ARC 1882, Birmingham RC 1873, Blyth RC 1874, Boston RC 1856, Bradford ARC 1867, Bradford-on-Avon RC 1873, Brighton Cruising Club 1892, Bristol Ariel RC 1870, Broxbourne RC 1860, Burton Leander RC 1847 (p. 166).

[43] Lowerson, *Sport and the English Middle Classes 1870–1914*, p. 23.

Specialist vocabulary is a pervasive and important feature of sporting groups. Obviously, one function is as an aid to manipulating and controlling a specific environment, be it the sea or the bowling green; but another important function is to signal membership of a group by the demonstration of easy familiarity with these arcane terms. Part of 'belonging' to a group is to utilise the correct emotional tone. For example, however frightened you may have been at the time, when recounting the sail, the gale becomes 'a hoolie' [hooligan], the sea became a bit 'lumpy' or 'naughty' and you 'took a bit of a dusting'.

These terms had the same function as the secret handshake. Indeed, the Freemasons in the period 1870–1912 founded 2,239 lodges, bringing their total to 3,630.[44]

The Growth of Yachting after 1865

> It was with a strange satisfaction I felt as I entered the Crouch again after four years' absence, and saw how literally fulfilled were all my ideas. Then the sunny, breezy anchorage was almost deserted; beyond the oyster dredgers and the barges there were next to no craft. Now the waters swarm with yachts. There are three yacht clubs ... [45]

We can try and specify why yachting might be one of the preferred sports of the new men.

Positive attributes that sailing shared with other prestige sports included: useful social networking, the involvement of Royalty, definition and confirmation of status by exclusion of the lower classes, submissive roles or exclusion for women, and health-giving exertion.

However, yachting also had distinctive, positive features, which were centred around the new definition of masculinity that it offered.

Yachting offered a new definition of masculinity, as it:
- Offered dangerous excitement, as the sailor pitted himself against the sea
- Was one of the few sports in which one could reach 'the sublime' (a peak experience in which one feels close to a higher power)[46]

---

[44] Lowerson, *Sport and the English Middle Classes 1870–1914*, p. 22.
[45] Frank Cowper, *Sailing Tours*, Part V, p. xiv. The (Royal) Corinthian, founded in 1872, moved from Erith on the lower Thames in 1892 because of the pollution and steamer traffic. The London Sailing Club, founded 1872, established a branch in Burnham in 1893. The (Royal) Burnham was founded in 1895 (Royal Burnham Yacht Club, *A History*, p. 2).
[46] This quasi-mystical/religious experience of union with nature was accompanied by terror, which is 'in all cases whatsever, either more openly or latently, the ruling principle of the

- Was more in tune with central Victorian values of gain through endeavour and discomfort; and frugality of life aboard
- Took place on the health-giving sea
- Offered a male-only environment[47]
- Was patriotic – a preparation for war service
- Had links with Navy
- Indicated greater wealth, if not also a higher social status, due to the high cost of purchasing and maintaining equipment.
- Was the subject of a range of books, creating a community of readers and discussants.There were a greater number of books – fictional and non-fictional – about yachting than was the case with other sports.

Among competing sports, mountaineering could offer both danger and the sublime, and alpine mountaineering became very popular, with steam ferries and the railways providing relatively quick access to the Alps. Among the yachting pioneers, both McMullen and McGregor were keen mountaineers.[48] However, since only the Alps, and not British peaks, were considered worth climbing, it could only be a holiday sport.

Canoeing was a contender among aquatic sports, and the two sports overlapped. Many canoes carried a simple lug sail, and many Victorian yachtsmen, including McGregor, Baden-Powell and Hamerton and the artist and yacht designer, Albert Strange, were also canoeists.[49] Dixon Kemp designed both yachts and kayaks.

There was a consistent rise in the number of yacht clubs after 1865. According to Trollope, who I have previously quoted, 'in 1867 there were

---

sublime'. This was expounded by Edmund Burke in *A Philosophical Enquiry into the Origin of Our Ideas of the Sublime and the Beautiful* (1756), p. 102.

[47] Whereas tennis was seen as a marriage market, with young ladies playing demurely so as to attract suitable young men (Ann Sumner *et al., Court on Canvas: Tennis in Art*; John Lowerson, *Sport and the English Middle Classes 1870–1914*, p. 98).

[48] In *Down Channel*, McMullen records climbing Hoy Hill '1500 feet of rugged climbing' (p. 59), the 'Rock of Quiraing' on Skye, another 1,500 foot summit (p. 60), and the 'Old Man of Storr' (p. 61) and Ben Nevis (p. 123). MacGregor climbed Mont Blanc, Vesuvius and Etna (Ransome, Introduction in John MacGregor, *The Voyage Alone in the Yawl 'Rob Roy'*, p. xv).

[49] There was a small canoeing literature. Warrington Baden-Powell, older brother of Robert, who founded the Boy Scout movement, sailed his 'Rob Roy' canoe by river, canal and lake across Sweden. He wrote up the trip in two issues of the *Cornhill Magazine* of 1870 and, in 1871, in book form as *Canoe Travelling: Log of a Cruise on the Baltic, and Practical Hints on Building and Fitting Canoes*. Canoeing trips on French rivers feature in P. G. Hamerton's *The Unknown River* (the Arroux), 1871. In 1876, Hamerton journeyed down the Saône in a barge and then in a steel-hulled catamaran, the *Arar*, a trip which he wrote about in *The Saône: A Summer Voyage*. R. L. Stevenson wrote of his 1876 canoeing in France and Belgium in *An Inland Voyage*, 1878. The reader interested in non-yachting aquatic recreation should consult R. A. L. Vine's *Pleasure Boating in the Victorian Era*.

thirty-one yacht clubs in the United Kingdom'.[50] By 1875, there were 75 clubs, 108 by 1895, by 1900, 152 and by 1914, some 200.[51] *Hunt's Universal Yacht Lists* recorded an increase in the number of yachts on its register from 3,096 in 1875 to 6,409 in 1900.[52] There was also a growth in the number of organised yacht races, so clearly both yacht cruising and yacht racing were becoming increasingly popular.

To give regional examples of this expansion: in the north-west in 1850, there were 3 yacht clubs; by 1870, only 2 more had been created – the Cheshire Yacht Club and the New Brighton Yacht Club. Between 1870 and 1900, another 16 were formed.[53]

Scotland, especially on the west coast and the Clyde, experienced a similar boom. Clydeside dealt with coal, iron, ship-building, cotton-spinning and thread-making, of which it was the world's largest producer.[54] An incomplete list includes the Clyde Model Yacht Club, founded in 1856 (soon to transmute into the Royal Clyde (see pp. 167–68)); the Mudhook Yacht Club formed to encourage 'non-serious' racing, with the owners helming, in 1873 at Fairlie – limited to forty-one members, who specialised in jolly japes, distilled through Scottish humour, such as round glasses and decanters which could not be put down; the (Royal) Western Yacht Club, Millport, Great Cumbrae, 1875; the Clyde Corinthian Sailing Club, formed in Dunoon in 1876 (its name changed to Yacht Club in 1888); the (Royal) Highland Yacht Club at Oban, in 1881; and the (Royal) Largs on the Lower Clyde 1882. The Gourock Sailing Club, formed 1894, became the Royal Gourock Yacht Club by 1908, and towards Greenock, Cardwell Bay Sailing Club was formed in 1906.

A sign of the growth was the creation of a new profession: yacht designer. Dixon Kemp (1839–1899) published his *Yacht Design* in 1876, heralding the profession's arrival. Its early practitioners, besides Kemp, were the lesser known St Clare J. Byrne (1831–1915), who designed Brassey's steam yacht

---

[50] Trollope, *British Sports and Pastimes,* pp. 201–202.

[51] After 1878, the figures should be accurate, as a list of yacht clubs was given in the annual publication, *Lloyd's Register of Yachts* (Ryan, *The West Lancashire Yacht Club,* pp. 2 and 138 n. 12).

[52] Cusack, 'The Rise of Aquatic Recreation and Sport, pp. 241–242.

[53] Ryan, 'The Emergence of Middle-Class Yachting in the North-West of England from the Later Nineteenth Century', p. 153, and John Millar, '*Anything but Sailing',* p. xv. Some of them are Rhyl YC (1880), West Lancs YC (1884), Blundellsands Sailing Club (SC) (1885), Royal Anglesey, Beaumaris YC (1885), Hoylake SC (1887), Tranmere SC (1892), West Cheshire SC (1892). West Kirby SC was formed in 1901 and Wallasey SC in 1903.

[54] The Coats sewing-thread business in Paisley employed 6,000 people in 1890; by 1896, through amalgamations, they controlled 80 per cent of the world's capacity. Their principal leisure interest was sailing and they were important customers of Fife and, especially, Watson.

Sunbeam, and G. L. Watson (1851–1904), who set up his Glasgow office in 1873.

We have reached the point where the two most influential sections of society were receiving a common education and induction into a world consisting of men, in which women were disturbing unknown quantities, and into the working philosophy of Athleticism. What we now need to explore is how these attitudes and experiences created a new type of yachting – the Corinthian.

CHAPTER NINE

The Enthusiastic Adoption of Yachting by the Mercantile and Professional Classes after 1870

PART TWO
A Philosophy of Yachting for the New Men

We know of no amusement that can offer such splendidly healthful adventure and at the same time so cheap, as cruising … All that is required is a boat that may range from £20 to £600 according to the purse of the adventurer.

…

The more one cruises the more friends one will have, and the more friends one has the better ought to be one's chances in life – provided they are of the right sort.[1]

The Corinthian Yachting Narrative

If the leaders in industry and manufacturing and their supporting professions were to be attracted to yachting, it had to be congruent with their core beliefs and values. Since Corinthian sailing is so central to the yachting narrative till well beyond the Second World War, I will first describe it and then examine it from a number of angles, such as its leading exponents, educative texts, and the implementation of class boundaries.

The origins of the application of the term 'Corinthian' to sport are somewhat vague but in *A Manual of Yacht and Boat Sailing* by Dixon Kemp, published in 1878, the author defined 'Corinthian' as:

---

[1] Frank Cowper, *Yachting and Cruising for Amateurs*, p. 166.

a term in yacht parlance synonymous with amateur. The name was adopted in consequence of the similarity between the fashionable young men of Corinth who emulated the feats of athletes and their modern prototypes. Some clubs in Corinthian matches do not allow any paid hands to be on board.[2]

The Corinthian spirit is well described in Cowper's introduction to his pioneering five-volume pilot for yachtsmen, published in1892:

> We write for that large and ever-increasing brotherhood of 'corinthian sailors' … A corinthian sailor, we take it, is one capable of managing a craft either single-handed (if she is small enough) or with the assistance of other amateurs, if she is from 5 to 30 tons.[3]

This passage includes most of the key values of Corinthian yachting – the small boat, manned exclusively by amateurs; a hardy activity which refreshes the soul; the soul being gender specific, since only men would be strong enough to undertake it; and also makes links with a glorious seafaring tradition and brotherhood of god-fearing, yet fearless, men.

Aristocratic and Corinthian Yachting: Differences and Similarities

The Corinthian approach, in large part, achieved its clarity of purpose by distancing itself from the Aristocratic style of yachting. The middle-class yachtsman could not afford the ostentatious displays which characterised Aristocratic yachting, and they did not want to be their scaled down cousins.

The most obvious differences related to size and comfort. In contrast to the ostentation and luxury of Aristocratic yachting, the Corinthian spurned comfort – his boat was small and Spartan.[4] There was a running Victorian sailing joke about the Corinthian yachtsman's stoical acceptance of the lack of headroom.[5] An early example comes from Rev. William Forwell's *A Thousand Miles' Cruise in the 'Silver Cloud' from Dundee to France and Back in*

---

[2] Dixon Kemp, *A Manual of Yacht and Boat Sailing*, 1878, p. 207. Peter Kemp in *The Oxford Companion to the Sea*, p. 206, adds that 'the term originated in the U.S.A in the mid-19th century to mean a rich amateur sportsman, and spread to Britain mainly in its yachting connotation'.

[3] Cowper, *Sailing Tours. Part 1: The Coasts of Essex and Suffolk*, p. xiv.

[4] Cusack, in her Ph.D., 'The Rise of Aquatic Recreation and Sport', studied yacht registers – the *Yachtsman's Annual General Register for 1845* (surely, Bonner's *The Yachting Season of 1845*) and *Hunt's Universal Yacht Lists* for 1851–1875. For 1845, she found 46 British yachts under ten tons (13 per cent) of the total. By 1875, there were 476 yachts under ten tons registered, making up 28 per cent of the total.

[5] Exceptions were studio boats, which needed headroom and light. Also, Arthur Ransome had *Racundra* deliberately built so that he could write in the saloon on a writing table (*Racundra's First Cruise*, p. 217).

a Small Boat (1878): 'Our cabin is at least 7 feet by 7; but there is only about four foot square in which you can sit straight, and even then you would be better without your legs'.[6] A little later, E. F. Knight, in his account of sailing to northern climes, *The 'Falcon' on the Baltic*, 1888, argued 'the smaller the boat, the better the sport'; and 'There was not much headroom in it, but I do not hold, as some do, that to be able to stand up in one's cabin is an essential on a small yacht. If one wishes to assume an erect position one can always go up on deck'.[7] F. B. Cooke bought the little, canoe-sterned *Snipe*. When a friend goes aboard for the first time to sail it round from Pin Mill to the Crouch, he goes below and exclaims 'Golly what a ship! Why! Look, Skipper, I can sit up with my hat on'.[8] Childers, in *The Riddle of the Sands*, 1903, mocks the aristocratic Carruthers' realisation that he is on a Corinthian's boat: '... I must have cut a ridiculous figure, peering awkwardly and suspiciously round, with shoulders and head bent to avoid the ceiling, which seemed in the half-light to be even nearer the floor than it was'.[9]

Because of the size of the Aristocratic yacht, a professional crew was needed. The owner might have only a hazy idea of how to sail. By contrast, the Corinthian sailor helmed his own boat. *Pluck* is a central feature and translates into discomfort and risk. Some of the Corinthian stance in yachting was inevitable, given the weight of the spars – gaff rig was the predominant mode – and the lack of weather forecasting until the 1860s when Captain Fitzroy, of the *Beagle*, and the first head of the Metereological Office, issued storm warnings and weather forecasts in newspapers. These, of course, were of little use once you had been at sea for any time.[10]

But some discomfort was sought for. The Corinthian sailor wanted to test the limits of his endurance and strength. He saw sailing as a struggle between the yachtsman and the sea, a struggle to be welcomed because the yachtsman could then demonstrate his pluck – his ability to accept discomfort, risk, danger, sweat and pain. This can be seen as one of the Ancient Greeks' representations of the sea – as a source of purification.[11]

[6] Forwell, *A Thousand Miles' Cruise*, p. 13.
[7] Knight, *The 'Falcon' on the Baltic*, pp. 23 and 27.
[8] F. B. Cooke, *Pocket Cruisers*, p. 177.
[9] Childers, *The Riddle of the* Sands, p. 14. This Corinthian yachting trope is used to amusing effect in Carol Mason's *Sea Fever*, 2007. The hero and heroine are lent a small, old yacht to allow them some privacy. They are talking in the saloon, when the man asks if they can go to bed as his (cricked) neck is killing him (p. 62).
[10] John Gribbin and Mary Gribbin, *Fitzroy: The Remarkable Story of Darwin's Captain and the Invention of the Weather Forecast*.
[11] Mack, *The Sea: A Cultural History*, p. 93.

Returning to the concept of *masculinity*, or to use the Victorian term, 'manliness', yachting provided an opportunity for the middle class professional to prove that he was no desk-bound, etiolated specimen. By going out in almost any weather on the sea, he was demonstrating his manliness.

The difference in the size of the vessels had another effect – the inclusion, or otherwise, of women. On the Aristocratic boat, the passengers did not help with sailing the vessel, so there was no call for 'unsuitable' female clothing. Also, the vessel was large enough to allow social distance and formality to be maintained. On the smaller Corinthian yacht, maintenance of separate space for the sexes was not possible. When a woman came aboard, the men, unused to and ill-prepared to be in the company of women, could either flee or fall in love with them, which is Davies' choice in *The Riddle of the Sands*. As a consequence, the Corinthian yacht was a male preserve.

The difference in the level of comfort sought expressed itself geographically, along a North/South axis. The Corinthians constructed an identity for themselves as Englishmen, which foregrounded ancient forebears, most notably the Elizabethan seadog (think of Newbolt's *Drake's Drum*, complete with cod Devon accent);[12] but also the Saxons and Vikings. Trollope becomes almost lyrical in his 1868 *British Sports and Pastimes*:

> It is to the Pagan pirates from the Saxon coasts and to the Slayers of the North, of the ninth and tenth centuries, and to the 'Brethen of the Coast' of the Tudor times, that the harmless yachtsman of the Solent or the Thames owes the passion that urges him afloat.[13]

The North Sea and the Baltic were the spiritual home of the Corinthian yachtsman – North, cold, rough, plucky. This is reflected in two of the Corinthians' prized texts – E. F. Knight's *The 'Falcon' on the Baltic: A Coasting Voyage from Hammersmith to Copenhagen in a Three-ton Yacht*, 1888; and Erskine Childers' *The Riddle of the Sands*, 1903. Childers had sailed to the Baltic and among the Frisian Islands in 1897.[14] In contrast, as shown in Chapter 5, the Squadron member headed south, sailing to the warm and soft.

---

[12] 'Drake's Drum' was published in Newbolt's best-selling poetry collection, *Admirals All*, 1896.

[13] Trollope, *British Sports and Pastimes*, p. 196.

[14] His pieces about the voyages were published mostly in the London *Times* and the *Cruising Club Journal* (see Hugh and Robin Popham, *A Thirst for the Sea: The Sailing Adventures of Erskine Childers*) The delay between the voyage and the novel is explained by Childers' participation in the Second Boer War.

Corinthian Yachting as a Demonstration of Core Victorian Values

The new way of sailing had a strong moral and emotional undertone, for it gained much of its attractiveness from its incorporation of key Victorian work-related values. As Lowerson put it, 'On to the great mid-century virtues of Work, Punctuality, Thrift and Respectability was grafted a sport ethic' – the sport should offer a stern test, a hair-shirted exertion that reaped the reward of achievement and earned relaxation only at the end of a testing passage.[15] For the middle class, yachting represented *working at leisure*, an incorporation of key workaday values into leisure.

It was because yachting could be shaped to incorporate these values, so clearly spelt out in Samuel Smiles' best-selling *Self-Help*, published in 1859, that it was so enthusiastically taken up. [16]

The Application of Core Victorian Values to Corinthian Yachting

Core Victorian Value	Corinthian Translation
Frugal with money	Owner owns a small, basically equipped craft
Hard work	Owner helms and skippers
Self-Help	Owner knows how to sail and maintain boat
Self-Education	Owner learns through Corinthian 'how-to' manuals, or from yacht club colleagues
Self-betterment	Yachting offers opportunities for demonstrating social worth and suitability, and for making useful contacts

---

[15] Lowerson, *Sport and the English Middle Classes 1870–1914*, p. 2.

[16] 'It [*Self-Help*] sold 20,000 copies in 1859, and another 130,000 during the next thirty years' (Thomson, *England in the Nineteenth Century*, p. 101). Despite the Victorian emphasis on reaping the rewards of hard work, it is telling in how few Victorian novels, hard work alone by a member of the working class or lower middle class reaps such a reward. Far more common is social advancement through an inheritance or gift, as in *Jane Eyre* and *Great Expectations*. *Jane Eyre* was criticised, by Elizabeth Rigby (later Lady Eastlake), since it was inappropriate for a governess to marry a gentleman. The situation may have been more open in the boom regions of Glasgow and Belfast later in the century.

Physical fitness	Owner demonstrates their fitness by handling heavy weather, heavy gear and long hours at the helm
Pluck	Owner goes out in all weather
Social Darwinian philosophy of survival of the (socially) fittest	Owner fights the sea and triumphs
Importance of improving one's standing	Yacht clubs as places to meet 'one's own' (and even one's betters) and make contacts
Relaxation only merited after hard work	Relaxation only valued after a hard sail

The term 'Corinthian' was highly valued by this new breed of yachtsman, and was included in the names of a large number of clubs created around the last quarter of the nineteenth century. Of the many examples, the Corinthian Club, London, was formed in 1852, with the aim of encouraging racing between owners who helmed their own small yachts. The Portsmouth Corinthian Yacht Club was formed in 1880.[17] In the southwest, the Plymouth Corinthian was created in 1877 by a boat builder and his friends as a small boat club; the Teign Corinthian Yacht Club in 1883; the Torquay Corinthian Yacht Club in 1895; and the Weymouth Corinthian Yacht Club in 1902.[18] Further east, the Orwell Corinthian Club was formed in 1888.[19] In Scotland, on the west coast, the Clyde Corinthian Yacht Club was created in Dunoon in 1876, while on the east, the Forth Corinthian Yacht Club was founded at Granton in 1880.

Few Corinthian yacht clubs started with a club house. They met in a pub or pubs, presumably in a back room – indeed some have never weighed themselves down with that worry and expense. What mattered was meeting one's peers. The club house only came later, when the membership had grown.

---

[17] Granted the Royal Warrant in 1880; merged with the Royal Albert YC in 1946, which merged with the Royal Naval YC in 1971.

[18] Cusack, 'The Rise of Aquatic Recreation and Sport'; Jim Hayes, *The History of the Weymouth Sailing Club*.

[19] David Chivers, *Austin 'Clarence' Farrar*, p. 9.

The Sea Gets (a Bit) Safer

The growth of yachting was aided by the fact that sailing was made safer in a variety of ways in the second half of the nineteenth century. The main impetus for such improvements was Britain's vast merchant fleet and sizeable Royal Navy.

Having a Trinity House pilot on board a commercial vessel, became compulsory between Orford Ness and the Isle of Wight in 1808. This rendered the movement of large vessels more predictable.

By 1811, the Coastguard service had mortars carrying a block and tackle that could be fired at a stranded vessel, creating a pulley rope link with the shore.[20] The Royal National Institution for the Preservation of Life from Shipwreck, which we now know as the Royal National Lifeboat Institution (the RNLI), was formed in 1824 by Sir William Hillary.

An Act of 1836 authorised Trinity House to purchase the patents of all the ten existing lighthouses and to erect lights where needed.[21] The Victorian age was the great era of lighthouse building by such engineers as the Stevensons and James Douglass. In Scotland, the Northern Lighthouse Board had been established in 1786, and four generations of Stevensons were the chief engineers, building lighthouses in such incredibly difficult and dangerous places as Bell Rock, guarding the Firth of Tay, and Skerryvore on the West coast.[22] The 1846 Steam and Navigation Act introduced Collision Regulations, which were then amended and widened over the next fifteen years.

In the 1860s, Darwin's captain on the *Beagle*, Robert Fitzroy, first head of the Meteorological Office, instigated a national system of weather data collecting, the information being sent by the recently invented telegraphy.[23] Synoptic charts and weather forecasts were published in the London *Times* for the first time in 1860, and Fitzroy set up a system of storm cone warnings at ports.[24]

In 1865, a set of Collision Regulations was published for the first time.

---

[20] William Webb, *Coastguard!*, p. 60.

[21] Christopher Nicholson, *Rock Lighthouses of Britain*, Chapter 1: 'Out of the Darkness', pp. 11–17. It was the Merchant Shipping Acts of 1854 which officially constituted Trinity House as the Lighthouse Authority for England, Wales, the Channel Islands, Heligoland and Gibraltar.

[22] Bella Bathurst, *The Lighthouse Stevensons*.

[23] Telegraphy was patented in 1837 by the physicists William Cooke and Charles Whealstone, and first used on the Great Western Railway in 1839.

[24] John Gribbin and Mary Gribbin, *Fitzroy: The Remarkable Story of Darwin's Captain and the Invention of the Weather Forecast*. By 1887, E. F. Knight:

   remembered having been told by someone that the Metereological Office would, if applied to, telegraph a weather forecast for the sum of one shilling.

In 1876, Thomas Walker introduced his trailing log with a taffrail recorder, the Cherub, taking the guesswork out of how far the boat had travelled through the water.[25]

Gaslit buoys became widely used around the British Isles by Trinity House in the 1880s. A system of buoyage to indicate the channels and safe water was introduced in the 1870s.[26] The International System of Buoyage was introduced in the 1890s.

The Admiralty started publishing tide tables in the 1840s and in 1850 issued them for twenty-four ports around the coasts of England, Scotland, Ireland and France.

The Admiralty had also produced a Channel Pilot as early as 1829, but this was for naval vessels, so it did not concern itself with small yacht havens.[27] Arthur Underhill, a founder member of the (Royal) Cruising Club, published *Our Silver Streak or The Yachtsman's Guide from Harwich to Scilly* in 1892; but the key figure who undertook the mammoth task of creating pilot books for yachtsmen for all of the United Kingdom and the East Coast of Ireland was Frank Cowper (1849 –1930). He published his 5-volume pilot of the British Isles, *Sailing Tours*, which included Ireland and the North Coast of France, between1892–1896.

Part One describes a two-week sail from Teddington to Aldborough [Aldeburgh] and the harbours in between. He was testing the market, and when it proved favourable, he set about his much larger undertaking. He accomplished this task in a variety of heavy vessels, such as a 48 foot ex-Dover fishing lugger, *Lady Harvey*, with, at the beginning, one young boy as crew; and later, increasingly, single-handed. It was an outstanding feat of seamanship, given that the main boom was 30 foot long; and, of course, he was without pilot information for many of the harbours he entered, and for which he created the pilot instructions.[28]

I telegraphed: 'What weather Harwich to Rotterdam tomorrow?' On calling at the telegraph-station in an hour's time, the following reply was handed to me: 'Light S. W. breezes, fine sea, nearly smooth'. (*The Falcon on the Baltic*, pp. 56–57)

However, Fitzroy's predictions were rather hit-or-miss, leading him to be ridiculed, which contributed to his suicide in 1865.

[25] Michael Richey, *The Shell Encyclopedia of Sailing*, p. 105. How far a boat has travelled 'across the ground' depends on the boat's relationship to the tide and the state of the relevant current or tide.

[26] There was an internationally agreed system of buoyage after the International Maritime Conference at Washington in 1889.

[27] Bill Young and Dudley Stamp, *Bude's Maritime Heritage*, pp. 14–15. The post of Hydrographer to the Admiralty was established in 1795 by George III. The first Pilot was issued by the second Hydrographer, Captain Thomas Hurd in 1829.

[28] Leather, Introduction to Cowper, *Sailing Tours*, Part One.

Sailing Tours opened up the prospect of yachtsmen safely entering hundreds of small harbours.[29] Pioneer English yachting authors, such as McMullen, MacGregor, Middleton and E. F. Knight expanded yachtsmen's imaginations and horizons, but it was Cowper's endeavours that allowed the Corinthian philosophy to be put into practice around the British, Irish and North Brittany coast.

Despite these improvements, the advent of steam brought new dangers to yachtsmen. The steamship made very rapid progress in terms of numbers, tonnage and the number of ports in which they were located. In 1815, there were 11 steamships in the UK with a total of 542 tons. By January, 1851 there were 1,181, with a total tonnage of 167,398 tons.[30]

This huge amount of traffic around the British coast all the year round inevitably led to many wrecks and loss of life, including the *SS Forfarshire* on the Farne Islands, Northumberland, famous for Grace Darling helping her father, the keeper of the Longstone Light, in his rescue mission, 7 September, 1838; and the *Deutschland*, wrecked on the Kentish Knock sandbank , 6 December, 1875, immortalised by Gerald Manley Hopkins' poem.

The very real fear of being run down is visible in texts across the period. McMullen, whose *Down Channel*, 1893, recounted his sailing experiences from 1850 onwards, wrote: 'the screw steamer, when carelessly handled, is a dreadful engine of destruction, and long ago earned the name of "Silent Deaths" bestowed upon them by the North Sea fishermen'.[31] John MacGregor, in *The Voyage Alone in the Yawl 'Rob Roy'*, noted how dangerous night sailing was.[32] E. E. Middleton, sailing from Limehouse down the Thames in 1869, wrote in *The Cruise of the Kate* of being anchored at night in 1869 in the Thames Estuary: 'The steamers from the Swin Channel that I saw, and I saw an immense number, steered straight on to the *Kate*'.[33] Small craft, of course, at that time, had no engine to help them get out of the way. At night, the situation was even more dangerous. The custom at night was only 'to exhibit a white lantern over the side of the vessel when another was approaching

[29] The harbours that the Royal Navy used extensively were often unwelcoming to yachts, whose dependency on wind strength and direction could inconvenience, if not endanger, their vessels. A private publisher, James Imray, was producing charts from the late 1850s, but these were also based on Admiralty surveys and on the needs of the coaster trade, not yachtsmen. Middleton complains about this in relation to British ports in *The Cruise of 'The Kate'*, p. 30; and E. F. Knight, in relation to the Baltic, in *The 'Falcon' on the Baltic*, p. 29.

[30] David M. Williams and John Armstrong, 'Changing Voyage Patterns in the Nineteenth Century: The Impact of the Steamship'.

[31] McMullen, *Down Channel*, p. 196.

[32] MacGregor, *The Voyage Alone*, p. 159.

[33] Middleton, *The Cruise of Kate*, p. 8.

– provided anyone had been able to detect its approach', a situation of much risk in bad weather or poor visibility, such as fog. [34]

There were no life jackets, no jackstays to clip onto, no stanchions, no lifelines on the boats and no flares. Despite innovations, the sea was, as ever, a dangerous place.

Corinthian Yachting Heroes

Victorians liked to elevate their best sportsmen into sporting heroes, such as the cricketer W. G. Grace and the jockey, Fred Archer. To give more of the feeling for the spirit of Corinthian yachting, we should meet Corinthian yachting's pantheon of heroes. Yachting's pioneering heroes are generally considered to be the quartet of R. T. [Richard Tyrell] McMullen, John MacGregor, E. E. Middleton and E. F. Knight. However, we need to be a bit careful about their representativeness. Their accounts are regarded today as sailing's canonical texts, but they were all chosen by Arthur Ransome after the Second World War for the publisher, Rupert Hart-Davis' forty-seven volume *Mariners' Library*. Ransome was very much a Corinthian with his accounts of sailing in what are now Latvia and Estonia, and this obviously affected the choices he made.[35]

The earliest exponent of Corinthian sailing, but not the first into print, was McMullen, a stockbroker and 'a stout, pugnacious Protestant, writing anti-Catholic tracts'.[36] McMullen started to cruise as early as 1850 and his *Down Channel* recounts cruises between 1850 and 1868. He started his serious cruising in the tiny cutter, *Leo*, just 6.1m (20 feet) long and weighing only 3 tons. With one 16-year-old paid hand, he sailed 8,222 miles between the Thames and Land's End between 1850 and 1857. In 1861 and 1865, he visited the south and west coasts of Ireland. During 1863, he sailed right round Britain in *Sirius*, a 9.8 metre (32 foot) gaff cutter.

His extensive cruising over many years was on a different scale to the other pioneers, so that 'Gradually other small boat sailors became aware of this veritable Messiah of cruising.'[37] He died in mid-Channel, helming his 27foot yawl, *Perseus*, thus adding to his lustre.

---

[34] Desoutter, 'The Old Yachting Days'.

[35] Ransome, *Racundra's First Cruise*, 1923; *Racundra's Third Cruise*. On Ransome's selectiveness, see my 'An Open Letter to the Editor'. For example, Ransome found no place for the Rev. William Forwell's *A Thousand Miles' Cruise in the 'Silver Cloud' from Dundee to France and Back in a Small Boat*, 1879 or Guy de Maupassant's *Afloat*, 1888.

[36] Ransome, Introduction, R. T. McMullen, *Down Channel*, p. 17.

[37] W. Nixon, *To Sail the Crested Sea*, p. 15.

8 *The* Orion *lying-to under head sail at midnight, 28 September 1868.* The standard engraving of Corinthian yachting, in this case off Dartmouth in a gale, that accompanied the pioneering Victorian accounts of cruising – in touch with the 'sublime' as the yachtsman challenges the sea.

McMullen's voyaging – or at least, his narrating of it – perfectly encapsulates the Victorian definition of leisure as an energy-sapping form of work. It is perhaps no surprise that he had little patience with an idle crew, sending them home from France and then single-handling his 48 foot gaff-rigged yawl back across the Channel.[38]

John MacGregor (1825–1892) was a typical Victorian sportsman in that he enthusiastically followed more than one sport. He was a proponent of the Rob Roy canoe, a sailing canoe that, with its bamboo pole, could carry a small gaff main and jib. When he sailed and paddled his kayak across Europe, he sent weekly reports on his progress to the *Daily Record*.[39] He wrote of the joys of transporting one's canoe abroad to sail on foreign waters in *A Thousand Miles in the Rob Roy Canoe on Rivers and Lakes of Europe*, 1866 (into its 21st edition by 1908). MacGregor founded the Canoe Club in 1866 and

---

[38] R. T. McMullen, *Down Channel: The 'Orion' 1877 – Thames to Cherbourg, and How I Came to Sail Alone, 1877*: pp. 138–199.

[39] George Drower, *Boats, Boffins and Bowlines*, p. 23. McGregor's account of his adventures is told in *A Thousand Miles in the 'Rob Roy' Canoe, 1883*.

soon got it made Royal, with the Prince of Wales as president, himself as Commodore and Warington Baden-Powell as Vice Commodore. 'I do not suppose any man ever sent so many of his countrymen to find pleasure on the water' wrote Ransome.[40] He was a superb showman. Albert Smith had given 2,000 performances about his ascent of Mont Blanc, using the new technology of the slide projector.[41] MacGregor gave a similar show concerning his canoe trip up the Nile in 1869.[42] He also gave innumerable lectures to enthusiastic and receptive undergraduates on the merits of canoeing.[43] This started a craze for undergraduates to transport their canoes by train upstream on European rivers and then paddle through mainly uncharted waters downstream – a dangerous activity for fragile craft in fast flowing rivers.[44]

In 1867, he sailed his 21 foot yawl, also named *Rob Roy*, to the Exposition Universelle in Paris. The voyage is described in *The Voyage Alone in the Yawl 'Rob Roy'*, 1867.

E. E. Middleton (1838–1916) read MacGregor's account and wanted to follow his example. In a boat a mere 21 foot long, he circumnavigated Great Britain via the Bowling (now called the Forth and Clyde) Canal.

Ransome tells of Middleton's pluck and determination in his circumnavigation of Britain:

> ... how resolutely he kept moving. Again and again he had to do with no more than two hours' sleep out of twenty-four. Day after day he would sail at whatever hour the tide served and was prepared, in order to reach a headland before the change of tide should make it impossible, to row himself to utter exhaustion ...[45]

E. F. Knight had also been influenced by hearing MacGregor speak, when he was an undergraduate in law at Cambridge. Knight made two important contributions. In his influential *The 'Falcon' on the Baltic*, 1888, he introduced the Baltic as the Corinthian yachtsman's natural cruising ground, where he would meet his Nordic ancestors.

---

[40] Ransome, Introduction, John MacGregor, *The Voyage Alone in the Yawl 'Rob Roy'*, p. xviii.
[41] Alan McNee, *The Cockney Who Sold the Alps: Albert Smith and the Ascent of Mont Blanc.*
[42] MacGregor's account is *The 'Rob Roy' on the Jordan: A Canoe Cruise in Palestine, Egypt and the Waters of Damascus.*
[43] Edward Hodder in his biography, *John MacGregor*, pp. 256–258, gives a detailed description of MacGregor's showmanship during one of his 'comedy lectures'.
[44] Vine, *Pleasure Boating in the Victorian Era.*
[45] E. E. Middleton, *The Cruise of the Kate*, p. xviii.

9 *The* Kate *in mid-channel, between Milford and Wexford, struck by a cross sea at the change of tide, 30 July 1869.* As with McMullen's image text (fig. 8), another early classic text of Victorian cruising, E.E. Middleton's small yacht is shown 'taking a dusting'. Relaxation has to be earned to be enjoyed.

Secondly, he wrote about long distance – ocean – sailing, such as his cruise lasting two years from Southampton to South America.[46] Believing stories emanating from a North Shields mariner about buried Spanish treasure on the South Atlantic, not the West Indian, island of Trinidad, he equipped an expedition in 1899 and recounted the fruitless quest in *The Cruise of the 'Alerte'*, 1890.[47]

Crossing the Atlantic Ocean in small boats became almost a regular occurrence during the 1860s and 70s.[48] Most were West to East to take advantage of the prevailing winds, and the majority by American sailors. David Klein and Mary Louise King comment that it descended into 'a circus sideshow'

[46] *The Cruise of the 'Falcon': A Voyage to South America in a 30-ton Yacht,* 1881. Mack, in *The Sea: A Cultural History,* p. 89, points out that ocean sailing has a quite different set of meanings, compared to coastal or offshore sailing, in terms of being sea-centred, not land-centred, and strange, as opposed to familiar.

[47] Buried treasure was in the air. R. L. Stevenson had published *Treasure Island* in 1883.

[48] The interested reader should consult Humphrey Barton, *Atlantic Adventurers.* Barton was well-qualified to write this book, having sailed the Atlantic himself in *Vertue XXXV* in 1950, a passage recounted in the book of the same name.

with smaller and smaller boats, and quite a few of the skippers being lost at sea.[49]

Frederick Norman, a Norwegian-born British national born in 1854, crossed with one crew in a 16 foot boat, *Little Western*, from Gloucester, Massachusetts to Cowes in forty-six days in 1880. East–West crossings were rarer. John Buckley and one crew sailed from Liverpool to Boston in *The City of Ragusa*, only 20 feet long, in 1870 in eighty-five days. They took a dog with them and the poor beast died seven weeks out. In 1881, Frederick Norman, after exhibiting *Little Western* in the Royal Aquarium, London, returned to Halifax, Nova Scotia in sixty-five days, remarkable times both ways.[50]

What Humphrey Barton shows clearly in *Atlantic Adventurers*, is the large amount of publicity such attempts generated, on both sides of the Atlantic, with the *Illustrated London News* especially diligent. This publicity for such dangerous feats would not have been lost on the generation of new Corinthian sailors.

The Texts the New Yachtsmen Learnt From

From around the 1860s, publishers realised that there was a new market of Corinthian yachtsmen wanting to learn the ropes, and released a veritable flood of annotated logs of voyages and self-help manuals.

These books not only taught the techniques and the appropriate vocabulary, but also the appropriate stances and emotions. Engravings of boats handling rough seas formed an important visual emphasis of the Corinthian philosophy, and encouraged a different kind of maritime art. In contrast to the Aristocrats' expensive and unique oil painting by a well-known marine artist, the Corinthian illustration in the iconic texts, such as those by McMullen, MacGregor and Middleton, was the simple engraving of 'Boat in gale at headland', usually off the Needles or the Lizard.

A very incomplete list of educative texts includes P. R. Marrett's *Yachts and Yacht Building*, 1856. Dixon Kemp published his *Yacht Designing* in 1876. *The Corinthian Yachtsman or Hints on Yachting*, 1881 and *Amateur Sailing in Open and Half-Decked Boats*, 1886, were both by Tyrell Biddle. By the early 1880s,

---

[49] Klein and King, *Great Adventures in Small Boats*, pp. 15–20. Quite often, following a successful crossing, men like William Andrews and Thomas Crapo set off in absurdly small boats and were never seen again. This sounds like playing with loaded suicide dice, as per Luke Rinehart's *Dice Man*. The same analysis is applicable to Joshua Slocum's final voyage in 1909.

[50] Norman returned to England and went to live in Hull, serving as a master mariner. He died in 1919, aged 65 (Barton, *Atlantic Adventurers*, pp. 52–54).

in the spirit of Corinthian self-sufficiency, he published *Hints to Beginners in Amateur Yacht Designing*, 1883, which must have sold well enough for him to revise, enlarge and re-title it as *Hints on Yacht-Building for Amateurs* in 1888. As well as writing about the delights of sailing on the Norfolk Broads, George Davies published *Practical Boat Sailing for Amateurs: Containing Particulars of the Most Suitable Sailing Boats and Yachts for Amateurs for Their Proper Handling* in 1886. R. C. Leslie built his yacht on the beach at Sidmouth, East Devon, and told readers how in *The Seaboat: How to Build, Rig and Sail Her* in 1892.

The titles of these manuals deliberately highlight the differences between the Aristocratic and Corinthian approaches. They emphasise the closeness to the elements and danger of an 'open-decked' boat. They invariably include the identifiers 'amateur', 'Corinthian' or 'practical', suggesting that the Corinthian yachtsman would maintain and repair his own boat.

With so many yachtsmen floating around, there was room for a book about *Yachting under Statute,* by Robert Preston, 1884, which went into a second edition, revised by Charles Jemmett in 1903.

The great majority of the Victorian texts aimed at the Corinthian sailor were concerned to teach the novice *cruising* skills. The Irish yachting journalist, William Cooper (1824–1872), who wrote as 'Vanderdecken', was unusual in advocating Corinthian *racing* as a new sport for the upper middle classes. After all, yacht racing in *small* yachts, either single-handed or with a mate or two, offered yachtsmen a readily useable and understandable definition of manliness, by offering competition and the opportunity to prove one's competence.

By the age of 26, Vanderdecken was the yachting editor of the periodical *Bell's Life*, and also wrote frequently on boat handling and boat maintenance for *Hunt's Yachting Magazine*. A compilation of his articles, *Yarns for Green Hands*, published in 1860, went into many editions – it was in its fifth edition by 1876 – being retitled, more weightily, as *The Yacht Sailor – A Treatise on Practical Yachtsmanship, Cruising and Racing*.[51]

---

[51] Sisk, *Dublin Bay, the Cradle of Yacht Racing*, pp. 8–9. He was also influential in the creation of the Royal Alfred along with George Thompson, Henry Crawford and James Lyle, and was made its chairman on its founding in 1857. He took his pseudonym from Hendrick van der Decken, the captain in Wagner's *The Flying Dutchman*.

Class Boundaries: Hobnobbing with One's Betters

It might appear that the Corinthian philosophy presented such a sharp break with the Aristocratic mode, that it would also change the value system of yachting and the yacht clubs. This was not the case, mainly because, as described earlier, the sons of the managerial and professional classes were sharing the same education and training as the sons of the landed gentry. There was unanimity among yacht club members concerning class boundaries. The Victorian yacht club was characterised by the two major aspects of snobbery: firstly, valuing the opportunities to socialise with those of a higher social status; and secondly, excluding those of a lower social status.

The landed gentry continued to possess a status separate from their economic standing. Although the power of the landed gentry was waning as a result of the 1832 Reform Act and the making the ballot secret by the Ballot Act of 1872, yet 'the years 1850–1880 were a splendid Indian summer of the landed gentry's "right to rule"';[52] and this provided social stability and harmony in the yacht club, and within the wider society.

The gentry might be non-sailing members. Any leisure activity club will always have many non-participating 'social members', for example, persons who have retired from the activity, or, in fact, have never actively participated, as long as they are people of some standing. The prestigious Bristol Channel Yacht Club, effectively the senior yacht club of the Bristol Channel, started in 1875 as an amalgam of yachtsmen and billiard players. (A billiard room, with a full-size snooker table, was a common asset of many yacht clubs, and can still be found in many of them.) By 1896, few members owned yachts.[53] At the North Devon YC, Instow:

> Many of these gentlemen had joined the Club principally to play Bridge and perhaps as a refuge from their ladies. They had no interest in sailing, and gradually, as the membership grew, the sailors became a minority group … Even the Sailing Sub-Committee, elected to look after races, was not wholly composed of sailors.[54]

Whether they were sailors or no, the presence of landed gentry would increase the desirability of membership of a yacht club for the aspiring middle-class professional.

[52] Bédarida, *A Social History of England,* p. 42.
[53] Austin, 'Yachting in Swansea Bay', p. 5.
[54] Peggy Lines, *I'm on Starboard!, The Story of the North Devon Yacht Club,* p. 19.

These two groups equitably shared the positions of power in the newly established yacht clubs, often with the gentry as the titular head (the 'commodore') and the majority of the committee being worthy burghers. The landed gentry might be able to enlist other worthies, and might even know members of the Royalty. *A History of the Royal Temple Yacht Club*, Ramsgate recounts:

> At the turn of the century, 2,000 members dined annually at the Hotel Cecil. The Commodore at the time was the Baron De Rothschild who was always accompanied by his close friend, the Prince of Wales.[55]

Status could be measured by the tonnage of a man's yacht, and also by knowing which yacht clubs he belonged to. As mentioned previously, he might belong to several but his peers would know which was the most prestigious and rank him by the highest. We shall see in the next section how quickly the Clyde Model Yacht Club, founded 1856, became a major player in Clyde yachting circles, but this did not stop the more staid, senior club the Royal Northern, founded 1824, being the more prestigious. The Royal Clyde had all the major designers – Watson, Fife and Mylne – as members, but when Watson married in 1903, he was elected to the Royal Northern, so that his new wife 'would find the society she sought'.[56]

So, while the 'Corinthian' was undoubtedly the dominant narrative concerning sailing and the sea, this should not be taken to mean that the existing status hierarchies had been abandoned or overturned. Rather, they were maintained through the processes of gentrification and of class exclusion.

Gentrification

The numerous 'Corinthian' clubs often advertised their founding with battle-cry like pronouncements about only accepting members with yachts of less than eight tons. However, some clubs with Corinthian credentials were set up by the very rich owners of large, professionally crewed yachts, who wanted to helm their own, smaller boat, as was the case with Squadron members and the Island Sailing Club, formed in 1889 at Cowes.[57] Other may have been formed by members of senior clubs, dismayed at their club's apathy. Since yacht club histories are invariably coy, we will not know. What we do know is that the dominant Corinthian narrative ran alongside the existing

---

[55] Royal Temple Yacht Club, *History of the Royal Temple Yacht Club.*
[56] Black, *G. L. Watson,* p. 303.
[57] The Island Sailing Club, *The Island Sailing Club 1889–2014.*

prestige system, and this is very clear in the frequent examples of gentrification seen in mid-century Victorian yachting.

Gentrification is *the abandoning of the original ideals in the search for greater prestige*, and occurs repeatedly in Victorian yachting. Whatever their original charter, as Janet Cusack showed, gentrification seemed inexorable and the desire for higher status quickly obliterated the original ideals.[58] To give just a few examples, the Arundel Yacht Club was formed by gentlemen from the Arundel Stairs on the Thames in 1838 for owners of boats between 5 and 7 tons.[59] In 1845, it became the London Yacht Club and became 'Royal' in 1849. It moved to Cowes in 1882 and is one of the most prestigious yacht clubs there.

> On 28th August, 1856, a number of solid and respectable citizens of Glasgow and parts adjacent met to consider the formation of what they proposed to call the Clyde Model Yacht Club. The appropriate minute runs thus:

> A number of Gentlemen connected with yachting propose forming a club under the above designation with the view of creating a greater amount of emulation among the proprietors of small craft. It is proposed to take in yachts under 8 tons only [25–28 feet long], being the smallest acknowledged by the Royal Northern Yacht Club [a senior club dating from 1824] ... [60]

'Model', in this context, means 'to be emulated'. The reference to the limitations imposed by the Royal Northern Yacht Club is clearly critical. Yet, the first Commodore of the club was James Smith, a founder member, many years earlier in 1824, of the Royal Northern.

By 1863, the Club was seeking a Royal prefix. This failed, but the club still changed its name to the 'Clyde Yacht Club', 'to get rid of an adjective no longer to be considered either useful or ornamental' – all in nine years.[61] Yet the narrative remained unchanged. In *Hunt's Magazine* for 1865, 'B', probably J. D. Bell, explained '... the Royal Northern Yacht Club has done honourable service in vindicating the taste, the wealth, and the hardihood of our titled and untitled aristocracy; but the influence of this club was hardly felt beyond the class who liked to own a floating palace ...'.[62] Very pointed and highly ironic with regard to the members' 'hardihood' of the members of the Royal

---

[58] Cusack has analysed this process in detail in South Devon 1875–1914, in 'The Rise of Aquatic Recreation', Chapter 6, pp. 240–308.
[59] Bonner, *The Yachting Season of 1845*, 1971, pp. 139–148.
[60] George Blake and Christopher Small, *Cruise in Company*, pp. 11–12.
[61] *Ibid.*, p. 40.
[62] *Ibid.*, pp. 42–44.

Northern. Yet the Clyde was already admitting owners of large yachts, and by the 1870s, it was agreed that an owner could employ one paid hand for every ten tons measurement, anathema to a true Corinthian.[63]

By 1871, it re-sought and gained the Royal Warrant, and, by 1900, it had the largest membership of any yacht club in the British Isles, with 1,100 members, and was among the most prestigious.[64]

Gentrification was the irresistible goal for many clubs. The Western Yacht Club was also formed in Glasgow in 1875 with the aim of encouraging small boat and dinghy sailing. In a vote of those present as to its name, the suggested 'Clyde Corinthian' lost by three votes. By 1885, it was running races for yachts 'of any rig or tonnage' and in that year, received permission to call itself 'royal' and fly a defaced ensign – all indications of its original aims being quickly forgotten.[65]

In Ireland, the Irish Model Yacht Club was formed around Dublin in 1857. It changed its name to the Alfred and thence to the Royal Alfred in 1872, and became the leading organisation of Irish Sea yacht racing, with excellent monetary prizes. The Munster Model Yacht Club was formed in Cork Harbour in 1872 to cater for the growing number of local small pleasure boats owned and sailed by the commercial and local professional businessmen of Cork, sailing their own boats. In 1886, it became the Munster Corinthian Yacht Club, suggesting it was catering for larger craft, and, in 1892, it became the Royal Munster.[66]

A side effect of gentrification was the replacement of wit by pomposity. The first club named after a one-design, the Water Wags, was formed at Dun Laoghaire in 1887. There was a pun on the word 'wags' (the numerous wagtails on Killiney beach, that the members originally launched from, and human jokers). The latter decided in 1889 to have a management committee made up of a King, Queen, two Bishops, two Knights and two Rooks, and the relevant personnel signed themselves accordingly. By 1895, 'King' and 'Queen' were renamed 'President' and 'Captain.'[67]

---

[63] *Ibid.*, p. 67.

[64] Black, *G. L. Watson*, p. 449.

[65] http://www.rwyc.org.uk/history.asp, accessed 11 April, 2016.

[66] Alicia St Leger, *A History of the Royal Cork Yacht Club*, p. 57. The failing Royal Cork and the flourishing Royal Munster amalgamated in 1966, under the Royal Cork's name.

[67] Delany and Delany, *The Water Wags*, pp. 12 and 32–35. Many decades later, this quirky humour is to be found in the Old Gaffers Association – in the name, in the ensign of a pitch fork, in using 'commodore' to mean the winner of the area's main race, and the Hidden Challenge trophy (Viv Head, *Sailing Gaffers*, pp. 43–44, 31, 45 and 93).

Class Boundaries: Yachtsmen and the Workers

Even more vital than mixing with one's betters was the exclusion of 'undesirables'. There was a near lower caste status attributed to trade and to people earning their living from the sea. Such people must not be allowed to join yacht clubs.

(1) Trade

The rapid expansion in the number and size of middle-class professions led to uncertainty about their relative social status. These newly arrived men required both affirmation of their status, and clarification of it. Fortunately for them, there was a complete consensus among both Aristocratic and Corinthian yachtsmen that their prestigious club should only accept 'suitable' members. Indeed, only suitable people, members or not, were to be allowed inside the club.

The (myth? of) 'pushing' of their goods and services by unsuitable members was a common source of Victorian yachting humour. For example, in Julian Gabe's 1893 *Sketches of Yachting Life,* the narrator goes to see the Hon. Secretary, the owner of a large furniture establishment:

> After having settled his business, Goddard was just going to leave the shop, when the secretary, probably from force of habit, said: 'Just one minute, sir, I wish to show you some patterns of a fresh consignment of curtains we have just received; they would do very nicely for bed curtains on your yacht.'[68]

A real life example of this almost phobic fear of contamination by trade is given by A. Fox-Geen, in his *Life and Times of the Royal Dorset Yacht Club*. Its minutes of its first year, 1875, record that a Mr. Edwards had to be reprimanded:

> The Chairman states that Mr Edwards had given a dinner to the GWR Directors and had invited as his own guests Mr Howard and Mr McLundie – the Secy said that Mr Edwards had said he had invited Mr McLundie as Mayor of Weymouth and did not see, until it was pointed out to him, that in entering the Club as his guest, he dropped his official capacity as Mayor of Weymouth and could only be recognised as one of the town's tradesmen.[69]

Mead in his *History of the Royal Cornwall Yacht Club,* recounts, disapprovingly, that in the 1890s, the RCYC was short of members and 'was somewhat

---

[68] Gabe, *Sketches of Yachting* Life, pp. 52–53. Johnson in *Yacht Rating,* p. 321, n.17, thinks that, at the turn of the century, Gabe was 'probably editor of *Yachting World* in those days of anonymous journalism.'

[69] Fox-Geen, *The Life and Times of the Royal Dorset Yacht Club,* p. 8.

catholic in composition, at least as regards local members … It is said that wealthy owners of visiting yachts using the club experienced no difficulty in finding persons on the premises eager to satisfy every need ranging from the supply of provisions to a simple hair cut'.[70] A group of higher class individuals broke away in 1894 and formed the Falmouth Sailing Club. By 1904, things had got so bad that members were having a sing-song, accompanied by the caretaker.[71] The Sailing Club members only returned in 1907 when they were in a sufficient majority to vote off the General Committee and engage in a process of excluding the 'undesirables'.

Tradesmen, *however financially successful*, were to be barred from membership of sporting clubs. Lipton, millionaire owner of a large chain of grocery stores, not being acceptable to the Squadron is probably the most famous example. Since income, of itself, would not exclude all 'undesirables', a variety of other methods were also used, as shown in the list that follows.

Means of Excluding 'Unsuitable' Persons
- High cost of joining
- Requirement of ownership of yacht of large tonnage
- High annual subscription
- Applicants recommended by existing members; application by invitation only
- Careful vetting
- Secret ballots
- Blackballing
- Multiple membership of yacht clubs increases information about candidates; and 'correct' procedures
- Cost of the various uniforms required for the various types of function
- Yacht Racing Association approval required the exclusion of 'artisans', 'tradesmen' and 'marine professionals'
- Fear of one's application being rejected; internalisation of the above values by would-be applicants

Blackballing was practised by clubs such as the Royal Western of Scotland and the Mudhook, who claimed to look after the interest of the small boat owners. Clearly, owning a small boat and the owner's class status were separate dimensions. An example of the ability of blackballing to limit the width

---

[70] Mead, *History of the Royal Cornwal Yacht Club*, pp. 81–82.
[71] *Ibid.*, p. 85.

of the intake is shown by North Devon Yacht Club, formed in Instow on the Torridge in 1905:

> One black ball in three being sufficient to reject a candidate. This ensured that the membership, both full and sailing, remained entirely constituted of officers of H.M. forces, members of the professions and landed gentry. The Club was thick with Colonels and Naval Captains and other officers and there was a good sprinkling of members of the Church.[72]

The Yacht Racing Association had an important national role to play in maintaining these class boundaries. The national organisation of yachting, in particular yacht racing, was part of a much wider range of similar developments in the 1870s, which involved the codifying of sports played or controlled by the middle classes. In a short period, around the 1870s, national rule-making bodies were set up. The Football Association was created in 1863; the Amateur Athletic Club in 1866; the Lawn Tennis Club in 1872; and the Amateur Rowing Association in 1882.

The Royal Alfred Yacht Club of Dublin Bay, probably the most active yacht racing club in the United Kingdom at the time, had sent out a proposal to unify 'Sailing Regulations' in 1872.[73] The YRA was formed to create and codify a single national set of yacht racing rules. It met in Willis' Rooms, in St James', London on 17 November, 1875 and adopted the Royal Alfred's proposals. 'In the chair was the Marquis of Exeter, then Commodore of the Royal Victoria Yacht Club, Ryde, the Isle of Wight, supported by thirty-five representatives from various clubs'.[74] However there was resistance from two of the most senior clubs, the Royal Squadron and the Royal Thames.[75] In 1874, the Prince of Wales was elected Commodore of the Royal Thames and in 1880 became the Patron of the YRA, and the following year, its President.[76] He had been a member of the Squadron since 1863 and when he was also elected Commodore of the Royal Squadron in 1882, 'it was assumed he would not tolerate any further dissension, and this indeed proved to be the case'.[77] In fact, the decision was forced on the Squadron, as, because most racing

---

[72] Lines, *I'm on Starboard! The Story of the North Devon Yacht Club*, p. 18.

[73] Sisk, *Dublin Bay: The Cradle of Yacht Racing*, p. 16 ff.

[74] Phillips-Burt, *The History of Yachting*, pp. 62–63.

[75] As did the Royal Clyde, objecting to the YRA telling it how to run races in Scottish waters, and also because the YRA rules concerned racing in shallow Southern waters, not the deep waters of the Lower Clyde (George Blake and Christopher Small, *Cruise in Company*, pp. 68–69).

[76] Ward, *The Chronicles of the Royal Thames Yacht Club*, p. 98; Gordon Fairley, *Minute by Minute: The Story of the Royal Yachting Association 1975–1982*, p. 16. The YRA was renamed the Royal Yachting Association in 1952.

[77] Dear, *The Royal Yacht Squadron 1815–1985*, p. 72.

yachtsmen supported the new body, the Cowes regatta of 1881 'was confined to three or four old schooner and a couple of cutters'.[78] Thus, after 1882, the YRA became the accepted rule-making body for yacht racing. The active role of the monarchy, in the form of the Prince of Wales, in the development of yachting, is very apparent here.

Ryan states its power clearly: 'No club could hope to survive for long without YRA recognition, which was only granted after a careful vetting of the new club's rule-book, membership and racing programme. Exclusiveness and social conformity was thereby maintained'.[79]

Dixon Kemp was the YRA's first secretary from 1876 to 1898. In his *Manual of Yacht and Boat Sailing,* he wrote that 'any yacht club is considered "recognised" which is "organised by yacht owners for the promotion of properly conducted yacht matches, and which do not enrol mechanics and labourers as members"'.[80] Clubs wanted to espouse the YRA guidelines as then they could race against other clubs with a common set of racing rules. Inter-club racing augmented the power of the YRA as it was the arbiter of racing rules and of suitable clubs that one could race against.

YRA control of the sport meant that more affordable yachting was not allowed to widen the class structure of yachting. Rather it was 'like tennis and golf, which recruited members from the same social background as yachting, including those with a modest income as long as they had a respectable middle class occupation'.[81]

(2) Artisans and Marine Professionals

Sailing clubs, which catered for the dinghy sailor, did not have either sufficient members 'of standing' or the tonnage to be acknowledged by the YRA, which did not recognise sailing (dinghy) clubs till just before the Great War. The Sailing Boat Association was founded in 1888 by clubs racing on rivers and estuaries, usually in dinghies. It was overtaken by the better organised Boat Racing Association, founded in 1913.[82]

---

[78] Guest and Boulton, *The Royal Yacht Squadron:Memorials,* p. 311.

[79] Ryan, 'The Emergence of Middle-Class Yachting in the North-West of England from he Later Nineteenth Century', pp. 153–155.

[80] *Dixon Kemp's Manual of Yacht and Boat Sailing,* 10th edn, p. 598. It had been first published in 1878.

[81] Ryan, 'The Emergence of Middle-Class Yachting in the North-West of England from he Later Nineteenth Century', p. 155.

[82] Ryan, 'Identifying the British Yachtsman, 1815–1839', pp. 68–69. The various organisations amalgamated with the YRA after the war.

However, again, any assumption that sailing clubs would widen the social basis of yachting is wide of the mark. True, the new clubs tended to be more locally based, but Cusack's data shows that there was little widening of the class basis, except to allow a few wealthier tradesmen in.

For example, the Dart Boat Sailing Club was founded in 1873 by the small tradesmen in the town, who were unable to become members of the Royal Dart, founded 1866. Its officers were Captain and Lieutenant. It had no clubhouse. However, while maritime trades such as sail making were admitted, professional seamen, watermen and fishermen were not; and the tradesmen were probably masters, not hired workers. By the 1880s, its officers were now Commodore, Rear Commodore etc. and the size of the craft increased.[83]

Yacht club members professed to despise 'trade' but they revealed an even greater fear of marine professionals. Probably this was because, as a newly arrived group, they were very sensitive to being made to look foolish by the superior sailing skills of their social inferiors. Since they could not voice this fear, they resorted to the dichotomy: 'professional vs. amateur'.

Huggins points out that, around 1800, 'professional' meant having a high level of expertise and 'amateur' 'an upper-class patron or sporting enthusiast (whether or not earning money from the sport'.[84] By the last quarter of the century, the term 'professional' had become much more negative. Since there was no rational basis for this dislike, an irrational one had to be created, stereotyping the professional, among other faults, as being violent, and likely to take 'dives', if paid sufficiently to do so.

Yachting shared this fear with other sports, such as Athletics and Rowing.[85]

Regattas would separate races for boats built for leisure from their working counterparts. So, at the Exmouth Regatta in 1877, a race for '… centre keel boats, kept for pleasure only, not to exceed 17 feet overall' was held.[86]

---

[83] Tim Bass, 'The Rise of Recreational Boat-Sailing', pp. 25–26.

[84] Huggins, *The Victorians and Sport*, p. 52.

[85] Thus, in 1866 the Amateur Athletic Club barred from membership anyone who 'is a mechanic, artisan or labourer'; and defined 'amateur' to exclude anyone who had competed in any competition, or for prize money, or for admission money' (Tranter, *Sport, Economy and Society*, p. 42). In rowing, the Henley Rules of 1879 excluded from its races anyone 'who had ever competed in an open competition for a stake, money or entrance fee' or 'competed with or against a professional for any prize', or 'ever taught, pursued or assisted in the practice of athletic exercises of any kind as a means of gaining a livelihood', or 'employed in or about boats for money or wages' (Cunningham, 'Leisure and Culture', p. 297; Huggins, *The Victorians and Sport*, p. 59).

[86] Bass, 'The Rise of Recreational Boat-Sailing', p. 41, quoting the *Western Times*, September 1877, p. 2.

Uniform or dress was helpful in distinguishing the owner from the worker, particularly where the activity was not expensive, as in model boating on the Serpentine.[87] Uniform or special kit functioned as a badge of belonging as well a way of exclusion.[88]

Mixing with the crew on the yacht itself was less of a problem for the aristocrat yachtsman, who had a crew of working men, allowing clear separation of role and rank. Even so, they usually wore a uniform, often with the name of the yachts sewn into their jackets or guernseys. 'Trousers and guernseys for hands could be had for as little as 20s a set' from Goy of London, 2 Praed Street, London. 'Embroidering the yacht's name on the Guernsey cost 1s 6d extra.'[89] Just in case there was still confusion, at the Royal Norfolk and Suffolk, 'paid hands ... wore gilt buttons on their reefer jackets to distinguish them from owners, who had black buttons'. [90]

At the Royal Cornwall, and doubtless at other senior clubs, boatmen were not allowed inside the club.[91]

The Corinthian yachtsman quite often needed one or two sailors as professional crew. The possibility therefore arose that anyone seeing them sitting cheek by jowl in their smaller yacht might jump to the horrific conclusion that they were friends. For this reason, if anyone took a photograph, the crew would be placed at the mast, with the owner back in the cockpit, helming.

The press was helpful:

> In cross-class sports like cricket, *Bell's Life* reports clarified this by the 1840s. Country and MCC players were variously titled, of military ranks, either 'Esquire' or 'Mr' if amateur, or given their surnames if professional.[92]

> Press reports of the day always described 'Waterman Ames' or 'Skipper Drake'.[93]

How did intelligent, successful men justify this fearful, caste-like behaviour?

H. C. [Henry Coleman] Folkard's classic *The Sailing Boat: A Description of English and Foreign Boats, their Varieties of Rig, and Practical Directions for*

---

[87] Ryan, 'Identifying the British Yachtsman 1815–1939', p. 71.
[88] Huggins, *The Victorians and Sport*, p. 194.
[89] A. W. Brian Simpson, *Cannibalism and Common Law*, p. 20.
[90] Jamie Campbell, *Royal Norfolk & Suffolk Yacht Club Founded 1859*.
[91] Mead, *History of the Royal Cornwall*, p. 102. Again, this problem was not confined to yachting. 'In cricket, gentlemen amateurs and working-class professionals did not meet socially. Professionals ate their own food with the spectators. Amateurs ate with the committee and members in the pavilion dining area' (Huggins, *The Victorians and Sport*, p. 54).
[92] Huggins, *Victorians and Sport*, p. 19.
[93] Campbell, *A History of the Royal Norfolk and Suffolk Yacht Club*, p. 233. Campbell is describing the situation as late as the 1930s.

Sailing, was first published in 1854 and went through many editions – by 1870, it was into its fourth. Folkard was clear that the amateur could not learn from the professional waterman because:

> No race of men are more coarse and uncouth in their language, or more uncultivated in their manners, than the fishermen and boatmen in many parts of our coasts; and they are generally reluctant to teach others the mysteries and accomplishments of their art.[94]

This is ironic since Folkard wrote the book because he was concerned about the increasing number of accidents in recreational boat sailing.

On the first page of the early *Yarns for Green Hands,* published in 1860, Vanderdecken declared: 'It is for the tyro [beginner] in the art, I have written, and to him addressed myself … A five-ton boat is the best to learn in, because in such a small yacht everything is so light that it is within the power of one man to take the entire management, and to handle her alone'.[95] He can learn by watching, or sailing with, more experienced racers. Frank Cowper, in *Yachting and Cruising for Amateurs* somewhat later in 1911, gives nearly identical advice:

> … no especial knowledge is necessary, anyone can pick it up with a little practice. Only when practicing have an odd boat, a safe place like the Crouch and plenty of room. In a week a learner will be fit to go anywhere, if he has managed his ship without professional assistance during that time.[96]

This is actively dangerous nonsense about yachting being easy, and easily taught to you by your yacht club mates. One wonders how many got injured or killed in acting out this dogma. It is all the more remarkable, since the Victorian yachtsman often played more than one game, and the same person was happy to learn from the club professional: '[In golf] There was none of the bland assumption that only a gentleman could teach another one how to play properly'.[97]

There were exceptions. The aristocratic Sir Edward Sullivan, introducing the *Badminton Library: Yachting,* Vol. 1 wrote: 'The chief peculiarity of all the seafaring class that I have been brought into contact with is their entire freedom from vulgarity. They are obliging to the utmost of their power, but

---

[94] Folkard, *The Sailing Boat,* 1854, p. x. Quoted by Bass, 'The Rise of Recreational Boat-Sailing', p. 16.
[95] Vanderdecken, *Yarns for Green Hands,* p. 4.
[96] Cowper, *Yachting and Cruising for Amateurs,* p. 166.
[97] Lowerson, 'Golf', p. 187.

never cringing or vulgar'.[98] Another was H. Lewis Jones, a pioneer in the use of electricity in medicine. Writing of his sails around the Thames Estuary in *Swin, Swale and Estuary*, 1892, he commends fishermen and bargemen, for their 'smartness and self-reliance'.[99] Somewhat later, the influential yacht designer, Albert Strange, writing in *Yachting Monthly* in 1911, wrote of the River Medway fishermen: 'They were all capital fellows, never letting me want for fresh fish (smelts included), and were not to proud or too shy to share a meal or a pipe when occasion gave the chance to invite them.'[100]

There must have been yet others who were fed up with the negative stereotyping of maritime professionals, for H. Fiennes Speed prefaces his logs of many voyages in small boats, *Cruises in Small Yachts*, 1883, with the lines: 'I don't want to give a dissertation on Religion … or cut yachts' hands to pieces with a wordy warfare as some sailing writers do.'

Some, or many, yachtsmen may have admired their skills, whilst agreeing that it would be quite unsuitable for them to join, or even be allowed to enter, a yacht club. For example, E. F. Knight was delighted when, short of crew, one John Wright arrives the night before departure: 'He had luckily had nothing to do with Cowes and yachts. His life is passed before the mast on foreign-going steams and sailing vessels'.[101] He is happy to eat with Wright on the boat, but ashore they always eat separately, and, it appears, in different establishments.

The good working relationship between the old and the new guard, their shared values, the unification of the rules of racing and of handicapping, due to the prestigious, active involvement of the future king, all helped yachting to prosper and, towards the end of the century, to enter its second Golden Period, often referred to as the Golden Age of Yachting.

---

[98] Sullivan, 'Introduction', p. 7.
[99] Jones, *Swin, Swale and* Estuary, p. 11. In a number of locations, maritime workers set up their own club. Hamworthy Sailing Club, Poole, was founded in 1898, because of '… the difficulty for artisans, such as paid professional skippers, paid hands, boat builders and sail makers and fishermen to become members of the more exclusive Yacht Clubs whose members consisted mainly of amateur sailing gentlemen' (http://www.pooleyc.co.uk/the-clubhistory/the early days). Other examples include the Leigh-on-Sea Sailing Club (Dent, *Not Quite at Sea*, p. 28) formed around the same time and the Burnham [-on-Crouch] Sailing Club, started in 1930 by men who worked in the boatyards (burnhamsc.co.uk, accessed 14 April, 2016).
[100] Quoted in John Leather, *Albert Strange*, p. 94.
[101] E. F. Knight, *The 'Falcon' on the Baltic*, p. 82.

CHAPTER TEN

The Golden Age of Yachting,
1880–1900

PART ONE
The Rich

… on one occasion when asked the Princes of Wales' whereabouts, the Kaiser replied that his cousin was sailing with his grocer, a reference to Sir Thomas Lipton. The Prince is rumoured to have shown his feeling about this remark by kicking a silver cup he had just won, which had been presented by the Kaiser, off the side of his boat.[1]

During the last twenty years of the nineteenth century, yachting achieved a higher level of social and cultural – and even, to a limited extent, political – centrality than before or since.[2] The next two chapters concern this centrality and examine it in six different areas:

- the sea, especially the English Channel, was central to the nation's anxieties and its imagery; and this importance extended to those who sailed on it, be they the Navy, merchant seamen or yachtsmen
- the leisure activity of the monarchy and the very rich
- the growth of yacht racing, as rich owners hired the best yacht designers, such as the Fifes of Fairlie and George Watson of Glasgow, to create winning yachts for them
- the attention paid to yachting in newspapers, magazines and in the cultural media – photography, art and novels
- the development of small boat racing. In this chapter, I discuss the development of keel-boat racing

---

[1] Knox-Johnston, *Robin Knox-Johnston's History of Yachting*, p. 76.
[2] I gave the defining characteristics when describing the first Golden Period in Georgian London (Chapter 4).

- a final factor, which I discuss in the following chapter, was the arrival of the dinghy, which allowed much cheaper sailing and which, because of its lightness, made successful small boat racing feasible for women sailors.

Yachting, Patriotism and the Navy

One major reason for the centrality of yachting was its links with the monarchy and the Navy. After the 1870s, national identity and the nautical became increasingly fused into a complex of public emotions concerning patriotism, the Navy and Englishness. For the empire to flourish, our seaborne trade required safe passage anywhere around the world. Naval supremacy was seen as the key to winning a major war, if not to the nation's very existence. British wealth, security and prestige depended on the effectiveness of our Navy. Till the First World War, the government aimed to keep its navy equal or superior to the next two largest navies combined – the so-called 'Two Power Standard', which had been codified in the Naval Defence Act of 1889, and which started 'the Great Naval Race'.[3] There was competition by the 1880s onwards from Germany as to who was building the larger and most modern fleet, creating an unstable situation.[4]

The sea was increasingly presented as a sanctified and highly cathexed British space. This sentiment made any seaborne activity, including yachting, merit worthy.

The prestige of all things nautical expressed itself in fashion in the years before 1914, whereby children of all classes were dressed in sailor suits, especially for the studio portraits of families.[5]

For their part, yacht clubs routinely allowed RN officers to use their facilities, without them needing to apply for membership. And the connection was more than gestures of hospitality. The Royal Naval Volunteer Reserve (the RNVR) was created in 1903, as the threat of war with Germany increased, to

---

[3] Tim Madge, *Long Voyage Home*, Part One; Behrman, *Victorian Myths of the Sea*, p. 128. The double standard was being suggested some time earlier. Behrman, p. 49, quotes 'a Naval Peer, writing anonymously in *Our Naval Position and Policy*, 1859, urging "a naval force superior to any other possible combination of enemy fleets"'. This policy put into practice the American naval historian, Captain A. T. Mahan's influential theory of the necessity of naval supremacy, expressed in his 1889 work, *The Influence of Sea Power upon History, 1660–1783*.

[4] Thanks in part to the activities of the Naval League, established in 1893, there was a vociferous popular demand for more battleships. These popular feelings and demands are sometimes referred to as 'navalism'. (*OED*: 'advocacy of or policy favouring naval power'. The first usage was in the *Nation*, New York, 1892; the first British usage in the *Daily News*, 1896). One of the popular slogans was 'We want eight [dreadnoughts] and we won't wait'.

[5] Walvin, *Leisure and Society*, p. 113.

attract yachtsmen into the navy.[6] By 1906, the RNVR had proved so success-ful with thousands enrolled, that a new journal, *Yachting Monthly*, was started for its members and quickly attracted a much wider readership. [7]

As the head of the Armed Services, it was important that the king was competent in naval matters. Victoria's son, Edward VII, and his son, George V were competent yacht sailors, the first since Charles II. The visible, and frequently photographed, presence of the future Edward the VII and then the future George V, the 'Sailor King', aboard *Britannia*, was useful evidence of their nautical prowess.[8] It also allowed the King to be seen mixing with commoners.[9]

We saw in the last chapter how the Prince of Wales, Edward, united the yacht clubs into accepting the jurisdiction of the YRA. He owned a succes-sion of seven racing yachts – in 1863, the 37 ton cutter, *Dagmar*, the 40 ton cutter *Alexandra* in 1871, the 40 ton cutter *Princess* in 1872, the 38 ton *Zenobia* in 1873, the 205 ton schooner *Hildegarde* in 1876, the 104 ton cutter *Formosa* in 1880 and the 210 ton schooner *Aline* in 1882. He had *Britannia* built in 1893 to revive large yacht racing and to compete against the Kaiser's *Meteor* (the re-named America's Cup Challenger of 1887, *Thistle*, which the Kaiser had bought in 1891); and also to aid Dunraven in his America Cup challenge.[10] Having sold *Britannia* in 1897, he bought her back in 1899 to act as a trial horse for Lipton's first America's Cup challenger, *Shamrock*.

The monarchy were not just involved in big yachts. In 1896, George, then the Duke of York had a little time off from naval duties and asked the yacht builder, Charles Sibbick, to build him a one-rater, to be delivered in one week. Working day and night – by acetylene lighting – *White Rose* hit the water six days later. Prince George won first prize at the Castle Yacht Club regatta two days later.[11]

Another monarch wanting to link yachting and the nation's navy was the Kaiser. Believing that yachting would make his nation more navy-orientated, the Kaiser encouraged the development of Kiel Regatta Week, which takes place in the last complete week in June. Yachts had gathered to race at Kiel for

---

[6] The RNVR should not be confused with the Royal Naval Reserve, created in 1859, which was composed of professional seamen and the Merchant Navy, who could be called on in times of war.

[7] Ryan, 'Identifying the British Yachtsman 1815–1939', p. 74.

[8] Derek Birley, *Land of Sport and Glory*, p. 146.

[9] Such royal mingling was taken as an indication of British classlessness praised by Arthur Lamsley (*Sea Lure*, p. 34); Barthes, in 'The "Blue Blood" Cruise' in *Mythologies*, pp. 32–33, more accurately, points out that by such mixing, the monarchy asserts its super-human status.

[10] Black, *G. L. Watson*, p. 186.

[11] http://www.sandemanyachtcompany.co.uk/blog/charles-sibbick

10 King George at the helm of *Britannia*. The monarchy was always keen to show
its close links with nautical activities. The amateurs are in white trousers, blazers
and club ties, the professionals in white cloth uniforms. King George is wearing a
sailor's beret to show his closeness to the professional seaman. This is a publicity
still from the 1930s – the King would not helm in a race.

some years previously, but after 1894, the regatta became called Kiel Week,
with the Kaiser becoming a regular visitor. How seriously he took yachting
is shown by the fact that G. L. Watson, the designer of his *Meteor II*, commu-
nicated directly with Admiral Baron von Senden, the Chief of the German
Imperial Naval Cabinet.

The Monarchy and the Season: Cowes Week

It became a social requirement for the aristocracy and those who aspired to the highest echelons of society to participate in yachting, preferably through the ownership of a racing yacht, or, at the very least, by attendance at Cowes week.

The prestige of Cowes Week reached its zenith during this period, when yachting literally became the sport of kings. The monarchs of Russia, Germany, Spain and Italy would come over to the Solent each summer to watch their yachts compete against the Prince of Wales' *Britannia,* as well as other 'big yachts' such as *Satanita, Navahoe* (an American yacht), *Calluna* and the unsuccessful challenger for the America's Cup in 1893, *Valkyrie II.* In 1899, the Squadron owned about 150 yachts and gave employment to over 2,000 seamen.[12] And, relative to other aristocratic sports, yachting was (apparently) not that expensive. Sir Edward Sullivan estimated the cost of racing large yachts in 1894:

> A modern racing yacht with a crew of 30 men may, if successful, easily knock a hole in 1,000 *l* [pounds] for racing wages alone to say nothing of cost of spars, and sails, and gear, & c. Of course, in comparison with keeping a pack of hounds, or a deer forest, or a good grouse moor, or to pheasant preserving on a very large scale, the expense of yacht racing, even at its worst, is modest.[13]

The Squadron had to widen its criteria for acceptability of source of wealth and type of vessel sailed. It was not possible to restrict its membership only to those who made their money from the land, and, slowly, industrial wealth had to be accepted. Also, the Squadron reluctantly came to terms with having to accept members whose vessel was a *steam* yacht. As early as 1829, Thomas Assheton-Smith had proposed that possession of a steam vessel should be acceptable for membership. When the Squadron had rejected this proposal, he resigned. But the Squadron could not hold their position. By 1842, steam propulsion was reliable enough for Queen Victoria to order her first steam yacht, the 1,034 ton paddle steamer, *Victoria and Albert,* to be built at Pembroke Dock, Milford Haven, and launched in 1843. It was replaced by the much larger *Victoria and Albert II,* of twice the tonnage, in 1855, but still a paddle steamer. The Squadron, with its close links with royalty, then had no option but to let in applicants who preferred steam to sail.

---

[12] Robert Simper, *Victorian and Edwardian Yachting from Old Photographs,* p. 3.
[13] Sullivan, Introduction, *The Badminton Library: Yachting,* p. 10.

Since such vessels only required an engine, not masts and rigging etc. – although, in the early days, they often had both – they could be far more luxurious, so steam yachts could incorporate banqueting or dance floors; or, for the owner that liked fresh milk, a small cow shed.[14] The social round was augmented in the last quarter of the nineteenth century by lavish hospitality on members' steam yachts.[15] In the first decade of the 1900s, the marginalised internal combustion engine, driven by petrol or diesel, appeared. This was quickly adopted by steam yachts, as the fuel was far less bulky and dirty than coal.[16]

The growth of the prestigious steam yacht detracted from the primacy of the sailing yacht, but not from the Squadron. By 1904, Sir Edward Sullivan, Bart, mournfully recorded that 'more than half the tonnage of the Club is in steamers'.[17]

In Cowes, the rich either bought or rented fine houses. Lillie Langtry, 'the Jersey Lily', a 'professional beauty' and astute social climber, was well aware of the symbolic value of yacht ownership. [18] At the time of their courtship in 1874, Edward Langtry was the owner of the luxurious 80-foot yacht *Red Gauntlet*. She half-joked: 'To become the mistress of the yacht, I married the owner'.[19] In her autobiography *The Days I Knew*, she recalled:

> Goodwood over, everyone who owned a yacht or who could, by hook or crook, manage to get on board one, went to Cowes ...

> The 'Cowes Week' with the daily sailing competitions ... the cruises in floating palaces by days and the dances on shore by night, became a whirlwind of gaiety.[20]

Sadly, for Langtry, this gaiety came at a heavy personal cost. Most of her autobiography is told in this breathy, naive style. The reality of her life style, of being involved with very rich, but often sadistic, men is told in Sonia Hillsdon's *The Jersey Lily*.

Photography had been created by Fox Talbot in England and Louis Daguerre in France in the late 1830s. By the second half of the century, pictures could be taken on plate glass slides by heavy cameras. This weight of

[14] See Drummond, *Salt-Water Palaces*.

[15] Guest and Boulton, *Memorials of the Royal Yacht Squadron*, pp. 319–320.

[16] Outboard engines made their appearance around this time. They were first developed by Evinrude of Milwaukee, Wisconsin, America, in 1907 but weighed 40 lbs.

[17] Sullivan, 'Introduction', Badminton Library: *Yachting*, Vol. 1, p. 4.

[18] The 'Jersey Lily', *Amaryllis Belladonna*, is a valued cut flower. It originates from South Africa.

[19] Sonia Hillsdon, *The Jersey Lily*, pp. 30–33.

[20] Langtry, *The Days I Knew*, p. 51.

gear and the difficulty of photographing moving objects from a moving platform delayed the advent of the photographing of yachts in motion till the
1880s.

Each major yachting centre had its professional photographers. The first at
Cowes were the Kirks. William Kirk had established himself as a leading maritime photographer by 1888. He used 10 x8 inch glass plates. Once inserted, he
could not see the image. With a moving boat, he had to guess where it would
be.[21] The same, of course, was true of the firm that is now synonymous with
yacht photography – the Bekens. Frank Beken first went out in his workboat
to photograph the Solent scene, especially the racing, from 1894 onwards.
He also used a bellows camera with glass slides. The shutter release was an
airbulb in his mouth. He could take some twelve pictures a day.[22] Further
east on the island, Arthur Debenham (1845–1936) had his premises in Union
Street, Ryde.

G. West & Son, of Southsea and Gosport, run by the brothers Alfred and
George, started offering yachting photographs from the 1880s.[23] Alfred West
(1857–1937) had a little yawl, in the well of which he placed a steel frame with
a heavy weight for stability.[24] On this frame was his camera, which could
rotate. He claimed to be the first photographer to capture racing yachts under
full sail in 1881. To do this, he invented the instantaneous shutter, needed to
capture motion.[25]

Down West, Mr Harrison was operating in Falmouth from the 1880s.[26]
On the Clyde were J. Adamson & Son of Rothesay, W. Robertson & Co. of
Gourock and Glasgow, and MacClure, MacDonald & Co. of Glasgow. Their
pictures, converted into postcards, were commercial ventures. The Adamsons
installed a dark room aboard their small steam yacht, so that prints would be
available to sell as soon as they returned to shore. They set up the Rothesay
Collotype Company to mass produce their images to the public, notably
passengers on the Clyde paddle steamers but also abroad.[27] Kirk of Cowes
was another leader in this field. ('... he was successful in capturing the Royal
Yacht *Alberta* steaming into Cowes at ten knots with Queen Victoria on

[21] Dear, *The Great Days of Yachting from the Kirk Collection*; David Couling, *Solent Yachting Scene
in Bygone Years 1890–1938.*
[22] Keith Beken, *The Beken File,* 1980.
[23] Simper, *Victorian and Edwardian Yachting from Old Photographs,* p. 5.
[24] Around 1898, it was wrecked in a storm off Southsea Beach and he replaced it with a steam
lauch, capable of 8 knots (Alfred West's unpublished autobiography, *Sea Salts and Celluloid,*
1936, p. 9).
[25] West, *Sea Salts and Celluloid,* pp. 6 and 7.
[26] Mead, *History of the Royal Cornwall,* p. 50.
[27] Black, *G. L. Watson,* p. 451.

board ... It was shown to Her Majesty, who said "We are pleased with it'").[28] Images of yachts racing sold in large numbers. For example, pictures of King George V on *Britannia,* or *White Heather II,* built in 1907 for Lord Waring, 95 foot long, carrying 8,000 square feet of canvas, sold well.[29]

Postcards, around the turn of the century, were very big business. Research by the Education and Social Research Institute, Manchester Metropolitan University, gives a figure of six billion postcards – an average of 200 per person – posted in Britain between 1901 and 1910.[30] With four postal deliveries a day, they were speedy communications, not like today when you are usually back at work a week before your postcard arrives through your friends' letterboxes.

Newspaper and magazine coverage of yachting was rendered more interesting and more immediate by the addition of photographs. Photography, as opposed to paintings, was instant – it recorded the present. It could provide multiple images of the various stages of a race, and could be available for distribution by newspapers the next day.

The increasing social centrality of yachting and the arrival of photography created a huge growth in its reporting. The *Nineteenth Century British Newspapers* data base cites 2,969 references to 'yacht' between 1801 and 1825; 13,456 from 1826 to 1850; 46,785 from 1851 to 1875; and 90, 219 from 1876 to the end of the century. The London *Times,* the *Daily Telegraph* and magazines like *The Field,* with its yachting section, had their yachting correspondents. Dixon Kemp, the first Secretary of the YRA, was at the *Field* from 1900 to 1928, and Brooke Heckstall-Smith, the second YRA secretary, at the *Telegraph,* gave detailed accounts, illustrated with photographs, of the major races. It is hard to imagine now, when the America's Cup is barely reported, but this extensive coverage included reports of local, mid-week races with just a dozen boats. There was also extensive reporting in local papers, such as in Swansea:

> Full accounts of all the races in the inaugural 1909 season are available. The local newspaper [the *Cambrian*] also kept the public informed about national yachting with, for example, accounts of events at Cowes.[31]

The *Yacht Racing Calendar and Review* provided a record of every British sailing event for the year, and this ran from 1888 to 1895, edited by Dixon Kemp,

---

[28] Couling, *Solent Yachting Scene in Bygone Years 1890–1938,* p. 8.
[29] *Ibid.,* pp. 34 and 40
[30] 'Is Tweeting One Hundred Years Old?' http://www.esri.mmu.ac.uk/news/news.php?id=1119
[31] Austin, 'Yachting in Swansea Bay', p. 23.

and from 1902 to1904, edited by Brooke Heckstall-Smith. These were hefty tomes, the 1894 edition running to 553 pages.

New media were coming on line. At the 1898 Royal St George regatta at Kingstown, Marconi followed the fleet in a tug, the *Flying Huntress*, and sent live reports by radio of a race to the Harbour Master's residence in Moran Park. From there, the results were immediately telephoned to newspaper offices. This form of 'instantaneous' communication, not surprisingly, was greeted with great excitement. In 1899, Marconi wirelessed the *New York Herald*'s reporter's account of one of the America Cup races from 'a specially fitted-up broadcasting plant on the steamer *Grand Duchesse*'.[32]

Silent film was also being developed. From 1895, the Boat race was a favourite topic and, at the turn of the century, short films were made of the Cowes and Carnarvon regattas.[33] In 1897, the innovative Alfred West moved from photography to moving film and made short films on nautical themes, such as *Our Navy*, which he showed privately to Queen Victoria in 1898 and Edward VII in 1901. It was first shown to the public at the cinema of the Regent Street Polytechnic in 1905 and, regularly updated, ran for fourteen years. It included:

> one particular film taken from the Warner lightship [off the east coast of the Isle of Wight] of yachts racing in rough weather. They came so close to the camera that, smothered in foam, they appeared to be sailing right out of the picture, and the effect on one member of the audience was so realistic that he was forced to leave suffering from acute sea-sickness![34]

In January, 1901, British Mutoscope and Biograph Co. released a short film, 'The Builders of *Shamrock II*', filmed at Denny's yard, Dumbarton. The boat's launch on 20 April was also filmed.[35]

Perhaps nothing illustrates better the cultural centrality of yachting during this period than the fact that so many leading painters and writers foregrounded yachting.

The first painters to frequently include yachts in their pictures were the French Impressionists, most notably Monet and Boudin in the 1860s, paint-ing the leisure activities of Parisians on Normandy beaches. Monet, Manet and Renoir painted riverine scenes with yachts on them.[36] After initial

---

[32] Lipton, *Leaves from the Lipton Logs*, pp. 98–99.
[33] Huggins, *The Victorians and Sport*, pp. 185–186.
[34] West, *Sea Salts and Celluloid*, p. 16.
[35] Black, *G. L. Watson*, pp. 336 and 18.
[36] See John House, *Impressionists by the Sea*. Monet painted at Sainte-Adresse in 1867. The oldest French yacht club still active, Société des Régates du Havre, organised prestigious regattas

hostility from art critics, Impressionist pictures became increasingly familiar to the British art public and, purchased by percipient Welsh (the Davies
sisters, daughters of the builder of Barry Docks, South Wales) and Scottish
shipping (William Burrell) families, rapidly increased in value, adding chic
and further prestige to leisure sailing.[37]

The Victorian gallery at Tate Britain shows how much the coast and
the sea was part of the painted Victorian landscape, with many works with
yachts in them by such leading painters as John Brett, R. C. Leslie, H. M.
Doughty, W. L. Wyllie, Philip Wilson Steer and James Tissot. These painters
frequently used sailing as the scene for their canvasses, presumably because
its popularity allowed ready sales. For example, Steer mainly painted around
Walberswick, Suffolk, but he spent the summers of 1888 and 1892 at Cowes.
His yacht paintings there include *Summer at Cowes*, 1888, and *Cowes Week*;
Yacht Racing on the Solent, and *A Procession of Yachts in Cowes* (our old friend:
the cruise in company?), which is in the Tate, all finished in 1893.[38] The most
eminent member of the group of major painters known as 'the Glasgow Boys',
John Lavery, found it useful to be a member of the Paisley Tennis Club and
the Royal Clyde Yacht Club in order to gain commissions. He painted Lady
Glen Coats (one of the two families with massive Scottish thread-making
concerns) yacht racing.[39]

Falmouth also had major yachting painters, namely Henry Scott Tuke
(1858–1929) and Charles Napier Hemy (1841–1917), while Percy 'Powder'
Thurburn painted yachting scenes on the nearby Helford River.[40] Hemy
was honorary artist to the Squadron from 1913 till his death. Marine artists
were expected to paint from seaward towards the land, and therefore major
Victorian and Edwardian marine artists – such as James Clark Hook, Henry
Moore, John Brett and Arthur Briscoe – all owned yachts and some of them,

---

there. Later, he lived in Argenteuil from 1871 to 1878. This town, on the banks of the Seine, was
home to the sailing club, the Cercle de la Voile de Paris, the prestigious Sailing Club of Paris,
the second oldest yacht club in France.

[37] See Frances Fowle, *Impressionism in Scotland*; Anne Sumner, *Colour and Light: Fifty Impressionist and Post-Impressionist Works at the National Museum of Wales*. For the London art scene
of the time, see Belinda Thomson, *Impressionism: Origins, Practice, Reception*. The collection
by the Courtauld family was much later, between the wars. For the Burrell Collection, see
Richard Marks *et al.*, *The Burrell Collection*.

[38] See Taylor, *Yachts on Canvas*; Laura Newton, ed., *Painting at the Edge: British Coastal Art Colonies 1880–1930*; Christiana Payne, *Where the Sea Meets the Land: Artists on the Coast in Nineteenth-Century Britain*; David Cordingly, *Marine Painting in England 1700–1900*, pp. 178–179.

[39] Ann Sumner *et al.*, *Court on Canvas*. Chapter 3; 'Tennis Parties', pp. 47–82 and Chapter 4:
'Tennis and the Artist', pp. 83–124.

[40] Tom Cross, David Hale and Pin Armitage, *The Artist Who Loved Boats: Percy 'Powder' Thorburn*.

such as Tuke, Wyllie, and Julius Olsen at St Ives, had them converted into floating studios.[41] Hemy converted a 40 foot seine fishing boat into a studio. He named her the *Vanderveld*, a nice homage to Charles II's yacht painters.

W. L. Wyllie (1851–1931) rose to considerable eminence, painting commercial craft and yachts on the Medway.[42] Arthur Briscoe (1873–1943), another internationally eminent maritime artist, was an active member of the Blackwater Sailing Club, which he helped found in 1899. His illustrations appeared regularly in *Yachting Monthly*.[43] Albert Strange (1855–1917), head of Scarborough School of Art, was a prime mover in the Humber Yawl Club. He is now best remembered as a yacht designer, but, in his time, was a respected maritime artist.[44]

Big Yacht Racing

Most boats were bought to cruise, but cruising is a relatively private business, and, as ever, popular attention and media reporting concerned yacht racing, the sport of the rich. A spectacular race was the Round Britain and Ireland of 1887 to celebrate the Queen's Golden Jubilee, organised by the Royal Thames. The first prize was £1,000 pounds (worth about £118,000 in 2016), raised by subscriptions from members. There were eleven entrants, from the 255 ton schooner, *Selene*, to the 40 ton cutter, *Sleuthound*, and a handicap system, time-on-distance, was used. *Sleuthound* came in, 1,500 miles later, only twenty hours behind the winner, another cutter, the 80 ton *Genesta*, the America's Cup challenger two years earlier.[45]

The spectacle of yacht racing was by no means restricted to the Solent. Cowes Week formed the high point of a circuit which, from the mid-nineteenth century, moved around from the East coast from early May. Racing for racers from 10 tons upwards started with the Thames matches, followed by the Down Swin from Southend to Harwich, which traditionally hosted the first regatta of the racing season; then the Up Swin back to near Southend; and the Nore to Dover, and so right round to the Clyde;[46] back via Belfast Lough for the Royal Ulster Regatta; and down to Kingstown (Dun Laoghaire)

[41] Payne, *Where the Sea Meets the Land*, pp. 55–59.
[42] Don Ellis, *Medway Yacht Club*. Famous Wyllie canvasses included *Toil, Glitter, Grime and Wealth*, 1895, concerning shipping in the Pool of London, and *The Opening of Tower Bridge*, 1895.
[43] Alex A. Hurst, *Arthur Briscoe: Marine Artist*, Brighton: Teredo, 1974.
[44] Leather, *Albert Strange: Yacht Designer and Artist 1855-1917*.
[45] Phillips-Birt, *The Cumberland Fleet*, pp. 92–98.
[46] Leather, *The Northseamen*, p. 116.

Regattas, organised by the Royal St George and the Royal Irish; to Cowes Week in the first week of August; and then down to the West Country, ending in Dartmouth early in September. This was the equivalent of the Formula One circuit. (There was some variation, with other yacht havens, such as Falmouth in 1894, and Swansea in 1909 and 1910, visited on occasion. Towns like Swansea would raise large sums by subscription towards expenses and attractive prize money. Swansea raised £1200 for the 1909 regatta).[47]

In addition, in the Spring, there was a Riviera Circuit in the Mediterranean, centred on Marseille, Cannes and Nice. By the 1890s, as mentioned, the Kaiser had created Kiel week at the end of June, and to encourage British participation, gave the Emperor's Cup for the winner of the Dover–Heligoland feeder race, which became an annual event from 1895.[48]

In her first season, 1893, *Britannia* scored thirty-three wins out of forty-three starts. In 1894, she won all seven starts for big yachts on the French Riviera. It was the sight of her racing the other big yachts that drew the crowds. However, these were just the largest class. There were a number of other classes at the major regattas.

Since the name of the game was winning, owners often had new boats built every year, creating a cycle of yacht development and sales. (Winning also helped offset the cost of running the yacht). The YRA periodically revised the rules for the various ratings, most notably in 1886, 1895 and 1901, and designers then had to work out how to get the fastest boat from the specifications, and how to take advantage of any vagueness in the specifications. The gain was that the lower the boat designer could make the rating, the greater the time allowance the yacht would receive. For example, narrowing the beam allowed for boats to get longer and/or more sail to be flown. So, boats became narrower and narrower. Johnson has a chart of this trend.[49] He gives the example of a 2½ rater in 1887, that was 20.94 long on the waterline and, by 1892, another boat with the same rating, which was 28 foot long.

---

[47] Mead, *The History of the Royal Cornwall*, p. 64; Austin, 'Yachting in Swansea Bay', p. 242. After 1910, the Bristol Channel YC, Swansea, had negotiated with the YRA to be part of a three year cycle, alternating with the Royal Mersey and Royal Cork regattas, but the War intervened (www.bcyc.co.uk/history). Cost of regatta: Austin, 'The Great Swansea Bay Regattas'.

[48] Dear in *Sailing in Eccentric Circles*, p. 33, gives 1897 as the start of this race. He tells of Squadron members racing their rather slow yachts: 'When one member entered with his old and extremely laggardly schooner, his son remarked, 'I'm sorry to see you going away, we always had such good Christmases together'; G. A. Henty, a member of the Royal Thames, took part a number of times. He died aboard his yacht, the *Egret*, in 1902 (Arnold, *Hold Fast for England*, pp. 11–12).

[49] Johnson, *Yacht Rating*, p. 46.

Since a big good boat beats a small good boat, obsolescence was being built in at the expense of the yacht owner.

These rule changes are difficult to comprehend in their complexity, and the reader may just find the table illustrative.[50]

Waterline Length	1881–1886	1886–1895	1896–1907	1907 International Rule
50 ft	20 tons	20 rater	52 ft rating	15-metre
60 ft	40 tons	40 rater	65 ft rating	19-metre
80 ft	85 tons	140 rater	75 ft rating	23-metre

Even more confusing, these changes also introduce terms, such as 'raters' that mean nothing to the non-racer, or change meaning of an ordinary word, such as 'metre'. These became class names **and do not refer to the boat length**.

An indication of international cooperation and coordination was the International Meridian Conference in Washington, DC, in 1884, which agreed that the prime meridian (0 degrees of longitude) should run through Greenwich. Further evidence of yachting's growing appeal was that races between boats of different nations were becoming increasingly common. With Brooke Heckstall-Smith, the recently appointed Secretary of the YRA playing a leading role, an international conference on yacht racing was held at the Langham Hotel, London in July, 1906, leading to the setting up of the International Yacht Racing Union.[51] The first International Racing Rule came into force from 1907 to 1920, and has been regularly revised since.[52]

Brooke Heckstall-Smith (Secretary, YRA) published a list of the numbers of sailing yachts in European countries valid for the time of the conference:

The numbers in Germany and Austria were 599, France 363, Norway and Sweden 300, Belgium and Holland 191, Denmark 107, but in the United Kingdom 2959 and her colonies 311 … with a tonnage of 57588 as against say, France with a total of 6300 tons.[53]

---

[50] Taken from *ibid.*, p. 81.

[51] The period 1890–1914 saw the creation of other international committees – the IOC (Olympics) in 1894, the International Association of Athletic Federations (the IAAF) 1912, FIFA (football) and ILTF (International Lawn Tennis Federation) both in 1913 (Horne *et al.*, *Understanding Sport*, p. 62). Note that these are *international* bodies, different from the *national* sporting bodies set up in the United Kingdom in the 1870s (see Chapter 9).

[52] For the convoluted history of yacht rating, see Johnson, *Yacht Rating: 170 Years of Speed, Success and Failure against Competitors – and the Clock.*

[53] B. Heckstall-Smith, *The International Yacht Racing Rules: The Helmsman's Handbook*, 1908, p. 8.

With such dominance, it is not surprising that for the first years, the IYRU was not much more than 'a file in a cabinet in the YRA office'; and the organisation was not very active till after the War.[54]

Whatever type of large boat racing the prospective owner wanted to engage in, he would invariably seek out one of four designers and builders – Watson and Fife on the Clyde;[55] Charles E. Nicholson of Camper and Nicholson at Gosport; and Mylne, initially an assistant of Watson, who set up his own yard on the Isle of Bute in 1896, and who built mainly smaller racing craft.[56]

If you went to the Clyde to get your boat designed and built, you went to North Essex for your skipper and crew – most notably Wivenhoe, but also Rowhedge, and Brightlingsea on the Colne, and Tollesbury on the Blackwater. The pattern was for the racing crews to fish in the winter, on the North Sea smacks, and crew the yachts in the summer.[57] The beginning of the connection between these Essex fishermen and yachting was through the Royal Thames, whose yachts raced the East Coast. By the mid-century, a number of their racers had men from these Essex villages aboard as crew. Later, they received a further boost as the boom in Scottish yacht racing demanded more good crewmen than could be found locally, so 'soft spoken' Essex men were signed on and yachting correspondents wrote of the Clyde racers being 'manned by smart and powerful English crews'.[58] The crew were poorly paid, their motivation improved by the fact that most owners shared out a proportion of the substantial prize money for finishing in the first three places among the crew. More was paid to the skilled, but dangerous, positions of bowsprit-end man, at the end of bowsprit some forty feet from the stem of the boat; and most dangerous, the masthead man (two on a large yacht), up to 180 feet above the water.

---

[54] Johnson, *Yacht Rating*, p. 79.

[55] 'He': Leather states that only two women ever ordered large yachts: Mrs Turner-Farley and Mrs Workman (*The Northseamen*, p. 159).

[56] Black, *G. L. Watson*; Franco Pace, *William Fife: Master of the Classic Yacht*; May Fife McCallum, *Fast and Bonnie: A History of William Fife and Son Yachtbuilders*; Ian Nicolson with David Gray, *Alfred Mylne: The Leading Yacht Designer 1896–1920*; John Nicholson, *Great Years in Yachting*, about his father, Charles Nicholson and his boatyard, Camper and Nicholson, which built *Shamrock IV* and *Shamrock V*, Lipton's America's Cup contenders in 1920 and 1930.

[57] The exception being crew from Largs who weaved (Leather, *The Northseamen*, p. 113).

[58] Leather, *The Northseamen*, pp. 97–99 and 114. Lord Brassey, a qualified master mariner, recruited Essex men for his yachts, 'as so many crews for yachts still are. It is the general experience of my yachting brethren that have seldom cause to complain of the men of Essex. They know their work and they do it'. When Lord Brassey circumnavigated in *Sunbeam*, his Captain, Isiah Powell, came from Rowhedge and he shipped 14 of his neighbours in a crew of 29 (Leather, *The Northseamen*, p. 193).

Outstanding skippers included Edward Sycamore (1854–1930) and Lemon Cranfield (1841–1912), one of five racing brothers, the others being William, Richard, John and George (skippers and crews frequently came from the same family).[59] Both Sycamore and Lemon Cranfield were Rowhedge men. The career ladder was to show sailing prowess as a member of the fishing fleet, since the first boat back got the best price for their catch. Then, the proving ground for yacht racing was to skipper in the 10 ton class, around 40 feet long, with two crew; and, with prowess demonstrated, to move on to skippering much larger craft.

When four 'Big Class' cutters were built in 1893, 'the command of all four of these big class racers was offered to racing skippers from Rowhedge, such was then the fame of the Essex village of only 1,000 inhabitants' (Thomas Jay, *Satanita*; William Cranfield *Valkyrie II*; John Carter was offered command of both *Calluna* and *Britannia* and chose *Britannia*, so Archie Hogarth from Port Ballantyne on the Clyde, sailed *Calluna*).[60] The crack skippers were well paid. They were much sought after, so would move upwards, changing if an owner sought them out and it looked like he had built a fast boat – or was having one built – and resigning if their judgement was crossed. They were the stars of their sport, akin to Formula One drivers today.[61] If a skipper made enough money to buy a new house or fishing boat, it was named after the yacht whose winnings had paid for it.[62]

In winter, the large yachts would come up the river on the equinoctial September tides, be laid up in the Tollesbury yards or on the mud, for safe keeping and to be worked on. The spars were removed into sheds and covered to maintain their varnish. The regattas were held then so that these skilled crews could participate and there would be a laying up supper. However, only the skipper was retained across the year, and perhaps the first mate to keep an eye on the boat. All the other crew, however skilled, had to go back to the fishing.

There were equivalent communities on the Clyde at Largs, Gourock and Port Bannatyne, and on the Solent, at Gosport, Hythe, Cowes and, best

---

[59] Leather, *The Northseamen*, pp. 85–251, and *The Salty Shore*, pp. 106–132.

[60] Leather, *The Northseamen*, p. 140.

[61] So, gossipy stories were told about them, as befits stars: 'In one of the early races [of 1893] the *Britannia* put the *Valkyrie II* about when she was on the starboard tack [i.e *Valkyrie II* had the right of way]. Lord Dunraven angrily asked Captain Cranfied his opinion. "Well, sir", replied the skipper, "I'm sorry for that. I'm afraid I can't ask the Prince [of Wales] to tea next time he comes to our village."' (Leather, *The Northseamen*, p. 208).

[62] Leather regrets that many of the house names in these villages have been changed by racing-ignorant incomers.

known, Itchen Ferry, on the eastern side of the river Itchen.[63] In that village, there were many households of racing professionals, of which the Diapers were the best known.[64]

The Growth of Keel Boat Racing

Hal Sisk has suggested that the growth in the popularity of yachting during the late Victorian period was not so much due to the uptake in yacht cruising.[65] Rather, it was due to the development of small yacht racing, both keel-boat and dinghy. He argues that you could crew on a racing yacht without cost. Also, until the end of the century, there was little leisure time, except for a privileged minority, to enjoy leisurely cruising holidays. One-design boats, which I discuss later in this chapter, would have further aided racing, since they significantly reduced the cost of owning a small racing boat.

In this interpretation, the iconic texts, which unite the yachting fraternity, are the annotated logs of innovative cruising yachtsmen, which the yacht racing community has to share, not having an equivalent shelf of books concerning yacht races.[66] He could well be partially right, in that there was active growth in both types of yachting, but considerable variation as to the take-up of each type, depending on locality. For example, in Dublin Bay, the very active Royal Alfred Yacht Club was dedicated to yacht racing, rather than yacht cruising.[67]

Independent of locality, there was another reason for the popularity of smaller boat racing: the expense of large boat racing. The YRA rules did not stop large yachts being structurally unsound ('plank on edge') or becoming ever narrower, carrying more and more lead in the keel allowing large amounts of sail. (The extreme of this trend was *Oona*, with a beam of only 5 feet 6 inches on a 33 feet 10 inch waterline, with a lead keel of 9.6 tons,

---

[63] Leather, *The Northseamen*, p. 102. Itchen Ferry no longer exists, having been bombed in Second World War.

[64] *Tom Diaper's Log* is, I think, unique in giving an Edwardian racing skipper's account of events. Written long after the actual happenings, he still grieved the loss of the 1920 challenge due to 'too many amateur sailing masters … The *Shamrock* lost the cup when she should have won it' (p. 123).

[65] Sisk, *Dublin Bay: The Cradle of Yacht Racing*; also personal communication 1 April, 2014.

[66] Yacht racing books tend to have their gravitas weakened by being coffee table size and laden with photographs, implying that the reader is nigh on illiterate.

[67] O'Sullivan, in *Dublin Bay: A Century of Sailing*, p. 74: 'In many respects Dublin Bay is perfect for racing and since we lack the inviting cruising grounds on our doorstep which Cork and Belfast yachtsmen enjoy, it is perhaps inevitable that the emphasis in Dublin is so much on day racing'.

setting 2,000 square foot of canvas. She was lost with all hands, sailing from Southampton to the Clyde, in a heavy gale off Malahide, in 1886.)[68] This trend towards ever longer and thinner yachts meant that a yacht could be hopelessly outclassed within a year, and owners either turned to steam yachts or to small racing classes. As an editorial in *Yachting World*, 21 September, 1894, recognised, racing yachts were so 'stripped down' that they were no use as cruising boats, so once they became non-competitive, they were near worthless; as a result 'racing is becoming confined to small boats, while in the larger classes, competition is lessening'.[69]

'Thalassa' (Col. John Townsend, R. E., of the Royal Victoria YC, IOW), in his chapter on 'Small Boat Racing in the Solent' in the Badminton volumes on *Yachting*, states that the pioneers of small boat racing on the Solent were the Royal Southampton (recommended for comfort and 'a fair cuisine') and the Portsmouth Corinthian in the 1880s; joined in the 1890s by the Royal Victoria ('the Red Squadron', at Ryde, IOW) and the Royal London.[70] His chapter is divided into 'rating' classes, the significance being that one-design classes had not 'arrived' by the time he wrote his chapter in 1894.[71]

The small boat classes were of two types: keelboat and dinghy.[72]

> The key criteria separating keelboats and dinghies from yachts are:
> a. *A dinghy or keelboat does not have accommodation.* It might be covered for part of its deck, but if you wanted to sleep on it, you'd have to sleep under the sky on the boards, perhaps with a tent strung along the boom.
> b. *A yacht should be capable of being lived on for a number of days*
> c. *A yacht should be able to withstand heavy weather at sea.* A dinghy or keelboat would be raced on a lake or river or inshore, so did not require the same solidity of build.

The difference between a dinghy and a keelboat is more self-evident. *A dinghy does not have a fixed keel*, but a lifting keel or centre board or centreplate. If it has *a fixed keel*, it is referred to as a *keelboat* (or sometimes, less exactly, as a *dayboat*), and most of the prestigious fleets raced in the Solent were keelboats, not dinghies. *Keelboats* had an iron or lead keel attached to their hull.

---

[68] Leather, *The Northseamen*, p. 120.

[69] Quoted by Johnson, *Yacht Rating*, p. 53.

[70] 'Thalassa', 'Small Boat Sailing on the Solent', pp. 224–226. 'Thalassa' means 'sea' in Greek. Thalassa's identity: Black, *G. L. Watson*, p. 432, n. 4. The 'red' Royal Victoria: it was unusual in having a defaced red, rather than blue, ensign.

[71] There seems to have been a ten-year delay on publishing these volumes. The Dedication to the Prince of Wales is dated May, 1885.

[72] Dear states that 'the word dinghy derives from the Hindi for a small open riverboat' ('Leisure Sailing in the Twentieth Century', p. 138).

The effect of a keel was that they were (and still are) heavy and cumbersome to get in or out of the water, so a hoist or a crane was needed. As a result, they had to be moored in sufficiently deep water.

One-Design Racing

A further refinement was *one-design* racing, defined by Folkard in his *The Sailing Yacht*, published in 1906:

> By a 'One Class One-Design' is meant a Class of sailing boats or small Yachts all of the same size and design: a form of boat chosen and adopted by the Club which institutes the Class, the object being that one and all competitors in the sailing matches of the Class, shall meet on fair and equitable terms.[73]

One-designs took off after 1890s. There were major benefits of a one-design class. Once sufficient members had agreed to purchase these vessels, they could negotiate reductions in build cost, by placing an order for a number of identical boats. They could then get a fleet together that avoided the arguments inevitable with handicapping. It also avoided the vagaries of rule changes by the YRA, as a one-design class, once adopted, was practically immune to changes in the rating rules.

Dixon Kemp neatly specifies the benefits of one-design when complimenting the original one-design, the Water Wags of Dublin Bay:

> This class is the germ of the One Model Club and has well carried out its initial objects viz.: restriction on an advantage of a long purse; preservation of selling value of the boat and the combination of a serviceable and a racing boat.[74]

Another benefit was that the club could specify a boat design that best suited their local conditions. So, Broad One-Designs, 'brown boats', sailed out of Lowestoft, with its sandbanks and breaking waves, and needed a long keel. Inland on the Broads, were 'the white boats' (the Yare and Bure OD), whose keels were shorter and which could carry more sail. Some boats needed to traverse a bar (for example, at Bembridge) whilst others had ready access to deep water (e.g. at Howth). So, there is wide variation between one-designs. A final benefit was that the successful adoption of a one-design class created a group of members committed to racing together, and using the club's facilities frequently and regularly.

---

[73] Quoted in Jack Coote, *Classic One-Designs*, p. 6.
[74] Delaney and Delany, *The Water Wags*, p. 32.

There was variability about how specific the building and rigging require-ments of a one-design class should be. Some one-design classes have very strict rules. The X One-Design was launched 1911 and today has one of the largest one-design fleets, with at least 70 boats, each with three crew, regu-larly at Cowes week:

> Besides strict measurement rules, the planking must be either pine or mahogany, and each boat must contain 13 or 14 planks. Each piece of timber must have 10 copper nails in it, keels must be cast iron with English elm or mahogany and masts must be fir or spruce.

> These tight and intolerant regulations ensure it makes no difference whether a boat is 25, 50 or 100 years old ... In 2010, the first two boats were built in the 1920s.[75]

Obviously, as one of the leading figures in contemporary yachting, Brooke Heckstall-Smith, wrote in 1912: 'If all yacht racing had been carried on between one-design classes, improvement in design would have come to a standstill'.[76] However, this comment is less true if the dinghy belongs to a 'restricted' class, a rather confusing term, which allows some changes within a specified range.[77] Even looser criteria are used with a dinghy in a 'develop-ment class', namely:

> A racing class in which certain measurements are limited such as maximum sail area, overall length or minimum weight, but others are left free for the individual designer to develop as he pleases – hull shapes, sail plans etc, but the boats race against each other without handicap. Some development classes are the International 14 and Moth, Merlin-Rocket, National 12.[78]

Some of the more conservative senior clubs refused to organise small boat racing. At Bridlington, the Royal Yorkshire, one of the early yacht clubs, mimicking the RYS' entry requirement of 30 tons, required their would-be members to own boats of at least 20 tons. The Pirate Yacht Club broke away in 1897 and ordered eight identical 25 ft. 6 in. keelboats from Field & Co. of Itchen Ferry, Southampton. These were the Yorkshire One-Designs.[79] The development of dinghy racing brought back racing to the Thames, with the

---

[75] Andrew Brook, 'X Hits the Spot', p. 62.

[76] Brooke Heckstall-Smith, *The Complete Yachtsman*, 1912; quoted without page number by Jack Coote, *Classic One-Designs*, p. 8.

[77] 'Restricted' because the specifications would give the lower and the higher range of a particu-lar measurement, i.e build must be within this restricted range.

[78] Schult, *The Sailing Dictionary*, p. 73.

[79] Coote, *Classic One-Designs*, p. 16.

Ranelagh Sailing Club and the London Corinthian Sailing Club, both established on the Hammersmith bank in 1889 and 1894, respectively.

The table indicates the keelboats that were created before the First World War and shows their widespread distribution across yacht clubs and areas of the country.[80]

One-design Keelboats Launched before 1914				
Type	Designer	Length	Year of Launch	Area of activity/ Yacht Club
Howth 17s	W. H. Boyd	17 ft	1895	Howth Sailing Club, nr Dublin
Solent One-Design	H. W. White	33 ft 3 in	1895/6	Solent Sailing Club
Bembridge Redwing	Charles E. Nicholson	22 ft	1896	Royal Victoria YC, Ryde; Bembridge Sailing Club
Yorkshire One-Design	J.S.Helyer	25 ft 6 in	1898	Pirate Yacht Club, Bridlington
Broads One-Design('Brown Boats')	Linton Hope	24 ft	1900	Royal Norfolk and Suffolk YC, Lowestoft
Fairy One-Design	Linton Hope	22ft 6 inches	1901	Belfast Lough; Lough Erne
Waverley One-Design	John Wylie	18 ft	1904	County Antrim Yacht Club, Whitehead, Belfast Lough
Yare and Bure One-Design ('White Boats')	Ernest Woods	20 ft	1908	Yare and Bure Sailing Club, Wroxham Broad
X Class One-Design	Alfred Westmacott	20 ft 3/8 in	1909	Motor Yacht Club, Netley*

*Now the Royal Motor Yacht Club, based in Poole Harbour.

The advent of small boat racing created a large number of designers and builders (often the same person). Leading designers of small boats, not necessarily racers, but racer-cruisers, or cruisers, included Linton Hope (1863–1920), Gilbert Umfreville Law (1870–1918), Albert R. Luke (1875–1930s),

[80] Source: Jack Coote, *Classic One-Designs*; Bird. *Classic Classes*. Since, as ever in yachting, primacy is highly valued, aficionados of a particular one-design will argue over dates of commissioning the design, the first completed build, the date of its launch and the first race in the class etc. to provide the most advantageous date.

Alfred Mylne (1872–1951), Arthur E. Payne (1858–1903), Charles Sibbick (1849–1912), and A. Westmacott (1868–1935). An esteemed builder of small sea-going yachts was Albert Strange (1955–1917), whose specialty was canoe yawls.[81]

Today, we know of one-designs that have celebrated their centenary, but the Victorian idea was that a club would change its fleet every decade or so. These small racing craft were built on the assumption that new designs would be developed to take advantage of advances in technology. So, they were built on the assumption that, before too long, they would be replaced, which helped keep costs down. Another reason for replacement was if one skipper kept winning

An early one-design, the Clyde 17/19 (17 feet waterline; 19 feet length, sail area not exceeding 530 square feet), sailing in the 1888 season if not before, demonstrated these features. It was developed by the Royal Western, Scotland. Unfortunately, *Hatasoo*, sailed by 'Duke' John H. Downes, won 100 prizes from 113 starts over four seasons. In addition, the boats were very wet and potentially dangerous. So the club replaced the 17/19 with the Clyde 19/24 in 1896.[82]

Whatever the pros or cons of one-design, their arrival shaped yacht and dinghy racing permanently. The advantages of doing away with handicapping, and the ill-feeling and continual arguments that go with it, were overwhelming. From here on in, yacht clubs had to work out what type of one-design their members wanted to sail, and try and create a decent sized fleet. They also had to keep a weather eye open for developments, so that they were not left with an unfashionable class, while a nearby yacht club benefited from a quicker change to a new class.[83]

They might also change their class to differentiate themselves from other local clubs. So, the Essex Yacht Club, Leigh-on-Sea, and the Alexandra, Southend, both developed fleets of Thames Estuary One-Designs, designed by Morgan Giles, before the First World War, but after it, the Essex, perhaps to distinguish itself from its lower class neighbour, the Leigh-on-Sea Sailing Club, ordered the rather similar, but somewhat faster, Essex One-Design, again from Morgan Giles.[84]

---

[81] John Leather, *Albert Strange*.

[82] http://scottishboating.blogspot.co.uk/2010/12/clyde-1719-foot-class, accessed 11 April, 2016.

[83] Graham Tracey, in *East Cowes Sailing Club 1912–2012*, p. 269, provides a useful chronology of adoption and then dropping of One-Design classes at that club.

[84] The Essex provided the navigator, its vice-commodore, Claude Hickman, and the helm, W. P. Burton, for Lipton's 1920 America's Cup Challenge in *Shamrock IV*. (Stuart Readman, *Four*

However, the price of a small yacht, be it for racing or cruising, was still considerable. Cusack comments: "'Thalassa' suggested in 1894 that a 'second hand 1-rater' [one of the smallest classes] would cost £50–80, and new £100–150. It should be noted that the cost of £100–150 for a new boat in 1894 has been calculated as equivalent to a 1995 expenditure of £24,000–36,000".[85]

There were additional requirements. A keelboat was cumbersome to winch in and out of the water after every race and needed a space-consuming cradle to lie in. So it needed to be moored in deep water, which was near the club or slip; and the racing area needed to be nearby, so could not be too busy with yacht or commercial movements.

With these limitations of cost and space, the dinghy, which could easily be stored ashore, was going to be by far the more popular choice, and its development is discussed in the next chapter.

Yachting Centres

The Crouch

The Solent saw a rapid growth in yachting activity in the last quarter of the century, and not just in Cowes, but also in Yarmouth, Isle of Wight, Southampton and Lymington. Cowes Week was the major yacht *regatta* of the season, but the most important *centres* for the racing yachtsmen were the Crouch in Essex and the Clyde.

The dispersion of city dwelling yachtsmen from London was accelerated by the state of the Thames, effectively London's sewer. The Royal Temple was founded in 1857, when lawyers from the Temple Chambers kept their boats at the nearby Temple Steps. The state of the Thames meant that their races were held at Gravesend and, by 1896, they had moved to their present location at Ramsgate, Kent.[86]

On the East coast, Burnham-on-Crouch, despite having marshes to the east and extensive sandbanks to the west, became a major yachting centre in a short space of time. The arrival of the railway from Wickford to Southminster, through Burnham, in 1889, underpinned this rapid growth.

Ships: One Hundred Years of the Essex Yacht Club, pp. 35–36 and p. 50; Graham Dent, *Not Quite at Sea*, pp. 28 ff.)

[85] Cusack, 'The Rise of Aquatic Recreation and Sport', p. 254. 'One-rater' refers to the Rating Rule of 1886 (Rating = Length x Sail Area/6000). A ½ rater would have a waterline length of 15 feet and a sail area of 200 square feet. A 1-rater would be about 20 foot long (Johnson, *Yacht Rating*, pp. 43–45).

[86] Johnson, *Yacht Clubs of the World*, p. 136.

The (Royal) Corinthian, created in 1872, found that the increasing traffic on the Thames at Erith required it to relocate. Remarkably, in 1892, it created not one, but two new clubhouses, one at Port Victoria, on the Isle of Grain, Kent, which was never very popular, and the other at Burnham-on-Crouch, a room at the 'White Harte', in 1892. (The Port Victoria clubhouse was taken over by the military in the First World War and the club never went back.)[87]

The London Sailing Club established a branch in the town in 1893, and was initially responsible for Burnham Regatta.[88]

The Burnham Yacht Club ('Royal' from 1927) was founded in 1895, with '51 members, forty of them London residents, including 18 gentlemen, 7 stockbrokers, 2 barristers, 2 solicitors, one medical doctor and 45 oyster merchants'. By 1900, it had 125 members and by 1910, 217 members 'after which the club could not really cope with further growth'.[89]

The North Fambridge Yacht Club, a few miles further up the Crouch, was founded in 1898, a key figure being Francis B Cooke. In his pilot guide, *London to Lowestoft: A Cruising Guide to the East Coast*, published in 1906, Cooke proudly asserts the Corinthian pedigree of the club, 'the members of which make a practice of fitting out their own craft … There is not a single paid hand employed in the whole fleet'.[90]

He was also pleased how popular yachting had become on the Crouch:

> As we approach the anchorage at Burnham we realize that it will be no easy matter to find a berth, for there is a huge fleet of yachts brought off the town. There is apparently no fairway kept … It is certainly a unique sight, as for a mile abreast in the town and from bank to bank, vessels of all sizes are moored in close company.

Clearly, such a density of yachts was unusual. Nor does it seem to have been much better further up the river, for *Yachting Weekly*, reporting the Crouch YC's first annual dinner in 1907, 'opined: 'The anchorage at both Burnham and Fambridge is already unduly crowded'.[91]

---

[87] http://royal Corinthian.co.uk/history, accessed 8 February, 2016.

[88] The London Yacht Club changed its name to the Eastern Yacht Club of England in 1907 and amalgamated with the (Royal) Corinthian in 1911, when the Corinthian joined them in their clubhouse (Wise, *A Century of Sailing*, p. 8).

[89] Lowerson, *Sport and the English Middle Classes*, p. 51. Clearly, the advent of the railway to North Essex was the key event, as the West Mersea Yacht Club was founded in 1898 and the Blackwater Sailing Club at Heybridge in 1899.

[90] Quoted by Wise, *A Century of Sailing*, p. 15.

[91] Both quotes from Wise, *A Century of Sailing*, pp. 19 and 16 respectively. The Crouch Yacht Club became the leading light in East Anglian offshore racing in the North Sea. See Wise, *50 Years of East Anglian Offshore Racing*.

Burnham Week, at the end of August, was the major East coast gathering of racing sailors. The organisers, from early on, were smart enough to welcome small boat racing, thus attracting members of both yacht and sailing clubs. For many, it was an annual 'pilgrimage', with which to end the season.[92]

The Clyde

Yachting on the East Coast of Scotland was centred on the port of Granton, east of Leith. Granton Yacht Club was founded in 1868 and became the Forth Yacht Club in 1872 ('Royal' in 1883). The Forth Corinthian Yacht Club was founded in 1880, also based at Granton, while the Almond Yacht Club was founded at Cramond in 1897, but moved a year later to Granton. Forth Week regatta started in 1908.[93]

The Firth of Forth was never part of the racing circuit, as it was a long way from any other yachting centres. It was on the West coast of Scotland that the great blossoming of Scottish yachting took place.[94]

Excepting Charles Nicholson in Gosport, the leading yacht designers were all on the Clyde. Fife and Watson were the acknowledged leaders, but with quite different backgrounds. The Fifes were a long established yard, whose ancestry came from a blacksmith, and their brilliance resulted from their ability to envisage the lines of a good fishing boat or yacht. Fife built *Shamrock I* and *III*, America Cup contenders in 1899 and 1903.

In contrast, George Watson was the son and grandson of a medical practitioner, and much more versed in scientific ideas, such as the use of testing tanks to compare hull speed.[95] Watson drew on the scientific experiments of William Rankine (1820–1872), professor of Civil Engineering and Mechanics at Glasgow University from 1855 to 1872, and the hydrodynamic research of William Froude and John Inglis.

We can give the date when Clyde yachtsmen knew that Watson was going to be a key figure in yacht design. A member of the Royal Alfred, W. M. Colhoun ordered the design of a 5-tonner, *Clotilde*, from him, when he was just starting out on his career. At the Clyde Regatta of July 1875, she beat *Pearl*, the crack boat of the previous two seasons, built by William Fife. She did not just win. In the first two races of three, her superiority was so crushing that

---

[92] Dartmouth Regatta, on a smaller scale, performed the same function of closing the season on the south coast.

[93] Further up the coast, the Royal Tay Yacht Club, Dundee, was founded in 1885.

[94] 'Edinburgh' and 'The Firth of Forth' do not feature in the indexes of McCallum's biography of Fife or Black's of Watson.

[95] Although he was a yacht designer, he also took commissions to supervise the building of his designs, using a small number of trusted Clyde boatyards (Black, *G. L. Watson*).

11 William Fife Sr.'s brother, Allan (right), waits for the tide to float off the 40-tonner *Sleuthhound* (1881). The cutter *Sleuthhound* was built for the Marquis of Ailsa. The Clyde was the most important location of Victorian yacht racing (Cowes was its social centre). The first major yard was Fifes at Fairlie, Argyllshire. After 1873, when George Watson set up shop as a yacht designer, the Clyde's eminence in yacht design and building was unchallenged.

Pearl was withdrawn from the third race to prevent further embarrassment.[96] Watson was on his way.

He designed *Thistle*, America's Cup contender in 1887; *Valkyrie II*, contender in 1893 and *Valkyrie III*, contender in 1897 for the Earl of Dunraven, and *Shamrock II*, Lipton's contender in 1901; *Britannia* for the Prince of Wales in 1893; and *Meteor II* for the Kaiser in 1896.

---

[96] Black, *G. L. Watson*, pp. 56 and 75.

The competition between Fife and Watson was amicable. Each designer kept an eye on the successful yachts from the other, so that they could offer the ambitious yacht owner a faster yacht, when he came back, as he was bound to do every few years.

Glasgow was, by far, the largest shipbuilding centre in the world, and yacht building developed as a specialised part of the industry in a number of yards; but it was in threadmaking that Glasgow had an even greater world share, thanks to the Clarks and the Coats. The rivalry between these two families provided a real stimulus to yachting. Both these families contained many dedicated yachtsmen, and there was keen competition between the two industrial clans, a competition that was keenly appreciated:

> ... dense crowd had stood at this [Bogany Point] and other viewing points on the Clyde and formed partisan loyalties to boats owned by Scotland's industrial plutocracy. Paisley's two formidable business dynasties, Clark and Coats, owned about 80% of the world's thread-making capacity, and when in 1885 they took their rivalry to sea in a yacht race that led them 60 miles around Ailsa Craig, two packed excursion steamers followed the race all the way even though the weather was bad enough to strand John Clark's boat on a reef.

> By 1897, Clyde regattas were covered by no fewer than nine yachting corre-spondents and several specialist photographers.[97]

The large amount of shipbuilding on the Clyde created a workforce that could appreciate the massively complicated machinery being manipulated with supreme confidence, daring and intuition. How profitable a good, topical picture postcard of Clyde racing was is shown by the fact that the Southsea professional photographer, George West, came up from Southsea annually for the Clyde Week.

Clyde Week, started in 1878, was the unifying of the regattas of the Royal Northern, the Royal Clyde, the Royal Western, the Royal Largs, Clyde Corinthian and the Mudhook Yacht Clubs. Key to its success was that the clubs accepted the YRA time allowances (handicap system), so that yachts, whatever their club or home port, were racing under the same conditions.[98] In 1891, this was extended to become the Clyde Fortnight, organised by the

---

[97] Ian Jack, *The Guardian*, 6 July, 2013, p. 41. Bogany Point is the headland of Rothesay, Isle of Bute. McCallum recounts that 'at one regatta after the First World War, no fewer than 20 boats, racing yachts or supporting steam yachts were flying either the Coat's or the Clark's house flags' (*Fast and Bonnie*, p. 144).

[98] McCallum, *Fast and Bonnie*, pp. 33–34.

Clyde Yacht Clubs' Conference. In providing eight days of racing, 'the organisers aimed to make it clear that the centre of gravity for racing in Britain was the Clyde rather than the Solent, with its traditional Cowes week'.[99] The Fortnight overlapped with Glasgow Fair Week, when the factories and shipyards were closed and families traditionally 'went doon the watter' i.e. along the coast or on a steamship, increasing the crowds who came to watch.

That the Conference carried clout cannot be doubted. In 1891, the YRA's measurer was resident in Edinburgh, so they wrote to the secretary, the eminent Dixon Kemp, expressing their concern. This resulted in a measurer being based on the Clyde and in 1900, the appointment of an official handicapper.[100] In 1894, the Clyde Clubs' representative, a Mr Hilliard, was instructed to inform the YRA meeting in London that the Clubs were entitled to 'the period from 29th June to 15th July inclusive' and carried the point![101] In 1900, the Royal Clyde wrote to the German Emperor, pointing out that the date he had fixed for the Kiel Regatta clashed with the Clyde fortnight.

Black states that 'The numbers of small raters on the Clyde (and on the Solent) reached record levels in 1893, spurred on no doubt by all the additional publicity in the press'.[102] The press was keeping its readers informed about the four First Class cutters being built. Mr A. D. Clarke had placed an order with Southampton based Fay & Co for *Satanita*. The other three were being built on the Clyde. D. & W. Henderson's Glasgow yard was building *Britannia*, for the Prince of Wales, and *Valkyrie II*, the American Cup Challenger, for the Earl of Dunraven. The Fife-designed *Calluna* was being built at J. and A. Inglis for a syndicate headed by Peter Donaldson.[103]

These were indeed 'big boats'. *Britannia* was 121 feet long, with a 175 foot mast, and *Valkyrie II*, 86 feet, and *Calluna*, 106 feet on the waterline. The size of these vessels and the need for crew are shown by the fact that: 'All handling and sheeting of sails was carried out by hand, winches were unheard of, and a 400 foot mainsheet took some overhauling and a 1 ½ ton mainsail some hoisting!'[104]

The next year, having beaten *Valkyrie* in the America's Cup of 1893, *Vigilant* sailed from America in time for Clyde Week, again emphasising its importance.

[99] Black, *G. L. Watson*, p. 169.
[100] http://www.Clydecorinthian.org./history
[101] George Blake and Christopher Small, *Cruise in Company*, p. 71.
[102] Black, *G. L. Watson*, p. 199.
[103] Such a large boat could not have been launched in the shallow waters off Fairlie.
[104] Leather *The Northseamen*, p. 232.

She was now about to take on the cream of British yachting. For weeks, the press had been trumpeting what promised to be a titanic struggle.

> Captain Carter, *Britannia's* skipper, remarked afterwards that when *Britannia* had raced against *Navahoe* [a crack American clipper] on the Solent the previous year, the spectating crowd had amounted to only a few hundred, not the tens of thousands that now lined the shores of the Clyde.[105]

These vast crowds, lining both sides of the Clyde, are reminiscent of the huge crowds seen at the start of yacht racing on the Exe and on the Thames towards the end of the eighteenth century, but they were not there just for the sight of clouds of white sails. They were cognoscenti of sailing, even if they themselves did not race, and their need for information was met:

> ... local lads were selling the Racing Programme for the day ... This, price sixpence, was a small masterpiece of the printer's art with, over and above the lists of entrants in the various classes, a tinted chart of the courses and, on the back, a glorious display in colour of the racing flags worn by all the yachts.[106]

I have already discussed the rapid rise of the Royal Clyde, as it took its place alongside the Royal Northern. By 1895, the Royal Clyde claimed to be the largest yacht club in the world, with 1,060 members. 'Very shortly afterwards, it became the largest in tonnage as well.'[107]

The width of the appeal of yachting is shown by a Para Handy story. 'Neil Munro' (Hugh Foulis) published his stories about a 'puffer' (small Clyde trading coaster) and its skipper, Para Handy, in the *Glasgow Evening News*. In 'Among the Yachts', the engineer slows down the puffer, so that they can watch a duel between *Shamrock* and *White Heather*. The tactics are carefully described. *Shamrock* winning would be popular with the readers, as Glasgow was Lipton's home town ('I would like, mysel', to see Sir Thomas Lipton winnin', for it's there I get my tea' says Dougie, the ship's mate).[108]

In the 1908 Olympics, the 12-metre class was held not on the Solent with the other classes, but on the Clyde, starting and finishing at Hunters Quay. There were only two entries – *Mouchette*, designed by Mylne, from the Mersey; and *Hera*, designed by its owner, Thomas Glen-Coats, of the thread manufacturing dynasty, who was able to devote himself full time to yacht

---

[105] Black, *G. L. Watson*, p. 226.
[106] George Blake and Christopher Small, *Cruise in Comfort*, p. 82.
[107] Black, *G. L. Watson*, p. 252 and Appendix E, p. 449.
[108] Neil Munro, *Para Handy Tales*, pp. 249–254. Munro published these 'tales' between 1905 and 1923. He seems to be describing a race during the 1907 Clyde fortnight.

racing, and who was a member of the Royal Clyde. *Hera* won the first two of the three-match competition, so the third race was not run.

A report from *New York Times*, 15 July, 1895, emphasises the international primacy of the Clyde racing scene. The interest of the American reader in British yachting was taken for granted; and it was also assumed that they knew their way round the Firth of Clyde. (Of course, quite a few of their readers may well have been of Scottish extraction, for the Glasgow manufacturers had set up offices and factories in New York, as well as the thousands of immigrants who had been driven out of their homes by the Highland Clearances).[109]

> The Clyde Fortnight entirely eclipses anything in yacht racing in the old world. The Royal Yacht Squadron Week in Cowes is a lame and tame affair alongside the Clyde Fortnight ... No doubt Cowes enjoys the summer smiles of numerous lords during the week, but the 'merchant princes' of Glasgow and Paisley have done more for the sport than all our aristocracy put together. The flotilla anchored in Rothesay Bay tonight is undoubtedly the most impressive ever seen in any yachting anchorage in this country.[110]

One-design classes developed as well. In 1895, the Clyde Sailing Club, Helensburgh, ordered five 18 foot centreboard dinghies from Linton Hope, to start a one-design fleet; and Allan's Club, a private club, ordered eight 1-raters from Sibbick. In 1896, the newly formed Inellan Corinthian Yacht Club, Argyllshire, created a fleet of a class of 17 foot boats, 15 on the waterline, which numbered 26 in 1896. Clearly, one-design sailing was taking root on the Firth.[111]

For the cruising man, the Hebrides provides spectacular cruising grounds, which were suitably challenging for the Corinthian soul. The Crinan Canal from Ardishaig to Crinan had opened in 1809 and after improvements, been travelled by Queen Victoria in 1850, making it both popular and 'royal'. It cut off having to go round the dangerous Mull of Kintyre, so allowing rapid access from the Clyde to the islands. By 1910, the Clyde Cruising Club was issuing Sailing Directions in its yearly journal, so opening up cruising on the West Coast, their 1910 directions, for example, being for the Mull of Kintyre to Ardnamurchan.[112]

---

[109] To make way for sheep, grouse and deer.

[110] Quoted by Black, *G. L. Watson*, p. 257, n. 20.

[111] *Ibid.*, p. 251.

[112] Its directions were considered of such high standard by the Admiralty that, in 1939, it requested the Club to provide it with all unsold copies and ask members to relinquish theirs (Nigel Sharp. *Troubled Waters*, p. 77).

In the years before the Great War, the Firth of Clyde, and the yacht clubs in it, could lay claim to be the leading location of British yachting.

Literature in the Golden Age of Yachting

Literacy only became widespread in England after compulsory education was introduced by the Foster Act of 1870. The Act could not be implemented till the schools required by the Act had been built over the next ten years. In 1903, Albert Mansbridge established 'An Association to Promote the Higher Education of Working Men', later renamed 'The Workers' Educational Association'. Its rapidly expanding number of branches demonstrated the thirst for literacy and literature among the working classes.[113]

A great number of people were engaged in trades relating to the sea. There were 170,000 merchant seaman in 1890 and 209,000 in 1912.[114] The building and repair of ships were major industries, focussed on the Clyde and Belfast, and also in the North-East of England. So, by the end of the century, there was a pool of literate sailors and marine employees, which created a consumer demand for suitable reading material. A maritime author was potentially assured of a large readership which was familiar with matters maritime.

It is therefore not surprising that many of the well-known sailing texts were published during this period. The period produced the only English maritime author whose work has become part of the literary canon. Conrad, a naturalised Pole, set *Heart of Darkness*, 1902, on a yacht, along with two of the three other Marlow tales, namely, *Youth* (1902) and *Chance* (1912).[115]

Three texts in particular – *Three Men in a Boat*, 1889, by Jerome K. Jerome, set on the upper Thames;[116] Joshua Slocum's *Sailing Alone Around the World*, 1900, an account of the first yacht circumnavigation; and Erskine Childers'

---

[113] Within the same philosophy, Ruskin Hall, Oxford University, was founded in 1899 for the education of working men. Mansbridge was also responsible for creating the Seafarers' Education Service, which, from 1919, placed libraries on merchant ships (Woodman, … *Of Daring Temper: A History of the Marine Society*, pp. 92–95).

[114] Madge, *Long Voyage Home*, p. 50. Some 50,000 were Lascars – seamen from the Indian sub-continent.

[115] The fourth, *Lord Jim*, 1900, is told on a hotel veranda in the Far East. See my 'Conrad, the Yarn and the Location of the Marlow Stories'.

[116] Despite being distrusted by reviewers for being seditious and lower class, the book sold in vast quantities. By 1894, it was in its 65th edition (Carolyn Oulton, *Below the Fairy City: A Life of Jerome K Jerome*, p. 75). Arrowsmith, his publisher remarked, 'I can't imagine what becomes of all the copies of that book I issue. I often think the public must eat them'. (Joseph Connolly, *Jerome J. Jerome: A Critical Biography*, p. 76). Concerning its rebellious undertones, see my 'Angry Voices on the River Bank'.

12 Joshua Slocum on *Spray*. Slocum was a beached skipper of commercial sail. His circumnavigation, 1895–1898, in the oyster boat *Spray*, that he had rebuilt, changed the boundaries of what was possible in yachting. This image is remarkable in how Slocum, in his 50s, represents a modern image of masculinity.

celebration of the Corinthian spirit, *The Riddle of the Sands*, 1903 – were megasellers.

Slocum's account of his circumnavigation in a yacht – to be exact, a rebuilt oyster boat, but he saved on harbour dues if he called it a yacht and, of course, accessed a much larger readership – was a paradigm changer, in terms of what could be achieved in a small craft, especially as he was single-handed. The book has been continually in print. Ransome made it the first volume to be published in the canonical Mariners Library.

In 1897, Erskine Childers sailed to the Baltic and the Frisian islands and then put his voyage to good account in his best-selling *The Riddle of the Sands*, 1903. It was not very well reviewed at the time of its publication. The heroine, who Childers, with little experience of the opposite sex, had put in

at the request of the publisher, was particularly criticised as a wooden creation. Yet it became an immediate best seller, going through three editions in
the first year, then a special cheap edition selling several hundred thousand
copies.[117] The yachtsmen heroes save England from invasion, and much of
its charm was that it was, in John Lowerson's apt phrase, an example of 'the
literary model which reinforced the sense of scruffy adventure and a defensive patriotism'.

Discussing these two books, Lowerson wrote 'it was in the wake of such
adventures that London's professionals and literary men took to lone sailing
in virtual droves'.[118] The literary men included Arnold Bennett and Hilaire
Belloc. But sailing's appeal was far wider than just to these groups. Nor was
it limited to rich yachtsmen. Although keel boat racing certainly greatly
reduced costs, it was still an expensive sport. It was the advent of the dinghy
that made yachting much cheaper and available to the less well-off, and the
lightness of its gear meant women started yacht racing in any numbers for
the first time.

---

[117] Leonard Piper, *Dangerous Waters: The Life and Death of Erskine Childers*, p. 72. Drummond, in
The Riddle, points out the quality of the writing about sailing: 'It is difficult to believe that any
writer has better the description of the torture wrought by weather on a small wooden yacht'
(pp. 98–99). The only modern author, in my opinion, who comes close is Frank Mulville,
who sailed old wooden boats, and seem to have rather bad luck in terms of strandings. Try
Terschelling Sands (1968) or *North Star to Southern Cross* (1993) – Mulville was in the merchant
navy as an apprentice, when his ship, the *Celtic Star*, on passage to Argentina, was torpedoed.
He retraces her passage in *Iskra*, an old gaff cutter, He writes well of the groans and creaks
inevitable when sailing wooden boats.

[118] John Lowerson, *Sport and the English Middle Classes 1870–1914*, p. 52. Sadly, both men came
to unhappy ends. Slocum never settled after his circumnavigation, regularly sailing *Spray* to
South America. In November 1909, he left Vineyard Haven, Massachusetts on another voyage
to the South, with *Spray* unprepared and in a very dirty condition. He was never seen again
(Teller, *The Search for Captain Slocum*). Teller ends his analysis with 'Every man tends to get
more or less what he wants. And at that point what was it Slocum wanted? Space, escape, adventure, danger, self-destruction, God, love – they all seem possible' (pp. 232–233). His words
equally apply to Childers, who fought in the First World War as a First Lieutenant of the Royal
Naval Volunteer Reserve and was secretary to the Irish delegation at the Anglo-Irish Treaty
negotiations. The Treaty was passed in 1921, but Childers joined the rebels rejecting the Treaty.
He made a suicidal return to Glendalough, his family home, in government held territory, was
captured and summarily executed in November, 1921 (Leonard Piper, *Dangerous Waters: The
Life and Death of Erskine Childers*).

CHAPTER ELEVEN

The Golden Age of Yachting
1880–1900

PART TWO
Small Boats and Women Sailors

The Golden Age of Yachting was not confined to the rich. There was a much larger group, which took up the new sport of dinghy sailing, among whom were a significant number of women sailors.

Lubbock's Bank Holiday Act, 1870, and the release of Saturday afternoons from work, allowed aquatic leisure activities to spread to the lower middle classes during and after the 1870s; and 'by the turn of the century even the poor came to assume that they had a right to leisure'.[1]

Cruising, in whatever size boat, has always been much more popular than racing. In the *San Francisco Call*, 22 May, 1904, there is an article on 'Ladies of High Station Who Love the Sea'. It starts by telling the reader that good women sailors are far more frequent among 'British sisters' than among American women. Three outstanding helmswomen are mentioned, but over twenty who enjoy cruising (these being high class ladies, they have crew).[2]

Unfortunately for the historian, it is hard to get a handle on yacht cruising. The tens of thousands who packed a hamper and sailed with friends and/or family a couple of miles down the river to their favourite picnic spot are unrecorded, and since they had no reason to join a yacht club, even assuming they would have been acceptable, there is even less record of their existence.[3]

---

[1] Walvin, *Leisure and Society, 1830–1950*, p. 63.

[2] The article mentions how Lady Margaret Crichton-Stuart, daughter of Lord Bute, tired of having her orders disobeyed on her steam yacht, the *Helliwake*. She passed her Board of Trade Master Mariner's certificate, which made disobeying her an act of mutiny. Note the American interest in British yachting.

[3] Ludwig Wittgenstein, in his unpublished study of the Imperial and Royal Yacht Squadron of Austria, expressed this frustration at the lack of data well: 'What you can't say, you can't say and you can't whistle it either'.

To cater for the needs of the cruising man, E. F. Knight, along with Claud Worth and his regular crewman, H. J. Hanson, created the Cruising Association in 1908, to counter the snobbishness and exclusiveness of the Royal Cruising Club. The Association, whose purpose was and is to offer support to the cruising yachtsman created a network of Boatmen, carefully selected and supervised by the Honorary Local Representative, who would go off to meet any incoming vessel flying the Association burgee.[4]

On the Clyde, the Clyde Cruising Club was formed on a November night in 1909, when four young men, standing on the starboard paddle box of the *Duchess of Montrose* heading for Wemyss Bay (on the mainland) from Rothesay (the Isle of Bute, and a major yachting haven) agreed to set up a club for the cruising man.[5] Within the year, the Club's journal was publishing 'Sailing Directions for the West Coast', and, unlike the Cruising Association, it went into racing. The creation of these two clubs for the cruising man at this time suggests a demand from an expanding number of cruising yachts and owners.

The cruising yachtsmen could now record their holiday, thanks to the arrival of the folding camera and roll film. The development of dry gel on paper ('film' replacing glass plates) by the American, George Eastman, allowed a portable camera to replace the bulky plate cameras. As photography became practical on a boat, the Corinthian memorialised his vessel and his ventures with his camera. H. Lewis Jones illustrated his voyages around the Thames Estuary, recorded in his *Swin, Swale and Swatchway*, published in 1892, with pictures from his box camera, 'the very convenient "Eclipse" Hand Camera made by Mr. Shew, of Newman Street, Oxford Street'.[6]

The Rise of the Dinghy and the Sailing Club

The move before the First World War towards greater take-up of sailing by lower income groups happened in two stages. First was the creation of sailing clubs, with mixed racing fleets of small boats; then the creation of single class 'one-design' fleets, i.e. made up of only one named type of dinghy, e.g. Waterwag, Seabird etc.

---

[4] Ian Griffiths, 'Sailing from Scratch', p. 13.
[5] Clyde Cruising Club from its website history, George Blake and Christopher Small, *Cruise in Company*, p. 113, state that six yachtsmen founded the club in the Argyll Arms, a small Rothesay hotel, known locally as the Gluepot.
[6] H. Lewis Jones, *Swin, Swale and Swatchway*, Preface.

In the first stage, after 1875, a number of *sailing* clubs were set up. 'Sailing' in their title indicated they were orientated towards the racing of small boats. A mixed fleet of different types of dinghies took part in races, with some form of handicap system. So, there was a growth of 'mosquito fleets' ('sailboats not exceeding 14 ft') in Dartmouth after 1868. The Torpoint Mosquito Yacht Club on the Tamar, founded in 1891 and still extant, is a reminder of that type of sailing.

By the late 1890s, the Solent had thirteen such clubs.[7] Southend's first yacht club, the Alexandra, was formed in 1873. The arrival of the London, Tilbury and Southend railway at Southend in 1856 transformed the area alongside the north bank of the Thames Estuary, because it encouraged the growth of commuter traffic up to town and the flow of leisure activity seekers from town. The growth of the towns to house the commuters meant that there were now a much larger number of people interested in sailing, living in the area. By 1913, the Southend area had five clubs, two of these in the small fishing town of Leigh-on-Sea.[8] These clubs would be the home of small racers, since the boats would be left on its drying sands, or, if the weather turned nasty, brought ashore to safety.[9]

This expansion of yacht clubs led to many harbour towns having two clubs – the prestigious *yacht* club and the more humble *sailing* club. The sailing clubs were, of course, cheaper to join. In 1905, the subscription for the Royal Torbay was four guineas, half a guinea for the Torbay Sailing Club; for the Royal Dart two guineas, for the Dart Boat Sailing Club, it was five shillings and stayed at that sum from the club's inception for the next 28 years till its demise in 1901.[10] On the east coast, the West Mersea Yacht Club was created in 1899 and the nearby Dabchicks Sailing Club in 1911. The Essex Yacht Club, Leigh-on-Sea dates back to 1890, the Leigh-on-Sea Sailing Club was formed in 1911, having had earlier manifestations dating back to the 1890s.[11]

[7] Lowerson, *Sport and the English Middle Classes 1870–1914*, p. 50.

[8] As well as the Alexandra, Essex Yacht Club, Leigh-on-Sea, 1890; Leigh-on-Sea Sailing Club, formed 1890s, but certainly by 1903; The Thames Estuary Yacht Club is a 1947 amalgamation of the Nore Yacht Club, Westcliff, 1895, which was created from the ashes of an earlier Minima Yacht Club, and the Westcliff Yacht Club, 1900. Incidentally, clubs continued to be created in this area after this period – the Benfleet Yacht Club, 1922, the Island Yacht Club, Canvey Island, 1936, and the Thorpe Bay Yacht Club, 1948.

[9] Lowerson, in *Sport and the English Middle Classes 1870-1914*, pp. 50–51. They would be racing *small dinghies*, as Southend does not have safe deep water moorings, so the craft have to be able to be brought ashore.

[10] Bass, 'The Rise of Recreational Sailing', p. 27, quoting the *Yachtsman*, Vol. 4, p. 209. The same situation applied on Bangor Lough, Ulster.

[11] Stuart Readman, *Four Ships*, p. 12; Graham Dent, *Not Quite at Sea*, p. 28.

Favoured inland locations for aquatic sport were the Broads, where boats could be hired from a number of locations;[12] but there were plenty of local sailors:

> Early in 1876 a meeting was held at Thompson's Boathouse in King Street, Norwich. As a result the Yare Sailing Club was formed, intended to cater for the more amateur sailors on the Broads, who sailed their own boats without the benefit of paid hands and some of whom were ordinary working men. Membership was set at five shillings, considerably less than the guinea demanded by the Norfolk and Suffolk Yacht Club, which aimed at the wealthier members of society. The newly formed club prospered and by 1897 it was claiming to be the largest sailing club in the world, with nearly 600 members.[13]

Sailing (dinghy) clubs had been started on inland waters, such as canal basins and reservoirs created by the construction of the canals in the Midlands.[14] The Midland Sailing Club was formed in 1893 at Edgbaston reservoir in the centre of Birmingham. The Barnt Green Fishing (and Sailing) Club on Barnt Green Waters, on the outskirts of Birmingham, was formed in 1911, among many.[15] The non-tidal Thames became a favourite weekend haunt for sculls, canoes and trips on motor launches.[16] The Thames Sailing Club was started up in Surbiton in 1870, and held its first regatta in 1871, attended by fifty-seven boats, indicating the considerable interest in dinghy sailing on the upper Thames. Chaplin lists the surge in Thames sailing clubs: the Thames Valley Sailing Club, founded at Hampton in 1876; the Upper Thames Sailing Club at Bourne End, with sailing matches by 1887; and the Thames United Sailing

---

[12] G. Christopher Davies, 'Sailing on the Norfolk Broads' in the Badminton Library; also his *Norfolk Broads and Rivers*, 1883; Ernest Richard Suffling, *How to Organize a Cruise on the Broads*, 1891. See also Henry Doughty, *Summer in Broadland*, 1899. Davies, the key figure in the popularising of the Broads, was 'a Norwich solicitor ... Clerk to Norfolk County Council and acknowledged as the first of the Broads photographers' (Campbell, *Royal Norfolk and Suffolk Yacht Club*, p. 61).

[13] www.Yaresailingclub.org.uk, accessed 7/4/2015. There is no contradiction between the Yare claiming to be the largest *sailing* club in the world around 1900, and the Royal Clyde claiming to be the largest *yacht* club in the world at that time.

[14] D. D. Gladwin, *Victorian and Edwardian Canals from Old Photographs*.

[15] Bernard T. Lee, *The History of Barnt Green Sailing Club 1918–1990*. (Thanks to ex-member, Mike Merritt for giving me a copy.) It is difficult to research dinghy clubs, since there are few histories of dinghy clubs, and their websites often omit any history.

[16] Peter H. Chaplin, *The Thames from Source to Tideway*; Bolland, *Victorians on the Thames*. According to R. T. Rivington's *Punting: Its History and Techniques*, p. 45, over 1,000 boats and 70 launches passed through Boulter's Lock on the first Sunday in August, 1880. These would predominantly have been day or weekend trippers, since the holiday of a week's length for all workers was not achieved till the 1938 Holidays with Pay Act.

Club at Egham, which is now the Laleham Sailing Club. 'Other clubs of similar vintage were the Tamesis Club and the Oxford University Sailing Club.
1896 saw the birth of the Henley Sailing Club'.[17]

One-Design Dinghies

To recap, the dinghy has no fixed keel but has a centreboard, which is lowered
to create a keel as required (when heading into the wind), and raised when
on a run (with the wind behind). The lifting centreboard was no recent innovation. Heaton found that the Royal Welsh had banned their use for racing
in 1863.[18] Because the centreboard comes up inside the dinghy, this allows
the dinghy to be dragged up a beach, saving on more expensive deep water
moorings, and on which the dinghy might get damaged in adverse weather.
So, for example, in designing the Water Wag, the brief specified that the
vessel had to be capable of being dragged up the pebble beach at Shankill
Beach near Dun Laoghaire.[19]

Moving onto the second stage – the arrival of the one-design dinghy, the
first race for 'dinghies' at Dartmouth was in 1890, and by 1894 there may well
have been a one-design dinghy, for it was recorded that there were four starters, 'built to a standard design for the new Dart Boat Sailing Club by W. J.
Hodge'.[20]

The table below lists some of the major 'one-design' dinghy classes that
were created before the Second World War.[21]

These boats are smaller than the keel boats, and, of course, without a
metal keel, cheaper. There is a cluster of one-designs around Lancashire harbours, in contrast to the keelboats being more often created by Southern and
Eastern yacht clubs. The creation of Marine Lakes at Southport in 1887 and
West Kirby in 1901 may be relevant to this local interest.

One-design helped encourage interclub competition, as all owners of a
particular class could compete at an agreed venue. Quite often, a regional
circuit was built up, so that various venues were used across the season.
Dinghies were transportable by horse wagon and train to other harbours and
launching points. Because dinghies had no inconvenient keels, and as long
as their length was less than fourteen feet, they could be transported in the

---

[17] Chaplin, *The Thames from Source to Tideway*, p. 137.
[18] Heaton, *Yachting: A History*, p. 104.
[19] Delaney and Delany, *The Water Wags*, p. 8.
[20] Davis, *Dartmouth Royal Regatta*, pp. 68–69.
[21] Source: Coote, *Classic One-Designs*; Bird, *Classic Classes*.

goods carriage of trains, or, if the distance was not too great, by sea towed behind a sympathetic member's motor boat.

Pre-First World War One-Design Dinghies

Type	Designer	Length	Year of Launch	Area of Activity/ Yacht Club
Water Wags	J. E. Doyle	14 ft	1887	Dublin Bay area; Dun Laoghaire
West Lancashire Seabird	H. G. Baggs and W. Scott-Hayward	20 ft	1898	West Lancashire Yacht Club, Southport; West Kirby YC
Hoylake Opera One Design	Alec Latta	16 ft	1902	Hoylake Sailing Club
West Kirby Star	George Cockshott	16 ft 9 inches	1906	West Lancashire Yacht Club
West of England Conference Dinghy	Morgan Giles	14 ft	1908	Devon and Cornwall
Thames Estuary One-Design	Morgan Giles	18 ft	1912	Southend, area clubs
International 12	George Cockshott*	12 ft	1912	West Kirby Sailing Club

* George Cockshott was a Southport solicitor and amateur yacht designer, when he entered a design competition organised by the Boat Racing Association in 1912, who wanted a sailing dinghy that could serve as a yacht tender. By 1920, it had international status, the first one-design to achieve this and was a class in the 1920 and 1928 Olympics.

An example of such a circuit occurred when the clubs in the West of England – from Portland to Land's End – set up the West of England Yacht and Boat-Sailing Conference in 1890 to coordinate small boat racing in the southwest. Agreement to use YRA national rules throughout the region opened up local races to visiting yachtsmen; and established a much wider area for buying and selling craft.[22] In 1898, it agreed a set of rules for a 14 ft. dinghy and in 1899, 'it "adopted" the class which became known as the W.E.C. dinghy'.[23]

---

[22] Davis, *Dartmouth Regatta*, pp. 74–75.
[23] Bass, 'The Rise of Recreational Boat-Sailing', p. 35. The class later became the National 14 foot dinghy class, which, in turn, became the International 14, and its prestige increased by the Prince of Wales providing a cup – the Prince of Wales Cup – for the winner of the annual championship, first competed for in 1927. This is often referred to as the most prestigious prize in the dinghy racing world.

The Thames 'A' Rater was designed for the upper Thames in the late 1880s. Eight metres long, with a three-man crew, they were shallow draught, with very tall rigs, which meant they could plane and were very fast. They competed at the Upper Thames Sailing Club's Bourne End week, an event that entered the aquatic social calendar along with Cowes and Henley. In 1893, Queen Victoria acknowledged its prestige by presenting the Queen's Cup for 'A' Class Raters to the Upper Thames Sailing Club.

The movement towards single class small boat racing was international. Both Canada and America had 14 foot fleets by the 1890s, and the first international competition for 14 foot dinghies, the Douglas Cup, took place between Canada and America in 1914. Canada won. Similar developments were going on in Australia.[24]

I showed, in Chapter 9, how the advent of Corinthian yachting did not greatly affect the social composition of leisure sailing. While the large expansion of sailing clubs might have threatened the status quo, an important mechanism for maintaining class boundaries was multiple club memberships: For example, in the Southwest, '... members of the RYS [the Squadron] and RWYC [Royal Western] affected the local sailing scene by being the stewards and sponsors of the smaller regattas away from Plymouth.'[25] Similarly, in the northwest:

> ... In 1907, the newly formed Blackpool and Fleetwood Sailing Club elected David Leadbetter, the Fleetwood Lifeboat coxswain to the membership.

Such an election would square well with Corinthian values of man fighting the waves. However, a more serious consideration had been overlooked – Leadbetter was a *professional* boatman.

And membership of senior clubs carried clout. So,

> ... An influential member who was also in the Royal Mersey Yacht Club advised the Blackpool & Fleetwood SC committee not to allow artisans to join. As the senior club in the North West, the RMYC was virtually duty-bound to follow YRA's [Yacht Racing Association] guidelines. The Blackpool & Fleetwood Committee obediently resolved 'that as an amateur Club it was not advisable to admit as members men who were engaged in the occupation of boatmen.' David Leadbetter, in turn, accepted the decision without protest: 'when the situation was fully explained to him' a week later, he obligingly

[24] http://www.international14.org/index.php?option=com_content&view=article&id=26
[25] Charlie Tolcher, 'The History of Organized Small Boat Racing'.

'agreed to withdraw his application for membership' and the club refunded his subscription.[26]

We see here a long chain of communication: from the YRA to the Royal Mersey; and through one of its members, to the Blackpool and Fleetwood SC; and on down to the obliging David Leadbetter. Two aspects of a dominant, or hegemonic, narrative – the explanation(s) of events preferred by the Establishment – are clearly illustrated.[27] First is the 'obviousness' of the 'right' course of action – to revoke the application of a maritime professional; and, secondly, the acceptance by the non-powerful of that narrative, so 'once the situation was fully explained to him', Leadbetter withdrew his application.

St Helier Yacht Club was formed in 1903 and the twelve founder members decided to form 'a working man's club ... [these members] were very independent and even refused to permit several moneyed yachtsmen to join, as they may have wanted the rules changed – arguably setting the egalitarian tone that prevails in the club today'.[28] A factor may have been the desire to differentiate themselves from the more exclusive Royal Channel Island Yacht Club, formed in 1862. However, more generally, the exclusion of artisans and those who worked for a wage remained basically unchanged. Cusack overviews the South Devon sailing clubs at the turn of the century:

> ... of the four small clubs examined, all of which had a majority of small yachts, one, at Salcombe, was socially exclusive, a second, the Torbay Sailing Club, started as an elite body and remained essentially a gentleman's club, although a limited number of wealthy yacht-owning tradesmen became members. In contrast, the Dart Boat Sailing Club started as a body with a

---

[26] Ryan, 'The Emergence of Middle-Class Yachting in the North-West of England from the Later Nineteenth Century', p. 169. Ryan is drawing on the Blackpool and Fleetwood Sailing Club Minutes, DDX 734 1/1, 7 April, 1908; 22 April, 1908, in the Lancashire Record Office.

[27] The power of narratives as a means of controlling the population and their voting preferences was first proposed by the Italian political philosopher, Antonio Gramsci (1891–1937). The narratives preferred and propagated by those in the power, usually those who are running the government, are termed *hegemonic narratives*. A key feature of narratives is that they *foreground* aspects of a situation that the Establishment wish to emphasise and value, and *background or minimise* features that are inconvenient or embarrassing. Gramsci's thoughts are contained in his *Selections from the Prison Notebooks* but, since Gramsci was imprisoned by Mussolini and in considerable pain when he wrote them, they are not an easy read. Hegemonic narratives occur not just in relation to governments, but wherever there is a power imbalance, as between a senior yacht club and a local sailing club, or between flag officers and member(s). A nice example of foregrounding and backgrounding is Stuart Readman, *Four Ships: One Hundred Years of the Essex Yacht Club*. The club's relationship with the Royal Burnham is frequently described as warm and close, while the less prestigious club, the Leigh-on-Sea Sailing Club, a few hundred yards away from the Essex, is not mentioned.

[28] Kevin Le Scelleur and Philip Jeune, *Sailing through a Century*, p. 27.

genuine wider social nature, but by 1900 was becoming a more select body. The Teign Corinthian Yacht Club, however, appears to have contained a combination of the town's most prosperous inhabitants.[29]

Overall, a little social broadening did occur in this period, but it was very limited. Yachting remained middle class in membership and its desire to exclude workers. All that had changed was that the middle class had expanded, so there were more of that class, probably mainly from the less affluent end, to join existing sailing clubs or form new ones. If the opportunity arose for gentrification and becoming a yacht club with larger yachts, it was eagerly taken.[30]

But what the greater numbers of sailors did do was attract magazine publishers. In the last quarter of the century, magazines combining how-to articles with news appeared for all major prestige sports. Some flourished while others floundered. In the late 1880s, the advent of mass-produced high quality white paper, on which excellent photographs and line drawings could be printed, opened the way for cheaper magazines with larger circulations.

In sailing, *Hunt's* had ceased publication in 1887, with the death of the founder of the firm. *Yachting News* and *Yachting Weekly* both only lasted from 1895 to 1897. *The Yachtsman* was founded in 1891 (and continued until 1950). At only 3d a week, The *Yachtsman* and *Yachting World* were certainly available to a wider audience.[31] *Yachting World* started in 1894, as a weekly magazine for the racing yachtsman; and *Yachting Monthly*, founded by the yacht designer G. L. Watson's friend, Herbert Reiach, started in 1906.[32] Its editorial for its first issue promised:

> We hope to make it a publication worthy of a sport which is healthy and pure
> – a sport which is to be fostered and encouraged for the development of all
> that is most manly in the human race.[33]

This is a statement of Athleticism with its valorising of masculinity, the fit male body, and also the implicit connection with the 'white man's burden', making it the duty of the English to impose their superiority on the inferior races.

---

[29] Cusack, 'The Rise of Aquatic Recreation and Sport', pp. 295–297.
[30] The Registrar General's first classification of classes was published in 1911, and differentiated between class III Non-Manual and III Skilled Manual, the key differentiation in determining yacht club membership (Mike Savage, *Social Class in the 21st Century*, pp. 32–35).
[31] Ryan, 'Identifying the British Yachtsman, 1815–1939', p. 68.
[32] Both are still published today.
[33] *Yachting Monthly*, May 1906, Vol. 1: 49.

About These Women

Women and Sport

Athleticism, the dominant form of masculinity and sporting philosophy, used the long-standing trope or cliché of 'the Angel in the House' – house-bound, kept innocent (ignorant), morally pure, to be worshipped. This worship ostensibly acted as protection against abuse by men of their near-complete economic and legal power – 'misogyny disguised as chivalry'.[34] Change was slow in coming. A wife had no legal personality – she did not exist as a person in her own right. Her property and possessions, her body (she could not be raped by her husband), her children (except when breastfeeding them) and her earnings all belonged to her husband on marriage. This was known as 'coverture' which was revoked by the Married Woman's Property Acts of 1870 and 1882. From 1884, she was no longer liable to imprisonment if she refused to return to the conjugal home, and shortly afterwards, a husband lost the right to confine her if she did run away.[35]

Exercise and sport might damage a woman's child-rearing potential.[36] Nothing should be done by women to damage their child-bearing potential (of preferably male children). Women of the middle and upper classes had a duty to marry and have a large number of children, to ward off the internal and external threats to the wellbeing of the empire. The greater fertility of the working class was seen as threatening the physical health and the intellectual fibre of the nation, and, later, fanned Francis Galton's Eugenic Movement.[37] The Irish migration into England to find work as navvies for the canals and railways accelerated after the Potato Famines of the 1840s.[38]

These concerns were increased by the very noticeable drop in fertility during the later part of the nineteenth century. In 1870, the average number of children per family was 6; in 1890–1899, it dropped to 4.3 and by 1915, it was 2.3. Birth control had become available – contraceptives could be ordered by post – and the drop in fertility among professional and salaried workers was even greater.[39] So, alongside the demand for the vote by the Suffragette

---

[34] The term 'Angel in the House' comes from the title of Coventry Patmore's poem, first published in 1854 and expanded till 1862. See Mary Poovey, *Uneven Developments*, for a lengthier discussion of the Victorian binaries concerning women.

[35] Bédarida, *Social History*, p. 122.

[36] Judith Rowbotham, *Good Girls Make Good Wives*, p. 124.

[37] See Angelique Richardson, *Love and Eugenics in the Late Nineteenth Century*.

[38] 800,000 living in Britain in 1901; but not just working as navvies but also as doctors, playwrights (Wilde, Shaw) and as administrators of the colonies (Linda Colley, *Acts of Union*, p. 199).

[39] Bédarida, *Social History*, pp. 113–114.

movement, women were taking greater control of their lives and one consequence was their participation in sport.

In an 1899 article, Dr Arabella Kenealy pronounced muscles to be 'the
stigmata of abnormal sex transformation'.[40] Dr James Cantlie (1851–1926)
repeated her arguments, in 1906, inveighing against the hockey boom, as this
was likely to develop shoulders, rather than the breeding parts of the anatomy,
as well as 'a mind at variance with womanly duties'. He was also concerned that
it would take five children per family to keep the empire (suitably) stocked.[41]
The male children of the middle class, suitably educated, would be needed
to maintain the colonies either peacefully or by military action, against the
indigenous population or against ambitious other powers. Women should
be brought up to be wives who would, of course, support their men in their
colonial ventures, and be able to handle with fortitude the anxiety and grief
that their fate might cause. 'From the 1880s ... British citizens both male and
female were viewed as the raw material of a new imperial race.'[42]

By the 1890s, these views were being contested. Women's participation
varied across sports. Women were permitted to hunt, but this was an aristocratic recreation, not a new, Victorian sport and they were not competing.
There was a woman's tennis championship at Wimbledon in 1877, but the
enforced dress code – reflecting concern regarding informal female dress –
meant that their freedom of movement was restricted.[43]

Although women were excluded from serious rowing competitions by the
national organisations, they were a common sight on the Thames – witness
Three Men in a Boat – and the ability to row was considered a desirable skill:

> Lady Greville, in *The Gentlewoman's Book of Sports*, published in 1880, sug-
> gested: 'It is essential for every English girl to learn to row; twenty years ago
> it was not considered "comme il faut" for a lady to row but now everything is
> changed and it is clearly to be seen that it is very best thing for her.'[44]

---

[40] Keneally, 'Women as Athlete: A Rejoinder', p. 927. See J. A. Mangan and Roberta Park, eds.,
From 'Fair Sex' to Feminism.

[41] Cantlie, *Physical Efficiency*, 1906. There was still a high infantile mortality rate which, of course,
affected his calculations. Infant mortality in London was 163 deaths per 1,000 births in 1895
and still 138 per 1,000 in 1905 (Ford ... *The Only Sailor in the Fleet*, p. 95).

[42] Harris, *Private Lives, Public Spirit: Britain 1870–1914*, p. 181.

[43] Ford, *This Sporting Land*, p. 55. Oddly enough, the mixed doubles championship only arrived
in 1913.

[44] Cusack, 'The Rise of Aquatic Recreation and Sport', pp. 342–343. Lady Greville was the editor
of the book, published c. 1890.

As Huggins points out, many women felt they had to be amateurish and not compete in a masculine style, so that they did appear to be feminine.[45] 'As late as 1903 the Mistress of Girton College, Cambridge was reported to have told students: "If you must play hockey, do try and hit the ball gently."'[46] For the more radical woman, the preferred sport to demonstrate the woman's independence was bicycling, using pantaloons as the dress of revolt.[47]

Women and Yachting

In trying to understand the treatment of women by yacht clubs, we need to distinguish four areas of contestation:

- racing small yachts, which was relatively quickly won
- cruising in mixed company
- access to all areas of the club house which, in most cases, took till after the Second World War
- serving on the committees and becoming flag officers of a club, which did not often happen till the 1970s or later.

While the more war-like 'fronts', rather than the clumsy 'areas of contestation' would seem initially appropriate, in fact in many clubs, women do not seem to have done any fighting for their rights. Where 'fronts' would be an appropriate metaphor, is that, as we shall see, advances gained one year could be lost the next.

Access to the yacht club can be broken down into a number of areas, such as lavatory, changing room, ladies room, dining room and bar, and the movement was often in this sequence, with the proviso that clubs very resistant to letting women in, such as the Squadron and the Royal Fowey, provided no female toilets.

Although many yacht club histories content themselves with describing physical barriers, *temporal barriers* were also manned. So, women were only to be admitted on certain days, such as regatta day or the annual yacht club dance; then as this weakened, they were only allowed on the premises at certain times of day, and had to leave by the early evening, so that the men could enjoy being blokeish and becoming intoxicated.[48]

---

[45] Huggins, *The Victorians and Sport*, pp. 79 ff.
[46] Kathleen E. McCrone, 'The "Lady Blue": Sport at the Oxbridge Women's Colleges from Their Foundation to 1914', pp. 191–215.
[47] Lowerson, *Sport and the English Middle Classes 1870–1914*, pp. 214–215.
[48] This duality of restrictions on time *and* space is valid for all difficult groups. Andrew Matthews' account of the Yealm Yacht Club, *The Bar and Beyond*, is interesting, as it started in 1933, and to a large extent continued as a social club for the villages of Newton Ferrers and

The power factor can be broken down into five stages: partial membership, full membership, voting rights, committees and flag officer status.

Allowing women access and equality in yachting was part of a slow, patchy progress across prestige sports. The use of the female body in active sports was contentious. Women exerting themselves and wearing less and looser clothing was certainly sexually arousing – witness Jerome K. Jerome's lascivious descriptions in *Three Men in a Boat* of ladies towing their skiff.[49] (Women swimming, playing tennis, bicycling or rowing was likewise titillating.)[50] Given the Victorians' confusion of love and lust, it is no surprise to find, in the proposal of marriage by a suitor in a letter to H. G. Wells' Ann Veronica:

> And how can I get into one brief letter the complex accumulated desires of what is now, I find on reference to my diary, nearly sixteen months of letting my mind run on you – ever since that jolly party at Surbiton, where we raced and beat the other boat. You steered and I rowed stroke.[51]

One more problem for women to overcome in yacht racing (and more generally) was that women should not have tanned or brown skin, as this linked them with poorer women who worked outdoors. So if they went into the sun – even when they sailed – they always used a bonnet reaching over their face. In the oil painting *Edwardian Yachts Racing* by Charles Murray Padday, circa 1910, Sheila, Duchess of Westminster is helming a yacht, Major Sir Philip Hunloke navigating. Her head, topped by a wide brimmed hat, is completely circled by a scarf. The Duchess won a bronze medal at the 1908 Olympics. Likewise, Anthony Heckstall-Smith in *Sacred Cowes*, recalled that at the turn of the century: 'Miss Barbara Hughes, together with her sister, Mrs Shenley, Babsy was in the first flight of small boat sailors and I always associate her with the parasol she invariably opened when at the tiller on a sunny day when the winds were light ... to make up a sunshade.'[52] The parasol was not to be

Noss Mayo. Women were admitted early on without hindrance, and also took an active part in the sailing committee by the early 1950s. The problem groups were dogs and cadets, whose permitted hours within the club Matthews carefully documents.

[49] Jerome J. Jerome, *Three Men in a Boat*, p. 109.

[50] In *Under Sail through Red Devon*, as late as 1937, R. B. Cattell, who would become a famous psychologist in America, is unable to sail his dinghy without going close inshore to view the lady swimmers. See Peter Kuhnst, *Sports: A Cultural History in the Mirror of Art*, particularly Chapters 5 and 6, to see how women at exercise excited the pornographic imagination across the twentieth century.

[51] H. G. Wells, *Ann Veronica*, 1909, p. 62. Another example of a woman's attraction when playing sport is John Betjeman's 'A Subaltern's Love Song' ('Miss Joan Hunter Dunn' in *New Bats in Old Belfries*) (1945).

[52] Heckstall-Smith, *Sacred Cowes*, p. 105.

parted with lightly. Watson designed *Eros* for the family of N. B. Stewart in 1874. It capsized, and Stewart Senior's wife was left swimming in the Clyde, with her parasol still held high to keep the sun off her face.[53] Pale skin started to lose its appeal when women working long hours in factories also had white faces, and Coco Chanel and Hollywood after the Great War made a tan an appealing feature of the chic woman of the 1920s.

From around the 1890s, women started to take part more frequently in dinghy and small boat sailing. Their participation was partly a statement of the independence of the New Woman, but was mainly a result of the development of small, open boats, especially lighter dinghies, which meant that single-handed racing, or with only one crew, became possible and muscle no longer determined outcome.[54] Mild steel wire in flexible forms replaced tarred rope rigging. Aluminium for some fittings made boats lighter and easier to handle.[55] Captain Edward du Boulay invented roller reefing in 1878, and Major Wykeham-Martin had introduced his jib-roller furling gear in 1903, so the foresail could be shortened from the cockpit. Initially, it was expensive, but it saved hauling sails up and down on a tipping foredeck, which was no easy task for a woman in a full length skirt or dress.

Another change was the replacement of the heavy gaff rig by the much lighter Bermudan. In the gaff rig, the main sail is split into two separate sails (main and topsail), separated by the gaff – a heavy wooden spar on which the top of the main and to which the topsail was attached.[56] Bermudan rigs have the triangular mainsail running up the mast. This rig became available in Britain shortly before the First World War. Because much less muscle is needed to raise a mainsail using a main halyard, compared with raising a gaff, women sailors now had a much better chance of winning. However, the switch from gaff to Bermudan was a lengthy process. Dear gives its acceptance in yacht racing as the 1920s, noting its use in the J Class in the 1930s. Maurice Griffiths, writing in 1922 about Burnham-on-Crouch, 'the principal yacht racing port on the East Coast ... not one of these yachts, nor any that I had seen at West Mersea, Maldon or elsewhere, was Bermudan rigged: that revolution in yachts' rigs was still to come.'[57]

---

[53] Black, *G. L. Watson*, p. 128, n. 2.
[54] Lowerson, *Sport and the English Middle Classes, 1870–1914*, pp. 203–220.
[55] Cusack, 'The Rise of Aquatic Recreation and Sport', pp. 246–248.
[56] Leather, *The Gaff Rig Handbook*.
[57] Dear, 'Leisure Sailing in the Twentieth Century', p. 139; Maurice Griffiths, *The First of the Tide*, p. 31.

In what follows, I am not distinguishing between dinghy and keelboat racing. As a rough rule of thumb, women were racing keelboats in the Solent, and dinghies elsewhere.

Women and Yacht Racing

The promotion of *ladies' races* (ladies only races) was relatively uncontroversial. Sufficient women took to racing in dayboats that a ladies' race was added to many regattas in the 1890s.[58] For example, by the 1890s, Topsham Sailing Club had an established Ladies race. In the July, 1898, race, seven took part.[59]

The Royal Plymouth Corinthian Yacht Club held annual races for the wives and daughters of members from 1889. Since they could not be members and only members could take part in club races, the Club graciously added to their rule book: 'Any lady assisting on board a yacht during a match shall be considered an Honorary Member for the day'. The 1894 ladies' race, using a shortened course of only two rounds in the Sound, instead of the usual three, attracted twenty entries. It was reported in *Yachting Monthly* that 'many more sailors could have requisitioned had there been yachts to compete'; and, in the *Western Morning News*, that 'the fair competitors, attired in pretty and appropriate costumes, handled their respective helms exceedingly well'.[60]

What raised male hackles was the fact that women were taking part in *races open to both sexes*. In many venues, they deliberately made yacht racing unpleasant for women, and on occasion, unfair, as protests were handled by committees made up solely of men. So, this was a case of 'be careful of what you wish for'. The hostility of male contestants discouraged less able women sailors, so that only very competent women racers had the confidence to compete and often win, much to male chagrin. This occurred country-wide.

The Dart Boat Sailing Club's first woman member, Ethel Tew, was in an 1888 race, finishing fourth out of eleven starters. Between 1890 and 1897, she was regularly among the placings in her two 14 foot dinghies, *Titwillow* and *Titwee*. It is clear that women winning was sufficiently common not to merit special reference. In 1894, she was commended 'after taking a very unconventional course, came up from behind to take the winning gun.'[61] She was sufficiently well known that 'the cover of the August 1894 issue of *Yachting*

---

[58] See Cusack, 'The Rise of Aquatic Recreation and Sport'. Also, Lowerson, *Sport and the English Middle Classes 1870–1914*, pp. 211–212.

[59] None of them were members, since women could not be members in their own right till after the Great War (Chris Williams, *125 Years: Topsham Sailing Club 1885–2010*, p. 4).

[60] *Yachting World*, 1, 1894: 388; *Western Daily Mercury*, 6 August, 1894.

[61] *Dartmouth Chronicle*, 22 June, 1894, quoted in Cusack, 'The Rise of Aquatic Recreation and Sport', p. 338.

Monthly is illustrated by a spirited drawing of what is thought to be Miss Tew sailing her boat, *Titwee*, a boat she had built for her'.[62]

Ivy Carus-Wilson (1887–1937) was a very successful dinghy racer from Teignmouth, who became a member of Shaldon Sailing Club around 1907. She had a 14 foot dinghy, *Myosotis*, designed for her by Morgan Giles, the eminent yacht designer and builder, and her future husband (they married in 1913). By the end of 1909 she was unbeatable, as she was racing a very early planning dinghy. She funded her sailing by her race winnings. As was common at the time, she transported her dinghy to regattas by train. Her unpublished journal (1906–1912) recounts the skulduggery and collusion by protest committees in male racers' attempts to beat her. Her reputation was such that she was the subject of 'Our Portrait Study' on the frontispiece of the November 1912 issue of *Yachting Monthly*, previous portraits invariably being of senior male members of the yachting establishment.[63]

Turning to the Solent, Mrs Allen was a faithful customer of Fife's. She was the only successful lady helm in larger boats, and was astonishingly dominant in the eight metre class – boats some 30 feet long – in the Solent, over a number of years in the early 1900s. She won 224 prizes in 286 starts, and 25 out of 25 starts in 1907.[64] 'Thalassa' in his chapter on 'Small Yacht Racing on the Solent', in the first of the two-volume Badminton Library *Sailing*, welcomed ladies racing and saw their participation as advantageous to the sport:

> The ladies who have taken an active part in the racing should also be mentioned, as their presence has done much to make the sport popular and fashionable.
>
> Prominent among them are Ladies Fanny and Blanche Stanhope [who had bought the 1-rater *Mahatma* from a Mr Flemmich, her designer and raced her in 1892 (p. 262)], Mrs. Sidney Watson, Mrs. Schenley and her sisters the Misses Hughes, Mrs. Rudston-Read and her sister Miss Cox, Mrs. H. Duff-Gordon and her sister Miss Hammersley, Mrs. Arthur Heygate, Mrs. Blair Onslow Cochrane, the Misses Sutton, and Colonel Bucknill's daughters.[65]

These women meant business. In 1891, Miss Schenley led her class, with 40 starts, 22 firsts and 12 other placings. *Wee Winn*, 15.5 feet on the waterline and 23.9 feet overall, was ordered by Miss Sutton from the top American yacht designer, Nat Herreshoff, and he built the boat and had it shipped over. In

---

[62] Bass, 'The Rise of Recreational Boat-Sailing, p. 51.
[63] *Ibid.*, pp. 72–74.
[64] McCallum, *Fast and Bonnie*, p. 96.
[65] 'Thalassa', *Small Yacht Sailing on the Solent*, pp. 277–278.

1892, in the ½ raters, 'the boat showed a clean pair of heels to the rest of the class in every sort of weather', and did so again in 1893, with 8 wins and 3 seconds in 11 starts.[66]

Guest and Boulton, in writing about an expert woman racer, show an acceptance of women racing:

> The pleasures of a small rater are perhaps best set forth in a very interesting article in the *Badminton Magazine* of June, 1892, written by a lady expert in the management and sailing of the small rater, Miss Barbara, or 'Bobsey' Hughes, one of three sailing sisters.[67]

Many of the successful Solent women racers were members of the Castle Club. 'Thalassa', having listed some of their successes, notes that in 1889:

> It really looked as if ladies were about to take an active part in Solent racing but next year … some owners objected, and this form of sport received a some-what rude and unexpected check from which it has never quite recovered.[68]

Again, we see that zones of contestation have fluctuating boundaries.

On the Medway, Marion Wyllie was considered nearly invincible.[69] An Australian, Mark Foy instituted the Anglo-Australian Challenge Match in 1898.[70] He challenged British yacht clubs to sail against his ex-champion 'A' class Sydney Harbour skiff *Irex*. W. L. Wyllie, the commodore of Medway YC from 1896 to 1904 (as well as being a famous maritime painter), accepted the challenge and had *Maid of Kent* designed by one of the crack designers of small racing yachts, Linton Hope, to the measurements laid down for the match. The match aroused considerable interest, with a special train running down to Rochester from London; steamers allowed spectators to follow the races on the Medway; and it was reported in the papers and the yachting press.[71] It was a five race series, and Wyllie's wife, Marion, aged 38 and the mother of their five children, helmed. The Brits won the first three, much to the Australian crew's disgust. But this was no fluke. Mrs Wyllie had won 21

---

[66] *Ibid.*, pp. 264 and 271.

[67] Guest and Boulton, *The Royal Yacht Squadron: Memorials*, p. 349. 'Bobsey': obviously, the same lady we met holding her parasol a few pages earlier. 'Babsy' is probably the correct nick-name. Women racers often seem to have been given nicknames during this period, possibly an upper-class habit.

[68] 'Thalassa', 'Small Yacht Racing on the Solent', p. 237. The club folded in 1947.

[69] Ellis, *Medway Yacht Club*, p. 14.

[70] Despite the implication in the title that this is an ongoing competition, this match was a one-off.

[71] Ellis, *The Medway Yacht Club*, pp. 11–17 (e.g. *Daily Graphic*, 19 September, 1898; *Yachting World*, 16 September, 1898).

13 Ladies Race, August 1895, off Cowes, possibly organised by the Royal London
Yacht Club. This was no half-hearted sop to female sailors. The race consisted of 4
laps, each of 4-miles length. Sail no. 2 is a Sibbick design.

out of 23 starts at the Royal Corinthian Yacht Club, Erith during the 1894–
1896 seasons. In 1897, the Medway Yacht Club adopted the Kittiwake 18 foot
dinghy as their one-design class, and she won 14 first places and a second out
of 16 starts in their inaugural season.[72]

On the east coast, the newly created *Yachting Monthly* in 1907 mentions
that 'the Orwell Corinthian Yacht Club is fortunate in the possession of skil-
ful yachtswomen who are sure to do well at Burnham'. Their reporter was
right. Sailing *June*, Misses C. Packard and N. Packard 'took seventeen prizes,
which included seven first prizes, and the Points Cup for Burnham Week'.[73]

Women and Yacht Cruising

As mentioned earlier, participation in sailing required freedom of dress and
movement, which made women particularly sexually arousing, an emotion

---

[72] John Basley, 'The Wyllies on the Medway'; Don Ellis, *Medway Yacht Club*, pp. 11–16.
[73] Renee M. Waite, *Pin Mill Sailing Club: Sixty Years*, p. 13; see also Chivers, *Austin 'Clarence'
Farrar*, pp. 10–12. Celia Packard was his mother. There is a nice picture on p. 12 of her, as an old
lady, helming a Harwich OD, hat firmly on head.

which the Victorian yachtsmen found difficult to handle. Educated in the all-male public school, a man's limited pre-marital experience of women provided only the binary of continence or the services of a prostitute. Interactions with women were, therefore, always at risk of descending into anxious chaos. So, as with Davies in *The Riddle of the Sands*, the men's choices were not to allow women on board; avoid them, either by fleeing or sailing away; or fall madly in love. Rare examples of women coming aboard were wives (Erskine Childers and Mary, called 'Molly'; Conor O'Brien and Kitty), but they were useful cover for the passage's real purpose – gun running into Southern Ireland in July 1914, in *Asgard* and *Kelpie*, respectively;[74] or sisters (H. Fiennes and Maud Speed; Conor and Margaret O'Brien; after the war, Ralph and 'Peter' Stock). If women did come aboard, the yachtsman's male buddies usually left.[75]

Women only came aboard in any numbers in the 1970s, most often as mothers of families (see Chapter 14).

Women at the Yacht Club

If women racing was grudgingly accepted, albeit often with ill grace, the boundary maintenance at the *yacht club* door was far more severe and lasted well into the twentieth century.

The rise of assertive New Women after 1880, even if only read about by the male members rather than directly experienced, probably only made the attitudes of the men who controlled entrance to sporting institutions such as yacht clubs more intractable – narratives tend to get more strident when their validity is being called into question.[76]

From mid-Victorian times, widows were allowed to retain their deceased husband's yacht club membership, if they retained their boat. Less commonly, if they were rich in their own right and owned a yacht, they could be elected. The Royal Mersey, formed 1844, never discriminated against

[74] *Asgard* was a 44 foot Colin Archer new build. Archer was Norwegian (a second-generation Scottish immigrant) with a yard at Narvik. According to Head, *Sailing Gaffers*, p. 102, she was built to accommodate Molly Childers' inability to walk due to tubercular abscesses, not remedied by a series of painful operations when she was a child (Piper, *Dangerous Waters*, p. 87). While important as gestures of defiance, these shipments pale into complete insignificance compared to the huge amount of weaponry pouring into Northern Ireland, with the connivance of the British government.

[75] Harry Speed and Maude Speed *Cruises in Small Yachts*, 1926, but mostly about cruises in the 1890s; Ralph Stock, *The Cruise of the Dream Ship*, 1922; Judith Hill, *In Search of Islands: A Life of Conor O'Brien*.

[76] For a discussion on 'the New Women', see Angelique Richardson and Chris Willis, *The New Woman in Fiction and Fact*, especially their Introduction. For their fiction, see Angelique Richardson, ed., *Women Who Did: Stories by Men and Women, 1890–1914*.

women members. Their first female member, Miss E. Fazakerley, of Denbigh Castle, owned both a steam yacht and the schooner *Fay* (64 tons). She was elected in 1877, as were two more women in the following two years.[77] The Island Sailing Club, Cowes, admitted women as members from its inception in 1889, and the Clyde Corinthian, founded 1902, did likewise.[78]

However, as Mead points out, it would take a brave woman to enter the club. Men relaxing with each other created an 'atmosphere of tobacco, strong drink, nautical language to match, and Rabelaisian anecdotes not unpopular with the seafaring male'.[79]

Generally, the sullying of their homosocial space was fiercely resisted. Men had to behave according to a completely different code of conduct when women were present, which demanded 'chivalry' and decorum, so it was far less relaxing for them.[80]

The much more common practice was to limit *when* women could enter the club – often restricted to regatta days; and *where*: which rooms they could enter – often just the balcony and the dining room, if accompanied by their husband, or, at the least, a (male) member. But again, these boundaries ebbed and flowed. This loosening and tightening up of controls on women members is explained by the volatility of AGMs. The success of the 'liberal' lobby one year at the AGM might cause a successful backlash among the more conservative members at the next.

For example, a portrait of the Royal Yacht Squadron's platform in 1870 shows women present; a portrait of the same location in 1880 shows none. Ian Dear, the Squadron's historian, notes 'the platform remained a male preserve for several decades'.[81] He lamely explains this as due to the abandonment of the Club Ball. It was only in 1932 that wives and daughters were permitted to dine with their husbands.[82] Prior to that, women were only allowed on the lawn, and, before the War, the Squadron did not provide any toilet facilities

---

[77] Brian Smith, *History of the Royal Mersey Yacht Club*, p. 9. Miss Fazakerley's portrait, with her yachts behind her, is on display at the club.

[78] Island Sailing Club, *The Island Sailing Club*, p. 23; George Blake and Christopher Small, *Cruising in Company*, p. 114. Miss E. Tew being appointed Race Officer at the Dart Boat Sailing Club in 1898, albeit for 'a minor fixture', was a first (Cusack, 'The Rise of Aquatic Recreation', pp. 341–342).

[79] Mead, *The History of the Royal Cornwall*, p. 39. The many verses of a ribald song, complete with chorus, are given on pp. 79–84(!) of Jan Wise, *A Century of Sailing: The Crouch Yacht Club 1907–2007*. Obviously, such singing endured as she quotes these verses when she is covering the period after the Second World War.

[80] Davidoff, *The Best Circles*, p. 25, speaks of 'the rigid formality of etiquette imposed by women'. She is referring to the formality imposed by their presence, not by their power

[81] Dear, *The Royal Yacht Squadron 1815–1945*, between pp. 40–41.

[82] Dixon, *The King's Sailing Master*, p. 249.

for them. The only option, if caught short, was to go behind the rose bushes, one's maid protecting one's modesty from view.

When the Countess of Cardigan collapsed and died on the Squadron lawn in 1907, a member was heard to remark 'These damned women have no respect for the Squadron'.[83]

A ladies' cloakroom was only created in 1928, by buying part of an adjoining property from Rosa Lewis, an ex-mistress of Edward VII. First renting and then getting a very good price, she sold the RYS her ballroom. 'As she caustically remarked: "While they won't 'ave me on their old lawn, I 'ave to let their lady friends into my garden to piddle"'.[84] Similarly, the Royal Fowey had no lavatories for women till 1931, and did not grant full membership to women till 1994.[85]

One could go on listing very similar behaviour at other senior clubs, such as the Royal Dart, where women were given very limited membership in 1894, only to have it withdrawn till 1936;[86] at the Royal Clyde;[87] and at the Royal Cornwall.[88]

Chapter 8 in Archer and Pearson's history of the Royal St George is titled 'Dogs, Strangers and Ladies'. 1861 was a bad year, for a Mr Irwin repeatedly brought his four-legged friend into the billiard room, while Mr Levinge, although allowed to bring a lady into the club, showed her around areas out of bounds to ladies, causing the House Steward to become so incensed, he swore. (He had to write to Mr Levinge apologising.)[89] The biographer of the Salcombe Yacht Club notes that, in 1908, 'ladies – like dogs – were not allowed on the Club's premises at this time'.[90] The linking of women and dogs is a feature of Jan Wise's history of the Crouch Yacht Club, *A Century of Sailing 1907–2007*, where the Committee seems to spend equal amounts of time discussing how to keep both out of the Club till well after the Second World War.[91]

---

[83] Dear, *The Royal Yacht Squadron, 1815–1895*, p. 100.

[84] Heckstall-Smith, *Sacred Cowes*, p. 132. Women were only permitted to lunch or dine in the club in 1939. From 1953, a wife could stay with her husband in the Castle but not enter through the main door. The class of 'lady associate member' was created in 1969 (Johnson, *Yacht Clubs of the World*, p. 66).

[85] Joan Coombs, *A Fowey Jig-Saw: The History of the Royal Fowey Yacht Club*, p. 165.

[86] Llewellyn, *A Brief History of the Royal Dart*, p. 4.

[87] George Blake and Christopher Small, *Cruise in Company*, p. 63.

[88] Mead, *History of the Royal Cornwall*, p. 108.

[89] Women were banned from the Reading Room till 1987.

[90] Sonia Parkinson, *Salcombe Yacht Club: The First Hundred Years*, p. 9. The club had no women committee members till the 1950s. This was not unusual.

[91] Wise, *A Century of Sailing*.

The Decline in Leisure Sailing after the Turn of the Century

From 365 yachts and 11 clubs in 1845, yachting grew to 3,096 registered yachts and 47 clubs in 1875, and to 3,889 and 143 clubs in 1914.[92] But such figures are misleading. The Golden Age ended quite sharply around 1900.

Hunt's Universal Yacht List records a drop from a peak number of 6,409 yachts registered in 1900 to 4,404 in 1914; *Lloyd's* records 2,352 yachts in 1890, a peak of 3,063 yachts registered in 1900 and a slight drop to 3,889 in 1914. The total tonnage – the size of the yachts – had dropped dramatically from 61,173 tons in 1890 to 59,420 in 1900 and to 37,594 in 1914.[93]

This national picture is mirrored in Devon, with severe losses of membership in the three 'royal clubs' in Devon after 1900.[94]

Number of Yachts on Devon 'Royal' Yachts Clubs' Books			
Year	Royal Western	Royal Dart	Royal Torbay
1890		112	59
1895	92	83	
1900	65		
1910	55		
1914		37	27

In Dun Laoghaire, the Royal St George closed its membership at 647 in 1873. By 1900, it had 380. There was a decline in racing in Dublin Bay after 1901.[95] By 1906, the Royal Irish was also worrying about the fall in membership. [96]

The peak of large boat racing was around 1895 and after 1900, racing circuit was declining.[97] Prince Edward stopped racing *Britannia* at the end of the 1897 season and sold her, thereby effectively killing Big Class racing. She lay unused in Cowes, passing through a number of owners, till he bought her back in 1902, but only to use as a cruising yacht till his death in 1910.[98] Phillips-Birt comments that there was little interest in big yacht racing after 1900 on the part of either the public or the owners:

[92] Cusack, 'The Rise of Aquatic Recreation and Sport', p. 411.
[93] Cusack, 'Yachting in Britain', pp. 167–169.
[94] Cusack, 'The Rise of Aquatic Recreation', p. 271.
[95] Archer and Pearson, *The Royal St George Club*, pp. 21 and 57; Boylan, *White Sails Crowding*, p. 82; O'Sullivan, *Dublin Bay: A Century of Sailing*, p. 37.
[96] Boylan, *White Sails Crowding*, p. 82.
[97] Leather, *The Northseamen*, pp. 147 and 157.
[98] Dear, *The Royal Yacht Squadron, 1815–1895*, pp. 79–80.

... The character of the years 1900–1914 was expressed in July, 1912, by the Editor of the *Yachting Monthly* in a survey of the Big Class yachting scene which concluded: 'Yacht racing does not appeal to the public, even the beautiful *Shamrock* and *White Heather* do not excite as much interest as a Punch and Judy show'. The trouble was that potential owners of Big Class yachts seemed to feel like the public.[99]

As with larger yachts, there was a decline in small boat racing after 1900. To give an example, on the Dart, the Dart Boat Sailing Club, founded 1873, had great success in the 1890s, but then started to lose members. It had talks with the local branch of the Minima Club, founded on the Hamble in 1889 – a group of nation-wide dinghy clubs, with clubs at Surbiton, Plymouth and Southampton – but these talks failed and both clubs closed in 1901.[100] The Start Bay Yacht Club was formed 1889 as a breakaway from the Royal Dart to exploit that the fact that the Royal Dart catered for the owners of the bigger yachts and, being on the Kingswear side of the river, was inconvenient for Dartmouth residents.[101] But Start Bay YC had to abandon its 1900 regatta and closed a few years later.

With three yacht clubs in difficulties or closing in the 1900s, the Dart Sailing Club was established to organise racing for smaller yachts. However, by 1907, there were insufficient competitors for a regatta and the outbreak of war in 1914 saw its closure.[102]

Why this severe downturn? There does not seem to be one single, over-riding explanation. For the landed gentry, relevant factors might have included the fact that during the last quarter of the century, agricultural prices were depressed. Death duties were introduced in 1894.

Another reason could be the greater attraction of alternative uses of surplus money and leisure. Other competing sports such as cycling, golf and tennis were growing rapidly but these had all been around since the 1870s.[103] Golf was enjoying a boom with the worldwide successes of James Braid, J. H. Taylor and Harry Vardon, 'the great triumvirate of British golf from 1894 to 1914'.[104] The motor car was the latest craze among the rich. (Witness Toad's

[99] Phillips-Birt, *The History of Yachting*, p. 113. Leather, *The Northseamen*, p. 162, states that big class racing was depressed between 1896 and 1908, but there does not appear to have been any clear signs of revival after 1908.

[100] The only surviving Minima Yacht Club is at Kingston-on-Thames, racing dinghies.

[101] Cusack, 'The Rise of Aquatic Recreation and Sport', p. 264.

[102] Davis, *Dartmouth Regatta*, pp. 75–79. A second yacht club on the Dart, the Dartmouth Sailing Club, was only formed in 1950.

[103] Bass, 'The Rise of Recreational Boat-Sailing', p. 76,

[104] Boylan, *White Sails Crowding*, p. 82.

fascination with motoring in Kenneth Grahame's *The Wind in the Willows*, 1908.)[105] King Edward was reported as having said in 1902: 'Everyone is going mad on motoring and apparently they enjoy it more than cruising in their yachts'.[106]

Then there was the increasing use of *motor* yachts by the rich to demonstrate their wealth, at the expense of the *sailing* yacht. The number of steam yachts in *Lloyd's Register of Yachts* rose from 735 in 1890 to 1,584 in 1914, from 24 per cent to 41 per cent of the total number.[107] The preference for steam yachts among the very rich and successful was becoming ever more marked. To some extent, this moved the wind-driven sailing yacht out of the limelight, or made the possession of one less exclusive. But since the majority of yachtsmen were from the middle class and could never aspire to a motor yacht, this can only be a small part of the explanation.

Yachting needs confidence and optimism concerning the future to flourish. This necessary condition was clearly lacking in the years before the Great War. The political situation was gradually worsening, on both the domestic and foreign fronts, The 'great unrest', with the army fighting workers, was around 1911–1912, but many of the relevant factors were already present many years earlier.

At home, unemployment and underemployment were recurring features, with cyclic depressions in 1879, 1885, 1894 and 1904.[108] 'Unemployment' first appeared in the *Oxford English Dictionary* for 1882 and 'underemployment' in 1888.[109] The unions were getting stronger – the matchgirls' strike was in 1888; the London dockers struck in 1889 and 1911. The Labour Party was formed in 1900 and won its first seat in 1903.

The Irish question was unresolved. It proved impossible to get home rule for Ireland through both Houses of Parliament, leaving the likelihood of an Irish rebellion an ever-present threat.

Another major political problem was votes for women. The National Union of Women's Suffrage Societies was formed in 1897; Emily Pankhurst's more militant Women's Social and Political Union in 1903; and the Women's Freedom League in 1908. Emily Davidson died at the feet of the king's horse in the 1913 Derby. By the 1910s, the suffragettes were using direct action, such

---

[105] Because of Ratty's remark about 'messing about in boats', *The Wind in the Willows* is often taken as a hymn to sailing. There is no sailing in the book. There is some rowing and sculling, but by far the most exciting form of transport Grahame describes is the motor car.

[106] Atkins, *Further Memorials of the Royal Yacht Squadron*, p. 53.

[107] Cusack, 'The Rise of Aquatic Recreation and Sport', p. 411.

[108] Bédarida, *Social History*, p. 103.

[109] *Ibid.*, p. 107.

as fire bombing buildings, and the State was responding by force feeding suffragette prisoners. Only the War and the national unity that followed broke
the deadlock.

Confidence in innate British superiority was severely dented by the long-
drawn-out Boer Wars. At the start of the first Boer War in 1899, many new
builds were cancelled on the Clyde, and many yacht owners went to fight as
officers in South Africa.[110]

The Second Boer War (1901–1902), where Britain overcame Dutch farmers, armed only with rifles,[111] with great difficulty and by the use of scorched
earth tactics and concentration camps, hardly squared with the rampant jingoism. Erskine Childers' letters home to his sisters were put together to form
the bestselling *In the Ranks of the CIV* [the City Imperial Volunteer Battery],
1900. As Childers bluntly put it, 'It took 450,000 British troops four years to
defeat 40,000 Boers'.[112]

Given we had difficulty winning a war against Dutch farmers, there had to
be pessimism as to whether Britain could win a war with Germany. As early
as 1887, in his account of his voyage from Hammersmith to Copenhagen in
1887, *The 'Falcon' on the Baltic*, E. F. Knight, an experienced political correspondent, was sure Germany was preparing for war, but was not clear as to
whom they intended to fight.[113] Erskine Childers' *The Riddle of the Sands*,
published in 1903, describes the build-up of naval resources on the German
West Coast; and the canals recently built to aid German naval movements –
the Ems-Jade between the naval port of Wilhelmshaven and Emden, finished
in 1888, and the Kaiser-Wilhelm (the Kiel) canal, completed in 1895 – and the
dangers arising from Admiralty complacency.[114] The novel describes how
our heroes prevent a well-planned invasion, aimed at landing thousands of

---

[110] Black, *G. L. Watson*, p. 327.

[111] The Mauser, the Boers' rifle, was the most up-to-date weapon available, provided by the Kaiser.

[112] Erskine Childers, *In the Ranks of the CIV*, 1900.

[113] E. F. Knight, *The 'Falcon' on the Baltic*, 1888. Would it be the Russians that had to be stopped in
its expansion; was it the British Navy that had to be challenged? Indeed, up to the 1880s, who
was plotting to invade England – France? Russia? German? Only around 1900 did the betting
shorten on Germany. See Adam Riches, *When the Comics Went to War*, pp. 44–69.

[114] Childers' voyage was from 4 August to 17 December, 1897, which is such a strange time to
cruise that one cannot help wondering if he was spying on German defences and updating
charts of the waters around the Frisian islands. The pun in Childers' title may be missed,
namely Matthew 7: 26. 'And every one that heareth these sayings of mine, and doeth them not,
shall be likened unto a foolish man, which built his house upon the sand'.

German troops in Norfolk. These authors were reflecting wider fears of a war with Germany.[115]

Doubts about England's ability to maintain its empire, or even its ability to prevent an invasion, grew. These are clearly expressed in *The Riddle* ... which is also full of criticisms of the organisation and running of the armed services. In the Epilogue, it reaches its zenith of despair:

> Cooperation between the army and the navy is not studied or practised ...
> Distracted by the multiplicity of its functions in guarding our colossal empire
> and commerce and *conspicuously lacking a brain*, not merely for the smooth
> control of its own unwieldly mechanism, but for the study of rival aims and
> systems.[116] (my italics)

That a best-selling book at home and across the empire by a senior Parliamentary clerk could, without apology, voice the seemingly traitorous dismissal of the hegemonic narrative concerning British supremacy indicates the serious unease about the reality of British imperial greatness.[117] In 1908, Admiral Fisher with chilling accuracy predicted that war with Germany would commence in August or September, 1914, as the Kaiser had to complete his programme of warship building, deepen the Kiel canal so that the warships could move easily from the Baltic to the North Sea, and get the harvest gathered in.[118] There was a strong underlay of paranoia and fear of British rigidity and incompetence, overlaid by a shouted chorus of British

---

[115] It was only one of a number of fictional accounts published around the same time that warned of the threat from the growth of German military might, such as William Le Queux's sensational *The Invasion of 1910*, published in 1906. See I. F. Clarke's compilation of such texts *The Great War with Germany 1890–19*. As early as 1871, Sir George Chesney had written an invasion story, 'The Battle of Dorking'. Successful invasions, beaten by the prompt action of farmboys and other worthy lads was a regular staple of end-of-century comics – see Riches, *When the Comics Went to War*. When, in one story from *The Boys Herald*, 1 May, 1909, our farmboy hero returns from alerting the authorities, he finds his father and brother dead. He asks: 'Tell me about the Navy. What has become of the North Sea Fleet? Why have they allowed the Germans to invade us?' (Riches, *When the Comics Went to War*, pp. 87–88). This plea is the same as Childers': why was there no naval base on the east coast, facing Germany? Our main naval bases, Portsmouth and Plymouth, were on the south coast, to face the old enemy, France. The creation of Rosyth naval base was announced in March, 1903 but it was not opened till 1915 (Drummond, *The Riddle*, pp. 162–163). (See Ruger, *The Great Naval Game*.)

[116] *The Riddle of the Sands*, p. 255. The passage is reminiscent of Kipling's contemporaneous 'The Islanders' (1902):

> Then you returned to your trinkets; then you contented your Souls
> With the flannelled fools at the wicket or the muddied oafs at the goals
> Given to strong delusion, wholly believing a lie,
> Ye saw that the land lay fenceless, and ye let the months go by

[117] It was 'hugely popular across the empire' (Riches, *When the Comics Went to War*, p. 67).

[118] Guy Crowden, 'Admiral of the Fleet, Lord Fisher: Technocrat Extraordinary'. That the Kaiser's *Meteor* was sailing to Cowes Week, just as war was being declared, was a bizarre feature of the

superiority (to be tragically acted out in the 'all over by Christmas' rush to enrol).[119]

The reader concerned with the causes of the First World War will want to read books on the subject; but it makes sense to think that the dismal showing in the Boer Wars, the threat from Germany and the knowledge that English jingoism was unfounded, may well have caused dismay among those with surplus income; and they, in senior management and in the professions, and well networked, were in a good position to separate the jingoistic chaff from the wheat of reality. Once the distant, but increasing, threat of war hung over the nation, yacht production and activity was always likely to suffer. Long before 1914, the Golden Age of yachting was a blur of hazily remembered summers.

In August 1914, Hilaire Belloc was sailing back East from picking up the *Nona* in Fowey. He had heard rumours of war in Plymouth. Now he was off the Start, sailing for the Dart:

> In this loneliness and content, as I sailed Northward, I chanced to look after an hour's steering or so, eastward again toward the open sea … . Like ghosts, like things themselves made of mist, there passed between me and the newly risen sun, a procession of great forms, all in line, ... hastening eastward. It was the Fleet recalled ... . Then I knew that war would come.[120]

Anthony Heckstall-Smith had come down to Cowes to report on the Regatta:

> … we took the paddle steamer from Ryde to Cowes on an August morning to witness the opening day of the regatta. The roadstead was crowded with yachts … . As for the war, well, Herr Krupp's *Germania* was lying in the roads and our own fifteen-metres had but recently returned from Kiel. What if the Kaiser's *Meteor* had not arrived? Even if the rumour was true that he had suddenly recalled her when she was halfway across the North Sea, he was probably only being truculent. There, too, in the roads was the *Victoria and Albert* with King George and Queen Mary aboard ... .

---

times. It is reminiscent of the Dutch giving Charles II yachts in 1660 and 1661, and being at war with him in 1665. It seems to be a small step to playing with yachts to going to war.

[119] An optimism shared by yachtsmen: 'Most yachts were quickly laid up in 1914 by owners convinced the war would soon be over' (Leather, *The Northseamen*, p. 170). In the winter of 1914, appeals were made to yachtsmen to contribute their wellies and their oilies to the ill-prepared troops at the Front (McCallum, *Fast and Bonnie*, p. 107).

[120] Hilaire Belloc, *The Cruise of the Nona*, 1925, pp. 149–150.

Then almost unnoticed by the holiday makers or the pretty ladies, a lean, grey destroyer came steaming into the gay and sunlit roadstead. Signals flashed between the bridges of the guardship and the Royal yacht. Launches and naval pinnaces sped like water beetle over the blue sea.

War had been declared ... .

All that afternoon the crews of the racing yachts and the steaming yachts were coming ashore with their kitbags ... By sunset that evening, many of the steam yachts had hardly enough hands left aboard to get underway ... .

By the following morning, there was scarcely a yacht left in the roadstead and the White Ensign no longer flew at the yard of the Squadron flagstaff.[121]

What happened to *Shamrock IV*, now in America? Sir Thomas Lipton had received a cable from New York regretting that Britain was at war, and Sir Thomas requested that the challenge be postponed for a month. If war continued the match should be postponed for a year.[122]

If any question why we died
Tell them, because our fathers lied[123]

But who shall return us our children?[124]

---

[121] Anthony Heckstall-Smith, *Sacred Cowes*, pp. 82–83. The use of the White Ensign had been granted to the R.Y.S. by William IV in 1833. At times of war, it can only be flown by ships of the Royal Navy.

[122] May Fife McCallum, *Fast and Bonnie*, p. 107.

[123] Kipling, 'Epitaphs of the War', 1914–1918. Kipling had encouraged his son, John, to enrol and used his influence to get him a commission, even though he had already been turned down by the Army because of his severe short-sightedness. He was commissioned as a second lieutenant in the 2nd Battalion, Irish Guards, on turning 17. After training, he went to France in August, 1915. John Kipling was killed at the Battle of Loos a month later.

[124] Kipling 'The Children', 1914–1918.

14 A powerful depiction of a classic yacht and an early submarine,
a few years before the outbreak of war in 1914

CHAPTER TWELVE

Between the Wars

War is coming. 1941, they say. And there'll be plenty of broken crockery, and little houses ripped open like packing cases, and the guts of the chartered accountant's clerk plastered over the piano that he's buying on the never-never.[1]

Britain and its allies had won the War, and the British empire had expanded still further, with the handing over of German East Africa and Mesopotomia (later Iraq), Palestine and part of Greater Syria from the Turkish (Ottoman) Empire. It now owned 30 per cent of the world's surface and controlled 25 per cent of its population; so winning the war could be judged, from that perspective, as a success. But this expansion was rendered problematic, as it required yet more troops and administrators to rule at a time when the British economy was much weakened by the colossal cost of the war effort in lives and money.[2]

Figures vary slightly concerning the carnage of the Great War, but, approximately, of 5,397,000 men mobilised, 703,000 were killed, and 1,663,000 wounded, giving a casualty rate of 44 per cent. Ten per cent of the British male population under 45 was dead.[3]

In the early part of the war, officers led their men 'over the top' (of the trenches) at the Front, wearing a different uniform and carrying a pistol, not a rifle. This made it easy for the German soldiers to carry out their orders to take out the officers in order to increase the chaos and demoralisation among the men. The average length of time before becoming a casualty as an officer in the trenches was six weeks.

The war was followed by the 1918–1920 pandemic of Spanish Flu, which killed some 40 to 50 million worldwide, and around 250,000 in Britain.

---

[1] George Orwell, *Coming Up for Air*, 1939, p. 223.
[2] Thus, John Illingworth, top post-war racing skipper, and Ransome's fictional father, Commander Walker, in *Swallows and Amazons*, were both in the Navy on the China Station during the inter-war period.
[3] Madge, *Long Voyage Home*, p. 89.

By 1920, many, many yachtsmen, and potential yachtsmen, were dead or invalided. I can find no figures for yachting, but in the neighbouring field of rowing, a quarter of the membership of Bradford Amateur Rowing Club on the River Aire were killed on active service.[4] The huge losses of men and their families' grief made enjoying leisure seem disrespectful into the mid-1920s.[5] There was little sailing in Swansea Bay, for example, till 1922, when its first post-war regatta was held.[6]

The RNVR's contribution to the war effort could not be doubted. Members of the yacht clubs belonging to the YRA received 'no less than twenty-four DSCs, seven DSOs, two Albert Medals and, most notable of all, three VCs'.[7]

During the war, yachts and fishing vessels had been used as Q ships – decoys to lure submarines to the surface, intending to sink the Q ship by gunfire, rather than use expensive torpedoes. But once surfaced, the British vessel would open concealed gun ports and attempt to sink the sub. In total, 366 Q ships were taken into service and 11 U boats sunk.[8]

There was a General Strike in 1926, polarising class divisions. The Great Depression, stemming from the Wall Street crash of 1929, stretched into the mid-1930s, with 2.7 million unemployed in 1932. The economy only recovered with re-armament.[9] Fear for Britain's economic future was quickly joined by fear about another world war. Hitler became Chancellor of Germany in 1933, and from then on in, war seemed ever more likely; while Britain could no longer depend on its navy to provide the continuation of the 'wooden walls'. As Stanley Baldwin, the prime minister, told the House on 10 November, 1932: 'The bomber will always get through.'

---

[4] Aylwin Sampson, *Winning Waters*, p. 18.

[5] 'After 1918 it was never quite the same again. Snobbishness and expensive habit came back, certainly, but they were self-conscious and on the defensive.' (George Orwell, 'Such, Such Were the Joys'.)

[6] Austin, 'Yachting in Swansea Bay', p. 245.

[7] Gordon Fairley, *Minute by Minute*, p. 55. Two members of the West Kirby YC alone gained VCs (John Millar, *Anything but Sailing*, pp. 85–100).

[8] Alston Kennerley, *The Maritime History of Cornwall*, pp. 379–380. On the German side, Felix von Luckner, captain of the *Seeadler* (Sea Eagle), a three masted commercial sailing ship with hidden armaments, became a legend for destroying Allied shipping, whilst always allowing the crew to disembark first (see Blaine Pardoe, *The Cruise of the 'Sea Eagle'*).

[9] Three great industries, namely coal mining, shipbuilding and, especially, cotton, declined severely. The industrial cities became characterised by their 'smokeless chimneys'. The severity was far greater in the north of the country and industrial Scotland. Sympathetic to the high unemployment among fishermen in Brixham, Devon, George V in 1930 requested that a proportion of *Britannia*'s crew be drawn from that port, and later, a few from Looe, Cornwall (Leather, *The Salty Shore*, p. 124).

The war had made a bitter nonsense of British racial superiority inevitably leading to a quick success; but when dominant narratives start losing their credibility and their 'naturalness' ('the ways things are'/ 'the way we've always done things'), they are trumpeted with increased noise and vigour, as if to drown out the citizens' doubts and decreased conviction. So, the major narratives pertaining to yachting, regarding patriotism, class and gender, in short Athleticism, continued to be applied more or less unchanged, especially as they might all need to be polished up and brought out again in the near future.[10]

The Anglo-Irish Treaty of 1921 at last resolved 'the Irish Question', but not before the Irish Civil War of 1922.[11]

During the war, many racing yachts were sold to Scandinavian countries. Many more yachts had had their heavy lead keels removed for making bullets.[12] The yachtsman seeking a new build could go to a number of respected yards – Hillyards in Littlehampton; Moody's at Swanick on the Hamble; Percy Mitchell at Mevagissey, and then in neighbouring Porthmellon, in Cornwall; and Woodnutts at Bembridge, Isle of Wight, whose managing director was Alfred Westmacott, a very respected yacht designer.[13] Often, these were yards whose reputation for building seaworthy fishing boats led yachtsmen to place orders with them. Albert Strange, working in Scarborough, was producing canoe yawls, capable of sailing in the North Sea.[14] Robin Balfour, later Lord Riverdale, designed and built himself a bilge keeler, *Bluebird*, and described it in *Yachting Monthly*, June 1929; however the bilge keeler only really took off after the Second World War.[15]

Fears of, and experiences with, steamers continued to be recorded, for example in Alker Tripp's *Shoalwater and Fairway*, 1924; and Griffiths' *The Magic of the Swatchways*, 1932. The totally inadequate practice of only showing a white light when you were aware of traffic coming up astern was still

---

[10] Hence the many Somerset Maugham short stories set in the colonies that feel very pre-First World War but are actually inter-war. In 'The Door of Opportunity', a cerebral district officer refuses to go with his police force into a plantation where the Chinese workers have rioted. When, reinforced by army troops, he eventually tackles the situation, he finds that a Dutch planter, armed only with a shot gun, and four assistants, have quelled the riot. He is sent home. His wife stands by him on the passage back home and then leaves him as she loathes him because 'I saw the fear in your eyes. I nearly fainted with horror' (p. 1,107).

[11] The effects of these years on the Royal Irish and the Royal St George are told in Boylan, *White Sails Crowding*, pp. 93–99 and Archer and Pearson, *Royal St George Yacht Club*.

[12] Leather, *The Northseamen*, p. 170.

[13] David Moody, *The Moody Legacy*; Percy Mitchell of Porthmellon. *A Boatbuilder's Story*.

[14] Leather, *Albert Strange*.

[15] Griffiths, *Swatchways and Little Ships*, p. 55; Lord 'Skips' Riverdale, *A Life, A Sail, A Changing Sea*.

current.[16] The inherent danger of being run down by the heavy steamer traffic in the Thames Estuary and the southern North Sea is vividly described in his *We Didn't Mean to Go to Sea*. Yachts rarely carried flares to seek help in distress.[17]

Developments in Yacht Cruising

There was a series of developments that made the cruising life a little easier. Pilot books for the cruising yachtsman helped him sail further afield. The Clyde Cruising Club published its first edition of *Directions to the West Coast* in 1922, and the Irish Cruising Club, founded in 1929, its pilotage of the Irish East coast in 1930. Adlard Coles published *Sailing the South Coast* in 1936.

The CQR (Coastal Quick Release) anchor was introduced in the 1930s by Sir Geoffrey Ingram Taylor. A single fluke anchor with a weighted tip, it represented a major advance on the fisherman's anchor, which had been in use up to then.[18] The RNLI motorised its lifeboats during the 1930s.

In the late 1930s, the first marina in England was created at Birdham near Chichester, by converting one of the last working tidal mill pools.

Sailing was undertaken with very basic equipment:

> as demonstrated by a 1938 inventory published by Francis Cooke ... No electrical instruments were listed, except a torch worked by dry batteries ... no signal lamps ... or even emergency rockets. Navigation was by compass, with a gimballed candlestick for night use, and there was a lead and line, but no trailing log ... Cooke suggested ... binoculars and, if there was sufficient room, a wireless receiver to obtain weather forecasts.[19]

To add to the list of equipment the modern yachtsman now takes for granted, there was no echo sounder. Accounts of sailing into shallows frequently have one crew man calling out the depths from the lead line, a piece of rope, at one end of which was a weight. When straightened out after it had hit the bottom, the crew man read off from the differing numbers of bits of leather

---

[16] Ransome describes this practice in an article for the *Cruising Association Bulletin* in 1937 (reprinted, 1996). Crossing the Thames at night: 'There was a good deal of traffic, and twice we had to show a light from the cockpit to steamers coming up astern' (p. 22). The system was inadequate because you could not locate an oncoming vessel in poor visibility.

[17] Griffiths, *Swatchways and Little Ships*, p. 66.

[18] Daria and Alex Blackwell, 'A Brief History of Anchors', pp. 44–46.

[19] Cusack, 'Yachting in Britain', pp. 175–176. She is quoting from Cooke's *Pocket Cruisers*, Chapter 13, pp. 126–135.

intertwined into the rope, and called out what the depth was in fathoms (6 feet, 1.83 metres).

Cooking was done on a paraffin stove, as gas bottles for cooking only came in after the Second World War. The Seagull outboard engine came on the market in 1931, but was expensive.

The petrol engine was available, and some yachts had them installed, but they were unreliable and low powered by today's standards.[20] Without an engine, yachtsmen had to sail off their moorings, or when they had raised the anchor. Until the boat gathers way, she is at the mercy of the wind and/ or tide. If the wind is strong, it is all too easy to lose control. In his autobiography, *Slide Rule*, Nevil Shute, a keen yachtsman and a novelist who often included yachting in his writings,[21] recalled, shortly after the first war, crewing in 'a heavy, straight, stem yawl of 28 tons':

> Getting that cumbersome old boat to sea under sail down the narrow river [the Hamble] was a nightmare for there was barely room for her to gather way upon one tack when it was necessary to come about again. Running on the mud and kedging off was normal and collisions with other boats moored in the river was so frequent that it was the usual practice for the owner to keep a supply of visiting cards handy near the cockpit. When you collided with another yacht and carried away his crosstrees or forestay you would apologise politely for what was an everyday occurrence and hand your card to the owner or his paid hand requesting him to send you on the bill, and go bumping your way out to sea. ... No bad feeling was engendered by these incidents, because they were normal to the sport of yachting in those days.[22]

While seemingly polite, this is actually rather cavalier behaviour, since if the forestay or crosstrees were carried away, it is likely that the mast would fall down.[23] Anchorages got more crowded as people recovered from the Great War. Francis B. Cooke, in *In Tidal Waters*, describes sailing with his friends and shareholders in an old bawley which, overwhelmed by a squall, runs

---

[20] Ian Nicolson, *Alfred Mylne*, p. 80.
[21] As in his first novel, a thriller *Marazan*, 1926, *What Happened to the Corbetts*, 1939 and *The Trustee from the Tool Room*, 1960.
[22] Shute, *Slide Rule*, pp. 42–43.
[23] Shute's anti-social behaviour may have contributed to his emigrating to Australia. 'He was very upset by a row at the [Hayling Island] Sailing Club, which led to him being rebuked by the Commodore for the unspeakable offence of untying a boat that had used his mooring without permission and letting it float out to sea ... He emigrated to Australia ...' (Tom Fort, *Channel Shore*, p. 134).

amok in the Gravesend anchorage, and Percy Woodcock several mishaps in *Looking Back*.[24]

Cruising Grounds

In the 1920s there were very few published accounts of yacht cruises. The three best known are Ralph Stock's *The Cruise of the Dream Ship*, 1922, G. H. P. Mulhauser's *The Cruise of the Amaryllis*, 1924 and Conor O'Brien's *Across Three Oceans*, 1927. All three had served in the war and two – Stock and Mulhauser – were recovering from its effects. Stock, invalided out of the trenches, sailed away in a converted fishing boat, with another demobilised officer and his sister, who was known as 'Peter'.[25] Via the Panama, they reached the Friendly Islands in the Pacific, where Stock, much to his crew's disgust, sold the boat. G. H. P. Mulhauser, his nerves in tatters after four years of minesweeping duties in the North Sea, circumnavigated with three crew in *Amaryllis*, a 52 foot yawl built in 1882, via the Panama and Suez canals, starting in September 1920 and returning in July 1923. He died within weeks of returning to Dartmouth and his log was published posthumously.[26] Conor O'Brien completed a circumnavigation in his 20-ton, 42 foot long overall ketch, *Saoirse* ('freedom' in Irish Gaelic) between 20 June, 1923 and 20 June, 1925, leaving from and returning to Dun Laoghaire. Yachtsmen stopped racing to escort him and a crowd, estimated at 30,000, cheered his homecoming.[27]

A few other long distance voyages worthy of note are Sidney Houghton's crossing from Burnham to Nova Scotia in 1921 in 25 days in a 21 ton (Thames Measurement) cutter *Neith*.[28] A retired naval commander, R. D.

---

[24] Cooke, *In Tidal Waters*, pp. 45–46, and Woodcock, *Looking Astern*, pp. 176–184.

[25] It was very common for women to be given nicknames from before the Edwardian era up to the Second World War. Women also commonly adopted masculine names. We will meet 'Peter Gerard', born Dulcie Kennard, later in this chapter.

[26] The boat had been lying in the mud of a Devon creek for fourteen years before, in 1919, E. G. Martin restored her superbly but then had to sell her (Clare McComb, 'George Martin, Founding Father of Restoration'). On Mulhauser's death, his sister gave *Amaryllis* to Britannia Naval College for use as long as she was seaworthy. In 1951, she was towed out to sea and sunk (Cyril King, 'Yachting at Dartmouth: An Outline History', p. 18).

[27] Boylan, *White Sails Crowding*, p. 100. For American Atlantic crossings, see Klein and King, *Great Adventures in Small Boats*. The Frenchman, Alain Gerbault, gained fame with his leisurely circumnavigation, 1923–1929, written up in his *In Quest of the Sun*.

[28] Jan Wise, *50 Years of East Anglian Offshore Racing*, p. 8.

Graham, sailed his small, 30 foot, 7 ton gaff cutter, *Emanuel*, from Ireland to Newfoundland and back to England in 1934.[29]

The Baltic continued its attraction for British yachtsmen. Arthur Ransome covered the Russian Revolution in Moscow as the foreign correspondent of the *Manchester Guardian*. He made the highly dangerous journey across the lines between the White and Red army lines to Estonia. There, in 1919, he took up sailing and his third boat was *Racundra*.[30] Adlard Coles bought *Racundra* from him in 1925 and, with his wife as his crew, brought her home from Riga, the account of the voyage being *Close Hauled* (1926). They explored Baltic water in a number of voyages till the beginning of the Second World War.[31] W. E. Sinclair, in *Cruises of the 'Joan'*, 1934, told of taking her to Greenland. On the return passage, she was overwhelmed and had to be abandoned.[32] Frank Carr's *A Yachtsman's Log*, 1935, records two voyages to the Baltic.

Nearer home, Hilaire Belloc's *The Cruise of the 'Nona'* is an enduring classic concerning a pre-war cruise from Holyhead to Shoreham, published in 1925.[33] His position is heavily Corinthian – *The Cruise* opens with a terrifying account of sailing through Bardsey Sound in a gale.

The Centrality of the Thames Estuary for the Cruising Man

The inter-war years highlighted relating to the sea and sailing as *the seeking of solitude and relaxation*. This emphasis is hardly surprising during a period of very high stress – grief at the loss of loved ones in the war, and the fear and anxiety about a second world war, which started long before 1939. The bombing of Guernica by German bombers on behalf of Franco's Nationalist movement in April 1937 during the Spanish Civil War, immortalised by Picasso's painting of the same year, would have removed any optimism.

---

[29] He wrote an account of his voyage in *Rough Passage*, 1936. He had promised to take his daughter, Helen, a competent sailor, as crew, but perhaps wisely in view of the rough weather he encountered, went back on his promise. She, Helen Tew, eventually sailed the Atlantic at the age of 88 in a 26 foot cutter with one of her sons. She tells her story in *Transatlantic at Last*.

[30] Ransome, *The Autobiography of Arthur Ransome*, pp. 279–307.

[31] Adlard Coles, *In Finnish Waters: From Estonia to Sweden*, 1932; *'Mary Anne' among 10,000 Islands: Cruising in the Finnish Archipelago*, 1938. Ransome asked Coles to change *Racundra's* name, as he was publishing *Racundra's First Voyage*, so Coles changed it to *Annette II*. He summarised his pre-war sails in his autobiography, *Sailing Years*.

[32] In his later *The Cruise of the 'Quartette'*, 1937, he wrote up his cruise to the west coast of Africa and South America.

[33] Belloc actually undertook the cruise in the summer of 1914 to help him get over the death of his wife, Elodie, in the February of that year. It is told as if it were a continuous cruise, but his biography indicates that there were quite long gaps while they left the boat in safe havens (A. N. Wilson, *Hilaire Belloc*, Chapter 9, pp. 203–215). Raban provides a good introduction to this mixture of sublime sailing writing and extreme right-wing politics in his Introduction to the Century edition.

Yachting as an escape from the city was almost a cliché of the yachting press and yachting writers. The pallid, etiolated existence of the city worker was contrasted with the freedom of the seas. For example, in his best-selling *The Magic of the Swatchways*, Griffiths describes how having arrived at the end of a weekend passage at his mooring at Heybridge:

> ... her owner was reluctantly making fast the last tier round the mainsail. On the cabin table a railway time-table lay open on the page on which read: 'Up trains, Maldon East and Liverpool Street.' The mate with shaven chin and stiff collar, was tragically hauling in the dinghy's painter bit by bit, while his hand ran affectionately along it and cleared it of clinging weed.[34]

Although there were more cars on the roads, this was not the main way of reaching one's boat. Rather, the yachtsman used his weekend pass on the railways, which the companies had introduced to encourage weekend travel at a much reduced rate, at the suggestion of the Cruising Association. This was particularly useful in the London sailors' favourite cruising ground – Essex, with its myriad small fishing ports, most of which had rail links to allow rapid transport of their catches.[35] The rail company's weekend pass was generous – from midday Friday to midday Monday.[36] If really late in reaching his port of destination, the yachtsman could take the milk train to work on Monday.

The possibilities of cruising were vastly expanded because the yachtsman did not have to return to his original port. He just had to pay the difference, if the journey was more expensive than that to his port of departure. So, in *June of Rochester*, published in 1939 but drawing on articles published previously in the yachting press, A. S. Bennett and his wife, Dorothy, are in their barge lying at Upnor on the Medway. She is content, he is restless:

> 'All right' she said with a smile 'When shall we go?'
> 'What about this weekend?'
> 'Where to?'
> 'Down Swin, somewhere or other. Maldon, if you like.'[37]
> 'M'm. Do you think we'd get there over the weekend?'

---

[34] Griffiths, *The Magic of the Swatchways*, p. 60.

[35] It would seem that creek crawling, per se, was attractive. In 1933, Adlard Coles published his *Creeks and Harbours of the Solent*, but the Solent is not usually viewed in this way. Rather, it is seen as a large expanse of relatively sheltered water, where you are never far from a harbour should the weather get rough.

[36] Dick Durham, *The Magician of the Swatchways*, p. 69.

[37] The West Swin runs up the side of the Foulness Sand, from where he can head for the Whitaker East Cardinal, giving him access to the Crouch, the Blackwater and the Colne.

'I reckon so. If not, there's Brightlingsea or Burnham. Might make
Battlesbridge with the wind easterly.[38] What does it matter?'
Which was true enough – so long as a morning train could be had for
London.[39]

The utility of the Cruising Association's Harbour Representative in pointing
one towards a reliable local to keep an eye on one's boat is evident. These
were 'registered boatmen' and there was a series of regulations governing the
contract between the visiting yachtsman and the boatman. One rather handy
one was 'Registered boatmen shall immediately go off to any vessel on which
they see the red rectangular flag with white diamond hoisted.'[40]

To aid the yachtsman, Stuart Messum provided a pilot, *East Coast Rivers*,
in 1903.[41] Francis B. Cooke published *London to Lowestoft: A Cruising Guide
to the East Coast* in 1906; and, in 1933, John Irving published his substantial
A Yachtsman's Pilot to the Rivers and Creeks of the Thames Estuary, an area
that conventionally stretched from North Foreland to Harwich (or even to
Orford Ness).

Sailing heavy boats among the sandbanks of the East Coast required
competent sailors and navigators. The Little Ship Club was founded in
central London, in 1926.[42] Leading figures behind its founding were Claud
Worth and Maurice Griffiths. It was an early provider of sailing instruction to
would-be yachtsmen, and, by 1927, was running courses on seamanship and
navigation for city workers, including women. Like the Cruising Association,
it ran a crew-finding service for skippers and sailors looking for a berth.

Worth was a busy man – ophthalmic surgeon, yacht designer, Commodore
of the Royal Cruising Club and, post-war, first President of the Little Ship
Club, and also a very influential writer on yacht design and construction.[43]
Both his *Yacht Cruising*, first published 1910, and *Yacht Navigation and
Voyaging*, 1927, went through many editions.

---

[38] Battlesbridge, on the Crouch, is ten nautical miles above Burnham and is the limit of navigation for a yacht.
[39] Bennett, *June of Rochester*, p. 219.
[40] Cooke, *Cruising Hints*, 6th edn, p. 436.
[41] Griffiths in *The First of the Tide*, 1971, p. 26, recalls its green cover from over fifty years ago but
gives the title incorrectly as *Thames Estuary Rivers*.
[42] The name of the club is a pun. A reader had written into *Yacht Sales and Charters*, which Griffiths edited before it amalgamated with *Yachting Monthly*, suggesting that there must be thousand of sea-starved, if not boat-starved, Londoners, and offered a room in the Ship Tavern,
Whitehall for a meeting (Griffiths, *Swatchways and Little Ships*, p. 80).
[43] His *Squint: Its Causes, Pathology and Treatment*, 1903, also went through many editions.

Halycon Days

The numerous accounts of sailing in the Thames Estuary, which includes North Essex, foregrounded the east coast with its creeks and mud and sandbanks, rather than the more riverine, deep water and class-conscious Solent. This difference is boldly stated by Francis B. Cooke in the first lines of the Preface to his *In Tidal Waters*, 1919, which concerns cruising in small boats in the Thames Estuary:

> Those whose ideas of yachting have been derived from lounging on the deck of a large steam yacht at Cowes during the Regatta Week, with an obsequious steward in attendance, will probably find little to interest them in these pages, as the cruises described were for the most part carried out in what the East Coast waterman usually terms 'little old tore-outs'.[44]

Accounts of 'creek crawling' had started with H. Lewis Jones' *Swin, Swale and Swatchway*, published in 1892. A key figure was Francis B. Cooke (1872–1974), author of many cruising books besides *In Tidal Waters*, which were concerned with sailing Essex waters.[45] This was published in 1919, with Hole Haven, behind Canvey Island, as the home of many of his tales. He then found the Thames too crowded with 'tea clippers, barges, collier brigs and those dirty new steamers' and moved to Fambridge, on the Crouch, where he founded the North Fambridge Yacht Club in 1892.[46] His was a Corinthian philosophy – being caught in a gale is referred to having 'a dusting'.

Alker Tripp (1883–1954), worked in the Metropolitan Police, so wrote as 'Leigh Hoe'. His first and best account of his cruising was *Shoalwater and Fairway: The Casual Explorations of a Sailing Man in the Shoal Seas and Tidal Waters of Essex and Kent*, published in 1924, which foregrounds yachting as a chance to relax. Tripp, unlike Cooke or Griffiths, saw little merit in seeking out rough weather.

---

[44] This is practically identical in tone to Carruthers' introduction to the *Dulcibella* in *The Riddle of the Sands*, comparing it to: '... Hazily there floated through my mind my last embarkation on a yacht: my faultless attire, the trim gig and obsequious sailors, the accommodation ladder flashing with varnish and brass in the August sun; the orderly snowy decks and basket chairs under the awning aft. What a contrast to this sordid midnight scramble, over damp meat and littered packing cases! (pp. 13–14). 'Tore-outs': Des Sleightholme uses the phrase in *A Funny Old Life*, p. 47, interchanging it with 'creaky-leakies'.

[45] He published some thirty books across seven decades (1900–1960s). He wrote all these books in his spare time, having a full-time job in banking.

[46] Quoted by Ian Griffiths in 'Sailing from Scratch', p. 12.

Griffiths was highly influential as a writer, yacht designer, and editor of *Yachting Monthly* from 1927 to 1965. He published his now canonical hymn of praise to these waters, *The Magic of the Swatchways*, in 1932.[47]

One of Griffiths' aims was to show that yachting was affordable and therefore to be enjoyed by a wide social spectrum, to be seen in his designing of small, affordable boats, 'sea-kindly, simple, shoal-draft little craft, ideally suited for the shallow waters of the creeks and estuaries that their designer understood so well and loved so dearly'.[48] Besides their shoal draft, they had lifting-keels and could be kept cheaply on moorings. He created 140 designs from which around 2,000 craft were built.[49] He explained his philosophy in many books about low-cost cruising, in *Yachting on a Small Income*, as he was starting out as a writer in 1920.[50]

The Magic of the Swatchways is incorrectly considered to be about peace, pipe smoking and sunsets in Essex creeks, and to epitomise 'messing about on the river' for successive generations. The magic and peace of the swatchways are there, but, in a direct continuation of Corinthian values, can only really be enjoyed after they have been earned by a battle with the sea.[51] The book starts with an account of leaving the fast ebbing Debden across a bar that is a mass of white water, on which they are nearly wrecked. In another chapter – an account of hauling up the anchor in a gale on the Stour – he writes 'There is something in a wind like this that holds out a challenge'.[52] Again, later, galebound on the Crouch, after a couple of days, 'the shrieking wind stirred up the waves the rain was trying to flatten out ... Bill and I looked at each other and the same thought occurred to us ..." Why not let's see what it's like outside, just for fun?"'.[53] So, the book is, in actual fact, about sailing in strong winds and difficult conditions; a philosophy of sailing that his wife, 'Peter Gerard', also a sailor, disapproved of. She was scathing about such combativeness:

---

[47] Swatchways or swashways are 'narrow channels through shoals or across a sandbank' (Joachim Shult, *The Sailing Dictionary*, p. 280). Griffiths' title indicates that the book is about inshore sailing.

[48] Frank Carr, Introduction, *The Magic of the Swatchways*, p. iii.

[49] Paul Gelder, '25 Cruising Heroes'.

[50] This became the better known as *Sailing on a Small Income*, published in 1953.

[51] The same frequency of derring-do in heavy weather is to be found in his edited collection, *Cruising Yarns from the 'Yachting Monthly'*, published in 1938.

[52] Griffiths, *The Magic of the Swatchways*, p. 92.

[53] *Ibid.*, pp. 118–119).

Only little, untried minds talk of *conquering* the sea ... No one CONQUERS Nature; you get by only through learning what you are up against and cooperating with her.[54]

The trope of the (earned) solitude and peace, letting the sailor get away from it all, was so well established that it could be lampooned. Griffiths recounts a sailing holiday with a friend and skipper in Hebridean waters:

> The wind fell and as twilight turned the hills of Skye into a sharp peaked jet black against the fading sunset, we stole quietly towards a light on shore and let go in seven fathoms.

> H. A. nodded to two white shapes that lay half a cable nearer the shore ... they appeared to be just little motor boats ... But my skipper liked them not. 'We'll clear out first thing in the morning, M. G.' he said. 'It's too crowded here'.[55]

And again, while clearly espousing Romantic concepts of one-ness with nature, he is prepared to parody this association:

> This was a night in a hundred, a soft refreshing night wherein the world and its haste and troubles seemed far away and insignificant. As I lay there and gazed up at the stars ... I felt supremely contented ... On a night such as this the soul of man is uplifted and he –

> 'Say, it's about time we had something to eat, don't you think? There are some cold sausages in the grub locker'.

> I could scarcely believe my ears as the mate's soulless voice broke in among my thoughts. His carnal desires, so brutally expressed, hurt my finer feelings ....[56]

A second author, this time of children's stories, fitted into both the mode of sailing for relaxation and calm, and also the joys of sailing the east coast waters. Arthur Ransome took a risk by retiring from being a foreign correspondent with the *Manchester Guardian*, for whom he had covered the Russian Revolution, and writing *Swallows and Amazons* in 1930. He wrote twelve volumes between 1930 and 1947, each being published in November in

---

[54] Peter Gerard, *Who Hath Desired the Sea*, p. 12, her emphasis.

[55] Griffiths, 'A Cruise in the Hebrides', in his *Little Ships and Shoal Waters*, pp. 146–170.

[56] *The Magic of the Swatchways*, pp. 102–103. Griffiths' attitude to boats was 'polygamous' (Stephen Pickard, *The 'Lone Gull' Files*, p. 26) – he was forever changing them, which lies uneasily on the easy-going persona he portrays in his writings. The West Mersea shipwright, Bill Wyatt, commented: 'Why, Mr Griffiths, I do believe every time you bring up in Mersea you come in a different bo't!' (*Swatchways and Little Ships*, pp. 32–33.)

time to be Christmas presents. The series became a major publishing success after *Peter Duck*, published in 1932.[57]

Ransome is so stereotyped as a gruff, uncle-figure, an embodied Captain Flint, that his importance as a writer is greatly under-rated.[58] Ransome, aware that another world war was coming, gave his readers a vision of England that was worth fighting and dying for. He also gave them a land, a geography to protect. So, he utilised the two most 'England-drenched' locations to be the backclothes of his novels – the Lake District and the Broads (*Coot Club*, 1934; *The Big Six*, 1940). Ransome also had the ability, after a series based on the Walkers in the Lake District, to create a whole set of new characters and use a new location: North Essex – Pin Mill and Harwich in *We Didn't Mean to Go to Sea*, and the Walton Backwaters in *Secret Waters*.

Remembrances of Craft Passed

Thames Barges

The iconic sight in the Essex maritime landscape was the Thames barge, carrying its hay to London and returning with horse-droppings (for manure) or bricks. The barges were a major form of transport before the Second World War. Griffiths counted thirty-five sheltering from a southwesterly gale in Harwich harbour in the early 1930s. As the wind turns westerly and eases, 'mainsails were unfolding like stage curtains, tops'ls were rising jerkily to mastheads … It was indeed a sight I have long since cherished in my sailing memories.'[59]

Yachtsmen greatly respected the bargemen for their skills. In Ransome's *Coot Club* (1934), a barge's mast is skilfully lowered before shooting a bridge and quickly raised after it, all by two men. *A Floating Home* (1918) by Cyril

---

[57] The 1930s was the decade when the sailing story, as opposed to the Sea Scout or Sea Cadet story, first appeared. Besides Ransome, two contemporary children's sailing authors were Conor O'Brien and Percy Woodcock. O'Brien had settled in Cornwall by the early 1930s and wrote *Two Boys Go Sailing* (1936), *The Runaways* (1941), *The Castaways* (1946) and *The Luck of the Golden Salmon* (1951). Yachting journalist, Percy Woodcock, like O'Brien, writing in the vein of 'good schoolchildren sailors vs. baddies', wrote *Sea Wrack* (1937), *Wreckers' Bay* and *Adventures Down Channel*, both published in 1938.

[58] For a more detailed discussion, see my 'Isn't It Time We Treated Arthur Ransome as a Grown-Up?' in which I suggest that Ransome is an important social commentator. For example, he gives girls leadership roles in the male world of sailing; and links children sailing dinghies with the adult world of yachting, most notably in *We Didn't Mean to Go to Sea*.

[59] Griffiths, *The First of the Tide*, pp. 66–68.

Ionides and J. B. Atkins, the latter a member of the Squadron, describes how Ionides bought a barge and made it his home. In their introduction, they:

> ... offer a tribute of praise to the incomparable barge skippers who navigate the busiest of waterways, with the smallest crews [the Thames estuary] and ... it [their book] is a study of dialect. It was impossible to grow in intimacy with the Essex skippers of barges without examining with careful detail the dialect which persists with a surprising flavour within a short radius of London.[60]

This desire to study and give value and validity to a regional and working man's dialect is highlighted by 'A glossary of Essex words and phrases' that occupies the last six pages of the book. A. S. Bennett's *June of Rochester* (1939) also is about buying a barge and living on it. It is also full of meetings with and advice from sailing bargemen. There were now 'crossover' yachts, because E. B. Tredwen had designed a barge yacht back in the 1890s, and quite a number were to be found on the east coast, tying up with the growth of Burnham as a yachting centre after the railway reached it in 1889.[61]

Sailorman (1933) by E. G. Martin, by now a leading light in ocean racing, recounts 'a winter spent working as a mate of a barge', and he also undertook a beautiful restoration of a Thames barge, *Memory*, which he then used commercially during the 1930s.[62]

Yachts and barges were frequently illustrated in the yachting press, and also in yachting books of the 1930s, by black and white drawings, and the magazines had covers by established artists. Griffiths, recalling his time at *Yachting Monthly*, wrote:

> I was in the enviable position of being able to reproduce the work of a number of fine illustrators whose pictures could be relied upon to capture the very essence of the sea and little ships and the kind of men who sailed on them. I recall with gratitude such names as W. L. Wyllie, Arthur Briscoe, Chas Pears, H. Alker Tripp, W. Edward Wigfull ... Robert E. Groves, George F. Holmes, Archie White, S. I. Veale, Winston Megoran, Leslie A. Wilcox, and Fid Harnack ...[63]

Some of these, such as Wyllie, Briscoe and Pears, were, and still are, considered eminent maritime artists. In addition to being a senior police officer in the Metropolitan force, Alker Tripp was also an accomplished artist, exhibiting

---

[60] Ionides and Atkins, *A Floating Home*, p. viii.
[61] Griffiths, *Swatchways and Little Ships*, p. 33.
[62] Clare McComb, 'George Martin Founding Father of Restoration'.
[63] Griffiths, *The First of the Tide*, p. 82.

at the prestigious Royal Academy summer shows. The illustrations of these artists gave visual evidence of the beauty of the swatchways and the craft that sailed along them. But, despite the large numbers still trading, already by the mid-1920s, Griffiths, looking back in *Swatchways and Little Ships*, wrote, 'But the beautiful sailing barges were beginning to die one by one. Here and there on the edge of the saltings you could come across a hulk alone, deserted and left to rot '.[64]

Recording the Death of Commercial Sail

By 1918, the golden age of the large commercial sailing ship had already passed.[65] In *Personal Record*, Conrad recalled sitting for his master mariner ticket. The month was November, 1886:

> The examiner pushed the signed blue slip across the table to me, and rose from his chair ... He offered me his hand and wished me well. He even made a few steps towards the door with me, and ended with good-natured advice.

> 'I don't know what may be your plans but you ought to go into steam. When a man's got his master's certificate it's the proper time.'[66]

Commercial sail was unable to compete with the motorised cargo ship. By the 1930s, only large bulk, low value cargoes, such as nitrates and wool, were still being transported by the clippers, and even here motorised vessels were making inroads. In 1927, Basil Lubbock attempted a retrospective study of

---

[64] Griffiths, *Swatchways and Little Ships*, p. 59. In fact, according to Leather, the peak time for barges had already passed. Writing about the Blackwater, he writes 'The local barge trade was at its peak about 1870–1914 ...' (*The Salty Shore*, p. 179).

[65] In fact, commercial sail was a long time dying. By the 1830s, regular steam ships were running on long distance routes, although they still kept their masts and sails. For inland and coastal work, paddle steamers were the preferred form of steam driven vessel (John M. Maher, *Channel Packets and Ocean Liners 1850–1970*). The nail in the coffin of commercial sail was the opening of the Suez Canal in 1869. The Canal was prohibitively expensive for sailing vessels, which had to be towed through it. Also, the shipping companies preferred younger men who only knew the ways of the steam vessel. There was a brief flurry during and for a while after the First World War, when the demand for the movement of freight and food caused decrepit ships to be brought back into service and some new building took place, but with the post-war slump, this upturn was short-lived (Basil Greenhill, *The Life and Death of the Merchant Sailing Ship*, pp. 51–57).

[66] Conrad, *A Personal Record*, p. 120. Conrad has been a little economical with the truth. This exchange – if it actually happened, for Conrad's 'factual reminiscences contain a fair amount of fiction' – occurred when he was re-sitting the exam (John Stape, *The Several Lives of Joseph Conrad*, p. 47). Conrad, like Slocum, could not continue in commercial sail, as it had so diminished by the turn of the century (Conrad did, initially, hope to get back to sea after starting to write novels).

the various types of boats in the various trades, such as wool, tea, nitrates, and jute, in his two-volume, thousand page *The Last of the Windjammers*.[67] A spectacular title, published in 1933 by John McCulloch, was *A Million Miles in Sail, Being the Story of the Sea Career of Captain C. C. Davis*. He achieved this incredible number of miles by being brought aboard his seafaring father's commercial sailing vessels.

Aware of the eminent demise of commercial sail, journalists, such as Eric Newby and the Australian, Alan Villiers, and the artist Claude Muncaster, signed on as ordinary seamen in order to gain an experience that would soon disappear. From their pens came Villiers' *Falmouth for Orders*, 1929, and Muncaster's *Rolling Round the Horn*, 1933.[68] Probably the most widely read was the journalist and travel writer, Eric Newby's *The Last Grain Race*, published in 1956, recounting his pre-war experience on the four-masted *Moshulu*, out and homeward bound from Australia with grain.[69]

These accounts were somewhat rose-tinted. As commercial sail declined, the profit margins were so small and the captain's wages so pitiful that corners were being cut, in terms of the ship's maintenance, the quality and quantity of the food, the number of crew and the very poor wages. When the pride of Eriksen's fleet, the *Herzogin Cecilie* foundered near Salcombe in April, 1936, he refused to spend any money salvaging her.[70]

---

[67] Ten years later, W. L. A. Derby undertook a similar task in a large, 400 page book with a similar era-defining title *The Tall Ships Pass*; and there were yet other commemorative texts, all with similar titles. Alan Moore published *Last Days of Mast and Sail* in 1925, and Ronald Pearse documented the surviving windships in three small books, starting in 1924 and published in one volume in as *The Last of a Glorious Era* in 1934. It has been said that Conrad was the narrator and Masefield the poet of commercial sail. Some of the appeal of Conrad's novels, such as *Youth* (1902) and *Typhoon* (1903) is due to evoking nostalgia; this is certainly true of Masefield's doggerel poems, such as 'Sea Fever' (1899) and 'Cargoes' (1902) and his boys' own stories of commercial sail, such as *The Bird of Dawning* (1933). The two poems are both in Masefield's *Salt-Water Ballads*, 1902. See Robert Foulke, 'Life in the Dying World of Sail, 1870–1910'. The English writers had the disadvantage of recalling the past. The great American sailing writers, such as Richard Dana (*Two Years before the Mast*, 1840) and Herman Melville (*Moby Dick*, 1851), were writing during the middle years of the nineteenth century and the heyday of American commercial sail (see my *Written on the Waves*).

[68] Other titles by Villiers include *By Way of Cape Horn*, 1930, and *Last of the Wind Ships*, 1934. Most of Villiers' books were well illustrated with his photographs.

[69] Newby's *The Last Grain Race* was undoubtedly helped by being added to the Mariners Library in the late sixties, when the list had been taken over by Adlard Coles. Some forty years later, he produced a book of the fine photographs he took during the voyage: *Learning the Ropes: An Apprenticeship in the Last of the Windjammers*, 1999. A female participant in these last days of commercial sail was Dorothy Laird (1912–2000), who, as a young journalist aged 22, made a voyage on the three-masted Finnish barque *Penang* in 1934. When she was working as an ordinary seaman, the ship was dismasted off Tasmania (Steve Humphries, *The Call of the Sea*, pp. 134–137). She wrote of her experiences in *Blackwood's* and *Chambers Magazine*.

[70] Greenhill and John Hackman, *Herzogin Cecilie*, pp. 165 ff.

The men who signed on under such conditions could, at best, move from one ship to another, if they could find one of the increasingly few commercial sail ships still carrying cargo. For such men, the pain of transition was acute and long-lasting. In Conrad's first maritime novel, *The Nigger of the 'Narcissus'*, the boat is drifting due to lack of wind. Able Seaman Belfast declares that he will 'chuck going to sea for ever and go in a steamer'.[71] Their wages, small as they were, were soon spent port-side on alcohol and women. Readers were consuming accounts of men they would never meet and would probably have shunned if they had.[72] But, as ever in yachting or sailing literature, the vast bulk of the readers had probably never sailed a boat, and for them, these accounts, with their deep masculinity, were seen as romantic.[73]

The Further Growth of Dinghy Sailing

To encourage a return to racing, in 1919 the YRA began to support Sunday racing, which had been taboo before 1914, due to pressure from the Church of England.[74]

The smallest YRA rated boat was selling at £900, well over twice its pre-war price.[75] As a result of such rising costs of yachting after the war, there was a downsizing in size of craft and 'the blossoming of small dinghy classes'.[76] Some of the one-design classes that came up between the wars are given in the table below.

The Weymouth Falcons are a good example of the benefits of a one-design. The problems with handicapping different types of boats were highlighted in 1904, when Mr Bussell, the Club Secretary, told the AGM of the Weymouth SC of his difficulty of handicapping fairly 'a Fife's one-design class racer sailing with a 14 ft. house-boat' and hoped the club would decide to adopt a one-design. Twenty-three years later, the club did agree on a one-design, designed by the good Mr Bussell. By ordering six at one go, the Club got the cost down to £40 for a sixteen-foot dinghy, and even negotiated hire purchase (£20 on delivery, £20 after the first year), and a sail-away cost

---

[71] Conrad, *The Nigger of the 'Narcissus'*, pp. 67–68.

[72] Peck, in *Maritime Fiction*, pp. 30–49, writes on the uneasy civilian construction of the sailor, for example, in Jane Austen's novels.

[73] The literature of the commercial 'wind ships' is discussed at greater length in my *Written on the Waves*.

[74] Ryan, 'Identifying the British Yachtsman, 1815–1939', p. 75.

[75] *Yachting Monthly*, 27 (159): 212; quoted by Ryan, 'Identifying the British Yachtsman, 1815–1939', p. 75.

[76] Dear, *The Great Days of Yachting*, p. 72.

of £42.50, which the Club's historian proudly claims makes it then and in 1955 when he was writing 'the cheapest O-D [one-design] on the market.[77]

Name	Designer	Comments
Shannon One-Design	Morgan Giles	18 ft dinghy with three crew. Commissioned by three yacht clubs on the Shannon – Lough Ree YC, Lough Derg YC and the North Shannon YC. First delivered 1921. (L. M. Goodbody. *The Shannon One-Design: A History*)
Sunbeam[a]	Westmacott	Solent and Falmouth classes formed 1923
Fowey Troy	Archie Watty in 1928	Only 21 ever built but still racing in Fowey. First race 1930
National 14, from 1927, International 14	Various – see text	Class formed 1923
Weymouth Falcons	Mr Bussell, sailmaker	First season 1927
Dart One-Design[b]	Morgan Giles	12 ft long, gunter rigged. First season late 1920s
Salcombe Yawl[c]	Design based on local fishing boats	First season 1935
National Twelve	Various – a development class	Spurred on by publication in *Yachting World*, March 1936, of Uffa Fox's 'Uffa King' design
Looe Redwing	Uffa Fox	Fox designed the 'Looe Redwing' as a 14 foot dinghy to cope with conditions off the South East Cornwall coast, at the request of the Commodore of Looe Sailing Club, Wilfred Neale. Eight were built in 1938[d]

a Peter Nicholson, *The Brilliance of Sunbeams*.
b Llewellyn, *A Brief History of the Royal Dart Yacht Club*, pp. 7–8.
c Parkinson, *Salcombe Yacht Club*, p. 21.
d Dear, *The Great Days of Yachting*, 127. See: http://www.looesailingclub.co.uk/redhistory.html

The Fourteens became a national class in 1923, through the combining of three existing fleets – the West of England Conference, the Norfolk Broads and a class sponsored by the Small Boat Racing Association. A Fourteen was the largest transportable dinghy, for its hull was the largest that could be transported by rail (for six shillings), and the mast was the longest that could be accommodated on a standard goods wagon.[78] It gained in prestige when,

[77] Hayes, *The History of the Weymouth Sailing Club*, pp. 7 and 59–62.
[78] Lavery, *In Which They Served*, p. 11.

'in 1927, His Royal Highness [the Prince of Wales] donated his famous cup to the 'Fourteens'.[79] It was first sailed for in 1927. In the same year, the YRA proposed to the International Yacht Racing Union that the Fourteen have international status, which was agreed. It was and is a restricted class, which meant that change and development was permitted within fixed guidelines. Uffa Fox (1889–1972) was a dinghy and yacht designer, who first saw most clearly the extra speed that would be created if a dinghy's bow could be made to lift from the water and plane. 'His 14s were vee'd in section rather than rounded, which, coupled with long, flat planning sections aft, gave them an excellent turn of speed off the wind.'[80] In 1928, his *Avenger*, out of 57 starts, claimed 52 firsts. By 1931, he gave up racing for the Prince of Wales Cup, saying, modestly, 'I can't go on beating all my customers if I am to go on selling them new boats'.[81] Actually, even more successful was Stewart Morris, twelve times winner of the Prince of Wales Cup between 1932 and 1965. He also won a gold medal at the 1948 Olympics, in the Swallow Class with David Bond.

Because the Fourteen could be built to improve on existing versions, this tempted the top small boat designers, such as Charles Nicholson, Morgan Giles and Alfred Mylne, as well as Fox, to design for this class, and it became quite an expensive pastime, only for the serious racer. So, Peter Scott, son of the Antarctic explorer, as he recalls in his biography, *The Eye of the Wind*, focussed on winning the Cup, knowing where next year's race would be, would rough up a design brief for a boat each year to take account of the local conditions. He then asked Uffa Fox to build it. The strategy worked. He won the Cup in 1937.

The 1938 Championships at Falmouth saw the first use of the trapeze, whereby the crew could sit further out than otherwise possible and keep the boat upright. Peter Scott, later to become a famous ornithologist, and John Winter used it as a secret weapon and won easily. The trapeze was promptly banned, only returning to the class in 1969, although allowed in the Flying Dutchman class by 1953 and by most of the other classes by then.[82]

The Sailing Olympics used the German Olympic Monotype- the Olympic Jolle – which were not sailed in England. The Commodore of the Royal Corinthian, Frederick G. 'Tiny' Mitchell obtained three of these boats

[79] Robin Steavenson, *Marks to Starboard*, p. 15; see also Thomas John Vaughan, *The International Fourteen Foot Dinghy, 1928–1964*.

[80] Bird, *Classic Classes*, p. 39.

[81] Lee, *The History of Barnt Green Sailing Club*, p. 11.

[82] Scott, *The Eye of the Wind*, pp. 243–247.

and held elimination trials at Burnham. Scott won these and went on to a bronze medal in Kiel in the summer of 1936.

Nationally, the sensation of the later 1930s was the National Twelve. The YRA, aware of the cost of the National 14, encouraged a smaller dinghy, but the 12 foot size did not take off till Uffa Fox published his design for *Uffa King* in the *Yachting World*, March 1936. N1 *Gipsy* was registered a month later. In September of the same year, 43 National Twelves gathered for the championship at Poole, racing for the first time for the Burton cup, donated by the top racing helmsman, Sir William Burton. By the end of the year, 175 were registered.[83]

There continued to be examples of members splitting away from an older, prestigious club to form a new club which was livelier and based around racing.[84] Salcombe Yacht Club had been created in 1894 as a place for well-heeled local gentlemen to meet. Salcombe Sailing club (SSC) was set up in 1922 'to suit the post-war situation. The younger element, male and female, and the local boat-building fraternity wanted a club of their own formed simply to provide facilities and organisation for racing, not the card room, the billiards etc. – and the high subscription – that went with a gentlemen's club'. Their clubhouse was an old paddle steamer, the *Ilton Castle*.[85]

Inshore Racing

The Seawanhaka International Challenge Cup for Small Yachts is the oldest yachting trophy originating in America, and also the oldest trophy for small yachts.[86] It originated in 1895 to encourage small yacht racing, usually in six-metre racers, and is held over five races between two yachts from a named yacht club of different nations. In 1922, after sailing a match of the British American Cup, F. J. ('Wee John') Stephen, of the Royal Northern YC on the Clyde, helming *Coila III*, which he designed, successfully challenged the holders, the Manchester YC, Massachusetts. The Royal Northern remained actively involved in this cup, in either six or eight metre boats up to 1947 – it had won the Cup in 1938 and defended it successfully on the Clyde in 1939. As usual on the Clyde, such racing was followed by large spectator fleets.

---

[83] Steavenson's *Marks to Starboard* is a detailed history of the 12s and 14s up to 1957.

[84] See my 'Concerning the Fragility and Future of Yacht Clubs'.

[85] Parkinson, *Salcombe Yacht Club: The First Hundred Years*, p. 15; Sharp, *Troubled Waters*, p. 74. The SSC and SYC amalgamated in 1964, the Sixties being a time of high inflation.

[86] Seawanhaka Corinthian Yacht Club, 'The History of the Seawanhaka Cup'. Seawanhaka YC is at Oyster Bay on the north side of Long Island, New York.

The Seawanhaka Corinthian Yacht Club was also responsible for the British–American Cup which was a team event and the first races were held in the Solent in 1921, in 6-metres, and on the Clyde in 1928. Four yachts were involved in each side. All the boats of the British team, the winners, were designed by Fife.[87]

The first Round the Island (Isle of Wight) Race was held on 11 July , 1931, the idea of Major Cyril Windeler of the Island Sailing Club, West Cowes. There were 25 starters, and the race was won by Captain R. T. Dixon's 10-ton cutter, *Lady Maud* in 6 hours, 10 minutes and 29 seconds. The club has organised the race ever since. It is claimed to be the most popular yacht race in the world. Usually, some 1,200+ boats, grouped into various starts, take part. The record is 1,875 yachts taking part in 2008.

The J Class

Large yacht racing never recovered to anything like its pre-war splendour. This was partly because ostentation was seen as bad form in the face of the nation's grief.[88] Also, after the war, there was a dramatic increase in the cost of running a large racing yacht. Before the war, a crewman's wage was 26 shillings a week. After the war, it was £3 17s 6d a week.[89]

George V relaunched *Britannia* as a racing yacht in 1920 in order to get yacht racing moving again. Regattas, and the racing circuit, slowly recovered.[90] An American Universal rule came into effect in 1930 – the size of a yacht was to be determined by its *waterline* length and 'J' signified yachts with a waterline length of between 75 and 87 feet and a Bermudan rig (*Britannia* had originally been gaff-rigged). These J Class yachts of the 1930s were some 130 foot overall length day racers, having no accommodation.[91] They needed a professional skipper and a crew of up to 24 men.

Ten J class yachts, six in America and four in England, were built and others converted. Four were designed by the now leading big yacht designer, Charles Nicholson from his Gosport yard – *Shamrock V* for Lipton; *Velsheda*, owned by Woolworths stores chairman W. L. Stephenson and named after

---

[87] Johnson, *Yacht Rating*, pp. 88–89; McCallum. *Fast and Bonnie*, pp. 115–117.

[88] The war also marked the end of the large, luxurious steam yacht, many of which had been volunteered or requisitioned by the Navy and lost in action (Couling, *Steam Yachts*, Introduction).

[89] Leather, *Northseamen*, p. 171.

[90] Occomore Sibbick, in *Lulworth Shared My Playground*, pp. xvii–xviii, gives practically the same regatta circuit in the 1920s as the pre-war one.

[91] Phillips-Birt, *The History of Yachting*, p. 167.

15 Charles Nicholson at the helm of the 23-metre class *Candida* in a two-reef breeze, up to weather of *Britannia* and with *Cambria* astern. J-class yachting in the first half of the 1930s attempted to recreate the glory of big yacht racing. *Candida* was designed and built by Charles Nicholson.

his three daughters, Velma, Sheila and Daphne; *Endeavour* and *Endeavour II*, both owned by aircraft manufacturer Tom Sopwith and built for the America Cup challenges of 1934 and 1937.

To compete with the J class, existing big class yachts had to be converted from gaff to Bermudan. These included *Britannia*, *Nyria*, Sir James Pender's *Brynhild*, *White Heather II*, *Terpsichore* (built in 1920 by R. H. Lee, later better known as *Lulworth*, when she was bought by Herbert Weld in 1924), *Astra* and *Candida*. TB Davis would race his schooner, *Westward*, against this fleet.[92]

---

[92] Despite being a good sailing friend of George V and his record of racing successes – *Westward* was nearly unbeatable when running – Davis was never proposed for the Squadron. His original trade was merchant seaman before a hugely successful career in stevedoring in Southern Africa. See Doug Ford. … *The Only Sailor in the Fleet*, the title being the compliment that the King gave Davis as an ex-seaman, the 'fleet' being the competing racing yachts.

In America, six J class yachts, were built. Four were built as contenders for the 1930 challenge of *Shamrock V*: *Enterprise*, the successful defender, and *Weetamoe*, from the Herreshoff yard; and from Lawley and Son's, Bristol, Massachusetts, *Whirlwind* and *Yankee*, the latter owned by Listerine mouthwash tycoon, Gerald Lambert; *Rainbow*, which defeated Sopwith's *Endeavour* in 1934; and *Ranger*, which defeated his *Endeavour II* in 1937.

Only *Yankee* ever sailed in British waters. Although, at most, six boats would be in any one race, their huge 'top hampers' made a dramatic sight and very large crowds would gather to watch them.

Neither of George V's sons, Edward VIII or George VI, was interested in yacht racing. So, the king instructed that, on his death, *Britannia* was to be scuttled. She was stripped of her gear and towed away from Cowes at night to prevent any public show of discontent, to the back of the Isle of Wight on 10 July, 1937 and dynamited. With that, the J class effectively ended.

Offshore and Ocean Racing

The Crouch Yacht Club, founded in 1907, claims its Houghton Cup, first raced for in 1911, to be the oldest established offshore race. Instigated by Sidney Houghton, it was an 80-mile *night* race from Burnham to the lightships and sand banks of the Thames Estuary.[93] From the same area, the Royal Corinthian Yacht Club's 95-mile Thames Estuary Race was inaugurated in 1932.[94] The Little Ship Club also organised North Sea races.[95]

In 1925, the first Fastnet race took place, organised by Weston Martyr (1885–1966), who had enjoyed taking part in the 1924 Bermuda Race, the 605-mile race from Newport, Rhode Island to Bermuda, organised by the Cruising Club of America, which had been founded in 1921. He organised it because the Royal Cruising Club (the RCC) refused to sanction what they saw as a dangerous event. It started at Ryde, Isle of Wight, went round the Fastnet Rock and lighthouse off the southwest coast of Ireland, and finished at Plymouth.[96] E. G. Martin had bought *Jolie Brise* in France in 1923, when she was a tunny fishing boat. He restored her in Teignmouth, close to his friend,

---

[93] It is still run, but is no longer a night race. One of the earlier competitors was run down by the Harwich train ferry (Wise, *50 Years of East Anglian Offshore Racing*, p. 8). The claim to be the oldest offshore race could be challenged by the Isle of Man Midnight Race, between Liverpool and Douglas, Isle of Man, organised by the Tranmere Sailing Club and first run on 24 May, 1907.

[94] Wise, *50 Years of East Anglian Offshore Racing*, p. 7.

[95] Cusack, 'Yachting in Britain 1890–1960', p. 171.

[96] Usually such events start from the Squadron line, so it is likely that permission was refused.

Morgan Giles' yard. She won the first Fastnet, with a time of 6 days, 2 hours and 45 minutes. (With Robert Somerset as skipper, she won this annual race again in 1929 and 1930.)

The skippers met after the race at the Royal Western, where Martin was Rear Commodore. He proposed they form the Ocean Racing Club – now the Royal Ocean Racing Club, and he was elected its first Commodore.[97]

Long-distance racing was initially criticised as too risky, for example by Claud Worth, as well as the RCC, but quickly developed a considerable following. By the 1927 race, there were fifteen starters. Only two boats finished and the winner was the gaff-rigged cutter *Betty*, later renamed *Tally Ho*, designed by Albert Strange. The Fastnet was soon established as a major race. The newly established American yacht design firm of Sparkman & Stephens produced *Dorade*, designed by Olin Stephens, which won the Transatlantic Race across in 1931, and then the Fastnet of 1931, steered by Olin, and the 1933 Fastnet, steered by by his brother, Rod. Olin Stephens' designs won all the races between 1931 to 1937, because he built to the rules to obtain the best rating possible, a manoeuvre considered unsportsmanlike by the Brits, till Charles Nicholson produced *Bloodhound* which won the 1939 race.

In 1928, the RORC began the annual Channel Race from Cowes to a mark off the French coast and back. In 1929, it organised the Cowes–Santander race. By 1938, it was running ten races.[98]

Yacht Clubs between the Wars: Unchanged Boundaries

There were more than 200 yacht clubs in Britain by 1936. Their structure of values remained basically unchanged from before the war.

There is a short story, 'Happy Ending', written in the 1930s, by Alfred Loomis (1890–1968), a leading American yachting journalist, who raced both in American and European waters. Tommy Wiley is an injured veteran of the First World War. Impecunious, he is forced to take paying guests on his yacht. This damages his 'amateur' status and he is expelled from his yacht club. He is unable to make ends meet. He has to downsize to a day boat, in

---

[97] The Royal Western clubhouse was then on the Hoe. One skipper was actually missing from the formation of the ORC. Ray Barrett's *Bamba IV* ran out of wind in the Sound, so anchored off Drake's Island, waiting for the tide to take it across the finishing line, which it did at 01:00 the following morning (Dear, *The Royal Ocean Racing Club: The First 75 Years*, p. 17).

[98] Johnson, *The Encyclopedia of Yachting*, p. 63. See also Phillips-Birt, *British Ocean Racing* and Dear, *The Royal Ocean Racing Club*.

which he dies while out sailing. The yacht club's fear of the contamination of amateurism by earning money has killed Wiley.[99]

The appeal of membership of the senior yacht club remained undimmed. Like other aspiring middle-class yachtsmen, Arthur Ransome, in 1924, had no doubts about what the implications of being accepted into the Royal Cruising Club were: 'Then we should have the right to fly a beautiful blue ensign and generally should have very much come up in the world.'[100] The beauty of the ensign – a rather mundane Maltese-type cross – clearly lay in its social cachet, not its aesthetic qualities.

Distancing from maritime professionals continued almost unabated. Besides being banned from the club, in 1935, the Royal Cornwall banned the hands from 'lounging about on the club terrace'.[101] However, there were signs of change. The Royal Gourack YC, on the Clyde, 'devoted itself among other things for the promotion and management of races for the King's Cup, given by George V in 1920, for craft belonging to "artisans and working men".[102] In Burnham-on-Crouch, paid crew and professionals were not allowed to take part in any of the YRA (and hence yacht club) races. They formed the Burnham Sailing Club in 1930 to organise their own dinghy races and enjoyed such success that in 1935, they built their own clubhouse.[103]

Where the yacht club incorporated dinghy sailors, they were likely to be treated as second-class citizens. At Whitstable, dinghy membership was introduced in 1934. Their five shilling annual fee only allowed these members in at certain times, did not permit them to use the billiards room or the bar, and did not afford them any voice in the management of the club.[104] The only two lady members had similar restrictions. Dogs were allowed in at any time.

However, there were some changes. The Essex Yacht Club, at Leigh-on-Sea, launched an innovative scheme to teach members' children to sail, with the first Cadet race run in 1922.[105] The idea was taken up at the Royal Corinthian, Burnham, where the energetic Tiny Mitchell and his wife started

[99] 'Happy Ending' can be found in Michael Gilkes, ed., *On the Water: The Yachting Muse*, pp. 85–94; and the *Marine Quarterly*, 11, Summer 2013: 48–57. The 'happy ending' is, presumably, that he dies at the helm and the boat magically sails itself back home.

[100] Roland Chambers, *The Last Englishman: The Double Life of Arthur Ransome*, p. 326.

[101] Mead, *The History of the Royal Cornwall*, p. 153.

[102] George Blake and Christopher Small, *Cruising in Company*, p. 112.

[103] http://www.burnham.org.uk/sailingclub, accessed 4 June, 2016.

[104] Wild, *A Handkerchief in the Rigging*, pp. 13–14. Note again the imposition of space *and* time boundaries. The title refers to the method of raising a protest during racing.

[105] Readman, *Four Ships*, p. 51; The Royal Corinthian Yacht Club Website: 'The Early Years 1930–1971', accessed 20 April, 2016.

the Corinthian Otter Club in 1930. By 1934, there were forty Otters. The West Mersea Yacht Club introduced cadet membership in 1932.[106]

Burnham was the base for the United Hospitals Sailing Club, which was the sailing club of the London medical schools, and also the Barts and London Sailing Club. The latter had links with the Royal Burnham.[107]

Another feature of the inter-war period was the growth of inter-club team races. With the popularity of one-design classes, it became easier for clubs with fleets of similar one-designs to hold meetings where a team from each club competed. In some instances, club members lent their boats so that there was no need for the visiting team to trail their vessels to the race. For example, Barnt Green Sailing Club sailed against Oxford University Sailing Club at home and on the Thames in the early 1930s. Using the Essex One-Design, the Essex Yacht Club, Leigh-on-Sea, staged ten annual team races in the 1930s, including one against the Cercle de La Voile, Paris.[108] At Whitstable Yacht Club, across the estuary, 'the Race Committee (Sailing Committee) would select the team from the best sailors in the Club; and owners were expected to lend their boats and not necessarily sail themselves'.[109]

Women and Yachting in the Inter-war Years

In the light of all their war work, the fight against giving women the vote was abandoned. In 1918, women over thirty were given the vote. In 1927, the grounds for divorce became the same for men and women; and in 1928, the Equal Franchise Act gave all women over 21 the vote. But their position in society was still clearly subservient to men, and many yacht clubs continued to exclude or restrict women's access and power till well after the Second World War. It is clear that many, if not most, members saw the yacht club as a 'men only' club first, and an institution to further sailing, a poor second. This stance was threatened during the inter-war years as the number of women interested in yachting was growing.

However, the financial downturn after the Great War caused women to be admitted as associate members, but with limited access to the rooms. For

---

[106] Greville, *The West Mersea Yacht Club*, p. 9.
[107] Since the London medical schools now seem to be in competitive, rather than cooperative mode, it is hard to get useful information from their websites as to the origins and histories of these clubs.
[108] Readman, *Four Ships*, pp. 62–64.
[109] Ian Wild, *A Handkerchief in the Rigging*, p. 11.

example, at the Royal St George, with a declining membership between the wars, this proposal, first put forward in 1926, was only accepted in 1932.[110]

There was, as ever, variation as to the freedom of women's access to yacht clubs, even in the same location. For instance, many of the members of the Clyde Cruising Club, which had been formed in 1909, and whose activities included both racing and cruising, were women. Lady members were admitted to the Royal Clyde in 1920, but were not permitted to use the clubhouse. At the Royal Burnham Yacht Club, a membership class of 'Lady Associate' was created in 1923, but with severe restrictions. They were limited to which parts of the clubhouse they could use. They could not attend meetings, nor serve on committees. Female members consistently represented one-third to one-quarter of the membership – 82 out of 259 members in 1930; 123 out of 456 in 1934. Yet, the detailed *History of the Club* gives no evidence of any protest.[111] One of the features of a successful hegemonic narrative – the narrative explanation of events preferred by the establishment – is that it is accepted by the non-powerful, with the women accepting their lowly position in the club, presumably because they did not want to embarrass their husbands or brothers.

Up to 1930, the Royal Corinthian operated a similar policy. 'It was said at the time that the only difference between dogs and lady members was that the dogs wore collars. Both were left to walk on the Quay outside the Clubhouse.'[112] The change came with the decision to build a new clubhouse, the 'movers' being the Commodore, Philip Benson, with Tiny Mitchell as Vice-Commodore. Anthony Heckstall-Smith commented favourably on the new club house, opened in 1931 in the International style (It is now a Grade II* listed building). He praises:

> ... the foresight of Tiny [who succeeded Benson as Commodore], who realised ... that if the pastime of yachting was to attract a new generation of young sportsmen and women, their tastes must be catered for. The days of old monastic yacht clubs with their gloomy smoking-rooms and libraries hung with portraits of dead commodores were over. The young people wanted cocktail bars, showers and rooms to dance. They certainly did not want their womenfolk shut off in a dingy harem, known as the Ladies Room, or forbidden access to the dining-room unless escorted by a male member.[113]

[110] Archer and Pearson, *History of the Royal St George*, p. 118.
[111] Royal Burnham Yacht Club, *A History of the Royal Burnham Yacht Club*, pp. 79 and 89.
[112] http://royalCorinthian.co.uk./history (accessed 27 January, 2016).
[113] Heckstall-Smith, *Sacred Cowes*, p. 123. 'Tiny' Mitchell (1885–1962) was quite a mover and shaker. His was a rags to riches story. Starting as a railway apprentice at 14, he ended up as head

There were limits to this vision. On the first floor was the men's dining room, a library and card room, with accommodation on the second. 'No ladies were allowed to venture up the staircase' the club website tells us.

Allowing women to become members was often a reluctant move required to remedy a poor financial situation, and was invariably accompanied by many restrictions. At Weymouth, the sailing club had a problem: more women wished to race, and, even more difficult, they wished to race in slacks, not trailing skirts, which were quite unsuitable for sailing. The underlying fear was that, by rejecting the male definition of appropriately 'feminine' dress, the women were demonstrating their independence, and the men could lose control of 'their' club.[114] By 1932, the club's finances allowed the building of a women's changing room as an extension. This led to the proposal in 1933 that they might attend the annual dinner. This, of course, meant that men could not get 'squiffy' or sing ribald songs. The motion was defeated 32–12.[115] The West Mersea, wishing to purchase, rather than rent, its clubhouse, in 1934, doubled the subscription for men, created a ladies' subscription, and one for unmarried daughters. The club had two bars, one Mixed and a separate Men's Bar.[116]

Quite often, as we shall see again after the Second World War, the liberal decision of one AGM was reversed within a short period of years. This to-ing and fro-ing of the space-time boundaries is probably more often the norm than a straight progression.[117]

Laura Mulvey (1975) coined the term 'the male gaze' which assumed heterosexual interest, power and superiority.[118] Unfortunately for the male members at the Royal Irish, there seemed to be an aberrant version – the female gaze. Until 1912, ladies could not eat in the dining room, but now, on certain 'Ladies' nights', male members could have female guests, who were

---

of Mitchell Construction, building power stations. Besides his role in the Burnham Royal Corinthian, he established the southern branch of the Royal Corinthian when he bought Rosa Lewis' house in Cowes in 1948; and then concerned that local yachtsmen were unable to afford the high cost of other Cowes yacht clubs, he created the Cowes Corinthian in 1952.

[114] The non-conformist Peter Gerard went further and encouraged her cadets to wear shorts when sailing. She tells of landing at Ryde Pier: 'It was only a stone's throw … to "Mike's" hotel; but an anxious and conventional husband had lugged a skirt and accessories down to the ferry waiting-room to meet us, and flatly refused to escort her a yard until she had "dressed herself properly". I left them arguing the point …' (*Who Hath Desired the Sea*, p. 42). Note the male name for the female cadet.

[115] Hayes, *The History of the Weymouth Sailing Club*, pp. 75–76.

[116] Greville, *The West Mersea Yacht Club*, pp. 36–37.

[117] This see-sawing is clearly shown by Ian Wild with regard to the Whitstable Yacht Club between the wars. See his *A Handkerchief in the Rigging*.

[118] Laura Mulvey, 'Visual Pleasure and Narrative Cinema'.

permitted to walk on the east side of the balcony, as if they strayed onto the west side, they could 'look into the reading room and observe the men there'. In 1924, the committee decided to put a rope across the balcony. In 1928, the same problem re-surfaced, but the lady guests' curiosity seems to have been insatiable, because, in the 1939, the flimsy red cord was replaced by 'an emphatic crimson rope'.[119]

A quite unusual event was the appointment of a lady commodore at the Aldeburgh Yacht Club, founded 1897. Yolande Faraday, born in 1904, was on the committee in her twenties. The Club History tells us that, in 1930, 'the Flag Officers declined to offer themselves for re-election, as they thought the Club would be best served if the Executive Officers lived in Aldeburgh or the immediate neighbourhood'. This explanation comes complete with bells, unless they had all moved home since their original election. Whatever the explanation, Ms Faraday, now married and now the titled Lady Eddis, was elected Commodore, almost certainly the first woman commodore of a yacht club.[120] Another formidable lady was Mrs H. S. C. Richardson, who, crewed by her husband, was in the prize list of nearly every Prince of Wales Cup in the 1930s.[121]

Novels by Women Sailors

What is interesting and new in this period is a number of novels by women sailors.

Virginia Woolf, a perceptive social commentator as well as an eminent novelist, saw yachting as evidence of male dominance and power.[122] In a 1926 article on 'The Cinema', she discusses how newsreels foreground activities undertaken by men, valued by powerful males:

> There is the King shaking hands with a football team; there is Sir Thomas Lipton's yacht; there is Jack Horner winning the Grand National.[123]

[119] Boylan, *White Sails Crowding*, pp. 102, 104, 110.
[120] Aldeburgh Yacht Club, *Against the Elements: Aldeburgh Yacht Club – The First One Hundred Years*, p. 57.
[121] Scott, *The Eye of the Wind*, p. 204.
[122] Sailing features in her *Jacob's Room*, 1922, where she describes a sail from Falmouth to St Ives by Jacob and his Cambridge friend, Durrant; and more prominently in *To the Lighthouse*, 1927, where the pre-war youthful wish to sail to Godrevy is only achieved after the war, which renders it meaningless. See my 'Why Move the Lighthouse?'
[123] Woolf is eliding time. George V was the first monarch to attend a football cup final, at Wembley in 1914; *Shamrock* was presumably *Shamrock IV*, unsuccessful contender for the 1920 America's Cup, and 'Jack Horner', ridden by Billy Watkinson, trained by Jack Leader, won the 1926 Grand National. While a woman, usually the owner's wife, might be seen giving out

In a society where sailing is socially relevant – i.e. provides a usable canvas – the author of sailing fiction has a considerable advantage: the sea and the shore line are *liminal spaces*: locations where people are in transition and temporarily in limbo.[124] They are spaces where conventional rules are less applicable, and therefore suitable locations for transgressive actions.[125] These women novelists used this liminality to explore the paradox that, while now enfranchised, if they did not marry, they were still trapped by the powerful social belief system that they were unfulfilled, pitiable spinsters.[126]

Elizabeth David, the famous cookery writer after the Second World War, left England in 1939 aged 25 in a yacht, the *Evelyn Hope*, that she had bought with her married lover, Gibson Cowan. They sailed to the Mediterranean. Looking back on an unsuccessful marriage, 'It's absurd of course', she would say, 'but a woman must marry'.[127] This is one of the major themes across Du Maurier's writings. She was a competent yachtswoman, having learn to sail on the Fowey River, when living there as a young novelist. She uses liminality with considerable skill as she explores female marital discontent.[128] Rebecca (*Rebecca* 1932) is a free spirit, with short hair, so that it didn't get in the way when riding or sailing.[129] She sails her boat single-handed and meets

---

prizes or christening his ship, they are acting as *meaning-carriers*, rather than *meaning-creators*. The symbolism of these activities demonstrating male power is shown by Emily Davison running out in front of the King's horse at the 1913 Epsom Derby, sustaining injuries that she died from four days later.

[124] 'Liminality' was termed by the Dutch anthropologist Arnold Van Gennep, in his 1908 book, *The Rites of Passage*, to describe the state of limbo of those going through a *rite de passage*, where they are neither who they were (boys) or who they will become (men). It was later widened by the English anthropologist Victor Turner to include marginal locations, where the usual laws and mores of society are poorly observed or ignored.

[125] We find such beliefs much earlier in Fielding's *Voyage to Lisbon*: 'It is difficult, I think, to assign a satisfactory reason why sailors in general should, of all others, think themselves entirely discharged from the common bands of humanity' (p. 215); 'men who live on the seashore are of the amphibious kind, and do not entirely partake of human nature ...' (p. 220); and 'Every commander of a vessel here [Deal] seems to think himself entirely free from all those rules of decency and civility, which direct and restrain the conduct of members of a society on shore' (p. 222).

[126] For a good overview of women writers of the 1930s, see Nicola Beauman, *A Very Great Profession: The Woman's Novel 1914–1939*, and Alison Light, *Forever England. Femininity: Literature and Conservatism Between the Wars*.

[127] The boat was impounded by the Italians. She lived in France, Italy, the Greek islands and Egypt, where she married Lieutenant-Colonel Anthony David during the war, but the marriage was short-lived. Quote from Artemis Cooper, *Written at the Kitchen Table*, p. 151.

[128] Du Maurier is often dismissed as a 'woman's writer', yet three of her books – *Jamaica Inn*, *Rebecca* and *The King's General* were given out to American troops as part of the Armed Services Edition scheme. *Frenchman's Creek*, again dismissed as 'a woman's novel' is centrally concerned with marital boredom vs. the cost of being a free spirit.

[129] One of the puzzles of *Rebecca* is that the reader's sympathy is with the murderer, not the murdered. To achieve this, a lesbian undertow is implied through her short hair and close

her lovers in a cottage by the shore. Her yacht – symbol of her freedom – becomes her coffin, after she has been murdered by her husband, Maxim.

E. A. Robertson was a well regarded 1930s novelist who used yachting as a location for a number of her novels, such as *Cullum*, 1928, in which the heroine is seduced by the bounder, Cullum, on a yacht. Ashamed, she rides a large, uncontrolled horse to hounds and is seriously injured. *Ordinary Families*, 1933, based around a sailing family living at Pin Mill on the Orwell, Essex, is a bitter recording of the emptiness of marriage for the young woman.

Peter Gerard's autobiography, *Who Hath Desired the Sea*, although published in 1962, is mostly concerned with the inter-war years.[130] She started as a cub yachting reporter at the same time as Maurice Griffiths and they got married in 1927. The same year, they had been crew for the Fastnet on O'Brien's *Saoirse*, and at the end of the cruise, 'he had exclaimed "You've all been good crew, but I'll tell you that Peter's been the best hand I've ever had!" ... At the end of the season, Peter said, "I shall never rest until I have a ship of my very own, to be my own skipper and sail her how and where I like".'[131] She also started a Women Sailors' Union but it failed to get off the ground, probably because of her autocratic style.

Encouraged by Frank Cowper, she started one of the first sailing schools, and, certainly, the first by some fifty years, for women. Griffiths, as editor, used *Yachting Monthly* to encourage women to sail. It carried articles about Gerard's sailing school, and, in 1938, an article advising women on which boat to buy for themselves.[132] However, Gerard's sailing school created marital difficulties, as he wanted a wife who organised dinner parties for his clients, while she wished to sail as often as possible. Also, her cruising ground was the

---

relationship with Mrs Danvers, when she should be monogamously devoted to the inadequate Max. The contemporary reader would have known that 'Mrs' did not necessarily indicate marital status, but was routinely used for the head of the female staff (Ella Westland, personal communication, June 2014).

[130] Gerard, *Who Hath Desired the Sea: Memoirs of Peter Gerard*, 1962.

[131] Griffiths, *Swatchways and Little Ships*, p. 110. Griffiths' feelings towards her are probably seen most clearly in his dire, sub-*Riddle of the Sands* novel, *The Sands of Sylt*, 1945, in which the hero falls in love with a young widow, clearly Gerard, who then in the last few pages, is transformed by the war into his second wife, Marjorie.

[132] Griffiths reported on sailing aboard the 28 foot Bermudan canoe yacht, *Elfin*, at the invitation of her owner, Mrs G. N. Findlay Smith of Hamble in *Yachting Monthly* (*YM*), March 1931. In a 1932 issue of *YM*, Mrs Findlay Smith wrote up her cruise in *Elfin* for a week in the Solent with a lady companion. *YM* also carried reports of pupils of Peter Gerard's Sailing School which was solely for women (J. Heath, 'Sail-training with a Woman Skipper', *YM*, March,1937; 'Taking the Plunge', *YM*, October and November, 1938). In May 1938, G.N.F.S. advised on 'Little Ships for the Woman Owner'.

16 Peter Gerard (in yachting cap) instructing a 'cadet' in her yacht *Juanita*. Peter
Gerard (Dulcie Kennard) founded one of the first sailing schools, certainly the first
for women, in the mid-1930s. She was Maurice Griffiths' first wife.

south coast from the Solent to the Scillies, while Griffiths sailed the Thames and the North Sea.

But there *was* a bond between sailors. Three chapters of Griffiths' *The Magic of the Swatchways* are given over to his agreeing to sail cross-channel as mate in Gerard's *Juanita*. On the passage home, they get caught in a fearsome North Sea gale. Gerard is violently seasick and incapacitated, and Griffiths, though affected as well, has to look after her and the boat. They eventually creep up the Orwell, *Juanita*:

> ... a tired, bruised thing coming back home ...
>
> The skipper [Gerard] opened the cabin door and let out a flood of yellow light, and I caught sight of a white table-cloth within and supper half laid,
>
> 'My God, what a passage!' she said. 'Thirty-six hours out from Ostend and the dinghy gone!' Then she closed the door behind her and I found her hand in mine.
>
> 'Glad to be back in your old river, mate man?'[133]

There is a loving empathy in Gerard's acknowledgement that she has returned Griffiths to his 'natural' haunt. No yachts*man* would have used a tablecloth and the yellow light from the oil lamp softens it further.

Sadly, these occasions were insufficient. They divorced in 1934, and Gerard married Charles Pears, the marine artist. Besides adoring him, his *Wanderer* and her *Juanita* were both based on the south coast, so they could anchor close to each other on occasion.[134]

Another woman sailor-writer with an unhappy marriage was skipper–owner, Dorothy Una Ratcliffe, who provided the paintings, poetry and word sketches in her *The Babes of the Sea*, 1929 and *Swallow of the Sea: Pages from a Yacht Log's*, 1937.[135]

---

[133] Griffiths, *The Magic of the Swatchways*, p. 204.

[134] While Griffiths continued to be feted till the end of his long life in 1997, Gerard's later years were sadder. Pears was much older than her and died in 1958. Griffiths' biographer records that Gerard moved to St Mawes, Cornwall with him, but never recovered when, while ashore, *Juanita* fell off her legs and stove in her bilge. A local shipwright described her in the 1970s: '... after *Juanita* was sold she got dirty and scruffy ... She started going down hill and wandered about crying all the time' (Durham, *The Magician of the Swatchways*, p. 166).

[135] The 38 ton auxiliary cutter yawl, *Sea Swallow* was the renamed *Tern IV*, designed and owned by Claud Worth, and built by Philips and Son, Dartmouth in 1924. The personal toll of the dilemma these novelists described was heavy. Woolf drowned herself in 1941. Robertson 'had always talked openly about suicide', her son said, 'and, when my father died [in 1961, drowned in a boating accident on the Thames] she simply felt that life wasn't worth living' and died from

Of course, not all sailing couples had such difficulties. Adlard Coles, the major yachting publisher after the Second World War, and his wife, Mamie, always sailed together in their cruises to the Baltic in the mid-1920s.[136] Very unusually, she is included in the title of his 1926 account: *Close-Hauled: Being the Adventures of the Author and His Wife Cruising Alone, in a 29-Foot Ketch, amongst the Lesser Known Islands of the Baltic during a Voyage from Latvia to England.*

As the Second World War approached, it was clear that more naval officers would be needed to bolster the peace-time numbers. In June, 1936, the secretary of the Royal Cruising Club wrote to the Admiralty, pointing out that many of its members would make good officers, but could not get to the few training centres run by the Royal Naval Volunteer Reserve. The Admiralty replied that it had such an idea in mind; and on 23 October, 1936, at the RNVR (Auxiliary Patrol) Club's Annual Dinner, Sir Ernle Chatfield, First Sea Lord, announced the creation of the Royal Naval Volunteer Supplementary Reserve (RNSVR). This initiative was received enthusiastically by yachtsmen. 'All' the yachtsman had to do was to volunteer and within a few days, 300 men, including Nicholas Monsarrat, Adlard Coles and Peter Scott, had done so.[137] Quite a few learnt their navigation at the Little Ship Club, founded 1926 in the City of London, which offered to train the RNVSR for free, for which the Admiralty, as a sign of thanks, offered them a defaced ensign.

The pleasures to be had in sailing the Thames Estuary chimed with the mood of the yachtsmen, for, since they did not have control over their future, and might well die in the next few years, they could at least gain respite by creek crawling. As the war clouds gathered, *Yachting Monthly* prepared yet once again to be the magazine of the Royal Naval Volunteer Reserve, thus gaining

---

an overdose (Polly Devlin, Introduction, Robertson, *Ordinary Families*, p. xvi); 'Du Maurier, later in her life, made at least one suicide attempt.' In 1960, Daphne had written to her cousin, Nico Davies, that she understood why his brother Peter had committed suicide, 'being myself, constantly, and for no earthly reason, a potential suicide' (Margaret Forster, *Daphne du Maurier*, pp. 403–404). When Ratcliffe's unfaithful husband gave her syphilis and rendered her childless, she went home to her parents who sent her back to her husband, so as to not to create a scandal for his politician father, Lord Brotherton.

[136] Adlard Coles, *Close-Hauled*, 1926; *'Mary Anne' among 10,000 Islands: Cruising the Finnish Archipelago*, 1938.

[137] Lavery, *In Which They Served*, pp. 9–17. Scott, a professional wildlife artist, designed the camouflage system used by all naval ships in the North Atlantic (Scott, *The Eye of the Wind*, pp. 392–395).

it the necessary supply of rationed newsprint. Its editor, Maurice Griffiths, and his colleague Norman Clarkson went off to serve on mine-sweepers, and, one of the many unmentioned heroines of yachting history, Kathleen Palmer, was left to produce the monthly number.[138]

[138] Griffiths acknowledged her work in a *Yachting Monthly* editorial, November, 1945; and was proud that 'not an issue was missed during the Second World War, just as none had been missed in the First' (Griffiths, *Swatchways and Little Ships*, pp. 130–131). Adlard Coles, the editor, and later in the war Eric Hiscock, kept *The Yachtsman*, reduced from monthly to bi-monthly, going (Sharp, *Troubled Waters*, pp. 106–110).

CHAPTER THIRTEEN

1945–1965:
Home-Built Dinghies and
Going Offshore

> Shortly after the war, I married and tried to settle down … Like most of my
> generation, though, I was infected by restlessness. … too much adrenalin had
> gone through our systems for them to adjust easily to the routine of 'nine to
> six' … London was strange and uneasy in those immediate post-war years.[1]

Once again, yachtsmen had played a significant part in the war. Dunkirk is
often represented as the high water of their involvement – when 700 'Little
Ships', working with the Navy, rescued more than 338,000 British and French
soldiers off the beaches between 26 May and 4 June, 1940. In fact, these
vessels were mainly motorsailers from the Thames and the South Coast,
volunteered, or requisitioned by the Government, and manned by Naval
personnel.[2] Less well known is 'Little Dunkirk', the evacuation of British
troops and personnel from St Malo by nineteen yachts, mostly sailing vessels, out of St Helier, Jersey in June 1940, for which the St Helier Yacht Club
was uniquely granted a defaced ensign for 'battle honours'.[3]

A Board of Trade Yacht Master's Certificate was an advantage for a candidate seeking a commission in the RNVR (the Wavy Navy – the RNVR
officers' stripes were wavy, while RN officers' were straight). Captain OM
Watts, later famous for his upmarket chandlers in Piccadilly, trained many
yachtsmen at Burlesdon; and the Little Ship Club, London did likewise.

---

[1] Ernle Bradford, *The Journeying Moon*, p. 29.
[2] In his 'Postscript to Dunkirk', broadcast 5 June, 1940, J. B. Priestley does not mention yachts.
 Instead, he eulogises the paddle steamer, the *Gracie Fields*. He is working to create an emotional link between the working man's seaside holiday and the war effort.
[3] See Leo Harris, *Lee Ho!*, pp. 22–40; Le Scelleur and Philip Jeune, *Sailing through a Century*,
 pp. 89–100, give a figure of 21,474 rescued from St Malo.

By the end of the war, there were approximately 30,000 ratings and officers in the RNVR.[4] Griffiths received a George Medal for his mine recovery work. Monsarrat was appointed to the new Flower-Class corvette *Campanula* in August 1940, experience he drew on when he wrote the first great maritime novel by an English-born author – *The Cruel Sea*.[5] He used himself as the model for Sub-Lieutenant Lockhart, a yachtsman and the son of a surgeon.[6] After two years as an engineer on inshore anti-submarine patrol, Eric Hiscock was medically re-assessed and discharged due to his poor eyesight. Later, he joined the Admiralty Ferry Service, which was set up to deliver old and new naval vessels around the coasts to wherever they might be required, and which developed into quite a flourishing branch of the merchant navy. The crews were made up of experienced amateur seamen, either too old or of an insufficient medical standard to qualify for regular service, and were called upon when needed. Passages were as far afield as to Malta and from America.[7] A less well known, individual contribution was made by Antony Bridges, who volunteered but was turned down because of 'a stiff leg'. After the sinking of the battleship *Royal Oak* in Scapa Flow in the Orkneys, 14 October, 1939, with the loss of 833 lives, it was decided to strengthen the Scapa Flow defences. Bridges used his 40 foot cutter yacht, *Mermaid*, to transfer detonators from Scrabster, across the very dangerous Pentland Firth, to the Orkneys.[8] Uffa Fox had not been idle during the war. He designed the airborne lifeboat that fitted beneath the wing of an aircraft, and which could be parachuted into the sea, complete with sail and engine. It saved the life of many airmen.[9]

Relevant developments in understanding yachting during this period include:

Civilian casualties, ruined cities: In the Second World War, Service casualties were very heavy but considerably less than in the First World War

---

[4] Sharp, *Troubled Waters*, pp. 115–116.

[5] Conrad was born in Poland. English was his third language, after French. His greatness is to use the sea and commercial sail as the backcloth to moral dilemmas, which makes him closer to Dostoyevsky than Dickens.

[6] Lavery, *In Which They Served*, p. 11 and Chapter 2, 'A Novelist at Sea', pp. 45 ff. The *Compass Rose*'s captain is Lieutenant Commander Ericson – the Nordic name highlighting the toughness of an English sailor. An equivalent major work by an American writer was *The Caine Mutiny*, by Herman Wouk, also published in 1951.

[7] 'Its foundations had been laid in some of the leading yacht-clubs, among them the Royal Ocean Racing Club, the Little Ship Club and the Royal Cruising Club, of which I happened to be a member' (Hiscock, *I Left the Navy*, pp. 145–147).

[8] Antony Bridges, *Scapa Ferry*, 1957.

[9] The airborne lifeboat is described in more detail in Sharp, *Troubled Waters*, p. 150.

(270,000 compared to 745,000). However, at the end of the First World War, the discharged servicemen came home to an intact England, its visual geography unchanged by the war. In the Second World War, Hitler's bombing campaigns against the cities had resulted in 60,595 civilians dying in air raids, and 86,192 wounded.[10] Many cities, among them Southampton, Plymouth and Coventry, were in ruins and required very extensive rebuilding. This reconstruction could only happen slowly, as the country was financially severely limited by fighting a second world war in the space of twenty-five years. Rationing of clothing and foodstuff was actually more severe after than during the war. Raw materials, including those needed for boat building, were strictly controlled. Clubs whose members needed to drive to them were particularly hard hit by the rationing of fuel. Those on the Clyde were severely affected by the rationing of petrol and also maritime fuel supplies, limiting steamer traffic on the Clyde.[11]

The situation was somewhat eased by the American assistance through the Marshall Plan, starting in 1948, but rationing of basic foodstuffs continued until 1954.

The Cold War and Nuclear Weapons: The peace settlement, as interpreted by the Russian leader, Joseph Stalin, created 'an Iron Curtain', the boundary of Russian influence, and the control of all the countries behind it by Russian troops. The development of nuclear weapons by the Americans and their use in Japan on Hiroshima, on 6 August and on Nagasaki on 9 August, 1945, led inevitably to the Russians developing nuclear weapons. The world watched in fascinated horror during the Cuban missile crisis in October 1962, when nuclear war was only just averted.

Nuclear testing led to a small number of protesting yachtsmen sailing to nuclear test sites, such as Ralph E. Lapp's *The Voyage of the 'Lucky Dragon'*, 1958, and Albert Bigelow's *The Voyage of the 'Golden Rule'*, 1959.[12]

The final factor affecting yachtsmen was *political change – the Welfare State*. The experiences of the men who fought the Second World War, and this time had the vote, led to a determination not to return to the old ways

---

[10] Bédarida, *A Social History of England 1851–1975*, p. 227. There had been a number of Zeppelin airship and some bomber raids during the First World War, causing much alarm but the number killed was in the hundreds.

[11] The Royal Largs Yacht Club was a casualty during this period. It was dissolved in 1975, but had ceased being active some years earlier.

[12] A more recent example is a fleet of New Zealand yachts protesting against French nuclear tests in the Pacific in 1995. Greenpeace's David McTaggart on NZ TV had requested New Zealand yachtsmen to 'just wander over' – a slight understatement for 'a winter Southern Pacific voyage of some 3000 nautical miles'! (Jon Tucker, 'A Voyage to Morurua', pp. 48–49).

of a society grossly divided by wealth and opportunity. The election of the Labour Party, the creation of a free National Health Service, free education, and the building of council houses were all results of that determination.

After fighting in a war, it is hard to readjust to returning back home, especially when major social and political changes are taking place.[13] Feeling cut off from, or unconnected to, one's society is termed *anomie* and the relationship *anomic*.[14]

Despite, or because of, these tensions, there was great interest in all things nautical. The most significant was the huge uptake in do-it-yourself boat building and dinghy sailing. Combined with a steady uptake in yacht cruising, this chapter describes the beginning of a surge in interest in yachting that was to grow right through till the end of the 1980s.

Veterans in Small Boats

> There were about 20 students [for Special Operations Executive training] ... And every one had a note on his records, saying 'This officer is unamenable to discipline'.
>
> ... After a while, we were sent to parachute school ... The girl behind the counter said 'If this one doesn't work, bring it back and we'll give you another' which she thought was funny, since we had no reserve chutes.[15]

In America and Australia, the railroad and the highway had taken over the psychological and metaphorical uses of the sea voyage. Englishmen could not discharge their post-war restlessness by travelling across their land, for it is too small. But an Englishman could *sail* away.[16] Perhaps they also wanted to reclaim the sea from its wartime representation as the killing fields – not just the North Atlantic convoys of *The Cruel Sea* but also the very high casualties of the Murmansk run to support the Russian war effort, which required rounding the North Cape to be attacked by waiting German submarines and

---

[13] A post-war novel that describes the adrenalin of war and the difficulties of peace-time resettlement well is Shute's *Requiem for a Wren*, 1955, the title a lift from William Faulkner's *Requiem for a Nun*, 1951.

[14] The term was introduced by the French sociologist Emile Durkheim (1858–1917), in his *Suicide* (1897).

[15] Patrick Ellam, *Things I Remember*, pp. 92–93.

[16] This had not happened after the First World War to any great extent, as so many of the would-be sailors were dead.

aircraft, to sail once again on 'the blue sea, the sure, the inaccessible, the uncontaminated and spacious refuge for wounded souls'.[17]

After the Second World War, there were a number of long distance voyages that bordered between the courageous and the foolhardy. They may have been influenced by the crossings of the Atlantic in Victorian times, though these were mainly West to East (see Chapter 9), whereas this time, the yachtsmen usually set out from England. They may also have been casualties of one war too many, their parents damaged by their experiences of the First World War, and they themselves suffering post-traumatic stress (PTSD) and survivor guilt.[18] Of course, this would be of relevance for some yachtsmen and not others, but it is a life history factor we shall observe through to the 1980s.[19]

In 1949, Stan and Colin Smith came from a family of Isle of Wight boat-builders and, like many other children, had been evacuated to Canada for safety during the war. They built the half-decked 20 foot *Nova Espero* in Halifax, Canada and then set off for Dartmouth, Devon.[20] Back in England, they strengthened the boat – the coachroof had been an upturned dinghy, and Stan Smith and Charles Violet sailed her back across the Atlantic to New York in 1951.[21] Smith designed a 14 foot cruising dinghy, called the Potter, and delivered one to Sweden under sail in November. This seems a rather odd time to sail so far North and Smith and his companion had to chop ice off the rigging in the Kattegut to prevent capsize.[22]

Ian Nicolson was one of a crew of three in a converted Norwegian lifeboat, the *Maken*, from Weymouth to Vancouver. Then, wishing to sail home, he hitchhiked across the continent to Halifax, Nova Scotia, but no-one was crossing the ocean that year, nor were there any suitable boats for sale.

---

[17] Conrad, *Chance*, p. 301.

[18] Bob Comlay, in 'Travels with Tilman', suggests that this was the case with Blondie Hasler, George Millar, Miles Smeeton and Bill Tilman. Modern clinical thinking is that PTSD is not a unitary condition, but comes in a variety of different, if overlapping forms. Alcohol abuse is a common response, and while there are recorded incidents of alcohol abuse among yachtsmen with PTSD, I have not named them, as there are doubtless many other yachtsmen with the same condition, whose alcohol intake has not been recorded.

[19] Another sign of unease and restlessness is the one million Britons who emigrated to Australia between 1945 and 1972 (the 'ten pound pommies' as the Australian government subsidised their travel). Twelve men and six women left Ilfracombe for Australia via the Panama Canal in 1955, in the *Agnes*, 72 ton ketch, officially built in 1903, but Grahame Farr (*Ships and Harbours of Exmoor*, p. 31) thinks she was a rebuild of the *Lady Acland*, built 1835.

[20] Stanley Smith, *Smiths at Sea*, 1951.

[21] Stanley Smith and Charles Violet, *The Wind Calls the Tune: The Eventful Voyage of the 'Nova Espero'*, 1952. The boat was freighted back to England.

[22] Tony Vasey, *The Ocean Cruising Club: The First Fifty Years*, p. 13. His first chapter summarises many of the voyages mentioned here.

After much searching, he found a 30 foot hull in Chester, 40 miles south of Halifax, and with the help of the yard, he built the boat, named her *Saint Elizabeth*, and, in 1952, unable to recruit crew, sailed her singlehanded back to Weymouth.[23]

Edward Allcard, a naval architect, sailed across the Atlantic in 81 days from Gibraltar to New York, in 1949, in *Temptress*, a 34 foot gaff yawl, built in 1910 by Celenick on the Fal. His return passage, via the Azores, gained publicity because of his unknowingly shipping a female stowaway.[24] In 1954, Allcard began a 16 year circumnavigation in *Sea Wanderer*.

Humphrey Barton, out of Falmouth bound for New York in a 25 foot boat, *Vertue XXXV* in 1950, survived a knockdown during a hurricane. (The Vertue, designed by Laurent Giles with the first prototype, *Andrillot* launched in 1936, is considered the iconic ocean-girding small boat).[25]

Barton, a partner in the leading yacht design firm of Laurent Giles in Lymington – no relation to Morgan Giles of Teignmouth – wanted to show one could safely cross the Atlantic in a stout, displacement boat.[26] Patrick Ellam 'decided to attack the problem from another angle: to produce a boat the size and weight of a dinghy, but modified so that it would be safe at sea in any weather while retaining the dinghy's high speed and manoeuvrability'.[27] He approached Colin Mudie, at 26, already a respected racing skipper and who also worked for Laurent Giles. They set off in 1951 from Falmouth in a strengthened and slightly enlarged, decked-in racing dinghy, the 20 foot *Sopranino*, also the title of their 1954 account of the crossing.

A little later, in 1955, John Guzzwell undertook a circumnavigation in a tiny – 20 foot 6 inches long – yawl. Born in England, he was brought up in Jersey. His father tried three times to get the family away in their yacht, but his engine failed. The Germans then invaded and the family was interned in Germany. After two and a half years, they returned to the island but his

---

[23] Ian Nicolson, *The Log of the 'Maken'* 1961; *Sea Saint*, 1957.

[24] Described in his *Single-Handed Passage*, 1950 and '*Temptress' Returns*, 1952. A rather cryptic entry in Vasey's *The Ocean Cruising Club: The First Fifty Years*, p. 26, states 'Hum (Barton) claimed to have known the true story but took it to his grave'.

[25] Humphrey Barton, *Vertue XXXV: An Account of the Author's Voyage from Lymington to New York*, 1950. Adrian Morgan, in 'The Vertue', tells the paradigmatic Vertue story: 'Apocryphally, a sign on the sea front of Durban [South Africa] forbids any yacht to put to sea in winds over Force 7, without the harbour master's permission, unless she's a Vertue'.

[26] For an overview of Laurent Giles' designs, see Adrian Lee and Ruby Philpott, *Laurent Giles: An Evolution of Yacht Design*.

[27] Patrick Ellam and Colin Mudie, *Sopranino*, pp. 10 and 34–35. (The book was written by Ellam, with comments from Mudie.) Humphrey Barton had not been so sure. 'I sailed *Sopranino* for a short time once in the Lymington River and I thought her quite an amusing toy but not a boat that I would take across the Solent on a windy day' (Barton, *Atlantic Adventurers*, p. 165).

father's health was 'wrecked' and he died in 1948. Guzzwell seems to have had his father's genes. His father had prospected for gold in Alaska and pearl fished in the South Seas. His son, fancying a long distance sail, reasoned that timber was cheap in British Columbia, so emigrated to Victoria, and built his boat, *Trekka*, at the back of a fish and chip shop, the drying glues causing some concern to the staff. Without much previous experience, he then set off round the world, stopping for sixteen months to crew for the Smeetons. In 1959, after four years away, he completed his circumnavigation by returning to Victoria.

A tragic example of anomic sailing is told in Ann Davison's *Last Voyage*. She and her husband, Frank, worked on rehabilitating a fishing boat in Fleetwood, Lancashire. When it was about to be impounded because of their debts, they sailed out of the harbour, hoping to make Cuba. The unreliability of the engine made them turn up-Channel and they reached Lyme Bay, where their sails were not equal to the high winds. Drifting for days, they were sucked into the Portland Race, where the boat was wrecked on the Bill. They took to their Carling lifefloat. Her husband, hallucinating that they were ashore, climbed overboard and was drowned. The lifefloat eventually crashed against the cliffs and Ann was thrown into a cave, from where she climbed up the cliffs.[28] Perhaps as some kind of reparation, Ann Davison went on to become the first woman to cross the Atlantic single-handed. In her small, 23 foot long *Felicity Ann,* she sailed down to the Canaries in 1952, and then, in November of that year, using the Northeast Trades, crossed to the West Indies and on to a rapturous welcome in New York.[29]

The equipment these yachtspeople crossing oceans had was primitive and little different from that of their Victorian forebears. They had no wind vane or autopilot to share the helming. Radar had been used in the war to warn of vessels in the vicinity but was not available on yachts.[30] There was no GPS (Global Positioning System) to determine position at the press of a button. There was no electronic chart plotter and no contact with meteorological information.

The sailor had to be familiar with the sextant and the mathematical calculations to make sense of its readings, to know where they were; and if the sun was hidden, he might not be able to take sunsights for days. (The sextant might well be a plastic Ebco, as many of the sailors could not afford the more

---

[28] Ann Davison, *Last Voyage*, 1951.
[29] Recounted in her *My Ship is So Small*, 1956.
[30] Radar initially became available for yachts in 1947; in 1949, the Kelvin Hughes radar set was selling for the prohibitive sum of £3,000 (Sharp, *Troubled Waters*, p. 60).

expensive ones made out of brass.) There were no autopilots or windvanes till the 1960s. Sometimes, they could gain some respite by leading the sheets back to the tiller, and tensioning them so that the boat held its course; but if that did not prove possible, they could be helming for days or weeks.

Gales make life difficult and dangerous. Humphrey Barton explains:

> Imagine yourself shut up in a box about 10-ft. long and 7-ft. wide [the saloon] and let a powerful crane pick it up at an angle and then raise and lower it fairly rapidly and erratically through distances from three to thirty feet. Alter the angle of heel, if possible from vertical to 40 degrees, very frequently while all this is going on and also try to introduce some fore and aft pitching movement. Now try moving about inside the box … Now try cooking a meal.[31]

I have pointed out some of the psychological aspects of these crossings, but one needs to separate motivation from competence. The sailors were often Naval veterans, who had endured discomfort for years at sea, so they 'knew' the sea far better than we do today. They were skilled and their boats were strongly built. The proof of the pudding is that there seem to be no accounts of tragedies during such voyages, which is ironic since, when ocean racing became professionalised and/or commercialised, there were deaths.

Barton ('Hum') founded the Ocean Cruising Club (OCC), in 1954, which embodies these post-war ideals. Disagreeing with the snobbery and selectiveness of the Royal Cruising Club, where membership was by invitation only, the sole criterion for membership of the OCC was, and still is, a non-stop 1,000 mile passage.[32] After his first wife died suddenly in 1959, 'over the next 15 years, Hum made 18 Atlantic crossings, routinely running down to the Caribbean for the winter and returning to Europe to collect his mail in the spring'.[33]

Down to the Mediterranean

Living in the Mediterranean was relatively cheap after the war. The weather was better than in England, and getting there did not necessarily require

---

[31] Barton, *Atlantic Adventurers*, p. 15.
[32] Mention must be made of OCC member, Peter Rose, who crossed the Atlantic in 1966 in a 23 foot boat. A man of the cloth, he secured a living at Feock on the Fal, 'where he could see his boat on her mooring from the pulpit' (Vasey, *The Ocean Cruising Club: The First Fifty Years*, pp. 103–104).
[33] Vasey, *The Ocean Cruising Club: The First Fifty Years*, p. 10.

crossing the dangerous Bay of Biscay.[34] It could be done in hops down the Biscay coast of France and Spain, or through the French canals.

George Millar was decorated after serving in the Special Operations Executive with the French Resistance in 1944.[35] Exhausted by the war, he and his half-Spanish wife, Isabel, decided to go on an extended cruise.[36] *Isabel and the Sea*, published in 1948, records sailing to the Med. in 1946 through the canals in a converted 1919 Looe Lugger, entering them via a war-torn Le Havre, where only a handful of houses were still standing.

Ernle Bradford had been stationed in Alexandria in the war as first lieutenant, gun crew, on a destroyer. After the war, Bradford and his wife sailed into Sestri Levante, Liguria, Italy and they were drinking in a wineshop with the owner and his wife, who had four sons, but now have only three. The fourth was sent down in a schooner, barely armed, to the African coast. Bradford's destroyer had first destroyed its Italian counterpart before sinking all the schooners.[37] He sailed to Malta with his wife in 1951 and, when she sailed away, settled there, living on his nautical writings, such as *Ulysses Found*, 1963, recording how he sailed in Ulysses' seasteps.

Charles Violet, who had sailed the Atlantic with Stanley Smith in *Nova Espero* in 1951, was unable to settle. So, within six months of their return to England, he took the boat, in which he had a half share, to the Med. to Sicily and back via Africa.[38]

By the 1960s, one could use Henry Denham's pilot books of the various parts of the Med. – *The Aegean*, 1963; *The Adriatic*, 1967. From the 1950s up to the present, large numbers of British sailors, often retired couples, kept their boats down in the Med., or cruised there for a few years.

Married Couples Go Blue Water – Long Distance Cruising

The first generation of British long-distance sailors – the Hiscocks, the Smeetons and the Pyes – were men sailing with their wives, highly competent first mates.

Eric Hiscock became the icon of the long distance sailor and those who dreamt that they might one day sail away. In the summer of 1952, Eric and Sue

---

[34] It is dangerous because the Continental Shelf changes from great depth to the relatively shallow hundred metre line quite deep inside the Bay, causing turbulence, which is combined with strong winds and can create perilous sea states.
[35] Described in his *Maquis*, 1945.
[36] Durham, *Amazing Sea Stories*, pp. 108–109.
[37] Bradford, *The Journeying Moon*, p. 67.
[38] Charles Violet, *Solitary Journey: Nova Espero's Third Voyage*.

Hiscock set off from Yarmouth, Isle of Wight, on their circumnavigation in a 30 foot sloop, *Wanderer III*. They returned three years and 32,000 miles later. They had become heroes and the boat was feted at the second London Boat Show at Olympia, 1956. Besides writing an account of the voyage, *Around the World in Wanderer III*, he also wrote how-tos: *Voyaging under Sail* and *Cruising under Sail*, which sold very well, despite the fact that only a handful of readers would actually follow in his seasteps. The Hiscocks set off again on a second circumnavigation in the same boat from 1959 to 1962.

The Smeetons were tough – they got dismasted twice whilst trying to round the Horn. Brigadier Miles Smeeton was 51 in 1957, when their boat, *Tzu Hang*, was overwhelmed in the Roaring Forties and pitchpoled, losing both its masts.[39] Beryl Smeeton's snap hook on her safety harness was sheered and she was thrown out of the boat and injured, but Miles and their crew, John Guzwell, managed to get her back aboard. With a jury (makeshift) rig, they limped to Chile six weeks later. Without Guzzwell, they tried again in their repaired boat, and again capsized. They eventually rounded the Horn in December 1968, at their third attempt.[40]

The third long-distance couple were Peter Pye, a GP, and his wife, Anne, sailing out of Fowey in their 29 foot converted Polperro gaffer, *Moonraker*, on long distance voyages.[41]

The Navigators

Thor Heyerdahl's *Kon-Tiki* (1948) described his attempt to prove that the Polynesian islands were colonised from South America – a now discredited idea, the accepted theory now being that they were colonised from Asia. His account of the 1947 passage of the balsa-wood raft, *Kon-Tiki*, with five crew, from Callao till it was beached on Raroia reef in the Tuamotos, was a phenomenal seller. By the time it came out in Penguin, in 1963, it had sold four million copies. It has been translated into seventy languages and was made into a film in 1951.[42]

---

[39] *Tzu Hang*: combines 'the name of a Chinese goddess, the protector of seafarers, with the word for a collection of people or a family group' in Mandarin (Miles Clark, *High Endeavours*, p. 102, the biography of Miles and Beryl Smeeton).

[40] Miles Smeeton, *Once is Enough*, 1959; *Because the Horn is There*, 1970.

[41] Peter Pye, *Red Mainsail*, 1952; *The Sea is for Sailing*, 1957; *A Sail in the Forest: Moonraker to the Baltic*, 1961; *Backdoor to Brazil*, 1986 (posthumous). Tom and Ann Worth sailed their 43 foot yacht, *Beyond*, from England to New Zealand, via Panama. They wrote two articles about the voyage in the Royal Cruising Club's *Journal* for 1953 and 1954.

[42] Durham, *Amazing Sailing Stories*, p. 121.

A less conventional crew was that of James Wharram's. Wharram was fascinated by Eric de Bisschop's *The Voyage of the 'Kaimiloa'*, his account of sailing across the Pacific and back to Cannes in a double canoe in 1937 – he didn't like the term 'catamaran'. Wharram built a 23 foot catamaran, *Tangaroa*, and sailed her across the Atlantic in 1956 with two young German women, Ruth Merseberger and Jutta Schultze-Rhonhof, as crew.[43] They reached Trinidad, and built a 40 foot catamaran, called *Rongo*, and sailed it back across the North Atlantic in 1959.

Wharram advocated a 'natural' style of sailing, based on his knowledge of Polynesian craft. He offered a design service and thousands of his Tika 30 foot catamarans have been built. However, his hippy life style and his determination to keep away from industrial production has deprived him of much of the high esteem he deserves.[44] Among eco-sailors, he is a legend, and an American magazine reported in 1987 that he had sold three times more plans than any other designer.[45] Wharram is also concerned with traditional ways of navigating.

David Lewis, born in Plymouth but raised in New Zealand and Rarotonga, was a GP in East Ham in the East End of London. He competed in the first OSTAR, then emigrated to New Zealand by sailing there with his wife and two small daughters, both under three years of age, via Cape Horn in a catamaran, *Rehu Moana*. He then studied the Pacific Islanders' navigational methods.[46]

---

[43] James Wharram, *Two Girls, Two Catamarans*, 1969. The long delay between voyage and publication is, at least, partially explained by Jutta dying 'of an inborn illness that none of us knew of', in the Canaries in 1960, at the start of a planned circumnavigation which the distraught James and Ruth abandoned (4th edn, p. 177).

[44] At Las Palmas, Gran Canaria, during his original crossing, 'the largest contingent of yachts was British ... these yachts without exception flew the blue ensign, the flag of the wealthy, privileged yacht clubs. They treated us like dirt... . In my previous happy wandering life, I had been free of the English 'social system' with its emphasis on the right regiment and public school, but in Las Palmas, I met the full force of it' (*Two Girls, Two Catamarans*, p. 71). At an Association of Yachting Historians meeting, Dartmouth, September, 2015, Wharram recalled that he had been refused membership of the Royal Cornwall, and his two sponsors were told that, if they persisted, their membership would be revoked.

[45] An important part of this success is his long-term partner and skilled draughtswoman, Hanneke Boon. See James Jermain, 'The Wharram Way'.

[46] David Lewis, *Daughters of the Wind*. This was the first circumnavigation by a catamaran. For his study of native Pacific navigational methods, see his *We, the Navigators*, 1972, and *The Voyaging Stars*, 1974. See also Stephen D. Thomas, *The Last Navigator*. Lewis later became fascinated by Antartic waters and completed a circumnavigation. *Ice Bird: The First Single-Handed Voyage to Antartica*, 1975.

Technological Advances

As access to raw materials eased in the second half of the 1950s, so, with so much interest in boating, technological innovations became more frequent. Aluminium spars were developed by Ian Proctor. Synthetic fibres entered the market – Dacron and Terylene were introduced by ICI (Imperial Chemical Industries) in the mid-1950s, and sails from these materials were pioneered by the famous sailmakers, Ratsey and Lapthorn of West Cowes. Terylene and nylon cordage for ropes (sheets, halyards) replaced manila. Stainless steel rigging replaced tarred rope or galvanised steel. The Avon Dinghy range – the Redcrest, the Redstart and the Redseal – was launched by the Avon India Rubber Company and exhibited at the 1960 London Boat Show.

Waterproof clothing to replace the oilskin with its limited protection was developed by John Baylay, head of Island Cruising Club, Salcombe; and by Henri Lloyd, a firm founded in 1963 by Angus Lloyd and Henry Strzelecki, who had fought in the Polish army in the war. Innovations in their clothing included using Bri-Nylon, non-corrosive zips made of nylon, and Velcro closures in waterproof garments.

There were a number of major innovations after the 1960s that made long-distance cruising and racing safer. Firstly, the *electronic echo sounder* was developed before the Great War, but required reduction in size and complete waterproof capability. These improvements were achieved by Brookes & Gatehouse, who in 1960 produced a cockpit repeater. It works by converting the time taken between an emission pulse and its return into a depth reading. It used electricity, but this became less of a problem as the engine, whose alternator charges the batteries, became standard in yachts after the Second World War. Its importance was two-fold: you knew when you were in water where you might ground, and by comparing the depth of the water you were in, you could compare that depth with what you would expect from the chart, so that you could get some idea of where you were (or where you weren't). But they didn't come cheap. Cusack quotes a 1956 advert for one at £75 (about £1,300 in 2016).[47]

The second innovation was the *Decca Radio-Direction finder*, which allowed the yachtsman some idea of where he was through a series of transmitting stations around England and the Channel coast. These were accessed through RDFs – radio direction finders – which picked up the signal from a series of overlapping radio beacons which were shown on the chart. You

---

[47] Cusack, 'Yachting in Britain', 1890–1960, p. 186.

listened with headphones, whilst turning the set till the morse code signal from a station disappeared ('the null point') and noted the compass reading on top of the finder. You then found a second transmitting station, and carried out the same procedure. Where the two direction lines from the stations crossed was your position. The receiver, developed by Heron, was pioneering, as it used transistors, which were claimed to be everlasting, rather than valves.[48]

The third innovation was *wind vane steering*, which was linked to a tab rudder, or to the existing rudder. First introduced in model boating, they started being applied to full size yachts around 1948. Their use was pioneered by Blondie Hasler, founder of the OSTAR (Observer Singlehanded Transatlantic Race), who developed the twin tab, which he used on *Jester* in the first OSTAR in 1960. In 1961, he invented the Pendulum Servo system, so that boats with counter sterns (sterns that cut back into the boat) did not need complicated modifications.

Vane steering allows the boat to be steered at a constant angle to the wind, thus alleviating the need for a human hand at the helm. So, in four Atlantic crossings adding up to some 12,000 miles, *Jester* was steered by hand for less than fifty. The vane steering mechanism revolutionised long-distance sailing, especially for single-handed or small crew sailing.

Where electric power was available, an *autopilot*, which steers the boat on the course set by the helmsman and then frees him for other activities, was launched by Raymarine in 1976.

A final innovation was the *Very High Frequency (VHF) Radiotelephone*, with a dedicated width of bands for marine use. The key one was Channel 16, International Distress and Safety. The yachtsman in distress could send out a Mayday (the vessel in peril) or a Pan Pan (a person requiring medical aid). They could also speak to the Coastguard, or the harbourmaster of a port they wished to enter.

Less spectacular but important was the improvement in the technology and efficacy of winches, which came in at the end of this period, when John Burton bought Lewmar winches in 1967 and then brought in the best machine tool designers to upgrade the product. By the 1970s, it was an international company. Another innovation was the development of clutches and stoppers by Spinlock, Cowes, with the lines all led back to the cockpit. Yet another was the flat stowing Danforth anchor, developed by the American Richard Danforth, as a stern anchor for landing craft; and for seaborne assault troops.

---

[48] *Ibid.*, p. 186.

In 1948, a Manchester company, E. Griffith Hughes, developed the sea sickness pill, Kwells.[49]

These innovations opened up long distance cruising and racing. And even if yachtsmen would never undertake such voyages, they added to the glamour and attractiveness of yachting, and raised its profile.

Yacht Racing

The large yacht crewed by a professional crew was now a thing of the past, due to the huge expense of a professionally crewed yacht after the War.[50] To fill the vacuum, ocean and offshore racing increased in popularity.

Ocean racing took the place of Big Class / J Class racing as the prestige sport of the very rich. The three key changes were: (1) races were offshore or ocean, not inshore and based around regattas; (2) the boats were smaller, usually around 50 or 60 feet long; and (3) they were crewed not by professionals, but by smaller numbers of amateurs who, obviously, were able to get the necessary time off from their work.

Wherever there was some action, John Illingworth (1903–1980) was there, either in person, or behind the scenes.[51] He was in Sydney, New South Wales in December 1945, when nine yachtsmen wanted to celebrate the end of the war with a passage to Hobart, Tasmania. Asked to join, he said he would if they made a race of it. They agreed and he skippered the winning boat, *Rani*, a 34 foot 8 inch canoe stern Bermudan cutter, the smallest boat in the fleet. This was the start of the now famous 630-mile Sydney–Hobart race that starts every Boxing Day. He was elected Commodore of the Royal Ocean Racing Club (the RORC) in 1948. The RORC was formed in 1925, but much of its growth was post-World War Two, so that by 1961, it had over 2,000 members.[52] Illingworth had a yacht design partnership with Angus Primrose, who designed Chichester's circumnavigating *Gipsy Moth IV*. [53]

---

[49] Sharp, *Troubled Waters*, p. 60. The interested researcher will wish to digest Charles Mazel's *Heave Ho!*

[50] T. B. Davis followed the example of his friend, King George V. Dying in 1942, in his will he offered *Westward*, his 97 foot schooner, to any organisation who would maintain her as a sea-going yacht. When no-one took up his offer, on the 15 July, 1947, following his instructions, she was taken to the Hurd Deep off Alderney and scuttled.

[51] His autobiography is *The Malham Story*. (All his boats had 'Malham' in their name, in honour of Hanlith Hall in Malhamdale, Yorkshire where he was brought up). The history of the Royal Ocean Racing Club is told by Ian Dear, *The Royal Ocean Racing Club: The First 75 Years.*

[52] Dear, *The Royal Ocean Racing Club*, p. 149.

[53] Primrose was lost at sea when cruising off South Carolina in his *Demon of Hamble* in 1980, the year Illingworth died.

'The first two post-war America's Cup challenges mounted by the British (1958 and 1964) were disasters and if the Australians had not intervened in 1962, the event might well have died out', wrote the well-placed Ian Dear, who suggests that the main focus of ocean racing became the Admiral's Cup, between nations fielding teams of three yachts. The key race in the Cup was the Fastnet.[54]

Illingworth instructed Laurent Giles, who was already famous for designing the Vertue, to design the 37 ft racer *Myth of Malham*, in which Illingworth won the 1947 and 1949 Fastnets. Illingworth was a stickler for weight – it has been said that he ordered crew to cut down their tooth brush handles![55] But a more substantial reason for his success was the ability of his favourite navigator, Mary Blewitt. She wrote the navigation texts that taught generations and were to be found on most yachts' bookshelf – *Celestial Navigation for Yachtsmen*, 1950 and *Navigation for Yachtsmen*, 1964. They were in the Fastnet Race of 1949. Somewhere near the Scillies:

> I was a little uncertain of my position, so I shook Maria the navigator. She was sleeping in one of the quarter berths, I remember her in her big duffle coat. I had felt this coat was too heavy and asked her to leave it ashore. We had had an up and a downer about this for a second or two, and she said, 'All right, if you don't want me, you needn't have me, but if I'm coming, I'm coming in my duffle coat' ... Anyway, I shook Maria who turned out pretty promptly, with a few f's and b's for good measure. It was a lovely moon horizon and a brilliant night, and in about twenty minutes, Maria had pulled down about five stars and we had a good fix.

In those twenty minutes, she had got up, cleared her head, got her sextant out of its protective box, run accuracy checks on the instrument, taken the sights, noted their time, done the necessary calculations from the Reduction Tables, plotted them on special graph paper and transferred the position to the boat's chart.[56]

The Observer Singlehanded Transatlantic Race started in 1960. It is discussed in the next chapter.

---

[54] Dear, 'Leisure Sailing in the Twentieth Century', pp. 146–147. The first race was only between Britain and America, for a racehorse trophy that Myles Wyatt, RORC Admiral, and his friends had bought. In 1959, the Cup races were opened to all countries.

[55] Dear, *The Royal Ocean Racing Club*, p. 104.

[56] Illingworth, *The Malham Story*, p. 98. 'Maria': It seems likely that Illingworth dictated *The Malham Story*, published in 1972, and used the name her husband called her after her marriage – in 1957, she married Gianni Pera, an Italian naval officer and keen sailor, and in 1969, she captained the first Italian Admiral's Cup team (Dear, *The Royal Ocean Racing Club*, p. 236, where she is listed as 'Mary Pera').

Offshore races are usually held over a long weekend, comprising one day's racing, one day for recuperation at the port of arrival's yacht club and repairs, and the third day cruising or racing home.

The East Anglian Offshore Sailing Association was formed in 1950, with fifteen clubs represented. Races included the Royal Corinthian YC's Thames Estuary Race, 95 miles long, and the long-standing Crouch Yacht Club's Houghton Cup, a hair-raising, 82-mile night race around the Sunk and Cork light vessels, among a number of other shorter races.[57] There were other races that contributed to Royal Ocean Racing Club (RORC) points, such as its North Sea race. Leading clubs were the Crouch Yacht Club and the West Mersea Yacht Club. Several of the West Mersea members were flag officers of both the club and the RORC. In 1949, the club first raced for the Pattison cup race (Burnham to West Mersea), for which there were fifty entries in 1961; and also for the Buckleys Goblets race (West Mersea to Oostende).[58] It is as if these racing yachtsmen, most of whom would have served in the war, wanted to reclaim the sea as a site of leisure and not the place to kill or be killed.

A leading designer in the 1950s was Kim Holman. He was still relatively unknown when his *Vie en Rose*, a 27 foot fractional sloop, was launched a day before the 1959 Burnham Week, which did not prevent her winning all her seven races, and winning them so conclusively that her fellow competitors demanded she be brought out of the water for her handicap rating to be checked – it was correct.[59] She was the prototype for the Stella class, apparently named after a beermat.[60]

The most important organisational advance in small boat racing was the Junior Offshore Group (JOG) started up in 1950, with Patrick Ellam, of *Sopranino*'s transatlantic crossing fame, being a key figure. Its aim was to encourage small boat racing when the Royal Ocean Racing Club refused to be interested in racing yachts below 30 feet. It is still going strong today.

At Cowes, the Round the Island continued to flourish, with 227 entries in 1953. In 1957, Peter Scott, by now a senior figure in the International Yacht

[57] Wise, *50 Years of East Anglian Offshore Racing*. Because of the dangers of night racing, it eventually became a daytime race during Burnham Week (p. 8).

[58] In the late 1970s, the Goblets went missing for five years, the holder apparently thinking they were glasses he had picked up at an auction (Greville, *The West Mersea Yacht Club*, pp. 7–8 and 28).

[59] Bird, *Classic Classes*, p. 149.

[60] A very similar 'foundation myth' concerns the Flying Fifteen. Apparently, its basic lines were drawn on a tablecloth by a group of International Fourteen sailors at the 1950 Olympic Class Championships in Holland. The story goes that the tablecloth found its way to Uus Van Essen, who created the definitive design (Chivers, *Austin 'Clarence' Farrar*, p. 164).

Racing Union (the IYRU), suggested that there should be catamaran racing during Cowes Week. Conservative suspicion of these craft was at least partially allayed by the Duke of Edinburgh sailing aboard Ken Pearce's catamaran, *Endeavour*.[61]

In 1964, the Duke of Edinburgh, as Commodore of the Squadron, suggested that Cowes Week, rather than consisting of one-day regattas organised by individual clubs, should be organised by a Cowes Combined Club Committee, which allowed a smoother and financially successful expansion of the week.

The Dinghy Explosion

While there was a blanket ban on yachts sailing in coastal waters, dinghy sailing, as along as it did not disturb naval or civil defence tasks, was permitted. It was seen as a useful recreation. It was permitted above Putney Bridge and two new sailing clubs – Goring Thames and Hampton Sailing Clubs – were formed in 1943 and 1944. Racing continued actively on the upper Thames during the war.[62]

The outstanding feature of the 1950s and the early 1960s sailing scene, and an important feature of people's leisure, was the building of literally tens of thousands of dinghies in people's houses and garages. This was actually the second stage of a huge explosion in dinghy production.

Phase One: Professional Build

The first stage after the war was the demand for, and increase in numbers, of professionally built dinghies. Traditional boat building woods, such as mahogany and teak, were unavailable, and the first boats were produced by Fairey Marine using ply left over from wartime aircraft manufacture by its parent company, Fairey Aviation. Plywood, the creation of a single thickness from multiple laminations, was a wartime innovation, which was successful because of the development of the glues needed.[63]

At a time when wood use was rationed, their supplies of marine ply gave them a head start, resulting in the launches of the highly successful Firefly, the Flying Fifteen and the Albacore, all designed by Uffa Fox.

---

[61] Scott, *The Eye of the Wind*, pp. 614–615.

[62] Sailing was banned in Burnham, from 1940, as it was in Plymouth Sound, but it was permitted on the nearby Yealm, inside the boom (see Sharp, *Troubled Waters*, Chapter 1: 'Sailing', pp. 11–62).

[63] Sharp, *Troubled Waters*, p. 160.

Their technique, developed for aircraft, involved using a hot-moulded construction of three layers of diagonally laid birch plywood. The hulls were built in moulds, covered with a vacuum bag made from surplus barrage balloon fabric, and put into an autoclave, which applied heat of 100 degrees centigrade and pressure in order to cure the waterproof glue.

Uffa Fox was Fairey's Design Consultant and the leading designer of dinghies before and after the war. First to come on line was the *Firefly*. He 'dusted off the design he had drawn before the war for a 12 ft. inter-college match racing dinghy' and developed it further with Charles Currey, sales director at Fairey.[64] They were the first dinghies to be mass produced. They were much lighter, being made of ply, rather than the heavier traditional woods, and because they had an aluminium, not wooden, mast.

Launched in the Spring of 1946, the Firefly's acceptance was almost immediate. In the Olympics sailing events in Torbay in August, 1948, the Firefly was the single-handed dinghy class.[65] Their initial price, in 1946, was £65 plus purchase tax.[66] 'Universities, schools, the armed forces and sailing associations everywhere opted for the Firefly and within a year or so she became the very epitome of one-design sailing.'[67] By the late 1940s, there was a fleet of some 50 at the Barnt Green club alone.[68] By midsummer 1949, 600 had been built, by 1956, 1,761; and in 1959, the class's national championship attracted 200 boats.[69]

In 1947, Fox designed a 20 foot keelboat, the Flying Fifteen, which became the largest keelboat class in the world, with over 3,700 built. In that year, Princess Elizabeth and Lieutenant Philip Mountbatten RN (created the Duke of Edinburgh just before their wedding) received two racing keelboats, a Dragon *Bluebottle* and a Flying Fifteen *Coweslip* as wedding gifts from the Island Sailing Club and the people of Cowes respectively. At the time of austerity after 1945, it might not have seemed the thing for the new member of the Royal Family to 'buy a yacht'.[70] Publicity and prestige was guaranteed

[64] Pickthall, *The British Marine Industry*, p. 43; Charles Lawrence, *Fairey Marine: Boats, Raceboats, Rivals and Revivals*, p. 16.

[65] The other four keelboat classes at the 1948 Olympics were the Star, the Swallow, the Dragon and the misleadingly named International 6-metre (actually 10–11 metres long). Great Britain won one medal. Stewart Morris and David Bond took gold in the Swallow class. The Dane, Paul Elvstrom, who was to become a legend in small boat racing, won the first of his four consecutive gold medals in the Firefly class, winning gold in the Finn class in 1952, 1956 and 1960.

[66] Cusack, 'Yachting in Britain', 1890–1960, p. 185.

[67] Johnson, *Boating Britain*, p. 31.

[68] Lee, *History of Barnt Green Sailing Club*, p. 20.

[69] Sharp, 'Boatbuilding in the Second World War', pp. 74–75.

[70] Johnson, *Boating Britain*, pp. 215–217.

17 Uffa Fox, with the Duke of Edinburgh and the 8-year-old Prince Charles in the Dragon class keelboat *Bluebottle*, Cowes, in 1957. It was a present from the Island Sailing Club, Cowes, to the Royal Family in 1948.

for this class, since the press always reported when Prince Philip was sailing *Coweslip* with Uffa Fox.

The Dragon, a 29 foot keelboat, was designed by the Norwegian John Anker, for a design competition organised by the Goteborg Yacht Club of Sweden in 1935, which he won. The first Dragon in British waters, *Anita*, appeared on the Clyde in 1935. After the War, Anker waived his royalty fees in recognition of what British seamen had done for Norway during the Second World War.[71] Also in its favour was that 120 were in Britain by 1939, and more available in Europe, so second-hand boats were available. If one was good enough to enter for the trials for the 1948 Olympics, one could have one built.[72] (Helen Pritchard, of the Royal Dart, reached the final selection trials in the Dragon Class, when, as her obituary in the Royal Dart YC Newsletter put it: 'as a lady, it was not the done thing to compete, and she was allowed

[71] For example, by running 'the Shetland bus', a group of fishing boats that ran men and supplies into occupied Norway between 1942 and 1945. See David Howarth, *The Shetland Bus*.
[72] Aldeburgh Yacht Club, *Against the Elements*, p. 84.

to go no further').[73] The Duke of Edinburgh presented the Edinburgh Cup, first raced for in 1949, and annually ever since. Blake and Small suggest that the Dragon, although expensive and a larger size of keelboat, represents the 'transition back from Big to Small yachting'.[74] Described by Vanessa Bird, in *Classic Classes*, as 'a pure racing thoroughbred, the sailing man's Bugatti', it was an Olympic class from 1948 to 1972 and the class is still flourishing.[75]

The single-hander Finn, designed by Rickard Sarby in 1949, has taken part in more Olympics than any other class. Elvstrom won three of his four successive gold medals in a Finn, and Charles Currey won a silver medal in a Finn at the 1952 Helsinki Olympics.[76] Fairey built hulls and complete boats.

The rather misleadingly titled *Yachts and Yachting* was launched in 1946, to cater for the racing dinghy and keelboat enthusiast. Joining it during this period was *Dinghy Sailing*.[77]

These professionally built dinghies were expensive. The Firefly was strictly one-design – the hull had to come from Fairey Marine, the sails from Ratsey, so clearly there was room for cheaper racing dinghies.

The Second Phase: In the Garage, or the Garden Shed, even the Spare Bedroom – the Home Built Dinghy Explosion

The home-built dinghy is almost the creation of Jack Holt (1912–1995) 'the father of dinghy sailing'. His ability to deliver designs for the various niches – the adult racer, the junior racer, the dinghy for father and child to sail in, and the dinghy for the child to learn in, is just remarkable and the work of a design genius. In 1946, he was approached by eight members of the Ranelagh Sailing Club, near his boatbuilding yard close to Putney Bridge, who asked him for a small racing boat, something like the club's existing National Twelves. He designed the 14 foot Merlin (later to amalgamate with the Rocket, designed in 1949 by Dick Wyche, to make the still very flourishing Merlin Rocket class). The Merlin could be built at home but few were.

Holt then moved to the second and far more successful stage of the explosive popularity of post-war dinghies. An important contribution to home build was the low cost, which was helped by the involvement of yachting magazines and competition between newspapers.

---

[73] Cusack, 'Yachting in Britain, 1890–1960', p. 180.

[74] George Blake and Christopher Small, *Cruise in Company*, p. 121.

[75] *Ibid.*, pp. 119–122; Bird, *Classic Classes*, p. 84.

[76] Ben Ainslie also won gold in a Finn in three consecutive Olympics, 2004, 2008 and 2012.

[77] The two titles combined in 2010, *Dinghy Sailing* being absorbed into *Yachts and Yachting*.

The iconic design of the Merlin came to the attention of the Editor of *Yachting World*, Group Captain 'Teddy' Haylock, who asked Holt to design a boat for children aged from 8 to 16 for home building, and the result was the *Cadet*, the pre-packed kits being created by Bell Woodworking of Leicester, who were later to be involved in the Mirror kits.[78] Before going into pre-packed dinghies, Bell had made beehives. At the time of its launch in 1946, the kit sold for £30. Parents clearly placed importance on using these home-built dinghies to teach their children how to sail. Sailing was moving towards being a family affair, rather than a men-only sport; but these dinghies were not that docile – they flew spinnakers downwind.

It is hard to realise how massive the sales of these various types of dinghy were. We shall be looking at successful types of cruising yachts in the next chapter, when a very successful run would be 500 of one type of yacht sold.[79] The first National Cadet Championship was held in 1966. By 1972, 185 boats lined up. Robert Lennox, of the Barnt Green Sailing Club, was a successful Cadet racer. He recalls that in 1970, in a club competition, his sister was racing in CK 6211! One just can't imagine any racing yacht class with anywhere near that number.[80]

One other dinghy that needs mentioning with the Cadet was the Optimist, because both were seen as excellent for teaching children to sail. The Optimist was an American design from Clark Mills, dating from 1947. Mills was asked to design 'a simple dinghy that could be built by a father and son at home which would cost less than $50 to produce'. The plans were taken to Denmark for European distribution. The European version was first introduced to the Hamble and then spread across the UK. At just 7 feet 7 inches (2.3 m) it was the smallest class dinghy you could buy. Its small size and design made it ideal for children to learn on. Its first international championship was held at Burlesdon on the Hamble in 1962.[81] By 1980, there were

---

[78] Rather confusingly, there is the Yachting World Cadet dinghy and also Cadet membership of yacht clubs. When reading of meetings and races, it can be confusing which meaning is being used.

[79] e.g. 'These early Westerlys sold in prodigious numbers. The 22/Nomad model alone lured around 622 new cruising families onto the water.' Taking all versions of the Moody 33, the status statement of yacht cruising (33, 33 Mk II, Moody 33S and 333) gives 494 boats built. In total, 364 Sigma 33s, *the* racing cruiser of the seventies, were built. Only the Westerly Centaur gets into the thousands. It sold 2,444. Westerly's second most popular model, the Konsort, sold 812. (See Brian Easteal and Peter Poland, *The Westerly Story*, pp. 7, 72–73, 84–85; Moody, *The Moody Legacy*, p. 141; Sigma 33 Association website, accessed 2 June, 2015.)

[80] Robert Lennox, 'Cadet Sailing'. In Lee, *The History of Barnt Green Sailing Club*, p. 40.

[81] Bird, *Classic Classes*, p. 54.

18 Jack Holt building one of his successful designs, the Enterprise. Jack Holt's
designs, most especially the Mirror and the Enterprise dinghies, were home-built
in their tens of thousands.

135,000 world-wide and the numbers were estimated to be increasing by
12,000 a year. Peter Johnson gives the total built as 250,000 in 1989.[82]

Holt followed up the Cadet with the Heron, launched in 1951. Originally
known as the 'Yachting World Heron (Cartop) Dinghy', the aim with this 11
foot dinghy was to obviate the need for a trailer whilst still being big enough
to carry two adults and two children. In fact, it couldn't easily go on top of a
car but it was a good two-hander and to date, 10,200 have been built.[83] This
was the dinghy *par excellence* for the children to learn to sail in.

These early models, such as the Cadet, were launched during the period of
post-war rationing, and part of their attraction would have been being able to
get hold of materials that would otherwise been very hard to buy. DIY skills
were at much higher level than today, when the term has been dumbed down
to mean little more than screwing together an IKEA bookshelf. Many of these

[82] Johnson, *The Encyclopedia of Yachting*, p. 233.
[83] Bird, *Classic Classes*, p. 45.

amateur boatbuilders had served in the Armed Forces, where they had been taught skills; and after the war and up to 1957, all healthy males, at age 17, had to do two years' National Service. Britain had a much larger manufacturing base, in metals, shipbuilding and car manufacture, where workers were using manual skills. Families tended to live closer to each other – to be extended rather than nuclear; and also to live in the same locality for generations. If you didn't have a relevant skill, a relative or a neighbour might well be able to help. So, building a dinghy was a far less daunting task for men who wanted to build them by themselves or with their children than it would be now.

An example of communal working was at the Topsham Yacht Club, on the Exe. Holt had designed the *Yachting World Hornet*, a small, 4 foot 7 inch dinghy, in 1952. Wally Beach, elected Commodore in 1952, reckoned they could be built for less than £100. Seventeen were built by the members working together in a church hall, for £69 each, and drawing lots at the end as to which they now owned. This resulted in Topsham Yacht Club having the largest Hornet fleet in the UK; a member, Tony Greenslade, won the World Hornet Championship in 1956 and 1957.[84]

Holt was asked by Group Captain Haylock, editor of *Yachting World*, to design a 14 foot boat that the dad could race on Saturday and potter about in with mother and two or three children on Sunday, say for a picnic.[85] To keep things nice and calm, it should have a smallish jib and no spinnaker. So, Holt created another design that could be built at home, the GP 14 (GP = General Purpose). The kit sold for £60. Some 25,000 have been built. Apparently, they were sold at a loss and contributed to the *News Chronicle*'s demise in 1960.

However, the GP 14 was a bit heavy and not surprisingly, given its design brief, was a bit staid. A more exciting boat, the Enterprise, was launched by the *News Chronicle* in 1956, as an affordable 'Everyman's' dinghy. It was 4 metres in length and was yet another Jack Holt design – he produced some 40 or so designs in his career. To launch the new dinghy, *Enterprise One*, crewed by Olympic dinghy sailor Bruce Banks and his wife Rosemary, and *Enterprise Two*, with Bobbie Prenger and Flavia Nunes, set off from Dover for Calais at 03:28 on 9 January, 1956, into a Force Four. The link with the sponsoring *News Chronicle* required that they delay their entrance into Calais harbour for an hour to allow the newspaper's photographer to arrive in a chartered

---

[84] Chris Williams, *125 Years: Topsham Sailing Club 1885–2010*, pp. 10–12.
[85] In all, *Yachting World* sponsored 23 designs (Sharp, *Troubled Waters*, p. 62).

aeroplane and take the photographs that would appear on the news that night, and in papers all over Britain the next day.[86]

For home build, the 1959 prices were £79 for the kit, £26 for racing sails. If you wanted terylene, not cotton, sails, add £6.00. Several boatyards could build you an Enterprise for about £146.00. It was an instant success. It sold about 1,000 a year and its blue sail gave it immediate 'brand recognition'. By the late 1950s, it had overtaken the Firefly in popularity, with its sales figures in five numbers, and was the top racing dinghy. By early 1968, at Frensham Pond Sailing Club, Keith Videlo and his brother, Ian, crewed for their father in his Enterprise sail number 10,117![87]

But it was with the Mirror Dinghy, developed with the DIY TV presenter, Barry Bucknell, that Holt hit the jackpot. Holt simplified Bucknell's original design so that it was a 'stitch and glue', hard chine 10 ft 10 inch (3.3 metres), gunter-rigged dinghy. The pram transom avoided the need for curved panels, which would be difficult to achieve at home. The kit cost £63.11s and was promoted as 'a boat for the people' in tune with the paper's socialist credentials, and it was the *Daily Mirror* staff who suggested the distinctive red sails.[88] The Mirror was launched at the 1963 London Boat Show. In its first year, it sold 800, and in its heyday, 400 kits were leaving the Bell factory each month.[89] By 1975, more than 47,000 had been built.[90]

This is one of the few times when television has played an important role in yachting. Television came in quickly after 1950: 'some tens of thousands of sets in 1950, 4 million in 1955, 10 million by 1960, and by 1970 the total was to reach 16 million'.[91] Programmes like *Coronation Street*, launched in 1960, and *Match of the Day* – first screened in 1964 and, from 1969, in colour, if you could afford the set – had massive audiences. Barry Bucknell was a TV 'face' at a time when TV personalities were major celebrities. In the late 1950s, he was presenting the series *Barry Bucknell's Do It Yourself*. Taken in conjunction with the fact that the *Daily Mirror*, which sponsored the dinghy, was the nation's best-selling paper, there was huge publicity for this new dinghy.[92]

---

[86] Steffan Hughes, 'Sixty Years Ago: Cross-Channel by Night in an Enterprise'. They eventually entered Calais harbour at 10:10. More than 23,000 Enterprises had been built by 2016.
[87] Donald Videlo, ed. *Frensham Pond Sailing Club. The First Fifty Years 1953–2003*, p. 94.
[88] Bird, *Classic Classes*, p. 52.
[89] Richey, ed., *The Shell Encylopedia of Sailing*, pp. 49–50.
[90] Lavery, *The Island Nation*, p. 131.
[91] Bédarida, *A Social History of England 1851–1975*, p. 241.
[92] See Sally Karslake, *Mirror Mania*.

19 Mirror Dinghy on top of a Mini. Unless one was a member of a club, the dinghy
still had to be transported to the water. The Mini was an iconic car of the sixties.
Note the child in the car, underlining the point that a dinghy was not just for racing
but could be used for family cruising. Photograph taken by Eileen Ramsay, pioneer
female yachting photographer and also a pioneer of 'action shots' of yachts.

The Sailing Club and the Reservoir

To enjoy sailing as a hobby, there had to be some surplus income, not just for
the dinghy but also for the car. If the inter-war sailor needed the railway, the
post-war sailor needed the car.

The car became ever more necessary for the leisure sailor, due to the 1963
Beeching plan and 'axe'. Beeching recommended the closure of 3,000 miles
of railtrack (30 per cent) in the next five years, and the closing of 2,363 stations (55 per cent of all stations). Most of these recommendations were acted
on. This was devastating for the sailor using the stations at the top of Essex
creeks and small harbours, traditionally used for returning to London after a
weekend sail.[93] Besides, reservoirs are not usually served by railways. So the
explosion in dinghy numbers was dependent on increasing car ownership. In
1939, there were 2 million privately owned cars, 2.25 in 1950, 3.5 in 1955 and 5.5
million in 1960.[94]

Of course, not all dinghy owners had a car, and for them, being able to
leave the dinghy at the club was a necessity. Also, trailing a dinghy to and

[93] The Beeching Report was titled *The Reshaping of British Railways*, 27 March, 1963.
[94] Chris Cook and John Stevenson, *The Longman Handbook of Modern British History 1714–1987*,
    p. 22.

from the nearest stretch of usable water was a chore, and required having somewhere to park it at home, so there was, not surprisingly, a huge growth in dinghy sailing clubs. 'Clubs were springing up on every available piece of water.'[95] The YRA recognised 321 clubs in 1946. (In 1953, it became the Royal Yachting Association (RYA) to indicate that it was now concerned with all aspects of the sport, not just racing.) During the 1952/1953 season alone, 150 small boat clubs were formed.[96] By 1958, the figure for clubs affiliated to the RYA was 831. In 1960, this figure had risen to 956.[97] While there was an increase in the number of yacht clubs, the main growth was in sailing clubs for dinghies.

Many new club houses started in a small way, with primitive facilities, often using surplus war material and Nissen huts. Wembley Sailing Club, set up in 1953 on the Welsh Harp, North London, started in a small Nissen hut with an Elsan toilet. It was the job of the racing officer to empty the Elsan on the nearby allotments.[98] The Island Barn Reservoir Club was initially formed in a gravel pit near Walton-on-Thames in 1959. The first club house was a tent on an island in the middle of the pit. Access was via a punt.[99]

But such was the demand that memberships grew rapidly. Sailing clubs had lower running costs than yacht clubs, and lower subscriptions. Many of the new members had received their education at state, rather than public, schools. One might have thought that, with this wider socio-economic base, they would wish to do away with the old protocols. But this does not seem to have been the case. Their practices and titles were borrowed from yacht clubs. If a prestigious person could be persuaded to be commodore, this was all to the good, and dinghy clubs kept the same nomenclature for flag officers as yachting clubs – commodore, vice-commodore etc.

To give one example, South Staffordshire Sailing Club was created in 1953 to cater for the workers in the booming engineering town of Wolverhampton. From thirty-nine people, who had paid a 10s note to join at the inaugural meeting at the Victoria Hotel, Wolverhampton on 3 September , 1953, the membership list rose so sharply it had to be closed after two years. There

[95] Videlo, *Frensham Pond Sailing Club: The First Fifty Years 1953–2003*, p. 6.
[96] A. R. Burrett, *Dinghy Sailing*, p. 9.
[97] By the 1980s, it was 1,400. Figures from Robin Steavenson, *Dinghy Sailor's Pocket Book*, p. 29.
[98] http://www.wembleysailingclub.co.uk/downloads/history written by John Sagues. The club chose the Gull, rather than the single person Cadet, as the junior training and racing boat. The Gull, launched in 1956 by Ian Proctor, was a gunter rigged, 11 foot dinghy, so was big enough for a parent to sail with and teach their child. The Gull was available as a kit boat and 'was well within the within the capability of most amateur boat builders'.
[99] http://www.islandbarn.org.uk/index.php/about-us/our-history, accessed 25 April, 2016.

was then a search for suitable water and Calf Heath Reservoir was located. A considerable coup was persuading 'yachting royalty', Uffa Fox, 'to perform the official opening and inspect the racing fleet of GP 14s and 12 ft. Fireflies ...', on 2 April, 1955.

The commodore, Victor Gough had arrived early in his chauffeur-driven Rolls-Royce:

> kitted out as one would have expected from the principal flag officer, complete with peaked yachting cap. In order to make sure the flag officers were correctly dressed, Victor had taken the precaution of writing to the Royal Yachting Association. Frank Usborne, the secretary had written back to say that peaked yachting caps were appropriate ... white caps could be worn during the summer season (May 1 to September 30) ... the RYA had stressed that it was not only the flag officers who could wear peaked yachting caps, with white covers in summer, it is 'the normal practice on the coast' for all members to do so.

> One summer morning, Josie Etchells ... rushed into the clubhouse to say how surprised she was that such a small sailing club like South Staffs had 'such a smart car parking attendant.' It turned out to be [one of either] two of the club's most immaculately turned out members who always wore smart blue suits and yachting caps with white covers.[100]

Thus suitably attired, they headed off to the dinghy park.

With a leadership structure and members keen to join, the club would enter 'the heroic phase', where improving facilities was done by the members pooling their skills. At Frensham, a Mr Wines, 'a first class dowser', was able to advise the club how to avoid building on marsh.[101] Accidents could happen. Wembley Sailing Club built its own clubhouse in the early 1950s. 'Partway through the building a party was held during which Bill Letten and Pete Smith danced a "flamenco" on the just laid floor – concrete paving slabs on pillars. The slabs broke and both dancers fell through'.[102]

The clubs would start with a motley collection of members' dinghies. At Frensham Pond, racing for prizes of teaspoons with the club burgee on them:

> Commander Morley had a National 12, there was a home built/designed 14 ft. Boat ..., an ordinary sailing dinghy with a red lugsail, there was our new

---

[100] Nicholas Jones, son of founder member, J. Clement Jones, in Carole Danbury, *SSSC: The First Fifty Years,* one of the few dinghy club histories available, the scarcity of which makes the job of the yachting historian difficult. The club moved to its present location in Gailey Lower Reservoir in 1971.

[101] Videlo, *Frensham Pond SC.* Water diviner, p. 8.

[102] John Sagues, 'The History of Wembley SC'.

Graduate (G11), a green boat with wooden sides and a canvas bottom ..., an old Sharpie ..., and a wooden single-handed Moth sailed by a lady called Biddy Bargrave-Deane.[103]

Obviously this was a handicapper's nightmare, so, as with the earlier sailing clubs, there was a push towards racing in one-design classes. By 1958, members would only be admitted if their boat was a National 12, Firefly, GP 14, Graduate, Cadet, Heron or Enterprise. To manage this system, class secretaries came into being. Because of the limit on membership size, you would be put on the list for the class of your boat, and throughout the 1960s at Frensham, there was a waiting list for most classes.[104]

The 'built in' redundancy of one-design through changes in taste and the desire for faster boats is nicely seen in sailing club histories. At Frensham, the Firefly class was phased out in 1963 and the National 12s would no longer have their own start in 1966, making way for the Lark and the Laser.[105]

Once these clubs were up and running, as before the war, inter-club team competitions became popular. Since many of the dinghies were one-design, they could be used by visiting helmsmen. After the war, while competing in the Midlands against South Staffs. and Rugby (for ladies), the Barnt Green Sailing Club competed as far away as West Kirby, the Royal Lymington and the Royal St George, Dun Laoghaire.[106]

Another feature common to sailing clubs was the provision of facilities to teach the members' children to sail, often in a dinghy their father had built. A major event was a National Cadets week at Burnham from the early 50s, attracting young sailors, and their parents, from all over the country. By 1953, there were 67 participants, by 1972, 185. The children were housed by the Burnham clubs, so one of the attractions was that, for many children, the Week was 'parent-free'.

The popularity of two-person dinghies, the weekend races and the Cadet classes brought the families into the clubs. To feed 'the inner man', the mothers would often run the kitchen. But one difference was that the restrictions on women members and their roles still current in the yacht clubs did not feature, at least overtly, in sailing clubs. As one Frensham member drily recalled: 'Equality came with the chemical toilets in open topped tin surrounds'.[107] And because dinghies did not have heavy gear, young girls were

---

[103] Videlo, *Frensham Pond Sailing Club*, p. 4. The 12′6″ 'Graduate' dinghy was sponsored by *Light Craft* magazine
[104] *Ibid.*, p. 52.
[105] *Ibid.*, p. 49
[106] Lee, *History of the Barnt Green Sailing Club*, p. 21.
[107] Videlo, *Frensham Pond Sailing Club*, p. 7.

encouraged to sail, especially in the Cadet class – and a few of their mothers also tried their hand in the family dinghy. The presence of families and the dinghy club acting as a social centre furthered the sense of community and common purpose of the club members of both sexes.

A densely populated area, such as the Midlands, with its reservoirs for the network of canals and for water supply, spawned many clubs. They varied in status, but all organised sailing all the year round, compared to the Easter fitting out and lifting out at the end of September of traditional yacht club seasons. The advent of dry suits in the 1970s helped prevent hypothermia, but were expensive.

Cruising yachts

Going abroad for a holiday was difficult after the war, as the amount of money you could legally take out of the country was strictly controlled. (When George Millar left to sail to Greece in 1946, 'any ordinary resident in Britain was allowed to take out only £75 out of the country to pay for his foreign travelling expenses for a twelvemonth').[108] So people looked to holiday in the UK. Dinghies were fine to potter around in or to race. However, for a holiday afloat, one needed a yacht but yachts were in scarce supply after the war. Some of the larger yachts with an engine had been taken into war service. Many had rotted in their mud berths. To make matters worse, yacht building was severely restricted by rationing and shortage of materials, such as timber and cotton sail-making material. 'In the first quarter of 1947, only 50 firms were licensed to build yachts and between them, they produced a mere 196 craft varying in size from a 40 ft. motor cruiser to an 8 ft. Dinghy'.[109] Supplies of material were released by the government only on condition that the finished product was sold abroad. Restrictions started easing in 1949.

Because of this shortage of yachts, skilled labour became much more expensive than before the war. Sharp gives a figure of three times the pre-war equivalent for a new boat.[110] The demand for new yachts greatly outstripped supply. This scarcity of boats for the home market continued into the 1950s and beyond. Into the 1980s, if you wanted a yacht, you paid a deposit and joined the queue.

One small source of yachts after the war was requisitioned Nazi yachts from Kiel, the German equivalent of Cowes, after the war. These 'windfall'

[108] George Millar, *Isabel and the Sea*, p. vi.
[109] Barry Pickthall, *The British Marine Industry*, p. 42.
[110] Sharp, *Troubled Waters*, p. 53.

yachts were split between the various victorious nations. The British yachts were given to service clubs, and were used to train a large number of service personnel in the skills of sailing.[111] All Naval officer recruits were taught to sail as part of their training.

Another source, especially for East Anglian sailors, were Dutch fishing boats. The Dutch had decided to reclaim the Zuiderzee, now called the Ijsselmeer, so there were fleets of soon to be landlocked fishing boats for sale. Mike Peyton recalls that 'On 5 November 1959, I bought a 40 ft. *botter* from a sad wooden-clogged fisherman for less than £400 and sailed her home the day after'.[112]

After the war, barges had ceased to be used as commercial cargo carriers, although commercial sail hung on in the Bristol Channel in such ports as Appledore, Velator Quay below Braunton and Ilfracombe, till the end of the 1950s.[113] Already romantic objects before the war, nostalgia at their passing induced a spate of books by people who had sailed in them, most notably Hervey Benham and Bob Roberts,[114] and a variety of preservation societies, such as the Thames Sailing Barge Association which was formed in 1952. Many were converted to be used for cruising purposes.[115]

Similarly, the replacement of the gaff rig with the Bermudan was also nearly complete by the 1960s. To keep gaff alive, a group was started in the Solent in 1959 and in Essex in 1963, coming together to form the Old Gaffers' Association in that year. By 1964, they were joined by enthusiasts from the Clyde and the Medway.[116]

As a consequence of this shortage, quite a few of the yachts sailed after the war were converted lifeboats from merchant navy vessels who had to renew their boats every few years, or even, if smaller, converted rowing boats. Sharp gives a figure of 700 ships' lifeboats sold as surplus after the war.[117] A standard text was C. Tyrell Lewis' *Lifeboats and their Conversion*, first published in 1935, and published in a number of editions after the war. Another well-thumbed text was Michael Verney's *Lifeboat into Yacht*, published in 1951.

---

[111] Michael Cudmore, *The Windfall Yachts*.
[112] Peyton, 'The Good Old Days', p. 91.
[113] Barry D. Hughes, *North Devon Barges*.
[114] Hervey Benham, *Last Stronghold of Sail: The Story of the Essex Sailing-Smacks, Coasters and Barges*, 1948; *Down Tops'l: The Story of the East Coast Sailing-Barges*, 1951; Bob Roberts, *Coasting Bargemaster*, 1949; *Last of the Sailormen*, 1960.
[115] Leather, *The Salty Shore*, Chapter 12 'The Malden Barges', pp. 179–189.
[116] Viv Head, *Sailing Gaffers*.
[117] Sharp, *Troubled Waters*, p. 199.

Maurice Griffiths' *Sailing on a Small Income* (1953) suggested ways of reducing costs. Yet another example of DIY tuition is R. M. Bowker and S. A. Budd's *Make Your Own Sails*, 1957. DIY skills were at a premium, if not an actual necessity. So, because of the limited resources, the Corinthian philosophy of maintaining one's own vessel lived on after the Second World War.

Not surprisingly, even after war-time conditions, family holidays in very cramped conditions did not have a wide appeal. However, the Greenways – 2 adults and 3 children in a 22 foot boat – ventured as far afield from Poole as France and Holland in the early 1950s.[118]

Edward Robinson's *Down River to the Sea* (1952) is symptomatic of the times. His career was in journalism, and he was in the RNVR during the war. The family – two adults, two children – sailed a 4 ton boat, some 21 feet long, with a tiny cabin with 4 foot headroom and a drop keel, for their holidays. This headroom was luxurious, as the children slept in the forepeak with 2 feet 6 inches headroom.

Lacking a dinghy, Robinson had to beg and borrow the materials, and made one with his children. When the engine played up, he stripped and rebuilt it. The boat was based at Winsford on the River Weaver, in Cheshire. Journeying down the navigation to the Mersey was an adventure, and a trip to the Menai Straits a major expedition, caution requiring the children be left with grandmother.

The Folkboat, a Swedish design, became the first popular and relatively inexpensive wooden yacht available after the war. It was 25 feet long, a pretty basic boat with little head room, but capable of long distance sailing.[119] They were built under licence in England. For example, *Martha McGilda* was built in 1953 at Chippendale's at Warsash for Noel Jordan, who then won the East Anglian Offshore Championship in 1954. Wishing to build a bigger yacht, he sold her to Roselle Raynes, who sailed in her along the North European coast to Finland and the border with Russia in 1959.[120] Hasler sailed a modified Folkboat, *Jester,* in the first OSTAR in 1960.

From 1954, Prouts, founded by Geoffrey Prout and his two sons, Roland and Francis, produced catamarans, originally from a small factory on Canvey

---

[118] Jocelyn M. Greenway, *Puffin's Log*, edited by Cathy Woodhead, her daughter, and there are lovely pictures and drawings by her father. Another family making do with little space on board were the Hellings – again two adults and two young children, this time going on a three-week holiday in 1946 in a small racing yacht, a Tumlare, with 4 feet 6 inch headroom in the saloon, and rather less in the forepeak (Dorothy Hellings, *Close Quarters*).

[119] See Dieter Loibner, *The Folkboat.*

[120] Rozelle Raynes, *Sea Bird.*

Island, for the upmarket cruising man and for the small group of racing cat-amaran sailors.

The first twin-keeled yacht, *Bluebird*, had been designed by Lord Riverdale in 1922. Twin or bilge keels allow yachts to take the ground without damage, which is not possible with a monohull, unless it has been provided with legs. Yachts with twin keels started being made by Fairey Marine in hot-moulded ply, in 1956.[121] They produced 186 26 foot Atalanta, conceived by one of Fairey's marketing directors, Alan Vines, and designed by Uffa Fox. These were advertised as trailable boats with two lifting cast iron centreboards. Altogether, some 291 of the three variants of the Atalanta were sold between 1956 and 1968.[122]

By 1963, the time of the launch of the Mirror dinghy, rationing was a thing of the past. There was full employment and a large growth in reasonably paid white collar jobs, with white-collar workers rising from 18.7 per cent of the workforce in 1911 to 35.8 per cent in 1961.[123] The economist Kenneth Galbraith's 1958 text, *The Affluent Society*, was about America, but the title became a catchphrase to describe the United Kingdom.[124] There was cer-tainly more optimism in the air.[125]

In the 1960s, bilge keelers started to be built in fibreglass, by firms such as Westerly and MacWester.[126] Westerly launched their Westerly 22 bilge keeler in 1963 and the Westerly 25, also a bilge keeler, a year later.[127] C.S.J. Roy, who had worked for Westerly, designed the bilge keeled MacWester 26 which was launched in 1964, for £1,695 new.

To check out the latest innovations, early each January, one took the District or Piccadilly Line to the Earl Court's Boat Show.[128] Again, this was a result of competition between newspapers. The annual Ideal Home

---

[121] Fairey adopted the technique from De Havilland, who had used it to build Mosquitos (Sharp, *Troubled Waters*, pp. 180–181).

[122] Charles Lawrence, *Fairey Marine: Boats, Raceboats, Rivals and Revivals*, p. 25. The book is a detailed history of Fairey Marine. Lawrence has also produced a facsimile copy of Fairey Ma-rine's 1958 catalogue for racing dinghies and utility boats. Fairey switched from the labour-in-tensive method of hot-moulded ply to GRP in 1965, and ceased leisure boat production in 1975.

[123] Bédarida, 'The Immutable Class System', Chapter 8 of *A Social History of England*, pp. 200–226; Cook and Stevenson, *The Longman Handbook of Modern British History 1714–1987*, p. 155.

[124] It was an academic text, albeit clearly written, but such was the appetite for the printed word, and the desire to achieve an understanding of what was happening, it was a best seller.

[125] Harold Macmillan, the Conservative prime minister, won the 1959 election with his slogan 'You've Never Had It So Good'.

[126] Andy Cunningham, 'The Truth about Twin Keels'.

[127] Brian Easteal and Peter Poland, *The Westerly Story*, pp. 68–69.

[128] No need to call it the 'London' Boat Show, as there was no Southampton Boat Show till 1969.

Exhibition, which had been started by the *Daily Mail* in 1908, drew huge attendances – it peaked in 1957 with 1.5 million people coming to Olympia.

Max Aitken, son of Lord Beaverbrook, the owner of the *Daily Express*, was the paper's chairman and a keen power boat sailor. The London Boat Show was started in 1955 by the paper with 120,851 visitors, and because of the large numbers of visitors, moved to Earl's Court in 1957, with 338,451 visitors that year. It was always held over the first two weeks in January. A central feature, besides the Guinness bars, was a pool area with a few yachts on it. The Boat Show was opened by a member of the Royal Family.[129] With its attendant publicity, it was an important part of keeping sailing in the national consciousness.

There were new sources of information. In 1960, the Royal Cruising Club made its annual collection of the last season's logs by members, previously only available to members, available to the general public. Since their members went far afield and included most of the famous names in long-distance cruising, these volumes offered wider horizons to the cruising fraternity.

The Cruising Association's (CA) Handbook was a pilot book with, after 1951, coloured charts. With its lectures, newsletter (the *Bulletin*) and clubhouse, the CA provided a focus and an identity for the cruising yachtsman, especially after it moved from Chiltern Court, Baker Street, to the prestigious Ivory House, in St Katherine's Dock in 1974. Its membership grew from 868 in 1956 to 1,000 in 1960 and 2000 in 1970.[130]

The first publishing house dedicated solely to yachting matters, such as 'how to' books, pilots etc. and the classic *Heavy Weather Sailing*, was founded in 1947 by Adlard Coles (1901–1983). Long before the Second World War, he had written books on finances and tax, drawing on his chartered accountancy training, and had written the *Shell Guide to the South Coast*. (A feature of the increasing interest in sailing, especially from the 1950s onwards, was the involvement of petrol companies in sponsoring pilot books and other sailing material.) After the war, besides being a keen racing skipper, he created a company to sell yachting books, called 'Robert Ross'.[131] In 1937, he bought *The Yachtsman* magazine. His book publishing grew slowly till he published Illingworth's *Offshore*, in 1949, which sold well. Then, as yachtsmen ventured

---

[129] Johnson, *Boating Britain*, pp. 108 ff.

[130] Fred Barter, compiler, *Cruising for a Hundred Years: The Centenary of the Cruising Association 1908–2008*, p. 23.

[131] 'the name being an amalgamation of the christian name of my father-in-law and the maiden name of my grandmother (after whom our own son Ross has been called)' (Adlard Coles, *Sailing Years*, p. 72). His account of the 1950 Transatlantic Race, in which he took part, *North Atlantic*, was published in 1950.

further afield, he moved into pilots. In 1952, he published *Harbours and Anchorages of the North Coast of Brittany*, by Blondie Hasler, the leader of the Cockleshell Heroes, but few yachtsmen sailed as far as Brittany at the time and the book sold slowly. Coles' own *Channel Harbours and Anchorages*, published in 1956, was a good seller, year on year.[132] 'Channel harbours' included those of Normandy and Brittany, indicating how the south coast sailors were gradually extending their horizons. For the first time, yachtsmen had a publishing house that was geared to providing for their needs. Coles changed its name from 'Robert Ross' to 'Adlard Coles' in 1953.

A little later, Coles was involved in creating the second major British yachting publishing house, founding the Nautical Publishing Company, Lymington, with Commander Erroll Bruce and Peter Johnson. In 1964, Stanford Maritime started up, publishing pilot books and how-to manuals.

Ransome wisely stopped his *Swallows and Amazons* series after the tired *Great Northern!* in 1947. There were a number of post-war writers of children's sailing stories, but none reached anything like Ransome's success. Of these, 'Peter Dawlish' (James Lennox-Kerr, 1899–1963) is the most interesting, as he tried to combine socialist principles with the sailing story. For example, in *Dauntless Takes Recruits*, 1950, with *Dauntless* lying in Bow Creek, Poplar, in the East End of London, the public school crew are pelted with stones by the local lads. The teenage skipper takes some of these locals on as crew and these boys claim salvage on a wrecked barge. The skipper, David, holds a full-scale court hearing to resolve the matter … [133]

Another feature of the post-war years was the creation of a canonical (definitive classic) series of cruising books. In 1946, Rupert Hart-Davis, junior partner at Jonathan Cape, the publisher of Ransome's *Swallows and Amazons* children's books, struck out on his own and set up his own publishing firm.

---

[132] He also published a number of the early Atlantic crossings, such as Smith and Violet, *The Wind Calls the Tune* and Barton, *Vertue XXXV*. He describes his early publishing ventures in his autobiography, *Sailing Years*, Chapter 20 'Publishing', pp. 134–139.

[133] Enid Blyton had published *The Adventurous Four*, 1941, where the children, aided by a 14-year-old Scottish fisherman's son as skipper, sail in his fishing boat to an island off Scotland's north-east coast. The Nazis are using it as a base, and of course, have to be outwitted. In the 1947 *The Adventurous Four Again*, the children come up against a Scottish smuggler. Aubrey de Selincourt wrote various titles such as *Three Green Bottles* and *One Good Tern*. Gilbert Hackforth-Jones wrote his *Green Sailor* series, which were published after they had been broadcast on *Children's Hour*; and 'Peter Dawlish' his *Dauntless* series. The yachting children's story died out at the end of the 1950s. These authors and Ransome are discussed in my 'Isn't It Time We Treated Arthur Ransome as a Grown-Up?' The genre was revived by Julia Jones in her *Strong Winds* trilogy: *The Salt-Stained Book*, *A Ravelled Flag* and *Ghosting Home* (2011–2012), which draws on Ransome; M. J. Vermeulen's *Islanders* trilogy (2009–2013), drawing on Blyton; and Alexander McCall Smith, *School Ship 'Tobymory'* (2015), using the school story format.

In 1948, he offered Arthur Ransome the task of selecting sailing texts to form the Mariners Library. Ransome recognised this as the unique opportunity it was, and asked for no payment.[134] He chose forty-seven titles, all relating to cruising, not racing. Megoran Winston, an accomplished maritime artist, designed many of the covers, adding to the books' attractiveness. There is little doubt that this list has, to a large extent, defined the yachting genre.[135]

At the Yacht Club

Griffiths, trying to help keep the cost of post-war sailing reasonable in *Everyman's Yachting*, 1952, still assumes yacht club membership. [136] 'Keep a steady pull on the paddles. Your little ship is on a mooring some way below the Yacht Club hard';[137] and the new member would be expected to 'muck in'. Given the shortage of materials and of skilled labour, many yacht clubs, as with sailing clubs had their 'heroic phase' when members mucked in and built the club house/the extension/ the car park/ the hard etc.[138] Even more than sailing clubs, because of their location in or near harbours that needed to be defended, yacht clubs were able to benefit from military surplus and, in quite a few cases, redundant buildings and slipways, erected during the war.

For a yacht club to take dinghy sailing on board, it had to have somewhere to park them, be that a dinghy park on spare land, trots of moorings, or the foreshore. Responses by established yacht clubs varied. Sometimes, a club bought land on which to build accommodation for dinghies. Such

---

[134] Rupert Hart-Davis in the Epilogue to *The Autobiography of Arthur Ransome*, records that 'He refused any sort of payment, so I gave him a set of the big Oxford Dictionary ...' (p. 354).

[135] Hugh Brogan, *The Life of Arthur Ransome*, 413–414. When the rights were bought by Adlard Coles in the late 1960s, they added a forty-eighth title, Eric Newby's *The Last Grain Race*. For a discussion of the series, see my 'An Open Letter to the Editor'.

[136] This was one of a number of teach-yourself texts available. C. Tyrell Lewis published *Teach Yourself Sailing* in the popular Teach Yourself series in 1947, and Percy Woodcock *Come Boating with Me* in 1953.

[137] Griffiths, *Everyman's Yachting*, p. 15.

[138] Among many examples: the long slipway into the Solent at the Gurnard Sailing Club was built by its members, as was the major extension to the Barry Yacht Club (Sheila Caws, *Gurnard Sailing Club 1931–2006*, p. 14; Norman Hockley, *Barry Yacht Club ... and 50 Years On*, p. 79). The 'pioneer' stage is the third stage. First is the 'founding myth' where a few local worthies gather in one of the town's hotels to form the club, call a meeting, create a rule book and a burgee, and appoint their first commodore. The second 'father figure' stage, is the reign of a commodore who holds office for decades. Examples of the latter are Underhill, Commodore of the Royal Cruising Club, 1888–1937; Hanson, Honorary Secretary at the Cruising Association for 45 years from 1908; Quiller Couch, Commodore at the Royal Fowey, 1911–1944; and W. S. Le Masurier, Commodore at the St Helier, 1925–1952. As soon as this figure retires, a rule is usually introduced limiting the Commodore's period of office to three years.

was the case with the Teignmouth Corinthian Yacht Club, which purchased land at Coombe Cellars up the Teign in 1965.[139] Some clubs had members who did not want to be swamped by these innumerable, lower-class sailors. The Royal Dart response was half-hearted. It could not decide on a dinghy wanted by any decent number of members, although it did commission the 16½ foot Royal Dart One- Design from Morgan Giles. The idea of converting its garden into a dinghy park, first suggested in 1951, was only achieved in 1964. Long before this time, two clubs focussing on small boat racing were formed in 1950 – the Dart Sailing Club (later Yacht Club) on the other side of the river by a member of the Royal Dart, Major Benson; and the Dittisham Sailing Club, which, with its ample space on the foreshore and immediate access to the wide Dittisham Pool, became the foremost dinghy club on the Dart.

If the yacht club did embrace dinghies, it tended to be the higher end, the Flying Fifteens, Dragon or Albacore. However, classes in Swansea Bay for this period included Enterprises (early 1950s), Albacores (early 1960s), GP 14s and Ospreys, and by the mid-1960s, Mirror dinghies (some 40 boats). By the 1960s, the Mumbles Yacht Club, effectively the sailing club for Swansea Bay, had over 800 members, and like a number of clubs that had embraced dinghy racing, had to close its membership list.[140]

The Mirror, with its socialist overtones as it was linked to the *Daily Mirror*, was not acceptable in a number of places, the line being drawn after welcoming Enterprises. Aldeburgh has two yacht clubs – the prestigious Aldeburgh Yacht Club, founded 1897, and the nearby Slaughden Sailing Club, founded in the 1970s, because, as their website delicately puts it: '… a small group of local people … some had built their own Mirror dinghy and they wanted somewhere to sail, rather than race, and there was no nearby club willing to host their needs'.[141] The two clubs are about 200 yards apart. The Aldeburgh Yacht Club had no need to accept them. Its membership rose from 580 in 1959 to 1,000 in 1969, and although it adopted the Loch Long class, it is clear that its growth was not due to active dinghy sailing, but to members either with cruising yachts and/or a large social element from the nearby prosperous town.[142]

With regard to maintaining boundaries, little was changed by the war. In the east of the Isle of Wight, 'to live at Bembridge and not be a member of the

---

[139] S. F. Thomas, *A History of the Teign Corinthian Yacht Club*, p. 33.
[140] Austin, 'Yachting in Swansea Bay', *Maritime South West*, 2014, pp. 2–33.
[141] www.slaughdensailingclub.co.uk/clubinfo/club history
[142] Aldeburgh Yacht Club, *Against the Elements*, pp. 73 and 78.

Bembridge Sailing Club would, I imagine, be a rather distressing experience. It is the centre of all things Bembridgian', reported Charles Pears in his guide to *Yachting on the Sunshine Coast*, 1932.[143] Distressing, certainly, to those who had their application for membership refused, and who, after the Second World War, in 1950, founded the Brading Haven Yacht Club. The title of the club's history is pithily to the point: *60 Years of Businessmen and Artisans*.[144]

The pre-war restrictions on women in the club did not greatly change till the late 1950s and 1960s. Thus, women were given full membership of Salcombe Yacht Club in 1947, but declared ineligible for the General Committee in 1948. This was relatively liberal.

Quite often, reading between the lines, it was financial necessity that allowed women in.[145] Readman gives a detailed example on the *Lady Savile*, the club house of the Essex Yacht Club. In 1948, it was agreed they could come aboard but (1) must board on the port side, but (2) only to the promenade deck, (3) not use the bridge, nor (4) remain later than one hour after sunset, (5) this is permissive at the discretion of the committee and (6) children are not permitted at the club.[146] The image of hand-to-hand fighting across the various spaces of the club between the various factions of the committee is irresistible, fighting concerned both with the control of time as well as space.

In 1947, at the Crouch Yacht Club, at Burnham, men had to bring their women guests (i.e. wives/sisters) drinks on the wall outside. When they were allowed on the balcony – not inside – there were complaints they could see in (the forbidden 'female gaze' again), so that liberalisation was withdrawn. More enlightened married men moved to the Royal Corinthian. A member of the Crouch Yacht Club told Wise, the club's historian, 'the club nearly died and would have done so unless it agreed to have ladies in …, "over my dead body" was the attitude, and it very nearly was …'. By 1953, the club's finances were in such a parlous state that it was agreed that they needed women members, yet in 1955, at the AGM 'it was minuted in capitals in case of any misunderstanding THAT LADIES SHALL BE EXCLUDED AT ALL TIMES FROM ALL PARTS OF THE CLUB EXCEPT THE MAIN CLUBROOM AND THEIR LAVATORY'. Women membership was finally only agreed in 1956.[147] It took another few years before they were free to move out of certain

---

[143] Chas Pears, *Yachting on the Sunshine Coast*, p. 42.

[144] Stephen de Boise, *60 Years of Businessmen & Artisans: BHYC 1950–2010*, 2010.

[145] One of the problems club faced was that, at eighteen, until 1960, men had to do two years' National Service, creating discontinuity in their lifestyle.

[146] Readman, *Four Ships*, pp. 96–97.

[147] Wise, *A Century of Sailing: The Crouch Yacht Club 1907–2007*, pp. 88–95.

defined areas in the club, the same situation applying till the end of the fifties at the Royal Dart.[148]

We should not be surprised by the heat generated. Economic necessity without attitudinal change creates severe *cognitive dissonance* – the tension caused by the discrepancy between behaviour and belief, which the person tries to reduce, in this case by minimising the amount of change.[149]

These restrictions were gradually withdrawn as the 1970s neared; but during this period, women very rarely broke the final barrier: committee membership and flag officer status.

Sail Training for Children and Young Adults

We have seen how dinghy clubs welcomed families and encouraged teaching children to sail. Many yacht clubs did the same. Cadet membership was introduced at the Whitstable Yacht Club as early as 1925. By 1938, the Norfolk Broads Yacht Club had younger members learning from more experienced members how to sail the class boat – the Yare and Bure One-Designs.[150] Following the success of the Corinthians' Otter Club at the neighbouring Royal Corinthian, in 1959 the Royal Burnham formed a Cadets section and taught members' children in West Wight Scows.[151] In Devon, the Yealm Yacht Club formed one of the first Cadet sections in the region, and by 1952, had 52 Cadets and held the first Cadet Regatta in the region, the BBC reporting the proceedings.

The ubiquitous Illingworth was a key mover in setting up the Sail Training Association (now the Tall Ships Youth Trust) in 1956, which offered holidays for inner city delinquents, idealistic middle-class children, and disabled people in the massive 153 foot three-masted topsail schooner *Sir Winston Churchill* or the *Malcolm Miller*. This move also tied in with keeping the memory of the large, commercial sailing ship alive.

Clearly, the idea was timely, for the Ocean Youth Club (OYC) was founded in 1960 by a Radley schoolmaster, Chris Ellis. Ellis had sailed with schoolboys from his public school and wanted to extend the experience to less privileged children. He teamed up with the Rev. David Tonkin, curate

---

[148] Llewellyn, *A Brief History of the Royal Dart Yacht Club*, p. 14.

[149] Leon Festinger, *A Theory of Cognitive Dissonance*.

[150] Ian Wild, *A Handkerchief in the Rigging*, p. 9; Pam Barnes, *The Norfolk Broads Yacht Club*, pp. 22–25.

[151] Jan Wise, *50 Years of Scows and the RBYC*. Readman, in *Four Ships*, p. 134, says girl cadets were introduced at the Essex Yacht Club in 1953 so this may well have been a common development at the time.

of the Eton (school) mission in Hackney Wick, London. The OYC's first vessel was *Theodora*, originally named *Kindly Light*, a 1911 Bristol Channel pilot cutter.

Also founded in 1960 was the Rona Sailing Project. Lord Amory, then Minister of Agriculture and Fisheries, didn't have time to use his yacht, *Ailanthus*, so he lent it to Commander Walter Scott, Sea Cadet Area Officer for London, who took eight lads sailing each weekend. After two years, Amory could see how much the lads were gaining and bought the 77 foot *Rona*, based at Portsmouth.[152] This has transmuted into the London Sailing Project, which is still active today. The various organisations got together for races, the first being from Torbay to Lisbon in 1956.[153]

Outward Bound centres were set up at the initiative of Kurt Hahn, the headmaster of Gordonstoun School, Elgin, to teach independence and survival training to teenagers through sailing at Aberdovey and the Moray Firth in the late 1950s, using a variety of craft.

The movement to offer sailing to children was international. A prestigious French school was Glenans Sailing School, started in 1947 on Ile du Loch, one of the Les Glenans group of islands off South Brittany, by a group of former French Resistance fighters. Its emphasis on simplicity and the relationship of sailing to nature has had a considerable impact. An Irish branch opened in Baltimore, County Cork. The *Glenans Manual of Sailing* was in its seventh edition and had sold 800,000 copies by 2010.

Another organisation that put teaching young people to sail high on its list of priorities was the Island Cruising Club, Salcombe (the ICC), which was both a yacht club and an early sailing school. It was founded by John Baylay and friends in 1951, with the explicit intention of helping people become members of the maritime community.[154] (It is called 'Island' because its offices were in Island Street). Learners became members of the Club, not merely customers, and were expected to help maintain the fleet. As its founder, John Baylay wrote concerning its guiding principle:

> The Club was founded on a single idea, 'That all could sail', no matter who, rich or poor, beginner or expert, and through all levels of society. Fortunately, people were fired by this ideal to make it practical. Just for once people had accepted the more one gave, the more one got back.

---

[152] John Hamilton, *Sail Training*, pp. 45–46.
[153] See Holly Hollins, *The Tall Ships Are Sailing: The Cutty Sark Tall Ship Races*.
[154] Key figures were Beth Baylay, John's wife, treasurer of the ICC for many years, and Anne Melville, in charge of the dinghy fleet, Helen Shaw, bursar, in the office, Des and Joyce Sleightholme (Des Sleightholme, Foreword, *When the Bug Bites*, p. viii).

While we can understand this as a statement of the basic principle of the Welfare State, Baylay himself thought of the Welfare state as undermining these principles by encouraging dependency. Rather, he believed the club's success was because 'the helping hand came from the people, not the Welfare State'.[155] Members could learn to sail with ICC and then return for a week or two to cruise in one of their cruising yachts. It obviously was in tune with its time, for by the end of its first year, it had 400 members.

Des Sleightholme was a key figure in the early years of the ICC. Baylay had been offered use of *Hoshi*, a large, 50-ton, Edwardian gentleman's schooner, which Sleightholme had skippered. Baylay lured him back from the Outward Bound School at Aberdovey, with the offer of re-uniting him with *Hoshi*. (Sleightholme was to go on to wider fame as the editor of *Yachting Monthly*, from 1966 to 1985 and as the author of the humorous 'Old Harry' series.) His wife, Joyce, was first mate. In order not to use a paying berth, they would sleep in the sail locker. (In an obituary, he is recorded as 'being sure his daughter was conceived 'between a stopped-up storm trysail and a schooner fisherman staysail').[156]

An innovation at the ICC was the development of syllabuses. If they passed, a certificate would be issued to the successful candidate. The certificates related to varying levels of seamanship. During the 1970s, the RYA was to develop this idea into the qualification system of 'competent crew', 'day skipper', 'coastal skipper', 'offshore yachtmaster' and 'ocean yachtmaster'.[157] The gaining of these certificates was to become the main purpose of a burgeoning number of sailing schools in this country in the 1960s, basing their classroom work on the theoretical qualifications, and their sailing around the practical certificates. Early examples of such schools are Plymouth Sailing School, started in 1957 and still going; and the Newton Ferrers School of Yachting, on the nearby Yealm, run by Lieutenant Commander Rab Moore and Dennis Montgomery, teaching both dinghy and yacht handling. The Pathe News for 30 July, 1956 gave it a 2 minute 45 second film. (Pathe had

---

[155] John Baylay, *When the Bug Bites*, pp. 42 and 44. Actually, Baylay's was and is quite a common stance. It values the spirit of community endeavour, seeing this not as a socialist value, but as a continuation of the war-time spirit (actually a myth, since air raid wardens' main task was to stop looting of bombed properties, and those with money were happy to use the black market; and the people voted out Churchill, the war-time leader, in 1945 to bring in the welfare state). At the same time, people like Baylay saw no reason to help the poor or disadvantaged, who, rather as today, were to be separated from the (worthy) ill or disabled.

[156] Anon., 'Obituary: Des Sleightholme', *Daily Telegraph*, 17 June, 2003.

[157] Fairley, *Minute by Minute*, pp. 163–164.

covered the 1955 National Twelves championships, with 130 dinghies taking part in Plymouth Sound in a five minute film.)[158]

Although yachting and dinghy sailing were becoming increasingly important leisure activities, television, especially as it was in black and white, had little use for sailing, as it is too slow to keep the audience interested. The music industry, however, did recognise the interest in things nautical. After the war, Charles Trenet's 'La Mer', in its original French, was frequently played on the radio. In 1959, Bobby Darin reached number 8 in the British hit parade in 1960 with an English version 'Beyond the Sea'. Josh MacRae had a hit in 1962 with 'Messing about on the River', complete with sploshes, presumably of somebody rowing. The title line comes, of course, from Kenneth Grahame's *Wind in the Willows*. It refers to home build: 'There are boats made from kits that'll reach you in bits/ For messin' about on the river'; and expects a fair knowledge of bits of a boat: 'Anchors and tillers and rudders and cleats/ Ropes that are sometimes referred to as sheets'.[159]

The post-war period was an important time for leisure sailing. Doubtless many dinghy kits stayed unbuilt and yet more unfinished, but the huge sales figures indicate that this was the highwater mark for boat ownership across the socio-economic classes in Britain, and this phenomenon deserves more research and discussion. Indeed, generally, the widespread development of dinghy sailing on reservoirs and rivers is a phenomenon that has evoked little interest and deserves more. It is also important for bringing women and children into the mainstream of yachting activity.

In 1962, the Duke of Edinburgh bought *Bloodhound*, a 63 foot racing yacht built by Camper and Nicholson in 1936, the winner of the 1939 Fastnet, so that he could go cruising with Charles and Anne, with two or three hands. Princess Anne became a keen sailor.

The same year, the traditional magazine *Country Life* thought it timely for its readers to understand sailing, so hired the best yachting photographer of the time, Eileen Ramsay, to pick the best of her catalogue, to create *The Country Life Book of Sailing Boats*, with an introductory text by Louise and

---

[158] The School closed around 2005. The ICC deserves a fuller treatment, which would look at the difficulties of a yacht club adopting its communal stance; and the financial difficulties that occurred in maintaining it. One problem was that its accommodation was provided by an old Mersey ferry, the *Egremont*, whose upkeep became increasingly prohibitive as it rusted away. The ICC went through many crises but kept going and, in fact, had a flourishing dinghy section when it collapsed in 2014.

[159] *Cleats* are shaped like cow's horns for tying a rope around so that it cannot slip; *sheets* control the angle of the sail to the wind, so are pulled tight when beating against the wind, and eased by reaching or running off the wind.

Roger Manvell, to allow the reader some idea of what yachting was all about – enough not to appear foolish at a dinner party. This was a much simpler introduction to sailing than the Puffin (Laurence Sandy, *Sailing*), published as early as 1953, or the Ladybird (Henry Marlow, *Sailing and Boating*, 1972), both of which would serve quite adequately for teaching at the RYA Competent Crew level.

Around 1960, small, twenty-foot cruisers – pocket cruisers – were brought onto the market, such as the Audacity, Silhouette and Caprice, initially in marine ply and later in GRP (glass-reinforced plastic).[160] They sold quite well but, not surprisingly, the number of families who wanted to holiday in these cramped conditions, was limited.

For yachting to really take off and a third golden period of yachting to blossom, ocean-girding exploits had to become mainline news, and cruising yachts had to become more available and more comfortable, which followed the replacement of wood with GRP. Boyle's Law states that if you heat a gas, the molecules bounce around faster, increasing the pressure. From the 1950s onwards, the sailing molecules were bouncing nicely.

---

[160] Peter Poland, 'Small is Beautiful'. They were proper boats – Shane Acton, an ex-marine commando, sailed his 18 foot Caprice 30,000 miles ending up in French Somaliland. (Acton, *Shrimpy*, 1981).

CHAPTER FOURTEEN

Yachting's Third 'Golden Period': Of Heroes and Heroines; Of Families and Marinas, 1965–1990

For boating people August is the height of the season, and the day after Blyth's triumphant return [6 August, 1971], in Cowes Road ... hundreds of men and a number of women plunged to windward at the start of the Fastnet race ... For many others that Saturday was the start of an annual summer holiday when the family would be off on some cruise ... For dinghy men, it was another weekend in a points series ... But suddenly everyone in Britain, who looked at a newspaper or a television screen, knew a bit about sailing. For five years, a procession of men alone against the sea had passed before their eyes: Chichester, Rose, Knox-Johnston, Blyth.[1]

The key phrase here is 'suddenly everyone ... knew about a bit about sailing'. In the 1970s, yachting events, such as single-handed circumnavigations, became headline news. An atmosphere was created whereby yacht sailing became an important statement of a person's values and social position – in short, this was yachting's third golden period.

The late 1960s and 1970s are often characterised as a period of 'flower power', 'hippies', and taking psychedelic drugs – relatively trivial fashion and lifestyle phenomena. Economically, the key event of this era was Britain joining the European Common Market in 1973, and the key social change concerned the radical improvement in the position of women, due to a number of important medical and legal changes, namely:

- the arrival of the birth pill – in the early 1960s, for married women and then in 1967, for all women, regardless of their marital status

---

[1] Johnson, *Boating Britain*, p. 28. 'Triumphant return': Chay Blyth, returning from his East–West circumnavigation.

- relaxation of the abortion law, much decreasing the fear of unwanted pregnancies (The Abortion Reform Bill, 1967)
- thirdly, the easing and the equalisation of divorce through the Divorce Law Reform Act of 1969, providing for 'no blame' divorce
- the impact of this legislation was strengthened by the Legal Aid Act of 1960, which made available legal services to those who could otherwise not afford it
- finally, sexual equality in the workplace. The 1970 Equal Pay Act made it illegal to pay women lower rates than men for the same work. The 1975 Sex Discrimination Act made it illegal to discriminate against women in work, education or training. (However, unlike the Race Relations Act, 1965, the legislation did not cover private organisations, such as yacht clubs.)

These measures, although not always adhered to, gave women control of their own bodies and much greater financial independence, and radically changed gender relationships.

With this surge of women's power, there was perhaps one short, tantalising period – one opportunity to pull out of the rat race and not define ourselves purely in terms of work. The tremendous advances in women's sexual and financial independence in the 1960s and 1970s coincided with the development of the computer. Some commentators, such as Clive Jenkins and Barrie Sherman, in *The Collapse of Work*, 1979, could foresee a society where there was insufficient work for the British population, because the computer could do much of the mundane administrative work. At that point in time, women could have said to the men: 'there's more to life than work and a career. Why can't we share parenthood and both of us work part-time (or, share any other activity or interest that we both consider worthwhile)?'

Instead, women joined the labour force. The long term effect, of course, was that there was much more competition for jobs as the labour pool got very much larger, driving down wages and salaries in the long term. It was an especially poor deal for the women, because they kept their childcare role in addition to working full-time.

Long-Distance Sailors: The Heroes and then the Heroines

Yachting in the late 1960s was continually in the news, including TV, for this period saw the start of the world-girdling exploits of *British* yachtsmen and women, which added patriotic fervour and excitement to yachting.

There were two breeds of 'heroes' during this period – long-distance dinghy sailors, and, receiving far more publicity, ocean racers.

The Ocean Races

The start of media attention to yachting in the 1960s can be dated from the Observer Transatlantic Singlehanded Race (the OSTAR). This singlehanded race from Millbay, Plymouth to New York first took place in 1960 and at four-yearly intervals thereafter, with a steady increase in the number of entrants.[2] The race was the idea of Blondie Hasler, creator of the windvane.[3] In a letter from Hasler to Lloyd Foster (later the Commodore of the Royal Western Yacht Club, Plymouth, that organised the race), he argued against making radio transmitters on racing yachts compulsory: 'He feared that if they got into difficulties, they would send out distress signals and cause a lot of trouble! He said; "It would be more seemly for the entrant to drown like a gentleman."'[4]

The first OSTAR was won by Francis Chichester, which was hardly surprising as his boat was far larger than those of the other four competitors. *Gipsy Moth III* was 40 feet long, the second boat home, Hasler's *Jester* 25 feet, with its distinctive Chinese lug sail.[5]

The 1964 OSTAR attracted more French entrants. Yacht racing has a far higher profile in France, so there was huge publicity when the race was won by the legendary ex-French naval officer, Eric Tabarlay in *Pen Duick II*. Tabarlay (1931–1998) was the first French yacht racing hero and he was instrumental in the French developing the best yacht racing skippers and new Ocean races.[6]

The 1968 race was won by Geoffrey Williams, helped by the fact that he was the only competitor with access to weather-routing (being informed

---

[2] For the history of the OSTAR, see Libby Purves and Trevor Grove, ed. *Single Handed: The Observer/Europe 1 Singlehanded Transatlantic Race*, 1984, and Lloyd Foster, *Ostar: The Full Story of the Observer Single-Handed Transatlantic and the Two-Handed Round Britain Races*, 1989.

[3] One wonders if such an attitude was, in part, the result of his experience as leader of the Cockleshell Heroes (Operation Frankton), 1942, which involved 6 canoes being unloaded from a submarine at the mouth of the Gironde estuary. One canoe was damaged in unloading, and the remaining five with ten crew started on their passage to Bordeaux harbour. Two canoes reached it and damaged six ships with limpet mines. Only Hasler and his crew, Bill Sparks, returned alive. cf. C. E. Lucas-Phillips, *Cockleshell Heroes*.

[4] Ewen Southby-Tailyour, *Blondie: A Life of Lieutenant-Colonel H. G. Hasler.*

[5] All the British competitors, except Hasler, wrote accounts of the race: Francis Chichester, *Alone Across the Atlantic*, 1961; David Lewis, *The Boat that Would Not Travel Due West*, 1961; Val Howells, *Sailing into Solitude*, 1966. The fifth competitor was the Frenchman, Jean Lacombe. (Hasler with J. K. McLeod did write about *Practical Junk Rig*.)

[6] Tabarley died in the boat his father had bought, *Pen Duick I*, a gaff-rigged cutter designed by William Fife in 1898. He never used a life jacket. On 12 June, 1996, while on passage in the Bristol Channel to the Clyde for a regatta of Fife built boats, he fell overboard and was drowned.

from experts on the land what and where the weather systems were going to be, so that one could plan one's route accordingly).[7] The OSTAR now became increasingly the province of heavily sponsored professional sailors, and Hasler's Corinthian ideals were washed away by the need for funds and sponsorship if one was to have any chance of winning.[8]

Even social science got in on the act. Previously, researchers into behaviour under extreme conditions had studied mountaineers and Arctic explorers.[9] David Lewis, GP and competitor, had asked his fellow competitors to keep a note of their physical wellbeing in the 1960 OSTAR and all, except Chichester, cooperated. Glin Bennet, consultant psychiatrist in Bristol, studied the 1974 OSTAR competitors for signs of stress and muddled thinking, by getting them to keep a log.[10]

The status of hallucinations had become ambiguous, thanks to the writings of the guru psychiatrist, Dr Ronald Laing, who argued that they contained a coded truth.[11] In yachting, they had currency due to Slocum's hallucinating during his circumnavigation. By the end of the 1980s, if a singlehander crossing the Atlantic didn't hallucinate at some point, he was disappointed. John Passmore neatly links Slocum with his own transatlantic experience of hearing someone whistling:

> The first thought, of course, was that this was the hallucination I had been expecting. All solo sailors worth their salt hope to experience their version of Slocum's Pilot of the *Pinta* appearing at the helm. The only trouble was that I had not been battling with a gale for three days ... and I doubted that even peanut butter and honey sandwiches [!] would produce the same effect.[12]

After the OSTAR was established, the next yachting challenge was to sail round the world. Chichester had broken various flying records as a young

---

[7] Geoffrey Williams, 'Sir Thomas Lipton' Wins.

[8] It seemed inevitable that any attractive race would become professionalised. Bob Salmon (1936–2014) started the Mini Transat[lantic] for boats only 6.5 metres long. The race started in 1977 from Penzance, moved to France in 1987 and is now a race for professionals on the way up.

[9] For example, Helen Ross, *Behaviour Perception in Strange Environments*, 1974. She quotes F. Chapman's *Watkins' Last Expedition*, where the expedition members fall out as to whether one should say 'bacon and eggs' or 'eggs and bacon' (p. 20).

[10] He wrote his findings up in a long article in *Yachting Monthly*, September 1973, in medical journals and then in a book *Beyond Endurance*, 1983. Michael Stadler, Professor of Experimental Psychology at Bremen University, joined in with *Psychology of Sailing*, in 1987.

[11] R. D. Laing, *The Divided Self*, 1958.

[12] John Passmore, 'Transatlantic Sailing', p. 90. See also my 'Yachting and Madness'. The *Pinta* was the fastest of the three ships Columbus used on his transatlantic voyage of 1492. Slocum had this vision, after a surfeit of plums and cheese, on leaving the Azores.

20 *Gypsy Moth* rounding Cape Horn, 21 March 1967. Chichester's 1966–1967 circumnavigation generated huge publicity, with some 30-odd reporters waiting at Punta Arenas for his rounding of Cape Horn. Murray Sayle got the image from a light aircraft, and it reached *The Times*, London, at 2.20 a.m., in time to appear on its front page that day.

man.[13] He had been diagnosed with cancer in 1958, which was in remission by the time for the first OSTAR. In 1966, now aged 65, he undertook a circumnavigation in *Gypsy Moth IV*, stopping only at Sydney. He chose Sydney as he wanted to beat the 100 days taken by clipper ships – Chichester always felt the need to set himself targets. He took a week longer, returning to the port he started from, Plymouth, to be greeted by huge crowds. Chichester was

---

[13] Francis Chichester, *Solo to Sydney*, 1930 (London–Sydney); *Seaplane Solo*, 1933 (1,450 miles in a frail seaplane); *Ride on the Wind*, 1936 (New Zealand–Japan).

knighted with great ceremonial pomp. He and his wife, Sheila, sailed the boat
to Greenwich, where, on 7 July, 1967, the Queen knighted him in the court-
yard of the Royal Naval College with Drake's sword – a nice intermingling of
our Elizabethan heritage, monarchy, war, being English and yachting.[14]

The same feat was undertaken in 1967–1968 by Alec Rose (1908–1991).
Whereas Chichester was from an aristocratic family and a member of the
Squadron, Rose's appeal was more that of 'the little man'.[15] From 1940, Rose
had served on the naval support for the Atlantic convoys, in the engine room,
a death trap if the boat was torpedoed. By 1944, 'my nerves were frayed and I
couldn't sleep …' and after several months of hospitalisation, he 'was invalided
out in 1945, with the rank of Lieutenant RNVR. The period of convoys had
taken its toll of my nervous system.'[16] He became a greengrocer in Southsea.
He bought *Lively Lady* in 1964. She had been built in Calcutta by her owner,
S. J. P. Cambridge, in very heavy timbers of paduak, which is harder than teak.
He went to Illingworth and Primrose to spruce up the boat. Rose took part in
the second OSTAR in 1964, coming 4th out of 15 starters. He had wanted to
undertake his circumnavigation, 'making a match' with Chichester, despite
Lively Lady being only 36 feet long, compared to Chichester's *Gipsy Moth IV*'s
54 feet.[17] A series of disasters – being hit by a steamer off Ushant; *Lively Lady*
falling off the wall at Mashfords Yard in Plymouth Sound – delayed him for a
year and his circumnavigation, with two stops at Melbourne and Bluff, New
Zealand for repairs, took place in 1967–1968. Within a few days of returning
to Southsea, *Lively Lady* was placed in the middle of Holborn Circus, outside
the *Daily Mirror* office. Rose was also knighted, but with less pomp.

The next logical target was a non-stop voyage around the world. The
Sunday Times, upstaged by its rival the *Observer* sponsoring the OSTAR,
learned that a number of yachtsmen were preparing to attempt this feat. They
decided to get in on the act. In March 1968, they offered the Golden Globe
and £5,000 (equivalent to about £60,000 in 2016) to the first singlehanded
non-stop circumnavigator home, and another £5,000 for the fastest. The only
proviso was that the boat had to have left its home port by 31 October, 1968.

[14] Both his autobiography, *The Lonely Sea and the Sky*, 1964, and his account of the circumnavigation, *Gipsy Moth Circles the World*, 1967, sold in very large numbers.

[15] To be exact, Chichester's father was a vicar in a parish that presumably was in the gift of the
Chichester who was the nearby lord of the manor at Arlington House, between Barnstaple
and Ilfracombe, Devon. Chichester took part in the 1972 OSTAR when his cancer was well
advanced, and he had no chance of winning. This suggests that he wished to use the sea for his
coffin, a wish denied by him by the pain of his illness and he turned back before being rescued
by personnel from HMS *Salisbury*.

[16] Rose, *My Lively Lady*, pp. 11–12.

[17] *Ibid.*, p. 30.

This was for three reasons. If they left it any longer, someone might go ahead and achieve a non-stop circumnavigation before then, leaving them with a non-event. They wanted the yachts to round the Cape of Good Hope and be in the Southern Ocean in time for the southern hemisphere summer. Finally, there is a limit to how long you can maintain interest in a forthcoming event. It was this viciously short lead-in time that was to play a crucial role in events, especially for Donald Crowhurst, who had yet to have his boat built.[18]

There were nine entries. Five retired early on – Chay Blyth, Commander Bill King, John Ridgway, Louis Fougeron and Alex Carazzo[19] Bernard Moitiessier, a very experienced French sailor was the favourite to win in *Joshua*, a 39 foot steel ketch. There were two catamarans: *Victress*, sailed by Lieutenant Commander Nigel Tetley, RN and *Teignmouth Electron* by Donald Crowhurst, which, if they came through unscathed, should be faster than the monohulls, and so win the £5000 prize for the fastest boat home.

Moitissier dropped out when he was likely to win. On 5 February, 1969, at Cape Horn, he did not turn to port but headed back across the Southern Ocean again, to Tahiti. He wrote in his journal:

> Plymouth so close, barely 10,000 miles to the north … but leaving from Plymouth and returning to Plymouth now seems like leaving from nowhere to go nowhere.
> […]
> I have set course for the Pacific again … last night was too hard to take. I really felt sick at the thought of getting back to Europe, back to the snakepit … the closer I got, the more disgusted I would be.[20]

Which left Knox-Johnston to pick up the Golden Globe for being first home. He had had his 32 foot *Suhaili* built in Bombay (Mumbai) whilst serving as second officer on a passenger ship sailing between Bombay and Basra. Building the whole boat out of Indian teak made her very solid but slow. He had hoped to use it to sail his wife, Sue, and children back to England, but by the time the boat was ready, they had separated. (They got back together, after his circumnavigation, in 1972.) So he, his brother Chris, and a friend,

---

[18] The same short time frame did for Pete Goss and the revolutionary carbon fibre boat *Team Phillips*, which broke up as it was being sailed to Barcelona for the start of The Race in 2000 and was caught in a storm.

[19] The English competitors, except of course Crowhurst, all wrote up their accounts: Chay Blyth and Maureen Blyth, *Innocent Aboard,* 1970; Bill King, *Capsize,* 1969; Nigel Tetley, *Trimaran Solo,* 1970; John Ridgway, *Journey to Ardmore,* 1971. For overviews, see Peter Nichols, *A Voyage for Madmen,* 2001 and Chris Eakin, *A Race Too Far,* 2009.

[20] Bernard Moitiessier, *The Long Way,* 1974, pp. 142 and 163.

21 Knox-Johnston in high spirits, singing a Gilbert and Sullivan tune as he nears home after his non-stop circumnavigation in a battered *Suhaili*, finishing in Falmouth on 22 April 1969. Chichester had stopped at Sydney. The Golden Globe trophy was for the first yacht to complete a non-stop circumnavigation. The £10,000 prize money attracted 9 entries. Only Knox-Johnston achieved a non-stop circumnavigation.

Heinz, sailed her back to England in 1963.[21] When he heard of the Golden Globe, he went to the yacht designer, Colin Mudie, who we last met crossing the Atlantic in *Sopranino* with Patrick Ellam in 1951. He drew the lines for a 53 footer for the race, but Knox-Johnston was unable to raise the funds, so had to make do with *Suhaili*.

Knox-Johnston, with Moitissier out of the race, was the first man back. He re-entered Falmouth on Tuesday 22 April, 1969:

---

[21] Knox-Johnston, *A World of My Own*, pp. 5–11.

The first people to board were Her Majesty's Customs and Excise officers …
As they jumped across, the senior officer, trying to keep a straight face, asked
the time-honoured question:
'Where from?'
'Falmouth' I replied.[22]

The huge publicity at Knox Johnston's arrival back at Falmouth after ten and
a half months, much of the time out of radio contact due to a flooded radio,
leading to an air search for him – publicity maximised by his literary agent,
George Greenfield – followed in the wake of the earlier British successes of
Chichester and Rose. Both Chichester and Knox-Johnston's voyages generated very considerable public interest. 'Children plotted his [Chichester's]
position on wall charts … our national, introductory topic of conversation,
the weather, made way for *Gypsy Moth* …'. Similarly, the *Sunday Times* had
given away a world chart, so that you could plot the Golden Globe competitor's position.[23]

All three, when finishing their circumnavigation, delayed their return to
port, so that they would enter it at the most convenient time for a welcome
party and the media, and were greeted by hundreds of craft and crowds estimated at quarter of a million, in Falmouth, Plymouth and Southsea respectively. Coupled with intense media coverage, these exploits raised public
interest in yachting to a new peak.

Greenfield made sure that Knox-Johnston was presented as the nice
young man you'd be proud to bring home to your parents:

> … the *Sunday Mirror*, in an effort to try to shed some light on my mental
> outlook, sent me to a psychiatrist in order that he could compare my state of
> mind before I left with my state when I returned. I am delighted to say that
> on both occasions he found me 'distressingly normal'. [24]

Implicit here was that the Golden Globe competitors were considered
unlikely to return, hence the suspicions about their sanity. This echoes
Slocum's circumnavigation and the first Fastnet, both ventures considered
foolhardy.

The race is also memorable for the tragic fate of Donald Crowhurst.
Crowhurst had mortgaged his house to take part in the race and hoped to use
it to advertise products produced by his electronic firm (Electron Utilisation).
He was sponsored by the Devon port of Teignmouth, hence the name of his

[22] Knox-Johnson, *A World of My Own*, p. 217.
[23] Peter Hambly, *Race under Sail*, p. 20; Kevin C. Crothers, *Salt in My Blood*, p. 77.
[24] Knox-Johnston, *A World of My Own*, p. 27.

boat *Teignmouth Electron*. However, his boat was desperately unprepared. He left on the last day allowed – 31 October, 1968. On 15 November, he took an inventory of his many problems. The most serious was that he could not pump out the forward floats. He knew that to sail his unseaworthy boat into the Southern Ocean meant almost certain death; but he felt he could not turn back, partly because he would have had been bankrupt, with a wife and four children to support. So, already off Portugal, Crowhurst was a dead man sailing. He got down to the Southern Atlantic and hung around off Brazil. He fabricated his log and transmitted false positions.

Crowhurst eventually decided to sail home, reckoning on being the third back, so no-one would look too closely at his logs, and he would get kudos as the plucky amateur sailor. Unfortunately, Tetley, acting on Crowhurst's transmission of fake positions, pushed his catamaran, *Victress*, too hard and she broke up. Tetley woke to find his port bow had floated away. The boat was reluctant to let go of the life raft's painter: 'Give over, Vicky, I have to leave you'.[25] This meant that Crowhurst would now win the prize for the fastest passage, and his log books would be carefully scrutinised. He was now faced with likely exposure as a fraud – Chichester, Craig Rich, Head of the School of Navigation, Plymouth Polytechnic, and Frank Page, the *Observer's* yachting correspondent, had all indeed become suspicious. Although Crowhurst could only guess this, it meant there was only one decision he needed to work out: the best time to die. On 1 July, 1969, he wrote 'I am what I am and I see the nature of my offence ... I will play this game when I choose. I will resign the game 11 20 40'.[26]

Madness at sea has long exerted a great fascination, buttressed by canonical works in many artistic forms – in poetry, Coleridge's 'Ancient Mariner' (1798); in literature, Herman Wouk's *The Caine Mutiny* (1951), made into a film with Humphrey Bogart in 1954; in opera, Wagner's *Flying Dutchman*, first performed in 1843, and Benjamin Britten's *Peter Grimes* (1945). Crowhurst is the most recent artistic lighting conductor. Tacita Dean, a leading post-modern British artist, produced a major exhibition at the National Maritime Museum in 1999, a book of photographs (1999) and a film showing *Teignmouth Electron* rotting in its last resting place on the Cayman Islands. There have been seven

---

[25] Tetley, *Trimaran Solo*, pp. 153–156. He was rescued by an Italian petrol tanker, *M. T. Pampero*.

[26] Nicholas Tomalin and Ron Hall, *The Strange Voyage of Donald Crowhurst*, pp. 273–274. See also Robert McCrum, 'Deep Water' and my 'How Strange Was "The Strange Case of Donald Crowhurst"?' and 'Yachting and Madness', for a discussion on Crowhurst's suicide. Teignmouth already had the bunting up and banners up to welcome his return. Knox-Johnston, on hearing the news of his loss, generously, immediately gave the £5,000 for the first boat home, which he had won, to the family.

22 The High Price of Failure. *Teignmouth Electron*, competitor in the Golden Globe, from the Royal Mail vessel *Picardy*, 10 July 1969, and a boarding party in a whaler. The boarding party will find no-one aboard. Crowhurst has stepped off his boat, after realising it could not survive the Southern Ocean.

plays, an opera, a book-length poem, two novels, six films, four of them full-length including a remarkable film made up of contemporary footage (*Deep Water*, 2005), all in addition to the contemporary biography and account of Crowhurst's race by Nicholas Tomalin and Ron Hall.[27] From Russia through

[27] Opera: *Ravenshead*, Steve Mackey, composer, libretto by Rinde Eckert 1998; Theatre: *The Lonely Sea*, by Jonathan Rich, 1979; *Daniel Pelican*, by Chris Van Strander, 1999; *Crowhurst*, script by John Harvey, performed by 'Benchtour', Scotland, 2007; *The Strange Voyage of Donald Crowhurst*, by Malcolm Hamilton, 2003, performed by Blue Raincoat Theatre Co., Sligo, Republic of Ireland; *Almost a Hero*, by Daniel Brian, 2004; and *Jet Lag*, performed by the Builders' Association, New York, 2007. Film: *The Roaring Forties*, French film, 1982; *Race of the Century*, Soviet film, 1986; *Teignmouth Electron*, 2000, and *Disappearance at Sea*, 2000, both created by Tacita Dean; *Deep Water*, directed by Louise Osmond and Jerry Rothwell, ATP Films, 2005; an as yet untitled biopic of Crowhurst, starring Colin Firth, filmed in 2015. Books: *The Strange Voyage of Donald Crowhurst*, by Nicholas Tomalin and Ron Hall, 1970; *Teignmouth Electron* by Tacita Dean, 1999; Fiction: *Outerbridge Reach*, by Robert Stone, 1998; *The Terrible Privacy of Maxwell Sim*, by Jonathan Coe, 2010; Poetry: *The Wake of the 'Electron'*,

Europe to America, the drama of Crowhurst's race, logs and death have clearly generated powerful emotional undertones. So, while Knox-Johnston represented the bluff Englishman 'who did it', Crowhurst represented glorious failure, and both were grist for publicity about yachting.

Chay Blyth, a Scottish ex-paratrooper, presented himself as the face of the non-posh yachtie. He had made his name rowing – not sailing some expensive yacht – across the Atlantic with John Ridgway.[28] After his unsuccessful venture in the Golden Globe, he decided to sail east around the world single-handed. He got sponsorship from the British Steel Corporation, hence the name of his boat – *British Steel.* The boat was designed by the top racing yacht designer, Robert Clark, who designed the cutters for the Ocean Youth Club and *Gypsy Moth III*, winner of the 1960 OSTAR.

The voyage was not particularly logical in its seamanship, as it meant beating against the prevailing winds in the Roaring Forties, which blow from the west. This was why the clippers coming back from Australia always went round the Cape of Good Hope on the way out and returned via Cape Horn. But it was a good example of British pluck and the voyage offered a new relationship with the sea – as the backdrop to the generation of publicity.

The Fastnet became included in the biennial Admiral's Cup competition between competing nations in 1965, each nation fielding three boats of different specified sizes. The Admiral's Cup's prestige in these years was such that 'in 1971, there are a nucleus of owners so bitten by the bug that they return with new boats, new designs, keen crews ... to battle in what is now Britain's big yacht racing.'[29] The numbers participating kept increasing from 185 in 1969 to 303 boats in 1979.

The 1979 Fastnet Race did not show yacht racing in a good light. On 11 August 303 yachts set out from Cowes for the rock lighthouse at the end of Southern Ireland and were hit by a fast-moving depression that changed direction, causing a maelstrom and triggering a huge rescue effort from both Irish and English services. Several boats were sunk and fifteen men died. One of the reasons for this carnage was that racing yachts were being built for speed, at the sacrifice of safety, and the sea had found them out.[30]

---

a book-length poem by Robert Finkel. The Wikipedia entry for Donald Crowhurst lists nine popular music songs concerning him. Only Slocum has generated a similarly large fictional wake, and Childers more accounts of his life.

[28] Captain John Ridgway and Sergeant Chay Blyth, *A Fighting Chance: How We Rowed the Atlantic in 92 Days,* 1966.

[29] Johnson, *Boating Britain*, p. 212.

[30] The most poignant personal account is Nick Ward, *Left for Dead*, which he was. The trauma of this is why the book only came out in 2007 and with a co-author to help in its production. The

The Search and Rescue helicopter service was crucial to the saving of lives. With their much wider field of vision than lifeboats and their skilled winch men, they recovered 74 survivors and 3 bodies.[31]

Round the world racing became a regular event, with the four-yearly Whitbread Round the World Race, the first race taking place in 1973/1974. The dangers involved in this competitive circumnavigation (with stopovers) was shown by the fact that three men were lost overboard in the initial race, including one from Chay Blyth's boat, *Great Britain II*, which was crewed by paratroopers. In the 1977/1978 race, *Heath's Condor* also lost a crew member, but he was saved because his position was marked by a group of albatrosses circling overhead.[32] Injuries, some of them serious, were common in this race, much of which was in the mountainous seas and high winds of the Roaring Forties.

Increasingly, long-distance races became dominated by catamarans and trimarans, which, because they are considerably faster, had to be in a separate class from the monohulls.[33]

Another racing event that also reached the front pages was the defeat of the Americans for the first time ever in the America's Cup. The Australian boat, *Australia 2,* with its secret keel, won from 3–0 down in a seven race series in 1983. *Australia 2's* skipper's account – *Born to Win* by John Bertrand – was a mega best-seller.

Once men had set the records, it made personal, and commercial, sense for women to try and gain the equivalent records. This became feasible because of changes in yacht design. The advent of Glass Reinforced Plastic and aluminium spars to replace wood had made sailing much less muscle-bound. Anne Davison had crossed the Atlantic, using the trade wind route in 1953. In 1971, Nicolette Milnes Walker was the first woman to sail straight across the Atlantic, from Dale, Milford Haven directly to Newport, a more dangerous route than going down to the North–East trades.[34]

Clare Francis was part of the first all-woman crew to take part in the Round Britain in 1974. She sailed the Atlantic singlehanded, and then was the

---

equivalent account in mountaineering concerns the choices made in *Touching the Void*, by Joe Simpson.

[31] John Rousmaniere, *Fastnet Force Ten*, p. 274, is probably the best account of the tragedy. The helicopter pioneer, Igor Sikorsky, neatly summed up their usefulness: 'If a man is in need of rescue, an airplane can come in and throw flowers at him … But a direct life aircraft could come in and save his life.'

[32] Bob Fisher and Barry Pickthall, *Ocean Conquest*, pp. 16–19; p. 37.

[33] Dear, 'Leisure Sailing in the Twentieth Century', p. 143.

[34] Nicolette Milnes Walker, *When I Put Out to Sea*, 1972.

first woman to enter an OSTAR in 1976. In 1977–1978, she skippered eleven men in a 65 foot yacht in the Whitbread Round the World race.[35]

Encouraged by her husband, the successful racing sailor Rob James, and Chay Blyth, Naomi James sailed from Dartmouth in 1977 and returned there 272 days later, to become the first woman to sail round the world with just two short stops. (The Australian, Kay Cottee, was to become the first woman to sail non-stop round the world in 1987–1988.)[36]

Inevitably, adventurousness being in the air affected cruising. The impoverished Rosie and Colin Swale took their daughter and 30-foot catamaran *Annelise* to Fiumicino, the port of Rome, where Colin delivered their second child. Then, with Eve, aged two and James, six months, they sailed to Australia via the Panama Canal, and back via Cape Horn, arriving back in Plymouth in July 1973, a voyage all the more remarkable for catamarans being a relatively untried mode of long ocean sailing.[37]

Clearly, long-distance women sailors had arrived, but they still had to handle the pre-feminist assumptions of the need to maintain being womanly and feminine at all times, as well as being sailors. 'To succeed as an athlete is to fail as a woman' was still the prevailing view.[38] Being 'the weaker sex', their results were inherently less valuable, if not an object of fun. The implication of being non-heterosexual lurked in the background. Francis wrote: 'People expect a singlehanded sailing lady to sport enormous biceps, baggy jeans and

---

[35] Clare Francis, *Come Hell or High Water*, 1977; *Come Wind or Weather: ADC Accutrac Races round the World*, 1978. Tracy Edwards skippered an all-women crew of *Maiden* in the Whitbread in 1989/90 (Tracy Edwards with Tim Madge, *Maiden*, 1990). Francis went on to become a very successful thriller writer. Her first was *Night Sky* (1983), about the French Resistance. *Deceit* (1993) is a return to the trope of 'the body in the sunken yacht', used so successfully in Du Maurier's *Rebecca*.

[36] Naomi James, *At One with the Sea: Alone around the World*, 1979; Kay Cottee. *First Lady: A History-Making Solo Voyage around the World*, 1989. Rob James tragically died overboard when bringing a large catamaran into Salcombe on 22 March, 1983.

[37] Rosie Swale, *Rosie Darling*, 1973; *Children of Cape Horn*, 1974. Some families who ventured into blue water were not so fortunate. Dougal Robertson, a master mariner and his wife Lyn sold their farm in North Staffordshire in 1970 and went off a leisurely circumnavigation with their four children. Days after leaving the Galapagos for the Marquesas, their boat, *Lucette*, was attacked by killer whales and sank. The family were thirty-eight days in a raft before rescue (Dougal Robertson, the father, wrote it up as *Survive the Savage Sea*, 1973 and years later, his son, Douglas, joined his father's account with his own memories of *The Last Voyage of the 'Lucette'*, 2005). The Baileys had an even more gruelling experience. Their boat, *Auralyn*, hit a whale north-east of the Galapagos, on 4 March, 1973 and rapidly sank. They spent the next 117 days adrift in a life-raft before being rescued. By 1975, they were on their way again to Patagonia in *Auralyn II* (Maurice and Maralyn Bailey, *117 Days Afloat*, 1973; *Second Chance: Voyage to Patagonia*, 1977).

[38] Paul Willis, 'Women in Sport in Ideology', p. 123.

a jolly yo-ho manner' – in short to be butch.[39] Rather, they should maintain an awareness of their sexuality. Both Clare Francis and Rosie Swale were photographed as desirable sex objects.[40]

Dinghy Heroics

The successors of the yachtsmen who crossed the Atlantic in small yachts after the Second World War, were a number of sailors who undertook long distance cruises in dinghies of around fifteen foot.

Frank Dye (1928–2016), on leaving school, worked in his father's Ford dealership selling cars, which hardly predicted his sailing exploits. With one crew, he crossed the North Sea in 1963, and again in 1964, in the 16 foot, Ian Proctor-designed, Wayfarer dinghy. This dinghy is famous for its stability, but is made of plywood, which could split under a heavy beating by the sea.[41] Dye had a well-thought-out philosophy, recalled by his companion on his 1964 voyage, Bill Brockbank:

> ... he should never call for help ... his radio could only receive and was not able to transmit a distress signal. He refused to take anyone who was married in case they were lost, and both crew had to do everything because their partner might be unconscious or dead. His medical kit included enough morphine to knock out a horse, as there was always a chance he'd need to amputate a limb at sea.[42]

The first passage was from Scotland to Iceland. The second, from Scotland to the Faroes and Norway, was particularly hazardous. In a Force 9, a severe gale, they were capsized and in the water three times. The mast was broken in the second capsize, and on the third, the boat rolled over, and by Dye's calculations they had 8 minutes survival time to right the boat and get aboard. They made a jury rig, with which they slowly made land.[43] Frank married

---

[39] Francis, *Come Hell or High Water*, p. 19.

[40] The pressure on them to do so would have been considerable. *Practical Boat Owner* published a fortieth anniversary edition in October 2007, with an article by Jake Kavanagh, appropriately titled 'Naughty but Nice', showing advertisements for sailing gear in the late 1960s and early 1970s. Most have a picture of a woman in a bikini in a suggestive pose, with the product. This trend continued into the 1980s.

[41] Peter Clutterbuck, *The Sea Takes No Prisoners*, p. 10.

[42] Charlie English, 'Sailing into Hell'; see Frank and Margaret Dye, *Ocean-Crossing Wayfarer*. The boat, *Wanderer*, can be seen in the National Maritime Museum, Falmouth.

[43] Eventually arriving in Norway, Brockbank got back to Liverpool five days after they landed. 'In Lime Street station, the first familiar surroundings he had seen since the gale ... he had a sudden, overwhelming realisation that he was alive, and started to cry' (Charlie English, 'Sailing into Hell').

Margaret in 1964 and their honeymoon was a dinghy sail to St Kilda, which lies about 110 miles off the Scottish mainland.

Peter Clutterbuck knew of Dye's voyages when he too took off in a Wayfarer in 1966. His account, *The Sea Takes No Prisoners*, tells of offshore and coastal sailing down to the Med. and up to Norway.

The Duxburys sailed their open, 8 foot Drascombe Lugger, *Lugworm* round Greece in 1971 and home to England in 1972.[44]

Shane Acton, unable to settle after leaving the Marines, kept having to come back to England from his roamings in America and England because he was penniless.[45] The thought struck him that if he had a boat, he could just sail to the next country (the logic isn't perfect). So he bought *Shrimpy*, a ten-year-old, 18 foot, plywood, bilge-keel, Caprice. Quite handy, one might have thought, for pottering down from his home town of Cambridge into the Broads, but one thing led to another and onto a world circumnavigation in the years 1973–1980, via the Panama and Suez Canals, returning to his home port of Cambridge.[46] He got various jobs, including painting rainbows on leather – only possible when there was no wind, as *Shrimpy* rocked too much when the wind blew; however, even a change of partner couldn't stop the restlessness, so by 1984, he, his new lady, Sandie Watts, and *Shrimpy* were off to the Caribbean and South America, via the traditional trade winds route from the Canaries.[47]

For seven seasons from the later 1980s, Frank Dye sailed up the American coast from Florida to the mouth of the St Lawrence and down to the Great Lakes. He called his account *Sailing to the Edge of Fear*. Obviously, that was what turned these dinghy sailors on. What kept them alive was their superb seamanship.

---

[44] Ken Duxbury, *'Lugworm' on the Loose*, 1973; *'Lugworm' Homeward Bound*, 1975.

[45] In his obituary in the *Cambridge Evening News*, 27 February, 2002, 'Debbie Watson, his sister, said: "He's always been a loner and gone off by himself. He used to go off in the school holidays and dad would drop him off at a river somewhere in Wales and he would come back six weeks later."'

[46] After Cristobal, Panama, he sailed with a Swiss lady, Iris Derungs. Iris had done very little sailing, but her 'provenance' was excellent: she had 'walked across the Sudan by herself, living with any of the wandering tribes of the Masai she met on the way' (*Shrimpy*, p. 45).

[47] Acton tells of his voyages in *Shrimpy*, 1981 and *Shrimpy Sails Again*, 1989. Acton decided to live in Costa Rica, *Shrimpy* was wrecked in a hurricane in the mid-1980s, and Acton returned to Cambridge. A similar venture was undertaken by A. J. Mackinnon in 1997. A 'couple of quiet weeks' pottering about on the Severn in a Mirror dinghy turned into a 4,900 kilometre navigation of the Danube to the Black Sea (see his *The Unlikely Voyage of Jack de Crow*).

Dinghies – the Laser Beam

The home-built kit phase had a final flourish with the Fireball, designed by Peter Milne, a designer of racing dinghies, the kit fabricated by Jack Chippendale: 'the boat caught the imagination immediately and throughout the winter hundreds of go-faster enthusiasts were cutting and gluing to produce the equivalent of a Formula One racing car'. Launched in 1962, this large, 18 foot dinghy spread internationally – 15,000 had been sold worldwide by 2012. It narrowly missed out on a being a 1972 Olympic class.[48] The Fireball marked the end of the era of home-build, wooden dinghies.

The world had moved on from a practical philosophy of 'mucking in together' to a more individualistic, achievement-oriented approach to life, and this fitted perfectly with an amazingly successful new dinghy: the single-handed Laser.

With GRP technology now readily available and the continued international interest in dinghy sailing, two Canadians, Bruce Kirby and Ian Bruce, worked up a dinghy you could stick on the roof of a car. It was launched at the New York Boat Show in 1971 as a 'pottering' dinghy and called 'the weekender' with a sail insignia TGIF (Thank God It's Friday).[49] It was only when keen racing sailors took it up that its phenomenal growth occurred, for the Laser, was, in fact, a fast boat. Another major plus was the careful achievement of identical boats, allowing less room for the rich owner to win. 'There were a limited number of moulds … every sail was cut identically and every fitting had to be bought from the same suppliers'.[50] It was simple to rig and launch. The hull, being of GRP, was hardwearing and low maintenance.

In this country, the launch of the Laser by Performance Sailcraft was linked to the creation of a large dinghy club on the huge, 700-acre Queen Mary Reservoir to the west of London. A change of government policy, telling the publicly-owned water companies to encourage recreational use of their reservoirs, was seized on by the founders of the Queen Mary Sailing Club, and access to this large reservoir achieved in 1972.[51] Performance Sailcraft encouraged the club to hold Laser races and by 1974, the club was the leading club for Lasers with a fleet of 60 to 70 lining up for a club race.

By 1974, the first World Championships were held in Bermuda, with competitors from 24 countries. It also received a boost by being chosen by the

[48] Johnson, *Boating Britain*, pp. 37–38; Bird, *Classic Classes*, p. 35.
[49] Bird, *Classic Classes*, p. 91.
[50] Videlo, *Frensham Pond Sailing Club: The First Fifty Years*, p. 144.
[51] The first use of a reservoir for sailing was by the Bristol Corinthian Yacht Club in the Cheddar Reservoir near Axbridge in 1931.

23 Lasers racing, Notts County Sailing Club. The Laser Dinghy, with its strict controls on building and sails to ensure uniformity, has become hugely popular as the dominant racing dinghy for the solo racer.

RYA for youth selection trials. By 1996, it was an Olympic class. By 2012, over 200,000 Lasers had been sold.[52]

To compete with the Laser in singlehanded dinghies, Ian Proctor, a well-established British dinghy designer, with the Merlin and the Wayfarer already to his credit, designed the 11 foot Topper, launched in 1977. Originally made out of GRP, production switched to injection moulding polypropylene, making it lighter – a mere 43 kilograms – after which sales really took off. By 2000, 50,000 of these singlehanded racers had been sold. The Topper is more suitable for learning to sail in than the Laser.

The Laser and the Topper were in tune with more individualistic times; but to somewhat counter that trend, the Lark dinghy, designed by Michael Jackson, launched 1967, enjoyed success as a two-person GPR dinghy, particularly among university clubs, as it is forgiving of crew weight. However, it has never approached anywhere near the success of the Laser or Topper.

Dinghies made out of GRP were considerably cheaper than their wooden equivalent. For example, in Devon, the GRP Devon Yawl was adopted by the

---

[52] There are three kinds of Laser: the original Standard, the Radial and the Laser 4.7. In 2012, Bird (*Classic Classes*, p. 91) gave the figures, for the next three most successful selling dinghies: Optimist 130,000, Topper 50,000 and Mirror 70,000.

Topsham and Yealm Yacht Clubs, as a 'plastic' version of the unaffordable wooden Salcombe Yawls.[53]

Families Come Aboard

The ocean racers and their achievements greatly elevated the profile of yachting and kept it in the news, but the key determinant was literally closer to home – *the expansion in yacht cruising by families.*

The number of white collar jobs greatly increased in the 1960s and 1970s, with expansion in the Health Service, Social Services and Education. As more people had surplus income, so they wanted to get out on the water and to take their holidays on boats. Some were dinghy sailors, now with the funds and the career stability to trade up and invest more heavily in their sport. The big change came in the 1970s, when men stopped going sailing solely with their male friends and instead, their families came on board. The rise of feminism meant that wives were less willing to play 'the little woman' and get left behind for weekends and during the summer weeks; and if they came, the children had to come too.

The arrival of the motorways changed the distribution of industry, but also of leisure. After the opening of the M6 Preston by-pass in 1958, the M1 was opened in stages throughout the 1960s and the M3, linking London to Southampton, in the seventies. The east coast yachting scene had already been weakened by the loss of the railway lines linking its harbours to London, due to the implementation of the Beeching Axe. The M1 only skirts eastern England (Essex, Suffolk and Norfolk), so the motorway network favoured north–south communication. These factors combined to create a decisive shift away from the east Coast as a key geographical and emotional centre of yachting towards the south Coast and its marinas.[54] There was also the frisson of 'going foreign' – the continent, and the Cotentin peninsula and Cherbourg, being only a day sail away from the south coast, compared with a 24 hour, 100-mile slog across the North Sea from the east – a day sail versus offshore night sailing among sandbanks

Families came on board because boating had become more comfortable, due to the advent of cruising yachts made of GRP, and not wood. This made them far easier to maintain, and they looked more modern and stylish. The other factor was the increasing availability of marina berths. This caused a

---

[53] Andrew Matthews. *The Bar and Beyond*, 149-151.
[54] For an overview of the period, see Johnson, *Boating Britain*, 1973.

circular upward movement – wives, bringing the children, came aboard, because the boat was comfortable and accessible – you could walk to it; and after sailing, walk to the showers to become human again and then go for a drink with friends at the bar. And this convenience created a demand for new boats and more marina berths.

By and large, families bought British-made cruisers. While not necessarily longer or faster, indeed without using the engine, probably slower than a Folkboat or a Contessa, they were beamier (wider), thereby creating more space, and had more headroom. The galley ceased to be a single burner but became well appointed, often with an oven, and the fittings aimed to be stylish and modern.

A prestige GRP yacht, the Nicholson 32, was moulded by Halmatic for the famous yard of Camper and Nicholson. The first was launched in 1963, and production stopped in 1981, after several modifications, at Mark IX, with 369 built; but this was an expensive, top of the cruiser range, boat.

Catamarans, twin hulled vessels, became more available after the 1950s. Catamarans were family-friendly, as they provide a more stable platform for cruising than monohulls. The problem was to find somewhere to moor them, as moorings became increasingly sought after and expensive, and many marinas charged double the monohull rate for a catamaran, since they often took up two berths.

It was the firms of Westerly and Moody which really opened the British family sailing market. Westerly was founded by Commander Denys Rayner in 1963 to start designing and building fibreglass yachts. His first, a triple keeler, the Westerly 22/Nomad model lured around 622 cruising families onto the water, and the following year, he lengthened it into the Westerly 25. The 26 foot Westerly Centaur, launched in 1969, was one of the few yachts to have sales of more than 1,000, selling 2,444. Westerly's second most popular model, the 28 foot Konsort, launched in 1979, sold 812.[55] Its flagship cruiser/racing cruiser, the Fulmar, designed by Ed Dubois, was launched in 1980 and sold over 400.

Moody's was a much older yard, dating back to 1827, and building wooden yachts before switching to GRP in 1973, when they started collaborating with Marine Projects, Plymouth. Taking all versions of the Moody 33, launched 1981, the status statement of yacht cruising (33, 33 Mk II, Moody 33S and 333), gives 494 boats built.[56]

[55] Easteal and Poland, *The Westerly Story*, pp. 72–73 and 84–85.
[56] Moody, *The Moody Legacy*, pp. 51–52, 141–142.

Sadler Yachts also got into the act. David Sadler, who had designed the Contessa, set up by himself with his son in 1974. His first designs, the Sadler 25, launched in 1975, and the Sadler 32, launched in 1979, were aimed more at the racing yachtsman. His next design, the Sadler 26, launched in 1981 and was aimed at the family market. It offered standing headroom right through the cabins, a separate toilet, and a dinette in the main cabin. Also very reassuring for the mother who had secret doubts about who would win if the going got rough, the sea or her husband, the yacht was rendered unsinkable by bonding a completely separate interior foam moulding onto the inside of the hull.

You needed a reliable engine to be in before nightfall – no more smug recounting of how you anchored on the lee side of some sandbank just off the shipping lanes in the Thames Estuary. Volvo, with their expensive engines and spare parts, did very nicely with their reputation for reliability. And if you did break down at sea, it was reassuring that inshore lifeboats had been introduced in 1963 and 'fast' (15 knot) all-weather lifeboats in 1967.

In the early 1970s, marinas began to be opened.[57] The first place to be dredged to make a marina of 200 berths was at Port Hamble, opening in 1964. By 1973, there were 35 marinas, containing 7,300 berths, 19 of them in the Solent area, 6 on the Hamble alone. Fees were far higher than those of the old river moorings, but such was the demand that berths were soon filled, and waiting lists developed.

The early investors were leisure industry firms, such as the Rank Organisation, Coral Bookmakers and EMI. Large scale builders such as Tarmac and Taylor Woodrow undertook marina development to provide prestigious settings for housing development.[58] With or without marinas – and many moorings were laid as they also became highly profitable – the number of boats in the Solent increased from 16,000 in 14 harbours in 1974 to 28,000 in 1989.[59]

As container ships needed deep water and Tilbury developed, the London Docks ceased trading. A number were converted to marinas, for example St Katherine's Dock, the old Surrey Docks (the 200 berth 'South Dock Marina'), the old Royal Albert Dock Basin (the 120 berth 'Gallions Point Marina') and the Limehouse Basin, Poplar, which was converted into a 450 berth marina.

---

[57] The first marina in England was at Birdham Pool, Chichester, which opened in 1937.
[58] Pickthall, *The British Marine Industry*, Chapter 6, 'Birth of the Marina', pp. 76–83.
[59] A similar growth of marinas further down the Clyde caused the Royal Northern and the Royal Clyde at Rhu, Helensburgh, to amalgamate in 1978.

The most remarkable development was at Brighton, where a marina was constructed between 1971 and 1979, by building out into the sea, protection coming from caissons the size of high rise tower blocks. When completed, it had 1600 berths.[60]

With families coming on board, things had to be easier, brighter, lighter, more comfortable and easier to maintain. GRP, being new, had the merit of novelty and being contemporary. Outfits got brighter and more designer-orientated. For years, wet weather gear had been the stiff, yellow 'oilie' (oilcloth) which did not keep out that much water. In its place came modern materials, designed by such firms as Guy Cotten, Gill, Helly Hansen, Henri Lloyd and Musto. All these firms were concerned to make their products attractive to get women to wear them, and worth the mark-up for things yachtie, and between them, their clothing came to define the active yachtsperson.[61]

The Victorian prioritising of male company and male friendship over the family was over. Modern yachting had broken away from the century-old Corinthian model and became family-centred. The table highlights these changes.

Modern vs. Corinthian Yachting

Corinthian	Family sailing
Yachting as an important aspect of identity	Yachting regarded as just one leisure activity among a number
One's yacht an important attribute of self	More peripheral – one's yacht an investment, to be used only when convenient
Yachting important in defining one's masculinity	Yachting important in defining one's social and familial status
Homosocial: male buddy-centred – sailing done with male friends	Family-centred – sailing predominantly done with family

---

[60] Johnson, *Boating Britain*, pp. 167–171.

[61] Helly Hansen is a Norwegian firm, founded in 1877. After the Second World War, it developed the fleece and later moved into the British yachting market. Guy Cotten was started by Guy and his wife in 1964, using a lightweight, waterproof cloth. Keith Musto was a silver medallist, Flying Dutchman class, in the 1964 Tokyo Olympics. By 1971, he had designed a three-layer system, the outside being waterproof Neoprene, the trick being not to allow any seams to be anywhere near where water could get in. Gill was started by Nick Gill in 1975 and specialised in heavy weather gear.

Risk-taking	Risk-averse
Uncomfortable	Comfortable
Little head room; narrow; open plan	Standing head room; beamy; separate cabins
Bucket-and-chuck-it 'sanitation'	Separate heads compartment, often another one en suite in the master cabin
Yacht to be used wherever possible	Yacht used only when convenient
Likely to be local	May well be coming from a distance
More likely to be a member of a local yacht club, as club likely to own suitable moorings; and friends members	Less need as using a marina berth (and, if travelling any distance, little time to use a yacht club)
Considerable DIY skills	Due to lack of skills and/or time limitations, more likely to be concerned to find reliable marine professionals to sort boat out, so can go straight off
If cannot 'sort the problem out', pool of skills available to them from other yacht members	Hires the various separate professional skills as and when required
Emphasis on keeping *absolute* cost low	Emphasis on value for money
Preferred length around 25 ft	At least 30 ft (by 2000s, 40 ft)
Deliberately cut off when at sea, as sailing's prime purpose is leaving work behind	Staying in touch with family and friends (and, increasingly, work) through onboard internet and mobile phone
Negative or ambivalent attitude to having, or using, an engine	Engine absolutely essential to get back to land-based engagements (work, school etc.)
Primitive navigation	Increasingly sophisticated navigation, e.g. autopilot, GPS
Reads *Practical Boat Owner* to improve DIY skills	Reads *Yachting Monthly* to find out new locations

The *Practical Boat Owner* (PBO) was launched at the (London) Boat Show in January 1967. The launching of *PBO* was clever marketing by IPC (International Publishing Corporation) which already owned established yachting titles, such as *Yachting Monthly* and *Yachting World*. As a guide to cheaper and Corinthian yachting, it had two target audiences – the still flour-ishing, if dwindling, group of ageing Corinthian, small boat, do-it-yourself, cash-limited sailors, seeking advice on repairs and maintenance; but also, it might well be bought by the more affluent middle-class sailor with a larger yacht, parked in one of the growing number of marinas, and serviced by the nearby marine workshops. Even if this new kind of boat owner had little understanding of how his boat worked, it did not mean he did not want to learn (or at least, talk the talk).[62] But this latter group would also buy *Yachting Monthly*, which told them about how to get to interesting places and gave hints on how to sail a bit more efficiently.

In 1968, a second Boat Show opened, not in London in winter, but in Southampton at the end of the sailing season in mid-September, with the boats on the water, not carpet. It quickly became an annual pilgrimage for yachtspeople to see the new boats and gear, get advice from experts, and, over lunch, meet friends.[63]

Once aboard, and after a couple of seasons without too many mishaps, families grew more adventurous, and the skipper-(usually) husband more ambitious. The classic account of family cruising with children was Libby Purves' *One Summer's Grace*, which described a voyage around the British Isles.[64] France, especially the Cotentin peninsula (Cherbourg and St Vaast-la-Hougue, a fishing port converted into a marina, much sought after for its delicatessen and restaurants) and the North Brittany coast, became very well used cruising grounds. So, there was a healthy market in pilot books, not just for the UK and the French coasts, but also further afield, the Mediterranean and the Baltic. Adlard Coles was the main publisher, and Rod Heikell and Philip Bristow wrote many of the pilots especially for those families that wanted to get to the Mediterranean and explore it. To get there, most used the French canals rather than cross Biscay and again a number of pilot books guided you through them.[65]

Family cruising, as ever in the unfamiliar and potentially frightening world of yachting, needed how-to books, teaching the apparently confident male skipper and the lucky wife and mother how to enjoy sailing. For the women, Joyce Sleightholme, wife of the *Yachting Monthly* editor, Des, wrote

---

[62] This educative function was exemplified by the diagrammatic 'How To' sections of Dick Ever-itt. My late friend Brian Biggs summed up the *PBO* as 'telling you how to make fenders out of lemonade bottles' (which it did!).

[63] Norman Kemish, *The First Twenty Years of the Southampton International Boat Show*.

[64] Libby Purves, *One Summer's Grace: A Family Voyage around Britain*, 1989.

[65] A nice 'how-to-get-there' pilot via the canals is *France: The Quiet Way* by John Liley, 1975.

The Sea Wife's Handbook, published in 1970, with a second edition in 1976.[66] There were also books that helped you come back with the same number of children as you left the marina with. Conrad Dixon and Edward Seviour's *Sailing with Children* was one of the first such books, but it was soon followed by, among many others, T. L. Kinsey's *Family Cruising*, 1975; David and Joan Hays' *The Handbook of Family Cruising*, 1977; and Pippa Driscoll's *Children Afloat*,1989.[67]

Their children might well be learning how to sail through dinghy lessons as cadets at the local yacht club, but the aspiring middle-class parent also purchased educative texts for them, such as Jeremy Howard-Williams' *Teach Your Child about Sailing*, 1963 or Gary and Steve Kibble's *Sailing for Kids*, 1987. For the exam-conscious parent, two grammar school teachers, W. B. Keeble and D. W. Cobden, offered 'twelve tests of sailing and seamanship' in *Cassell's Young Mariners' Guide*, 1962.

Tall Ships were in their heyday, with the organisations founded after the war now flourishing. Geoffrey Williams won the 1968 OSTAR and was appointed Director of Development at OYC. He set about raising funds for a fleet of purpose-built ketches. During the 1970s, its fleet reached eleven vessels, including nine Robert Clark designed 72 foot ketches, such as *Master Builder*, built at Penryn, Cornwall.[68] From its start, the OYC 'sailed with mixed crew at a time when ladies on boats were considered an affliction'.[69] Sail Training organisations continued to be created into the 1980s – the Jubilee Sailing Trust was founded in 1978, the Cirdan Sailing Trust in 1983 by Bill Broad. Tower Hamlets Council had the *Larvik*, an old Norwegian pilot-cutter, and chartered her out to various charitable organisations, so that children could have a holiday on her.[70]

An innovative training of children is described in Rozelle Raynes' *The Tuesday Boys*. She had a much-loved Folkboat, *Martha McGilda*, but since

---

[66] By 1991, the title was passé and it was changed to *The Cruising Mate's Handbook*. There are changes in the cover too. The fifty-something lady is replaced by one at least ten years younger; the tiller has been replaced by a rather large wheel, suggesting the boat is both more modern and larger. The stowage of some rather Sleightholme type cans on the lazarette have gone, but still the red duster flies over the smiling ladies. Chapter 1: Coming to Terms with Yachting' has been replaced by the more egalitarian 'Women and Cruising', and the chapter 'Beauty Care and Clothes' has completely disappeared.

[67] By 1990, Lyndsay Green was telling mothers how to keep *Babies Aboard* and happy. John Mellor talks directly to the teenage sailor in *Young Crew*, 1993.

[68] Hamilton, *Sail Training*, pp. 76–77.

[69] Hambly, *Race under Sail*, p. 35.

[70] This is perhaps the most inclusive leisure sailing got – as if every child had a right to at least experience sailing for a week.

her husband could not sit up in it, they decided to trade up. *Martha* objected strongly and started behaving strangely. Besides, a third share of her was owned by Noel Jordan, her original owner. Jordan died of a heart attack during this period, and his widow, Ursula, having scattered his ashes from the boat, was unwilling to agree a sale. Faced with the prospect of two boats, in discussion with Newham Social Services, key figures being Ken Boyce and, especially Peter Cobb, the idea was sounded that perhaps it could be used to sail train deprived children in one of the borough's children's homes.[71] Peter Cobb approached the house-mother, Emily Murphy, of Edith Morley House, Forest Gate, and she was enthusiastic. The eight boys, all devastated by their rejection by their parents, for whatever reasons, and mostly poor scholars, needed much structured loving. They were taught, in two groups of four, on alternative Tuesday afternoons in 1975 and 1976, first in the London Marina, Woolwich, and then out in the Thames, Rozelle often being helped by both Ursula and Emily.

Raynes arranged for the Tuesday boys to learn the ways of the tall ship on *Larvik*, on *Thalatta*, an ageing Thames sailing-barge owned by the East Coast Sail Trust, and *Arethusa*, not the Shaftesbury Society base, but an Ocean Youth Club ketch.[72] In the November of 1976, they were examined in Seamanship by Captain Ian McClaren, Extra Master Mariner, Deputy Head of the School of Navigation.[73] Three of the eight passed with a distinction and five with a merit.

Raynes kept in touch with the boys after they left the home, noting for some their successes and for some their difficulties. This remarkable initiative seems to be unique in yachting in reaching out for the disadvantaged, not just for a week or two, but over a period of time.[74]

New Races for the New Yachtsmen

GRP made single class racing much simpler with every boat coming from the same mould. (These 'single class' racers were the successors to the

---

[71] The connection was that her husband, Dick, was the Deputy Medical Officer of Health for the borough.

[72] Raynes, *The Tuesday Boys*, pp. 113–115.

[73] Situated on Tower Hill, this was a noted navigation training school and also ran evening classes for yachtsmen.

[74] Rozelle Raynes died in 2015 and all the Tuesday Boys who were still living came to her funeral (Peter Cobb, personal communication 14 February, 2016). Peter Chilvers, the inventor, at the age of 12 when living at Hayling Island, of the windsurfer, opened a sailing and windsurfing school for underprivileged children in the East End in the 1970s, in the Royal Victoria Dock.

'one-designs'.) In 1970, Jeremy Rogers, using GRP, built the 26 foot Contessa to a design by David Sadler, who he had asked to design a GRP version of the Folkboat. The boat's name is a pun on David Sadler's wife's name, Tessa, and 'con' meaning 'with' in Italian, the first boat built being called *Contessa of Parkstone* (Poole Harbour). In total, 350 were built. Following the success of the 26, they worked together to create the iconic Contessa 32, launched in 1972, which was even more successful, especially with the racing fraternity, and 700 were built. The racing boys did not want much comfort, which was a good thing because they didn't have it.

Another very successful racing yacht, again GRP, was the Sigma 33, designed by David Hunter. This was launched in 1978, and the last one, no. 364, was built in 1991. This was somewhat more suitable for family cruising ('a cruiser-racer').

The racing bug was caught by more ordinary sailors who had raced inshore or coastal and now wanted a piece of the action, but could not afford the time off work, nor the expense of ocean racing, nor commit to a *series* of races, where boats had to be delivered to the start lines of different clubs and brought home from harbours where the race had finished.

So attractive, new 'stand alone' races were added to the racing calendar. The Helford–L'Aberwrach race had been run since 1959 by the Helford River Sailing Club. On the Norfolk Broads, the Three Rivers Race was started in 1961, organised by the Horning Yacht Club, with David Hastings and friends as the creative force. It is a 50 mile race along the Rivers Bure, Yare and Waveney, involving four mast lowerings and overnight sailing.

The Falmouth–Azores and Back (the AZAB), a four-yearly solo non-stop race, originally for singlehanded sailors in boats of less than 38 feet (11.58m), had been mooted by Chris Smith, a Dorset dentist. The first race was organised by the assistant editor of *Yachting Monthly*, Andrew Bray, and Colin Drummond, another dentist, practising in Falmouth.[75] It was, and is, sponsored by the Royal Cornwall Yacht Club, Falmouth. The first race left Falmouth with forty-nine starters on 7 June, 1975, the entry cost being £15. The race really took off in 1979 when it allowed two-handers, a more popular option, and eighty-nine boats started.[76] A year later, the Sussex Yacht Club, Shoreham, organised the first Royal Escape race from Brighton to Fécamp,

---

[75] Michael Hutchinson notes 'There used to be a phenomenal number of dentists in the sailing world – to the extent that a dentists' journal once had a cartoon of two miners at the coalface, captioned 'Well, my mother wanted me to be a dentist, but I simply couldn't stand the sailing' (*Hello Sailor*, p. 114).

[76] Mark Fishwick, 'A Taste of the Ocean Deep'.

to commemorate King Charles' escape from England by that route in 1651. It is claimed to be the largest yacht race in the south of England outside the Solent.

The Three Peaks Yacht Race combined competitive sailing and mountain climbing. Dr Rob Haworth, a GP in Barmouth, West Wales, enjoyed talking to Bill Tilman, one of his patients. Tilman had climbed high peaks in the Himalayas and later made long voyages to polar waters. Haworth talked to his partner, Merfyn Jones. They came up with the idea of sailing with a crew of three, plus two climbers scaling the highest peaks in England (Scafell), Wales (Snowdon) and Scotland (Ben Nevis). The first race was run in 1977 and is an annual event.[77]

Among the dinghies, the Round the Island Race, organised by the Isle of Sheppey Sailing Club, near Sheerness, is a forty mile circumnavigation of the Isle of Sheppey. It has attracted 200 to 300 racing dinghies of any class since its inception in 1959.

A dramatic new race was the non-stop 24 hour (12:00–12:00) race at Southport Marine Lake, hosted by the West Lancashire Yacht Club from 1967, and spurred on by the Liverpool University Sailing Club, who had a representative on the club's committee. The students wanted the race in early September, before they went back to college, and this has always been its date. Crew size is up to the individual club, and can vary from a rather tired two to twelve. It was open to Fireflys, Enterprises and GP 14s.[78] Interest was considerable from the first year, when fifty teams took part. Bolton Sailing Club, home base Belmont Reservoir, have an active GP 14 fleet, which may account for it being the most successful club in this race.

Another major dinghy race was the Bloody Mary race, organised by the Queen Mary Sailing Club every January since 1973. This is a pursuit race, so the dinghies start at staggered times. By 1976, it had 274 entries in 60 classes from 123 clubs.

At the Yacht Club

The move to family cruising was not an innovation driven by yacht clubs, who did not have much to offer the cruising family and many of whom were

---

[77] The biggest change was in 1980, when the Scafell leg began to be started from Whitehaven, and no longer Ravensglass, in whose shallow waters too many boats had fallen over. This move meant that a 15-mile cycling leg had to be added.

[78] Ryan, *A History of the West Lancashire Yacht Club*, pp. 132–137. After five years, the Fireflys were withdrawn.

not keen on having children running around their hallowed portals. The last barrier – to allowing women on committees and being flag officers – fell, albeit slowly. Women did not get full membership and voting rights in the Royal Cork till 1991. At the Royal Fowey, it took till 1994, and at the Royal Squadron till 2014;[79] but the game was up. Members were now husbands and parents, rather than male buddies, and would not tolerate discrimination against their family members.[80] Besides, there were economic drivers. Oil prices tripled in 1973/1974, inflation reached 26 per cent in 1975 and interest rates 15–20 per cent. Not surprisingly, any source of increased membership was very welcome, and this time, if they wanted, women could seek to become flag officers.

What clubs could do well was organise races, as we have seen with the OSTAR, organised by the Royal Western, and the AZAB, organised by the Royal Cornwall. The huge classes of dinghies led to large national championships. Most reservoirs were too small to handle these numbers. Indeed, the championships could only be held in a limited number of locations, which had to be free of commercial traffic, have weak tides, should not advantage the local sailors too much, had to have sufficient parking for boats and cars and places for the competitors to stay. This led to only a few centres being used on a regular basis: Weymouth (used most frequently, as it has a small tidal range), Plymouth, Falmouth, Llandudno on the north coast of Wales, Helensburgh on the Forth of Clyde, Scarborough, Yorkshire, Thorpe Bay, Southend and Whitstable in Kent.[81] Clubs in these locations built up their expertise in running national events.

At Cowes, the ever increasing demand of marinas and moorings led, in 1964, to the Cowes Combined Clubs, who organised Cowes week, giving up trying to organise the Dinghy Racing Week in the increasingly narrowed and congested river. A new group of clubs, including the Island Sailing Club, organised the week till 1972, when it was moved to the end of August and organised solely by the Gurnard Sailing Club, two miles outside the town.[82]

---

[79] Coombs, *A Fowey Jig-Saw*, p. 165. Other prestige sports were only a little less tardy. No women were permitted to row in Henley regatta till 1981, some years after the Sex Discrimination Act of 1975 (Christopher Dodd, *Henley Royal Regatta*, pp. 184 and 209). Women were not able to join the Royal Alpine Club, formed 1857, till 1975.

[80] The question of dogs lived on. Dogged debates concerning allowing dogs in the bar continued at the Cowes Corinthian at least up to 2007, when Diana Cave finished her history of the club.

[81] Johnson, *Boating Britain*, p. 50. More recently, one would add Abersoch and Pwllheli in Tremadog Bay, North Wales, and Portland Harbour, where, once the Navy left, the Weymouth and Portland Sailing Academy opened in 2005, hosting the sailing Olympics in 2012.

[82] Caws, *The Gurnard Sailing Club 1931–2006*, p. 32.

By 1973, the RYA had created its series – theoretical and, separately, practical – of levels of competence (Competent Crew, Day Skipper, Coastal Yachtmaster, Offshore Yachtmaster and Ocean Yachtmaster); and an equivalent set of grades for dinghy sailors. There was a considerable uptake in RYA courses at sailing schools and yacht clubs. Many sailing and yacht clubs offered lessons to members' children and to schools to teach dinghy sailing. Since, increasingly, people wanted to be assessed and given a certificate, this greatly strengthened the role of the RYA as the accrediting body. Yacht clubs strove to become accredited teaching/ training establishments for RYA certificates. The RYA developed a range of booklets, one or more for each of the many syllabuses, plus videos, films etc. The National Sailing Centre was opened in West Cowes in 1969 by the Duke of Edinburgh as the prestige 'university' of sail, where one could learn to race, cruise or dinghy sail with the best instructors. A similar Scottish centre, the Scottish National Centre, was opened on Great Cumbrae Island in 1976, and, in Wales, the Plas Menai National Outdoor Centre, on the Menai Straits near Caernarfon, was opened in 1983.

The Yachting Culture Whirlpool

In times of cultural centrality, yachting will be a prestige activity supported by royalty and leading members of the Establishment. Prince Philip was the Commodore of the Squadron from 1961 to 1968.[83] When Chay Blyth returned from his West-about circumnavigation:

> On Friday, August 6th, 1971, I walked on to the quay of the Royal Southern Yacht Club at Hamble 292 days after I'd left. The Prince of Wales, Princess Anne, the Duke of Edinburgh, the Prime Minister (Edward Heath), a host of other notable people, and a great crowd of those who would call themselves ordinary people, but who are the backbone of the country, were there to meet me.[84]

Clearly, people right at the top of the social hierarchy wanted a piece of the action.[85]

Edward Heath, leader of the opposition and then prime minister from 1970 to 1974, won the tough Sydney–Hobart race in *Morning Cloud* in 1969,

---

[83] Princess Anne has been the president of the RYA since 1997.

[84] Blyth, *The Impossible Voyage*, p. 210.

[85] Despite all this acclaim, Blyth is careful to line himself up with the common people, 'who are the backbone of the country'.

three years after taking up yacht sailing. In a different boat with the same name, he captained Great Britain to victory in the 1971 Admiral's Cup. [86] One could argue that what he did well was picking good crew, but he helmed his boats and still is unique in winning the highly prestigious Gold Roman Bowl for the winner, on corrected time, of the Round the Island Race four times (1971–1973 in *Morning Cloud II*; 1980 in *Morning Cloud IV*).[87]

By this date, the 'establishment' had widened to include leading figures in pop culture, for example Elton John, who would sing 'Goodbye England's Rose (Candle in the Wind)' at Princess Diana's funeral in Westminster Abbey on 6 September, 1997. Another pop star, Simon Le Bon, lead singer with the group Duran Duran, became a keen racing yachtsman. His maxi racer, *Drum*, was in the 1985 Fastnet when its keel fell off and the boat turned turtle. Le Bon and five of the other off watch crew were trapped in the hull for forty minutes. Forty days later, it was at the start line for the Whitbread.[88]

Yachting also attracted one of the very few Englishmen to win the Nobel Prize for literature – William Golding in 1983.[89] During the war, he had been in charge of an LCT(R) – a landing craft, with a rack of powerful rockets, equivalent to a frigate's fire power. After D-Day, the Allies had taken Antwerp, which they needed for the push on Germany, but they could not access it by sea because the Germans occupied the island of Walcheren in the Scheldt and were heavily fortified there. Golding trained with lightly armed yachts in Poole and knew the crew. In the actual operation in November 1944 (Operation Infatuate), the yachts went inshore and Golding realised that

---

[86] He had sailed dinghies before switching to yacht racing. In all, he raced five yachts, all called *Morning Cloud*. Two were wrecked on the same night, 2 September, 1974. The first *Morning Cloud* which he had sold was wrecked on her mooring in Jersey. The third *Morning Cloud,* on passage from the Burnham regatta to the Solent, was wrecked six miles from the Ower's Light Vessel. Two crew, Nigel Cumming and Heath's godson, Christopher Chadd, were drowned. Heath had a very rough Fastnet in 1979. His *Sailing: A Course of My Life.* 1975, pp. 154–158, describes the wrecking of *Morning Cloud III.* Heath's sailing master, Owen Parker, describes sailing with Heath in *Tack Now, Skipper.*

[87] Gold Roman Bowl: A golden Roman bowl had been dredged from the Thames and put on display at a goldsmith near Roman Wharf, London. Major Windeler, who had the idea for the Round the Island Race, so loved the design, he ordered a replica from Bruce Benzie, the Cowes jeweller, and presented it to the Island Cruising Club for the fastest boat on corrected time. (Handicapping is needed in the race, due to the greatly varying size and speed of the yachts taking part.) Windeler won his own trophy in 1939, sailing the 7-ton auxiliary cutter, *Kalliste*, designed by Jack Giles.

[88] For an account of preparing for and sailing the race, see the project manager, Skip Novak's *One Watch at a Time: Around the World with 'Drum' on the Whitbread Race.*

[89] The only other fiction authors, who won the prize, are Kipling (1907) and Galsworthy (1932). Embarrassed patriots pad out the numbers with non-fiction prize winners (Bertrand Russell for his philosophical writing and Churchill for his historical works) and immigrants (the American, T. S. Eliot and Doris Lessing from South Africa).

they were being used as defenceless decoys to draw German fire. All the crews were killed. He had also been led to believe that the Dutch civilians had been evacuated. They hadn't, so his considerable firepower killed and injured many civilians. Golding's work was undoubtedly affected by his war experience. In *Lord of the Flies*, 1954, he inverts Ballantyne's *Coral Island*, which concerns a group of shipwrecked youths, who teach Christian principles to the natives. On his island, Golding has a church choir among the schoolboys, survivors after a nuclear war, and they become psychopathic killers. The book was a literary success, a best- seller and the basis of Peter Brooks' film. With the profits from *Lord of the Flies*, he bought a Dutch barge, *Tenace*, and was crossing the Channel in the summer of 1967, when, in poor visibility, it was run down by a Japanese freighter. Fortunately, the family were not hurt and the freighter took them on board. Golding never sailed again.[90]

When yachting is culturally central, it is utilised by and promoted through a wide variety of media, and this period was no exception, with books, soaps, films and records all featuring it.

In terms of visual media, the return of the circumnavigators received considerable coverage on T.V, showing the fleets of welcoming boats and the huge crowds welcoming the heroes.

The traditional print media did very well from the yachting boom. Each achievement, or even apparent achievement, resulted in an account being quickly produced, doubtless sometimes ghosted. This would come out in hardback, and a year later, in paperback. Book clubs would bring out cheap hardback editions, so sales could be even larger. Even a talking, existentially aware, seagull got into the act. Richard Bach's *Jonathan Livingston Seagull*, 1970, concerning this exceptional avian, was a world-wide mega-seller and was made into a film in 1973.

The BBC had made a six-episode version of *Swallows and Amazons*, screened in 1963. Ransome clashed repeatedly with the BBC during its making, and in his diaries describes it as 'a ghastly mess' and 'ham'. He died in 1967, so he didn't have to see the butchered and unfaithful film version of *Swallows and Amazons* that was released in 1974. In 1979, *The Riddle of the Sands* was made into a successful, atmospheric and beautifully photographed film with Michael York as Carruthers and Simon MacCorkindale as Davies.

---

[90] John Carey, *William Golding*, Chapter 9., 'The War', pp. 82–110; *Tenace*: Judy Golding, *The Children of Lovers*, pp. 1–7; Carey, *William Golding*, pp. 311–313. (A similar intrusion of the author's war-time experience into his writing is to be found in Henry Williamson's *Tarka the Otter* (1927), where the random and brutal, mass killings of the First World War trenches are transferred to the rivers of North Devon.)

An interesting first was a long running nautical soap, *Howard's Way* (six series, 1985–1990). That a soap could be based around sailing and a boat-yard clearly shows the centrality of yachting to the nation's imagination in this period. The series even had a racing yacht designed for it – the Sadler Barracuda, a 46 foot ultra-light displacement boat. Sadly, it was poorly marketed, only nineteen were sold and, by 1988, Sadler was in receivership.

In the 1960s, Michael Green had produced the best-selling *The Art of Coarse Sailing*, which was an amusing account of sailing on the Norfolk Broads, but Green spread his humour across a number of sports. Thelwell, mainly famous for his cartoons of children on ponies, drew boating cartoons, but his subjects are too manic to ring true.[91] Jack Giles ('Giles') drew cartoons for the *Daily* and *Sunday Express* from 1943 for the next half century. While mainly concerned with Grandma and her family, a number of his cartoons feature sailing, some of which can be seen at the Sir Max Aitken Museum and the Island Sailing Club, Cowes, of which he was a member.[92]

The increased interest in yachting and yachting magazines meant that there was sufficient demand for a group of specifically yachting humourists to flourish in the 1980s: Bill Beavis' *Looking Around* column in *Yachting Monthly*, and put together into books, and Des Sleightholme's *Old Harry* column and books usually concern gaff rig and old boats. Perhaps with their heavy gear and a more Corinthian stance, such as self-help and sailing in heavy weather, they offered more opportunity for humour.[93] We might call this 'East Coast humour', in tune with the barges, bawleys and smacks of the Thames Estuary. Mike Peyton's pithy cartoons also were often concerned with old boats, which is not surprising as he lived near, and sailed from, a small tributary of the Crouch. His second daughter's bunk was created by inserting a berth above his first daughter's bed. This new berth had eighteen inches of head-room, and the first words she apparently uttered were 'Mind my head!' as she was lifted out.[94] But Peyton was much more in tune with family yachting and its tribulations. His cartoons usually involve two people – husband and wife; skipper and a crewman. Whereas Giles provided a comforting sense of oddball continuity, Peyton was much more aware of social change. So, he often contrasts east coast vs. southern sailing. For example, one of his

---

[91] Thelwell, *Three Sheets to the Wind*, 1973.
[92] Three yachting cartoons are also shown on pp. 167–169 of Peter Tory, *Giles: A Life in Cartoons*.
[93] Bill Beavis, *Bows Amidships*, 1984; *The Best of 'Looking Around with Bill Beavis' 1970–1976*, 1987; Des Sleightholme, *Old Harry's Bunkside Book*, 1978; *Up the Creek with Old Harry*, 1979. Peyton has many volumes of cartoons, among them *The Pick of Peyton*, 1983; *Quality Time: His 50 Years of Sailing plus 80 Cartoons*, 2005, and *Ever Wonder Why We Do It?*, 2007.
[94] Durham, *Peyton*, p. 59.

cartoons concerns 'a snotty yachtie' going across the Essex foreshore with an east coaster, who is suitably kitted out in thigh length waders. The southerner is wearing shorty boots and saying 'That's alright. I don't mind a bit of mud. We have it on the South Coast too'.[95]

Because Giles' talent was spotted early and his humour is that of a united, if disparate and slightly wacky war-time Britain, similar to that of *The Goon Show*, it is easy to think he must be of a much earlier generation.[96] In fact, they were near contemporaries, Giles born in 1916, Peyton in 1921. Giles was a war artist, seeing the fiasco and the heavy losses of Arnheim, and the horrors of freeing Belsen concentration camp. 'Not a day or even a night goes by now when I don't think of Belsen. It was the most dreadful, terrible thing in my life.'[97]

Similarly, while it is easy to see Peyton as highlighting yachtsmen's foibles and pretensions, his own life does not lie easily with this reading. His mother 'had lost her first husband, John Kells – one of five brothers, all killed, three on the same day'.[98] (They had been in a Pals battalion, all from the same town, which was supposed to improve morale, till it went horribly wrong.)

Peyton was lucky to be alive. He fought in the African campaign in the Fourth Battalion of the Northumberland Fusiliers. By the time they were overrun by German tanks, 'just four officers and 106 men' of the original 800 were left. As a prisoner of war in Germany, he escaped at the end of the war and became a ping-pong ball between the Russian, German and American lines. Fifty years later, round the cabin stove, the conversation turns to the best meal the various participants have ever had ... wild strawberries ... lobster thermidor ... We then both turned to Mike ... "The best meal I ever had was Alsatian in a POW camp"'.[99]

Peyton came to the forefront as yachting was expanding both in terms of numbers and the professions joining in, just as it had done a century before when the new professions took up Corinthian yachting. Such a rapid expansion creates insecurity as to one's position and status and uncertainty about that of the others around one. It might be more accurate to see Peyton as yachting's Gilbert and Sullivan, concerned with debunking pretensions.

---

[95] *Ibid.*, p. 109.

[96] Eric Sykes wrote for *The Goons*, and Michael Bentine acted in the radio show. Both were close friends of Giles (Peter Tory, *Giles: A Life in Cartoons*).

[97] It may be the explanation of why Giles rarely went to bed before 3 a.m. (Peter Tory, *Giles: A Life in Cartoons*, pp. 50 and 59).

[98] Durham, *Peyton*, p. 8.

[99] *Ibid.*, p. 152.

They say that the year before a tree dies, it produces luxuriant blossoms. Maybe, the offshore racers – small groups of men competing against each other, often in very difficult conditions – were a similar statement with regard to Corinthian sailing and a defiance of the supposed joys of family life. Certainly, it was in sharp contrast to the marinas and the GRP boats going out into the Solent or cross-channel to Brittany. Maybe it divides those who fought in the war and those that were too young to do so.[100] The Corinthian lives on, as ways of relating to the sea cannot die, but this was the time when the predominant mode switched from Corinthian to family yachting.

---

[100] If a date and a person are needed for this change, Bill Tilman might fill the bill. He had fought in both wars, going from school to fight in the trenches in the First and with the Albanian resistance in the Second. When, in 1955, he got too old to climb mountain peaks, he sailed in Bristol pilot cutters to polar wastes (see his *The Eight Sailing/Mountain-Exploration Books*). His famous advert for crew ran: 'Hands wanted for long voyage in small boat: no pay, no prospects, not much pleasure'. In November, 1977, aged 79, he left Rio in *En Avant*, Simon Richardson skipper, for the South Shetland islands and neither boat nor crew were ever seen again. (See Tim Madge, *The Last Hero: Bill Tilman*; Dorothy Richardson, *The Quest of Simon Richardson*.)

CHAPTER FIFTEEN

The Summer Before the Dark:
Yachting in Post-Modern Times
1990–2007

The Summer …

This time period was characterised by the accelerating development of
neo-liberal capitalism: the unfettering of restraints on big business, through
laissez-faire policies, privatisation and deregulation. This policy was developed and carried out by Ronald Reagan, President of the United States from
1980 to1988, and Margaret Thatcher, British prime minister from 1979 to 1990.

On the surface, the yachting scene of the 1980s and 1990s appeared
healthy. Marinas were full. A small number of companies gained control of
most of the marinas, the industry leader being Marina Development Limited
(MDL), with eighteen marinas in the UK. Prices were increased regularly.
The pricing was such that only those in good jobs could afford their berths,
but there were enough people willing and able to pay marina prices to keep
them full.

Yachtspeople benefited, as competition was now international. They
could get more boat for their money by buying French made boats. Jeanneau
introduced the Sun-Fizz, a 44 foot Cruiser, in the early 1980s and Dufour
introduced their Gib'Sea range in the mid-1980s, with aggressive marketing
and promotion in the UK. Another successful French range was the Feelings,
made by Kirie of Les Sables D'Olonne (later taken over by Kelt Yachts),
coming onto the market in 1980. Beneteau, with its factory line production of
Firsts, became the market leader.

Internet shopping was coming online by the end of the 1980s, obviating
the need to be overcharged by the local monopoly chandler. With the deregulation of industry, the first years of neo-liberal capitalism seemed liberating.
People talked of the age being 'ironic', 'fragmenting into minority interests'

and tolerant of experimentation in the arts and in gender behaviour. This chapter shows that yachting reflected this diversity and diversification.

The Second Generation of Women Racers

There were international races around the world, such as the three-yearly, crewed Whitbread, which started in 1973, and which Volvo took over in 2001, and the brutal, single-handed, non-stop Vendée Globe. The Vendée, founded by Philippe Jeantot, was first raced in 1989 and then four-yearly from 1992.

With the much greater range of lighter materials, a new generation of successful women sailors emerged. Whereas the previous generation of women racers could not compete with the men's physical strength, this new generation could. The outstanding example was Ellen MacArthur. In 1995, aged 19, she sailed a Corribbee, a 20 foot yacht, around Britain. She was seventeenth in the Mini Transat of 1997 and won the OSTAR for a monohull in 2000. Her breakthrough came when she was second in the Vendée Globe in 2001 in *Kingfisher*. She was the youngest competitor, at 24, to ever complete the course. Not surprisingly, the Kingfisher corporation kept up their sponsorship, this time on the non-stop circumnavigation time record.[1]

While she was having the Nigel Irens designed, 75 foot trimaran *B&Q* built in Australia and was preparing for her circumnavigation, a French sailor, Francis Joyon, reduced the time by an amazing 20 days to 72 days. Just after 10 pm, 7 February, 2005, MacArthur came back in 71 days, 14 hours, 18 minutes, taking a further day off the time.[2] I have commented on the pressures of the previous generation of female yacht racers to appear feminine. Since MacArthur did not play up to this expectation, sadly, her standing as a national hero contains a goodly degree of ambivalence. She is far more revered in France – she can speak fluent French – than in England.[3] She was lampooned by the satirical TV show, *Dead Ringers*, for her emotional webcam transmissions – presumably crying is not allowed for yachties.[4] Bob Fisher, an eminent yachting correspondent, at the time of her triumphant return in 2005, accused her of sailing by numbers, and contended that most

---

[1] She recounts her early sailing career in *Taking on the World*, 2002.
[2] *Race against Time*, 2005; video with the same title.
[3] 'Loved by the French': Yacht racing skippers have near rock star status in France. MacArthur was called 'the little sparrow' and Samantha Davies 'la petite Anglaise'.
[4] It can be argued that *Dead Ringers* lampooned everyone in the news, such as other sportsmen and politicians, so this was no different.

24 Ellen MacArthur (furthest astern) sailing with young people from the
Ellen MacArthur Cancer Trust. MacArthur, after her record-breaking non-stop
circumnavigation in 2004, gave up competitive racing in 2009. She set up a trust
for children recovering from cancer in 2002, and the Foundation to increase
environmental awareness in 2010.

of her admirers were French, not English.[5] I am reluctant to repeat this bile-
filled nonsense – having French admirers of her sailing ability is apparently a
negative. No-one can sail round the world non-stop 'mechanically'. Clearly,
MacArthur's success did not fit easily into at least some commentators'
assumptions about gender roles. A reflection of this is the organisation that
helps women learn to sail. Quite a few women sailors prefer to learn with just

---

[5] Stephen Moss, 'Against the Wind', 8 February, 2005. Libby Purves countered in *Yachting
Monthly*, May 2005: 23. Fisher also accused MacArthur of never having sailed in a crewed boat.
She had, for example in the Jules Verne trophy for 2003. He issued a retraction, but clearly has
a problem.

women present, so such an organisation, created in 1999, makes sense. What is rather disturbing is that it is called 'Girls For Sail'.

MacArthur opened the door for a generation of women sailors who competed in the same, prestigious ocean races as men – Emma Richards, Dee Caffari and Samantha Davies.[6] In 2009, MacArthur announced her retirement from yacht racing to focus on helping children with cancer to sail and on green issues.[7]

Staying with ocean sailing, Chay Blyth was canny enough to spot the economic opportunity to be gained by offering yachting to a wider audience. If they could raise the money, members of the public, of either gender, could train and then race around the world on one of his identical Challenge yachts against the prevailing winds, but with a number of stops, thereby demonstrating the slogan 'no guts, no glory'.[8] The first British Steel Challenge was in 1993. Robin Knox-Johnston copied the idea with his Clipper Yacht race, but going east around, which started in 1996.

Selling Up, Sailing Away

a strain of discontent of lamentation, a sullen growl of resentment … a querulous murmur of distress.[9]

During the Thatcher years, there seemed a pervasive discontent among her middle-class followers, as if, like King Canute, she was doing her best but could not stop the greatness of Great Britain leeching away. The theme of disenchantment with their home country was reflected in the escape of the 'young old' to 'sell up and sail away' (rather than buy a villa in Spain). This mood was represented in the best-selling *Sell Up and Sail*, 1986, by Bill and Laurel Cooper, who themselves sailed away, mainly to the Mediterranean; in the book by blue water sailors Bill and June Raper, *Sail to Freedom*, 1993, a 'practical guide to extended cruising'; and the sailing account and fiction,

---

[6] Emma Richards, *Around Alone*, 2004; Dee Caffari, *Against the Flow*, 2007, which described her leaving her career as a teacher and her east–west circumnavigation. She has since completed a west–east circumnavigation; Samantha Davies came 4th in the 2009 Vendee Globe and was dismasted in the 2013 race.

[7] She set up the Ellen MacArthur Cancer Trust in 2003; and the environmental Ellen MacArthur Foundation in 2010.

[8] The title of Barry Pickthall's account of the 1992/1993 race. Chay Blyth and Elaine Thompson give the background to the race in *The Challenge: The Official Story of the British Steel Challenge*, 1993.

[9] Samuel Johnson on Dryden in *The Lives of the British Poets*, Vol. 3, p. 377.

Foreign Land (1985)and *Coasting* (1986), by Jonathan Raban, who emigrated to Seattle in 1990.[10]

This move was helped by sailing becoming considerably safer. The period saw remarkable developments in communication technology. Mobile phones meant that you could now have a phone in your pocket. Satellite communication meant that you could know your position within ten metres, through GPS (Global Positioning System). You could set an anchor watch using it, so if you moved more than ten metres, an alarm went off. Satellites also meant that you could phone from anywhere in the world to anywhere in the world. You could get up-to-date weather charts and forecasts for several days ahead. Electronic chart plotters, as long as you were confident your batteries wouldn't stop working, got rid of the need for paper charts, and allowed you to plot a course on your computer and get instantaneous feedback about where you were, boat speed, boat direction, distance to the next way point etc. EPIRBs (Emergency Position Indicator Radio Beacons) transmitted your position and activated rescue services. Almost all yachts carried a radar reflector, so that larger vessels with radar could 'see' them. With increased uptake among yacht persons, radar came down in price, so many, especially if going long distances, carried a radar receiver, so that they could be aware of the presence of other vessels and their course. When they reached a port, a bow thruster, allowing the bow to be pushed in the desired direction, made coming alongside a berth or mooring buoy much easier. If you got into difficulties, the Lifeboat and the Search and Rescue services were available 24/7 and, in the Solent area, from Chichester to Poole, there was even a breakdown service for yachts, Sea Start, created in 1994 by Nick Eales.

Besides getting safer, boats also got larger. Whereas thirty years earlier, a couple's 'entry' (first) boat might be 26, perhaps 30 feet long, now it was 40 feet long, and harbours started to be filled with the best-selling, mass-produced 40 to 44 feet long Beneteaus.

As a result of all these improvements in safety, sailors felt confident to travel further.

Blue Water Live Aboards

The yachtsman and his wife, in their sixties in the 1990s, had lived through the period of the welfare state, with free education and health services, stable

---

[10] An interesting feature of Bill Cooper and Raban is that both carried large libraries on their boats, as if their identity resided in their reading 'self' or persona, rather than in their national identity.

careers, protected by strong unions, permitting the purchase of houses that greatly increased in value and good pensions. Their children, especially if they went to university, were likely to be in well paid jobs and be financially independent. Their parents were eligible for free social care in residential or nursing homes. They took up sailing in the context of these positives. In their middle age, having paid off most of the mortgage, and looking forward to a final salary pension, they bought a yacht. They could then decide to go sailing either more frequently, or, perhaps upgrading their boat, go further afield, leave their boat in the Med., or even try some long-distance sailing.[11]

As a consequence, married couples going long distance sailing, spending years in the Med. or the Caribbean, became an increasingly common occurrence. The technological advances made it less risky and easier for them to sail these longer distances. The greater use of electric appliances meant the anchor could be raised, or lowered, at the touch of button, and, likewise, the mainsail reefed or furled, without leaving the cockpit.

Of course, the amount of electrical and electronic gear on board required a generator, although electricity could now be generated by the new technologies of wind turbine, water turbine and solar panel. But these were insufficient, and the boat had to be plugged in as soon as it came alongside a marina berth. Peter Poland, in an article praising the flexibility of German yachtbuilders Hanse towards customer needs, writes:

> To get an idea of just how complex and comprehensively equipped a modern cruiser can be, options they [the couple ordering the boat] selected include washer/dryer, extra refrigeration and freezer, wine refrigerator, microwave, coffee machine, generator, reverse-cycle air-conditioning, electric winches, three-cabin/three en-suite layout, upgraded sail selection, large screen pop-up LED TV in the saloon, air compressor in the RIB's dinghy garage, electric tables in the cockpit, water maker, bow and stern thrusters, upgraded navigation package (two 12in. plotters and one 8in. plotter), broadband radar, AIS [automatic identification system], autopilot … larger generator …[12]

This may be an extreme example but a high degree of dependency on electric and electronic gear seems to characterise this mode of sailing.

Many cut their teeth on cruises in company across the Atlantic, or, in stages, around the world. The market leaders in catering to, and writing for,

[11] Claire James, *Sail for the Mediterranean: How to Prepare for Your Dream Cruise*, 2003, was a fairly typical primer.
[12] Peter Poland, 'The Hanse Story', p. 28. It is highly likely that the boat would also have had solar panels, but these do not merit a mention.

this group were Jimmy and Gwenda Cornell, with their Around the World rallies, their books of advice on type of boat, gear, routes etc.[13] Some did take children, often pre-school, but the majority were couples by themselves.[14] Not surprisingly, there was a growth in books on long-distance sailing, often in the manner of 'you can do it too'. These included Anne Hammick's *Ocean Cruising on a Budget*, 1990, and Annie Hill's *Brazil and Beyond*, 2000.

The Corinthian Lives On

The Corinthian model of racing in small boats lives on in the Junior Offshore Group, founded in 1950 to race small boats offshore, and which was, and still is, flourishing.

The OSTAR had become commercialised and professionalised by crack French skippers with very expensive boats. Lt Col. Ewen Southby-Tailyour, biographer of Blondie Hasler, the creator of the OSTAR, was himself a renowned yachtsman who charted the Falklands, conveniently just before the Falkland War, April–June, 1982 – his charts were used during the campaign.[15]

He suggested the Jester Challenge be a race for boats between 20 and 30 foot (the 'correct' Corinthian length?), with no prizes and no rescue boats. Hasler had sailed *Jester* in the first OSTAR and then sold her to Michael Richey, who competed in her in every OSTAR till the 1998 one in which, 500 miles northeast of Halifax, Canada, she was wrecked in a storm and sank, Richey getting off safely. The yacht was commemorated in the race title, the Jester (Transatlantic) Challenge, in alternate years leaving Plymouth for the Azores or heading across the Atlantic.[16]

The tradition that Corinthian sailors show their spartan qualities by heading in small boats to the purity of Northern waters lived on with the exploits of Bob Shepton and Willy Kerr, who, with Tilman, make up the holy trinity of Greenland sailors. Cape Farewell at the Southern tip is 'probably one of the worst capes in the world for bad weather'.[17] The Rev. Bob Shepton regularly took a bunch of disadvantaged pupils from Kingham Hill School to

---

[13] Jimmy Cornell, *Ocean Cruising Survey*, 1987; *Around the World Rally*, 1993.

[14] In a survey of 40 women involved in long-distance sailing, 11 were travelling with their children. Of these 20 children, 14 were under the age of ten (Jimmy Cornell, 'Partners Afloat', 1986). Gwenda Cornell offered advice in *Cruising with Children*, 1986.

[15] Ewen Southby-Tailyour, *Falkland Island Shores*, 1985.

[16] Richey died in December 2009. Trevor Leck, who had built a replica of *Jester* and sailed in the 2010 Jester Challenge, offered to take some of his ashes to the spot where *Jester* sank, and the family accepted his offer.

[17] David Cowper, 'The North West Passage, 1986–2012', p. 27. Cowper has gone through the North West Passage twice in a converted and toughened lifeboat.

Arctic waters. He undertook the North West passage in a modified Westerly 33 sloop from east to west in 2012, and from west to east in 2013.[18] He was sailing these waters and climbing cliffs in Greenland into his seventies in 2014. Willie Kerr, who saw action in Burma in the Second World War, has sailed 100,000 miles, mostly single-handed and mostly in Arctic waters, but also Antarctic waters.[19] Tom Cunliffe, his wife Ros and their four-year-old daughter, Hannah, followed the route of tenth-century Vikings from Norway, past Greenland, to Newfoundland, in his 75-year-old Bristol Cutter, *Hirta,* in 1983.[20] More recently, Roger Taylor, with his concept of 'minimal sailing', has written two books about sailing his 21 foot junk rigged boat, *Mingming II,* to Iceland and Greenland.[21]

Les Powles has circumnavigated three times. The third time, aged 70, he had been given up for dead, till he was found on his pontoon at Lymington four months later than expected. He had lost five stones, and had been living on a handful of rice a day.[22]

James Wharram and Hanneke Boon, building on their knowledge of Polynesian catamarans, kept developing the no-frills Tiki design of catamaran, which sold primarily as plans for self-build. The 36 foot version was launched in 1997. Rory McDougall, then aged 22, built himself *Cooking Fat,* a Tikka 21, in a barn near Newton Abbot, Devon, and set off on a circumnavigation from Totnes. He took one year to get to New Zealand, and, after a four-year break, sailed her home in 1997.[23]

In 2008, Wharram, now aged 80, with Hanneke Boon undertook a 4,000 mile voyage along the island chains of the Philippines, Indonesia, New Guinea and the Solomons in a double sailing canoe.[24]

Knox-Johnston has stayed a much revered figure in yachting, and probably more widely, due to his continued sailing ventures, such as replicating Columbus' voyage, using the instruments that Columbus used. With Peter Blake, in *ENZA,* he gained the record for the fastest non-stop circumnavigation

---

[18] Shepton, *Addicted to Adventure.*

[19] Willy Kerr, 'Refurbishing a Legend', 2014. Kerr is the author of the pilot guide to *Faroes, Iceland and Greenland.* You can hear him talk on You Tube. There is no recording of the taciturn Tilman.

[20] Cunliffe, *Topsail and Battleaxe.* One of his crew was Chris Stewart, the original drummer in the band, Genesis. Part Three of his *Three Ways to Capsize a Boat,* rather twee till then, is strong on the Vinland Voyage.

[21] Taylor, *Mingming and the Art of Minimal Ocean Sailing,* 2010; *MingMing and the Tonic of Wildness,* 2012; *Mingming II and Islands of the Ice,* 2016.

[22] Les Powles, *Hands Open,* 1987; *Solitaire Spirit,* 2012.

[23] www.jesterinfo.org/rorymcdougall

[24] Wharram, *Lapita Voyage,* CD.

in 1994 (seventy-four days) so he could joke that he held the records for the slowest (in *Suhaili*) and the fastest non-stop circumnavigations.[25]

At the institutional level, the Classic Boat Museum, Cowes, with its fine collection of yachts, opened in 1996; the impressive Jersey Maritime Museum at St Helier in 1997; and the National Maritime Museum, with its collection of historic craft used for leisure, at Falmouth in 2003. All are engaged in restoration work of old craft.

The loving restoration of old, wooden boats, the deliberate use of simple techniques, and the spurning of modern materials tie in with a number of nostalgia-utilising organisations, such as the Old Gaffers, Sail Training, Barge associations etc. There are a number of yards in Cornwall, especially around Penryn, which retain shipwright skills. The tradition is also continued by retro designs such as the Cornish Shrimper, built by Cornish Crabbers in fibreglass, at Rock, Cornwall.[26]

As mentioned earlier, another development using GRP, rather than the much more expensive build in wood, was the Devon Yawl, which uses the lines of the Salcombe yawl. This class was developed at Topsham Sailing Club in the early 1990s, with another fleet on the Yealm.[27]

At the other end of expense and ostentation, the restoration of old classic boats, such as original Fife and Watson yachts, became an industry, mainly for mainland European firms, supported by the super-rich. True, there is Cowes Classic Week at end of July, but the real place to show them off was and is the Mediterranean circuit.[28] The La Nioulargue regatta was started in 1991, but after a serious racing incident, where two boats rammed each other, it was suspended in 1995. In 1999, it was relaunched as Les Voiles de St Tropez. This regatta marks the end of the classic boat racing season, which includes the Regates Royales at Cannes.[29]

---

[25] Robin Knox-Johnston, *The Columbus Venture*, 1991; *Beyond Jules Verne*, 1995, the name of the trophy they won. Peter Blake, an America's Cup skipper, retired from racing and became an expedition leader. He was shot and killed by a pirate on the Amazon, 6 December, 2001 (see Alan Sefton, *Sir Peter Blake: An Amazing Life*).

[26] Sharp, 'Birth of a Modern Classic'.

[27] Chris Williams, *125 Years: Topsham Sailing Club 1885-2010*, pp. 19-21.

[28] See Nic Compton, *The Great Classic Yacht Revival*. The Mediterranean yachting scene of the very rich is now a quite large source of employment, with training courses available, for example at the National Sailing Academy, Cowes to teach you the relevant skills.

[29] It is not just competition between owners. Boat crews, for all the season having to act as flunkeys at the whim of their owners, have the opportunity to show their sailing skills during the races. To get the flavour of life on these classic yachts, see David Shalleck, *Mediterranean Summer: A Season on France's Cote d'Azur and Italy's Costa Bella*.

There was a revival of the J class, which now number some six boats. Most are replicas, but *Velsheda* was rescued after years in a mud berth in Hamble and, after major reconstructions, is now owned and raced by the Dutch businessman, Ronald de Waal.[30] These restorations are lovingly recorded and photographed under sail in *Classic Boat*, aimed squarely at the luxury retro end of the boat market. Started in 1996, in 2011 it celebrated twenty-five years of publication concerning the beautiful people and their boats, and is still being produced.[31]

Back home, texts for courses leading to RYA accreditation also sold well, in an increasingly exam-orientated world, the leader being Tom Cunliffe with his *The Complete Day Skipper* and *The Complete Yachtmaster*, to get you through the practical exams. Cunliffe, a Yachtmaster Examiner, writes with a light touch and is a leading yachting journalist. He also is the author of the *Shell Channel Pilot*. While most skippers have equipped their cruisers with electronic chart plotters, a pilot book is still reassuring. We first met the *Shell Channel Pilot* before the Second World War, when its author was Adlard Coles. He had handed it over to Jack Coote, so Cunliffe is only the third compiler in getting towards a century.[32]

A final trend of note is the active interest in Sailability – helping disabled people sail – among yacht clubs, strongly sponsored by the RYA. Some of the impetus for this has undoubtedly come from the National Lottery, which insists on equal opportunity and wheelchair access in allocating funds. A dramatic example of disabled sailing was in the round the world BT Global Challenge Race of 1996/1997. Skippered by James Hatfield, whose heart condition required eight operations before he was twenty-one, this mixed crew included amputees, people with hearing or sight loss, and two with cerebral

---

[30] Adrian Morgan, *The Trouble with Old Boats*, 2008, p. 18.

[31] In 2015, its long-term editor, Dan Houston left to start a new magazine *Classic Sailor*, with much the same material, but less obviously aimed at ' the beautiful people'. The Chelsea Magazine Company, which publishes *Classic Boat*, also publish *Sailing Today*, aimed at the cruising sailor seeking fresh waters (by chartering?) and the revamped *Yachts and Yachting*, aimed at keelboat and yacht racers. It may be that niche publications can survive better than newspapers in lean and internet-centred times, but the thinness of the major yachting magazines suggests otherwise. The 'niche' explanation would certainly seem useful in understanding the survival of the *Marine Quarterly*, a four times a year 'journal', only available on subscription, quirkily edited by Sam Llewellyn, which contains the best of past and present maritime writing.

[32] One sometimes fears that Cunliffe – perhaps Cunliffes is a better term, as he freely admits to his wife, Ros' organisational and business acumen – could be referred to the Monopoly Commission for he has written a book for each group with any growth. In the slot vacated by the late John Leather (1928–2006) and his *The Gaff Rig Handbook*, Cunliffe provides the basic text for retro sailors, *Hand, Reef and Steer*.

palsy.[33] More locally, there are over 200 RYA Sailability sites and hundreds of sailing and yacht clubs have taken part, most usually with modified dinghies. There are also specialist organisations for particular disabilities, such as Blind Sailing. Wetwheels Foundation modifies boats so that they are suitable for wheelchair sailors. Its CEO is Geoff Holt, who became paraplegic in 1982 as the result of a swimming accident. This has not stopped him sailing round Britain and across the Atlantic.[34] Holt has been very influential and active in Sailability, and his voyages have certainly raised public awareness. When fed up with being stuck in Abersoch, West Wales, for three weeks by bad weather, he checked and found that, since departing the Hamble, 'my website was averaging nearly 30,000 hits a day'.[35]

The Paralympics were organised immediately after the Olympic Games from 1988 onwards, getting ever bigger. Clubs supported the sailing competitors. For example, a disabled crew of Andy Cassell, Kevin Curtis and Tony Downes from Cowes Corinthian Club competed in the European Disabled Championships in Spain in 1995 and won, but needed Sonars to compete in the 1996 Paralympics in Atlanta, USA. The club raised the necessary funds. The team won a gold medal.[36] In 2000, sailing became a full part of the Paralympic programme.[37]

---

[33] Maria Cantacuzino, *On Equal Terms: The First Disabled Crew to Sail round the World*.

[34] Geoff Holt. *Walking on Water*, 2008, covers his voyage round Britain. Preface by Princess Anne, a rare modern day example of the monarch–yachting link; Digby Fox. 'A Remarkable Voyage' concerns Holt's Atlantic crossing, using *Impossible Dream*, an 18 metre carbon catamaran, designed by Nic Bailey for Mike Browne, also a disabled sailor, paralysed after a skiing accident. Fox takes his hat off to Susana Scott, the nurse who looked after Holt, having to move him on the rolling, pitching platform of a rigid catamaran. She had been partly chosen because of her lack of sailing experience. Besides the nursing, she spent the first week and then later two days upside down in the engine compartment, sorting out filthy fuel.

[35] Holt, *Walking on Water*, p. 224.

[36] Cave, *Cowes Corinthian Yacht Club*, pp. 24–25.

[37] In February 2015, the International Paralympic Committee announced that sailing was not being included in the Tokyo 2020 Paralympics.

... Before the Dark

Margaret Thatcher, prime minister from 1979 to 1990, broke the coal miners strike in 1984, as part of a general strategy of creating a malleable, docile workforce by reducing union power.[38] Partly as a result of this strategy, there was a recession from 1980 to 1985, with unemployment reaching 3 million. This was largely in the heavy industries, such as coalmining, shipbuilding and steel, which lost much of their capacity, and much of their skilled workforce. North Sea gas and oil, coming on line towards the end of the 1970s, concealed this major downturn in the nation's industrial production.

The British merchant navy had flourished after the war. However, lack of investment, the lower wages paid by non-British shipping lines, and ships travelling under 'flags of convenience', poorly supervised by the issuing countries, caused its decline and near demise within the space of a few years. In his book on the subject, *Long Voyage Home*, Tim Madge points out: 'It was only in 1975 that Britain had the greatest ever tonnage on her register ... from a peak tonnage of about thirty-three million gross registered tons in 1975, the British fleet fell away until by 1991 it reached 6.2 million gross registered tons' (147).[39] The number of professional fishermen was reduced by the Cod Wars with Iceland (1958–1976) and by the exhaustion of the fishing stock and quotas. In 1997, according to the Ministry of Fisheries and Agriculture, there were some 18,000 people employed fishing. By 2000, that had dropped to 17,000 and by 2006, to 13000. The shrinking of the Royal Navy was shown during the Falklands War (1982), when commercial ferries had to be requisitioned to take the troops to the South Atlantic. By 2014, the Royal Navy had only 33,000 men, the merchant marine 23,000.

As a result, the country's connection to the maritime world has nearly completely gone – a condition that has been referred to as 'sea blindness'.

Economically, the 1990s onwards were disastrous for the British yachting industry. From its peak in the 1970s and 1980s, British yacht production collapsed, under the onslaught from much larger French factories, with their economies of scale, such as Beneteau and Jeanneau. They, in turn, were undercut by German marques, such as Dehler, Bavaria, and especially Hanse,

---

[38] Thatcher could not convince the population of the rightness of the hegemonic narrative regarding this new economic system. As a result, her premiership was punctuated with examples of physical and legal domination which include the battle of Orgreave Colliery, where the police charged striking miners (18 June, 1984); the Battle of the Beanfield where the police charged travellers heading for Stonehenge (1 June, 1985); and colluding in the covering up of police negligence at the Hillsborough Stadium disaster (15 April, 1989).

[39] Madge, *Long Voyage Home*, p. 147.

benefiting from building in the old East Germany, and who later took over Dehler.[40] All these were seen as giving more value for less money, and also more modern designs. One by one, British manufacturers stopped production. Westerly went into administration for the first time in 1980, was sold, was back in receivership by 1991 and finally died in 2000. Moody was sold to the group that included Dehler and Hanse, but does not produce boats in any quantity. A similar fate befell Hunter Yachts, once the acme of well-produced, small to medium sized British yachts, taken over and the name retained in 2003, but not much else. By around 2000, there was little left of the British yachtbuilding industry, except at the luxury end, such as Rustler Yachts, Falmouth, and Oyster, Ipswich.[41] North Shore, who had seemed the height of British success, making the upmarket Southerly yachts, which could take the ground, and the sturdy Fisher motor sailers at Itchenor, Chichester Harbour, went into receivership in 2012 and died in 2014. Raymarine, makers of a wide range of electronic equipment for the nautical market, went into administration in 2010, and was bought by American firm, FLIR. Brookes and Gatehouse, now a subsidiary of the Norwegian company, Navico, transferred its production to Mexico in 2013. Sails are increasingly being ordered from Far Eastern factories, where labour costs are lower than in this country.[42]

The RYA began to license sailing schools in countries such as Portugal and Spain where one could learn to sail in more clement conditions. As a result, the number of sailing schools in the UK fell sharply during this period.

There was also a large expansion in chartering yachts abroad. Companies, such as Sunsail, operate in most areas of the world, but much of their business is in the Mediterranean. They offer tuition to the newcomer, both in the Solent before their holiday, and during the flotilla week and also at their holiday water activity centres.

The Boat Show moved to ExCeL in London's Dockland in 2004, with an attendance, curious to see the change from Earl's Court, of 213,000. After the financial crash of 2008, it stabilised at around 100,000, down from 154,211 in 2002. In 2015, it attracted only 92,000.

---

[40] 'Old East Germany': After the collapse of the Berlin Wall in 1989, West and East Germany were re-united in 1990. East Germany was far poorer, so received subsidies.

[41] See Rupert Holmes, 'Best of British', 2014, who adds Petticrows of Burnham-on-Crouch, who have built 700 Dragons over the past 25 years; Green Marine, Hythe built VO65s for the Volvo Ocean Race; Discovery Yachts, Southampton, build half-a-dozen top end cruising yachts each year; Cornish Crabbers, Rock, Cornwall, have now sold over 1,000 Shrimpers.

[42] Holmes, 'Best of British', p. 43.

Sailing organisations fared little better. Chay Blyth's 'The Challenge Business', ran for its fourth and final time in 2004/2005 and went into administration in October 2006.

The Ocean Youth Trust (previously Club) was operating from various bases across the country when, due to financial difficulties in 1999, it had to close its central office in Gosport and become a cooperative of four separate sail training charities (OYT South, OYT Scotland, OYT North East and OYT Ireland).[43]

Yacht club membership was declining. For example, in South Wales, in 1974, Barry Yacht Club's membership reached 887 and the list was closed. In 1998, the club had 515 members. In 2013, it had 273.[44] The Yacht Club offers moorings in soft mud and the mooring area is highly tidal, so it may well have lost out to Penarth marina, which opened in 1987 and the Cardiff and the Cardiff Bay Yacht Clubs, whose pontoons were safely behind the Barrage by 1999. However, it is likely that such a decline in membership was not unusual, the reason being that people's leisure time was getting more restricted – a theme I will return to in the final chapter.

In accord with the greater competitiveness, by the end of the 1970s, there was a decline in inter-club *team* racing competitions, and an increase in open races where the best helmsmen competed, bringing their own boat to race in a single class race; and the RYA was becoming increasingly active in encouraging competitiveness and 'excellence'.[45]

Not surprisingly with the downturn in interest, yachting became of less interest to the media. An indication of this comes from Dun Laoghaire. The history of the Water Wags records that Jack Kennedy, a keen local sailor, 'was most efficient at ensuring that all sailing results [in Dublin Bay] appeared in all the national Irish newspapers'. He died in 1991 and 'After Jack's passing, sailing results [in Dublin Bay] were only printed intermittently and Water Wag Club results never'.[46]

Yachting publications showed a sharp decline. Yacht racing had never attracted the newspapers or publishers, except for coffee table accounts of the major races. The major exception is dramatic rescues. There were two of these in the Southern Ocean in the Vendée Globe of 1996/1997. Peter Goss

---

[43] Ocean Youth Club–Ocean Youth Trust, *50 Years of Adventure under Sail*
[44] Norman C. Hockley, *Barry Yacht Club … and 50 Years On*; also data kindly provided by the Club Archivist, Mike Righton. Quoted in my 'Leisure Sailing on a Hostile Shore', p. 302.
[45] Videlo, *Frensham Pond Sailing Club: The First Fifty Years*, p. 53.
[46] Delaney and Delaney, *The Water Wags 1887–2012*, p. 94.

sailed 160 miles beating into a hurricane to rescue Raphael Dinelli,[47] and Tony Bullimore spent five days in an air pocket in his upside down catamaran, *Exide Challenger*, surviving on small bits of chocolate, till rescued by the Australian navy.[48]

Minor exceptions to this trend were that a number of sailing thrillers were published, most notably by Sam Llewellyn and Bernard Cornwell.[49] Also, a small group of women humorists were published. First on the scene was Lesley Black, her position summed up in the title of her first book, *Must I Go Down to the Sea Again?* 1983. Libby Purves had been writing a humorous column for *Yachting Monthly* for some years; the best were collected into her *This Cruising Life* in 2001. Purves has done some serious sailing, so her writing is more about the exasperating side of sailing. Finally, Hilary Harron looks at the trials of a yachting couple in *Right to the Bitter End*, 1995.[50]

By the 1990s, books about voyages were only published if the book had novelty value. Stanford Maritime closed in 2007. Adlard Coles, the defining publisher of yachting books of importance, was taken over by A & C Black, who did have nautical publishing expertise, in 1990. Black, in turn, was taken over by Bloomsbury, rich from the profits of the Harry Potter books, in 2000.

Yachting is a sensitive thermometer of national wellbeing. Its activity level, the type of activities and the ownership structure all relate to the wider economic and political context. Something was happening or about to happen, and the signs in all areas of yachting activity were there for some years before 2008, just as the late Victorian boom in yachting finished some fifteen years before the outbreak of the First World War. British yacht building, yachting publishing, and yacht club memberships were all in sharp decline. Long before the 2008 crash, British yachting, along with much of British industry, was being eviscerated, a hollowed shell, a shop front for imported goods. Yachting activity had clearly contracted quite dramatically, which was not surprising, as yachtspeople – actual or potential – were in posts and positions that meant they knew that the system was unsustainable, and changed their leisure patterns accordingly.

---

[47] In 1997, Goss received the Légion d'Honneur for this rescue (Peter Goss, *Close to the Wind*, 1998).

[48] Tony Bullimore, *Saved*, 1997.

[49] Desmond Lowden, *Cry Havoc*, 1984; Sam Llewellyn. Quite a number including *Dead Reckoning*, 1987 and *Riptide*, 1992; Bernard Cornwell. *Wildtrack*, 1988; *Sea Lord*, 1989; *Stormchild*, 1991. Cornwell then decided to focus on historical adventures, with his *Sharpe* series.

[50] Black also wrote *Still Wet Behind the Ears*, 1986 and Harron *Involuntary Jibes*, 1998.

CHAPTER SIXTEEN

After the Crash

Billy Connolly, in his funeral oration for the shipbuilders' union leader, Jimmy Reid, on 20 August, 2010, described walking through Govan, Glasgow, with him. Connolly recalled Reid's words:

> You look at these housing estates, and these high rise flats. Look at all these windows, he says, and behind every one of those windows, there's somebody who might be a horse-jumping champion, a Formula One racing champion, a yachtsman of great degree, but you'll never know because he'll never step on a yacht or in a Formula One car, or that. He'll never get the chance.[1]

In this chapter, I bring the narrative of British yachting into the present and look at pointers towards its future. While I am confident of the trends I suggest, I can be less precise about timing, and recognise that there will be some regional, and even local, variations.

The 2008 Banking Crisis and financial crash were caused by reckless mortgage lending and other risky financial behaviours by British bankers. The taxpayers had to lend (give?) billions of pounds to the banks to bail them out, resulting in the longest economic slump in modern British history.

The grounds for such an event had been created from the 1980s onwards, as successive governments believed that the economy could only flourish if they gave the multinationals all they demanded in terms of a docile workforce.[2] This required that they provided a cheap workforce, and a fearful one, by removing the financial and legal safety nets for anyone who was not working – mothers who believe that bringing their children up is a full-time job, the poor, the ill, the old.

---

[1] Billy Connolly, Oration at Jimmy Reid's Funeral, 20 August, 2010. www.stv.tv/video Redirect. cfm?refid ... connollyfull

[2] This chapter was written before the June 2016 referendum on the UK's membership of the European Union. The decision to leave probably strengthens the predictions made in this chapter.

The impact of political or social issues on yachting is not discussed in the yachting press. There are three large-selling magazines in the United Kingdom: *Practical Boat Owner,* catering for the smaller boat sailor who wishes to undertake his own maintenance; *Yachting Monthly*, aimed at the cruising, middle-size, yacht owner; and *Yachting World*, concerned with yacht racing and super yachts. All are owned by the same company, IPC (International Publishing Corporation, now part of Time Inc. UK), and editorial staff move freely between them. Given this near monopoly situation, there is a lack of alternative views or vision. The stance is staunchly apolitical, so that they do not comment on the political context of sailing.

As a result, they do not reflect social changes. The rigidity of traditional class, sex roles and orientation boundaries remains.[3] The economics of sailing have always discouraged members of the lower socio-economic classes from participating. During their teens, they might have experienced a free or subsidised week on a Sail Training vessel but there seems little provision for any affordable follow-up.

The rigidity of traditional sex roles remains. The RYA magazine, Summer 2016, looked at four ladies-only sailing groups.[4] Two of the four emphasised their femininity – the Torbay Tiller Girls, a pun on the troupe of dancing girls nationally popular between the 1900s and 1950s, and the Ditsum (Dittisham, South Devon) Belles, whose officer of the day is called the Belle of the Day. The need to avoid being seen as butch, as with the previously discussed Girls for Sail, still seems to resonate.

Civil partnerships for gay men and women were enacted in 2004, and commenced in 2005. The Equality Act of 2010 made any discrimination illegal. Gay marriage was legalised in 2014. Despite this legislation, there is almost no evidence of gay men or women, let alone mention of people who are bisexual or transgender, in yachting. magazines. In 2005, the Gay Sailing and Cruising Association celebrated its first twenty-five years of catering for gay and lesbian yachting people. It has a membership of about 400.[5] However, at least till recently, its visibility was very muted among the 'straight' and the yachting press.

---

[3] In yachting magazines, sex does not seem to happen, except as adolescent excitement, e.g. ladies in negligees on deck when a wind shift causes the boats in a popular anchorage, usually Newtown Creek, Isle of Wight, to drag in the middle of the night ('My powerful flashlight picked out the Commodore's wife ...' etc.)

[4] RYA Magazine, Summer 2016: 58–59.

[5] www.gaysailing.org.uk

Regarding race, judging from the yachting magazines' pictures and stories, yachting appears almost 100 per cent white. Presumably this is due to a mixture of self-selection and well- or ill-founded fear of racial prejudice. Certainly, yachting does not have the stigma of anti-semitism that golf clubs did. A reasonable hypothesis is that immigrant families, even when second or third generation, do not feel that the world of yachting is for them.

The Future: 'Being for the Most Part Puppets'[6]: Time the Contested Resource

Clearly, in an economic depression, people will not have the money to buy yachts. Since poorer people have smaller yachts, what will be most visible will be the sharp decrease in the number of small boats. However, we need to try and be more specific as to the key aspects raised by the advance of neo-liberal capitalism, so that we can see how they affect yachting.

The central relationship is buyer–seller. So, a person, however well trained, however well paid, and in whatever occupation, is not treated as a professional who is best placed to decide how a task should be tackled. Rather, they are construed as selling their time and skills to achieve goals set by managers. *Neo-liberal capitalism defines a person's sole relevant identity as that concerning work.* It insists that the work identity is the only one of any importance, and roles such as parent, child of one's parents, follower of a religion, holder of positions of responsibility in civic or professional organisations, are all of minor importance, and an irritating irrelevance (unless they can be shown to bring benefits to the employer). The employer has no responsibility, unless legally required, to support such roles, such as giving time off for caring for a sick relative or to attend a funeral.

The central issue in the continuation of leisure sailing is not money, but time. Wealth and plentiful leisure time used to be linked, so that the rich disappeared for long summer holidays. The 'comfortably off' professional middle classes took a two- or three-week, or longer, summer cruise. This has changed. Banks and investment houses etc. are still prepared to pay very high wages and bonuses but now expect the worker to devote themselves to their job.

Sailors are not in control of the weather (or the tide), so, if they go sailing any distance, they cannot guarantee to get the boat back to its base. But not showing up on time for the first day of return to work could prove very costly.

---

[6] The title of a book by William R. Torbert. The quote is from 'An Athenian Stranger' in Plato's *Laws*.

The worker – however well trained – is no longer trusted to make up lost time and catch up with any backlog. This fear must limit the freedom with which the person sails.

I have not mentioned 'global warming' or to be more exact, global meteorological instability. The effect of this is that summers offer less predictable weather, stronger winds, and less guaranteed sunshine, and therefore yet further reduction in the number of days available for sailing.[7]

I have pointed out, throughout this book, that there are several ways of relating to the sea, which co-exist, though one may be dominant at a given time. It is not so long ago that people went sailing 'to get away from it all', following in the wake of the inter-war Essex creek-crawlers, like Maurice Griffiths. Mairi Hedderwick wrote an account of a six-week cruise around the West of Scotland, *Sea Change*, in a 26 foot boat, with the line 'Everything within hand's reach and me outwith anyone's reach'. Although it was published as recently as 1999, such a long time away from work is of a different, bygone era.[8]

In contrast, neo-liberal capitalism is offering a new relationship to the sea and sailing, and is something of a paradigm change. It competes with, and to large extent replaces, the use of the yacht to escape, highlighted in the inter-war period; or the location of quality family time, practised as families came aboard in the 1970s and 1980s. Instead, *the yacht becomes a twilight zone between work and leisure,* the interface mediated through the mobile and computer, now combined in the smart phone, and using satellite communication – not so much rest and relaxation, but recharging and readiness. If both of the adults in a partnership are working, their freedom is even more compromised. (But one might, almost perversely, argue that it is only by allowing

---

[7] An indicator of global warming is that yachts can now sail both the North West passage (through Canadian waters) and the North East passage (from the Atlantic to the Pacific above Russia) – see Andrew Wilkes, *Arctic and Northern Waters*, 2014. Leading yachtsmen who have commented on their experience of how global warming is making sailing less predictable and often more dangerous include David Cowper, who took three seasons to get through the North West Passage starting in 1986; in 2012, he did it in nineteen days. See his 'The North West Passage 1986–2012'. Jimmy Cornell, in *Yachting World*, February 2016: 36–42, likewise comments on the unpredictability of Arctic sailing, while Rod Heikell describes the increasing turbulence of Atlantic and Pacific waters (*Sailing Today,* January 2014: 21).

[8] Mairi Hedderwick, *Sea Change: The Summer Voyage from East to West Scotland of the 'Anassa',* p. 98. It is, incidentally, also out of date in terms of valorising a twenty-six foot yacht, when the contemporary 'entry' boat (into yacht ownership) is now forty foot. The 1999 publication date might seem to contradict my assertion in the last chapter that accounts of cruising became unpublishable, but Hedderwick is the best-selling author of the *Katie Morag* children stories and her fine pen and ink illustrations adorn the book.

themselves to be accessible at all time to their work that they can go sailing at all).[9]

There may be a temptation on the part of readers to see the present difficulties as part of the normal stop–go of the economy. Slumps have, traditionally, been ended by increased productivity in the manufacturing sector; but this sector is showing a continual decline in this country, as we saw, in the previous chapter, when considering firms relating to yachting. So, the mechanisms, the levers, by which the country moves out of recession are no longer available.

The problem is deeper than another boom–bust cycle. The economic script has been re-written. The government, of whatever hue, is relatively helpless to stop multi-nationals moving production to wherever they deem is most profitable. Likewise, the attempt to ensure the availability of a low paid and docile workforce is doomed to failure, because there will always be Far Eastern or South American countries with even lower wages for work in poorer conditions than in Britain.

The facts and figures available from yachting offer no comfort to an optimistic view.[10] A survey by the British Marine Federation, reported in the *Practical Boat Owner*, showed a vacancy rate of marina berths of 20 per cent.[11] Out of a possible 29,118, 23,462 berths were occupied. Arkenford, a social research company, provide a yearly market report on yachting. Between 2002 and 2012, the numbers taking part in yacht cruising went down from 433 to 333k; in yacht racing from 153 to 106k; in small boats from 606 to 388k; and small boat racing from 333 to 165k.[12] In 2002, 154,000 people, according to an ABC audit, attended the London Boat Show. In 2016, the unaudited attendance was 90,328.[13]

---

[9] I am grateful to Alison Bender for making this rather sobering point to me.

[10] Similar downturns are reported in other prestige sports. In England, golf club membership dropped 20 per cent between 2004 and 2013, from 882,184 to 707, 424, and in Scotland by 14 per cent to 227,292 during that period (Kate Youde, 'Rough Time for Golf', *Independent on Sunday*, 24 August, 2014). According to BBC Sport, 9 May, 2011, the numbers playing rugby union at least once a week decreased from 230,000 in 2009 to 177,900 in 2015. The English and Wales Cricket Board reported a drop of 908,000 playing the sport in 2013 to 844,000 in 2015. The main reason seemed to be that league matches take up too much time (Nick Hoult, *Daily Telegraph*, 19 November, 2014).

[11] *Practical Boat Owner*, June 2013: 7.

[12] Tim Bartlett, 'What's the Future of Sailing?' 2013.

[13] *All at Sea*, February 2016: 4.

What Happens Now? Who Survives?

I will divide my analysis into the situation of two generations, those who are working in well-paid jobs and who, it might be thought, would find yachting an attractive pastime; and the older generation, moving towards retirement.

Let us examine the decision matrix of the person who is attracted to the idea of sailing. If we return to the necessary conditions for a sailing community to flourish (p. 97), the potential sailor(s) must have sufficient leisure time, under their control, to make sailing worthwhile. It is highly likely that, if married/in a partnership, both salaries are needed. They must also have confidence in their future, secure employment. All these conditions are being continually undermined. They are dealing with much higher levels of uncertainty and lack of control than the previous generation.[14] If in their twenties and thirties, they have to pay back their education costs (plus compound interest) if they are earning a reasonable wage; they have much less job security, and no comeback if the minimal legal requirements for removing them have been adhered to; and cannot look forward to a generous pension. The demands on the leisure time that is available – the children's sports day, visiting their parents, going to the theatre or cinema, the meal with friends etc. – all compete, further reducing boat use, a situation that may well be complicated by both working, both with different demands from work, and separate primary familial responsibilities. It is hard to see, in this scenario, how they will become proficient in yachting, and even less likely that they will purchase a yacht.

While the number of days' leave may not have changed that much, the content of that leave has changed radically. The relevant dimension is the *impermeability vs. permeability of leisure time (work intrusion)*. As electronic communication has become ever faster and more pervasive, so workers are expected to respond with less and less time delay. To achieve this, they need to be available, so the boundaries of the eight-hour day, the five-day week, the weekend and the holidays, including Bank holidays, become increasingly open to intrusion from work. This is happening on a very large scale, as people take work home with them, and contact people via the internet on work matters from home during the evening and at weekends.

---

[14] As Suzanne Moore, *Guardian, Review*, 20 May, 2015: 5 put it, 'So often when I am talking to young people I realise that it is now utterly pointless to speak about what it was like for me. It is now a different world, and yet the fundamental myths, the founding stories, if you like, of what it is like to be grown up have not shifted.'

As a result of these changes, leisure sailing is shrinking, and there have been major changes in types of aquatic leisure activity. *A major resultant of decreased leisure time is the need to reach relaxation or enjoyable stimulation quickly.* This is doubtless some part of the motivation behind binge drinking of spirits, and of recreational drugs (reaching a 'high' quickly); and, on the water, for adrenalin-rush adventure sports, such as kite-surfing. The water sports enthusiast must grab their opportunity when, and only when, work permits, and often this is not under their control. They need sports they can pick up, enjoy for a few hours and put down, with minimal preparation and maintenance.

So, the very merit of sailing – slow relaxation – may well be antithetical to the needs of the younger generation.

Because time has become tied to the demands of work, so the activity has to be predictable and controllable as to time use. Dinghy racing fulfils these conditions far better than yachting. A dinghy race in the evening or at weekend is time-limited. It allows competition on the water, and conviviality at the bar afterwards. The dinghy can, usually, be safely left in the dinghy park till needed.

However, dinghy sailing may also be suffering from time constraints. It also may be too staid. If the person wishes for an adrenalin rush, they may well have to buy the latest, and most expensive, model. Another risk is that clubs use development or restricted classes of dinghies, where money talks and wins through buying better designed models, sails are changed more often etc. If clubs allow such moves, they will lose one of their strengths – skill, not money, as the determinant of winning, and members will lose interest.

Pilot gig racing has become very popular, especially in southwest England, with an annual World Championship in the Scillies, and Wales. You step into the boat, you row for a certain amount of time, you step out and are free to go home or to work after that. Both gig racing and dinghy racing allow for the expression of competitiveness within a group setting. They have the further merit of being more (apparently) classless, both of which attributes are in tune with the modern business psyche.[15]

Another challenge to sailing is from kayaking. Here is a highly mobile form of aquatic activity, and one which provides the Corinthian challenge of being close to, and battling with, nature.

---

[15] In making sense of the class structure in today's Britain in *Social Class in the 21st Century*, Savage and his colleagues use the variables of social capital, cultural capital and age, as well as economic capital. Social capital is partially measured on the range of people one knows.

But the big challenge is from water sports that use boards rather than sails, or more exactly, boats, since windsurfers and kite-surfers use sails. It feels almost evolutionary the way in which sail is dying as board sports take over, which is not surprising, as the various forms of surfing are far more flexible than sailing. Wet suits and dry suits have both been around for a long time but are now made of better quality material and are cheaper and more fashion-conscious. Also, with a surfboard or a kayak, you are, unlike a yachtsman, not making a large, initial investment, second only to the cost of property, not tied to a single location where the yacht is moored; and the maintenance costs – both in terms of time and money – are much less.

Unlike sailing, these sports can be engaged in all the year round. In contrast, there is no point a yacht owner thinking in December that it would be a nice day to go for a sail if their boat is laid up on a hard.

These competing aquatic sports give rise to yet another cause for concern for the longer term well-being of yachting. Most children, I suspect, learn their leisure pursuits from their parents. *Their parents socialise them to become potential sailors.*[16] One might call this process *intergenerational legacy* – the unspoken handing down of the enjoyment and skills of sailing. If their parents are not sailing, because they have preferred, and become skilled in, other aquatic sports such as board sailing, then it is unlikely that their children will take up yacht sailing 'from cold' when they are older.[17]

And the future is not bright. If we bear in mind Roger Ryan's dictum that yachting is the sport of the middle class, then yachting's well-being and middle-class 'health' are interrelated. But the problem for yachting is that *the middle class is shrinking*, especially for its younger members, as part-time, zero hours 'self-employment' and unpaid 'internships' eat away at the entry jobs into the professions – the apprenticeships, the jobs on probation.[18] For the established professionals, the professions are continually having the simpler tasks – or even, not that simple tasks – being given to a burgeoning

---

[16] Horne *et al.*, *Understanding Sport*, Chapter 5: 'Approaches to Socialisation', pp. 129–140.

[17] To be more exact, parents set an example in showing to them the pleasures of family sailing. Then, after a gap of some years to establish an independent identity and probably go to university, they consider what form of leisure activity they want to take part in and choose sailing.

[18] Savage, in *Social Class in the 21st Century*, points out that many students, unable to get good jobs after graduation, become part of the 'precariat', working in fast food outlets or pubs. They may find this environment remarkably 'sticky' and, if not escaped from quickly, difficult to extricate themselves from. Regarding shrinkage of career opportunities, in universities, much of the teaching is done by Ph.D. students, or graduates hired only to teach a specific course, so neither group is being offered any job security. In quite a number of our universities, including leading ones, the great majority of the staff are not on permanent contracts (Aditya Chark-abortty, 'Dawn Cleaning Shift, Shower, then Teach: Survival as a Lecturer').

army of assistants, who stand little chance of joining those professions. With a shrinking professional class, social mobility from below becomes reduced, and these may well be the people most concerned with their new status, which yacht club membership and boat ownership used to confer and confirm. So yachting's constituency is getting smaller, and it is shrinking further as potential constituents prefer more immediate, more exciting and less costly sports.

Let us turn to the members of the older generation, retired or moving towards retirement. It is received wisdom that the person buying a yacht used to do this towards the end of their forties or in their fifties, as the mortgage on their house became paid off. The scenario I outlined in the previous chapter, concerning ocean cruising, is now becoming history for a number of reasons. Years of very low interest rates means that the retired persons' savings are earning far less than they used to. Even more important is the desire of the older generation to support their children from the effects on their income and time use of the neo-liberal economy. There is an ever-expanding intergenerational black economy. Even if older parents are able to save, the need to contribute to the living standards of their offspring decreases their spending power. Again, *time is the key variable*. Their free time is restricted. A key part of this black economy is the 'free' childcare they offer, especially crucial with the high rate of divorce. The Office of National Statistics in 2013 gave the divorce rate as 42 per cent, and presumably the frequency of break-up of non-married, but long-term, partnerships is equal or greater, and the time needed to support a working single parent with one or more children may be considerable. But divorced or not, the long hours worked mean that much of the salary earned would go in childcare, if it were not for the grandparents' free childcare. So, a generation that might have thought they would be sailing whenever they wanted to, is having their ability to get afloat restricted.

It is the older age-group of yachtspeople that provides the volunteers on committees and work parties, and would-be flag officers. The lack of people coming forward for these roles and positions is already a problem for many clubs, making the very running of the club itself difficult.

Combining the choices facing the two generations, people may hold onto their yachts, even when they use them infrequently. So, yachting activity – the number of boats moving on the water – will decline much more sharply than the number of boats in marinas and on moorings. This will have a number of effects.

Rapid access to the location of the leisure pursuit will be an increasingly important determinant in the choice of leisure activity. Clubs on the Isle of Wight are inconveniently distant for mainland sailors, and the Royal Corinthian 'merged' with the Royal Ocean Racing Club in 2014. On the Clyde, the population, in Glasgow, is some distance from the yachting centres. The clubhouse of the Royal Northern and Clyde at Helensburgh was put up for sale in February, 2016. This is a major club – the Royal Northern going back to 1824, and the Royal Clyde having the largest membership and the largest tonnage of any yacht club in Britain around 1900. In the Republic of Ireland, the historically important Royal Alfred Yacht Club has amalgamated with the Dublin Bay Sailing Club. It is hard to believe that all the clubs on the Crouch can survive.[19]

Inevitably, leisure cruising for more than two weeks will decrease, and sailing will be squeezed into the weeks of school holidays. Another visible trend in yachting havens is the considerable increase in small motorboats, the so-called 'pêche plaisir' (fishing/recreation). Since the largest producer of such vessels is Beneteau, this switch again weakens yachting and creates little industry in Britain.

Additionally, many people who know how to sail are chartering abroad. That way, they do not have the expense of maintaining a yacht, and there is a better chance of good weather. The flotilla holiday village in the Med. may also cater much better for the differing needs and wishes of the various family members.[20] Both trends have serious consequences for the British yachting industry, in terms of people buying boats, doing them up, renting marina berths etc.

Ocean racing, already dominated by professionals, will become a purely professional circuit, akin to Formula One racing.[21]

Long-distance racing by amateurs will sharply decline, although the one-off, prestige race, for which leave can be booked months in advance, whether for yachts or dinghies, will still attract large numbers. For example, the Round the Island (Isle of Wight) Race regularly has some 1,700 entries, involving some 16,000 sailors, making it the fourth largest participation sporting event in the UK after the London Marathon, the Great North and the Great South

---

[19] Amalgamations will certainly not be without pain. John Basley, archivist of the Medway Yacht Club (personal communication, 14 January, 2017) pointed out that 'on the stretch between Rochester Bridge and Sheerness (about 13 miles) there are 14 Yacht Clubs, 5 Marinas and 4 training and/or education centres. Some have proud traditions that they would be loath to surrender. Others have been founded to meet the needs of local yachtsmen and in consequence offer different services and charge varying fees.'

[20] Rupert Holmes, 'Families Afloat'.

[21] George Corlett, 'FI Factor'; GAC Pindar and Jane Hyde, 'Secret Scenes behind Racing'.

Runs.[22] However, yacht racing at club level, especially among larger yachts requiring a number of crew, will decline quite rapidly. Racing series over a number of evening and/or weekends will suffer much decreased numbers, as the unpredictable nature of work demands force non-attendance by would-be competitors. That strange hybrid, cruiser racing, will disappear.

What may survive are fleets of one-designs, especially keelboats. These are very clearly status symbols, as they are expensive to buy new, and expensive to maintain with any realistic chance of winning, especially in restricted or development classes.

Yacht clubs are an important part of sailing. Certainly, what has been lost is the feeling of *belonging* to a yacht club, of mucking in, of community. In my research, I visited a lot of clubs, and, frequently, members would proudly tell of the pioneering days – when they built the extension, created a car park over the river mud, came together to rebuild after a fire. Some clubs try to replace this integral or integrated community spirit with demands for episodic help with members agreeing to pay so much to club funds if they cannot make their four half days per annum etc., but this indicates that these *episodic acts of community* are now having to be phrased in economic terms; and, at the larger yacht clubs, no such demands are made, as the relationship is seen as a financial transaction.[23]

Also, if people are sailing less, they will use their yacht club less, decreasing its takings, and also increasing the member's unit cost per use, so that they may decide they are not getting value for money. An even more severe problem in many yacht clubs is the ageing membership, which is not being replaced. Most yacht clubs are seeing a decline in the size of their racing fleets and declining member activity, if not membership numbers; and, of course, the smaller the yacht club, the more serious any loss of membership is.

A sharp decline in members of a yacht club who are racing is more serious than reduced numbers of members cruising. It is the racing crowd that both needs the organisation the yacht club provides – the races, the safety boats, referees ('officers of the day'), the courses to be sailed and often marker buoys, etc.; and it is they who energise the club and who pile into the bar after races. They are younger and livelier. Without them, the club is a much duller and financially poorer place.

---

[22] *All at Sea*, June 2016: 24.

[23] The sociologically minded will recognise the dichotomy of *gemeinschaft* (community) versus *gesellschaft* (economic ties), written about by the German sociologists, Ferdinand Tonnies and Max Weber.

But there is more than just the financial view. An important aspect of being part of a yacht club is the networking and friendships formed there. A declining membership, which is getting older and less willing to go out in the evenings, leads to the club only being opened at certain times on certain days, and means that its utility and relevance as a place to meet and network social and business contacts, decreases. At this point, the greater ease of access and more frequent opening of clubs concerned with other prestige sports, such as racket sports or golf, may cause a yet further loss of membership.

Many yacht clubs, for a long time, have been encouraging cadet sailing – teaching youngsters how to sail. Watching a long row of dinghies go past, interspersed every so often by a father in a large safety RIB, is an impressive sight. Aspiring parents encourage such activity as offering 'value' to their child's CV – a commercial exchange, rather than sailing for its own sake.[24] Talking to instructors of such schemes, the problem is that the 'conversion rate' of these youngsters to yachting is low, and they get 'lost' as they progress through 'A' levels and university and do not return.

The day of reckoning might be delayed by horizontal integration with other water sports, so that links could be made with sub-aqua and fishing,[25] and by incorporating the members of the ever expanding gig racing organisations. Kayakers, board and windsurfers likewise could also be admitted. Though the yacht club may keep its name, it would be, in effect, a water sports centre.

A few of the senior clubs may have a future, with less emphasis placed on sailing activity, but with the yachts providing a mobile, prestigious, visual backdrop to entertain the members' bosses, the owners and major shareholders, from China, the Middle East or America. Effectively the yacht club becomes a high-class dining club, although their house magazine will foreground their handful of racing members, with glossy pictures of their boats under full sail. Likewise, in some coastal villages, the yacht club will continue primarily as a prestigious social club for incomers and second-homers, with a small yachting fraternity attached.

Peter Poland, visiting France, reports that town councils often own the beach, where dinghies can be left for free. Learning to sail in a French sailing school costs half what the same course would cost in England.[26] Many of the marinas are defunct fishing harbours which the community developed and run, charging half the fees of an English equivalent. So, sailing is affordable

[24] Corlett, 'School Colours'.
[25] For example, the Swansea Yacht and Sub-Aqua Club.
[26] Poland, 'Broadside', 2014.

by, and belongs to, the community. It is hard to see that this model could be used in this country, where most of the land is privately owned and councils do not have the money, nor are encouraged, to run such schemes.

Rather, the situation is running downhill. Harbours or yacht club moorings that are not accessible for the great percentage of the time are not fit for contemporary purpose. Similarly, those where a sand bar limits access, will suffer from decline. Large coastal areas of the British Isles, such as the Bristol Channel and West Wales, have problems with silting by silt or mud. Dredging is very expensive. Without sufficient income, the companies or councils will not have the money to dredge, rendering their harbours or marinas inoperable.

Where the harbour or marina is within commuting distance of work, one likely use, or re-use, is for it to become a floating village of live-aboards.[27]

As all these factors kick in, there comes a tipping point where fewer and fewer people are using the resources of a club or marina, so those resources become more expensive and fewer and fewer people can afford them. This may eventually mean that only the elite, and the senior managers and professionals who help them maintain their wealth, will be able to afford marinas, which will be, effectively, gated communities. This is likely to go hand in hand with a smaller number of locations, and for any given location, a few successful organisations or clubs. So, yachting, not surprisingly, will mimic the economy, with a few, select, large organisations, while many other clubs going to the wall.

There may be regional differences. The momentum behind sailing in the Solent area – say, from Weymouth and Portland to Chichester – is far greater than in the rest of the country; and this momentum is based on the acknowledged advantages of networking, with so many people in one's business area engaged in the same sport and using the same yacht clubs as oneself. It may be that the Solent area will maintain a yachting culture, whilst it becomes rudimentary in other areas of the country.

Throughout this book, I have suggested that yachting, as an activity, is given its personal importance, its emotion pull, by the meanings the sailor gives to sailing and the sea. Yachting has been underpinned and supported by four key areas, so that, when one sails, one engages in an activity with powerful associated imagery. But in the last thirty or so years, the relationship

---

[27] Bristol's Floating Harbour is full of such live-aboard yachts. Of course, this response to a severe housing shortage is not a new phenomenon. After the Second World War, with so much housing in ruins, many ex-military craft were converted into houseboats (Sharp, *Troubled Waters*, p. 201).

between the people and the maritime has diminished greatly.[28] The emotional power of the cluster of values which infused yachting with meaning – masculinity, patriotism, class and links with the Navy – now seem out of date and unfashionable. Considering each in turn:

Masculinity: Once women came on board, and especially once they raced and won races, the relationship of masculinity to sailing was always going to become more complicated. It is doubtful whether being a yachtsman is seen as a useful definition of masculinity by today's younger generations. It is too rigid. It carries too much baggage. The teenager who board sails well is surely acting out a much more potent definition of masculinity. Also, defining oneself so clearly by membership of an upper-class sport may not be seen as a very intelligent move, when one needs to have the flexibility to adapt to one's boss' definition of a valued identity. Indeed, such an identity may cause particular irritation.

Patriotism: The Royal family, with the exception of Princess Anne, does not sail. It is no longer the must-do sport of senior Establishment figures, whether of the old or new elites. The portrait of the young, tiara-ed, queen on the wall is almost the only reminder of this once powerful sentiment.

Class: Yachting has always been characterised by being exclusive. The excluded will never sit in the cockpit of a yacht watching the sun go down, or beat to windward. Abroad, the indigenous population, with the rare exception of a very few, very wealthy or powerful 'native' members, were excluded. At home, those earning a wage were kept out. Given falling standards of living, it seems unlikely that yachting can now reverse this history, even if there was the will do so.

Links with Professional Seamen: The idea that the sea is in every Englishman and woman's blood now seems farfetched, because the number of British men and women who work on the sea are so few in number. No more do men come home from the sea, drop their kitbag in the hall, and over a cup of tea, regale their long un-seen children, sitting wide-eyed on their knee, with tales of far-off lands and storms survived. Instead, the sea is now little more than the medium in which car ferries take them quickly to the continent;[29] or which provides a floating holiday aboard a stabilised cruise liner.

---

[28] The closure of museums, due to cuts in councils' budgets, will make maritime history even less visible (David Henshall, 'Saving History').

[29] Which is why the Zeebrugge Ferry Disaster of 6 March, 1987, with 193 passengers killed when the bow doors were left open, was so shocking – conveyor belts aren't supposed to behave like that.

When a narrative is dying, it can generate regretful sentimentality, for example, in suggesting that everyone hums 'Sailing By'; but this is empty rhetoric.[30] Charlie Connelly, in *Attention All Shipping*, visited every sea area mentioned in the shipping forecast and the sea-side towns in them. Yet, except for two brief mentions, yachting doesn't exist in his travels. Connelly must have gone past thousands of yachts, yet he didn't see them.[31] Belloc ends *The Cruise of the 'Nona'* with a hymn to yachting: 'Sailing the sea, we play every part of life: control, direction, effort, fate; and there we can test ourselves and know our state. All that which concerns the sea is profound and final.'[32] These sentiments make little sense today. If the vast majority of the population continue to have neither the means, or the time, or the desire, to sail, or any interest in it, then yachting will surely fall on the wrong side of history.

---

[30] Carolyn Brown, a radio announcer who had read the shipping forecast, tells us: 'non-sailors ... go all misty eyed at the mention of the shipping forecast and start softly humming *Sailing By*. I think it is because subconsciously us Brits can never forget we are an island nation ...' ('Sailing by ... Or Not'). Again, the rhetoric of a united, seafaring nation has split from the reality, if it ever existed. 'Sailing By' is played before the 00:48 shipping forecast, so it is hardly listened to by a large number of people. Much more realistic is the response of Anusha, the intelligent heroine of Chris Speyer's story, *Devil's Rock*. The hero, Zaki, tells her they have to hurry if they are to see his boat builder grandfather: 'Grandad likes to finish work before the shipping forecast'. 'Whatever that is', said Anusha, as she followed him into the shed' (p. 101).

[31] Charlie Connelly, *Attention All Shipping, A Journey around the Shipping Forecast* (Cowes, p. 175; Kilrush, p. 290).

[32] Belloc, *The Cruise of the 'Nona'*, p. 346.

Epilogue:
Fair Winds

There is a huge amount of research and study still needed into yachting history, which should be rewarding, because, as I hope I have shown, yachting holds up a mirror to its society and has been an important part of this nation's social history for centuries.

I am all too aware of the many unanswered questions in this text, unanswered because the data was not there. There is an additional urgency for two reasons. Many of the original shipwrights who built wooden yachts, and many of the sailors who cruised and raced in them, are now getting on in years. A second, more recent, overlapping watershed concerns those who sailed by compass, log and sextant, before the advent of Global Positioning Systems, that started coming into civilian use in the late eighties. There is so much yachting history that urgently requires recording and researching.

In a book of this length, covering such a long period of time and so many types of sailing, there are bound to be factual errors, misunderstandings and misinterpretations. If you spot one, please contact the publisher who will pass your comments on to me. Thank you.

Mike Bender

Bibliography

Note: Where the original date of publication differs substantially from the edition quoted, or the original date is of particular interest, it is noted after the title.

Acton, Shane. *Shrimpy*. Cambridge: Patrick Stephens, 1981
——. *Shrimpy Sails Again*. Wellingborough, Northants.: Patrick Stephens, 1989
Adams, James Eli. *Dandies and Desert Saints: Styles of Victorian Masculinity*. Ithaca, NY: Cornell University, 2005
Adburham, Alison. *Silver Fork Society*: *Fashionable Life and Literature from 1814 to 1840*. London: Constable, 1983
Adlington, Lucy. *Stitches in Time: The Story of the Clothes We Wear*. London: Random House, 2015
Aiken, J. *Description of the Country from 30 to 40 Miles Round Manchester*. 1795
Aldeburgh Yacht Club. *Against the Elements: Aldeburgh Yacht Club – The First One Hundred Years*. Aldeburgh, Suffolk: Aldeburgh Yacht Club, 1997
Allcard, Edward. *Single-Handed Passage*. London: Putnam, 1950
——. *'Temptress' Returns*. London: Putnam, 1952
Anderson, Benedict. *Imagined Communities: Reflections on the Origin and Spread of Nationalism*. Rev. edn. London: Verso, 1991
Andrews, Brothers. *A Daring Voyage across the Atlantic by Two Americans, the Brothers Andrews, The Log of the Voyage*. Introduction and Notes by Dr Macaulay. New York: Griffiths and Farran, 1880
Anglesey, The Marquess FSA (Paget, George Charles Henry Victor). *One-Leg: The Life and Letters of Henry William Paget, First Marquess of Anglesey K.G. (1768–1854)*. London: Cape, 1961
Anon. 'Obituary: Des Sleightholme'. *Daily Telegraph*, 17 June, 2003
Anson, Lord. *A Voyage Around the World MDCCXL (1740), I, II, III, IV by George Anson; Compiled from Papers and Other Materials of the Right Honourable George Lord Anson and Published under His Direction by Richard Walter*. London: Printed for John and Paul Knapton, 1748
Archer, Stella and Peter Pearson. *The Royal St George Yacht Club: A History*. Dublin: Royal St George Yacht Club, 1987
Arnold, Guy. *Hold Fast for England: G. A. Henty, Imperialist Boys' Writer*. London: Hamish Hamilton, 1980
Arnold, John H. *History: A Very Short Introduction*. Oxford: Oxford University Press, 2000

Arnold, Thomas, D. D., Headmaster of Rugby School. *Christian Life, Its Hopes, Its Fears and Its Close: Sermons Preached Mostly in the Chapel of Rugby School.* London: B. Fellowes, 1842

Ashley, Maurice. *England in the Seventeenth Century.* Harmondsworth, Penguin, 1977

Atkins, J. B. *Further Memorials of the Royal Yacht Squadron (1901–1938).* London: Geoffrey Bles, 1939

Auden, W. H. *The Enchafed Flood or The Romantic Iconography of the Sea.* 1950. New York: Vintage, 1967

Austen, Jane. *Persuasion.* 1818. Harmondsworth: Penguin English Library, 1965

Austin, Ronald L. The Archive of the Bristol Channel Yacht Club. *Annual Report of the County Archivist, 2006–2007.* Swansea: West Glamorgan Archive Service, 2007: 33–36

——. 'The Great Swansea Bay Regattas, 1896–1929: the Large Yachts'. *Gower,* 7, 2007: 23–36

——. 'Yachting in Swansea Bay'. *Maritime South West,* 2014: 200–263.

Ayton, R. *A Voyage around Great Britain Undertaken in the Summer of the Year 1813.* Paintings by William Daniell. 4 vols. 1814–1825

Bach, Richard. *Jonathan Livingston Seagull.* New York: Macmillan, 1970.

Baden-Powell, Robert. *Scouting for Boys.* 1908. Oxford: Oxford University Press, 2004

Baden-Powell, Warrington. *Canoe Travelling: Log of a Cruise on the Baltic, and Practical Hints on Building and Fitting Canoes.* London: Smith, Elder & Co., 1871. Also in two issues of the *Cornhill Magazine* of 1870 and in 1871

Bailey, Maurice and Maralyn Bailey. *117 Days Afloat.* Lymington: Nautical, 1973

——. *Second Chance: Voyage to Patagonia.* London: Weidenfeld and Nicolson, 1977

Ballantyne, R. M. *Coral Island.* 1858. Edinburgh: T. Nelson and Sons

Barnes, Pam. *The Norfolk Broads Yacht Club – A Short History.* Norwich: Norfolk Broads Yacht Club, 1982

Barter, Fred, compiler. *Cruising for a Hundred Years: The Centenary of the Cruising Association 1908–2008.* London: Cruising Association, 2009

Barthes, Roland. 'The "Blue Blood" Cruise'. In *Mythologies* by Roland Barthes. Selected and trans. from the French by Annette Lavers. 1957. London: Cape, 1972, 32–33

Bartlett, Tim. 'What's the Future of Sailing?' *Yachting Monthly,* August 2013: 10–12

Barton, Humphrey. *Vertue XXXV: An Account of the Author's Voyage from Lymington to New York.* London: Robert Ross, 1950

——. *Atlantic Adventurers: Voyages in Small Craft.* London: Adlard Coles; George G. Harrap, 1953

Basley, John. 'The Wyllies on the Medway'. *Newsletter of the Association of Yachting Historians,* Winter 2011: 1–4.

Bass, Tim. 'The Rise of Recreational Boat-Sailing in South Devon from the Mid-Nineteenth Century to 1914'. University of Exeter MA Thesis in Maritime History, 2000

Bathurst, Bella. *The Lighthouse Stevensons.* London: HarperCollins, 1999

Baylay, John. *When the Bug Bites.* Warkworth, New Zealand: John Baylay, 1998

Beard, Mary. 'Move over History Boys'. *Guardian Review,* 6 February, 2016: 2

Beauman, Nicola. *A Very Great Profession: The Woman's Novel 1914–1939*. London: Virago, 1983

Beavis, Bill. *Bows Amidships*. London: Adlard Coles, 1984

——. *The Best of 'Looking Around with Bill Beavis' 1970–1976*. London: Yachting Monthly, 1987

Bédarida, François. *A Social History of England 1851–1975*. Trans. A. S. Forster. London: Methuen, 1979

Bedford, Jacey. 'Dorothy Una Radcliffe, Yorkshire Poet, 1887–1937'. www. Artisan-harmony.com (accessed 27/12/2015)

Beeching, Richard. *The Reshaping of British Railways* (*The Beeching Report*) London: HMSO, 1963

Behrman, Cynthia. *Victorian Myths of the Sea*. Athens, OH: Ohio University Press, 1977

Beken, Keith. *The Beken File*. Aylesbury: Channel, 1980

Belloc, Hilaire. *Cautionary Tales for Children: Designed for the Admonition of Children between the Age of Eight and Fourteen Years*. London: Eveleigh Nash, 1908

——. *The Cruise of the 'Nona'*. 1925. Intro. Jonathan Raban. London: Century, 1983

Bender, Mike. 'Why Move the Lighthouse? Virginia Woolf's Relationship with St Ives'. *Cornish Studies*, 13, 2005: 53–69

——. 'A Brief History of the British Yachting Narratives 1604 –2005'. *Maritime South West, Journal of the Southwest Maritime History Society*, 22, 2009: 18–114

——. 'The Yachting Narrative with Particular Reference to Cornwall'. *Troze*, the Online *Journal of the National Maritime Museum Cornwall*, 1(4), June, 2009

——. 'A Brief History of the British Yachting Narratives 1604–2005. Part Two – Additions, Corrections and References'. *Maritime South West, Journal of the Southwest Maritime History Society*, 23, 2010: 178–200

——. 'Written on the Waves: British Yachting Literature and Codes of Masculinity 1888–1945'. Exeter University Ph.D. Thesis, 2011

——. How Strange Was 'The Strange Case of Donald Crowhurst'? *Maritime South West*, 25, 2012: 97–120

——. 'An Open Letter to the Editor'. *The Marine Quarterly*, 7, Autumn 2012: 99–104

——. 'Yachting and Madness'. *Journal for Maritime Research*, 15 (1), May 2013, 69–82

——. 'Conrad, the Yarn and the Location of the Marlow Stories'. *Mariner's Mirror*, 100 (2), 2014: 168–185

——. 'Isn't It Time We Treated Arthur Ransome as a Grown-Up?' *Maritime South West*, 27, 2014: 137–172

——. 'Angry Voices on the River Bank: A Reinterpretation of Two Aquatic Classes'. *The Mariner's Mirror*, 101 (2), 2015: 135–155

——. 'Leisure Sailing on a Hostile Shore: Yachting in the Bristol Channel and its "Mudhole" Yacht Clubs'. *Maritime South West*, 28, 2015: 280–322

——. 'Concerning the Fragility and Future of Yacht Clubs'. *Maritime South West*, 29, 2016: 182–215

Benham, Hervey. *Last Stronghold of Sail: The Story of the Essex Sailing-Smacks, Coasters and Barges*. 1948. London: George G. Harrap, 1948

——. *Down Tops'l. The Story of the East Coast Sailing-Barges*. London: George G. Harrap, 1951

Bennet, Glin. 'Medical and Psychological Problems in the 1972 Singlehanded Transatlantic Yacht Race'. *Lancet*, 1973: 747–754

——. 'The Tired Sailor and the Hazards of Fatigue'. *Yachting Monthly*, September 1973: 1393–1400.

——. 'Psychological Breakdown at Sea: Hazards of Singlehanded Ocean Sailing'. *British Journal of Medical Psychology*, 47, 1974: 189–210

——. *Beyond Endurance: Survival at the Extremes*. London: Secker & Warburg, 1983

Bennett, A. S. *June of Rochester*. Illustrated from Photographs by the Author. London: Edward Arnold, 1939

Benson, E. F. *David Blaize*. London: Hodder and Stoughton, 1916

Bertrand, John, as told to Patrick Robinson. *Born to Win: A Lifelong Struggle to Capture the America's Cup*. London: Sidgwick and Jackson, 1985

Bestic, A. A. *Kicking Canvas: The Ordeal of the 'Denbigh Castle'*. London: Evan Brothers, 1957

Betjeman, John. *New Bats in Old Belfries*. London: John Murray, 1945

Bickerdyke, John. *The Best Cruise on the Broads. With Useful Hints on Hiring, Provisioning and Manning the Yacht; Clothing, Angling, Photography etc.* London: Bliss, Sands & Foster, 1895

Biddle, Tyrell E. *The Corinthian Yachtsman or Hints on Yachting*. 1881. London: C. Wilson, 1881

——. *Hints to Beginners in Amateur Yacht Designing*. London: Norie and Wilson, 1883

——. *Amateur Sailing in Open and Half-Decked Boats*. London: Norie and Wilson, 1886

——. *Hints on Yacht-Building for Amateurs*. London: George Wilson, 1888

Bigelow, Albert. *The Voyage of the 'Golden Rule': An Experiment with Truth*. Garden City, NY: Doubleday Anchor, 1959

Bird, Vanessa. *Classic Classes*. London: Adlard Coles Nautical; Classic Boat, 2012

Birley, Sir Derek. *Land of Sport and Glory*. Manchester: Manchester University Press, 1995

Black, Jeremy. *A History of the British Isles*. Basingstoke: Palgrave Macmillan, 2003

Black, Lesley. *Must I Go Down to the Sea Again?* 1983. London: Adlard Coles; Fernhurst, 1985

——. *Still Wet behind the Ears*. Steyning, Sussex: Fernhurst, 1986

Black, Martin. *G. L. Watson: The Art and Science of Yacht Design*. Limerick: Peggy Bawn Press, 2011

Blackwell, Daria and Alex Blackwell. 'A Brief History of Anchors'. *Cruising*, September 2015: 44–46

Blake, George and Christopher Small. *Cruise in Company: The History of the Royal Clyde Yacht Club 1859–1959*. Glasgow: Royal Clyde Yacht Club, 1959

Blake, John. *The Sea Chart: The Illustrated History of Nautical Maps and Navigational Charts*. London: Conway, 2009

——. *Sea Charts of the British Isles: A Voyage of Discovery around Britain and Ireland's Coastline*. London: Conway, 2009

Blewitt, Mary. *Celestial Navigation for Yachtsmen*. London: Iliffe, 1950

——. *Navigation for Yachtsmen*. London: Iliffe, 1964

Blyth, Chay. *The Impossible Voyage*. London: Pan, 1972

Blyth, Chay and Maureen Blyth. *Innocent Aboard*. Lymington: Nautical, 1970

Blyth, Chay and Elaine Thompson. *The Challenge: The Official Story of the British Steel Challenge*. 1993. London: Hodder and Stoughton, 1993

Blyton, Enid. *The Adventurous Four*. London: George Newnes, 1941

——. *The Adventurous Four Again*. London: George Newnes, 1947

Bolland, R. R. *Victorians on the Thames*. Tunbridge Wells: Midas, 1974

Bone, David. *Landfall at Sunset: The Life of a Contented Sailor*. 1955. London: Gerald Duckworth, 1955

Bonner, George Frederick. *The Yachting Season of 1845*. 1845. Lymington: Nautical, 1971

Boswell, James. *The Journal of a Tour of the Hebrides*. London: Charles Dilly, 1785. Ed. with an Introduction and Notes by Peter Levi London: Folio Society, 1990

Bowery, Thomas. *The Papers of Thomas Bowery, 1669–1713*. Ed. Richard C. Temple. Hakluyt Society, Series 2, 58, 1927:1–109

Bowker, R. M. and S. A. Budd. *Make Your Own Sails: A Handbook for the Amateur and Professional Sailmaker*. London: Macmillan, 1957

Boylan, Henry. *White Sails Crowding: A History of the Royal Irish Yacht Club*. Dublin: A. and A. Farmar, 1994

Bradford, Ernle. *The Journeying Moon*. London: Jarrold, 1958

——. *Ulysses Found*. London: Hodder and Stoughton, 1963

——. *Three Centuries of Sailing*. London: Country Life, 1964

Brassey, Lady Anna (1839–1887). *A Voyage in 'The Sunbeam': Our Home on the Ocean for Eleven Months*. 1878. London: Longmans, Green and Co., 1907

Bray, David. *The Story of the Norfolk Wherries*. Norwich: Jarrold & Sons, c. 1978

Brian, Daniel. *Almost a Hero*. Play, 2004

Bridges, Antony. *Scapa Ferry*. London: Peter Davies, 1957

Briggs, Asa. *Victorian People: A Reassessment of Persons and Themes*. London: Odhams Press, 1954

Brogan, Hugh. *The Life of Arthur Ransome*. London: Hamish Hamilton, 1985

Brook, Andrew. 'X Hits the Spot.' *Practical Boat Owner,* December, 2011: 62–64

Brookes, C. *English Cricket – The Game and Its Players through the Ages*. London: Weidenfeld and Nicolson, 1978

Brown, Caroline. 'Sailing by … Or Not'. *Yachting Monthly*, December 2014: 83

Brown, Geoffrey. *The Deben Yacht Club and the Deben Sailing Club, 1838 to 1988*. Woodbridge, Suffolk: Deben Yacht Club and Friends, 1988

Bullimore, Tony. *Saved*. London: Little Brown, 1997

Burke, Edmund. *A Philosophical Enquiry into the Origin of Our Ideas of the Sublime and the Beautiful*. 1756. London: Penguin, 2004

Burnell, Richard. *Henley Royal Regatta: A Celebration of 150 Years*. London: Heinemann; Gieves and Hawkes, 1989

Burney, Frances. *Journals and Letters*. Selected with an Introduction by Peter Sabor and Lars E. Troide. London: Penguin, 2001

Burrett, A. R. *Dinghy Sailing*. St Ives, Huntingdon: Colourmaster

Burstall, Patricia. *The Golden Age of the Thames*. Newton Abbot: David & Charles, 1981

Bush, Geoff. *Of Merlins, Mirrors and Darts: Whitstable Yacht Club, 1952–2002*. Whitstable: Friends of Whitstable Museum and Gallery, 2006

Butler, Marilyn. *Romantics, Rebels and Reactionaries: English Literature and its Background 1760–1830*. Oxford: Oxford University Press, 1981

Butler, T. Harrison. *Cruising Yachts: Design and Performance*. London: Adlard Coles, 1945

Caffari, Dee. *Against the Flow*. London: Adlard Coles, 2007

Campbell, Jamie. *Royal Norfolk and Suffolk Yacht Club*. Lowestoft: Hamilton, 2009

Cannadine, David. 'The Context, Performance and Meaning of Ritual: The British Monarchy and the 'Invention of Tradition',c. 1820–1977'. In *The Invention of Tradition*. Ed. Eric Hobsbawm and Terence Ranger. Cambridge: Cambridge University Press, 1984: 100–138

——. *Aspects of Aristocracy: Grandeur and Decline in Modern Britain*. London: Penguin, 1994

Cantacuzino, Maria. *On Equal Terms: The First Disabled Crew to Race around the World – Racing in the BT Global Challenge*. London: Simon & Schuster, 1997

Cantlie, Dr. J. *Physical Efficiency: A Review of the Deleterious Effects of Town Life upon the Population of Britain, with Suggestions for Their Arrest*. London: G. P. Putnam's Sons, 1906

Carey, John. *William Golding, The Man Who Wrote 'Lord of the Flies': A Life*. London: Faber and Faber, 2009

Carr, Frank G.G. *A Yachtsman's Log*. London: Lovat, Dickson & Thompson, 1935

Castle, Edward Walter, Robert Castle and R.T. Pritchett. *The Thames Clubs and Windermere*. Ed. His Grace the Duke of Beaufort. The Badminton Library. *Yachting*, Vol. 2, pp. 152–189. London: Longmans, Green and Co., 1894

Cathcart, Brian. *The News from Waterloo*. London: Faber and Faber, 2015

Cattell, Raymond B. *Under Sail in Red Devon: Being the Log of 'Sandpiper'*. London: Alexander Maclehose, 1937

Cave, Diana. *Cowes Corinthian Yacht Club: 55 Years of History*. Cowes: Cowes Corinthian Yacht Club, 2007

Caws, Sheila. *Gurnard Sailing Club 1931–2006*. Freshwater, IOW: Coach House, 2006

Chakrabortty, Aditya. 'Dawn Cleaning Shift, Shower, then Teach: Survival as a Lecturer.' *The Guardian*, 17 November, 2016: 8–9

Chambers, Roland. *The Last Englishman: The Double Life of Arthur Ransome*. London: Faber and Faber, 2009

Chaplin, Peter H. *The Thames from Source to Tideway*. London: Whitter, 1988

Chapman, F. Spencer. *Watkins' Last Expedition*. London: Chatto and Windus, 1934

Chedzoy, Alan. *Seaside Sovereign*. Wimborne: Dovecote, 2003

Chesney, George Tomkyns. *The Battle of Dorking: Reminiscences of a Volunteer*. 1871. Edinburgh: W. Blackwood, 1871

Chetwood, W. R. *A Tour through Ireland, 1748*. Printed by J. Roberts in Warwick Lane, London

Chichester, Francis. *Solo to Sydney*. London: John Hamilton, 1930

——. *Seaplane Solo*. London: Faber and Faber, 1933 (Later Re-titled *Alone Over the Tasman Sea*)

——. *Ride on the Wind*. London: Hamish Hamilton, 1936

——. *The Spotter's Handbook*. London: George Allen & Unwin, 1941

——. *Alone Across the Atlantic*. 1961. London: George Allen & Unwin, 1961

——. *The Lonely Sea and the Sky*. London: Hodder & Stoughton, 1964

——. *Gypsy Moth Circles the World*. London: Hodder & Stoughton, 1967

Childers, Erskine. *In the Ranks of the C.I.V.: A Narrative and Diary of Personal Experiences with the C.I.V. (Honourable Artillery Company) in South Africa by Driver Erskine Childers, Clerk in the House of Commons*. London: Smith & Elder, 1900.

——. *The Riddle of the Sands*. 1903. Woodbridge: Seafarer, 1998

Chivers, David. *Austin 'Clarence' Farrar: An Eye for Innovation 1913–2004*. Shepperton, Middlesex: Bosun, 2007

Clark, Arthur Hamilton. *The History of Yachting 1600–1815*. 1903. Nabu Public Domain Reprints, 2014

Clark, Miles. *High Endeavours: The Extraordinary Life and Adventures of Miles and Beryl Smeeton*. London: Grafton, 1992

Clark, Wallace. *Sailing around Ireland*. 1976. Londonderry: North-West Books, 1990

Clarke, I. F., ed. *The Great War with Germany 1890–1914*. Liverpool: Liverpool University Press, 1997

Clutterbuck, Peter R. *The Sea Takes No Prisoners: Offshore Voyages in an Open Wayfarer Dinghy*. Clutterbuck, 2015

Clyde Cruising Club. *Sailing Directions and Anchorages West Coast*. Glasgow: Clyde Cruising Club, 1923

Cobbett, William. *Rural Rides*. 1830

Coe, Jonathan. *The Terrible Privacy of Maxwell Sim*. London: Penguin, 2010

Coleridge, Samuel. 'The Ancient Mariner'. In William Wordsworth and Samuel Coleridge. *The Lyrical Ballads*. Bristol: Joseph Cottle, 1798

Coles, K. Adlard. *In Broken Water: Being the Adventures of a Six-Tonner through Holland and among the Frisian and Danish Islands*. 1925. Southampton: Adlard Coles; 2nd edn. London: George G. Harrap, 1956

——. *Close-Hauled: Being the Adventures of the Author and His Wife Cruising Alone in a 29-Foot Ketch, among the Lesser Known Islands of the Baltic during a Voyage from Latvia to England*. London: Nautical, 1926

——. *In Finnish Waters: From Estonia to Sweden*. London: Edward Arnold, 1932

——. *Creeks and Harbours of the Solent. With Langstone and Chichester Harbours and the Isle of Wight*. London: Edward Arnold, 1933

——. *Sailing the South Coast* (Retitled 1939 *Pocket Pilot for the South Coast: A Shell Guide*). London: Faber and Faber, 1936

——. *'Mary Anne' among 10,000 Islands: Cruising the Finnish Archipelago*. London: H. F. and G. Witherby, 1938

——. *North Atlantic: Boat against Boat over 3,000 Miles*. Southampton: Robert Ross, 1950

——. *Channel Harbours and Anchorages: Solent to Portland–Barfleur to St Malo, Including the Channel Islands*. London: Edward Arnold, 1956

——. *Heavy Weather Sailing*. London: Adlard Coles, 1967

——. *Sailing Years: An Autobiography*. London: Adlard Coles Granada, 1981

Colley, Ann. *Victorians in the Mountains*. Farnham: Ashgate, 2010.

Colley, Linda. *Britons: Forging the Nation 1707–1837*. New Haven: Yale University Press, 1992

——. *Acts of Union and Disunion: What Has Held the UK Together – And What Is Dividing It Now?* London: Profile, 2014

Comlay, Bob. 'Travels with Tilman'. *Cruising*, December 2010: 40

Compton, Nic. *The Great Classic Yacht Revival*. London: Mitchell Beazley, 2004

Condy, Flora Ross. *Reminiscences of a Yachting Cruise*. London: Ackerman & Co., 1852; London: British Library, 2010

Connelly, Charlie. *Attention All Shipping, A Journey around the Shipping Forecast*. London: Little Brown, 2004

Connolly, Billy. Oration at Jimmy Reid's Funeral, 20 August, 2010. www.stv.tv/video Redirect.cfm?refid...connollyfull

Connolly, Joseph. *Jerome J. Jerome: A Critical Biography*. London: Orbis, 1982

Conrad, Joseph. *The Nigger of the 'Narcissus'*. London: Heinemann, 1898

——. *Lord Jim*. 1900. Ware, Hertfordshire: Wordsworth Classics, 2002

——. *Heart of Darkness*. 1902. London: Penguin, 1994

——. *Youth*. 1902. London: Heinemann, 1954

——. *Typhoon*. 1903. London: Heinemann, 1954

——. *A Personal Record*. 1906. with *The Mirror of the Sea*. London: Dent, 1946

——. *Chance. A Tale in Two Parts*. 1913. London: Penguin, 1974

Cook, Chris and John Stevenson. *The Longman Handbook of Modern British History 1714-1987*. London: Longman, 1988

Cooke, Francis B. *London to Lowestoft: A Cruising Guide to the East Coast*. London: Imray, Laurie, Norie & Wilson, 1906

——. *In Tidal Waters*. With Illustrations by C. Fleming Williams. London: Chapman and Hall, 1919

——. *Pocket Cruisers*. London: Edward Arnold, 1938.

——. *Yachting Yarns*. London: Herbert Jenkins, 1944

——. *Cruising Hints*, 1904. 6th edn rev. London: Edward Arnold, 1948

Coombs, Joan. *A Fowey Jig-Saw: The History of the Royal Fowey Yacht Club*. Fowey: Royal Fowey Yacht Club, 2000

Cooper, Artemis. *Writing at the Kitchen Table: The Authorized Biography of Elizabeth David*. London: Michael Joseph, 1999

Cooper, Bill and Laurel Cooper. *Sell up and Sail: Taking the Ulysses Option*. London: Stanford Maritime, 1986

Coote, Jack. *Classic One-Designs*. Shrewsbury: Waterline, 1994

Copping, A. E. *Gotty and the Guv'nor*. London: Grant Richards, 1907; Lavenham, Suffolk: Mallard Reprints, 1979

——. *Gotty in Furrin Parts*. London: Chapman & Hall, 1908

Corbin, Alain. *The Lure of the Sea: The Discovery of the Seaside 1750-1840*. 1988. Trans. Jocelyn Phelps. London: Penguin, 1995

Cordingly, David. *Marine Painting in England 1700–1900*. London: Studio Vista, 1974

Corlett, Georgie. 'School Colours'. *Yachts and Yachting*, no. 1678, October 2014: 56–59

——. 'FI Factor'. *The Yachting Year 2015*: 68–70

Cornell, Gwenda. *Cruising with Children*. London; Adlard Coles, 1986

Cornell, Jimmy. 'Partners Afloat', *Yachting World*, Febuary 1986: 57–61

——. *Ocean Cruising Survey: An Appraisal; of Boats, Gear and Crew*. London: Adlard Coles, 1986

——. *Around the World Rally*. London: Adlard Coles, 1993

Cornwell, Bernard. *Wildtrack*. London: Michael Joseph, 1988

——. *Sea Lord*. London: Michael Joseph, 1989

——. *Stormchild*. London: Michael Joseph, 1991

Cottee, Kay. *First Lady: A History-Making Solo Voyage around the World*. Sydney, Australia: Pan, 1990

Couling, David. *Steam Yachts*. London: B. T. Batsford, 1980

——. *Solent Yachting Scene in Bygone Years 1890–1938*. London: Stanford Maritime, 1984

Cowper, David. 'The North West Passage, 1986–2012'. *Marine Quarterly*, 18, Summer 2015: 26–35

Cowper, Frank. *Sailing Tours*. 5 vols. 1892–1896. Southampton: Ashford, 1985

——. *Sailing Tours. Part I. The Coasts of Essex and Suffolk Containing Descriptions of Every Creek from the Thames to Aldborough*. 1892. Southampton: Ashford, 1985

——. *Sailing Tours. Part II. From the Nore and Swin Middle Lightships to Tresco, Isles of Scilly*. c.1893. Southampton: Ashford, 1985

——. *Sailing Tours. Part III. Falmouth to the Loire*. c. 1894. Southampton: Ashford, 1985

——. *Sailing Tours. Part IV. Land's End to the Mull of Galloway, including the East Coast of Ireland*. c. 1895. Southampton: Ashford, 1985

——. *Sailing Tours: The Yachtsman's Guide to the Cruising Waters of the English and Adjacent Coasts. Part V. The West Coasts of Scotland, the Orkneys and the West Coast of the North Sea. Containing Descriptions of Every Creek, Harbour, and Roadstead, Suitable for Yachting Purposes from the Mull of Galloway to Duncansby Head, with Brief Account of the Coast from the Orkneys to the Thames*. 1896. Southampton: Ashford, 1985

——. *Yachting and Cruising for Amateurs: Being Practical Directions upon All Matters Connected with Fore-and-Aft Sailing Craft; with Detailed Suggested Cruises round the British and Adjacent Coasts*. London: 'The Bazaar', 1911

——. *The Vagaries of Lady Harvey: The Meanderings of a Freak among the Orkneys and Elsewhere*. Kirkwall: W. R. Mackintosh, the Orcadian Office, 1930

Crane, John, Resident Physician at Weymouth. *Cursory Observations on Sea-Bathing; the Use of Sea-Water Internally, and the Advantages of a Maritime Situation, as Conducing to Health and Longevity*. To which is added, *A Concise History of Weymouth*. Weymouth: Sold at Lowe's Circulating Library, 1795

Cross, Tom, David Hale and Pin Armitage. *The Artist Who Loved Boats: Percy 'Powder' Thorburn*. Tiverton: Halsgrove, 2006

Crothers, Kevin C. *Salt in My Blood*. Dublin: Original Writing, 2014

Crowden, Captain Guy, R. N. 'Admiral of the Fleet, Lord Fisher. Technocrat Extraordinary'. *Maritime South West*, 20, 2007: 47–58

Cudmore, Michael. *The Windfall Yachts: A Legacy of Goodwill*. Stoke sub Hamdon: Topsy, 2007

Cunliffe, Tom. *Topsail and Battleaxe: A Voyage in the Wake of the Vikings*. Newton Abbot: David & Charles, 1988

——. *The Complete Yachtmaster: Sailing Seamanship and Navigation for the Modern Yacht Skipper*. London: Adlard Coles, 1994

——. *The Complete Day Skipper: Skippering with Confidence Right from the Start*. London: Adlard Coles, 2002

——. *Hand, Reef and Steer: Traditional Skills for Classic Boats*. London: Adlard Coles Nautical, 2004

——. *The Shell Channel Pilot: South Coast of England, the North Coast of France and the Channel Islands*. 7th rev. edn. St Ives, Cambs.: Imray Laurie Norie and Wilson, 2013

——. *In the Wake of Heroes*. London: Adlard Coles Nautical, 2015

Cunningham, Andy. 'The Truth about Twin Keels'. *Practical Boat Owner*, 479, November 2006: 50–55

Cunningham, Hugh. 'Leisure and Culture'. In *The Cambridge Social History of Britain 1750–1950. Volume 2: People and Their Environment*. Ed. F. M. L. Thompson. Cambridge: Cambridge University Press, 1990

Cusack, Janet. 'The Rise of Aquatic Recreation and Sport: Yachting and Rowing in England and South Devon, 1640–1914'. University of Exeter Ph.D. Dissertation, 1996

——. 'The Rise of Yachting in England and South Devon Revisited, 1640–1827'. In *Recreation and the Sea*. Ed. Stephen Fisher. Exeter: Exeter University Press, 1997: 101–149

——. 'Yachting in Britain, 1890–1960'. In *Exploring the Sea. Aspects of Britain's Maritime Economy since 1870*. Ed. David J. Starkey and Alan G. Jamieson. Exeter: Exeter University Press, 1998

——. 'Yachting in Cornwall before the First World War'. In *The Maritime History of Cornwall*. Ed. Philip Payton, Alston Kennerley and Helen Doe. Exeter: Exeter University Press, 2014: 307–317

Dalton, Tony. *British Royal Yachts: A Complete Illustrated History*. Tiverton: Halsgrove, 2002

Dampier, William. 'An Account of Captain William Dampier's Voyage round the World'. 1705 folio. In John Harris, DD, FRS *Navigantium Atque Itinerantium Bibliotheca*, etc. Vol. 2, pp. 865–906.

Danbury, Carole. *SSSC: The First Fifty Years: The History of the South Staffordshire Sailing Club 1954–2004. htttp://www.southstaffsailingclub.co.uk/page/page.php?editorial_id=74*. Accessed 28 May, 2015

David, Elizabeth. *A Book of Mediterranean Food*. London: John Lehmann, 1950

——. *French Country Cooking*. London: John Lehmann 1951

Davidoff, Leonore. *The Best Circles: Social Etiquette and the Season*. London: Croom Helm, 1973

Davies, G. Christopher. *The Handbook to the Rivers and Broads of Norfolk and Suffolk*. London: Jarrold and Sons, 1882

——. *Norfolk Broads and Rivers, or the Water-ways, Lagoons and Decoys of East Anglia*. Edinburgh and London: Blackwood, 1883

——. *Practical Boat Sailing for Amateurs: Containing Particulars of the Most Suitable Sailing Boats and Yachts for Amateurs and Instructions for Their Proper Handling, & c.* Illustrated with Numerous Diagrams. London: Upton Gill, 1886

——. 'Sailing on the Norfolk Broads'. In *The Badminton Library: Yachting*, 2 vols. Vol. 2. Ed. His Grace the Duke of Beaufort. London: Longmans, Green and Co., 1904, pp. 190–226

Davies, J. David. *Pepys' Navy: The Ships, Men and Organisation*. Barnsley: Seaforth, 2008

Davies, Peter. 'The Discovery of the *Mary*, Charles II's Yacht'. *International Journal of Nautical Archeology and Underwater Archeology*, 11 (1), 1973: 59–60

——. 'The Discovery and Excavation of the Royal Yacht, *Mary*', *Maritime Wales*, 1979, pp. 25–32

Davis, Gordon. *Dartmouth Royal Regatta from 1834 to the Present*. Dartmouth: Harbour Books, 1987

Davis, John. *A History of Britain, 1885–1939*. New York: St Martin's Press, 1999

Davison, Ann. *Last Voyage*. London: Peter Davies, 1951

——. *My Ship is So Small*. London: Peter Davies, 1956

Dawlish, Peter. *Dauntless Takes Recruits*. With Line Decorations by P. A. Jobson. Oxford: Oxford University Press, 1950

De S. Honey, J. R. *Tom Brown's Universe: The Development of the Victorian Public School*. London: Millington, 1977

Dean, Tacita. *Teignmouth Electron*. London: Book Works; National Maritime Museum, 1999

Deane, Sir Anthony. *Deane's Doctrine of Naval Architecture, 1670*. Intro. Brian Lavery. London: Conway Maritime, 1981

Dear, Ian. *The Royal Yacht Squadron 1815–1985*. London: Stanley Paul, 1985

——. *The Great Days of Yachting from the Kirk Collection*. London: B. T. Batsford, 1988

——. *Sailing in Eccentric Circles*. London: Nautical, 1989

——. *The Royal Ocean Racing Club: The First 75 Years*. London: Adlard Coles Nautical, 2000

——. 'Leisure Sailing in the Twentieth Century'. In *The Conway History of Seafaring in the Twentieth Century*. London: Conway Maritime, 2000, pp. 134–149

De Bisschop, Eric. *The Voyage of the 'Kaimiloa'*. London: G. Bell and Sons, 1940

De Boise, Stephen. *60 Years of Businessmen & Artisans: BHYC 1950–2010*. Bembridge: Brading Haven Yacht Club, 2010

Deep Water. Dir. Louise Osmond and Jerry Rothwell. ATP Films, 2005

Defoe, Daniel. *Robinson Crusoe*. 1719

——. *A New Voyage around the World*. 1725

——. *A Tour through the Whole Island of Great Britain*. 1724–26. London: Everyman's Library, 1928

Delany, Alfred and Vincent Delany. *The Water Wags 1887–2012*. Dun Laoghaire: The Water Wags, 2012

Denham, Henry. *The Aegean: A Sea-Guide to Its Coasts and Islands*. London: John Murray, 1963

——. *The Adriatic: A Sea-Guide to Its Coasts and Islands*. London: John Murray, 1967

Dent, Graham. *Not Quite at Sea*. Bakewell, Derbyshire: Ashridge, 2003

Derby, W. L. A. *The Tall Ships Pass: The Story of the Last Years of Deepwater Square-Rigged Sail Embodying therein the History and Detailed Description of the Finnish Four-Masted Steel Barque 'Herzogin Cecilie'*. With an Introduction by Basil Lubbock. London: Cape, 1937

De Selincourt, Aubrey. *One Good Tern*. Illustrated by Guy de Selincourt. London: George Routledge & Sons, 1943

——. *Three Green Bottles*. Illustrated by Guy de Selincourt. London: George Routledge & Sons, 1943

Desoutter, Denny. 'Command or Request?' *Practical Boat Owner*, 292, April 1991

——. 'The Old Yachting Days'. *Practical Boat Owner*, 303, March 1992: 60–62

De Souza, Philip. *Seafaring and Civilization: Maritime Perspectives on World History*. London: Profile, 2002

Devitt, Jerome. The 'Navalization' of Ireland: The Royal Navy and Irish Insurrection in the 1840s. *Mariner's Mirror*, 101 (4), 2015: 388–409

Diagonal White. *By Ocean, Firth and Channel: Amateur Cruising on the West Coast of Scotland and North of Ireland*. London: 'The Yachtsman', 1894

Diaper, Captain Tom. *Tom Diaper's Log: Memoirs of a Racing Skipper*. Southampton: Robert Ross, 1950

Dickens, Charles. *Dombey and Son*. 1848. London: Collins, 1954.

——. *David Copperfield*. 1849–1850. London: Penguin English Library, 1966

Disappearance at Sea. Film by Tacita Dean, 2000

Dixon, Conrad and Edward Seviour. *Sailing with Children*. London: Adlard Coles, 1969

Dixon, Douglas. *The King's Sailing Master: The Authorized Story of the Life of Major Sir Philip Hunloke, G.C.V.O., Légion D'Honneur, etc. and the House of Yvere, the Family of Hunloke in Derbyshire, Together with a History of Yachting*. London: Harrap, 1948

——. *Return to Gallipoli*. Ipswich: East Anglian Magazine, 1965

Dodd, Christopher. *Henley Royal Regatta*. Rev. edn. London: Stanley Paul, 1987

Doughty, Henry Montagu. *Summer in Broadland. Gipsying in East Anglian Waters*. Illustrated by the Gypsies. 1889. 6th edn. London: Jarrold & Sons, 1899

Driscoll, Pippa. *Children Afloat*. Hove: Fernhurst, 1989

Drower, George. *Boats, Boffins and Bowlines: The Stories of Sailing Inventors and Innovations*. Stroud, Gloucestershire: Sutton, 2006

Drummond, Maldwin. *Salt-Water Palaces*. London: Debrett, 1979

——. *The Riddle*. London: Nautical, 1985

Dufferin, Lord. *Letters from High Latitudes: Being Some Account of a Voyage in the Schooner Yacht 'Foam' 850.m to Iceland, Jan Meyen, and Spitzbergen in 1856*. 3rd edn. London: John Murray, 1857

Du Maurier, Daphne. *Jamaica Inn*. 1936. Intro. Sarah Dunant. London: Virago, 2003
——. *Rebecca*. 1938. London: Pan, 1976
——. *Frenchman's Creek*. London: Gollancz, 1941. Intro. Julie Myerson. London: Virago, 2003
——. *The King's General*. London: Gollancz, 1946

Dun Laoghaire Harbour Co. 'The Construction of Dun Laoghaire Harbour', download, n/d (accessed September 2015)

Dunning, James. *The Maritime History of Southern England*. Ed. Ronald Elliot. Tavistock, Devon: Heritage Publications; Southern Tourist Board, 1982

Durham, Dick. *The Magician of the Swatchways: A Biography of Maurice Griffiths*. London: Yachting Monthly, 1994
——. *Peyton: The World's Greatest Yachting Cartoonist*. London: Adlard Coles Nautical, 2009
——. *Amazing Sailing Stories*. Chichester: Wiley Nautical, 2011

Durkheim, Emile. *Suicide: A Study in Sociology*. 1897. Trans. John A. Spaulding and George Simpson. London: Routledge & Kegan Paul, 1952

Duxbury, Ken. *Lugworm on the Loose*. London: Pelham, 1973
——. *Lugworm Homeward Bound: Greece to England in an Open Dinghy*. London: Pelham, 1975

Dye, Frank. *Sailing to the Edge of Fear*. London: Adlard Coles Nautical, 2000

Dye, Frank and Margaret Dye. *Ocean-Crossing Wayfarer*. Newton Abbot: David & Charles, 1977

Eakin, Chris. *A Race Too Far*. London: Ebury, 2009

Easteal, Brian and Peter Poland. *The Westerly Story: A History of the Company and the Boats*. Westerly Owners' Association, 2006

Education and Social Research Institute, Manchester Metropolitan University. 'Is Tweeting One Hundred Years Old?' 2012. http://www.esri.mmu.ac.uk/news/news.php?id=1119

Edwards. Philip. *The Story of the Voyage: Sea-Narratives in Eighteenth-Century England*. Cambridge: Cambridge University Press, 1994.

Edwards, Tracy with Tim Madge. *Maiden*. London: Simon & Schuster, 1990

Egan, Pierce. *Pierce Egan's Book of Sports and Mirror of Life, Embracing the Turf, the Chase, the Ring and the Stage, Interspersed with Memoirs of Sporting Men*. London: Thomas Tegg and Son, 1836

Ellam, Patrick. *Things I Remember*. 1998. New York: iUniverse, 2010.

Ellam, Patrick and Colin Mudie. *Sopranino*. 1954. London: Hart-Davis, 1954.

Ellis, Don. *Medway Yacht Club: The First Hundred Years 1880–1980*. Maidstone: South Eastern Magazines, 1979

Engels, Friedrich. *The Condition of the Working Class in England in 1844*. 1845

English, Charlie. 'Sailing into Hell: Two Men, A Dinghy and One of the Luckiest Escapes Ever'. *Guardian*, 21 June, 2014

Evelyn, John. *The Diary of John Evelyn*. Now printed in full from the manuscripts belonging to Mr. John Evelyn and edited by E. S. de Beer in 6 volumes. Vol. 3. Kalendarium 1650–1672. Oxford: Clarendon Press, 1955

Fagan, Brian. *Beyond the Blue Horizon*. London: Bloomsbury, 2012

Fairley, Gordon. *Minute by Minute: The Story of the Royal Yachting Association 1975–1982*. Woking: Royal Yachting Association, 1983

Falconer, William. *An Universal Dictionary of the Marine or, A Copious Explanation of the Technical Terms and Phrases Employed in the Construction, Equipment, Furniture, Machinery, Movements and Military Operations of A Ship*. 1780. Newton Abbot: David & Charles, 1970.

Farr, Grahame. *Ships and Harbours of Exmoor*. 2nd edn. Dulverton, Somerset: Exmoor Press, 1974

Faulkner, William. *Requiem for a Nun*. New York: Random House, 1951

Ferris, Richard. 'The Most Dangerous and Memorable Adventure of Richard Ferris, One of the Five Ordinarie Messengers of Her Maiesties Chamber, Who Departed from Tower Wharfe on Midsommer Day Last Past, with Andrew Hill and William Thomas, who undertooke in a Small Wherry Boate, to Rowe by Sea to Bristowe, and are Now Safely Returned'. London: Printed by John Wolfe for Edward White, and are to be Sold at His Shop, Being at the Little North Door of Pauls at the Sign of the Gunne. 1590. In J. Payne Collier. *Illustrations of Early English Popular Literature*, Vol. 2. London: Privately printed, 1863

Festinger, Leon. 'A Theory of Social Comparison Processes'. *Human Relations*, 7, 1954: 117–140

——. *A Theory of Cognitive Dissonance*. Stanford: Stanford University Press, 1957

Fielding, Henry. *The Journal of a Voyage to Lisbon*. 1755 (with *Jonathan Wild*) London: Dent, 1932

Fincham, John. *The Royal Yacht Squadron: Its Yachts: and a Scientific Basis for their Improvement*. G. Clayton, 1855

Finkel, Donald. *The Wake of the 'Electron'*. New York: Atheneum, 1987

Fisher, Bob. *The Great Yacht Races*. London: Orbis, 1984

Fisher, Bob and Barry Pickthall. *Ocean Conquest*. London: Little, Brown and Co., 1993

Fishwick, Mark. 'A Taste of the Ocean Deep'. *Yachting Monthly*, August 2011: 74–75

Fleming, Fergus. *Killing Dragons: The Conquest of the Alps*. London: Granta, 2000

Folkard, H. C. *The Sailing Boat: A Description of English and Foreign Boats, their Varieties of Rig, and Practical Directions for Sailing*. 1863. London: Chapman & Hall, 1906

Ford, Doug. ... *The Only Sailor in the Fleet: TB Davis (1867–1942)*. St Helier: Jersey Heritage Trust, 2014

Ford, John. *This Sporting Land*. London: New English Library, 1977

Forster, E. M. *Maurice*. 1914. Harmondsworth: Penguin, 1972

Forster, Margaret. *Daphne Du Maurier*. London: Chatto & Windus, 1993

Fort, Tom. *Channel Shore: From the White Cliffs to Land's End*. London: Simon & Schuster, 2015

Forwell, William. *A Thousand Miles' Cruise in the 'Silver Cloud': From Dundee to France and Back in a Small Boat*. 2nd edn. Glasgow: Blackie & Son, 1879

Foster, Eric K. 'Research on Gossip: Taxonomy, Methods and Future Directions'. *Review of General Psychology*, 8, 2004: 78–99

Foster, Lloyd. *Ostar: The Full Story of the Observer Single-Handed Transatlantic and the Two-Handed Round Britain Races.* Yeovil: Haynes, 1989

Foulke, Robert. 'Life in the Dying World of Sail 1870–1910'. *The Journal of British Studies*, 3 (1), November 1963: 105–136

——. *The Sea Voyage Narrative.* New York: Trayne, 1997

Fowle, Frances. *Impressionism in Scotland.* With Contributions by Vivien Hamilton and Jennifer Melville. Edinburgh: National Galleries of Scotland, 2008

Fox, Digby. 'A Remarkable Voyage'. *Practical Boat Owner*, 520, April 2010: 96–99

Fox-Geen, A. *The Life and Times of the Royal Dorset Yacht Club 1875–1975.* Gillingham, Dorset: Blackmore, 1975

Francis, Clare. *Come Hell or High Water.* London: Pelham, 1977

——. *Come Wind or Weather. ADC Accutrac Races round the World. 1978.* London: Pelham, 1979

——. *Night Sky.* London: Heinemann, 1983

——. *Deceit.* London: Heinemann, 1993

GAC Pindar and Jane Hyde. 'Secret Scenes behind Racing'. *All at Sea*, July 2015: 18

G.N.F.S. 'Little Ships for the Woman Owner'. *Yachting Monthly*, no. 385, May 1938: 21–27

Gabe, Julius. *Sketches of Yachting Life.* London: 'The Yachtsman', 1893

Galbraith, Kenneth. *The Affluent Society.* London: Hamish Hamilton, 1958

Garrett, Alisdair and Trevor Wilkinson. *The History of the Royal Cruising Club 1880–1980.* London: Royal Cruising Club, 1980

Gay Sailing and Cruising Organisation. www.gaysailing.org.uk. Accessed 16 February, 2014

Geertz, Clifford. 'Thick Description: Towards an Interpretative Theory of Cultures'. In Geertz. *The Interpretation of Cultures: Selected Essays.* New York: Basic Books, 1973, pp. 3–30

Gelder, Paul. '25 Cruising Heroes'. *Yachting Monthly*, March, 2012, pp. 22–31

Gerard, Peter (Mrs Charles Pears). *Who Hath Desired the Sea.* London: Arthur Barker, 1962

Gerbault, Alain. *In Quest of the Sun: The Journal of the 'Firecrest'.* London: Hodder and Stoughton, 1929

Gladwin, D. D. *Victorian and Edwardian Canals from Old Photographs.* London: Fitzhouse Books, 1976

Glenans Sailing School. *The Glenans Manual of Sailing.* Trans. Peter Davison and Jim Simpson with Ruth Bagnall and Catherine du Peloux Menage. Newton Abbot: David & Charles, 1992

Goffman, Erving. *Asylums: Essays on the Social Situation of Mental Patients and Other Inmates.* Chicago: Aldine, 1962

Golding, Judy. *The Children of Lovers: A Memoir of William Golding by His Daughter.* London: Faber and Faber, 2011

Golding, William. *Lord of the Flies.* London: Faber and Faber, 1954

Goodbody, L. M. *The Shannon One-Design: A History*. Shannon One-Design Association, c. 1971

Goss, Peter. *Close to the Wind*. London: Headline, 1998

Gower, Francis Leveson, Lord, afterwards Earl of Ellesmere. *Mediterranean Sketches*. London: J. Murray, 1843

Graham, Michael. *The Troy Boats of Fowey*. 2nd rev. edn. Perranporth, Cornwall: Windjammer, 1997

Graham, Commander Robert D. *Rough Passage: Being the Narrative of a Single-handed Voyage to Newfoundland, Labrador and Bermuda in the Seven-Ton Yacht 'Emanuel' and the Subsequent return to England with a Soldier Crew*. Intro. Claud Worth, Vice-Commodore of the Royal Cruising Club. Edinburgh: William Blackwood, 1936

Grahame, Kenneth. *The Wind in the Willows*. 1908. London: Methuen, 1951

Gramsci, Antonio. *Selections From the Prison Notebooks*. Ed. and trans. Quentin Hoare and Geoffrey Nowell Smith. London: Lawrence and Wishart, 1971

Graves, S. R. *A Yachting Cruise in the Baltic*. London: Longman, Green, Longman & Roberts, 1863

Green, Lyndsay. *Babies Aboard*. Camden, Maine: International Marine, 1990

Green, Martin. *Dreams of Adventure, Deeds of Empire*. London: Routledge & Kegan Paul, 1980

Green, Michael. *The Art of Coarse Sailing*. London: Hutchinson, 1962

Greenhill, Basil. *The Life and Death of the Merchant Sailing Ship*. London: HMSO, 1980

Greenhill, Basil and John Hackman. *Herzogin Cecilie: The Life and Times of a Four-Masted Barque*. London: Conway Maritime, 1991

Greenway, Jocelyn M. *Puffin's Log*. Ed. Cathy Woodhead. Porthmadog: Delfryn, 2009

Greville, N. R., *The West Mersea Yacht Club*, Colchester: privately published, 1999

Greville, Lady Violet, ed. *The Gentlewoman's Book of Sports*. London: Henry & Co., c. 1890

Gribbin, John and Mary Gribbin. *Fitzroy: The Remarkable Story of Darwin's Captain and the Invention of the Weather Forecast*. London: Review, 2003

Griffiths, Ian. 'Sailing from Scratch'. *Cruising*, December 2010:12

Griffiths, Maurice. *Yachting on a Small Income: A Talk with the 'Man in the Street'*. London: Hutchinson & Co., 1953

——. *Little Ships and Shoal Waters*. 1937. London: Conway, 1985

—— (ed.) *Cruising Yarns from the 'Yachting Monthly'*. London: Peter Davies, 1938

——. *The Sands of Sylt: An Episode of the North Sea Before the War*. London: Rich & Cowan, 1945

——. *Everyman's Yachting*. London: Hutchinson's, 1952

——. *Sailing on a Small Income*. London: Hutchinsons, 1953

——. *Swatchways and Little Ships*. London: Allen & Unwin, 1971

——. *The Magic of the Swatchways: Cameos of Cruising in Small Yachts*. 1932. London: Futura, 1978

——. *The First of the Tide*. London: Conway Maritime, 1979

Grosvenor, Earl. *The Narrative of a Yacht Voyage to the Mediterranean during the Years 1840–1841*. London: John Murray, 1842

Guest, Montague and William B. Boulton. *The Royal Yacht Squadron: Memorials of its Members, with an Enquiry into the History of Yachting and its Development in the Solent; and a Complete List of Members with Their Yachts from the Foundation of the Club to the Present Time from Official Records.* London: John Murray, 1903

Guzzwell, John. *Trekka round the World.* London: Adlard Coles, 1967

Hackforth-Jones, Gilbert. *The Green Sailors.* Illustrated by Jean Main and David Cobb. London: Hodder & Stoughton, 1951

Hakluyt, Richard. *Divers Voyages Touching the Discoverie of America and the Ilands Adjacent unto the Same, Made First of all by our Englishmen and Afterwards by the Frenchmen and Britons.* 1582

——. *The Principall Navigations, Voiages and Discoveries of the English Nation.* 1589; 3 vols. 1598–1600

Hambly, Peter. *Race under Sail.* London: Stanford Maritime, 1978

Hamerton, P. G. [Philip Gilbert]. *The Unknown River. An Etcher's Voyage of Discovery.* Illustrated with 37 etchings by the Author. Boston: Robert Brothers, 1871

——. *The Saône: A Summer Voyage.* London: Seeley & Co., 1887

Hamilton, Ian. *A Gift Imprisoned: The Poetic Life of Matthew Arnold.* London: Bloomsbury, 1998

Hamilton, John. *Sail Training: The Message of the Tall Ships.* Wellingborough, Northants.: Patrick Stephens, 1988

Hamilton, Malcolm. *The Strange Voyage of Donald Crowhurst.* Play, performed by Blue Raincoat Theatre Co., Sligo, Republic of Ireland, 2003

Hammick, Anne. *Ocean Cruising on a Budget.* London: Adlard Coles, 1990

Hansen, Peter. 'Albert Smith, The Alpine Club, and the Invention of Mountaineering in Mid-Victorian Britain'. *Journal of British Studies,* 34, 1995: 300–324

Harding, Diane. 'So What Did the Yacht Club Do for Cowes?' Unpublished talk, n/d

Harris, Jose. *Private Lives, Public Spirit: Britain 1870–1914.* London: Penguin, 1994

Harris, Leo. *Lee Ho! 50 Years Sailing around the Channel Islands.* St John, Jersey: Channel Island Publishing, 2008

Harrison, Brian. *Drink and the Victorians: The Temperance Question in England 1815–1872.* London: Faber and Faber, 1971

Harron, Hilary. *Right to the Bitter End: A Survival Guide for Sailing Couples.* London: Adlard Coles Nautical, 1995

——. *Involuntary Jibes.* London: Adlard Coles Nautical, 1998

Harvey, John. *Crowhurst.* Play, performed by 'Benchtour', Scotland, 2007

Haslam, S. Alexander. *Psychology in Organizations: The Social Identities Approach.* 2nd edn. London: Sage, 2004

Hasler, H. G. ('Blondie'). *Harbours and Anchorages of the North Coast of Brittany.* Southampton: Robert Ross, 1952

Hasler, H. G. and J. K. McLeod. *Practical Junk Rig: Design, Aerodynamics and Handling.* London: Adlard Coles, 1988

Hay, David and Joan Hay. *The Handbook of Family Cruising.* 1977. London: Paul Elek, 1977

Hayes, Jim. *The History of the Weymouth Sailing Club: The First Fifty Years.* Weymouth: Weymouth Sailing Club, c.1994

Head, Simon. 'Children of the Sun', *Review Saturday Guardian*, 2 October, 2010

Head, Viv. *Sailing Gaffers: Stories from 50 Years of the Old Gaffers Association*. London: Quartet, 2013

Heath, Johanna. 'Sail-training with a Woman Skipper'. *Yachting Monthly*, 62 (371), March 1937: 383–390

——. 'Taking the Plunge – with Some Sound Advice over the Water'. *Yachting Monthly*, 65 (390), October, 1938: 487–491

——. 'Taking the Plunge. II – First Lessons in Cruising under Convoy'. *Yachting Monthly*, 66 (391), November 1938: 26–31

Heath, Ted. *Sailing: A Course of My Life*. London: Sidgwick & Jackson, 1975

Heaton, Peter. *Yachting: A History*. London: B.T. Batsford, 1955

——. *A History of Yachting in Pictures*. London: Tom Stacey, 1972

Heckstall-Smith, Anthony. *Sacred Cowes*. 2nd edn, rev. London: Anthony Blond, 1965

Heckstall-Smith, Brooke. *The International Yacht Racing Rules: The Helmsman's Handbook*. London: Horace Cox, 1908

——. *The Complete Yachtsman*. London: Methuen, 1912

Hedderwick, Mairi. *Sea Change: The Summer Voyage from East to West Scotland of the 'Anassa'*. Edinburgh: Canongate, 1999

Hellings, Dorothy. *Close Quarters*. London: Robert Ross, 1947

Henshall, David. 'Saving History'. *All at Sea*, August 2015: 30

Henty, G. A. *With Clive in India*. London: Blackie & Son, 1884

——, *With Kitchener in the Soudan*. London: Blackie & Son, 1903

Heriot, Geoff. 'Australia's First Ocean Race'. *Marine Quarterly*, 15, Autumn 2014: 14–23

Herman, Camilla. 'From Bluebacks to Chart Apps'. *Cruising*, September 2015

Herreshoff, L. Francis. *Captain Nat Herreshoff, the Wizard of Bristol*. Dobbs Ferry, New York: Sheridan 1996

Herring, P. M. *A Memorandum and Some Reminiscences*. Burnham-on-Crouch: P. M. Herring, 1976

Heyerdahl, Thor. *The Kon-Tiki Expedition: By Raft across the South Seas*. 1948. London: Allen & Unwin, 1950

Hickey, William. *Memoirs*. 4 vols. London: Hurst & Blackett, 1948

Hill, Annie. *Brazil and Beyond: Long Distance Voyaging with Annie Hill*. 2000. Bradford-on-Avon: Thomas Reed, 2000

Hill, C. P. *British Economic and Social History 1700–1964*, 3rd edn. London: Edward Arnold, 1970

Hill, Judith. *In Search of Islands: A Life of Conor O'Brien*. Cork: Collins Press, 2009

Hillsdon, Sonia. *The Jersey Lily: The Life and Times of Lillie Langtry*. Bradford-on-Avon: Seaflower, 1993

Hiscock, Eric C. *I Left the Navy*. London: Edward Arnold, 1945

——. *Cruising under Sail*. Oxford: Oxford University Press, 1950

——. *Voyaging under Sail*. Oxford: Oxford University Press, 1959 (combined with *Cruising Under Sail* in one vol., Oxford University Press, 1981, as *Cruising under Sail*)

——. *Around the World in Wanderer III*. London: Oxford University, 1956

Hobsbawm, Eric and Terence Ranger, ed. *The Invention of Tradition*. Cambridge: Cambridge UP, 1983

Hockley, Norman C. *Barry Yacht Club … and 50 Years On: A History of Barry Yacht Club.1928–1978*. Barry: WAP Printers, 1978

Hodder, Edwin. *John MacGregor ('Rob Roy')*. London: Hodder Brothers, 1895

Hollins, Holly. *The Tall Ships Are Sailing: The Cutty Sark Tall Ship Races*. Newton Abbot: David & Charles, 1982

Holmes, Richard. 'Death and Destiny'. *Guardian, Review*, Saturday 24 January, 2004

Holmes, Rupert. 'Families Afloat'. *Yachts and Yachting*, 1678, October 2014, 77–82

——. 'Best of British'. *Yachts and Yachting*, Nov. 2014: 40–43

Holt, Geoff. *Walking on Water: A Voyage round Britain and through Life*. Woodbridge: Seafarer, 2008

Holt, Richard. *Sport and the British: A Modern History*. Oxford: Clarendon Press, 1992

Hooft, C. G't. 'The First English Yachts'. *Mariner's Mirror*, 5, 1912: 108–123

Horlock, Christopher. *The Neat and Nippy Guide to Brighton's History*. Brighton: S.B. Publications, 2003

Horne, John, Alan Tomlinson and Garry Whannel. *Understanding Sport: An Introduction to the Sociological and Cultural Analysis of Sport*. London: Spon, 1999

House, John. *Impressionists by the Sea*. London: Royal Academy of Arts, 2007

Howard-Williams, Jeremy. *Teach Your Child about Sailing*. London: Pearson, 1963

Howarth, David. *The Shetland Bus*. Edinburgh: Nelson, 1957

Howells, Val. *Sailing into Solitude*. 1966. London: Temple, 1966

Huggins, Mike. *The Victorians and Sport*. London: Hambledon and London, 2004

Hughes, Barry D. *North Devon Barges*. Appledore: North Devon Museums Trust, 2015

Hughes, John Scott, ed. *MacPherson's Voyages*. London: Methuen, 1944

Hughes, R. E. *Two Summer Cruises with the Baltic Fleet, 1854–5. Being the Log of the 'Pet' Yacht, 8 Tons, R.T.Y.C.* London: Smith, Elder, 1855; Nabu Public Domain Reprints

Hughes. Steffan. 'Sixty Years Ago: Cross-Channel by Night in an Enterprise'. *Classic Boat*, 333, February 2016

Hughes, Thomas. *Tom Brown's Schooldays*. 1857. Ed. Andrew Sanders. Oxford: Oxford University Press, 1989

——. *The Manliness of Christ*. 1879

Humphries, Steve. *The Call of the Sea: Britain's Maritime Past 1900–1960*. London: BBC Books, 1997

Hurst, Alex A. *Arthur Briscoe: Marine Artist*. Brighton: Teredo, 1974

Hussey, Frank. *The Royal Harwich: A Short History of the RHYC*. Ipswich: Boydell Press, 1972

——. *Old Fitz: Edward Fitzgerald and East Coast Sailing*. Ipswich: Boydell Press, 1974

Hutchinson, Michael. *Hello Sailor: A Year Spent Adrift and All at Sea*. London: Yellow Jersey, 2009

Hutton, M. *The Cruise of the 'Humming Bird', 1864, to Ireland or Notes near Home*. London: Tinsley and Co., 1864; Forgotten Books, 2015

Illingworth, John. *Offshore: A Complete Introduction to Ocean Racing and Cruising, Modern Yacht Handling and Equipment*. London: Robert Ross, 1949 (6th edn retitled *Further Offshore*, London: Adlard Coles, 1969)

——. *The Malham Story*. Lymington: Nautical Publishing Co., 1972

Ingenhousz, John. 'On the Degree of Salubrity of the Common Air at Sea Compared with that of the Seashore and that of Places Far Removed from the Sea'. *Philosophical Transactions of the Royal Society*, LXX (1780), 375

International 14s. 14s website, http://www.international14.org

Ionides, Cyril and J. B. Atkins. *A Floating Home*. Illustrations by Arnold Bennett. 1918. London: Chatto & Windus, 1918

Irish Cruising Club. *Sailing Directions for the East Coast of Ireland*. Dublin: Irish Cruising Club, 1930

——. *Sailing Directions for the South and SouthWest Coasts of Ireland*. Dublin: Irish Cruising Club, 1930

Irving, John, Lieut.-Commander. *The Yachtsman's Pilot Volume I: Rivers and Creeks of the Thames Estuary*. London: Captain O.M. Watts, 1933

Irving, John and Douglas Service. *The Yachtsman's Week-End Book*. With Illustrations by Beryl Irving. London: Seeley Service, 1938

Island Sailing Club. *The Island Sailing Club 1889–2014*. Cowes: Island Sailing Club, 2015

Jack, Ian. *Guardian*, 6 July, 2013: 41

Jacobs, W. W. *Many Cargoes*. 1896

——. *Night Watches*. Illustrated by Stanley Davis. London: Hodder & Stoughton, 1914

James, Claire. *Sail for the Mediterranean: How to Prepare for Your Dream Cruise*. London: Adlard Coles Nautical, 2003

James, Naomi. *At One with the Sea: Alone around the World*. London: Hutchinson/ Stanley Paul, 1979

Jenkins, Clive and Barrie Sherman. *The Collapse of Work*. London: Eyre Methuen, 1979

Jermain, James. 'The Wharram Way'. *Yachting Monthly*, January, 2006: 98–102

Jerome, Jerome K. *Three Men in a Boat (To Say Nothing of the Dog)*. 1889. London: Collins, 1957

Jet Lag. Play. Perf. The Builders' Association, New York, 2007

Jonathan Livingston Seagull. Film. Perf. James Franciscus, Philip Ahn. Dir. Hall Bartlett. Paramount, 1973

Johnson, Peter. *Boating Britain*. Lymington, Hants.: Nautical Publishing Co., 1973

——. *The Encyclopedia of Yachting*. London: Dorling Kindersley, 1989

——. *Yacht Clubs of the World*. 1994. Shrewsbury: Waterline, 1994

——. *Yacht Rating: 170 Years of Speed, Success and Failure against Competitors - and the Clock*. Lymington: Bucksea Guides, 1997

Johnson, Samuel. *A Journey to the Western Islands of Scotland*. 1775. London: Philip Allan & Co., 1925

——. *The Lives of the British Poets*, Vol. 3, 1781

Jones, H. Lewis, MA, assisted by C. B. Lockwood. *Swin, Swale and Swatchway or Cruises down the Thames, the Medway and the Essex Rivers.* London: Waterlow & Sons, 1892. London: Lodestart, 2014

Jones, Julia. *The Salt-Stained Book.* Vol. 1 of the 'Strong Winds' Trilogy. Pleshey, Essex: Golden Duck, 2011

———. *A Ravelled Flag.* Vol. 2 of the 'Strong Winds' Trilogy. Pleshey, Essex: Golden Duck, 2011

———. *Ghosting Home.* Vol. 3 of the 'Strong Winds' Trilogy. Pleshey, Essex: Golden Duck, 2012

Joyce, James. *Dubliners.* 1914. London: Grant Richards

Karlsson, Elis. *Mother Sea.* London: Oxford University Press, 1964

Karslake, Sally, ed. *Mirror Mania: An Illustrated Guide to Building, Cruising and Racing the World's Most Popular Family Centreboard Dinghy.* Mirror Class Association, 1976.

Kavanagh, Jake. 'Nautical but Nice'. *Practical Boat Owner,* 490, October 2007: 62–64

Keeble, W. B. and D. W. Cobden. *Cassell's Young Mariners' Guide.* London: Cassell, 1962

Kember, Frank. 'To Us It's Sport … To the Americans It's War'. In The Royal Burnham Yacht Club. *A History of the Royal Burnham Yacht Club,* 2nd edn. Burnham-on-Crouch: Royal Burnham YC, 1995: 229–262

Kemish, Norman. *The First Twenty Years of the Southampton International Boat Show.* Hants.: Norman Kemish, 2003

Kemp, Dixon. *Yacht Designing: A Treatise on the Practical Application of the Scientific Principles upon Which Is Based the Art of Designing Yachts.* Illustrated with Numerous Drawings of Celebrated Yachts. London: 'The Field' Office, 1876

———. *A Manual of Yacht and Boat Sailing.* 1878. 10th edn (ed. B. Heckstall-Smith), 1904

Kemp, Peter, ed. *The Oxford Companion to Ships and the Sea.* London: Oxford University Press, 1976

Kemp, Peter and Richard Ormond. *The Great Age of Sail.* Oxford: Phaidon, 1986

Kenealy, Dr. Arabella. 'Woman as an Athlete: A Rejoinder'. *Nineteenth Century,* April 1899: 643

Kerr, Willy. *RCC Pilotage Foundation: Faroes, Iceland and Greenland.* 3rd edn. St Ives, Cambs.: Imray Laurie Norie and Wilson, 2004

———. 'Refurbishing a Legend'. *Practical Boat Owner,* 579, October 2014: 82–85

Kibble, Gary and Steve Kibble. *Sailing For Kids.* First published in 1987 as *The Prudential Book of Sailing.* Brighton: Fernhurst, 1989

King, Bill. *Capsize.* Lymington: Nautical, 1969

King, Cyril. 'Yachting at Dartmouth: An Outline History'. *Maritime South West* 24 (2011): 5–22

Kinsey, T. L. *Family Cruising.* London: Stanley Paul, 1975

Kingsley, Charles. *Westward Ho!* 1855. London: Robinson, 1989

Kipling, Rudyard. *Stalky and Co.* 1899. Oxford University Press, 1987

———. *The Collected Poems of Rudyard Kipling.* Ware, Hertfordshire: Wordsworth, 1994. ('The White Mans Burden', 1899, p. 334; 'The Islanders', 1902, pp. 312–314; 'The

Dykes', 1902, pp. 315–317; 'Epitaphs of the War', 1914–1918, p. 399; 'The Children', 1914–1918, p. 544)

Klein, David and Mary Louise King. *Great Adventures in Small Boats*. (Original Title: *They Took to the Sea*). 1948. New York: Collier Books, 1963

Knight, E. F. *The Cruise of the 'Falcon': A Voyage to South America in a 30-ton Yacht*. 1881. London: Longmans, Green & Co., 1904

——. *The 'Falcon' on the Baltic*. 1888. London: Rupert Hart-Davis, 1951. The Mariners Library no. 15

——. *The Cruise of the 'Alerte'*. 1890. London: Rupert Hart-Davis, 1952. The Mariners Library no. 2

——. *Small-Boat Sailing. An Explanation of the Management of Small Yachts, Half-Decked and Open Sailing-Boats of Various Rigs; Sailing on Sea and on River, Cruising, etc.* London: John Murray, 1901

Knox-Johnston, Robin. *A World of My Own: The Single-Handed, Non-Stop Circumnavigation of the World in 'Suhaili'*. London: Cassell, 1969

——. *Robin Knox-Johnston's History of Yachting*. Oxford: Phaidon, 1990

——. *The Columbus Venture*. London: BBC, 1991

——. *Beyond Jules Verne*. London: Hodder & Stoughton, 1995

Kuhnst, Peter. *Sports: A Cultural History in the Mirror of Art*. Dresden: Verlag Der Kunst, 1996

Laing, R. D. *The Divided Self: A Study of Sanity and Madness*. London: Tavistock, 1960

Lamsley, Arthur. *Sea Lure*. London: Heath Cranton, 1935

Langtry, Lillie. *The Days I Knew*. 1925. St John, Jersey: Redberry Press, 1989

Lapp, Ralph E. *The Voyage of the Lucky Dragon*. London: Frederick Muller, 1958

Laver, James. *A Concise History of Costume*. London: Thames and Hudson, 1969

Lavery, Brian. *The Island Nation: A History of Britain and the Sea*. London: Conway Maritime, 2005

——. *In Which They Served. The Royal Navy Officer Experience in the Second World War*. London: Conway, 2008

Lawler, Ray. *Summer of the Seventeenth Doll*. Play. London: Samuel French, 1957

Lawrence, Charles. *Fairey Marine – Racing Dinghies and Utility Boats 1958*. Charleslawrencechiswick.co.uk, 2014

——. *Fairey Marine: Boats, Raceboats, Rivals and Revivals*. Chiswick: Charles Lawrence, 2014

Leather, John. *The Northseamen: The Story of the Fishermen, Yachtsmen and Shipbuilders of the Colne and Blackwater Rivers*. Lavenham, Suffolk: Terence Dalton, 1971

——. *The Salty Shore: The Story of the River Blackwater*. Lavenham: Terence Dalton, 1979

——. *Albert Strange: Yacht Designer and Artist 1855–1917*. Edinburgh: Pentland Press, 1990

——. *The Gaff Rig Handbook: History, Design, Techniques and Development*. 2nd edn. London: Adlard Coles Nautical, 2002

Lee, Adrian and Ruby Philpott. *Laurent Giles: An Evolution of Yacht Design*. London: A and C Black, 1990

Lee, Bernard T. *The History of Barnt Green Sailing Club 1918–1990*. Barnt Green Sailing Club, 1991

Lee, Hermione. *Penelope Fitzgerald: A Life*. London: Vintage, 2014

Leger, Alicia St. *A History of the Royal Cork Yacht Club*. Cork: Royal Cork Yacht Club, 2005

Le Queux, William. *The Great War in England in 1897*. London: Tower Publishing Co., 1895

———. *The Invasion of 1910, with a Full Account of the Siege of London*. Naval Chapters by H. W. Wilson. Introductory Letter by Field-Marshal Earl Roberts. 1906. London: Eveleigh Nash, 1906

Le Scelleur, Kevin and Philip Jeune. *Sailing through a Century … A Story of Maritime Pleasure, Competition and Bravery*. St Martin, Jersey: PJ News and Publishing, 2003

Leslie, Anita. *Francis Chichester: A Biography*. New York: Walker and Co., 1975

Leslie, Robert C. *The Sea-Boat. How to Build, Rig and Sail Her: Including Practical Directions for Handling Small Boats in Launching or Landing through a Surf*. London: Chapman & Hall, 1892

L'Estrange, The Rev. A. G. *Yachting around the West of England*. London: Hurst and Blackett, 1865

———. *From the Thames to the Tamar*. London: Hurst and Blackett, 1873

Lewis, C. E. Tyrell. *Lifeboats and Their Conversion*. London: H. F. & G. Witherby, 1935

———. *Teach Yourself Sailing*. London: English Universities Press, 1947

Lewis, David. *The Boat that Would Not Travel Due West*. London: Temple, 1961

———. *Daughters of the Wind*. London: Gollancz, 1967

———. *We, the Navigators: The Ancient Art of Landfalling in the Pacific*. Canberra: Australian National University Press, 1972

———. *Ice Bird: The First Single-Handed Voyage to Antartica*. London: Collins, 1975

———. *The Voyaging Stars: Secrets of the Pacific Island Navigators*. Sydney/London: Collins, 1978

Light, Alison. *Forever England: Femininity, Literature and Conservatism Between the Wars*. London: Routledge, 1991

Liley, John. *France – The Quiet Way*. London: Stanford Maritime, 1975

Lines, Peggy. *I'm on Starboard! The Story of the North Devon Yacht Club*. Instow: North Devon Yacht Club, 1986

Lipton, Sir Thomas, Bt. *Leaves from the Lipton Logs*. London: Hutchinson, n/d [1931]

Llewellyn, L. R. *A Brief History of the Royal Dart 1866–1983*. Dartmouth: Royal Dart Yacht Club, 1983

Llewellyn, Sam. *Dead Reckoning*. London: Michael Joseph, 1987

———. *Riptide*. London: Michael Joseph, 1992

Loibner, Dieter. *The Folk Boat: From Cult to Classic – The Renaissance of a Legend*. Dobbs Ferry, NY: Sheridan House, 2002.

London, Jack. *Sea Wolf*. New York: Macmillan, 1904

Loomis, Alfred F. 'Happy Ending'. In *On the Water: The Yachting Muse*. Ed. Michael Gilkes. Brighton: Book Guild, 2009, pp. 85–94; *Marine Quarterly*, 11, Summer 2013: 48–57

Loughran, Tracey. 'Masculinity, Trauma and "Shell-Shock". *The Psychologist*, 28 (3), March, 2015: 250

Lowden, Desmond. *Cry Havoc*. London: Macmillan, 1984

Lowerson, John. 'Golf'. In Tony Mason, ed. *Sport in Britain: A Social History*. Cambridge: Cambridge University Press, 1889: 187–214

——. *Sport and the English Middle Classes 1870–1914*. Manchester: Manchester University Press, 1993

Lubbock, Basil. *The Last of the Windjammers*. 2 vols. Glasgow: Brown, Son and Ferguson, 1927

Lucas-Phillips, C. E. with H. G. Hasler. *Cockleshell Heroes*. London: Heinemann, 1956

Mac Annaidh, Seamas. *Irish History*. Bath: Paragon, 2005

MacArthur, Ellen. *Taking on the World*. London: Michael Joseph, 2002

——. *Race against Time*. London: Michael Joseph, 2005

MacGregor, J. *A Thousand Miles in the Rob Roy Canoe on Rivers and Lakes of Europe*. London: Sampson, Low and Marston, 1866

——. *The Voyage Alone in the Yawl 'Rob Roy' from London to Paris*. 1867. Introduction by Arthur Ransome. London: Rupert Hart-Davis, 1954. The Mariners Library no. 24

——. *The 'Rob Roy' on the Jordan: A Canoe Cruise in Palestine, Egypt and the Waters of Damascus*. London: Murray, 1869

Mack, John. *The Sea: A Cultural History*. London: Reaktion Books, 2013

Mackinnon, A. J. *The Unlikely Voyage of Jack de Crow: A Mirror Odyssey from North Wales to the Black Sea*. Woodbridge, Suffolk: Seafarer, 2002

MacRae, Josh. *Messing About on the River*. Comp. Tony Hatch and Les Reed. Pye, 1962

Madge, Tim. *Long Voyage Home: True Stories from Britain's Twilight Maritime Years*. London: Simon & Schuster, 1993

——. *The Last Hero. Bill Tilman: A Biography of the Explorer*. London: Hodder & Stoughton, 1995

Mahan, Captain A. T. *The Influence of Sea Power upon History, 1660–1783*. 1889

Maher, John M. *Channel Packets and Ocean Liners 1850–1970*. London: HMSO, 1980

Malthus, Thomas. *An Essay on the Principle of Population as It Affects the Future Improvement of Society*. 1798

Mangan, J. A. *Athleticism in the Victorian and Edwardian Public School*. Cambridge: Cambridge University Press, 1981

——. *The Games Ethic and Imperialism*. London: Viking, 1985

——. 'Social Darwinism and Upper-Class Education in Late Victorian and Edwardian England'. In *Manliness and Morality: Middle-Class Masculinity in Britain and America 1800–1940*. Ed. J. A. Mangan and James Walvin. Manchester: Manchester University Press, 1987: 135–159

Mangan, J. A. and Roberta Park, ed. *From 'Fair Sex' to Feminism: Sport and the Socialization of Women in the Industrial and Post-Industrial Eras*. London: Frank Cass, 1987

Mangan, J. A. and James Walvin, ed. *Manliness and Morality: Middle-Class Masculinity in Britain and America 1800–1940*. Manchester: Manchester University Press, 1987

Manvell, Louise and Roger Manvell. *The Country Life Book of Sailing Boats.* Photographs by Eileen Ramsay. London: Country Life, 1962

Marks, Richard *et al. The Burrell Collection.* London: Collins, 1983

Marlow, Henry. *Sailing and Boating.* Loughborough: Ladybird, 1972

Marrett, P. R. *Yachts and Yacht Building: Being a Treatise on the Construction of Yachts and Other Matters Relating to Yachting.* London: E. & F.N. Spon, 1865

Martin, E. G. *Sailorman.* Illustrated by the Author. London: Oxford University Press, 1933

Masefield, John. 'Sea Fever'. 1899. In *Salt-Water Ballads.* London: Grant Richards, 1902

——. 'Cargoes'. In *Ballads and Poems.* London: Elkin Matthews, 1910

——. *The Bird of Dawning.* 1933. London: Methuen, 1933

Mason, Carol. *Sea Fever.* London: Sphere, 2007

Matthews, Andrew. *The Bar and Beyond: The Story of the Yealm Club 1933 to 2006.* Newton Ferrers: Andrew Matthews, 2007

Maugham, W. Somerset. 'The Door of Opportunity' in *W. Somerset Maugham. The Complete Short Stories.* Vol. 3. London: Heinemann, 1951, pp. 1078–1108

Maupassant, Guy de. *Afloat.* With a Selection of Drawings by E. Riou. 1888. Trans. from the French *Sur L'Eau* by Marlo Johnston. London: Peter Owen, 1995

Mazel, Charles. *Heave Ho! My Little Green Book of Seasickness.* Shrewsbury: Waterline, 1993

McCallum, May Fife. *Fast and Bonnie: A History of William Fife and Son Yachtbuilders.* Edinburgh: John Donald, 2002

McComb, Clare. 'George Martin, Founding Father of Restoration'. *Classic Boat,* June 2015: 50–54

McCrone, Kathleen, E. 'The "Lady Blue": Sport at the Oxbridge Women's Colleges From their Foundation to 1914'. *British Journal of Sports History,* 3 (1986): 191–215

McCrum, Michael. *Thomas Arnold, Headmaster: A Reassessment.* New York: Oxford University Press, 1989

McCrum, Robert. 'Deep Water'. *Guardian,* 5 April, 2009

McCulloch, John Herries. *A Million Miles in Sail: Being the Story of the Sea Career of Captain C. C. Dixon.* London: Hurst & Blackett. The Paternoster Library, no. 5, 1933.

McMullen, R.T. *Down Channel.* 1869. 2nd edn, 1893. The Mariners Library no.7. London: Rupert Hart-Davis, 1949.

McNee, Alan. *The Cockney Who Sold the Alps: Albert Smith and the Ascent of Mont Blanc.* Brighton: Victorian Secrets, 2015

Mead, Lt Col. C. J. H. *History of the Royal Cornwall Yacht Club, 1871–1949, Including a Contemporary Account of the Falmouth Sailing Club and Items of Interest concerning Yachting in General.* Plymouth: Underhill, 1951

Mellor, John. *Young Crew.* Shrewsbury: Waterline, 1993

Messum, Stuart Victor Seymour Craigie. *East Coast Rivers: Charts and Sailing Directions for the Rivers Crouch, Roach, Blackwater, Colne, Stour, Orwell, Deben, Ore and Alde; Together with General Charts from the Thames to Southwold.* London: J. D. Potter, 1903

Middleton, E. E. *The Cruise of the 'Kate'*. 1870. The Mariners Library no. 23. London: Rupert Hart-Davis, 1953

Millar, George. *Maquis*. London: Heinemann, 1945

——. *Isabel and the Sea: A Voyage through the Canals of France to the Mediterranean*. London: Heinemann, 1948

Millar, John. *'Anything but Sailing': A History of West Kirby Sailing Club*. Holyake, Wirral: John Millar, 1985

Mitchell, Percy of Porthmellon. *A Boatbuilder's Story*. Mevagissey: Kingston, 1968

Moitessier, Bernard. *The Long Way*. London: Granada, 1983

Monsarrat, Nicholas. *The Cruel Sea*. London: Cassell, 1951

Moody, David. *The Moody Legacy: An Illustrated History 1827–2005*. Warsash: Warsash Publishing, 2008

Moore, Alan. *Last Days of Mast and Sail: An Essay in Nautical Comparative Anatomy*. 1925. Newton Abbot: David & Charles Reprints, 1970

Morgan, Adrian. 'The Vertue'. *Yachting World*, November 2004, 59–63

——. *The Trouble with Old Boats*. London: Adlard Coles Nautical, 2008

——. 'The Schooner America'. *Marine Quarterly*, 23, Autumn, 2016, 67–75

Morris, James. *Farewell the Trumpets*. London: Penguin, 1979

——. *Heaven's Command: An Imperial Progress*. London: Penguin, 1979

——. *Pax Britannica: The Climax of an Empire*. 1968. London: Penguin, 1979

Moss, Stephen. 'Against the Wind'. *Guardian*, 8 February, 2005

Mount, Ferdinand. 'Lumpers v. Splitters'. *London Review of Books*, 31 March, 2016: 31–33

Mulhauser, G. H. P. *The Cruise of the Amaryllis*. 1924. With a Memoir by E. Keble Chatterton. London: Hart-Davis, 1950

Mulvey, Laura. 'Visual Pleasure and Narrative Cinema'. *Screen*, 16(3), Autumn 1975: 6–18

Mulville, Frank. *Terchelling Sands*. London: Herbert Jenkins, 1968

——. *North Star to Southern Cross, by Steam and Sail to Argentina*. Leatherhead: Ashford, Buchan & Enright, 1993

Muncaster, Claude. *Rolling Round the Horn*. London: Rich & Cowan, 1933

Munro, Neil. 'Among the Yachts'. In Neil Munro. *Para Handy Tales*. Edinburgh: Blackwood, 1969, pp. 249–254

Newbolt, Henry. *Admirals All*. London: Elkin Matthews' Shilling Garland no.8, 1896

——. *The Island Race*. London: Elkin Mathews, 1898

——. *Clifton Chapel and Other School Poems*. London: J. Murray, 1908

Newby, Eric. *The Last Grain Race*. London: Secker & Warburg, 1956

——. *Learning the Ropes: An Apprenticeship in the Last of the Windjammers*. 1999. London: John Murray, 1999

Newton, Laura (ed). *Painting at the Edge: British Coastal Art Colonies 1880–1930*. Bristol: Sansom, 2005

Nichols, Peter. *A Voyage for Madmen*. London: Profile, 2001

Nicholson, Christopher. *Rock Lighthouses of Britain*. Cambridge: Patrick Stephens, 1983

Nicholson, John. *Great Years in Yachting*. Lymington: Nautical, 1970

Nicholson, Peter. *The Brilliance of Sunbeams: A Celebration of the Classic Keel Boat.* Bosham, Chichester: Solent Sunbeams, 2005

Nicolson, Ian. *Sea Saint.* London: Peter Davies, 1957

——. *The Log of the 'Maken'.* London, Peter Davies, 1961

Nicolson, Ian with David Gray. *Alfred Mylne: The Leading Yacht Designer 1896–1920.* Stroud, Gloucester: Amberley, 2015

Nicolson, Marjorie Hope. *Mountain Gloom and Mountain Glory: The Development of the Aesthetics of the Infinite.* 1959. New York: Norton, 1963

Nixon, James. *Royal Ulster: A Yacht Club and Its House.* Bangor: Royal Ulster Yacht Club, 1999

Nixon, W. M. *To Sail the Crested Sea: The Story of Irish Cruising and the First Fifty years of the Irish Cruising Club.* Dublin. The Irish Cruising Club, 1979

——. *Howth: A Centenary of Sailing.* Dublin: Howth Yacht Club, 1995

North, Roger. *Notes of Me: The Autobiography of Robert North.* Ed. Peter Millard. Toronto: University of Toronto Press, 2000

Novak, Skip. *One Watch at a Time: Around the World with 'Drum' on the Whitbread Race.* Newton Abbot: David & Charles, 1988

O'Brien, Conor. *Across Three Oceans.* 1927. London: Granada, 1984

——. *Two Boys Go Sailing.* London: Dent, 1936

——. *The Runaways.* London: Harrap & Co., 1941

——. *The Castaways.* Dublin: Browne & Nolan, 1946

——. *The Luck of the Golden Salmon.* London: Nelson & Son, 1951

Ocean Youth Club–Ocean Youth Trust. *50 Years of Adventure under Sail.* Gosport: Ocean Youth Trust South, 2010

O'Connell, Adrian. 'Royal Western Yacht Club of Ireland – Club History'. http://www.westernyachtclub.com/cms/index.php?page=club-history. Novembe, 2004 (accessed October 2015)

Ogilvie, Vivian. *The English Public School.* London: Batsford, 1957

Orford, Lord. *Lord Orford's Voyage round the Fens in 1774.* Intro. H. J. K. Jenkins; Notes Mary Liquorice. Peterborough: Cambridgeshire Libraries, 1988. Facsimile of edn. Printed Doncaster: Edwin White, 1868

Orwell, George. *Coming Up for Air.* 1939. Harmondsworth: Penguin, 1962

——. 'Such, Such Were the Joys'. *Partisan Review*, Sept.–Oct., 1952. Reprinted in Orwell. *The Penguin Essays of George Orwell.* London: Penguin, 1984, pp. 416–452

O'Sullivan, Daniel (compiler). *Dublin Bay: A Century of Sailing 1884–1994.* Dublin: Dublin Bay Sailing Club, 1984

Oulton, Carolyn. *Below the Fairy City: A Life of Jerome K. Jerome.* Brighton: Victorian Secrets, 2012

Owen, Jamie. *Magic Islands.* Llandysul, Ceredigion: Gomer, 2002

Pace, Franco. *William Fife: Master of the Classic Yacht.* Brooklin, Maine: Wooden Boat Books; London: Adlard Coles Nautical, 1998

Pardoe, Blaine. *The Cruise of the 'Sea Eagle': The Amazing True Story of Imperial Germany's Gentleman Pirate.* London: Crecy, 2009

Parker, Owen. *Tack Now, Skipper.* London: Adlard Coles Granada, 1979

Parker, Peter. *The Old Lie: The Great War and the Public-School Ethos.* 1987. London: Hambledon Continuum, 2007

Parkinson, Sonia. *Salcombe Yacht Club: The First Hundred Years.* Privately printed, 1995

Parsons, Timothy. *The British Imperial Century 1815–1914: World History Perspective.* Oxford: Rowman and Littlefield, 1999

Passmore, John. 'Transatlantic Sailing'. *Yachting Monthly,* 1989

Patmore, Coventry. 'The Angel in the House'. Boston: Ticknor & Fields, 1856

Payne, Christiana. *Where the Sea Meets the Land: Artists on the Coast in Nineteenth-Century Britain.* Bristol: Sansom & Co., 2007

Payton, Philip, Alston Kennerley and Helen Doe, ed. *The Maritime History of Cornwall.* Exeter: Exeter University Press, 2014

Pears, Chas. *Yachting on the Sunshine Coast.* Southern Railway Company, 1932

Pearse, Ronald. *The Last of a Glorious Era.* 1934. London: Syren & Shipping, 1934, p. 96

Peck, John. *War, the Army and Victorian Literature.* Basingstoke: Palgrave, 1998

——. *Maritime Fiction: Sailors and the Sea in British and American Novels, 1719–1917.* Basingstoke: Palgrave, 2001

Pemble, John. 'Golden Dolly: Review of William Rubinstein, *Who Were the Rich?*' *London Review of Books,* 24 September, 2009: 23–24

Pepys, Samuel. *The Diary of Samuel Pepys: A New and Complete Transcription.* Ed. Robert Latham and William Matthews. London: Bell & Hyman, 1985

——. *The Tangier Papers of Samuel Pepys.* Ed. J. Chappel. London: Naval Records Society, 1935

Pett, Phineas. *The Autobiography of Phineas Pett.* Abbreviated version edited by Rev. S. Dunne in *Archeologia,* 12, 1796. Full version ed. W. G. Perrin. London: Naval Records Society, 1918. Miami: Hard Press Publishing, n/d.

Peyton, Mike. *The Pick of Peyton.* London: Macmillan, 1983

——. *Quality Time: His 50 Years of Sailing plus 80 Cartoons.* Arundel: Fernhurst, 2005

——. *Ever Wonder Why We Do It?* London: Adlard Coles, 2007

——. 'The Good Old Days'. *Marine Quarterly* 18, Summer 2015: 88–92

Phillips-Birt, Douglas. *British Ocean Racing.* London: Adlard Coles; George Harrap, 1960

——. *The History of Yachting.* London: Elm Tree; Hamish Hamilton, 1974

——. *The Cumberland Fleet: Two Hundred Years of Yachting 1775–1975.* London: Royal Thames Yacht Club, 1978

Pickard, Stephen. *The 'Lone Gull' Files.* Shepperton: Bosun Publications, 2007

Pickthall, Barry. 'No Guts–No Glory': *The Dramatic Story of Chay Blyth's British Steel Challenge Yacht Race around the World.* Abingdon: Carfax, 1993

——. *The British Marine Industry: A Century of Development and Growth.* Egham, Surrey: British Marine Industries Federation, c. 1998

——. *A History of Sailing in 100 Objects.* London: Adlard Coles Nautical, 2016.

Piper, Leonard. *Dangerous Waters: The Life and Death of Erskine Childers.* London: Hambledon and London, 2003

Poland, Peter. 'Small Is Beautiful'. *Practical Boat Owner* 572, April 2014: 24-28

——. 'Broadside'. *Sailing Today*, September 2014: 22

——. 'The Hanse Story'. *Practical Boat Owner*, 587, June 2015: 24–28

Poovey, Mary. *Uneven Developments: The Ideological Work of Gender in Mid-Victorian England*. Chicago: Chicago University Press, 1988

Popham, Hugh and Robin Popham. *A Thirst for the Sea. The Sailing Adventures of Erskine Childers*. London: Stanford Maritime, 1979

Porter, Bernard. *British Imperial: What the Empire Wasn't*. London: I. B. Taurus, 2015

Powles, Les. *Hands Open: Twice round the World Single-Handed East-to-West and West-to-East*. Emsworth, Hants: Kenneth Mason, 1987

——. *Solitaire Spirit; Three Times around the World Single-Handed*. London: Adlard Coles Nautical, 2012

Preston, Robert. *Yachting under Statute: The Principal Provisions of the Maritime Law Applicable to Pleasure Yachts Practically Arranged as a Handbook for the Use of Yacht-Owners*. London: Norie & Wilson, 1884. 2nd edn, rev. Charles Jemmett. London: Sweet & Maxwell, 1903

Priestley, J. B. 'Postscript to Dunkirk'. *BBC Broacast*, 5 June, 1940

Pritchett, R.T. 'Irish Clubs'. *The Badminton Library. Yachting*, Vol. 2, ed. His Grace the Duke of Beaufort. London: Longmans, Green and Co.,1894, pp. 99–151

Purchas, Samuel. *Purchas His Pilgrimes. In Five Bookes. The First, Contayning the Voyages ... Made by Ancient Kings ... and Others, to and thorow the Remoter Parts of the Knowne World etc.* 4 vols. London: Printed by William Stansby, for Henrie Featherstone, 1625

Purves, Libby. *One Summer's Grace: A Family Voyage around Britain*. London: Grafton, 1989

——. *This Cruising Life*. London: Adlard Coles, 2001

Purves, Libby and Trevor Grove, eds. *Single Handed: The Observer/Europe 1 Singlehanded Transatlantic Race*. London: 'The Observer', 1984

Pye, Peter. *Red Mainsail*. London: Herbert Jenkins, 1952 (London: Rupert Hart-Davis Mariners Library no. 44, 1961)

——. *The Sea is for Sailing*. London: Rupert Hart-Davis, 1957

——. *A Sail in the Forest: Moonraker to the Baltic*. London: Rupert Hart-Davis, 1961

——. *Backdoor to Brazil*. In *The Peter Pye Omnibus*. Southampton: Ashford, 1986

Raban, Jonathan. *Foreign Land*. London: Collins Harvill, 1985

——. *Coasting*. London: Collins Harvill, 1986

——. *Passage to Jeanneau: A Sea and Its Meanings*. London: Picador, 1999

Race of the Century. Soviet Film, 1968

Rai, Gulshan. *The History of the Royal Bombay Yacht Club*. 2nd edn. Mumbai: Gulshan Rai, 2011

Ransome, Arthur. *Racundra's First Cruise*. London: George Allen & Unwin, 1923

——. *Swallows and Amazons*. London: Cape, 1930

——. *Swallowdale*. London: Cape, 1931

——. *Peter Duck*. London: Cape, 1932

——. *The Coot Club*. London: Cape, 1934

——. *We Didn't Mean to Go to Sea*. 1937. London: Cape, 1963

——. *Secret Waters*. London: Cape, 1939

——. *The Big Six.* London: Cape, 1940

——. *The Autobiography of Arthur Ransome.* Ed. with Prologue and Epilogue by Rupert Hart-Davis. London: Cape, 1976

——. *Racundra's Third Cruise.* Ed. and Compiled by Brian Hammett. Arundel: Fernhurst, 2002

——. 'Saturday by Saturday'. *Cruising Association Bulletin,* 1937. Reprinted, *Cruising Association Bulletin,* 35 (3), Autumn, 1996: 22–24

Raper, Bill and June Raper. *Sail to Freedom.* Brighton: Fernhurst, 1993

Ratcliffe, Dorothy Una. *The Babes of the Sea: Being an Account of their First Voyage in 'Sea Swallow'.* Leeds: North Country Press, 1929

——. *Swallow of the Sea: Pages from a Yacht's Log.* 1937. Illus. by Margaret Dobson. London: Country Life, 1937

Ravenshead. Opera. By Steve Mackey. Libretto Rinde Eckert,1998

Raynes, Rozelle. *The Sea Bird.* London: Springwood, 1979

——. *The Tuesday Boys.* Ormskirk, Lancs.: Thomas Lyster, 1991

Readman, Stuart. *Four Ships: One Hundred Years of the Essex Yacht Club.* Leighon-Sea: Essex Yacht Club, 1990

Revell, Roger. *Yacht and Rowing Club Buttons for the British Isles, 1750–1950: Descriptions, Histories and Values.* Lulu, 2010.

Rhinehart, Luke. *The Dice Man.* London: Grafton, 1972

Rich, Jonathan. *The Lonely Sea.* Play, 1979

Richards, Emma. *Around Alone.* London: Macmillan, 2004

Richards, Jeffrey. ' "Passing the Love of Women": Manly Love and Victorian Society'. In *Manliness and Morality: Middle-Class Masculinity in Britain and America 1800–1940.* Ed. J. A. Mangan and James Walvin. Manchester: Manchester University Press, 1987, pp. 92–122

Richardson, Angelique, ed. *Women Who Did: Stories by Men and Women, 1890–1914.* London: Penguin, 2002

——. *Love and Eugenics in the Late Nineteenth Century. Rational Reproduction and the New Woman.* Oxford: Oxford UP, 2003

Richardson, Angelique and Chris Willis, ed. *The New Woman in Fiction and Fact. Fin-de-Siècle Feminism.* Basingstoke: Palgrave, 2001

Richardson, Dorothy. *The Quest of Simon Richardson.* London: Gollancz, 1986

Riches, Adam. *When the Comics Went to War.* Edinburgh: Mainstream, 2009

Richey, Michael W., ed. *The Shell Encyclopedia of Sailing.* London: Stanford Maritime, 1980

The Riddle of the Sands. Directed by Tony Maylam. Perf. Michael York, Simon McCorkindale, Jenny Agutter and Alan Badel. National Film Finance Consortium, 1978

Ridgway, John. *Journey to Ardmore.* London: Hodder & Stoughton, 1971

Ridgway, Captain John and Sergeant Chay Blyth. *A Fighting Chance: How We Rowed the Altantic in 92 Days.* London: Paul Hamlyn, 1966

Riverdale Lord 'Skips'. *A Life, A Sail, A Changing Sea.* Beverley, Yorkshire: Hutton, 1995

Rivington, R.T. *Punting: Its History and Techniques.* Oxford: R. T. Rivington, 1982

The Roaring Forties ('Les Quarantièmes Rugissants'). French Film. Dir. Christian de
   Chalonge. Perf: Jacques Perrin, Julie Christie and Michael Serrault, 1982
Robbins, Michael. *The Railway Age*. Harmondsworth: Penguin, 1965
Roberts, Bob. *Coasting Bargemaster*. 1949. Lavenham, Suffolk: Mallard Reprints, 1984
——. *Last of the Sailormen*. London: Routledge & Kegan Paul, 1960
Robertson, Dougal. *Survive the Savage Sea*. London: Elek, 1973
Robertson, Douglas. *The Last Voyage of the 'Lucette'*. Woodbridge, Suffolk: Seafarer,
   2005
Robertson, E. Arnot. *Cullum*. 1928. Intro. by Rachel Billington. London: Virago, 1989
——. *Ordinary Families. A Novel*. 1933. Introduction by Polly Devlin. London: Virago,
   1982
Robinson, Edward. *Down River to the Sea: Family Adventures in a Small Yacht*.
   Altrincham: John Sherratt and Son, 1952
Roch, Jeremy, R.N. 'The Journals of Jeremy Roch'. In *Three Sea Journals of Stuart Times,
   Being, First, the Diary of Dawtrey Cooper, Captain of the Pelican … Secondly, the
   Journals of Jeremy Roch, Captain of the King's Navy … Thirdly, the Diary of Francis
   Rogers, London Merchant*. Ed. and Transcribed from the Original Manuscripts by
   Bruce S. Ingram. London: Constable & Co., 1936
Roper, Michael and John Tosh, eds. *Manful Assertions: Masculinities in Britain since
   1800*. London: Routledge, 1991
Rose, Sir Alec. *My Lively Lady*. Lymington: Nautical; London: Harrap, 1968
Ross, Helen. *Behaviour and Perception in Strange Environments*. London: George
   Allen & Unwin, 1974
Rousmaniere, John. *Fastnet Force Ten*. Lymington: Nautical, 1980
Rousmaniere, John and the Editors of Time-Life Books. *The Luxury Yachts*.
   Amsterdam: Time-Life, 1982
Rowbotham, Judith. *Good Girls Make Good Wives: Guidance for Girls in Victorian
   Fiction*. Oxford: Blackwell, 1989
Royal Burnham Yacht Club. *A History of the Royal Burnham Yacht Club*. Burnham-
   on-Crouch: Royal Burnham Yacht Club, 1995
Royal Temple Yacht Club. *History of the Royal Temple Yacht Club*. http://www.Rtyc.
   com/history.htm. Accessed 12 November, 2009
The Rubaiyat of Omar Khayyám (Edward Fitzgerald)
Rubinstein, W. D., ed. *Wealth and the Wealthy in the Modern World*. London: Croom
   Helm, 1980
——. *Who Were the Rich? A Biographical Dictionary of British Wealth-Holders*. London:
   Social Affairs Unit, 2009
Ruger, Jan. *The Great Naval Game. Britain and Germany in the Age of Empire*.
   Cambridge: Cambridge University Press, 2007
Ruskin, John. *The Harbours of England*. London: George Allen, 1907
Russell, Richard. *A Dissertation on the Use of Seawater in the Diseases of the Glands,
   Particularly the Scurvy, Jaundice, King's Evil, Leprosy and the Glandular Consumption*.
   Trans. from the Latin of R. Russell, M.D by an Eminent Physician. London, 1752
Ryan, Roger. *The West Lancashire Yacht Club 1894–1994: A Centenary History*. Preston:
   Carnegie, 1993

——. 'The Emergence of Middle-Class Yachting in the North-West of England from the Later Nineteenth Century'. *Recreation and the Sea*. Ed. Stephen Fisher. Exeter: Exeter University Press, 1997: 150–180

——. 'Identifying the British Yachtsman, 1815 to 1939'. In *Entertainment, Leisure and Identity*. Ed. Roger Spalding and Alyson Brown. Newcastle: Cambridge Scholars, 2007: 66–82

Ryan, W. F. 'Peter the Great's English Yacht: Admiral Lord Carmarthen and the Russian Tobacco Monopoly'. *Mariner's Mirror*, 69, 1983: 65–83

Sagues, John. 'The History of Wembley Sailing Club'. http://www.wembleysailing-club.co.uk/downloads/history_of_club accessed 27 May 2015

Sampson, Aylwin. *Winning Waters: The Homes of Rowing*. London: Robert Hale, 1986

Sandy, Laurence. *Sailing*. Puffin Picture Book, no. 95. Harmondsworth: Penguin, 1953

Savage, Mike *et al. Social Class in the 21st Century*. London: Pelican, 2015

Scott, Peter. *The Eye of the Wind*. London: Hodder and Stoughton, 1961

Schult, Joachim. *The Sailing Dictionary*. Trans. and Extensively Rev. by Barbara Webb. London: Adlard Coles Granada, 1981

Seawanhaka Corinthian Yacht Club. 'The History of the Seawanhaka Cup' archive. www.sailingscuttlebutt.com/news/09/0929a/

Sefton, Alan. *Sir Peter Blake: An Amazing Life*. The Authorized Biography. London: Penguin, 2006

Seligman, Adrian. *The Voyage of the Cap Pilar*. London: Hodder & Stoughton, 1939

Shalleck, David with Erol Munuz. *Mediterranean Summer: A Season on France's Cote d'Azur and Italy's Costa Bella*. New York: Broadway, 2007

Sharp, Nigel. 'Boatbuilding in the Second World War'. *Marine Quarterly*, 17, Spring 2015: 68–76

——. 'Birth of a Modern Classic'. *Classic Boat*, July 2015: 38–42

——. *Troubled Waters: Leisure Boating and the Second World War*. Stroud, Gloucs.: Amberley, 2015

Shaw, Frank H., Capt. *White Sails and Spindrift*. London: Stanley Paul, Shaw 1946

Shepton, Bob. *Addicted to Adventure*. London: Bloomsbury, 2014

Shute, Nevil. *Marazan*. 1926. London: Pan, 1964

——. *What Happened to the Corbetts*. 1939. London: Pan, 1965

——. *Slide Rule: The Autobiography of an Engineer*. 1954. London: Mandarin, 1990

——. *Requiem for a Wren*. London: Pan, 1955

——. *Trustee from the Tool Room*. London: Heinemann, 1960

Sibbick, Occomore. *Lulworth Shared My Playground*. London: Minerva, 1996

Simper, Robert. *Victorian and Edwardian Yachting from Old Photographs*. London: B. T. Batsford, 1978

Simpson, A. W. Brian. *Cannibalism and Common Law: A Victorian Yachting Tragedy*. London: The Hambledon Press, 1994

Simpson, Joe. *Touching the Void*. London: Cape, 1988

Sinclair, W. E. *Cruises of the 'Joan'*. London: Edward Arnold, 1934

——. *The Cruise of the 'Quartette'*. London: Edward Arnold, 1937

Sisk, Hal. *Dublin Bay: The Cradle of Yacht Racing*. 2nd edn. Limerick: Peggy Bawn Press, 2014

Sleightholme, Des. *Old Harry's Bunkside Book.* London: Adlard Coles, 1978

——. *Up the Creek with Old Harry.* London: Adlard Coles, 1979

——. *A Funny Old Life.* London: Adlard Coles Nautical, 2001

Sleightholme, Joyce. *The Seawife's Handbook.* 1st edn. 1970, 2nd 1976. London: Angus and Robertson. Retitled: *The Cruising Mate's Handbook: A Guide to Good Crewing.* London: Adlard Coles, 1991

Slocum, Captain Joshua. *Sailing Alone around the World.* London: Sampson, Low, Marston & Co., 1900. *The Original Edition.* Intro. by Walter Magnes Teller. Dobbs Ferry, NY: Sheridan, 1954

——. *The Voyages of Joshua Slocum.* Ed. with commentaries Walter Magnes Teller. 1958. New York: Sheridan, 1985. (Includes *The Voyage of the Liberdade,* 1890; and *The Voyage of the Destroyer,* 1894.)

Smeeton, Miles. *Once is Enough.* London: Rupert Hart-David, 1959

——. *Because the Horn is there.* Lymington: Nautical, 1970

Smiles, Samuel. *Self-Help.* London, 1859

Smith, Alexander McCall. *School Ship Tobermory.* Edinburgh: BCBooks, 2015

Smith, Brian. 'History of the Royal Mersey Yacht Club'. Unpublished, undated

Smith, Stanley. *Smiths at Sea.* Southampton: Robert Ross, 1951

Smith, Stanley and Charles Violet. *The Wind Calls the Tune: The Eventful Voyage of the 'Nova Espero'.* London: Robert Ross, 1952

Smollet, Tobias. *The Adventures of Roderick Random.* 1748

——. *The Adventures of Peregrine Pickle.* 1751

Sobel, Dava and William J. H. Andrewes. *The Illustrated Longitude.* London: Fourth Estate, 1998

Southby-Tailyour, Ewen. *Falkland Islands Shores.* London: Macmillan/ Nautical, 1985

——. *Blondie: A Life of Lieutenant-Colonel H. G. Hasler DSO OBE RM, Founder of the SBS and Modern Single-Handed Ocean Racing.* 1998. London: Leo Cooper, 1998

Southgate, Beverley. *History Meets Fiction.* Harlow: Pearson Education, 2009

Spavens, William. *Memoirs of a Seafaring Life.* 1796. N. A. M. Rodger, ed. London: Folio Society, 2000

Speed, H. Fiennes and Maude Speed. *Cruises in Small Yachts by H. Fiennes Speed and a Continuation, entitled More Cruises by Maude Speed.* 1926. London: Imray, Laurie, Norie & Wilson, 1926. 1st edn of *Cruises in Small Yachts,* 1883

Spencer, Herbert. *Progress: Its Law and Cause.* 1857

Speyer, Chris. *Devil's Rock.* London: Bloomsbury, 2009

Stadler, Michael. *Psychology of Sailing: The Sea's Effects on Mind and Body.* London: Adlard Coles, 1987

Stalkartt, Marmaduke. *Naval Architecture, or, The Rudiments and Rules of Ship Building: Exemplified in a Series of Draughts and Plans: with Observations Sending to the Further Improvement of That Important Art.* 1781

Stanley, Arthur Penryn. *The Life and Correspondence of Thomas Arnold, D.D., Sometimes Head-master of Rugby School, and Regius Professor of Modern History in the University of Oxford.* London: Fellowes, 1844

Stape, John. *The Several Lives of Joseph Conrad.* London: Arrow, 2008

Steavenson, Robin. *Marks to Starboard.* London: Herbert Jenkins, 1958

——. *Dinghy Sailor's Pocket Book*. London: Evan Brothers, 1961

Stephen, Fitzjames. 'Liberalism, Patriotism and English Liberty'. *Edinburgh Review*, 1858

Stevenson, P. L. *How the Jubilee Fleet Escaped Destruction and the Battle of Ushant*. Hertford: Stephen Austin & Sons, 1898

Stevenson, R. L. 'The English Admirals'. *Cornhill Magazine*, 38, July 1878: 36–43

——. *An Inland Voyage*. London: C. Kegan Paul, 1878

——. *Treasure Island*. London: Cassell & Co., 1883

Stewart, Chris. *Three Ways to Capsize a Boat*. London: Sort Of Books, 2009

Stock, Ralph. *The Cruise of the Dream Ship*. London: Heinemann, 1922

Stone, Robert. *Outerbridge Reach*. Boston: Mariner, 1998

Stopes, Marie. *Married Love: A New Contribution to the Solution of Sex Difficulties*. London: A. C. Fifield, 1918

Suffling, Ernest Richard. *How to Organize a Cruise on the Broads*. London: Jarrold & Sons, 1891

Sullivan, Sir Edward. 'Introduction'. *The Badminton Library: Yachting*, 2 vols. Vol. 1. Ed. His Grace the Duke of Beaufort. London: Longman, Green, and Co., 1904, pp. 1–17

Sumner, Ann. *Colour and Light: Fifty Impressionist and Post-Impressionist Works at the National Museum of Wales*. With contributions by Louisa Briggs and Julia Carver. Cardiff: National Museum of Wales, 2005

Sumner, Ann with Kenneth McConkey, Susan J.Elks and Robert Holland. *Court on Canvas: Tennis in Art*. London: Philip Wilson, 2011

Swain, Henry. *Return to Murmansk*. London: Seafarer, 1996

Swale, Rosie. *Rosie Darling*. London: Pan, 1974

——. *Children of Cape Horn*. London: Paul Elek, 1974

Swallows and Amazons. Film. Dir. Claude Watham, 1974

Taking on the World: Ellen MacArthur. Video. Offshore Challenges, 2001

Taylor, Captain H. N. *A Captain's Tale*. Lavenham, Suffolk: Terence Dalton, 1984

Taylor, James. *Yachts on Canvas: Artists' Images of Yachts from the Seventeenth Century to the Present Day*. London: Conway, 1998

Taylor, Roger. *MingMing and the Art of Minimal Ocean Sailing*. Waltham Cross, Herts.: Fitzroy, 2010

——. *MingMing and the Tonic of Wildness*. Waltham Cross, Herts.: Fitzroy, 2012

——. *Mingming II and Islands of the Ice*, Waltham Cross, Herts.: Fitzroy, 2016

Teignmouth Electron. Film by Tacita Dean, 2000

Teller, Walter Magnes. *The Search for Captain Slocum*. 1956. London: Andre Deutsch, 1959

Tetley, Nigel. *Trimaran Solo: The Story of Victress' Circumnavigation and Last Voyage*. Lymington: Nautical, 1970

Tew, Helen. *Transatlantic at Last*. Woodbridge: Seafarer, 2004

'Thalassa' [Col. John Townsend]. 'Small Yacht Sailing on the Solent'. *The Badminton Library: Yachting*, 2 vols. Vol. 1. Ed. His Grace the Duke of Beaufort. London: Longmans, Green and Co., 1904, pp. 222–294

Thelwell. *Three Sheets to the Wind: Thelwell's Manual of Sailing*. London: Eyre Methuen, 1973

Thesleff, Holger. *Farewell Windjammer: An Account of the Last Circumnavigation of the Globe by a Sailing Ship and the Last Grain Race from Australia to England*. London: Thames and Hudson, 1951

Thomas, Pascoe. *A True and Impartial Journal of a Voyage to the South-Seas and Round the Globe in His Majesty's Ship the Centurion*, 1745

Thomas, S. F. *A History of the Teignmouth Corinthian Yacht Club*. Published by the Author, 1999

Thomas, Stephen D. *The Last Navigator*. London: Hutchinsons, 1987

Thomson, Belinda. *Impressionism: Origins, Practice, Reception*. London: Thames & Hudson, 2000

Thomson, David. *England in the Nineteenth Century*. Harmondsworth: Penguin, 1950

Tilman, H. W. *The Eight Sailing / Mountain - Exploration Books*. London: Diadem Books; Seattle: Mountaineers, 1987

Tolcher, Charlie. 'The History of Organized Small Boat Racing'. *Maritime Southwest*, 24, 2011: 34–99

Tomalin, Claire. *Samuel Pepys: The Unequalled Self*. London: Viking, 2002.

Tomalin, Nicholas and Ron Hall. *The Strange Voyage of Donald Crowhurst*. London: Hodder & Stoughton, 1970

Torbert, William R. with Malcolm P. Rogers. *Being for the Most Part Puppets: Interactions among Men's Labor, Leisure and Politics*. Cambridge, MA: Schenkman, 1973

Tory, Peter. *Giles: A Life in Cartoons*. London: Headlines, 1993

Tracey, Graham. *East Cowes Sailing Club 1912–2012*. East Cowes: East Cowes Sailing Club, 2012

Tranter, Neil. *Sport, Economy and Society in Britain 1750–1914*. Cambridge: Cambridge University Press, 1998

Travis, John F. 'Devon Seaside Tourism and the Coastal Environment 1750–1900'. *Man and the Maritime Environment*. Ed. Stephen Fisher. Exeter: Exeter University Press, 1994: 160–179

Trease, Geoffrey. *The Grand Tour*. New York: Holt, Rinehart and Winston, 1967

Tripp, Alker ('Leigh Hoe') *Shoalwater and Fairway: The Casual Explorations of a Sailing Man in the Shoal Seas and Tidal Waters of Essex and Kent*. Illustrated by the Author. London: John Lane The Bodley Head, 1924

Trollope, Anthony. *British Sports and Pastimes*. London: Vertue, 1868. Facsimile copy: Forgotten Books, 2012.

Trunnion. *Sporting Annals*, October 1822; quoted by Ian Dear. *The Royal Yacht Squadron 1815–1985*, London: Stanley Paul, 1985, p. 27

Tucker, Jon. 'A Voyage to Morurua'. *Marine Quarterly*, 20, Winter 2015, 48–57

Underhill, Sir Arthur, Ll.D. *Our Silver Streak or The Yachtsman's Guide from Harwich to Scilly*. London: Norie & Wilson, 1892

——. *A Short History of the Royal Cruising Club MDCCCLXXX–MCMXXX*. 1930. London: Royal Cruising Club, 1930

Vance, Norman. 'The Ideal of Manliness'. In *The Victorian Public School: Studies in the Development of an Educational Institution.* Ed. Brian Simon and Ian Bradley. Dublin: Gill and Macmillan, 1975, pp. 115–128

——. *The Sinews of the Spirit: The Ideal of Christian Manliness in Victorian Literature and Religious Thought.* Cambridge: Cambridge University Press, 1985

Vanderdecken (William Cooper). *Yarns for Green Hands: A Treatise on Practical Yachtmanship.* London: Hunt & Co., 1860

——. *The Yacht Sailor – A Treatise on Practical Yachtsmanship, Cruising and Racing.* 1861. London: Hunt, 1862

——. *Yachts and Yachting, being a Treatise on Building, Sparring, Canvassing, Sailing and the General Management of Yachts.* London: Hunt: Simpkin, Marshall & Co., 1873. Introduction by John Leather. London: Scolar, 1979

Van Duzer, Chet. 'On the Origins of Sea Monsters'. *Marine Quarterly*, Winter 2013: 86–92

Van Gennep, Arnold. *The Rites of Passage.* Trans. Monika B.Vizedomand and Gabrielle L.Caffee. Intro. Solon T.Kimball. Paris, 1909. London: Routledge & Kegan Paul, 1960

Van Strander, Chris. *Daniel Pelican.* Play, peformed 'Frying Pan Lightship', New York, 1999

Vasey, Tony. *The Ocean Cruising Club: The First Fifty Years.* Alton, Hampshire: Chalvington Press, c. 2005

Vaughan, Thomas John. *The International Fourteen Foot Dinghy, 1928–1964.* Norwood: International Fourteen Dinghy Class Association of Great Britain, 1964

Veblen, Thorstein. *The Theory of the Leisure Class.* 1899. London: Viking Penguin, 1979

Vermeulen, M. J. *Adventures of the Islanders.* Bradford-on-Avon, Wilts.: ELSP, 2009

——. *Islanders Adventures in Sark.* Bradford-on-Avon, Wilts.: ELSP, 2010

——. *Islanders go to Jersey and Alderney.* Bradford-on-Avon, Wilts.: ELSP, 2013

Verney, Michael. *Lifeboat into Yacht: Practical Hints for the Amateur on Conversion of Ships and R.N.L.I. Lifeboats.* London: Yachting Monthly, 1951

Vickery, Amanda. 'From Whigs to Wigs'. *Guardian*, 26 October, 2013, p. 18

Videlo, Donald. *Frensham Pond Sailing Club: The First Fifty Years 1953–2003.* Frensham: Author's Estate, Frensham Pond Sailing Club, c. 2003

Villiers, A.J. *Falmouth for Orders: The Story of the Last Clipper Ship Race around Cape Horn.* 1929. London: Geoffrey Bles, 1929

——. *By Way of Cape Horn.* London: Geoffrey Bles, 1930

——. *Windjammer.* Film 1930.

——. *Last of the Wind Ships*, 1934. London: George Routledge & Sons, 1934

——. *The War with Cape Horn.* London: Pan, 1971

Vine, P. A. L. *Pleasure Boating in the Victorian Era.* Chichester: Phillimore, 1983

Violet, Charles. *Solitary Journey: 'Nova Espero's Third Voyage.* London: Adlard Coles, 1954

Waite, Renee M. *Pin Mill Sailing Club: Sixty Years.* Ipswich: Pin Mill Sailing Club, 1995

Walker, Nicolette Milnes. *When I Put out to Sea.* London: Collins, 1972

Walton, John K. *The English Seaside Resort: A Social History 1750–1814.* Leicester: Leicester University Press, 1983

Walvin, James. *Leisure and Society 1830–1950*. London: Longman, 1978

Ward, Captain A. R. *The Chronicles of the Royal Thames Yacht Club*. Arundel: Fernhurst, 1999

Ward, Nick with Sinead O'Brien. *Left for Dead*. London: A. & C. Black, 2007

Ward-Jackson, C. H. *Ship Portrait Painters*. Greenwich: National Maritime Museum Maritime Monographs and Reports No.35, 1978

Warner, Oliver. *An Introduction to British Maritime Painting*. London: B.T. Batsford, 1948

Waugh, Alec. *The Loom of Youth*. London: Grant Richards, 1917.

Webb, William. *Coastguard!: An Official History of HM Coastguard*. London: Her Majesty's Stationery Office, 1976

Weeks, Jeffrey. *Sex, Politics and Society*. London: Longman, 1981

Wells, H.G. *Ann Veronica*. 1909. London: Penguin Classic, 2005

West, Alfred. 'Sea Salts and Celluloid'. Unpublished, 1936. http:// user29269.vs.easy. co.uk/seasalts.pdf

Wharram, James. *Two Girls, Two Catamarans*. London: Abelard-Schuman, 1969; 4th edn. Bologna: Crociera Totale Edizioni, 2001

———. *Lapita Voyage*. Devoran, Cornwall: James Wharram Designs. CD, 2009

Whitehead, Alfred North. *Science and the Modern World*. The Lowell Lectures, 1925. Cambridge: Cambridge University Press, 1926

Wigfull, W. E. 'The Yacht Clubs of the Southend District'. *Yachting Monthly*, 15, 1913

Wild, Ian. *A Handkerchief in the Rigging: Whitstable Yacht Club – The First Fifty Years*. Whitstable: Friends of Whitstable Museum and Gallery, 2002

Wilde, Oscar. *The Picture of Dorian Gray*. London: Ward, Lock & Co., 1891

Wilkes, Andrew. *Artic and Northern Waters*. St Ives,Cambs.: Imray, Laurie, Norie and Wilson, 2014

Williams, Chris. *125 Years: Topsham Sailing Club 1885–2010*. Topsham, Devon: Topsham Sailing Club

Williams, David M. and John Armstrong. 'Changing Voyage Patterns in the Nineteenth Century: The Impact of the Steamship'. *International Journal of Maritime History*, 22 (2), 2010: 151–170

Williams, Geoffrey. 'Sir Thomas Lipton' Wins. London: Peter Davies, 1969

Williamson, Henry. *Tarka the Otter*. London: G. P. Putnam, 1927

Willis, Paul. 'Women in Sport in Ideology'. In *Sport, Culture and Ideology*, ed. Jennifer Hargreaves. London: Routledge & Kegan Paul, 1982, pp. 89–135

Wilson, A. N. *Hilaire Belloc*. London: Hamish Hamilton, 1984

Winterbottom, Derek. *Henry Newbolt and the Spirit of Clifton*. Bristol: Redcliffe Press, 1986

Wise, Jan. *50 Years of East Anglian Offshore Racing: A Tribute by Jan Wise*. Benfleet: Brent, 2001

———. *A Century of Sailing: The Crouch Yacht Club 1907–2007*. Burnham-on-Crouch, Essex: Crouch Yacht Club, 2007

———. *50 Years of Scows and the RBYC Cadets 1959–2009: How the West Wight Scow Came to Burnham on Crouch*. Lemon Cat, 2009

Woodcock, Percy. *Sea Wrack*. London: Nelson, 1937

——. *Adventure Down Channel*. London: Nelson, 1938

——. *Wreckers' Bay*. London: Peal Press, 1938

——. *The Surprise*. London: Frederick Muller, 1949

——. *Looking Astern: A Ditty Bag of Memories*. London: Frederick Muller, 1950

——. *Come Boating with Me*. London: Frederick Muller, 1953

Woodman, Richard. *Keepers of the Sea: A History of the Yachts and Tenders of Trinity House*. Haversham, Suffolk: Terence Dalton, 1983

——. *Of Daring Temper: A History of the Marine Society*. London: The Marine Society and Sea Cadets, 2006

——. 'A Brief History of Cargo Liners'. *Marine Quarterly*, 20, Winter 2015: 69–76

Woodman-Smith, Cecil Blanche. *The Great Hunger*. London: New English Library, 1964

Woolf, Virginia. *Jacob's Room*. London: Hogarth, 1922

——. 'The Cinema'. *Arts*, June 1926

——. *To the Lighthouse*. 1927. Ed. Stella McNichol. Intro. Hermione Lee. London: Penguin Classic, 2000

Worth, Claud. *Squint: Its Causes, Pathology and Treatment*. London: John Bale, Sons & Danielsson, 1903

——. *Yacht Cruising*. London: J. D. Potter, 1910

——. *Yacht Navigation and Voyaging*. London: J. D. Potter, 1927

Wouk, Herman. *The Caine Mutiny*. Garden City, NY: Doubleday, 1951

The Yachtsman. *British Yachts and Yachtsmen: A Complete History of British Yachting from the Middle of the Sixteenth Century to the Present Day*. London: Yachtsman Publishing Co., 1907

Young, Archibald, Advocate. *Summer Sailings by an Old Yachtsman*. Edinburgh: David Douglas, 1898

Young, Bill and Dudley Stamp. *Bude's Maritime Heritage: Past and Present*. Bude: Bill Young, 2001

Index

This index lists all events, people and boats named in the text. It also lists all yachts, yacht clubs and sailors mentioned in the footnotes. Authors mentioned in the main text are listed, but not those only named in footnotes.

Names of yachts, book and magazine titles are italicised, with book titles being followed by the name of the author in brackets.

419